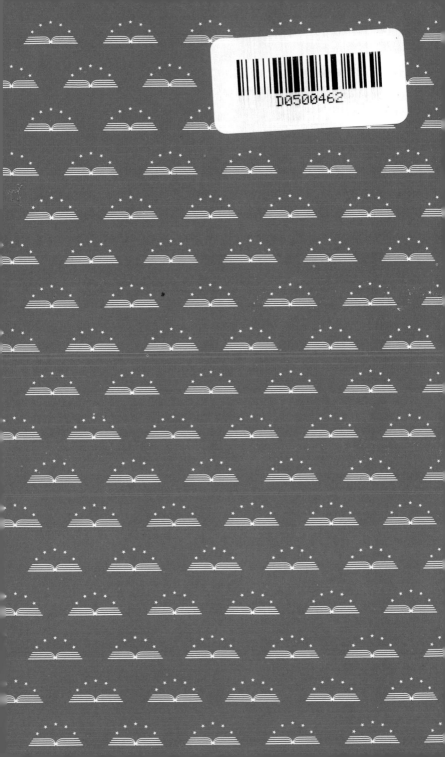

REPORTING VIETNAM
PART TWO

REPORTING VIETNAM

PART TWO

AMERICAN JOURNALISM 1969–1975

THE LIBRARY OF AMERICA

The paper used in this publication meets the
minimum requirements of the American National Standard for
Information Sciences—Permanence of Paper for Printed
Library Materials, ANSI z39.48—1984.

Distributed to the trade in the United States
by Penguin Putnam Inc.
and in Canada by Penguin Books Canada Ltd.

Library of Congress Catalog Number: 98–12267
For cataloging information, see end of Index.
ISBN 1–883011–59–0

First Printing
The Library of America—105

Manufactured in the United States of America

Advisory board for *Reporting Vietnam*

Contents

A Long, Leisurely Drive Through Mekong Delta Tells Much of the War

by Peter R. Kann

SAIGON—The war drags on. President Nixon has ruled out any quick withdrawal, and enemy attacks seem to be increasing once again. No progress is reported in Paris. But if there is no progress at the peace table, is there at least progress on the battlefield?

There isn't a clear answer. "Progress" is measured here in many ways. The Air Force computes the tonnage of bomb-loads dropped. The Army tots up enemy bodies. Pacification planners neatly categorize hamlets on computerized evaluation charts. Psychological warriors conduct mini-Gallup Polls among taxi drivers. Economists plot curves on the shipments of rice. Embassy officers sip tea with Saigon legislators and seek to divine their Delphic utterances.

And still, Vietnam seems to defy analysis. The Vietnam war remains a kaleidoscopic conflict over a splintered society in a fragmented nation, and the bits of Vietnam that one man sees probably are no more typical—and no less valid—than the fragments perceived by another.

With such thoughts in mind, three Americans recently set out in a 1954 Volkswagen on a week-long drive through the Mekong Delta, that densely populated rice bowl of Vietnam where, it has often been said, the war ultimately will be won or lost. The trip covered some 400 miles by road, with side trips on motor launches, sampans and helicopters. The route ran from Saigon southwest to Can Tho, the administrative hub of the Delta; then westward through the tranquil province of An Giang and on to Chau Doc province along the Cambodian frontier; then back through one-time Vietcong base areas of Sandec province and finally northeast back to Saigon.

I

The trip offers some glimpses of recent progress and of perennial problems, of new threats like North Vietnamese battalions and of more esoteric dangers like a nine-nostriled water monster allegedly loose in the Mekong River. The trip provides no grand conclusions, only the observation that three unarmed Americans were able to spend a week driving through rural Vietnam without being shot at. That, perhaps, is progress.

Scenically, the Delta is both beautiful and boring, a lush green blanket of marshy rice paddies stretching to the horizon. The flat monotony sporadically is broken by small mounds of earth encasing tombs, by narrow belts of palm trees and by the small clusters of thatch houses that constitute Vietnamese hamlets. Less frequently, one passes larger villages, usually with an aluminum-roofed schoolhouse (courtesy of U.S. aid), a pastel pagoda and a bustling marketplace crammed with delicacies like river eel and skinned paddy rat. Crisscrossing this landscape at intervals of every few miles are the French-built canals, which, far more than the potholed roads, serve as the Delta's economic lifelines.

Despite the war, there is an overwhelming sense of peacefulness and prosperity about the Delta. The Delta has a way of enveloping, almost swallowing up, the war. Conflict seems to encroach upon the peaceful Delta setting only as isolated incidents—here a Vietcong raid on a mud-walled militia outpost, there a string of U.S. helicopters swooping down to strafe a tree line. Unlike the dusty plateaus and jagged hills of the northern areas, the placid green Delta seems unsuited to a war.

The Delta traditionally has been an area of "low profile" U.S. involvement, with Americans serving only to advise and support Vietnamese troops in a slow-paced struggle against locally recruited Vietcong. In mid-1968, this pattern was jarred when the U.S. Ninth Division moved into the upper Delta, chalking up staggering (some skeptics say unbelievable) Vietcong body counts. Then, this past summer, the Ninth was shipped home as the first instalment on President Nixon's troop-withdrawal promise.

Wherever two or more American officials gather together these days the talk is of "Vietnamization," the turning over of a greater share of the war burden to the Vietnamese. So it goes in Can Tho, the Delta administrative center, where visitors can be briefed on everything from Vietnamese adaptation to the M-16 automatic rifle to Vietnamese receptivity to participatory democracy. The prevailing new theme is sounded by Maj. Gen. Roderick Wetherill, ranking American in the Delta, who says: "The Vietnamese have just about everything we can give them. Now it's up to them, and we're confident they can hack it."

But if the talk of Can Tho is Vietnamization, the visible evidence still bespeaks Americanization. The massive USO building near the center of town has just unveiled a new barbecue pit, dedicated with military honors. Down the street is the even busier Hollywood Bar where GIs can buy "Saigon tea" from miniskirted, de-Vietnamized girls. Nearby is Palm Springs, a Hawaiian-style enclave for U.S. civilian advisers on everything from hog raising to intelligence gathering. Like the American military compound across town, Palm Springs boasts a well-chlorinated swimming pool.

Driving west out of Can Tho you pass several miles of impressive testament to American logistical capabilities: An airbase, warehouses, storage depots, helicopter fleets, truck yards, a naval support base, office buildings for civilian contractors. Scores of American trucks and jeeps clog the narrow road. A giant American road grader rumbles along, its treads cracking the pavement of this road even as it heads off to build a new road somewhere else. For perhaps five miles the Vietnamese are visibly represented only by a few militiamen rooting through the American tin cans on a roadside garbage heap.

A few miles farther on, the rural Delta re-emerges, and the view once again is of small boys draped over the backs of water buffalo, which are wallowing in the wet green paddies. A two-hour drive over relatively smooth road (potholes no deeper than six inches) brings you into An Giang province, heartland of the Hoa Hao religious sect. This sect's militant anti-Communism (the result of the sect's founding father's having been decapitated by the Vietminh) makes An Giang the most pacified province in Vietnam.

Indeed, the senior American adviser in An Giang, an

Agency for International Development official named Bill
Small, sleeps alone in an unguarded house on the outskirts of
the province capital. (He's considerably more confident than
several dozen U.S. military advisers working under him; they
live in a well-armed, walled compound defended by a platoon
of Vietnamese militiamen, a minor incongruity in light of the
American priority program to get Vietnamese troops off static
defense.)

Mr. Small has been seeking to reduce the U.S. advisory
presence in An Giang, but with limited success. One problem:
The An Giang advisory team is required to file 144 separate
reports to Can Tho and Saigon every month, and many Americans are needed here just to fight this paper war. Another
problem is the "adviser cult" that has developed among Government of Vietnam (GVN) officials. "To rate a U.S adviser
means status to a Vietnamese. To be Vietnamized out of your
adviser is to lose much face," explains a young American.

With Mr. Small, the American visitors board an outboard
motor launch for a spin through An Giang's inland waterways.
There's a stop in a Cho Moi district capital where Lt. Col.
Nguyen Quang Hanh, the urbane district chief who holds a
French passport and has a son studying in Paris, welcomes
visitors to his office, its walls gaily decorated with red, yellow
and green paper flowers of the sort associated with the Eugene
McCarthy campaign.

Breaking out a sealed bottle of Chivas Regal shortly before
10 a.m., Lt. Col. Hanh volunteers the view that because of
the death of Ho Chi Minh, the war will be over by the end
of this year. "There will be a couple of months of power struggle in Hanoi and then the war will end, militarily and politically, end completely," he says with absolute assurance.

Cho Moi district has been peaceful recently—except for the
appearance several months ago of the nine-nostriled water
snake. The snake is said to have been raised by a Cho Moi
necromancer who let it loose in the Tien Giang River. The
snake rapidly grew to a length of 15 feet, and it is rumored
recently to have gobbled up an old fisherwoman. Reports on
the river monster have circulated as far as Saigon. To many
Vietnamese, magic and monsters remain far more interesting
subjects than politics and war.

Taking a shortcut down a network of narrow canals, the motorboat runs afoul of some floating weeds and the engine jams in reverse. Luckily there's a Vietnamese Popular Force (PF) militia outpost nearby, and the boat backs over for assistance.

It's a fairly typical PF outpost, thick mud walls built around a tin-roofed shack in which the 12 PF soldiers and their families all live together. Startled by this surprise mid-afternoon visit, the PF scurry off to locate their new M-16s, to strap on ammunition belts and to don their steel helmets (most of which had been put to use collecting rainwater).

The PF return and try to look vigilant. One is asked if the outpost has had any contact with the Vietcong. "Oh, yes." When was the most recent contact? "The VC fired a mortar at us two years ago." (To be a PF in An Giang province is to be a lucky PF. In less secure provinces, the PF take heavier casualties than any other allied unit.)

The outpost is hardly equipped to handle motor repairs, and so, to the delight of laughing PF lining the mud walls, the Americans begin backing their way home. Pride is forgotten soon enough, and the costly American speedboat is strapped to the side of a Vietnamese sampan with a tiny put-put engine and is towed on home.

The next morning's drive brings the Americans into Chau Doc province, which has a common border of nearly 50 miles with Cambodia. Chau Doc is often called Vietnam's "Wild West" because it was one of the last Vietnamese frontier areas to be settled and because it has a tradition of professional banditry, smuggling and general lawlessness that predated the present war and no doubt will continue long after it is over.

Cambodia and South Vietnam have no diplomatic or legalized trade relations, but there is a considerable cross-border commerce greased by bribes to Vietnamese, Cambodian and Vietcong officials. At the small village of Nui Sam, some 500 beef cattle are milling and mooing as local merchants negotiate sales with Saigon buyers. The cows have recently been smuggled into Chau Doc from Cambodia through a complex procedure involving cross-border communication by coded message and Indian-style smoke signals.

At Nui Sam's only soup kitchen–coffee house, one can

watch the last coats of grease being applied to the cattle smuggling operation. The Cambodians and Vietcong already have been paid off. The GVN district chief at the crossing point has pocketed 200 piasters ($1.60) per head (enough money so that after three months in his lucrative job he is said to have built new homes in Chau Doc, Saigon and the seaside resort of Vung Tau).

In the soup kitchen, official papers are now being drawn up for the approval of the local GVN police chief, tax agent, economic service chief, animal husbandry representative and village chief—all of whom are accustomed to a small gratuity for their services. The room is crowded with old women clutching sheafs of paper, young clerks with stamps and chops, buyers and sellers exchanging wads of cash. Vietnamese soldiers meander among the tables cadging cigarets. Under the table, dogs, chickens and pigs poke around on the earthen floor looking for scraps of food. Perhaps $150,000 of business will be transacted here today. And as a result Americans and wealthy Vietnamese will continue to be able to buy beefsteak in Saigon restaurants at $10 a plate.

But cattle and other commercial commodities being smuggled across the border are of little concern to U.S. officials. "Hell, it's just honest smuggling," says a military officer in Chau Doc. American concern is focused on the infiltration of enemy troops and supplies across the border, and this sort of smuggling is on the rise.

In recent months, nearly two North Vietnamese regiments—up to 3,000 men—have crossed into Chau Doc from their Cambodian sanctuary. This represents the first appearance of regular North Vietnamese Army (NVA) units in the Mekong Delta and is doubly significant, and doubly dangerous, since it has occurred hard on the heels of the withdrawal of the U.S. Ninth Division. Some of the NVA troops are ensconced in cave and tunnel complexes on several of the heavily forested "Seven Sister" mountains, which dot the otherwise flat riceland of Chau Doc; others have moved south of Chau Doc into the swamp areas of the lower Delta.

There are conflicting interpretations on practically everything in Vietnam, and the NVA influx is no exception. In Saigon, some American military officers believe the Delta Viet-

cong have been so badly battered in the past year or so that
the NVA have been called in as a "desperation move." Some
U.S. diplomats think the NVA are moving in to solidify enemy
control of long-time base areas in anticipation of a future
cease-fire and territorial settlement. In Can Tho, senior U.S.
officers suggest the NVA may move up into the eastern Delta
and attempt to overrun several district capitals—a sort of
"mini-Tet" campaign—and thereby score a propaganda coup.

In Chau Doc, some officials believe the NVA may break
down into small units and spread across the Delta, combining
with local VC forces to attack targets far more diverse and
widespread than a few district capitals. "We better get over
this Tet-mini-Tet psychology because I think Charlie has,"
says one Chau Doc officer.

In any case, whichever tack the NVA take, it likely would
serve the political and psychological purpose of demonstrating
South Vietnamese military vulnerability at a time of perhaps
too much, too optimistic talk about Vietnamization. It could
also serve to warn President Nixon that Hanoi isn't about to
make American withdrawal pains any easier.

How the NVA are infiltrating the Delta is seen next day at
a small village near the border. It's 9 a.m., and a military operation is in progress. Vietnamese Regional Force (RF) troops
in helmets and flak jackets are cautiously moving up a hillside
just off the road. They're searching for the remnants of a Vietcong unit that in the early morning hours overran a PF outpost on the hilltop, killing four PF along with a PF wife and
four children. The PF had deployed no troops to set up night
ambushes outside their outpost, a move that might have in-
tercepted the enemy attack.

Lying at the edge of the road, caked in dust and crusted
blood, are a wounded PF and a little girl, her face split open
by a grenade fragment. Three-wheeled Lambretta buses,
packed with passengers and sacks of brown sugar smuggled
from Cambodia, rattle down the road. The war-hardened passengers barely bother to glance at the wounded or at the RF
troops moving up the hillside 20 yards away.

The significant thing about this Vietcong attack isn't the
body count. The VC attack was merely one of a dozen en-
counters around Chau Doc province the previous night with

the aim of diverting allied forces—and particularly helicopter gunships—from border surveillance to defensive support. The local VC were attracting allied attention so the NVA regulars could slip smoothly across the border. The plan succeeded: An NVA battalion crossed from Cambodia during the night, it was later learned.

American military men have long been frustrated by the sanctuary that enemy troops have in Cambodia. A helicopter flight along the Vinh Te canal, which separates Chau Doc from Cambodia, illustrates the point. A mile or two inside Cambodia are several clusters of buildings considerably larger than thatched peasant huts. "That over there is an NVA supply depot. And that one there is a VC training center," says a young American major, casual as a tourist guide.

Allied military forces, of course, aren't permitted to attack enemy troops or facilities in Cambodia. This is partly to avoid angering Cambodia and forcing it actively into the war on the side of the Communists. And, while allied strikes might yield instant tactical dividends, the longer range result likely would be to widen the scope of the war and necessitate still more U.S. troops.

The chopper swings away from the border and lands at Tre Ton, one of five district capitals of Chau Doc province. A district is the smallest military-administrative division of Vietnam, and it is the American advisory team at this level (generally four to eight men) that has the worm's eye view of how the war is going. The senior U.S. district adviser in Tre Ton is Maj. William R. Fields, an exceptionally able two-year veteran of Vietnam.

The town of Tre Ton lies in the shadow of Nui Co To, one of the dark, forbidding Seven Sister mountains. Nui Co To is both Tre Ton's most dramatic success story and one of its most persistent problems. For nearly two decades, the Vietcong dominated the mountain. Last year the allies mounted a major campaign for Nui Co To and by April of this year succeeded in capturing the enemy's vast cave and tunnel complexes. Some 250 allied troops, many of them Cambodian mercenaries working for the U.S. Special Forces, died in the campaign.

Next, the allies tried to render the caves and tunnels uninhabitable, by pounding them with B52 air strikes, by exploding tons of TNT, by trying to fill the holes with motor oil and even snakes. The rock vaults proved indestructible. Consequently, to keep the 100 or so VC who still roam the mountainsides from moving back into their former refuges, Vietnamese troops are occupied in static defense positions in the caves, a waste of much-needed mobile manpower.

An intense pacification program in hamlets at the base of Nui Co To has made modest gains. Most of these hamlets were solidly controlled by the Vietcong seven months ago but now have at least a daytime GVN presence. Driving through these hamlets one is met by sullen stares. "These people don't know yet if the GVN is here to stay or if the VC are coming back. They haven't decided which way to lean yet, but at least they're debating it for the first time," says Maj. Fields.

It's dusk, and along the road a thin line of peasants, many leading cows or water buffalo, is moving away from the mountainbase hamlets and toward the town of Tre Ton. These people feel reasonably secure farming their fields by day but dare not sleep in their home hamlets for fear of VC reprisals or allied artillery fire. It's a chancy business being a Vietnamese civilian in a "contested" area. This same morning, for example, two civilians had been killed by an American helicopter as they ran across a rice paddy to try and retrieve a parachute that had been used to drop a flare the night before.

Throughout the district, the most significant progress, says Maj. Fields, has been in providing village and hamlet security through the Popular Self Defense Force (PSDF) program. Begun last year, this program provides minimal training and hand-me-down weapons to the residents of villages and hamlets and thus, for the first time since the war began, permits them to defend their homes and families.

"PSDF is the single best investment ever made in this country. Most people here wouldn't support the VC if they had a reasonable choice. PSDF gives them that choice. It lets them make and defend that choice," the major says. He recounts the case of a VC tax collector who sauntered into a long-compliant village one recent night to pick up monthly tax revenues. He was nabbed by the newly formed PSDF unit and hacked to death on the spot.

While the PSDF gets rave reviews from Americans here, Vietnamese army units seem more of a mixed bag. Regular army troops (ARVN), who operate only sporadically in the district, haven't been noticeably aggressive in seeking out enemy forces on the mountains. The district's Vietnamese Regional Force companies generally operate only by day and return to static defense positions at night.

And in the critical struggle to root out the Vietcong infrastructure, it's the U.S.-controlled Provincial Reconnaissance Units (PRU) that have proved highly effective at unorthodox night strikes, while the GVN-controlled National Police Field Force operates only in the late afternoon between the end of siesta and dinnertime.

Thus, here in Tre Ton, as elsewhere, the truth about the Vietnamese armed forces lies somewhere between the view of a Can Tho colonel who calls them "a bunch of little tigers" and the opinion of a Chau Doc sergeant who says "the only way to get them to move is to stick a bayonet up their rear ends."

The small U.S. advisory team in Tre Ton has one domestic problem all its own. As told by Sgt. James Smith: "We had the mother of all rats living in our outhouse. That damned rat must have measured three feet long, weighed maybe 40 pounds. It flipped our big, old tabby cat half way 'cross the compound. Haven't seen that cat since. Dogs were scared to go near that mother rat. We had this master sergeant visiting one time, and he went out to the outhouse at night, and next thing we hear is pots flying and water splashing and old sarge comes screamin' out of that outhouse. From then on that mother rat owned that outhouse after dark. Man, that rat used to eat poison like it was bread. We finally got the mother, but it took enough poison to kill a couple of cows."

If U.S advisers at the district level get thoroughly involved in both the mundane and arcane aspects of Vietnamese life, there are other American units that could profit by a bit more contact with the Vietnamese.

For example, back in Chau Phu, capital of Chau Doc province, the U.S. Navy, which helps patrol the Delta's rivers and canals, has arranged a demonstration of military gadgetry to impress the Vietnamese province chief. The gadget is an MSD (mine sweeper drone), an unmanned, remote-controlled, armor-plated boat about 15 feet long. Directed by radio waves from a black control box, the MSD can drag a chain across waterways to cut enemy mines. ("We could also use it to ram and explode enemy sampans, but that would get pretty expensive," says a Navy officer. An MSD costs about $45,000, he adds.)

The province chief and entourage are welcomed aboard a U.S. Navy patrol boat by a natty USN lieutenant commander and his well-starched staff. The black control box is unveiled and the MSD is made to loop, circle, turn right-angle corners and zig-zag back and forth across the river. The province chief, a worldly colonel who has spent the better part of three years studying in the U.S., including a term at the National War College, and who consequently speaks fluent English, is in excellent humor. At least he is until the lieutenant commander calls on a young U.S. seaman to explain the MSD controls.

"You see boat. Hard work boat. Boat go far away. No good. Boat go quick quick. Good. Stop boat push button. Box make stop go. Make boat go. Quick quick. Same same other boat no men . . ." rattles off the proud young seaman in flawless pidgin English of the sort that snows Vietnamese bargirls but not Vietnamese colonels. The innocent U.S. Navy officers smile on happily. The province chief manages a forced smile. And so ends the U.S. Navy's public relations program for this particular day.

The return trip to Saigon is remarkably uneventful, interesting only in that the road through Sandec province is now considered reasonably safe whereas 10 months ago it assuredly was not. At mid-afternoon, nearing Saigon, the Americans drive past three companies of regular ARVN soldiers, accompanied by armored personnel carriers, marching down the middle of the road—hardly the place to locate and engage enemy forces. "Maybe it's a parade," murmurs an optimist.

It's nightfall, and the dusty Volkswagen rolls into downtown Saigon. At the city's busiest intersection, directly in front of the colonnaded National Assembly Building, a beefy American construction worker in a gray Chevrolet collides with two Vietnamese soldiers on a Honda who are trying to run a red light.

The American rolls up his windows and accelerates, dragging along the battered Honda that has hooked on the Chevy bumper. The two Vietnamese soldiers give chase. They run alongside the moving car, pounding on the windshield and screaming "dirty American bastard! stinking American son of a bitch!"

Downtown Saigon's normal assemblage of dirty picture peddlers, sidewalk money changers, barhopping GIs, prostitutes, pickpockets and beggars go on blissfully about their business. Home again.

The Wall Street Journal, November 10, 1969

The My Lai Massacre

by Seymour M. Hersh

Lieutenant Accused of Murdering 109 Civilians

FORT BENNING, Ga., Nov. 13—Lt. William L. Calley Jr., 26 years old, is a mild-mannered, boyish-looking Vietnam combat veteran with the nickname "Rusty." The Army is completing an investigation of charges that he deliberately murdered at least 109 Vietnamese civilians in a search-and-destroy mission in March 1968 in a Viet Cong stronghold known as "Pinkville."

Calley has formally been charged with six specifications of mass murder. Each specification cites a number of dead, adding up to the 109 total, and charges that Calley did "with premeditation murder . . . Oriental human beings, whose names and sex are unknown, by shooting them with a rifle."

The Army calls it murder; Calley, his counsel and others associated with the incident describe it as a case of carrying out orders.

"Pinkville" has become a widely known code word among the military in a case that many officers and some Congressmen believe will become far more controversial than the recent murder charges against eight Green Berets.

Army investigation teams spent nearly one year studying the incident before filing charges against Calley, a platoon leader of the Eleventh Brigade of the Americal Division at the time of the killings.

Calley was formally charged on or about Sept. 6, 1969, in the multiple deaths, just a few days before he was due to be released from active service.

Calley has since hired a prominent civilian attorney, former Judge George W. Latimer of the U.S. Court of Military Appeals, and is now awaiting a military determination of whether the evidence justifies a general court-martial. Pentagon offi-

cials describe the present stage of the case as the equivalent
of a civilian grand jury proceeding.

Calley, meanwhile, is being detained at Fort Benning, where
his movements are sharply restricted. Even his exact location
on the base is a secret; neither the provost marshal, nor the
Army's Criminal Investigation Division knows where he is
being held.

The Army has refused to comment on the case, "in order
not to prejudice the continuing investigation and rights of the
accused." Similarly, Calley—although agreeing to an interview—refused to discuss in detail what happened on March
16, 1968.

However, many other officers and civilian officials, some
angered by Calley's action and others angry that charges of
murder were filed in the case, talked freely in interviews at
Fort Benning and Washington.

These factors are not in dispute:

The Pinkville area, about six miles northeast of Quang
Ngai, had been a Viet Cong fortress since the Vietnam war
began. In early February 1968, a company of the Eleventh
Brigade, as part of Task Force Barker, pushed through the
area and was severely shot up.

Calley's platoon suffered casualties. After the Communist
Tet offensive in February 1968, a larger assault was mounted,
again with high casualties and little success. A third attack was
quickly mounted and it was successful.

The Army claimed 128 Viet Cong were killed. Many civilians
also were killed in the operation. The area was a free fire zone
from which all non-Viet Cong residents had been urged, by
leaflet, to flee. Such zones are common throughout Vietnam.

One man who took part in the mission with Calley said that
in the earlier two attacks "we were really shot up."

"Every time we got hit it was from the rear," he said. "So
the third time in there the order came down to go in and
make sure no one was behind.

"We were told to just clear the area. It was a typical combat
assault formation. We came in hot, with a cover of artillery in
front of us, came down the line and destroyed the village.

"There are always some civilian casualties in a combat operation. He isn't guilty of murder."

The order to clear the area was relayed from the battalion commander to the company commander to Calley, the source said.

Calley's attorney said in an interview: "This is one case that should never have been brought. Whatever killing there was was in a firefight in connection with the operation."

"You can't afford to guess whether a civilian is a Viet Cong or not. Either they shoot you or you shoot them.

"This case is going to be important—to what standard do you hold a combat officer in carrying out a mission?

"There are two instances where murder is acceptable to anybody: where it is excusable and where it is justified. If Calley did shoot anybody because of the tactical situation or while in a firefight, it was either excusable or justifiable."

Adding to the complexity of the case is the fact that investigators from the Army inspector general's office, which conducted the bulk of the investigation, considered filing charges against at least six other men involved in the action March 16.

A Fort Benning infantry officer has found that the facts of the case justify Calley's trial by general court-martial on charges of premeditated murder.

Pentagon officials said that the next steps are for the case to go to Calley's brigade commander and finally to the Fort Benning post commander for findings on whether there should be a court-martial. If they so hold, final charges and specifications will be drawn up and made public at that time, the officials said.

Calley's friends in the officer corps at Fort Benning, many of them West Point graduates, are indignant. However, knowing the high stakes of the case, they express their outrage in private.

"They're using this as a Goddamned example," one officer complained. "He's a good soldier. He followed orders.

"There weren't any friendlies in the village. The orders were to shoot anything that moved."

Another officer said "It could happen to any of us. He has killed and has seen a lot of killing . . . Killing becomes nothing in Vietnam. He knew that there were civilians there, but he also knew that there were VC among them."

A third officer, also familiar with the case, said: "There's this question—I think anyone who goes to (Viet) Nam asks it. What's a civilian? Someone who works for us at day and puts on Viet Cong pajamas at night?"

There is another side of the Calley case—one that the Army cannot yet disclose. Interviews have brought out the fact that the investigation into the Pinkville affair was initiated six months after the incident, only after some of the men who served under Calley complained.

The Army has photographs purported to be of the incident, although these have not been introduced as evidence in the case, and may not be.

"They simply shot up this village and (Calley) was the leader of it," said one Washington source. "When one guy refused to do it, Calley took the rifle away and did the shooting himself."

Asked about this, Calley refused to comment.

One Pentagon officer discussing the case tapped his knee with his hand and remarked, "Some of those kids he shot were this high. I don't think they were Viet Cong. Do you?"

None of the men interviewed about the incident denied that women and children were shot.

A source of amazement among all those interviewed was that the story had yet to reach the press.

"Pinkville has been a word among GIs for a year," one official said. "I'll never cease to be amazed that it hasn't been written about before."

A high-ranking officer commented that he first heard talk of the Pinkville incident soon after it happened; the officer was on duty in Saigon at the time.

Why did the Army choose to prosecute this case? On what is it basing the charge that Calley acted with premeditation before killing? The court-martial should supply the answers to these questions, but some of the men already have their opinions.

"The Army knew it was going to get clobbered on this at some point," one military source commented. "If they don't prosecute somebody, if this stuff comes out without the Army taking some action, it could be even worse."

Another view that many held was that the top level of the military was concerned about possible war crime tribunals after the Vietnam war.

As for Calley—he is smoking four packs of cigarettes daily and getting out of shape. He is 5-foot-3, slender, with expressionless gray eyes and thinning brown hair. He seems slightly bewildered and hurt by the charges against him. He says he wants nothing more than to be cleared and return to the Army.

"I know this sounds funny," he said in an interview, "but I like the Army . . . and I don't want to do anything to hurt it."

Friends described Calley as a "gung-ho Army man . . . Army all the way." Ironically, even his stanchest supporters admit, his enthusiasm may be somewhat to blame.

"Maybe he did take some order to clear out the village a little bit too literally," one friend said, "but he's a fine boy."

Calley had been shipped home early from Vietnam, after the Army refused his request to extend his tour of duty. Until the incident at Pinkville, he had received nothing but high ratings from his superior officers. He was scheduled to be awarded the Bronze and Silver Stars for his combat efforts, he said. He has heard nothing about the medals since arriving at Fort Benning.

Calley was born in Miami, Fla., and flunked out of the Palm Beach Junior College before enlisting in the Army. He became a second lieutenant in September 1967, shortly after going to Vietnam. The Army lists his home of record as Waynesville, N.C.

An information sheet put out by the public affairs officer of the Americal Division the day after the March 16 engagement contained this terse mention of the incident: "The swiftness with which the units moved into the area surprised the enemy. After the battle the Eleventh Brigade moved into the village searching each hut and tunnel."

St. Louis Post-Dispatch, November 13, 1969

Hamlet Attack Called "Point-Blank Murder"

WASHINGTON, Nov. 20—Three American soldiers who participated in the March 1968 attack on a Vietnam village called Pinkville said in interviews made public today that their Army combat unit perpetrated, in the words of one, "pointblank murder" on the residents.

"The whole thing was so deliberate. It was point-blank murder and I was standing there watching it," said Sgt. Michael Bernhardt, Franklin Square, N.Y., now completing his Army tour at Fort Dix, N.J.

Bernhardt was a member of one of three platoons of an Eleventh Infantry Brigade company under the command of Capt. Ernest Medina. The company entered the Viet Cong–dominated area on March 16, 1968, when on a search-and-destroy mission. Pinkville, known to Vietnamese as Song My village, is about six miles northeast of Quang Ngai.

The Army has charged Lt. William L. Calley Jr., Miami, one of Medina's platoon leaders, with the murder of 109 South Vietnamese civilians in the attack. A squad leader in Calley's platoon, Sgt. David Mitchell, St. Francisville, La., is under investigation for assault with intent to murder.

At least four other men, including Medina, are under investigation in connection with the incident. Calley and his attorney, George W. Latimer, Salt Lake City, have said that the unit was under orders to clear the area.

Bernhardt, interviewed at Fort Dix, said he had been delayed on the operation and fell slightly behind the company, then led by Calley's platoon, as it entered the village. This is his version of what took place:

"They (Calley's men) were doing a whole lot of shooting up there, but none of it was incoming—I'd been around enough to tell that. I figured they were advancing on the village with fire power.

"I walked up and saw these guys doing strange things. They were doing it three ways. One: They were setting fire to the hootches and huts and waiting for people to come out and then shooting them up. Two: They were going into the hootches and shooting them up. Three: They were gathering people in groups and shooting them.

"As I walked in, you could see piles of people all through the village . . . all over. They were gathered up into large groups.

"I saw them shoot an M-79 (grenade launcher) into a group of people who were still alive. But it (the shooting) was mostly done with a machine gun. They were shooting women and children just like anybody else.

"We met no resistance and I only saw three captured weapons. We had no casualties. It was just like any other Vietnamese village—old Papa-san, women and kids. As a matter of fact, I don't remember seeing one military-age male in the entire place, dead or alive. The only prisoner I saw was about 50."

An Army communique reporting on the operation said that Medina's company recovered two M-1 rifles, a carbine, a short-wave radio and enemy documents in the assault. The Viet Cong body count was listed as 128 and there was no mention of civilian casualties.

Bernhardt, short and intense, told his story in staccato fashion, with an obvious sense of relief at finally talking about it. At one point he said to his interviewer: "You're surprised? I wouldn't be surprised at anything these dudes (the men who did the shooting) did."

Bernhardt said he had no idea precisely how many villagers were shot. He said that he had heard death counts ranging from 170 to more than 700.

Bernhardt also said he had no idea whether Calley personally shot 109 civilians, as the Army has charged. However, he said, "I know myself that he killed a whole lot of people." Residents of the Pinkville areas have told newspapermen that 567 villagers were killed in the operation.

Why did the men run amuck?

"It's my belief," the sergeant said, "that the company was conditioned to do this. The treatment was lousy . . . We were always out in the bushes. I think they were expecting us to run into resistance at Pinkville and also expecting them (the Viet Cong) to use the people as hostages."

A few days before the mission, he said, the men's general contempt for Vietnamese civilians intensified when some GIs walked into a landmine, injuring nearly 20 and killing at least one member of the company.

Why didn't he report the incident at the time?

"After it was all over, some colonel came down to the firebase where we were stationed and asked about it, but we heard no further. Later they (Medina and some other officers) called me over to the command post and asked me not to write my Congressman."

(The Army subsequently substantiated Bernhardt's accusation. In a private letter dated Aug. 6, 1969, Col. John G. Hill Jr., a deputy for staff action control in the office of Army Chief of Staff William C. Westmoreland, wrote that Medina acknowledged that he had requested Bernhardt to wait until a brigade investigation of the incident was completed. Nothing came of the investigation.)

Bernhardt said that about 90 per cent of the 60 to 70 men in the short-handed company were involved in the shootings. He took no part, he said. "I only shoot at people who shoot at me," was his explanation.

"The Army ordered me not to talk," Bernhardt told the interviewer. "But there are some orders that I have to personally decide whether to obey; I have my own conscience to consider.

"The whole thing has kind of made me wonder if I could trust people any more."

His opinion, he said, is that a higher ranking officer must have ordered the destruction of Pinkville. "Calley's just a small fry," he said.

Bernhardt said the Army must have known at high levels just what did happen at Pinkville.

"They've got pictures. Some dude went along on the mission and shot pictures," he said.

Bernhardt said the photographs were shown to him in the Article 32 proceeding, which concluded that the charges against Calley were justified.

"They showed a mass of people . . . this pile-up of people. I don't see how anybody could say it was artillery or crossfire that killed those people," he said.

(The Cleveland Plain Dealer printed today photographs showing South Vietnamese civilians allegedly killed in the incident. It said the photographs came from a former Army combat photographer, Ronald L. Haeberle, Cleveland.

(Haeberle said in a copyright story that he joined the company just before it entered the village and heard from the men that the villagers were suspected of being Viet Cong sympathizers. He said he saw men, women and children killed.)

Another witness to the shootings was Michael Terry, Orem, Utah, then a member of the C Platoon of Medina's company and now a sophomore at nearby Brigham Young University. Interviewed at his home, Terry said he, too, came on the scene moments after the killings began.

"They just marched through shooting everybody," he said. "Seems like no one said anything . . . They just started pulling people out and shooting them."

At one point, he said, more than 20 villagers were lined up in front of a ditch and shot.

"They had them in a group standing over a ditch—just like a Nazi-type thing . . . One officer ordered a kid to machine-gun everybody down, but the kid just couldn't do it. He threw the machine gun down and the officer picked it up . . ." Terry said.

"I don't remember seeing any men in the ditch. Mostly women and kids."

Later, he and the platoon team he headed were taking a lunch break near the ditch when, Terry said, he noticed "some of them were still breathing . . . They were pretty badly shot up. They weren't going to get any medical help, and so we shot them. Shot maybe five of them . . ."

Why did it happen?

"I think that probably the officers didn't really know if they were ordered to kill the villagers or not . . . A lot of guys feel that they (the South Vietnamese civilians) aren't human beings; we just treated them like animals."

Apparently one officer, who was not from Medina's company, attempted to halt the shootings. Terry and Bernhardt both reported that a helicopter pilot from an aviation support unit landed in the midst of the incident and attempted to quell it.

The officer warned that he would report the shootings. On the next day, the pilot was killed in action and the subsequent investigation started by officials of the Eleventh Brigade was dropped after one and a half days because of insufficient evidence.

Terry said he first learned of the present investigation when he was interviewed last spring by a colonel from the Army Inspector General's office. Bernhardt was not questioned until a team from the Army's Criminal Investigation Division visited him two months ago.

The third witness to the Pinkville shootings cannot be identified. He is still on active duty with the Army on the West Coast. But he corroborated in detail the Bernhardt and Terry descriptions of that day in March 1968.

"I was shooting pigs and a chicken while the others were shooting people," he said. "It isn't just a nightmare; I'm completely aware of how real this was.

"It's something I don't think a person would understand—the reality of it just didn't hit me until recently, when I read about it again in the newspapers."

All three GIs were read key excerpts from a three-page letter sent in March by a former GI, Ronald Ridenhour, to the Army and 30 other officials, including some Senators. The letter outlined the Pinkville incident as he understood it. It was Ridenhour's persistence that prompted the Army to begin its high-level investigation in April.

Ridenhour, now a student at Claremont (Calif.) Men's College, was not in Medina's company and did not participate in the shootings. He relied on information from Terry and Bernhardt, among many others, to draft his letter.

Calley's attorney refused to comment on the new charges brought out in the interviews. But another source, discussing Calley's position, said, "Nobody's put the finger yet on the man who started it."

The source said also that he understood that Calley and other officers in the company initially resisted the orders but eventually did their job. Calley's platoon led the attack on the village, with the other units forming a horseshoe-shaped cordon around the area, to prevent enemy troops from fleeing.

"I don't care whether Calley used the best judgment or not—he was faced with a tough decision," the source said.

St. Louis Post-Dispatch, November 20, 1969

Ex-GI Tells of Killing Civilians at Pinkville

TERRE HAUTE, Ind., Nov. 25—A former GI told in interviews yesterday how he executed, under orders, dozens of South

Vietnamese civilians during the United States Army attack on the village of Song My in March 1968. He estimated that he and his fellow soldiers shot 370 villagers during the operation in what has become known as Pinkville.

Paul Meadlo, 22 years old, West Terre Haute, Ind., a farm community near the Illinois border, gave an eyewitness account—the first made available thus far—of what happened when a platoon led by Lt. William L. Calley Jr. entered Pinkville on a search-and-destroy mission. The Army has acknowledged that at least 100 civilians were killed by the men; Vietnamese survivors had told reporters that the death total was 567.

Meadlo, who was wounded in a mine accident the day after Pinkville, disclosed that the company captain, Ernest Medina, was in the area at the time of the shootings and made no attempt to stop them.

Calley, 26, Waynesville, N.C., has been accused of the premeditated murder of 109 civilians in the incident. Medina, as commander of the Eleventh Infantry Brigade unit, is under investigation for his role in the shootings. Last week the Army said that at least 24 other men were under investigation, including Calley's chief noncommissioned officer, Sgt. David Mitchell, 29, St. Francisville, La., who is being investigated for assault with intent to commit murder. Calley was ordered yesterday to stand general court-martial.

Here is Meadlo's story as given in interviews at his mother's home near Terre Haute:

"There was supposed to have been some Viet Cong in Pinkville and we began to make a sweep through it. Once we got there we began gathering up the people . . . started putting them in big mobs. There must have been about 40 or 45 civilians standing in one big circle in the middle of the village . . . Calley told me and a couple of other guys to watch them.

" 'You know what I want you to do with them' he said," Meadlo related. He and the others continued to guard the group. "About 10 minutes later Calley came back. 'Get with it,' he said. 'I want them dead.'

"So we stood about 10 or 15 feet away from them, then he (Calley) started shooting them. Then he told me to start shooting them. . . . I started to shoot them, but the other guys (who had been assigned to guard the civilians) wouldn't do it.

"So we (Meadlo and Calley) went ahead and killed them. I used more than a whole clip—actually I used four or five clips," Meadlo said. (There are 17 M-16 shells in a clip.) He estimated that he killed at least 15 civilians—or nearly half of those in the circle.

Asked what he thought at the time, Meadlo said, "I just thought we were supposed to do it." Later, he said that the shooting "did take a load off my conscience for the buddies we'd lost. It was just revenge, that's all it was."

The company had been in the field for 40 days without relief before the Pinkville incident on March 16, and had lost a number of men in mine accidents. Hostility to the Vietnamese was high in the company, Meadlo said.

The killings continued.

"We had about seven or eight civilians gathered in a hootch, and I was going to throw a hand grenade in. But someone told us to take them to the ditch (a drainage ditch in the village into which many civilians were herded—and shot).

"Calley was there and said to me, 'Meadlo, we've got another job to do.' So we pushed our seven to eight people in with the big bunch of them. And so I began shooting them all. So did Mitchell, Calley . . . (At this point Meadlo could not remember any more men involved). I guess I shot maybe 25 or 20 people in the ditch."

His role in the killings had not yet ended.

"After the ditch, there were just some people in hootches. I knew there were some people down in one hootch, maybe two or three, so I just threw a hand grenade in."

Meadlo is a tall, clean-cut son of an Indiana coal mine worker. He married his high-school sweetheart in suburban Terre Haute, began rearing a family (he has two children) and was drafted. He had been in Vietnam four months at the time of Pinkville. On the next day, March 17, his foot was blown off, when, while following Calley on an operation, a land mine was set off.

As Meadlo was waiting to be evacuated, other men in the

company had reported that he told Calley that "this was his (Meadlo's) punishment for what he had done the day before." He warned, according to onlookers, that Calley would have his day of judgment too. Asked about this, Meadlo said he could not remember.

Meadlo is back at a factory job now in Terre Haute, fighting to keep a full disability payment from the Veterans' Administration. The loss of his right foot seems to bother him less than the loss of his self-respect.

Like other members of his company, he had been called just days before the interview by an officer at Fort Benning, Ga., where Calley is being held, and advised that he should not discuss the case with reporters. But, like other members of his company, he seemed eager to talk.

"This has made him awful nervous," explained his mother, Mrs. Myrtle Meadlo, 57, New Goshen, Ind. "He seems like he just can't get over it.

"I sent them a good boy and they made him a murderer."

Why did he do it?

"We all were under orders," Meadlo said. "We all thought we were doing the right thing. . . . At the time it didn't bother me."

He began having serious doubts that night about what he had done at Pinkville. He says he still has them.

"The kids and the women—they didn't have any right to die.

"In the beginning," Meadlo said, "I just thought we were going to be murdering the Viet Cong." He, like other members of his company, had attended a squad meeting the night before, at which time Company Commander Medina promised the boys a good firefight.

Calley and his platoon were assigned the key role of entering the Pinkville area first.

"When we came in we thought we were getting fired on," Meadlo said, although the company suffered no casualties, apparently because the Viet Cong had fled from the area during the night.

"We came in from this open field, and somebody spotted this one gook out there. He was down in a shelter, scared and huddling. . . . Someone said, 'There's a gook over here,' and asked what to do with him. Mitchell said, 'Shoot him,' and he did. The gook was standing up and shaking and waving his arms when he got it.

"Then we came onto this hootch, and one door was hard to open."

Meadlo said he crashed through the door and "found an old man in there shaking.

"I told them, 'I got one,' and it was Mitchell who told me to shoot him. That was the first man I shot. He was hiding in a dugout, shaking his head and waving his arms, trying to tell me not to shoot him."

After the carnage, Meadlo said, "I heard that all we were supposed to do was kill the VC. Mitchell said we were just supposed to shoot the men."

Women and children also were shot. Meadlo estimated that at least 310 persons were shot to death by the Americans that day.

"I know it was far more than 100 as the U.S. Army now says. I'm absolutely sure of that. There were bodies all around."

He has some haunting memories, he says. "They didn't put up a fight or anything. The women huddled against their children and took it. They brought their kids real close to their stomachs and hugged them, and put their bodies over them trying to save them. It didn't do much good," Meadlo said.

Two things puzzled him. He vigorously disputes the repeated reports of an artillery barrage before the village was approached.

"There wasn't any artillery barrage whatsoever in the village. Only some gunships firing from above," he said.

The South Vietnamese government said Saturday that 20 civilians were killed in the Pinkville attack, most of them victims of tactical air strikes or an artillery barrage laid down before the U.S. troops moved in. The government denied reports of a massacre.

Meadlo is curious also about the role of Capt. Medina in the incident.

"I don't know if the C.O. (Company Commander) gave the order to kill or not, but he was right there when it happened. Why didn't he stop it? He and Calley passed each other quite a few times that morning, but didn't say anything. Medina just kept marching around. He could've put a stop to it anytime he wanted."

The whole operation took about 30 minutes, Meadlo said.

As for Calley, Meadlo told of an incident a few weeks before Pinkville.

"We saw this woman walking across this rice paddy and Calley said, 'Shoot her,' so we did. When we got there the girl was alive, had this hole in her side. Calley tried to get someone to shoot her again; I don't know if he did."

In addition, Calley and Medina had told the men before Pinkville, Meadlo said, "that if we ever shoot any civilians, we should go ahead and plant a hand grenade on them."

Meadlo is not sure, but he thinks the feel of death came quickly to the company once it got to Vietnam.

"We were cautious at first, but as soon as the first man was killed, a new feeling came through the company . . . almost as if we all knew there was going to be a lot more killing."

St. Louis Post-Dispatch, November 25, 1969

The Moratorium and the New Mobe

by Francine du Plessix Gray

ONE MORNING shortly after the Vietnam Moratorium demonstrations around the country last October, three of the young coördinators of the Vietnam Moratorium Committee—Sam Brown, David Mixner, and David Hawk—sat down at a table behind a bank of microphones in a room at the Ambassador Hotel in Washington and held a press conference for more than a hundred newsmen. The three young men belonged to the generation of activists who had played a role in forcing a President into retirement, thereby acquiring a strong sense of their own political power, and the success of their first Moratorium had exceeded all their hopes; they had an air of shy earnestness that morning, the self-conscious candor of men trying to handle sudden fame with modesty. To the right of the microphones was David Mixner, twenty-four, a hefty young man with a ready smile, who had organized caucuses in non-primary states for Eugene McCarthy's Presidential campaign in 1968; he had been on crutches for three months after the police threw him through a hotel window during the Chicago Convention, and he later suffered a heart attack, partly from the sheer exhaustion of his campaign work. At the left was David Hawk, twenty-six, a former divinity student with a pale, handsomely chiselled face, who had worked for McCarthy in New Hampshire and was facing trial in the near future for resisting the draft. In the center was Sam Brown, twenty-six, a slight, elegant man with a cinnamon-colored mustache, also a former divinity student, who had been chief student coördinator for the McCarthy campaign. Although Brown, Mixner, and Hawk were unusually poised for their age, they fidgeted uneasily before the microphones, looking uncomfortable over what they had to say. For one of the reasons they had called the conference was to announce the Moratorium Committee's endorsement of a vastly more

28

controversial group, called the New Mobilization Committee to End the War in Vietnam—a coalition of some sixty organizations, ranging in ideology from the Episcopal Peace Fellowship to the Socialist Workers' Party, which was proposing to bring several hundred thousand Americans to Washington in November for another large protest against the Vietnam war. The Moratorium was backed by many cautious liberals who regarded mass demonstrations as both too radical and rather obsolete and preferred quiet grass-roots organization. It may be for this reason that each of the three young leaders looked somewhat sheepish that day, as if he was about to announce his marriage to an older woman of doubtful reputation.

The television cameras started whirring, and Brown, the official spokesman for the group, rose and began to read in a soft voice from a prepared text: "The second series of activities of the Vietnam Moratorium is scheduled for November 13th and 14th. On these dates, local committees around the country will be continuing the efforts which got off to such a tremendous start on October 15th." Brown enumerated the various local activities planned for the November Moratorium: educational programs, such as canvassing and meetings with congressional leaders; community referendums and resolutions on immediate-withdrawal plans; symbolic activities, such as reading the names of the war dead, the wearing of black armbands, and church memorial services. But there was a distinct note of uneasiness in his voice as he began to read the last part of his text: "On November 13th and 14th, the New Mobilization Committee to End the War in Vietnam is sponsoring a March Against Death—a Vietnam memorial. Many supporters of the Moratorium will be participating in this solemn event. . . . On November 15th, the New Mobilization is sponsoring a peaceful and legal mass march and Rally in Washington, D.C. The four coördinators of the Vietnam Moratorium Committee, as well as many Moratorium supporters from around the country, plan to march. We will provide support for local Moratorium groups who will be coming to Washington and encourage others to join the March in Washington."

Brown sat down with an air of relief, and fielded the newsmen's questions in careful sociologese. "Our November activities will be of higher intensity and lower visibility. . . . The general term of response is that last month we had a significant new segment of the American community joining us. . . . We view our actions as complementary, not contradictory, to those of the New Mobilization."

The Moratorium's press conference ended a little before eleven o'clock, at which time a press conference called by the co-chairmen of the New Mobilization Committee to End the War in Vietnam—known as the New Mobe—was scheduled to take place in the same room. The next group of individuals who settled before the microphones were considerably older than the Moratorium leaders, and they had the weighty self-assurance of men who were veterans rather than newcomers in the business of demanding peace. At the table this time were Stewart Meacham, an imposing silver-haired former Presbyterian minister and union official, who was at present the Peace Education Secretary of the American Friends Service Committee; the Reverend Richard Fernandez, a minister of the United Church of Christ, who was director of Clergy and Laymen Concerned About Vietnam; Sidney Peck, swarthy and intense, a professor of sociology at Case Western Reserve University, in Cleveland; Cora Weiss, a handsome Riverdale housewife, who was a leader of Women Strike for Peace; Ron Young, a pacifist and draft-resister; and Sidney Lens, pacifist, trade-unionist, and prolific historian of the labor movement. Two other New Mobe co-chairmen were unable to attend the meeting—Douglas Dowd, a professor of economics at Cornell University, and David Dellinger, a pacifist who began his career by studying for the ministry at Union Theological Seminary, and who was standing trial in Chicago on a charge of conspiring to incite riot at the Democratic Convention of 1968.

The New Mobe leaders had a much more pronounced taste for political analysis than the preceding group, and they expounded it as from a pulpit or a union-meeting platform. "The present war strategy includes three distinct elements," Sidney Lens declaimed in a powerful voice. "One: U.S. military and economic aid to the Thieu-Ky government. Two: U.S. combat forces, which do the actual fighting. Three: U.S.

bombing and logistical support. The Nixon strategy proposes to eliminate only the ground combat troops supplied by the United States and continue the other two elements of the strategy unchanged. Mr. Nixon has no intention of ending the war but merely of changing assignments between the United States and its puppet allies. . . . Unfortunately for Mr. Nixon, as for Mr. Johnson, the American people want to get out of Vietnam. They are sick of the deaths, sick of the inflation, sick of the cut in living standards, sick of the tension, sick of confronting the danger of an enlarged war. To appease the American people, therefore, Nixon is seeking to reduce casualties by disengaging from ground combat. But he has no intention to disengage from the war itself unless and until he wins the political objectives the American ruling circles have demanded from the beginning—military bases, spheres of influence and trade, the continued presence of puppet regimes—in short, an iron ring around China." Lens ended with a demand for a cease-fire accompanied by withdrawal of American troops from Vietnam "as soon as boats and planes can take them out."

A reporter asked whether the speech that President Nixon had scheduled for November 3rd might not negate the purpose of the November demonstrations.

"Just as the deception of Nixon's policy as announced on his election platform created the Moratorium," Lens replied, "so the deception we anticipate on November 3rd will be an incentive for larger groups in Washington on November 15th."

The reporters pressed the New Mobe leaders much harder than they had the coördinators of the Moratorium.

"If this war could be won by either side, which side would you be on?" one newsman asked.

"We're on the side of the American people winning honor by getting out!" Lens roared.

"Is there not a member of the Communist Party on your steering committee?" asked another newsman.

Stewart Meacham answered, "We are a broad coalition of individuals connected with some sixty organizations, and one of the members of our coalition is Mr. Arnold Johnson, peace secretary of the American Communist Party. The only two principles at work in the composition of Mobe are: one, the principle of non-violence; two, the principle of non-exclusion, which we believe essential to a rich, free society."

But the principle of non-exclusion was far from settled, and was to come up repeatedly as the two groups coöperated in preparing for the November demonstrations.

The Moratorium, which represents a tradition of political centrism, is made up largely of Americans who are against the war but are still determined to work within the two-party system. The New Mobe is in the tradition of American radicalism which—whether practiced by Thoreau, by William Lloyd Garrison, or by Eugene Debs—has been forced by the very nature of our two-party system to operate outside of the political mainstream. Considering the long-standing distrust between the two traditions, the alliance worked out between the left and the center of the peace movement for the November demonstrations was a remarkable achievement.

The origins of the Moratorium are recent and relatively uncomplicated. In the spring of 1969, Jerome Grossman, a fifty-two-year-old Massachusetts envelope manufacturer who had been active in the McCarthy campaign, suggested to Sam Brown that a series of nationwide strikes, increasing by one day a month, should be organized in protest against the war. The word "strike" seemed too radical to Brown, but he adapted Grossman's ideas to a program under which peaceful pauses in "business as usual" would be coördinated across the nation as long as the Vietnam war continued. Brown pulled into the program some friends who had been active in the Presidential campaigns of both McCarthy and Robert Kennedy, Grossman helped in raising seed money for the project, and the Moratorium began operations in midsummer, in offices on the eighth floor of the building at 1029 Vermont Avenue, four blocks from the White House. Right from the start, the Moratorium was marked by the same romantic improvisation and youthful enthusiasm that had characterized the McCarthy campaign. Its October 15th success was as unexpected and exhilarating as that of the New Hampshire primary, and its later deflation proved again that charm and idealism are not enough to keep a nationwide political movement successful.

The origins of the New Mobe, which has always stayed aloof from electoral campaigning, are older and more complex. They are rooted in the work of the great American pacifist A. J. Muste, a Protestant minister, who died early in 1967, six months after laying the groundwork of the Mobilization to End the War in Vietnam. Muste—to cite only a few of his activities—was the leader of the textile workers' strike in Lawrence, Massachusetts, in 1919, an official of the Brookwood Labor College in the nineteen-twenties, and a founder in the nineteen-thirties of the Trotskyites' American Workers Party. In the nineteen-forties, Muste was a pioneer in the agitation for nuclear disarmament and for repeal of the draft laws. In the nineteen-fifties, he played a crucial role in various civil-rights organizations, particularly in the direction of CORE, and had a large influence in the formation of Martin Luther King's and Bayard Rustin's philosophies of non-violence. Throughout these decades, Muste was also an active leader in the Fellowship of Reconciliation, an international pacifist organization founded during the First World War. Although he went through a two-year Marxist period in the nineteen-thirties with the American Workers Party, he came to believe, in the last two decades of his life, that in a nuclear age it was the peace movement, not the working class or any political grouping, that would be the most important force in reforming society. But Muste argued that pacifism could only attract a sizable number of converts if a committed minority called dramatic attention to its principles. It was his contention that the peace movement could only affect the uncommitted by "mobilizing" people, by getting them out into the street to confront authority, and that only men "acting with their bodies" in non-violent demonstrations could create enough radical change in individuals' consciences to bring about a just and warless society. Muste's politics of the street, which blended the techniques of labor protest with the principles of non-violence advocated by Tolstoy and Gandhi, had already been widely and effectively used in the civil-rights movement when the United States became heavily involved in the Vietnam war in 1965, and hundreds of Americans turned to Muste for leadership. It was a motley group that sought him out, for throughout his career Muste had been stern in his assertion that peace groups must remain non-exclusive, that any man who wished to work for peace—be he a conservative Episcopal minister, a Communist, or a student activist—must be admitted into the peace movement as long as he was willing to abide by the rules of non-violence. "If what we believe is not strong enough to absorb all these people," Muste said, "then it is not entirely real."

The first Mobilization meeting, which Muste presided over in Cleveland in July, 1966, was attended by Quakers and Trotskyites, liberal academics and campus rebels, morally-outraged Methodist ministers, and glandular leftists rooting for the Vietcong. Cleveland had been chosen as a meeting place because some of the nation's first anti-Vietnam teach-ins had been held there, at Case Western Reserve University, in the spring of 1965, and also because two prominent members of the University's teach-in Committee—Sidney Peck, of the Sociology Department, and Benjamin Spock, of the Medical School—were eager to have it meet there. The peace movement was badly split at that time over the problems of whether to include the far left in its activities and whether to demand immediate withdrawal from Vietnam. Indeed, these two issues divided and almost destroyed SANE in 1966. Under Muste's guidance, the first Mobilization convention dealt forthrightly with both problems, affirming his principle of non-exclusion and setting forth more strongly than ever the thesis that Vietnam was not an accident or a miscalculation but a symptom of a deep sickness in American foreign policy.

Muste died, at the age of eighty-two, in February of 1967, after returning from a trip to Hanoi. He had gone there with David Dellinger, leading a delegation of pacifists. And after Muste's death it was Dellinger who became the moving spirit of the Mobilization, and a chief tactician for the increasingly turbulent peace demonstrations of the next two years: the New York rally of April, 1967, the March on the Pentagon in the following fall, and the demonstrations at the Chicago Convention in the summer of 1968. The violence that occurred in Chicago alienated a great many Americans from peace demonstrations, and, largely because of this new national mood, Sidney Peck invited a number of people who had been associated with the Mobilization to meet in Cleveland in July, 1969, to discuss which way the peace movement should go next. It was decided that all future protests were to be both legal and non-violent in nature, and great emphasis was placed on drawing new support from four groups in which anti-war sentiment had been growing: the labor movement, the armed forces, high-school students, and the religious community. The New Mobe of 1969 was an infinitely broader and less radical coalition than the first Mobe of 1966 had been. There was still a motley variety of Old and New Leftists on the New Mobe's national steering committee, notably half a dozen Trotskyites, who got on it by packing the convention with their followers. But it also incorporated a wide variety of middle-of-the-road religious, pacifist, political, and labor groups, including the National Council of Churches, the United Methodist Church, the New Democratic Coalition, and District 65 of the A.F.L.-C.I.O.'s Retail, Wholesale, and Department Store Workers' Union. The only significant New Left groups not included were those which refused to pledge themselves to legal and non-violent tactics, such as the Yippies and the Weatherman faction of S.D.S. (which had announced that its slogan was not "End the War" anymore but "Bring the War Home"). One member of the New Mobe's steering committee, Irwin Bock, who posed as a representative of the Veterans for Peace group, later surfaced at the Chicago conspiracy trial as an undercover policeman, which prompted Sidney Lens to say, "We're a *really* broad coalition. We range from the Trots to the Chicago police."

The New Mobe met in Cleveland just four days after the Vietnam Moratorium Committee made the first public announcement of its existence. Right from the start, there was at least one link between the two groups in the person of David Hawk, a coördinator of the Moratorium, who attended the New Mobe convention, received its enthusiastic backing of the Moratorium, and was elected to the New Mobe's steering committee. But in the months that followed the relationship between the two organizations, whose headquarters were only a floor apart at 1029 Vermont Avenue, were often strained. The powerful and distinguished company of Americans who had expressed their support of the Moratorium by the end of September—including John Kenneth Galbraith,

Richard Goodwin, Walter Reuther, Republican Party Chairman Representative Rogers Morton, and Democratic Party
Chairman Senator Fred Harris, along with some forty other
members of Congress—made it difficult for the Moratorium
to be officially affiliated with a group that contained a sizable
sprinkling of the Old and New Left and that denounced the
imperialist nature of American foreign policy in its entirety.

A typical example of the Moratorium backers' uneasiness
about the New Mobe was a phone call made early in October
by Adam Walinsky, a former Kennedy aide who was directing
Moratorium activities in New York City, to Richard Fernandez, a member of the executive committee of the New Mobe.
Walinsky suggested that if Arnold Johnson, the one Communist Party member on the New Mobe's steering committee, would "step down," the New Mobe would be "more
acceptable" to the Moratorium. "Wisdom might indicate that
to retain your following this might be necessary," Walinsky
said. Fernandez reacted to this pressure against Johnson, a
sixty-five-year-old graduate of the Union Theological Seminary who had been a close friend of Muste's, with a burst of
quixotic humor. "My inclination," Fernandez said, "would
be to add ten C.P.s to the steering committee, to provide a
front for Arnold Johnson." According to Fernandez, Walinsky
was not amused. Some leaders of the New Mobe have said
they find it symptomatic that one member of the American
Communist Party, a conservative and impotent organization
of a few thousand members (a fifth of whom are estimated to
be F.B.I. men), which preaches peaceful coexistence and
whose radical potential is about that of the Salvation Army,
still elicits panic from some of the highly educated men who
have endorsed the Moratorium. The issue produced friction
between the two groups. And many New Mobe people accused the Moratorium backers of encouraging Red-baiting by
the right-wing press—which has often referred to the New
Mobe as "Communist-led" and "Communist-inspired"—and
of further aggravating the Red-baiting tendencies of the
Nixon Administration.

It could be argued that the Moratorium's original program
of coördinating nationwide walkouts and shutdowns, aug-

mented by a day a month until the war came to an end, was
actually much more revolutionary than the New Mobe's plan
to assemble half a million Americans in Washington for one
peaceful afternoon. Like most under-thirty activists, the young
men and women who devised the Moratorium's low-keyed
style of selling peace tend to regard the warmed-up Marxist
rhetoric of the Old Left not with fear but with a mixture of
humor and disdain. The Moratorium leaders are convinced
that strident demonstrations can only alienate the broad middle-class constituency from which they hope to win a symbolic
vote for peace. Although the young Moratorium leaders come
from vastly different backgrounds, they are all advocates of
what they call the "politics of low visibility," which is the
direct opposite of the high-visibility politics that A. J. Muste
had hoped would change the consciences of men. Sam Brown,
whose father runs a chain of shoe stores in the Midwest, who
speaks constantly of the need to maintain close liaison with
"the Hill," and who is said to have congressional ambitions
himself, is extremely sensitive to what people will think back
in his home town of Council Bluffs, Iowa. "The very people
whom the movement is trying to bring in have become wary
of demonstrations," he says. "We have to go back to a slow,
tough building operation." David Mixner, the son of a warehouse worker, started organizing migratory farm workers at
the age of fifteen, and specializes in getting labor backing for
the Moratorium. "We are trying to create a non-partisan base
in every congressional district," he says. "We're going to a
broader coalition with new and different entry levels. For my
father, who is a member of the Teamsters' Union, wearing a
black armband to work on October 15th was a major event.
He debated it for days. He's not ready to march in Washington." David Hawk, son of a Pennsylvania electronics sales-
man, was an all-American diver at Cornell and describes
himself as having been brought up in a "Nixon–Billy Graham
sort of home." The fourth coördinator of the Vietnam Moratorium Committee, Marge Sklencar, daughter of a Chicago
research chemist, spent a year in a convent of Franciscan nuns
before going to Mundelein College, in Chicago, where she
was president both of the student body and of the S.D.S.

chapter. Like the others, she is convinced that the Moratorium's grass-roots tactics are "more difficult, radical, and effective" than any demonstration.

The atmosphere of the Moratorium offices is characterized by collegiate cheerfulness and miniskirted volunteers wearing shiny buttons that say "McGovernment" and "You're a Good Man, Charlie Goodell." Larry Kudlow, one of the Moratorium's fifteen regional organizers, is typical of the young Moratorium activists searching for a new style in politics. Kudlow, who is twenty-five, worked for McCarthy in the early months of his campaign, became disillusioned, switched to the Kennedy campaign, and, after the assassination, "freaked out" and joined the S.D.S., because it seemed to be "the only ballgame in town." He dropped out of S.D.S. when the most violent splinter group in that organization—the Revolutionary Youth Movement I, or RYM I, now known as the Weatherman faction—took over the national S.D.S. office. Kudlow spent the summer of 1969 doing odd chores in Representative Allard Lowenstein's office, but became disillusioned there, too, and joined the Moratorium staff after a brief stint at the office of Senator Goodell. Despite the many disappointments he has suffered, Kudlow's criticism of the New Mobe is based on a kind of buoyant optimism that seems to be shared by many young activists who found state-primary politics surprisingly easy and enjoyable. "Demonstrations were a minority tactic that were good for '66 and '67," Kudlow said recently. "We have a majority now, and have to do grass-roots organizing on that assumption. The days of symbolism are over." He is also wary of the broad coalition composing the New Mobe. "It includes too much of the Old Left to attract the middle ground," he explained. "I'm a history major, and *I* know how hopelessly conservative the American C.P. and Trotskyites are, but the American people and lots of congressmen are not ready to hear it. Our only hope is with a centrist movement, rather than with the New Mobe's popular front." As an example of how cautiously the Moratorium handles its constituents, Kudlow cited a controversial group in a conservative area of the country which, although it is most enthusiastic about the Moratorium, has organized under the name Committee for the Celebration of Peace and Life, because the

Moratorium is considered too controversial for that area. "In a few months, they'll surface as Moratorium," Kudlow said, with parental pride, "and then I'll send them pins and bumper stickers."

The atmosphere of the New Mobe headquarters, one floor above the Moratorium offices, had the helter-skelter austerity of an emergency-relief station. In this setting, Stewart Meacham, managing to look like an affable bank president, explained why he had taken to the politics of the street at the age of fifty-nine. "We at Mobe are more disillusioned with electoral politics than the Moratorium kids," he said. "We believe that we're in a deep Constitutional crisis, and we're wondering whether our system of government is elastic enough to allow the voice of the people to be effective. I campaigned for Eugene McCarthy and ended up voting for Dick Gregory. To carve out a distinction between Nixon and Humphrey was meaningless. Our Constitutional system not only failed us last year in Chicago—it also failed us when our courts refused to hear evidence on issues raised by young resisters claiming Nuremberg principles to not go to war and commit crimes against humanity in Vietnam. How do you deal with structures that violate the legal authority of our society? Street politics is the last Constitutional means we have left—our assertion of the rights of free speech and assembly. I have been lecturing to businessmen's clubs all over the country recently, saying, 'The most conservative thing you can do is to engage in the politics of the street—it is the only way to conserve our Constitutional system.'" Meacham, who became a pacifist and a Quaker in 1950, holds firmly to the Muste principle of non-exclusion. "Non-exclusionism is not only morally right from the pacifist point of view, it also has pragmatic validity. I believe that the most dynamic periods of our country's history were the periods when all sections of the political spectrum were working together—the years when the C.I.O. was founded, the first two decades of our century when the greatest humanitarian advances were gained by the workers, the years when Eugene Debs got six per cent of the Presidential vote and there were seventy-nine Socialist mayors in our country, the early years of the New Deal when a very wide variety of political ideologies were represented in Roosevelt's

Cabinet. Once you start excluding, you have to start setting standards for purity, and you end up in an emasculated left or centrist segment." Meacham gave a sly smile and added, "The only trouble I have with the Trotskyites and the Communist member of our coalition is that they advocate more strongly than any other groups that demonstrations be kept not only non-violent but legal. That gives me trouble because we Quakers do not link non-violence with legality. On the contrary, we believe that we often have to make our moral points by going to jail. Non-violence needs civil disobedience, and any Communist or Trots sees red at the mention of civil disobedience. They don't want to alienate the middle and lower classes. In terms of public image, it's often easier to accommodate to the Trots than to the Quakers."

In the first weeks of October, while the Moratorium was still hedging on its endorsement of the New Mobe, some New Mobe leaders were practicing their own brand of exclusionism toward the Moratorium. For several of the New Mobe leaders exhibited a holier-than-thou attitude about having come out against the war in 1965, which was as divisive as the Moratorium's prudent centrism. The congressmen and academics who turned out in large numbers to back the Moratorium in the second week of October were referred to by some New Mobe leaders as "Johnny-come-latelies hitching on to the peace bandwagon" and "Kennedy liberals responsible for the Vietnam war." "Forty-five thousand dead later they come out against the war," some New Mobe people muttered. And many of them were worried that the Moratorium's pending endorsement of the November demonstrations would sully the radical purity of their own program. "I'd feel bad if Walter Reuther spoke at our November rally, even if he asked for immediate withdrawal," Dellinger said at one of the New Mobe's executive-committee meetings. "Some people come in so soiled and opportunistic they have no right to be with us. If we fly with Reuther, it's like supporting Humphrey— we'll convince students that we are bourgeois and coöpted, and they will increasingly go toward the Weathermen."

"The New Mobe thinks that the congressmen and other leaders who have recently come out against the war are traitors because they have not opposed it since 1965," Sam Brown remarked that same week, "whereas we at Moratorium are looking for just that kind of congressmen." Throughout the country, there were Moratorium organizers who feared that the New Mobe's uncompromising rhetoric and the possibility of violence at the November rally would undo all the Moratorium's cautious grass-roots work. "We are trying to reach out to little people in the little towns of Iowa," one New England Moratorium organizer said. "We believe in soft, persuasive rhetoric for the heartland of America. Moratorium kids don't want to be responsible for November. They're scared. Every peace freak in America is going to be there. Dellinger, and even Coretta King, are going to put people off. I know the New Mobe people are pure, but purity can mean bringing the whole thing down on your head."

A New Mobe organizer holding the opposite point of view replied, "If the Moratorium can't adjust itself to people who were against the war in 1965, and has to adjust itself to those late-comers who are making political hay out of the peace issue in 1969, then the Moratorium is not morally supportable."

It has been said that the New Mobe leaders have the arrogance of prophets and the Moratorium leaders have the cautiousness of politicians. It took a housewife and a clergyman—both members of the New Mobe—to fuse the two organizations into a united front. The first was Cora Weiss, a thirty-six-year-old mother of three, a woman of remarkable energy and uncompromising candor. The second was Richard Fernandez, thirty-five and also the parent of three, a short, powerful man who attributes his own remarkable energy to a passion for basketball. (Wherever he travels, Fernandez packs an uninflated basketball in his suitcase and plays on the nearest court he can find.) Mrs. Weiss, whose visceral views on peace transcend all political ideology, was less adamant than most of her colleagues in the New Mobe about preserving radical purity, and was more sympathetic toward the Moratorium's problems. As for Fernandez, he insists, as did A. J. Muste, that "a radical change in society will not come from the political system but from a change in the moral consciousness of men." And, like Muste, Fernandez has the ability to push a program through against embattled opposition while retaining the affection of all his opponents. For five weeks before the Moratorium endorsed the New Mobe, Cora Weiss and Richard Fernandez worked unceasingly at healing divisions between the two groups, by stressing to other New Mobe leaders the absolute folly of not coöperating with the Moratorium, and by convincing the Moratorium that the November rally would be legal, respectable, and non-violent. "We've got to discuss this a bit more among ourselves," Sam Brown, the most political and cautious of the four Moratorium leaders, would say when Mrs. Weiss phoned with her daily plea for endorsement. "Hurry up, cookie," she would answer. "The nation is ahead of you." ("They're just the victims of liberal Red-baiting," she would explain. "Congressmen should know that it's not chic to Red-bait anymore.") Actually, Brown and his colleagues had been planning all along to make an alliance with the New Mobe, but they wanted to make sure it was done without antagonizing their supporters. The success of the October Moratorium may have made the endorsement easier.

The two camps finally came together on the evening of October 20th—the night before the press conferences—and the meeting went much more smoothly than either side expected. The Moratorium agreed easily to the New Mobe's two basic principles: there was to be a demand for immediate withdrawal, and the peace coalition was to be kept non-exclusive. The New Mobe invited the four Moratorium coördinators to be on its executive committee, and offered them ten seats on its national steering committee. The Moratorium asked that two senators, one from each party, be invited to speak at the November 15th rally in order to make it a bipartisan program. There was some tension when the Reverend Joseph Duffey, chairman of the A.D.A. and one of the Moratorium's "adult advisers," objected to the rhetoric of the anti-imperialist position paper put forward by the New Mobe. "We can't support *this* awful stuff," Duffey said. "It's just a lot of radical noise. Who wrote it?" "*I* wrote it," Sidney Lens roared, "and I think *your* stuff is awful. We show it to our kids and they vomit." But the alliance had been formed by the time the meeting broke up at 1 A.M.

The agreement still had to be ratified by the New Mobe's national steering committee, and its next meeting—the first to include the Moratorium—was held in Chicago on November 2nd, two weeks before the rally. This meeting can only be described as a valiant exercise in participatory anarchy. What else could be expected from a caucus attended by representatives of the Unitarian Universalist Association, the Liberation News Service, the RYM II faction of S.D.S., District 65 of the Department Store Workers' Union, and sixty other groups, each claiming a constituency of thousands and wanting to speak his piece? The mayhem was aggravated by the sectarian quibbling of the Old Left and the totalitarian self-righteousness of the New Left campus radicals. Little progress would have been made without Fernandez, who, as chairman, handled the tempestuous crowd with the authority and skill of a lion tamer. ("Sit down and shut up, RYM II. We're going to listen to the sister from the Ohio Peace Council.") The first order of business was to win approval of the new alliance with the Moratorium from the clamoring group, half of whom were muttering about being "coöpted by the liberals." Sidney Lens, who was chosen for the task because of the respect he commanded with wide sections of the left, said, "We woke up on October 16th lyrically elated, with a historically new situation. No anti-war action in history has had the impact that Moratorium has had." But his motion to seat the four Moratorium coördinators on the New Mobe's executive committee was followed by pandemonium. Phil Hutchins, a former leader of the Student National Coordinating Committee, accused the New Mobe chairmen of having made a deal with right-wing liberals. The editor of the radical weekly *Guardian* spoke angrily of "bourgeois coöptation." "You're ending up with the left wing of the Democratic party!" a campus activist shouted. At that point, the women's-liberation groups and several of the New Mobe's co-chairmen threatened to resign if the Moratorium was not immediately seated. Dellinger offered a motion that four "more radical" members of the coalition be picked for the executive committee to "balance out" the Moratorium four. The Moratorium, which was represented at the meeting by Marge Sklencar and David Hawk—Brown and Mixner having shied away—threatened to walk out if Dellinger's motion was passed. "We're playing games trying to be ideologically pure while people are dying!" shouted Terrance Hallinan, a young San Francisco lawyer who was co-chairman of the New Mobe for the West Coast. "Our task is not to go to meetings we dig but to get peace, and for that we've got to unite with the Moratorium!" There were cries of "Right on!" from some members of the caucus, boos and hisses from others. "The last thing we want is a walkout by the Moratorium," warned the Trotskyite leader Fred Halstead, who had been a chief marshal for many of the peaceful protest marches of past years and was again chief marshal of the November 15th rally. "The real problem we want to concentrate on is how to avoid any civil disobedience, any politics of confrontation." Finally, after three hours of debate, the alliance with the Moratorium was approved by a small margin.

The next order of business was to persuade the national committee to accept the speakers' list that had been drawn up for the November 15th rally. The most prominent names on it were Senator McGovern, Senator Goodell, Coretta King, George Wald, David Dellinger, Teamsters' International Vice-President Harold Gibbons, and former Under-Secretary of Commerce Howard Samuels.

"You've become the imperialist, élitist Mobe!" a RYM II girl shouted from the back of the hall after Cora Weiss had finished reading the list. "Those congressmen and businessmen are war criminals!"

"Right on, sister!" some campus radicals yelled.

"I want none of that!" Cora Weiss bellowed in the voice of an angry schoolmarm. "Keep quiet or get out of here!"

"Those who want a RYM II show are the worst exclusionists of all!" Lens cried out. "If I'm not going to be coöpted by McGovern, I'm not going to be coöpted by the S.D.S., either!"

But there were still dozens of complaints to be heard— protests that there were no Puerto Rican or Asian-American speakers on the list, demands that "multi-issues of imperialism" be proclaimed from the platform by Trotskyite anti-war G.I.s, accusations that the platform was "male chauvinistic" because only four out of the twelve speakers were women. Before the vote was taken, a last, passionate plea that the list of speakers be accepted without modifications was made by a benign, grandfatherly man with pink cheeks and a tuft of silvery hair, who was generally considered the most conservative member of the New Mobe coalition. "You guys get moving instead of bickering!" he pleaded. "How can November 15th surpass October 15th? What a tremendous task! Senator Goodell had a hundred thousand in Boston! Our job is to create a massive political movement and force our government out of war!" This was Arnold Johnson, the gentleman from the Communist Party.

Toward the end of the meeting, which lasted ten hours, Abbie Hoffman, the Yippie leader, came to the front of the room to speak. A man with a disproportionately long torso, short bowed legs, and a wild head of coarse black hair tied at the nape, which looked like a periwig worn askew, Hoffman had jotted down some notes with a ballpoint pen, in minuscule script, on the very small, pudgy palm of his left hand. Referring to these notes, he asked the New Mobe to endorse an action he was planning in support of the Chicago conspiracy-trial defendants at "the Department of Injustice" on the evening of the November 15th rally.

There was a groan of displeasure from all over the hall, and Arnold Johnson said over and over, "Oh, no, no, no, no."

Hoffman leered and said, "Well, it's going to happen whether Mobe and Agnew endorse it or not."

Harry Ring, the aging gray eminence of the Socialist Workers' Party, rose to say, "This is just what we don't want. The government is looking for every reason it can find to propagandize this as a violent demonstration. It is the most effective weapon the ruling class has."

A motion to the effect that there would be no announcement from the platform at the November 15th rally of any event not endorsed by the New Mobe was carried by a bizarre alliance for law and order that included the Socialists, the Trotskyites, Arnold Johnson, various middle-of-the-road groups such as SANE and the National Council of Churches, and the new right wing of the New Mobe—the clean-for-Gene Moratorium kids who shared with the Old Left a horror of confrontation politics. Abbie Hoffman was to stage his demonstration at the Justice Department without the New Mobe's official endorsement, thus providing just about the only evidence Attorney General Mitchell was able to cite when he claimed that the November 15th rally could not be "characterized as peaceful."

During the days that preceded the Washington demonstration, the Justice Department refused to approve a permit for a march down Pennsylvania Avenue, predicting violence on November 15th, and made vigorous attempts to divide the alliance that had been worked out between the Moratorium and the New Mobe. The New Mobe alone was in charge of negotiating for the march permit. Yet right in the middle of the negotiations John W. Dean III, a Justice Department official who was referred to by demonstration leaders as "a very pleasant Humphrey-Lindsay type of liberal" but was obviously following orders from less friendly superiors, invited Sam Brown and David Hawk to the Department to discuss the route of the march. The New Mobe's negotiating team—composed of Richard Fernandez, Stewart Meacham, and Ron Young—had an appointment at the Justice Department just afterward and arrived a little early. When Dean heard that the New Mobe delegation was outside, he asked the Moratorium leaders if they wouldn't prefer to go out his side door, so that they wouldn't be seen. But the Moratorium people chose to go out by the front door, pausing to shake hands with the New Mobe leaders, and later that afternoon Brown and Fernandez agreed that the Moratorium leaders should not accept any further invitations to the Justice Department. Four days later, Brown and Hawk were again invited to go there and discuss the permit issue, this time with Deputy Attorney General Richard G. Kleindienst. They declined.

The Monday morning before the November 15th rally, the New Mobe's negotiating team had its only face-to-face meeting with Kleindienst. The march permit still had not been granted and time was running out for both sides; according to Fernandez, Kleindienst's language was rough as he made his last attempt to have the New Mobe accept Constitution Avenue instead of Pennsylvania. "I don't want to have to shoot any demonstrators on the White House lawn," Kleindienst told Fernandez. "I'll have to line both sides of Pennsylvania Avenue with American soldiers shoulder to shoulder."

But that afternoon the District's Mayor, Walter Washington, intervened directly with President Nixon, and the following day a march permit for Pennsylvania Avenue was granted. Fernandez' explanation of the Justice Department's tactics is that "Kleindienst tried to gain a personal victory by scaring us before being overruled by his bosses. But we're not the kind who scare quickly."

Preparations went smoothly after that, although one potentially divisive issue had to be resolved at the last minute. Late in October, Senator McCarthy had been invited to speak at the New Mobe's California rally and declined. However, he had let it be known, partly through remarks he made to people in the peace movement, that he was intending to speak at the Washington rally. Since Senators Goodell and McGovern had been approved as speakers by the New Mobe's national steering committee only after turbulent debate, adding a third senator to the afternoon program was clearly out of the question. But it was evident that a special spot had to be devised for McCarthy in some other part of the program. The final decision was to schedule him for nine-thirty in the morning, at the very beginning of the march. He would be getting, as some New Mobe leaders put it acidly, "prime visibility time." Richard Fernandez and Stewart Meacham went to see McCarthy on Thursday to offer him the nine-thirty spot, and after reading them some of his new poetry McCarthy readily agreed to speak at nine-thirty on the Mall below the Capitol, where the march was to begin.

A crowd of some twenty-five thousand had gathered when McCarthy arrived, hatless and with his coat open in the sun-drenched but freezing morning. The demonstrators' placards, bobbing against the sky like sails on a blue bay, were exceedingly cheerful. "Free Kim Agnew," "Young Hegelian Society for Peace," "Snobs for Peace," "Jesus Christ Did Not Carry a Draft Card," "Support Your Local Planet." In the pleasant, flat voice that always sounds as if he were about to come down with a cold, McCarthy spoke of "the cases in which political leaders, out of misjudgment or ambition, in ancient times and in modern times, basing their action on the loyalty of their people, have done great harm to their own countries and to the world." At the end, he quoted some Gide. "Last year, it

was Péguy," a girl in the crowd said. "Next year, St. John
Perse." After the applause, the crowd began to chant "Peace
now! Peace now!"—at first slowly, but accelerating in tempo
and volume like a football cheer. McCarthy gave his cold,
wide smile, and the largest peace march in the history of the
nation began.

Later that afternoon, the colorful carpet of humanity that
stretched up the gentle greensward of the Mall would grow
to at least half a million. Some of the New Mobe leaders said
they regretted that Muste had not lived to see all this humanity asking for peace together; it was the apotheosis of everything he had preached for sixty years. And many of the
demonstrators regretted the passing of an era—a decade of
marching had come to an end. Given the way the nation's
present leaders were polarizing Americans' emotions, some
found it doubtful whether such huge and visible expressions
of conscience could remain peaceful in the future.

The Moratorium activities across the nation in December
were extremely quiet compared to the October turnouts. As
it enters the sixth month of its existence, the Moratorium is
carefully evaluating its original tactics. For the time being, the
original plan calling for nationwide shutdowns to be expanded
by one day each month has been abandoned. In January, February, and March, one "peace day" a month is to be dedicated
to grass-roots educational campaigns, stressing the impact of
the war on taxes and inflation, and the dangers of a possible
recession. "If we can demonstrate to Americans that nineteen
cents out of their every tax dollar goes into the Vietnam war
and fifty-four cents of it into military expenditure, we can have
a real taxpayers' revolt," David Hawk has predicted. A good
deal of effort will also be concentrated on getting peace candidates elected in the 1970 congressional elections.

The Moratorium coördinators have various explanations as
to why they have been unable to carry out their original, more
radical program. "We peaked too early," Sam Brown says.
"October was too big for our own good, because the nation
had not had a chance to demonstrate its anti-war sentiment
for a whole year. It would have been healthier and simpler for
us to start slowly and grow month by month." Marge Sklen-

car believes that the Moratorium overestimated the country's activist potential. "We were using our own five-year committedness as a standard for the nation, and too many people are still indifferent," she says. "The obstacle to getting peace is not the silent majority but the indifferent majority." David Hawk stresses the placating effects of Nixon's November 3rd speech. "Nixon's speech was a moral disaster, but it was very brilliant, and it will make us lie low for a few months," Hawk says. "However, in the long run it will help us, because the peace movement had not taken Nixon's politics serious until November 3rd. Now we know that his true intention is to continue a pro-West client state in Vietnam, and we can fight back more accurately." The Moratorium leaders estimate that it will take the nation three or four months to realize that Nixon's November 3rd speech was "a public-relations coverup for a continued war." On the basis of this prediction, the Moratorium plans to hold its next round of substantial, high-visibility activities on April 15th, with demonstrations at Internal Revenue Service centers in dozens of cities throughout the nation. In April, it will also support three-day fasts on university campuses, and thousands of non-students are expected to join. "The self-denial involved in fasting will stress the immorality of the war," David Hawk says. "And the immorality of this war is one thing that cannot be coöpted."

The New Mobe has also selected April as the time for new demonstrations across the country. Whatever their ideological differences may be, the Moratorium and the New Mobe agree that the peace movement in 1970 will tend strongly toward local actions rather than huge rallies in Washington, Los Angeles, or New York. "The new phenomenon of the movement is decentralized demonstration," says Ron Young, of the New Mobe, "and that's an evidence of the enormous growth of anti-war sentiment. A year or two ago, you could never have pulled anything off outside of the major cities." And Sam Brown adds, "Thirty people meeting in a church basement in Peoria to protest the war for the first time may be infinitely more important than thirty thousand people converging on Washington."

The New Yorker, January 3, 1970

Massacre at Takeo

by T. D. Allman

Yesterday's Prisoners Lie Dead in
Bloody Cambodian Schoolyard

TAKEO, Cambodia, April 17—Before, there had been about 200 Vietnamese men and boys crowded into the enclosure. Now there were less than 50.

Bodies lay to one side.

"They killed them last night at 7:30," a Vietnamese man told us.

We had driven our small car into the school compound. From a distance of 40 feet, we could see the blood-stained walls.

We jumped out of our car and ran, nearly slipping in the blood, into the enclosure.

"Where are the others?" I asked an old Vietnamese man with a wispy Ho Chi Minh beard.

"They killed them all last night. They will kill us all tonight. They say we are Vietcong. But we are just shopkeepers," the man said.

It was the third mass killing of ethnic Vietnamese discovered in Cambodia in recent days.

I and another reporter found it today after we had recalled seeing 200 Vietnamese men and boys crowded into an open-walled building yesterday and decided, "Let's go see those Vietnamese to see if they're all right."

The hour's drive from Phnom Penh to Takeo passes through tranquil countryside, with jitney busses competing with cows and bullock carts for a place on the road.

Except for a convoy of ammunition trucks near Phnom Penh, we saw nothing to remind us that Cambodia is at war.

Even in Takeo, there was the typical air of peace that characterizes the tranquility of a lazy afternoon in a Cambodian market town.

And then we found the scene at the school.

"They took the bodies away at 2 in the morning. Two truckloads of the dead and badly wounded—150 in all," a Vietnamese said.

"Can you save my brother?" he pleaded. A man about 30 with at least five bullet wounds in him lay on the concrete floor, the straw mat upon which he lay soaked with blood. He and the others had received no medical attention although Takeo has a hospital.

Near him lay a boy, about 10 years old, with two bullet wounds in his mangled leg.

Cambodian soldiers came up and motioned us away. They seemed tired and scared.

"Are you Vietcong?" I asked the Vietnamese.

"We have lived here all our lives. We are not Vietcong," said the old man. "Stay with us, or they will kill us too."

The old man and his friends spoke calmly and with no emotion in their voices.

My companion, Time correspondent Robert Anson, talked to the guard while I planned.

"Can we take the child?" I asked.

Answered another man, "Take all the wounded, or they will die."

We took the child and lay him on the back seat of the car.

"We'll be back in two hours," we said. "Before dark."

"If you don't," the old man answered, "you will find us dead."

We roared back to Phnom Penh, not stopping at any of the checkpoints. The Vietnamese boy held my hand tightly. Anson kept asking, "He's not dead is he?"

We stopped at the first Catholic church we found in Phnom Penh. The French priest led us to a French hospital near the Hotel Le Royale.

After fretting about who would pay the bills for the boy, the nurses finally let him in.

Then a French doctor came.

"Who are you?" he asked. "Who are his parents? He has a gun wound."

"You know," he said as he gave the child oxygen, "you must not think it is only the Cambodians who do this. I was down in Takeo last week and I patched up 15 Cambodians wounded by a Vietcong grenade."

I ran out to get back in the car to reach Takeo by dark. Already the journalists had heard Anson, and were rushing to their cars.

At Takeo, I asked one of the soldiers, "Was there an attack here? Is that why you killed them?"

He seemed ashamed, but said: "No, we were ordered. The Vietcong are our enemies and all Vietnamese are Vietcong. They were ready to help the Vietcong if they came."

The madness of the catastrophe that has overtaken Cambodia since March 18, in a way, is summed up in the tall, unshaven and totally placid exterior of a Cambodian paratroop captain who so far has refused to give his name to the press.

The man stands more than six feet tall, rare for a Cambodian, and he describes military events tersely and unemotionally, like a professional.

But in less than one month, he has ordered the deaths of about 40 Vietnamese civilians—men, women and children. Journalists interviewed him following the Prasaut massacre in Svay Rieng province nearly two weeks ago.

At that time, he admitted ordering the mass slayings there "because they were Vietcong."

The officer was transferred to the until now placid little provincial capital of Takeo, 50 miles south of Phnom Penh and about the same distance from the South Vietnamese border.

It is the major town in the province, which has an estimated 10,000 North Vietnamese and Vietcong troops dug into sanctuaries along the border.

Takeo was also the scene of major pro-Sihanouk demonstrations in the days immediately after the March 18 coup. Officials estimated that there were almost 4,000 pro-Sihanouk demonstrators at one time or another.

One of the first acts by the tall Cambodian captain after his transfer to Takeo was to order the 200 Vietnamese men and boys rounded up and held in detention.

It was after a sumptious French lunch, topped off with a

chocolate souffle, by the palm-fringed swimming pool at the venerable Hotel le Royale that we had decided today to drive out to visit the Vietnamese prisoners and the paratroop captain whom we had jokingly called "Killer."

The paratroop captain was nowhere in sight during our brief, rushed visit to Takeo, but Cambodian soldiers lounged around eating bananas just 50 yards from where the bodies lay.

I must stop writing now, fill my car with gas and get back to Takeo before dark.

"We will take all the wounded you can bring us," said the French doctor. If we are lucky tonight, we shall have more wounded for him to stitch up. If we are not, all we will have are dead Vietnamese shopkeepers and small farmers, all born and raised in Cambodia, for the photographers to take pictures of.

The Washington Post, April 18, 1970

The Aftermath of a Massacre: Newsmen Rescue 7

TAKEO, Cambodia—"Please rent a truck in Phnom Penh to take us away," the old Vietnamese pleaded.

He was one of the 50 survivors of the Thursday night massacre of 140 Vietnamese in a walled schoolyard here.

It was now after dark Friday, and the old man was watching me and my colleague, Robert Anson of Time Magazine, prepare to head back to Phnom Penh with seven other survivors, four little boys and three wounded men.

I asked a Cambodian if he would rent us a truck, but he wanted 12,000 riels (over $200) and we didn't have enough.

"Get out of here before the police stop you," other Western newsmen who were staying behind told us.

We started off in our car with the seven survivors. It was the second such trip of the day. Earlier, after coming upon the bloody massacre site almost by accident, Anson and I had rushed back to the capital with a wounded 8-year-old boy.

We had also rallied several of our colleagues from the Royale Hotel to get them to go to Takeo in hopes their presence might be protection for the remaining Vietnamese.

Over the past several days, several Cambodians had told me that they considered all Vietnamese to be Vietcong, the hated invaders of the country.

During the 50-mile ride to Phnom Penh on the second trip, the Vietnamese showed no emotion at all. The least wounded of the men told me his life story:

"I was born in Takeo 42 years ago. I am not a Vietcong. None of us are. I passed the eighth grade and I have the certificate. In 1942, I worked for the French officers in Takeo. That is why I can speak to you now.

"I had a small shop.

"They came and took all the men and boys—from six up to the old grandfathers. Then they shot us. My sons are dead. This is my brother on the seat. Are they killing Vietnamese in Phnom Penh too?"

We passed a convoy of Cambodian recruits, singing and shouting on buses in the darkness, as we headed north to the city.

On the outskirts of town, the car engine failed, then started, then failed and started again. It was the spark plugs. We inched along a little further and then police surrounded us.

"These are Vietnamese," said one policeman. "I want to see their identity cards."

"They are all wounded, let me pass," I said. The other journalists had stopped too, and while they distracted the police I drove off, but the car would not go faster than 25 miles an hour.

A police motorcycle overtook us, and as we passed by the airport, one of the policemen was waving an automatic pistol.

"Don't you know we have orders to shoot?" he asked. "You all could have been shot dead."

The police captain arrived. "These people were badly hurt in an accident," I shouted. "If you do not let us pass, I will tell your superiors and they will punish you."

"What kind of an accident?" the police chief wanted to know.

He finally agreed to let us proceed, on the condition that we went to the commissariat of police in town. I agreed, but had no intention of going anywhere but to the hospital.

At the main intersection in Phnom Penh I turned left, toward the hospital, rather than going straight on to the police station.

The police blew their horns and pulled out their guns. I slammed on the brakes and ran over to the police chief's jeep.

"Go ahead, shoot me," I shouted in French. "Right here in the heart. But I am going to the hospital."

It was an utterly calculated move, which I had been planning for about ten minutes—and utterly devoid of risk. The Cambodian police would never have shot a white man down on the main boulevard of Phnom Penh. They followed us to the hospital.

At the hospital, the Vietnamese were all taken, where they joined the other little boy I had brought up earlier. Two hours later, they were still operating on the most seriously wounded man. The others seemed in good shape.

After a drink, about 20 of us went to the sumptuous suburban villas of the minister of information, Trinh Hoanh, and of the deputy prime minister, Prince Sisowath Sirik Matak.

At both places, the leaders refused to see us, though at the deputy prime minister's house, I was allowed to talk to the head bodyguard, a young Cambodian army officer, fluent in French, who wore his revolver in a holster belt around his waist, like an American cowboy.

"The deputy prime minister will give a press conference on April 20," he said. "You can see him then."

He added, "All the time the press harps on the fact that we massacre Vietnamese. You never report that the Vietnamese are attacking us, that they kill us."

"The men in Takeo killed no one," I said. "This will hurt you in America now that you want arms," I said.

He answered: "They are all Vietnamese. The Germans bombed London, didn't they?"

"But there was no fighting at Takeo," I said. A simple telephone call to Takeo could save those still living.

He replied: "It is all the same." As for telephone calls, the days of one-man rule are over in Cambodia. The provincial authorities are in charge.

It was, of course, those same provincial authorities who had ordered the massacre. The local commander, who refused to give his name, had claimed the victims were killed in a crossfire during a Vietcong attack, but even his own soldiers denied this. "There was no attack," one sergeant told me. "We just shot them."

We walked back to my car. "I can only tell you this will hurt you in world public opinion and in the United States," I said.

"We still find out who our friends are," the captain said. "Prince Sirik Matak talked for an hour yesterday with your charge d'affaires, Monsieur Rives. He was very sympathetic."

Indeed, many diplomats in Phnom Penh have attempted to make allowances for or otherwise explain the killings.

"These things happen," one Western ambassador told me. "War is new to Cambodia. There's bound to be some initial fumbling."

On the morning before we discovered the Takeo massacre, an American official told me, "All this can be exaggerated. I have the feeling these incidents are going to die down."

Indeed, Western officials, in their enthusiasm for the new anti-Communist government here, seem unwilling or unable to accept the fact that slaughters of innocent civilians are taking place, seemingly with government encouragement.

"Did you really see all these alleged killings?" a Western diplomat demanded of me irritably today. "Some of you people will do anything for a story."

At the gate, the Cambodian bodyguard of the deputy prime minister said, "We want the journalists to see everything. We have nothing to hide. Come to the press conference on the 20th. You can ask any question you want."

The Washington Post, April 20, 1970

from
Kent State: What Happened and Why

by James A. Michener

What happened on Monday

THE CRUCIAL EVENT at Kent State was, of course, the action of the National Guard on Monday, May 4. Here is what happened.

At 11:00 in the morning of a bright, sunny day, students began collecting on the commons as their 9:55–10:45 classes ended. They came casually at first, then in larger numbers when some of their 11:00–11:50 classes dismissed early because the confusion on campus made it too difficult to teach. Many students wandered by, as they always did, to check on what might be happening. Another set of classes, 12:05–12:55, would soon convene, and it was traditional for students who were involved either in leaving one class or heading for another to use the commons as their walkway. Without question, they had a right to be on the commons. But were they entitled to be there this day? A state of emergency had been declared by Satrom, presumably outlawing any unusual gatherings. Classes would meet, and that was about all. Yet testimony from students is overwhelming that they believed their campus to be operating as usual. On Friday a rally had been openly announced for Monday noon, and invitations to attend it had been circulated on succeeding days; in fact, announcements for this rally had been scrawled on certain blackboards and were seen by students when they reported for classes on Monday. Furthermore, those students and faculty who had left the campus Friday afternoon could not have listened to local radio stations and would have had no personal knowledge of what the situation was. Later we shall watch several professors, absent over the weekend, as they specifically instruct their students, with the most laudable intentions, to leave class and

57

observe the campus rally. The rally may have been forbidden, but there were too many who either were not aware of this fact or did not believe it.

At 11:15 leaders of the National Guard, in discussion with school officials, became aware of this confusion and asked that the university radio station WKSU and the school intercom announce: 'All outdoor demonstrations and gatherings are banned by order of the governor. The National Guard has the power of arrest.' This was repeated several times but reached only a small proportion of the students, because the intercom system operated in only certain classrooms and none of the dormitories. But the rally had been forbidden; everyone knew it except the students.

At 11:30 General Canterbury, fresh from the inconclusive and even contradictory meeting with university and town officials, arrived at the burned-out ROTC building, surveyed the commons which lay before him, and concluded that the crowd was orderly and did not constitute any kind of significant threat. He could not at that moment have known that the impending dismissal of the 11:00–11:50 class would promptly crowd the commons.

At 11:45 General Canterbury, unaware that the radio broadcast canceling the rally had been heard by so few people, and not knowing about the normal movements of students going from class to class, was astonished to see so many students proceeding as if the rally were still authorized. The crowd was growing larger every minute. He saw about 600 students massing not far from his troops and became justifiably concerned. Giving a clear order, he commanded that the students be dispersed. This order was given before any rocks had been thrown.

At 11:48 someone began ringing the Victory Bell. Two students climbed onto its brick housing to issue frenzied calls to action. The bell continued clanging intermittently during the next fifteen minutes, and this coincided with the end of another class period, so that a constant press of new arrivals kept pouring onto the commons, while a much larger group watched from various walkways, driveways and porches of classroom buildings.

At 11:49 Officer Harold E. Rice, of the campus police, stood by the ruins of the ROTC building and read the riot act over a bullhorn: 'Attention! This is an order. Disperse immediately. This is an order. Leave this area immediately. This is an order. Disperse.' Unfortunately, he was so far away from the students that they could not hear him, and his words had no effect.

At 11:50 a National Guard jeep was driven up, with a driver at the wheel and two armed Guardsmen perched high atop the rear seat. Officer Rice climbed into the right front seat and with his bullhorn proceeded to read the riot act repeatedly as the jeep moved slowly along the edges of the crowd: 'This assembly is unlawful. This crowd must disperse immediately. This is an order.' (Later, certain students would claim that Rice *asked* them to break up the crowd but did not *order* them to do so, and it is possible that in one or another of the repetitions he may have used those words, but the evidence is overwhelming that he recited the version, as given, at least eight times.) The jeep was greeted with catcalls, boos, cursing and a shower of rocks; few of the latter reached the jeep and none appear to have struck any of the four passengers.

At 11:52, as the jeep made its slow progress, with Rice still shouting over the bullhorn, he spotted in the crowd someone he recognized as a leader of riots on the two preceding nights, and he wanted to arrest him. So the driver edged the jeep right into the edge of the crowd, but the young radical saw what Rice was up to and slipped away. So that all students might be properly warned, the jeep made three complete circuits.

At 11:55 the order was passed to the Guardsmen: 'If you have not already done so, load and lock. Prepare for gas attack. Prepare to move out.'

At 11:58 it was obvious that Rice in the jeep was accomplishing nothing, so Major Harry Jones ran out, banged on the jeep with his baton, and ordered it to return to the ROTC building.

At 11:59 General Canterbury gave the order: 'Prepare to move out and disperse this mob.' There is considerable variance in published reports as to the number of troops he had at his disposal. Inaccessibility of accurate records makes any estimate arbitrary; some seem much too low. It would appear that the total contingent contained 113 Guardsmen, disposed as follows: three senior officers, Brigadier General Robert H. Canterbury, Lieutenant Colonel Charles Fassinger, Major Harry D. Jones in command of three units of troops arranged in this order. On the left flank, nearest to the tennis courts, Charlie Company, First Battalion, 145th Infantry, consisting of two officers (Captain Ron Snyder, Lieutenant Herthneck) and 34 enlisted men; in the center, headed for Taylor Hall, G Troop, Second Squadron, 107th Armored Cavalry Regiment, consisting of two officers (Captain Raymond J. Srp, Lieutenant Stevenson) and 16 enlisted men; on the right flank, headed toward Johnson Hall, Alpha Company of the 145th, consisting of three officers (Captain John E. Martin, Lieutenant Klein, Lieutenant Fallon) and 51 enlisted men, but to Alpha Company, two members of Charlie Company (Richard Love and Richard Lutey) had attached themselves because their own unit had moved out before they could catch up with it. The contingent therefore included 10 officers and 103 enlisted men.

According to the plan that General Canterbury had worked out with his commanders, the Guardsmen were to sweep the commons toward the southeast, driving all demonstrators across the crest of Blanket Hill, keeping Taylor Hall on their left, the pagoda on the right. The troops would then push the students down the far slope of the hill toward the practice football field, and the operation would be completed. Captain Snyder had suggested an additional detail: his left-flank Charlie Company would sweep left of Taylor Hall and take a holding position between it and Prentice while the center and right flank completed the main sweep on the other side of Taylor. To this General Canterbury assented, adding, 'Before you step off, fire a barrage of tear gas.'

It is important to visualize the number of students confronting the Guard. At 11:45 Colonel Fassinger had estimated the number of students on the commons—that is, in position to constitute a threat of some kind to the Guard—as 'more than 500.' In the interval this number had grown to 600 and then to something over 800. Now it might number as high as 1,100; for students were piling in from all directions as their classes ended. But a much larger crowd had assembled on the terraces of halls like Johnson and Stopher to the west, Prentice and Engleman to the east. And the largest group of all filled the open spaces directly in back of ROTC toward Administration. All of these must be considered as spectators only, and they could have numbered as many as 2,500. Included among them were townspeople, high-school children, professors and, of course, university students. As they were situated that morning they formed a gigantic amphitheater focusing upon a small stage of green.*

At 12:00 sharp, before the order to march could be given, an unidentified spokesman for the students, perhaps a faculty member, ran up to Canterbury and said, 'General, you must not march against the students,' to which the general replied that the students congregated illegally. 'These students,' he told the intercessor, 'are going to have to find out what law and order is all about.' Then he nodded to his commanders; the first slim gray tear-gas canisters popped out in their long parabolas toward the demonstrators, and 103 Guardsmen plus 10 officers stepped off into the history of contemporary America. The three senior officers, apparently by accident, distributed themselves among the units: Major Jones stayed with Charlie Company on the left flank; Colonel Fassinger marched with G Troop in the center; General Canterbury went with Alpha Company on the right flank.

At 12:01 Captain Snyder positioned himself on the extreme right of his men, so that when the gas stopped and his troop broke off from the other units for the drive to the east end of Taylor Hall, he would be anchor man on the right flank. Following his custom, he kept up a barrage of tear gas. A tear-gas canister launched by an M-79 is a most effective crowd-control device; if fired on a level trajectory (none were), it has sufficient velocity to kill a man at twenty-five yards. A sudden cross wind blew up to spread it across the field and up the Taylor Hall slope—before long the smoke would be inhaled

---

*Eszterhas and Roberts believe the crowd to have been much larger: 'By a few minutes before noon nearly fifteen hundred students had gathered around the bell. Another two thousand to three thousand students were assembled on the opposite side of the commons behind the National Guard lines. Another two thousand were on the northern edge of the commons near the tennis courts.' One member of the research team, working independently, came up with almost these same estimates, but other members, reviewing each available photograph, convinced him that his figures were too high.

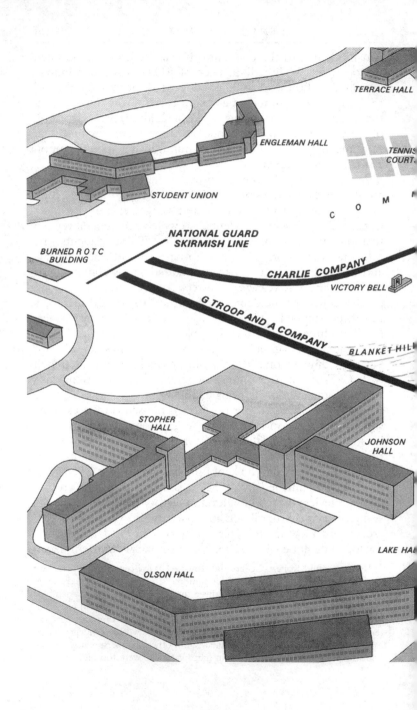

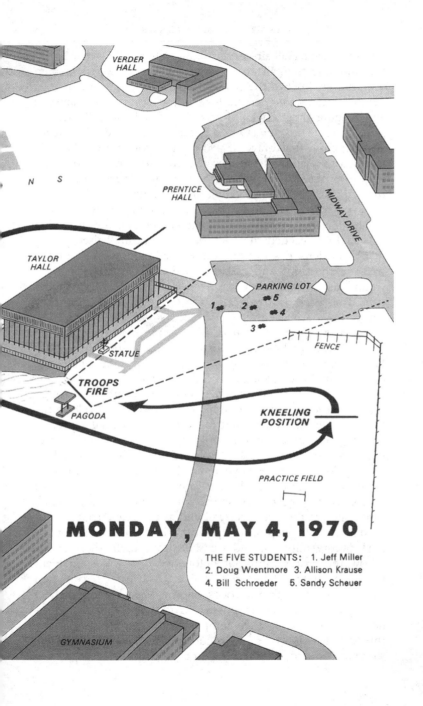

MONDAY, MAY 4, 1970

THE FIVE STUDENTS: 1. Jeff Miller
2. Doug Wrentmore 3. Allison Krause
4. Bill Schroeder 5. Sandy Scheuer

into the Taylor Hall air-conditioning system, filling that building and affecting all those inside. Now, as Snyder's men
moved ever closer to the crowd, those among the more daring
demonstrators came darting forward, seizing the hot canisters
and flinging them back. Most of these fell short of the approaching Guardsmen. One says *most* because certain unusually aggressive—or brave, if you prefer—young men not only
grabbed the canisters but also ran good distances with them
back toward the troops, throwing them from such short range
that canisters sometimes landed in the ranks.

At 12:02 Snyder's men reached the point at which they
would detach themselves from the center unit for the swing
left. As they reached the Victory Bell a 'bushy-haired young
man' (Snyder's description) came darting down out of the
trees on the slope and gave the bell a final swing. Then he
wound up and hurled a fistful of small stones. Ron Snyder
turned his back on the stones, spun around and brought his
baton down across the boy's shoulders with such force as to
snap off the tip of the baton. The young man then reached
in his pocket and brought forth a piece of metal with four
finger holes—a brass knuckle. Snyder hit him again. He
dropped the piece of metal and dashed back up the hill.

At 12:03, as Charlie Company began to climb up through
the trees, they could see a number of demonstrators along the
brow of the hill. They fired more tear gas in that direction
and kept climbing. At the top they beheld an even greater
number of students gathered below them in the Prentice Hall
parking lot, and here Snyder decided to form his line. He
placed his men in a single row from the northeast corner of
Taylor toward the nearest corner of Prentice, leaving twenty
yards open at the Prentice Hall end as an escape route.

At 12:04 they were in the position they would hold for the
next twenty minutes, and we shall leave them there as we
follow the center unit, but before we do so, one incident
should be noted. Clustered in front of Snyder's formation
were a number of frantic coeds, and he began calling to them
through the voice emitter in his M-17-type gas mask (all officers and non-coms were equipped with these special masks,
through which voice instructions could be issued). He
shouted to them, 'Come on, come on! It's safe.' Like a herd

of frightened deer, the girls suddenly made their decision and bolted through the opening and around the side of the building. In the next few minutes Snyder estimates that he let upward of 100 students pass, all trying to escape the agony of drifting tear gas.

At 12:04, as Captain Snyder's troops were reaching their final position at the east end of Taylor, Captain Srp's center unit of eighteen soldiers was approaching the pagoda, undergoing as they marched a heavy barrage of curses and their own tear-gas canisters thrown back at them by determined students. The canisters were of little consequence to the Guardsmen, who, having anticipated this maneuver, were wearing gas masks, but this in itself posed a problem. As one Guardsman says, 'It was a hot day, and this was the hottest part of the day. The gas masks were heavy, and as soon as you put yours on, you were hemmed in and sweating. Your vision was restricted to a narrow field and sometimes you couldn't even see the man next to you. It was like being tucked away in a corner . . . sweating.' To the outsider, seeing a Guardsman in mask evoked a sense of the unreal, the mechanical, the monster from outer space, and this was an advantage, for it frightened the observer; but to the man inside the mask, there was a sense of remoteness, of detachment, of being alone in a crowd, and that was a disadvantage, for it cut a soldier off from his fellows and from reality.

At 12:05 the unit reached the pagoda, where it was met by a good deal more than returning gas canisters. Students began throwing rocks at them, and chunks of wood studded with nails, and jagged hunks of concrete. Where did they get such missiles? At least two witnesses swear they saw girls carrying heavy handbags from which they distributed rocks to men students, and some photographs would seem to substantiate this charge. At a nearby construction site some students had picked up fragments of concrete block. And some of the students had armed themselves with bricks. In addition, there were a few—not many—small stones and pebbles available on the campus itself, but these were inconsequential; on a normal day one could have searched this commons fairly carefully, without finding a rock large enough to throw at anyone.

Did any of the missiles hit the troops? Not many. The distances between the mass of the students and the Guards were later stepped off by expert judges, who concluded that students would have required good right arms like Mickey Mantle's to have reached the Guardsmen with even small stones. But as with the canisters, some students were bold enough to run back down the hill and throw from close range, and their stones did hit.

Worse, in a way, than the missiles were the epithets, especially when launched by coeds. A steady barrage of curses, obscenities and fatal challenges came down upon the Guard, whose gas masks did not prevent their hearing what they were being called. Girls were particularly abusive, using the foulest language and taunting the Guardsmen with being 'shit-heels, motherfuckers and half-ass pigs.' Others called them less explosive but equally hurtful names: 'toy soldiers, murderers, weekend warriors, fascists.' During the half hour that the Guardsmen were in action, this rain of abuse never let up.

In addition, a special few among the students—perhaps a dozen men and four girls—kept running at the Guardsmen, daring them to retaliate. One young man, with extremely long hair held in place by a beaded band, displayed a large black flag at the end of a pole, and with extreme bravado waved it at critical moments at the troops, almost in their faces, retreating to eight or ten yards at other times. Guardsmen behind their masks were unsure whether it was a Vietcong flag or not. Certainly it was not any with which they were familiar.

As this central detachment reached the top of Blanket Hill, they found that the mass of students had melted away before them. Never were the students very close, except for the daring ones, and people who have studied the facts and the photographs become irritated when someone asks, 'Why didn't the Guard surround the students and arrest them?' The Guards were never within a hundred yards of being able to surround this ebbing and flowing mass of people, and besides, there were not nearly enough men to have done so had they desired. It was like asking a group of six people why they didn't surround a flock of pigeons who kept flying in all directions.

At 12:06, with the central unit perched atop the hill, the officers faced an awkward decision. They now stood between

Taylor Hall on their left and the cement pagoda on their right, with almost the whole body of students, who a few minutes ago had been on the commons, facing them in the various open spaces that lay ahead. Also, many hundreds of additional students who could have known nothing of the preceding sweep, now arrived from their 11:00–11:50 classes, which had been held in buildings at distant parts of the campus, or were on their way to 12:05–12:55 classes in buildings nearby. For anyone to say of these students 'They had no right to be on the campus' is to misunderstand the nature of a university; they had every right to be precisely where they were, but they did add to the visual confusion. If at this crucial moment the Guard had returned to their ROTC station, they would have had an absolutely clear escape route, but in all likelihood the radical students would have followed behind them, so that the situation would have wound up exactly as it started, with the Guard at ROTC and the students occupying Blanket Hill.

So an understandable decision was reached that the Guard would push on and try to clear the large area that lay ahead, an open field used for practice football, with a soccer goal at the south end and a baseball diamond at the north. What none of the Guardsmen apparently realized was that along the eastern side of this field, ran a sturdy six-foot-high chain-link fence, topped by three strands of heavy barbed wire. What was worse, at the baseball end this fence took a right-angle turn to the west to form a catcher's backstop; it would be difficult to find on the campus a more perfect cul-de-sac. It was inconceivable that soldiers would march with their eyes open into such a trap, where they would be subjected to hostile students who would have large numbers of rocks at their disposal. But this is what happened.

At 12:07 the center unit, led by Colonel Fassinger and reinforced by large numbers from Captain Martin's Alpha Company on the right flank, marched down from the pagoda and smack against the steel chain-link fence. They had placed themselves in a position from which they could escape only by retreating, which, when it happened, would have to be interpreted by the watching students as a defeat for the Guard. How large was this combined unit? Photographs show at least 69 Guards against the fence, but one meticulous investigation augments that number. There were 75 Guards present, comprised as follows: two senior officers (Canterbury, Fassinger) with 53 men from Alpha Company, including three officers, plus the two casuals from Charlie Company, to which were added 18 men from G Troop, including two officers. However, Major Jones now ran across the grass to join the group. We have seen that he started with Charlie Company, which halted at the far end of Taylor Hall, so that during the first few minutes when the Guard stood penned against the fence, he had been with Captain Snyder. But quickly he discerned what was developing; elbowing his way through the crowd of students, he joined the larger contingent at the fence, where he would play a conspicuous role in what was to follow. The unit therefore consisted of 68 enlisted men led by 8 officers.

As soon as the students saw that the Guard was pinned against the fence, they began to close in from the parking lot to the north, cursing, throwing rocks, waving flags and tossing back gas canisters. The word *surrounded* has often been used to describe the Guard's condition at this moment. Nothing could be more inappropriate. To the east, across the fence, there was no one but Mike Alewitz, the socialist leader whose presence there will be explained later. To the south—that is, behind the Guardsmen on the practice field—there was no one for more than a hundred yards, as numerous photographs attest. And to the west, over the path to the pagoda which the Guard had just traversed, students had not yet re-formed. Far from being surrounded, the Guard had empty space on all sides.

At 12:10 the Guard underwent a heavy assault from the north, where students had grown bolder and were dashing in close to unload. What happened next remains obscure, but the sixteen enlisted men of G Troop, plus one other, believing their supply of tear gas to have been exhausted, knelt on one knee and assumed a firing position, aiming their rifles directly at the gadfly students who were pestering them. It appears that they must have been ordered by some officer to assume this frightening and provocative position, and if a further command had been given at this moment, students on the parking lot would have been mowed down, but no such command was uttered. (Actually, the beleaguered troops had more gas. Specialist Russell Repp of A Company still carried eight canisters, a fact known by his immediate superiors, Srp and Stevenson, but not by those in command.)

The brazen young man with the black flag ran close and waved it before the silent rifles, daring the Guardsmen to fire. When they refrained, he and others were convinced that they would never shoot, that even if they did, the bullets were blanks. That much of the situation is ascertainable; what is still unknown is what took place at the core of the unit, where General Canterbury discussed this dangerous and ridiculous situation with his officers.

At 12:18 Colonel Fassinger issued the order: 'Regroup back at ROTC.' And the contingent began to form up for retreat, assuming the pattern of a flying wedge, point foremost and flanks trailing, with officers inside the V. (It may seem strange that a colonel should have been issuing orders to the troops when a general was present, but this was not unusual. In the navy, for example, it is customary for a five-star admiral attended by three- and two-star admirals to choose some warship as headquarters afloat; when they do so, they are technically under the command of whatever captain is in charge of the ship they occupy, and all personnel attached to that ship take their orders from the captain and not from the admirals.)

At 12:19 Fassinger radioed: 'For the third time I am asking for more tear gas.'

At 12:22 Fassinger gave the order to march, and his unit left the fence, where they had suffered much humiliation, some of it at their own hands, crossed the service road, and at an increasing speed, hurried back up to the pagoda. They were hot, and angry, and disgusted at having been pinned down against the fence, infuriated by the students who had challenged them, and bitterly resentful of the girls who even now trailed them up the hill, cursing and reviling them. Their gas masks prevented them from seeing just what was happening, and they were only vaguely aware of students still massed on their right flank. They had a long hot hill to climb and they were sweating. Were they in danger? On their left flank there was nobody except a few Guardsmen stationed at Johnson

Hall. In the rear there was a handful of gadflies, mostly girls, who posed no threat at all. Straight ahead the commons was almost empty. At Taylor Hall the porches were crowded with students, at least half of them girls, and some teachers who were observing the scene. On the right flank, however, at a distance of seventy yards, there was a large mass of students, including many of those who had been pestering the Guard at the practice field but also many who were merely passing by between classes. The closest student seems to have been at least twenty yards away; the bulk were more than a hundred yards distant. But there was movement, and in the confusion of the march, it could be interpreted as hostile.

At 12:24, with the escape route back to ROTC completely unimpeded and with alternate ones available either to the left flank or to the rear, some Guardsmen on the trailing right flank suddenly stopped, wheeled 135 degrees to the right—that is, they turned almost completely around—faced the students who had collected on the south side of Taylor Hall, and dropped their rifles to a ready position. It so happens that three tape recorders, operated by would-be reporters from the School of Journalism, were running at this moment, and their testimony as to what happened next is incontrovertible.

There was a single shot—some people heard it as two almost simultaneous shots—then a period of silence lasting about two seconds, then a prolonged but thin fusillade, not a single angry burst, lasting about eight seconds, then another silence, and two final shots. The shooting had covered thirteen seconds, which is a very long time under such circumstances, and fifty-five M-1 bullets seem to have been discharged, plus five pistol shots and the single blast from a shotgun. Twenty-eight different Guardsmen did the firing, but this fact should be remembered: If each of the men had fired his weapon directly at the massed students, the killing would have been terrible, for a steel-jacketed M-1 bullet can carry two miles and penetrate two or four or six bodies in doing so. Fortunately, many of the men found it impossible to fire into a crowd and pointed their rifles upward—avoiding what could have been a general slaughter.

But some Guardsmen, fed up with the riotous behavior of the students and in fear of their lives, did fire directly into the crowd, and when the volley ended, thirteen bodies were scattered over the grass and the distant parking area. Four were dead, and nine were wounded more or less severely.

On the afternoon of the shooting, a governmental agency took careful measurements (which have not previously been released); here are the dry statistics. Thirteen young people shot: eleven men, two girls. All were registered at the university and all were attending classes formally. If the wounded were arranged in order of their nearness to the Guard, the closest young man was 71 feet away from the rifles, the farthest 745 feet away, or nearly two and a half football fields. The seventh body—that is, the median one—happened to be Doug Wrentmore, who was 329 feet away. The distances of the four dead at the time they were hit are as follows:

Jeffrey Glenn Miller, fifth closest	265 feet
Allison B. Krause, eighth closest	343 feet
William K. Schroeder, tenth closest	382 feet
Sandra Lee Scheuer, eleventh closest	390 feet

Of the thirteen who were struck by bullets, two were shot in the front, seven from the side, and four from the rear. Ten of the wounded were struck directly, three by ricochets. We came upon fairly strong evidence that a fourteenth student was hit in the left arm, but not seriously; he fled the area with his wound concealed, apprehensive lest he become involved with police or FBI investigations. He was more than 600 feet away when hit, and obviously not involved in the immediate action, though what he might have been doing earlier, we have no way of knowing.

Ascertaining the correct time of the firing is difficult, for whereas most of the other events can be confirmed with minute accuracy, often by three or four people, it is impossible to state precisely when the shooting occurred, even though hundreds of eyewitnesses observed it. The time indicated here is by no means a consensus, but it does represent the best-educated guess. Estimates vary from 12:12, which hardly gives the Guard time to cover the distances involved, let alone take action at any of the resting points, to 12:45, which is the solid report of one of the most careful investigating committees but which seems ridiculously late to those who participated. A highly placed Guard officer who was in position to know what was happening, who looked at his wristwatch at the moment of firing, and who was responsible for calling the information in to the command post, affirms, 'The shooting took place at exactly 12:20, for I checked it as it occurred.' But the official log of the action recording his report times it at 12:26. The apparent impossibility of determining a precise time is not critical; if an early time is used, it means only that the Guardsmen had conducted all their operations on the practice field in less than three minutes, which seems impossible; if a late time is used it means that they dallied there for more than half an hour, which seems contrary to evidence and common sense. The time given here was noted by a journalism student at Taylor Hall, who made no great claim for its accuracy, but it does conform to the judgment of many.

At 12:25 (or 12:46, if the extreme time is accepted) the firing ceased, thanks to the energetic efforts of Major Jones, who can be seen in photographs beating his troops over their helmets with his swagger stick, pleading with them to stop. General Canterbury can also be seen, turning in surprise from the direction in which he had been heading—down the hill to safety—which lends credence to the theory that if an order of some kind had been given to fire, he at least had not been informed of it.

At 12:29, after a lapse of at least four minutes, during which frantic officers did their best to restore order, the unit reformed, retreated in orderly fashion to their staging area at ROTC, and surrendered their guns for registry and inspection. Jack Deegan, a Marine Corps reservist majoring in history, who had followed the unit at extremely close range all the way from the link fence, reports, 'I saw one young Guard lying on the ground, tossing himself back and forth in hysteria and moaning something I couldn't hear.' He may have been William Herschler, whom the FBI reported as having cried, 'I just shot two teenagers.' At this point a veil of silence descended over the Guard.

Letters to the editor

WHEN Harold Walker left the field of the dead, he suspected that on his many rolls of film he might have captured some compelling shots, but like John Filo, he could not be sure until he saw them developed. So he did what he had been taught in journalism: 'If you think you have a scoop, get in touch with the newspaper you know best.' In his case it was *The Gazette and Daily*, of York, Pennsylvania, one of America's real odd-ball journals. Operating in the heart of the conservative Pennsylvania–German country and surrounded by people who vote Republican, it is liberal and outspoken. It is also interesting in that it is edited on a devil-may-care basis, with the editor saying pretty much what he likes. Among the American newspapers from cities its size, it has no peer. That many of its subscribers consider it communistic is a cross it has to bear.

Its reaction to the Walker photographs was typical. Calling Walker on the phone as he worked at Kent State, the editor said excitedly, 'These photos are too good to waste on a small-town paper like this. I've alerted the *Washington Post* and they want you to fly to their offices immediately.'

With some excitement young Walker caught a plane at Akron, and entered the *Post* editorial offices to find the entire staff gazing in bewilderment at the shots which he himself had not yet seen. 'How did you get such photos?' some of the older men asked in admiration, but before Walker could explain, one of the senior editors delivered the crushing decision: 'We're not going to use any of them.'

'Why not?' several assistants asked.

'Because we think they may have been faked.'

'What do you mean?' Walker cried.

'I mean these. The ones showing the National Guard marching up the hill away from the football field.'

'What's wrong with them? I couldn't have got any closer.'

'Yes, but these photos don't show any students following the Guardsmen, and we know from all the news stories that there were students there.'

'Look at the negatives,' Walker pleaded, 'they're in sequence.'

'Yes, but we think you may have spliced in a series of shots taken on Sunday afternoon. There ought to be students visible.'

Walker, exhausted from tension and lack of sleep, looked at his amazing shots of what had happened. Of all the photographs taken that day, they best illustrated the needlessness of the tragedy. Then he looked at the disbelieving experts from the great newspaper. Then he packed up his pictures and went back to York, where they appeared in the *York Gazette and Daily.* It scooped the world.

The York editor came up with the logical idea of having Walker accompany his photographs with a verbal account of what had happened, and the young newsman ended his essay in the way most sensitive men his age would have done: 'I think that when people look at the situation—students shot without warning; the dead and the wounded—there will be sympathy across the nation, no matter what the political beliefs. As for the city of Kent, the whole town seems to be in sympathy with the students.' He concluded: 'I believe the incident may bring the student and the adult communities together. It may bring about mutual understanding.'

Never in his future career as newspaperman will Harold C. Walker, Kent State 1970, be more completely wrong, for even as the paper in York was printing these hopeful and constructive words, the newspaper in Kent was being forced to find space for what will be remembered as one of the most virulent outpourings of community hatred in recent decades. It seemed as if everybody in the Kent area suddenly wanted to unburden himself of resentments against young people, colleges and education which had been festering for years. The paper had to reserve a full page, day after day for several weeks, for this violent outburst, and anyone who wishes to explore the Kent phenomenon more deeply than this book allows, is directed to those terrifying broadsides, printed solid in compact type. They give a portrait of Middle America at the beginning of the 1970's that is frightening. The first group requires no comment.

Authority, law and order are the backbone of our society, for its protection. Would you want authorities to stand by if your home were threatened? Well, Kent State is my home by virtue of taxes spent funding it. What's more, it's their home by virtue of tuition paid. Playful children destroying a disenchanting toy.

How dare they! I stand behind the action of the National Guard! I want my property defended. And if dissenters refuse to obey the final warning before the punishment, hurling taunts, rocks (stones, they say), sticks, brandishing clubs with razor blades imbedded, then the first slap is a mighty sting.

Live ammunition! Well, really, what did they expect, spitballs? How much warning is needed indeed.

Hooray! I shout for God and Country, recourse to justice under law, fifes, drums, martial music, parades, ice cream cones—America, support it or leave it.

Ravenna housewife

When radical students are allowed to go through a town smashing windows, terrifying the citizens, and are allowed to burn buildings belonging to the taxpayers to the ground, I think it is high time that the Guard be brought in to stop them—and stop them in any way they can.

The sooner the students of this country learn that they are not running this country, that they are going to college to learn, *not teach*, the better.

If those students don't like this country or our colleges, why don't they go to the country from which they are being indoctrinated?

Concerned citizen

A surprising number of the writers referred to property rights and taxes. If there had been any doubt as to what values many citizens in this part of Ohio placed in paramount position, these letters settled that question.

We are paying a large percentage of our hard-earned money to support and educate these young people. For what? To let them burn and destroy property that more of our tax money has paid for? Who paid for the hose that was cut while our firemen were trying to stop a fire, set deliberately, all the while being pelted with rocks. Some innocent person's home could very well have burned while our firemen were busy fighting a fire on campus.

Concerned resident

I, and thousands of other old-timers, have been paying taxes for many years—even before some of the present troublemakers were born. These taxes were used, and are being used, to erect and equip modern campus buildings and to pay the salaries of professors (even those who support and condone the actions of the troublemakers) who have such a vital role in the educational process. How many buildings were erected and equipped from taxes paid by campus vandals? How many professors and other university personnel received salaries from taxes paid by campus vandals? This property does not belong to them. It belongs to me and thousands like me who have paid taxes for twenty, thirty and even forty years to provide the money for these facilities. We are lending them OUR facilities and we expect them to take care of OUR property. We do not expect these temporary occupants to burn, damage or destroy that which they have borrowed. We will gladly pay for these buildings, but we see red when OUR property has to be repaired or replaced because of the actions of a few irresponsible misfits who only want to damage or destroy.

A concerned old-timer

Only a small percentage of the letters printed in that period can be reproduced here, but each one chosen represents a score or more. On no subject was the comment more unanimous than on the right of the National Guard to do whatever was required to enforce discipline.

Some have questioned the need of the National Guard on campus and throughout our city. However, I shudder to think of the condition of our city today had they had not been present to protect and preserve what so many have labored endlessly to build.

Kent citizen

Are we the citizens of this fine town going to sit back and allow certain officials to persecute the National Guard for doing their duty? Are we going to accept the theory that these ones involved in this rioting and burning were JUST children?

Since when is rioting, looting, burning, assaulting a town called academic freedom? Is it freedom of expression? Why do they allow these so-called educated punks, who apparently know only how to spell four-lettered words, to run loose on our campuses tearing down and destroying that which good men spent years building up?

I plead with the citizens of Kent to take a stand, don't allow these tragic deaths to go for naught. Make your voice heard. Do not let the National Guard be blamed for something they did not create.

> Signed by one who was taught
> that 'to educate a man in mind
> and not in morals is to educate
> a menace to society'

Congratulations to the Guardsmen for their performance of duty on the Kent University Campus. I hope their actions serve as an example for the entire nation. The governors of our states cannot waste the taxpayers' money playing games. These men were alerted as a last resort to control mob action.

I extend appreciation and whole-hearted support of the Guard of every state for their fine efforts in protecting citizens like me and our property.

> Mother of Guardsman

Not included in this sampling are the numerous letters, submitted by committees, with hundreds and even thousands of names, approving the behavior of the Guard. One of the most interesting themes was the recrudescence of an idea that had been born many years ago and which had enjoyed frequent revival through the decades. In April, 1933, at the depth of the depression, Representative William R. Foss, of the Ohio legislature, proposed that in view of the current oversupply of teachers, more than four thousand of whom were unable to obtain work, it would be a good idea to convert one of the four large colleges—Ohio State University was excluded—into a mental asylum. 'We intend to investigate this proposition thoroughly,' Foss warned, 'and to determine which college can most readily be converted. We're not bluffing.'

After a visit to Kent on May 4 of that year, Foss reported: 'Kent State has the finest, most modern buildings and, therefore, is most adaptable to welfare work. There would be no fire hazard in connection with the structures, and this is an important feature.' Later, referring obliquely to Kent, he said that 'one of the institutions visited was so adapted to welfare needs that it would be difficult to distinguish it from those built for that specific purpose.' The proposal came to naught and Kent State was spared.

However, two years later the idea of converting the college into an asylum surfaced again, and once more, serious consideration was given to closing down the college, but an improvement in the economy saved it. Now, after the riots of 1970, the project was reopened.

I have one possible solution to the problem. Build a fence completely around KSU, put President White and his 550 faculty members inside along with all the agitators that they understand so well and let them do their thing. We could also change the name from KSU to 'Idiot Hill.' Then Dr. White and his faculty and students could assemble and throw rocks at each other and play with matches and burn things down, because they understand each other's reasoning and don't want to be bothered. So be it! I have more ideas, but what's the use. In fact, who needs KSU? Not me.

Kent taxpayer

Letters abusing student behavior were numerous. Their endless and bitter barrage startled the students and saddened the professors, who felt that a whole society was turning against the youth who would soon be constituting that society. One of the reasonable complaints against students follows:

Last night on TV were several shots of protesting students and a leader of these talked for some time about continuing the protest into the summer. The TV program showed pictures and named the student leader.

This student leader was not a student during 1968 and to October, 1969. Girls, wild parties, filthy living conditions and failure to pay bills featured this man; an acme of unreliability. Another man, said to be a leader of Kent SDS, lived with him for a time. His fine parents came to pay the bills he owed us when he disappeared. Word is that other creditors in the area were not so fortunate. Yet, this man is shown as depicting an important trend in our times.

Ravenna citizen

A surprising number of the letter-writers, and among them the most vehement, referred to themselves as members of the silent majority. Two examples follow:

When is the long-silent, long-suffering majority going to rise up in force to show the militant minority on the KSU campus exactly how they feel about them? It's hard to believe that the surly, foul-mouthed, know-nothing punks that have raised so much hell in this town the past few days are speaking for all of us, or half of us, or even one tenth of us. Yet, like any mob, they've got you outnumbered, and any sort of ideology is completely lost in the sadistic pleasure of sheer destruction. In other words, the would-be heroes are behaving exactly like the criminals they are.

As a person young enough to be more a member of their generation than that of their parents, I reject these creeps.

Anti-violent

Kent has tolerated these so-called misunderstood students long enough. The city of Kent should be off-limits to students. Keep them on the university grounds, and when they have completely destroyed it, they can go home and we will be rid of them.

If the National Guard is forced to face these situations without loaded guns, the silent majority has lost everything. The National Guard made only one mistake—they should have fired sooner and longer.

As for the parents of the dead students, I can appreciate their suffering, they probably don't know the truth. A dissident certainly isn't going to write home about his demonstration activities. Parents are learning the hard way and others should take heed. The high school photos that appeared in the paper were all very nice, but how do you explain the mother who refused to identify her own son at the hospital because of his appearance. This same boy had refused to go home on holidays.

I only hope the National Guard will be here the next time we need them. I am fully prepared to protect what is mine—property, home and life—at any cost against these mobs of dissidents in the event our law enforcement is prohibited to do what is necessary.

Ravenna citizen

Numerous letters spoke of the need for instituting some kind of vigilante movement to combat the students. Sometimes this was intimated; often it was spelled out.

There has been no other issue in recent years that has raised my wrath as much as student demonstration, including SDS leadership, against the Vietnam war and against anything else that occurs to the demonstrators.

So, it was refreshing to see a group of hard-hatted construction workers in lower New York do something about it. They went through
those demonstrators like Sherman went through Atlanta, leaving sixty
or seventy injured. That's exactly what we need . . . a harder line
with demonstrators, not the easy, 'pat on the wrist' punishment for
their crime.

I'm for raising a counterforce to neutralize the efforts of sometimes
silly, and sometimes dangerous, and always unthinking students who
want to go to a school without abiding by its rules.

Aurora citizen

My first reaction, and again I have been thinking of this for some
time, was to arm both my home and my office. But during moments
of more rational thought, I realize that probably all I would accomplish is to shoot myself in the foot. I abhor violence and I have no
desire to traipse all over the country protecting other people's property. However, I feel an immediate and compelling responsibility to
protect my own locality. I am thinking in the direction of a kind of
citizens committee, under appropriate professional direction, who
would bear arms against these people to protect our families and
property. Further, I will support taxation to raise the funds to provide
a capable effective force to deal with this problem.

Kent citizen

Many persons in the Kent area felt that students who
dressed oddly or who wore their hair long ought to be disciplined. In fact, the bitterness which such appearance created
was one of the recurrent themes in discussing the shooting.
Several intimated that the penalty for non-conformity should
be death.

It is too bad that a small minority of students feel that these damnable
demonstrations must take place. If the slouchily dressed female students and the freakishly dressed, long-haired male students would
properly dress and otherwise properly demean themselves as not to
make show-offs of themselves, such trouble could be and would be
avoided. It is difficult to understand why female students must get
out and make such fools of themselves as they do, but it is understandable that male students do so largely to get their screwball mugs
on television and in the press.

If the troublemaking students have no better sense than to conduct
themselves as they do on our university and college campuses, such

as throwing missiles, bottles and bullets at legally constituted police authority and the National Guard, they justly deserve the consequences that they bring upon themselves, even if this does unfortunately result in death.

                                                                Attorney-at-law

There were, of course, several letters which challenged the headlong rush to law and order. These writers endeavored to explain that the phrase required careful definition.

Where are the voices of 'law and order' when construction workers in New York City attack a peaceful, non-violent demonstration of anti-war protesters? I would suspect that the lawless action of the construction workers is condoned by the 'silent majority' because they aren't members of the 'effete corps of impudent snobs,' or they aren't 'bums.'

You see, the voices of the silent majority chose to remain silent on those issues. It would appear to me, then, that a double standard exists when people call for law and order—it's a good phrase when applied to young, long-haired dissidents and radicals, but it's a meaningless phrase when applied to the silent majority. I would submit that just as students are not above the law, neither are members of the 'silent majority.'

                                                                Ravenna citizen

And from time to time isolated writers would remind the public that four young people were dead, that something had gone fearfully wrong. They sounded like lost voices, except for the eloquence they sometimes introduced into their letters.

I am a KSU student. I am not a radical, but to quote Albert Camus, 'I should like to be able to love my country and to love justice, also.'

The letters I've been reading about the Kent deaths, and the people I've heard saying that the demonstrators deserved to be shot, frighten me. Many justify the slayings because of the property damage that had been done. But the crowd Monday was attacking no buildings. Did they shoot to avenge the burning of the ROTC building?

Revolutionaries and SDSers don't frighten me, nor do squads of police or National Guards. I am afraid of the people who say 'kill the demonstrators, because they destroyed our property.' I am afraid of these people who value property over human life. I am not afraid for my life, but for my soul, and for the sensitivity and humanity that is slowly being erased from our society.

Jesus said that no one can truly love God if he cannot love his fellow man. You people with the 'mow 'em down' philosophy, can you love God without loving Jeffrey, Bill, Sandy and Allison?

Ravenna student

On Monday, May 4, I witnessed the KSU killings. As horrible and frightening as the memories of those experiences are, they are not nearly so terrifying as the hostility that has been revealed in their aftermath. I am not a radical. I do not believe that arson and violence should go unpunished, but I know of no state in which arson carries a death sentence, and there are certainly none in which 'illegal' assembly is punishable by execution.

I have recently heard a multitude of comments such as, 'They should have mowed them all down' or 'I'll bet they think twice next time' or 'They got what they deserved.' It is in the people who make these statements that the real violence is to be found. They seem to be permeated with an intense desire to see destroyed or shackled anything they do not understand or anyone who does not concisely conform to their glorious social ideals about what is 'American.'

They are to be feared far more than are the campus dissidents, for they would destroy something far more precious than property, or even life—they would destroy freedom! And is not freedom supposed to be what America is all about?

Kent State student

It would be fruitless to reproduce all the savage attacks that were visited upon the faculty. The unfortunate resolution adopted in the Akron Church on Tuesday afternoon was referred to in a score of letters, with citizens rebuking them in harsh terms for their one-sided interpretation of what had happened on the campus. Only three letters need be cited here, a typical one of rebuke, and two reflections by university members on the tragedy that had overtaken a notable institution. They represent the kind of reevaluation that was being undertaken across the nation.

I do not understand why the teacher who was convicted of first-degree riot is permitted to teach at the university during the week and serve her time on weekends. She shouldn't even be allowed on the campus, much less be permitted to teach.

Ravenna resident

The meeting of the faculty of Kent State University held on Tuesday [in the Akron church] was deeply disturbing to me. The tone of the meeting seemed to me emotional and rhetorical—in short a mob. And I am sick of emotionalism, mobs and violence.

What is truly academic must be personal and humble. As I recall hearing it read, one of the items in the resolution stated that we will not teach under military coercion. Similarly, I don't see how we can teach under the social pressure of our own desire to reach unanimous decisions.

I want my students back, but I do not want to unite them behind any social issue or against any issue, such as the war in Indochina, even though I abhor that war. I want my students to wander a free campus, and I only want those who are 'academically inclined' to contemplate with humility and with intricacy. I am frightened of the mob—the mob in me.

Kent professor of English

The statement issued [by the faculty] from an Akron church Tuesday correctly expresses the angry mood of the majority of the faculty, but it is not enough. If academic democracy is to work, it must be self-enforcing. We must demonstrate clearly that we understand and are able to assume the responsibility for conduct of our university.

It is imperative that we defend academic freedom, which includes the right to dissent, as we have undertaken to do, but we must insure that the freedom we defend is clearly differentiated from license to destroy by violence. Our campus must remain open to those who would express unpopular ideas, but it must not be a sanctuary for those who commit felonious acts, no matter what purpose they avow.

I am not making just another appeal to 'law and order.' My position is that unless we insist upon the maintenance of orderly processes, the tragic circumstances of last Monday are the eventual and inevitable result.

All who have contributed to the blurring of the connection between the rights and responsibilities of free people must share in the guilt for the deaths of our students: those who have engaged in civil disobedience and have refused to accept the consequences, those who have cried for amnesty for those who have criminally violated the rights of others in pursuit of a worthy cause, those who have failed to understand that destroying a building is not a legitimate exercise of freedom of expression, and those who have stood silently by while this tide of passion has engulfed us in its tragic whorl.

Kent professor of journalism

The most deplorable aspect of these letters was not the explosive outpouring of hatred (which could be forgiven as an autonomic response to phenomena not understood) nor the obvious obsession with property values as opposed to human life (which is often observed in American life) but rather the willingness to condemn all students, perceiving them as a mass to be castigated. Nothing can excuse this error. We must constantly remember that only a small percentage of the Kent student body was involved. The following table has been revised continuously from the day this study started; it was refined whenever new police reports were made available or new photographs came to light. As it now stands, it incorporates the best guesses of many experts but reflects the personal conclusions of none. It is a composite.

Percentage of Student Body of 21,186 Participating in Disturbances

Incident	Total Persons Involved	Non-university Persons	University Persons	%age of Total Student Body Participating
Friday night downtown	1,000	600	400	01.9
Saturday night ROTC fire				
Passive spectators	1,500	250	1,250	05.9
Active participants	500	250	250	01.2
Sunday night sitdown	700	150	550	02.6
Monday noon rally				
Distant spectators	2,500	400	2,100	09.9
Passive on Blanket Hill	650	150	500	02.3
Active on Blanket Hill	450	50	400	01.9

from *Kent State: What Happened and Why*, 1971

"I think we have a very unhappy colleague-on-leave tonight"

by Mike Kinsley

FRANCIS BATOR leaned back in his Littauer Center office a few days after the excursion to Washington. "You might ask me," he suggested, " 'Why not get an appointment with the President?' " I obliged.

He answered, "Well, my strong view is that in the Oval Office one is the guest of the President and he conducts the conversation. And the discourtesy involved in trying to override his management of the conversation is too much when dealing with the President of the United States. So you see for our purposes Henry Kissinger wasn't second-best. He was the absolute best we could have done—he was the closest we could get to the President without having to feel like guests. But even in our meeting with Kissinger there was nothing harsh, but rather the tone was muted and painful. You see we broke two long-standing rules: First, one doesn't announce such a meeting in the papers ahead of time. (I feel this especially strongly given that I too was special assistant to the President for National Security Affairs. I won't dissociate myself with Johnson's Vietnam policy even though I wasn't on that particular area. It wasn't even my part of the world—it was Rostow's. But I knew what was happening, so I won't dissociate myself.) And second, the fact that we were thinking seriously about Congressional restraints. I had always thought of Congress as at best a nuisance, sometimes an adversary, often the enemy. But now my fear is that Nixon may believe that Eisenhower ended the Korean war by making a nuclear threat. It's the fear of the process, rather than of the discrete decision, that forces myself and these others to break these two rules."

Thomas Schelling, professor of Economics and organizer of the group, said at dinner that night in Washington, "Not that all our other meetings weren't helpful, but the crucial purpose in coming here was really to communicate something important to Henry Kissinger. I would guess that Henry's boss will hear of this meeting with a group that has affected him so much. We have all known Henry and—to the extent that this is possible—loved him. That's the one that mattered and that went as well as it could have gone."

According to the participants, the meeting with Kissinger was one of intense emotions painfully suppressed. "We made it clear to Henry from the beginning," Schelling said, "that we weren't here lunching with him as old friends, but were talking to him solely in his capacity to communicate to the President that we regard this latest act [the invasion of Cambodia] as a disastrously bad foreign policy decision *even on its own terms.*"

As reported by one member of the group, Schelling then turned to Dean May, who had flown down especially for the Kissinger confrontation and would have to return immediately afterwards, for a comment. May is a professor of History at Harvard and has worked as a military historian for the Defense Department. "Ernest told Henry, 'You're tearing the country apart domestically.' He said this would have long-term consequences for foreign policy, as tomorrow's foreign policy is based on today's domestic situation.

"Then Bator and Westheimer [Frank H. Westheimer, Morris Loeb Professor of Chemistry] chimed in with an explanation of how difficult it was for us to have Henry read in the newspapers beforehand of our coming. Bator said it was especially painful for him since he had held part of the same portfolio Kissinger now handles, back in 1965 through 1967. But despite that, they explained, we felt that the only way we could shock him into realizing how we felt was not to just give him marginal advice. We wanted to shock him into realizing that this latest decision was appallingly bad foreign policy in the short run.

"At this point Henry got called out to see the President. He asked to have someone explain to him when he returned what short-term mistake the Nixon policy made. We decided to let Tom do it, as he was the one who organized us and he was Henry's closest academic colleague in the group. So when

Henry returned after a few minutes, Schelling gave him the Monster Speech."

Schelling's Monster Speech was one he used frequently during that day. It's a metaphorical analysis similar to those he uses frequently in his undergraduate course on game theory and decision-making, Ec 135. The speech goes something like this: "It's one of those problems where you look out the window, and you see a monster. And you turn to the guy standing next to you at the very same window, and say, 'Look, there's a monster.' He then looks out the window—and doesn't see a monster at all. *How do you explain to him that there really is a monster?*

"As we see it, there are two possibilities: Either one, the President didn't understand when he went into Cambodia that he was invading another country; or two, he did understand. We just don't know which one is scarier. And he seems to have done this without consultation with the Secretary of Defense or the Secretary of State, or with leaders of the Senate and House. We are deeply worried about the scale of the operation as compared with the process of decision."

Bator reportedly continued, "We are full of anxiety about what more things Nixon could do. And if we're scared, then the people in London, Paris, Moscow and Bonn that we care about must really be concerned. It's a scary situation—that's the foreign policy consequence. The hawks in Moscow can now say that the Americans occasionally go nuts. What does that mean for the SALT talks?" Bator gave two explanations of Nixon's behavior. The first he called the "Kennedy-Vienna syndrome." When President Kennedy returned from his Vienna talks with Khrushchev in 1961, Bator said, he was afraid he had given Khrushchev the impression he was soft. ("Some say this is the explanation of the Cuban Missile Crisis of 1962," Bator now says, "but I doubt it.") Bator said, "Maybe Nixon is also afraid of appearing weak."

But the more likely explanation of the sudden invasion of Cambodia, Bator said, is the enormous leverage the military field commander has over the President. "The field commander can tell the President that he will be carrying the blood of American soldiers on his conscience unless he backs him. And if pressure from the field commanders can create an invasion of Cambodia in 10 days—well then, what next."

According to one of the group, Richard Neustadt (expert on the Presidency) then added, "What this is going to signal to American senior military officers—and the Saigon government—is that, if you put enough pressure on Nixon by emphasizing that 'American boys are dying,' you can get the President to do very discontinuous things. And this makes his whole promise of withdrawal open to question. It's not that we doubt his intention; it's just that we're unsure of the pressure available to field commanders."

"Each of us spoke to Henry at least once," the member reported. "Michael Walzer [professor of Government], told him that as an old dove, he was impressed by the intensity of the concern of us old government boys. Gerry Holton [professor of Physics] talked generally about the lack of restraint in Nixon's policies. Adam [Yarmolinsky, professor of Law] questioned the credibility in Saigon of the withdrawal strategy.

"When we were all through, Henry asked if he could go off the record. We said no. Schelling said one reason we had brought non-ex-government types like Walzer was to keep us honest. Henry replied that the nature of his job as an advisor to the President was such that he never spoke on the record."

Kissinger did tell his colleagues three things.

"First, he told us that he understood what we were saying, and the gravity of our concern. Second, he said that if he could go off the record he could explain the President's action to our satisfaction. And third, he said that since we wouldn't let him go off the record, all he could do was assure us that the President had not lost sight of his original objective or gone off his timetable for withdrawal.

"Bator muttered something about the interaction of means and ends, and how he doubted whether with even the best of intentions Nixon and Kissinger could control the process Johnson and Bundy couldn't. Schelling ["Wisely, I think," Bator said later] told him to be quiet and let Henry go on. But there wasn't much else to say.

"So afterwards we all got up and shook hands, with a sense of sadness. It was painful for us, but it wasn't a personal thing.

It was an impersonal visit—to try to save the country. I think Henry fully understood the gravity of what we were talking about."

Back in their headquarters—a room in the Hay-Adams Hotel across Lafayette Park from the White House—the professors discussed their confrontation lunch with Kissinger.

Holton said, "It was not exactly what I would call a love-feast. He said that he was moved by our visit, that he felt that it's all a tragic situation. But he refused to speak on the record, and we refused to go off, so we had an hour-and-a-half of presenting views."

Bloch said, "Kissinger told us 'When you come back a year from now, you will find your concerns are unwarranted.'" Holton: "But he doesn't understand that the end-justifies-the-means philosophy is exactly the problem, and what is antagonizing the large part of the population. Kissinger just did not realize that we'd crossed the threshold. He said our concerns would be brought to attention upstairs."

Westheimer: "He said the invasion of Cambodia will not affect the withdrawal of troops from Southeast Asia, that Nixon's withdrawal schedules will eventually be met. Someday that statement will be true like the stopped clock which is true twice a day."

Schelling said, "We had a very painful hour and a half with Henry, persuading him we were all horrified not just about the Cambodia decision, but what it implied about the way the President makes up his mind. It was a small gain to be had at enormous political risk. He refused to reply on-the-record, therefore he had our sentiments heaped upon him, sat in pained silence, and just listened."

"He did just right with his response, actually," Bator commented. "He could have done two other things that would have scared me more: He could have said things on-the-record that he shouldn't have said, or he could have given us a canned war briefing, which would have demeaned whatever relation we have with him. If he'd tried to dissociate himself with the policy, I would have walked out. But he behaved with great grace and dignity and courage under intense emotional pressure from his peer group."

Seymour Martin Lipset, professor of Government and Social Relations, said, "I think we have a very unhappy colleague-on-leave tonight."

Schelling added, "I hope so." Then, as with a flushing of toilets and a straightening of ties the professors swirled out of the room to catch cabs for the Pentagon and a meeting with Undersecretary of State David Packard, he turned back into the room and perspired, "You know, this is hard work."

One of the purposes of the Harvard professors' trip to Washington was to get publicity for the anti-war campaigning then going on. But the kind of publicity they got was not what they expected. The first person to pick up the story (besides the CRIMSON, which had it a day and a half earlier) was Mary McGrory of the Washington *Star*. McGrory wrote Friday that the professors were "descending" on the White House "with blood in their eyes" to tell Henry Kissinger that "if he doesn't quit soon—or reverse policy—Harvard will never have him back again." The same story was reprinted in McGrory's syndicated column, and appeared in Saturday's Boston *Globe*. Last week's *Time* magazine improvised further on the same theme. *Time* had Kissinger replying to this threat, "quietly" (if somewhat disingenuously): "I want you to understand that I hear you."

McGrory called Neustadt at the Hay-Adams Thursday night with this interpretation already uppermost in her mind. Neustadt told her that the group was talking to Kissinger purely as a surrogate for the President, and that his relation to Harvard would not enter the discussion at all. Unsure that he had communicated this to her, he had Bator call her back again with the same story. Then Yarmolinsky called her too, for good measure. After this final phone call, Yarmolinsky told the group, "Mary's message is that no one else needs to call her."

"But she printed the story exactly the way she wanted to anyhow," Bator said.

The story was picked up by the Montreal *Star*, and following his return from Washington Bator received an incensed phone call at his home from a professor at McGill University. "He asked if we had lost our wits, and if we had no respect for academic freedom," Bator said. Then the Washington editor of the (London) *Sunday Times*, a friend of Bator and Neustadt, called Bator at 11:45 Monday night to say he had heard that at a lunch Sunday at the home of Katherine Graham (publisher of the Washington *Post* and *Newsweek* magazine), someone had alleged that the Harvard group had arrived at Kissinger's office Friday with a tape recorder.

"Imagine myself and Dick Neustadt and all the others arriving at the basement of the White House with a tape recorder!" Bator sputtered. "It's grotesque! It's incredible how utterly grotesque paranoid rumors circulate as reality. Reston's column Monday suggested that in the end we protected Henry's confidences. But there were no confidences! The idea that this has to do with Kissinger's relation to Harvard is grotesque on its face."

The professors returned to the Hay-Adams from their meeting with Packard—barely an hour after they'd left—in a highly agitated state. William Capron, associate dean of the Kennedy School and former assistant director of the Budget, complained, "He gave us the straightforward party line—he sounded just like John Foster Dulles. It was nothing like Kissinger in terms of emotional content. We gave it to him very hard and he said to please wait six weeks and we'd see, that everything will turn out all right. He said he understood our concern, but asked for our *forebearance*! In six weeks, he said, we'll be out and it will be a great victory! We were just talking past each other."

Neustadt (author of *Presidential Power*): "Mr. Packard heard us out, then responded in a perfectly canned way that we should be patient. His explanation was irrelevant to our concern. It was a matter of our reporting our feelings to him and hearing no attempt at exchange. Perhaps we underestimated the credibility gap. Ghastly. The President's credibility is hopeless. And nobody can call us radicals, either. The purpose of giving our views was precisely that. We're not voicing our concern because of Harvard or the domestic impact. We were offering our professional judgment as former advisors to Presidents that it was a horrendous act of foreign policy.

"We said to Henry, we said to Mr. Packard, that the military-civilian imbalance today is the greatest threat to the Presidency since McCarthy's challenge to Johnson in 1968. I myself don't see anything that can restore military credibility."

Bator said, "From Packard we got a canned speech—a casual, pat speech about his administration and Vietnamization and wiping out a few bases. He said it would all please us in just another six weeks. He seemed very aware of our campus origins. We reacted quite strongly."

Konrad Bloch, Higgins Professor of Biochemistry, said, "It was the straightforward drivel. It's like leaving the radio on. He coldly misinterpreted what we had to say. It was hard to know how to explain our position, although Schelling put on a great performance with his Monster Speech when Packard was finally through. Later Packard started talking about Stanford—he said it is infiltrated by a hard core that will have to be eliminated. He said tension in this country will have to come to a head some day, and it might as well be now."

Walzer commented, "It's one of the most frightening things we heard all day."

A bellhop brought Pepsi and Michelob for the overheated professors. Bator had iced coffee. The phone rang. Bator answered it.

"Hello, Averell!" He smiled. "Well hello governor! Yes governor, I'm here. This is Francis." As Bator talked to Harriman, Yarmolinsky dashed to the extension phone in the bathroom to listen. "Yes governor, well Scotty said . . ." When Bator finished, Yarmolinsky started talking on the bathroom extension. Neustadt quickly established possession of the bedroom phone. Alarmed to discover the conversation wasn't over, Bator scurried to the bathroom to listen in when Yarmolinsky was finished. Finally they all said goodbye and hung up. "That was Averell," Bator explained. The professors nodded appreciatively, put on their coats, and poured back out of the room for their meeting with Undersecretary of State Elliot Richardson, muttering at McGrory in the *Star* over each other's shoulders.

The meeting with Richardson was long, but uninspiring. It began at 5:30 and the professors did not return to the Hay-

Adams until ten minutes of 8 P.M. All the professors except
Yarmolinsky, Lipset and Neustadt were trying to catch a
9 P.M. plane. These three had promised to appear at a meeting of Everett Mendelsohn's larger Harvard student-Faculty
delegation—the Peace Action Strike—at the Cleveland Park
Congregational Church that evening. So the professors
washed up, took their messages (Max Frankel of the New York
Times for Yarmolinsky; National Educational Television,
which wanted Schelling to debate Herb Klein on T.V. about
the strategic implications of the invasion), and rushed down
to dinner as Bator reserved a cab to take them to the airport.
A sign in the elevator warned guests that all the hotel's vital
functions would be shut down and guards placed at every
door in preparation for the huge anti-war demonstration Saturday. Over double martinis for most and Caesar Salad (the
quickest thing on the menu), they summed up the day.

"Richardson was different from Packard because many of
us knew him," Bator said. Richardson '43 is former Lieutenant Governor of Massachusetts. "But he was different from
Kissinger because no one knew him really well, and we didn't
regard him as a stand-in for the President."

Schelling said, "I used my lugubrious pitch—words like
'horror' and 'monster.' I think he felt we were overreacting,
therefore he felt he could go back and try to convince us that
the foreign policy was not wrong, but maybe merely mistaken.
It was late in the day; perhaps we did get carried away. But
he was his usual urbane, deft, intelligent self—a fine human
being. He can disguise his pain."

Capron: "We all share the impression that he seized on the
ground rules of not talking about domestic consequences.
This was clear. He talked about tactics of battle. Packard had
talked about the 'problems of liberals'—as if he were going
to end the war to do you a favor."

"I found our meeting with Kissinger deeply moving. It
went better than I could have hoped for. It must have impressed him deeply—it did me. Did it make any difference? I
don't know," Schelling said.

Bator continued, "In the executive branch we've shot the
bolt today. From now on we just have to work on Congress.
If these guys get us all out of Vietnam in 90 days, we'll have

the biggest crow dinner—and we'll all vote for Richard Nixon in 1972." Nervous laughter all around.

Bator flew out the door with a cheery "Goodbye, Gentlemen." Others followed, including Schelling, who instructed Neustadt to take care of the bill, saying they would straighten out the finances Monday. Yarmolinsky left for the church.

Neustadt and Lipset relaxed briefly over strawberries and cream.

"You know," Neustadt said, "one of the most remarkable developments of going public like this—this is the first time in years that I've come to Washington and stayed at the Hay-Adams and had to pay the bill out of my own pocket."

He continued, "Elliot Richardson told us this afternoon, 'I'm still a rational man.' I wanted to say, 'But so was Mc-George Bundy.'

"Many of us will now have to decide whether we will resign from all our consulting positions with the government. It's sort of silly. I have some on which I haven't been consulted for two years. But it's hard after a thing like today to keep operating in the executive branch. Doris Kearns [assistant professor of Government, who taught Neustadt's course on the Presidency this year], who's been down here with Everett Mendelsohn's group, resigned today from the White House Fellows Commission, despite the fact that final selections are this weekend and she had considered her appointment a great honor. People whose advice was being asked on a number of issues have now cut themselves off by announcing that they're going to the Hill to lobby. But there's so much disaffection within government that us academics resigning will be no big deal. That's why we put so much emphasis today on those of us who were ex-officials of government. We were trying to distinguish ourselves—today at least—from those who are 'merely' professors."

Lipset said, "Packard today dismissed us as 'professors' and 'liberals'—same thing." He shrugged.

They asked me to call the CRIMSON to find out what was happening in Cambridge. I returned to report that a group of 500 had left the stadium meeting and had trashed the CFIA, and was now heading for the Square.

Lipset, a CFIA associate, sighed. "I don't leave anything important there anymore. I just hope Schelling remembered to take his stuff out before he came down here yesterday."

They paid their bill, and caught a cab to the Cleveland Park Congregational Church, to continue the fight against the war in the best way they know how.

The Harvard Crimson, May 19, 1970

Dawn at Memorial: Nixon, Youths Talk

by Don Oberdorfer

AFTER a nearly sleepless night in an empty and barricaded White House, President Nixon emerged early yesterday morning to talk to student demonstrators about "the war thing" and other topics.

"Sure, you came here to demonstrate and shout your slogans on the Ellipse. That is all right. Just keep it peaceful," Mr. Nixon told the students on the steps of the Lincoln Memorial as dawn was breaking over the city.

As the President related his surprise visit later for the benefit of reporters, "I told them that I know you think we are a bunch of so-and-sos—I used a stronger word to them. I know how you feel—you want to get the war over.

"I told them that I know it is awfully hard to keep this in perspective. I told them that in 1939 I thought Neville Chamberlain was the greatest man living and Winston Churchill was a madman. It was not until years later that I realized that Neville Chamberlain was a good man but Winston Churchill was right," Mr. Nixon said.

After relating the conversation, he shrugged and said, "I doubt if that got over."

According to the President, he talked about pollution, race relations and parts of the world he has seen and would recommend including Japan, Mexico City, India, Iran, Bali, Budapest, Prague and Siberia.

"There were no TV cameras, no press. They (the students) did not feel the awesome power of the White House. I was trying to relate to them in a way they could feel that I understood their problems," he said.

If the comments of some of the students to newsmen later are any guide, Mr. Nixon failed to bridge the communications gap.

"It was unreal. He was trying so hard to relate on a

personal basis, but he wasn't really concerned with why we were here," said Ronnie Kemper, a Syracuse University sophomore.

"I hope it was because he was tired, but most of what he was saying was absurd," said Joan Pelletier, also of Syracuse University. "Here we had come from a university that's completely uptight, on strike, and when we told him where we were from, he talked about the football team. And when someone said he was from California, he talked about surfing."

After his news conference Friday night, Mr. Nixon had stayed up until about 2:30 a.m., reading and talking on the telephone.

The President slept only an hour. About 3:45 a.m. he telephoned Helen Thomas, a United Press International reporter covering the White House, to chat about the late Merriman Smith.

About 4 a.m., the President awakened his valet, Manolo Sanchez. The two men picked up a hasty Secret Service escort—the agents were "petrified," according to Mr. Nixon—and the group left the White House in darkness at 4:55 a.m.

About eight students here to demonstrate were napping at the Lincoln Memorial when the President arrived. As he talked, the crowd grew steadily to about 50 students. More Secret Service agents, roused from sleep, joined the original three.

After speaking to the students for 55 minutes, the President, accompanied by his valet and a few White House aides who had joined the group, drove to the Capitol. They walked through the nearly deserted building, with Mr. Nixon pointing out the sights.

Just before 7 a.m., Mr. Nixon and his party drove to the Mayflower Hotel, where the President had corned beef hash topped with an egg in the Rib Room.

Mr. Nixon returned to the White House, which was cordoned off by buses parked bumper-to-bumper and heavily guarded by police, at 7:37 a.m. He spent the rest of the day in one of his offices or at the Executive Residence.

He did stop to chat with Army troops who were stationed

as extra security in the area, but otherwise saw no other outsiders during the day, according to aides.

A total of 60 to 80 demonstrators, some dressed in sneakers,
dungarees, T-shirts and beads, were invited into the White
House for chats by various Presidential aides. Seven students
who were invited by Donald Rumsfeld, who is director of the
poverty program as well as a presidential assistant, also had
talks with Henry A. Kissinger and Ambassador Ellsworth
Bunker while in the White House.

Nancy Shalala and Dee-Dee McCabe, two nursing students
at Marymount College of Virginia in Arlington, said they were
walking near the White House yesterday morning when a man
asked them if they'd like to speak to a White House aide. They
agreed and were escorted to the office of Raymond K. Price
Jr., one of Mr. Nixon's speechwriters.

According to Miss Shalala, Price explained that the White
House wanted to know what they thought, in the interests of
bringing students and the government together.

"The meeting was really interesting," she added. "It was a
nice thing to see and it's too bad it had to come so late."

The Washington Post, May 10, 1970

Hard-Hats: The Rampaging Patriots

by Fred J. Cook

ON MAY 8 a band of hard-hat construction workers, pliers, hammers and wire snippers concealed in their overalls, assaulted peace demonstrators in Wall Street. They roared up Broadway to City Hall and invaded the Hall itself, then smashed their way into Pace College and beat up students there. On May 20, the hard-hats, some 100,000 strong, surged through the streets of the city in a denunciation of Mayor John V. Lindsay and in support of the Nixon Administration and its war in Cambodia and Vietnam.

Television commentaries and most of the accounts in the daily press have pictured these massive performances—and a series of rallies and marches in between—as spontaneous demonstrations of patriotism by the blue-collar workers of New York. Nothing could be more untrue. The fact is that these events were organized and promoted—and permitted to happen—in a pattern that contains the classic elements of Hitlerian street tactics.

Fascism is a word to be used with discretion—particularly in times of social crisis—but it is undeniable that its elements could be felt in New York last month. The hard-hat workers, many fearing the incursion of Negroes in their white union ranks, formed the nucleus of a marching army, the kind of army that thinks with its muscles and is easily aroused to passion. A second ingredient—the propagandist and instigator—was provided, much evidence indicates, by agents of a small right-wing sheet, the New York *Graphic*. And behind these, giving the hard-hats their indispensable support, were powerful groups of the establishment. In the New York demonstrations, this vital support came from two sources: from construction firms that promoted and encouraged the demonstrations by in effect closing down their jobs and paying the hard-hats, not for working but for marching; and from the police, who cheered the hard-hats on.

Administration demagogy and the pressures of the most un-popular war in American history are today rendering this country incapable of sane debate. On the extreme Left is the relative handful driven to insensate acts of violence by detestation of the war in Southeast Asia and by the deprivations at home which stem from it. From this extreme toward the Center, protest ranges in all gradations from long-haired youths and sober college types to 1,000 lawyers from Wall Street and college administrators, respectable segments of the normal Establishment that have tried to impress upon Mr. Nixon the serious plight of the nation. These essentially middle-of-the-road voices of responsible protest are now being drowned out by the raucous shouts of the extreme Right, by the super-patriots whose sentiments are expressed in the bumper sticker: "America: Love It or Leave It." Anyone who opposes the war automatically becomes "a Commie" who "ought to go back to Russia."

This explosive atmosphere is ideal for the gut thinkers. As one construction worker himself says: "These are touchy, tough, excitable guys. They can't discuss an issue except with their fists. If they can't find a peace guy to fight with, they'll get in a bar and end up starting a fight among themselves. They put all college kids in one category. To them, they are all pot smokers, rabble-rousers, faggots, and they deserve anything they get. They ought all to be beaten up."

It was among a contingent of such men that the events of New York began to unfold. The first incident, almost unnoticed, occurred on Wednesday, May 6, two days before the big bust in Wall Street. A new construction job is under way in the Whitehall Street area, and the steelworkers had erected an American flag. Some medical students from the nearby Whitehall Medical Center held a small peace demonstration in Battery Park. Someone ripped down the steelworkers' flag. "The steelworkers piled out of the building and pitched into them," one union man says. "Several were beaten up, though nothing much about it got into the papers."

The only forecast of events to come was written by Pete

Hamill, columnist of the *New York Post*, the following day. There had also been a peace demonstration in Wall Street that same Wednesday afternoon, and afterward the college types who had participated in it marched up Broadway. Hamill, who circulated in the watching crowds and tagged along with the marchers, recorded the hate. He wrote:

"Listen to their language," said a 40ish man in a wrinkled suit standing next to me. "Those goddam bums *should* be shot. I wishta Christ I was in the National Guard."

"What would you do?" I asked him.

"Shoot them, mow them down. If they don't like this country let them go back to goddamned Russia!"

As the marchers went up Broadway toward City Hall, Hamill wrote, "some gutless construction workers started throwing beer cans and clumps of asphalt at them from a building at the corner of Maiden Lane. A woman passerby was hit and the construction workers stood up there, bellies bulging defiantly.

" 'Jump! Jump! Jump!' one group yelled. I went to see Inspector [Harold] Schryner who was heading the police escort and asked him if he was going to make arrests. 'Don't worry about it,' he said.

" 'You expect these kids to respond to law and order and you won't go up and make arrests?' I said. 'Law and order,' said Schryner. 'These bums don't respect anything. . . .' "

Two days later, the permissiveness of police on the command level was to allow the hard-hats to rampage unhindered for four hours, even bashing through the portals of City Hall.

The steam for the explosion that was to come built up slowly after the events at the Battery. The steelworkers who had bloodied medical students returned to their jobs and began to talk among themselves. As one worker says, "They began to psych themselves up. A lot of them feel strongly about the situation, no doubt about that. Their attitude was that not enough was being done about these goddam kids. They knew there was to be a peace rally in Wall Street the next day, and they decided to stage a counter demonstration. They took off about 12:30, made a show, and were back on the job shortly after the lunch hour ended. This had been an entirely spontaneous demonstration, no question about it; but after they came back, they kept talking, kept psyching themselves up. They weren't satisfied they'd done enough, and the word began to go around that the next day they would really do it up right.

"The word circulated on all the jobs in the area. It was a planned thing. They were going out, and they were really going to bust some heads."

The man who tells this story has credentials of credibility. "I'm a veteran," he says, "and I believe in the flag, too. But I can't go along with all this stuff." Worried, he telephoned the office of Rep. Allard K. Lowenstein, the liberal Nassau County Democrat, to warn that construction workers were planning to turn the Friday peace rally into a blood bath. The word was relayed to Mayor Lindsay's office. Tom Morgan, the Mayor's press secretary, said later that this was only one of several tips received Thursday night and Friday morning—and that the Police Department had been alerted well in advance. Nevertheless, they permitted all hell to break loose on the streets of lower Manhattan.

The worried worker who had tipped Lowenstein's office was waiting on the steps of the old Sub-Treasury Building (now known as the Federal Hall National Memorial Building) in Wall Street before the hard-hats arrived. What follows is an account of the action as he saw it.

The men left their jobs and marched up Broad Street. The police were already there. I was standing behind the police lines myself, and I saw what happened. All of a sudden flags broke out everywhere, and handbills appeared as if by magic. They were being distributed by this guy from the New York *Graphic*, and he had some helpers with him. When you saw that happen, you knew that this had to be a planned thing.

What made me sick was the police. The kids were already spread all over the steps of the old Treasury Building, and the police lines were out in front. The fellows came marching up and were stopped by the police. Then they began to shove against the police lines. They were pushing, pressing, and not a night stick was raised in anger. Suddenly the whole left side of the police line just melted away, and those yellow hats charged up the steps and began to beat up students.

I ducked around through a nearby underpass to get on the other side of the crowd, and as I was hurrying through a policeman stopped me. "Did Twin Towers get here yet?" he asked. [This was a reference to the large number of workers employed on the new trade center being built nearby.] I said: "No, they haven't come yet." And he said: "Gee, I wish they'd hurry up and get here." That, in itself, just goes to show that the police knew all about it.

When I got back up to the street again, I was just in time to see the Twin Towers guys come charging up, and as soon as they joined forces with the others, the police line just melted away. The police didn't try to do a thing.

This account is supported in its major points by the television cameras and the reports of newsmen who were on the scene. About five minutes after noon the first contingent of some 200 construction workers, waving their suddenly unfurled flags and chanting "All the way U.S.A." and "Love it or leave it," surged against the virtually unresisting police lines. "All we want to do is put our flags on those steps," one yellow-helmeted worker told Inspector Schryner.

"If you try, there'll be blood to pay," the inspector replied.

Meaningless words—and the construction workers must have known it. In less than two minutes, they had shoved the police aside, with never a drop of their own blood spilled, and went to work with their brawny arms, spilling the blood of the peaceful peace demonstrators.

Newspapers the next day reported that the workers beat the students with their helmets, but more than helmets were used—pliers, wrenches, wire snippers all came into play. And the burly super-patriots enjoyed nothing so much as ganging up on a single victim.

"I tried to raise the peace flag on the steps of the building after they came up," said Michael Doctor, 19, a student at Pace. "Some guy belted me in the face and I threw him down the steps; then I got hit from all sides." Doctor spoke through a gap in his teeth, a front tooth having been broken off about halfway down.

Another victim of the assault was Drew Lynch, 19, slightly built, a teacher in the Human Resources Administration's Brooklyn street program. He had been beaten so badly about the face that both eyes were flecked with blood, the skin beneath them was black and blue, and his mouth was swollen and bleeding. Lynch said that "at least four workers" had ganged up on him, pummeling and kicking. "They beat me for a long time," he said, "and then a cop I know, a very together person, kicked one of them and dragged me out. He got me away and told me to 'get the fuck out of here.'"

Between forty and sixty beaten, bloodied victims were treated at a first aid station set up inside historic Trinity Church, on Broadway almost opposite Wall Street. They slumped in the church aisles, bandages pressed to bloodied heads, and they told, sometimes between angry curses, similar stories of brutality. Harry Boles, a stocky 21-year-old film student from New York University, had been filming the scene with two fellow students when the hard-hats got him. They beat him until his face was covered with cuts; they smashed his $3,000 camera; and then they tried to kick his ribs in.

Even as these victims were being treated, Trinity Church itself became the target for assault. Twice the frenzied hard-hats tried to break through the iron gates and invade the church itself. They ripped down a Red Cross banner, and they tried to tear down the Episcopal flag. "I don't think they really knew what the Red Cross means," said Father John Corn. And Father Donald Woodward, vicar of Trinity, added: "I never thought I'd live to see the day when I would stand behind the door of my church and see it stormed."

There is considerable evidence that this mob scene was expertly stage-managed. From his 32nd floor office at 63 Wall Street, Edward Shufro, a partner in the brokerage firm of Shufro, Rose & Ehrman, watched through his binoculars the activities of two men in gray suits and gray hats. "These guys were directing the construction workers with hand motions," he said flatly. According to a witness on the street, the men wore yellow patches in their coat lapels, matching the color of the helmets.

It is impossible to say with certainty who these men were, but Lowenstein's informant insists that "the man from the *Graphic*" (he does not know him by name) had been active in helping to whip up passions for the big Friday bust. The man, always accompanied by one or two others, had circulated

around the construction jobs all day Thursday and again on
Friday morning, "passing out his hate literature and talking
to the men," this witness says. Others were to call attention
to the mysterious role of the right-wing *Graphic*.

After the violence on Wall Street and the surge against the
iron gates of Trinity, the hard-hats, now some 500 strong with
the addition of the Twin Towers contingent, stormed up
Broadway to City Hall. "The police were there," says the informant, who went along with the marchers. "They even had
some mounted cops on hand, and you know what they can
do in a crowd with those horses. But they just didn't seem to
make any real effort to stop the construction men, and the
first thing I knew there were those hard-hats charging up the
steps to the very door of City Hall."

The City Hall flag was being flown at half-staff on Mayor
Lindsay's orders in memory of the four students, none of
them militants, who had been killed by the National Guard
at Kent State University. This gesture apparently enraged the
marchers and gave them their pretext for a direct assault on
City Hall. After they had burst through the first restraining
police lines, an unidentified letter carrier (how he got into the
act no one seems to know) went to the roof and raised the
flag to full staff. Moments later, Sidney Davidoff, an aide to
Mayor Lindsay, stalked out onto the roof and lowered it again.

The workers reacted with fury. Fists flailing, they stormed
the police again and rushed the City Hall doors. Police officials, having done little or nothing to prevent all this, be-
seeched city officials to raise the flag, and Deputy Mayor
Richard R. Aurelio, in charge in the absence of Mayor Lindsay, capitulated. The flag was raised, and the hard-hats cheered
and began singing the *Star-Spangled Banner*. A construction
worker yelled to the police detail: "Get your helmets off."
And this command, too, was obeyed as the police sheepishly
doffed their helmets in subservience to mob rule.

With City Hall conquered, a new target now offered itself.
Across Park Row from City Hall is Pace College, and there
some peace-minded students had unfurled a large banner on
the roof. "The men saw it," says the informant. "I was standing right next to this man from the *Graphic* when he pointed

out the sign and shouted to the workers, 'Let's get them at Pace.' That was all they needed, and they charged off across the street, breaking through the entrance of Pace, smashing the glass doors, and beating up any students they could get their hands on. It's just lucky they never caught those students on the roof or they would have thrown them off."

Miss Susan Harman, 29, who works as an administrative assistant in Mayor Lindsay's office, was at a municipal workers' rally on Foley Square when she heard about the onslaught on City Hall. She hurried back and arrived just as the hard-hat mob was flowing back and forth between City Hall and Pace. She heard shouts of "Get the hippie! Get the traitor!" She described what happened next:

> Then I saw one construction worker arm himself with a pair of iron clippers and head towards a student already being pummeled by three workers. I shouted to him, "Don't," and grabbed hold of his jacket to stop him. He yelled at me, "Let go of my jacket, bitch"; and then he said, "If you want to be treated like an equal, we'll treat you like one." Three of them began to punch me in the body. My glasses were broken. I had trouble breathing, and I thought my ribs were cracked.

She was taken to Beekman-Downtown Hospital and was later released, cut and bruised but with her ribs still intact.

At City Hall, when the hard-hats began chanting, "Lindsay's a Red," Donald Evans, a Lindsay aide, told a construction worker: "Stop being juveniles." He was punched on the jaw. A Wall Street lawyer, Michael Belknap, 29, a Democratic candidate for the state Senate, was trapped near City Hall by several workers and was beaten and kicked while his assailants shouted, "Kill the Commie bastards!" He also was treated at Beekman-Downtown Hospital. His right eye was completely closed, he had a large welt on his head, and five boot marks were imprinted on his back where he had been stomped after he was down.

An observer of much of this action was Deputy Manhattan Borough President Leonard H. Cohen. He was enraged by what he saw and offered to testify to the "gross negligence" of police. When the hard-hats charged across the street to attack Pace, he said, he "shrieked" to police to follow and stop them, but he added that the police "joined ranks with the attacking workers and laughingly watched students brutally beaten. . . . Construction workers and police had literally joined hands."

It was not until 2:30 P.M., having chased and beaten up some seventy persons, that the hard-hats trooped back into Wall Street, massing again at the Sub-Treasury. Here Richard Schwartz, a reporter for the *New York Post*, observed a man in a gray business suit addressing the rioters with the aid of a bullhorn.

"I am glad to see all of us here, and three cheers for the construction workers!" the man with the bullhorn shouted. He continued: "I must tell you something. They [the antiwar demonstrators] are all Socialists. All right now, we've proven our point. Let's go. We've shown we are behind the Presidency of the United States. Now, before you all create a riot here [one has to wonder what the man thought *had* just taken place] we must go home. And let's have a wonderful weekend." It was as if the commander of the recent fracas had spoken to his troops. After some milling around, the hard-hats gradually drifted off to the bars to celebrate their victory.

The following Monday, reporter Schwartz was in the City Hall press room when he was startled by the entrance of the man whom he had seen using the bullhorn to such good effect. The man was distributing copies of the New York *Graphic*. Attached to the copies was a mimeographed leaflet dedicated to: "The Courageous Construction Men" and addressed to "fellow Americans." The leaflet called Lindsay a "One World Socialist Mayor," and the author wrote: "Last week I spoke to you from the steps of the Federal Hall Memorial on Wall Street. I congratulated you on your victory against Mayor Lindsay. I congratulate you again." The letter closed with the words, "For God and Country," and was signed "Ralph L. Clifford, publisher."

Schwartz followed Clifford to the *Graphic* office at 33 Park Row, only a short distance from City Hall. Clifford, 53, a former editor of the Watertown (Mass.) *Times*, denied he had had any part in planning the Friday demonstration. He described himself as "a true-blue American." A headline in the May 23, 1968 issue of his paper read: "Sainthood Proposed for Senator Joseph McCarthy."

Clifford acknowledged that he thinks highly of the John Birch Society, but he has doubts about William F. Buckley, Jr. "I think he's some sort of internationalist we haven't found out about yet," he told Schwartz. A man who was obviously far to the right of even Buckley, Clifford hadn't seen anything to worry about in the storm-trooper antics of the hard-hats. Their demonstrations, he said, marked "the beginning of the end of Fabian socialism" in the United States, and he added: "I liked what happened. I was very thrilled. I've been waiting for this to happen for some time." He refused to discuss his activities further, but he did say he was "planning and organizing for a later date."

Reporter Schwartz pressed him about his role in the Friday riot. How did he come to be in the line of march? It was "impulsive," Clifford said; he'd just seen the workers trooping by and had become so carried away by their patriotic demonstration that he had joined them. How had he come to have a bullhorn in his hand? "It was given to me by the Police Department," Clifford said. "I was asked to speak to the crowd." Who asked him? A police captain. Why would a police captain single him out? "I have no idea," Clifford said. Nor, at this point, does anyone else.

After the super-patriotic blood bath, a shocked and angry Mayor Lindsay called police brass on the carpet. Only six arrests had been made, and four of these had resulted from cross-complaints that individuals had filed against one another—arrests, in other words, that had been practically forced on the Police Department. Mayor Lindsay said bluntly that the police had not done their job, that there had been in his words "a breakdown of the police as the barrier between the public and wanton violence." Acknowledging that police forces had been spread thin trying to cover a number of demonstrations in the city, the Mayor said "none of this alters the fact that a roving band of 500 construction workers were allowed to move at will . . . beating up people all along the way."

Police Commissioner Howard R. Leary presented what must be described as a lame and not entirely candid defense. He contended that the first attacks in the Wall Street area had occurred "out of the immediate view and control of the police"—a statement at variance with reports by virtually all eye-witnesses. The commissioner advanced the claim that the department had "no reason to anticipate violence or dis-orders," ignoring the well-established fact it had been alerted to just what was going to happen hours in advance of the event. Leary argued further that his police had been spread too thin covering various demonstrations, and that in Wall Street and at City Hall his inadequate forces had been over-whelmed by the mass of demonstrators—a contention at odds with the reports of eyewitnesses that the police made no effort to stop the hard-hats.

In fairness to the police, says one long-time observer of the cops in action, there were probably several reasons for the police collapse on Bloody Friday. "Hindsight is a wonderful thing," he says. "Yes, the police were warned in advance, but remember nothing like this has ever happened here before and no one could conceive the scope of this thing. It was much like the time Watts went up in flames. People said in shock: 'Why, they're burning their own houses!' And so here the reaction was: 'Why, they *are* actually beating up people!' Then, too, a lot of cops have the same thoughts and emotions about demonstrators that the hard-hats have, and there may have been this reluctance to beat up a brother. I think the police, despite the warnings, were caught by surprise at what they had on their hands, but I doubt if there was any collu-sion, any prior understanding between police and hard-hats."

The American Civil Liberties Union refused to accept the police alibis and called on U.S. Attorney Whitney North Sey-mour, Jr., to make a federal investigation. The ACLU referred to the "shameful inaction" of police and added: "Reports we have received make it clear that police stood around passively and in some instances joined in the assaults on the anti-war demonstrators." Aryeh Neier, executive director of the New York Civil Liberties Union, said he was furnishing Seymour with the names of witnesses.

Peter I. Brennan, president of the 200,000-member Building and Construction Trades Council of Greater New York, insisted that union leadership had had nothing to do with the Friday demonstration. "The men acted on their own," Brennan said. "They did it because they were fed up with violence by anti-war demonstrators, by those who spat on the American flag and desecrated it." Brennan added that union headquarters had been deluged with messages "from all over the country" running 20 to 1 in praise "of the workers for their patriotism"—not a fantastic circumstance in a nation in which the White House can be inundated with praise for a speech by President Nixon before the speech has even been delivered.

Little noted at the time, submerged under the attention given more dramatic events, was the alarming fact that the Mayor was defied by spokesmen for five Police Department organizations. They bluntly accused him of "undermining the confidence of the public in its Police Department." Edward J. Kiernan, president of the powerful Patrolmen's Benevolent Association, went further and charged that the confrontation between students and workers "was brought about by remarks of people in city government. We can no longer afford the luxury of self-serving appeals to one group or another, made for the cynical and calculated purpose of securing a fleeting political advantage." The police are, of course, a brotherhood in blue, and they band together by automatic reflex whenever any one of them is criticized. This much is routine, but it is not routine—and it says much about the authoritarianism of the times—for spokesmen for line organizations representing the entire department to make a political attack upon the mayor in terms that the John Birch Society might have employed.

The gauge of battle had been flung down to City Hall, but Lindsay did not pick it up. Instead, he did what he could to mollify a force that all evidence says cannot be changed or mollified. On Monday, May 11, the hard-hats marched again in a contingent 2,000 strong, roaming the streets of the financial district from Bowling Green to City Hall. This time police were out in force, and there was no violence comparable to that of Bloody Friday. However, there was some. At one point, a bystander on the curb behind the wooden barricades raised his hand in the peace sign, and a hard-hat reached across the barricade and punched him in the mouth. "The new Nazis; they're here," murmured a woman spectator.

The language of the super-patriots supported her. Some of their signs read: "Impeach the Red Mayor." "Lindsay, Liar, Leftist, Lunatic." "Impeach Lindsay, Commie *Rat*." Inevitably: "America, Love It or Leave It." Passing Pace, where students appeared at the windows, the marchers waved signs saying: "Don't worry, they don't draft faggots." And, arrived before City Hall, the hard-hats gave eloquent voice to their emotions, chanting, "Lindsay is a bum" and "Lindsay is a faggot."

In response to all this, Mayor Lindsay tried first to soothe the bruised feelings of the Police Department by praising it for "alertly, skillfully and professionally" controlling the crowds and acting in the best professional tradition. He then urged tolerance and restraint upon those holding opposing viewpoints. "The divisions over the Vietnam war—not only here but across the country—are the results of a controversy over the war that engages the interest and the efforts of vast numbers of citizens, and the parallel neglect of the needs of the people in the cities and elsewhere here at home," Lindsay said. "These feelings will not soon be dispelled. The frustrations and grievances on all sides are real." It was an appeal that could hardly be expected to register with those whose visceral impulses reduced all argument to the level of shouted epithets like "Commie rat" and "faggot."

The hard-hat suddenly became a symbol of patriotism. At a Madison Avenue rally on May 14, promoters for a big Conservative Party affair scheduled for Manhattan Center on May 22 appeared wearing hard hats decorated with flag symbols. It was the first occasion on which so-called responsible politicians were to adopt the hard hat as a badge of honor.

As the hard-hats continued to claim the center of the stage, questions arose. What was behind these demonstrations? What forces in union ranks had led to the Bloody Friday outbreak? What impelled the unions to keep up the pressure? The answers are to be found on two levels—the low level of the

ordinary construction worker, the high level of union leadership. As for the first, one observer comments:

A lot of these guys feel they have legitimate grievances. They are
almost the only segment of the population government hasn't paid
much attention to. People whom they feel beneath them, the blacks
and Puerto Ricans, for instance, demonstrate and get attention. The
college kids, the more violent of them, spit on the flag and burn
buildings; others demonstrate and cause upheavals—and they, too,
get attention. These construction men got the feeling they were in a
kind of limbo, with nobody paying much attention to them. Obviously, there is a lot of frustration here.

Then, remember that a lot of these workers who were demonstrating against Lindsay don't even live in New York. In one union a good
40 per cent of the men working here, in another at least one-third,
are not New Yorkers at all. They come here from Tennessee, from
the Carolinas and Pennsylvania. Why? Because most of the high construction jobs in the nation are being built in New York. Last year
25 per cent of all the office space in the country was built in Manhattan. . . .

So you have this situation: you have construction workers from all
over the nation east of the Mississippi coming here to work—and
they belong to unions that are predominantly white. Some unions
are all white. I doubt if any of these unions has more than 15 percent
blacks or Puerto Ricans among its members, and there has been enormous pressure from minority groups, from government and from
John Lindsay himself to open up the union rolls. Obviously, if this
were done, if the city were training its own available labor, there
wouldn't be jobs here for construction workers from all over the
nation. And it was no secret to these men, or to anybody else, that
John Lindsay is determined to do all he can to open up these kinds
of jobs to minorities in this town.

The union leadership has other problems. Early this year
the labor publication *Labor Today* carried this headline:
"Building Trades in Crisis." It wrote: "The year 1970 will be
a crucial period for the building trades unions. Many of their
contracts come up for renewal in the spring and summer. At
this time, when the building trades unions should direct their
main efforts to secure a broad range of benefits, job security
and a wage increase to offset the rising cost of living, they are
being boxed into a defensive position by the strongly united
Contractors' Association, bolstered by sharpened attacks by

the Nixon Administration." Considered especially threatening by the building trades was the Administration's "Philadelphia Plan" that would compel the hiring of fixed percentages of minority people.

Such was the situation when President Nixon extended the war into Cambodia and precipitated a national crisis. With colleges across the nation erupting in protest, with even usually conservative professional groups deciding that this was just too much and we must get out of Southeast Asia, the President turned for support to one source that has never failed the military-industrial complex—the labor leadership of George Meany, president of the AFL-CIO. On May 12, the President went to AFL-CIO headquarters in Washington and addressed the executive council, and Meany let it be known that he was 100 per cent behind the Administration in its Cambodian adventure.

Following this soul meeting, the New York building trades made the hard-hat demonstrations official policy. Peter Brennan circulated a letter to building trades councils throughout the nation, outlining his plans and urging them to spread the hard-hat demonstrations nationwide. He wrote that the building trades leadership in New York was planning a mass rally "to show our support to our country and our boys in Asia." This was to be done "in a proper and nonviolent manner," Brennan wrote, and he urged his fellow union leaders to "have similar demonstrations in your cities" to "let anti-Americans know where the construction workers stand."

These moves would seem to indicate that some kind of tacit understanding had been reached with the Administration. But what about the Contractors' Association whose united front had seemed so menacing? There was every indication that now, as far as the demonstrations were concerned, the contractors and the hard-hats were as one. It should be noted that the building trades, management and workers alike, are traditionally the very good friends of state and federal administrations (George Meany himself comes out of the building trades). The reason is normal self-interest: directly or indirectly, much of the money that goes into modern construction comes from the public purse.

After the hard-hats had been marching almost daily for

some ten days, the New York *Post* tried to unravel an obvious
mystery: who was paying the marchers for demonstrating instead of working? Most construction men gross around $300
a week, yet here they were knocking off their jobs to demonstrate for hours at a time. "Workers . . . have freely admitted taking time from their jobs to join demonstrations or
battle with students, and they say they have not lost pay," the
Post wrote. But the contractors, when asked, spoke with one
voice. Every firm in the business said it had not noticed any
of *its* men absenting themselves from work; those demonstrators must have come from some other fellow's project.

Such pretenses became ridiculous when the building trades,
joined by the Longshoremen's union, held the mass rally
about which Brennan had written in advance. It took place
on Wednesday, May 20. Almost every major construction project in Manhattan was shut down, and the hard-hats and their
cohorts, in a sea of flags and banners, massed more than
100,000 strong around City Hall. This huge turnout was pictured on television and in the press as a spontaneous demonstration of patriotism, but it was nothing of the sort. It was
a command performance.

Here is how it looked to one union man who *had* to
march:

After that Friday rally where there was so much violence, the union
leadership evidently started to worry about the reaction. The word
came down to cut out the rough stuff. Then they began to plan for
this big rally. Originally, it was supposed to be held the next Friday,
but the plans were changed and it was put off to Wednesday.

The word was passed around to all the men on the jobs the day
before. It was *not* voluntary. You *had* to go. You understand these
are all jobs where the union controls your employment absolutely. If
you're on a job where there's a lot of overtime and you stand in well
with your shop steward, you get the overtime. If you make trouble,
you're shifted to a job where there is no overtime—or maybe you
don't get any job at all.

We were told that if we got back to the job a half-hour after the
parade ended, we'd be paid for a full day's work. Of course, the
parade lasted until 3:30 and by the time the guys got back, the day
was done. But everybody got paid.

That raises the question. The unions could order the men to march, but the unions don't pay them—the contractors do. "Sure," says this union man. "That in itself shows there had to be collusion somewhere."

"The man from the *Graphic*" was not to be seen at this peaceful mass rally. "There was this moment," the union eye-witness says, "when the men marched past Pace, and they saw some students standing there. The men paused for a moment as if they were going to go after them, and it was almost funny. This time, there was no one to shout orders, no one to spark them, and so they just stared at the students, not knowing quite what to do, and the police urged them along and got them moving again."

Mayor Lindsay and his City Hall spokesmen continued to try to cool tempers, praising the orderliness of the mass rally and the work of the thousands of police who kept it under control. But there are still some indications that the police force is not an impartial arbiter of peace, that it and the hard-hats think as one, and that, as a result, there is one standard of police conduct for hard-hats and quite another for peace demonstrators.

This became evident on Thursday, May 21, when about 1,000 peace demonstrators held a rally at City Hall and then marched up Sixth Avenue to Bryant Park. The demonstrators had no permit to march, but all was peaceful until they neared Bryant Park. Leonard Kolleeny, an American Civil Liberties Union lawyer who was at the scene, said that he had reached an agreement with the police command to permit the demonstrators to go into the park, hold their final rally there and disperse.

"There was never any question about it," Kolleeny said. "The officials on the scene had walkie-talkies to check out the plan with their superiors at headquarters. We even reached an agreement on which staircase the marches would use to get into the park."

But when the peace demonstrators reached 39th Street, the police suddenly assaulted them, night sticks flailing. "The police just waded into the crowd without warning," Kolleeny said. "Kids were beaten and an elderly woman and other innocent bystanders were trampled in the crush." At least nine persons were injured, and sixteen complaints of police brutality were filed with the department's Civilian Complaint Review Board.

What wasn't realized at the time was that the violence might have been much worse had the impromptu march turned in another direction. According to one union member, a large group of hard-hats, chafing at the restraints that had been imposed upon their conduct, had gathered in the Wall Street area, anticipating that the peace marchers would come that way. The police were standing behind wooden barricades erected to contain the sidewalk crowds, and their attitude, this observer says, was made clear in their badinage with the hard-hats. "When you start throwing things, remember we're here," he quoted one cop as saying. "Just keep it from curb to curb." Another commented: "I'm here guarding this lamp-post, and I'm not going to leave." The mood was the mood of Bloody Friday, this worker says, but nothing happened because the march went uptown.

That is the story—except for an epilogue that gives it a national frame. The quality of the forces that were unleashed in New York was perhaps most vividly expressed in the hate-filled signs the hard-hats prepared for their peaceful mass rally at City Hall. One sign that they especially liked, but were dissuaded from carrying read: "National Guard, 4; Kent, o." A sign that was actually waved on high in front of Pace said "Lindsay Eats Here"—and underneath there was the crude drawing of a toilet. Another sign underwent some modification. It originally read: "LINDSAY SUCKS." After someone pointed out that you couldn't carry *that* through the public streets, it was amended to: "LINDSAY SUCKS . . . lollipops."

One might have thought that this kind of stuff would have disgusted even the most insensitive of men, but our national leaders have strong stomachs. Vice President Agnew sent Brennan a letter commending "the impressive display in patriotism—and a spirit of pride in country that seems to have become unfashionable in recent years." And President Nixon wrote: "I want you and all members of the building and construction trades to know how pleased I was to see the tremendous outpouring of support for our country demonstrated in your orderly and most heartening rally May 20. This means a great deal to our men fighting for peace in Southeast Asia, and, needless to say, it means a great deal to me."

To express his gratitude to the hard-hat super-patriots, the President called Peter Brennan and twenty-two other union leaders to the White House on Tuesday, May 26. They sat around the President's giant new Cabinet table and discussed the affairs of the nation for forty-seven minutes. Then the President held still while Brennan presented him with a hard-hat and pinned an American flag in his lapel.

The only sign of embarrassment at the White House was that the television camera crews and press photographers were not allowed to record the historic hard-hat crowning of the President of the United States.

The Nation, June 15, 1970

The American Class System

by Stewart Alsop

WASHINGTON—Last week's Supreme Court ruling on draft exemptions for conscientious objectors will make this country's system of military recruitment even more discriminatory than before. And even before the decision, the system was one of blatant class discrimination. This fact probably has at least as much to do with the radicalization of the campuses as the Vietnam war itself.

The Court upheld the appeal of a California intellectual who claimed status as a conscientious objector, not on the accepted basis of "religious training and belief"—he had crossed out that phrase on his application—but as a result of "reading in the fields of history and sociology."

As Selective Service Director Curtis Tarr has pointed out, the ruling will be of no use to the uneducated—it will be useful only to a would-be conscientious objector who has "sharpened his intellect in the matter of religion and philosophy." Selective Service anticipates a flood of CO applications from college graduates who have been busy sharpening their intellects.

Even before the decision, a college man had a far better chance of avoiding the draft, one way or another, than the poor clod who only finished high school. Last year, for example, out of 283,000 men drafted only 28,500 were college men—just over 10 per cent. Well over 40 per cent of the college-age young now go to college. The figures speak for themselves—if you can manage to go to college, your chances of not being drafted are quadrupled.

A system which produces this result is quite clearly based on class discrimination. But the story does not really end there. The radical young, especially in the prestigious Eastern Ivy League colleges, talk as though they were a lost generation, condemned by the system to be hauled away to Vietnam, and killed or wounded—this has been the theme of many a youthful valedictorian. But it is nonsense.

Yale, Harvard and Princeton, to cite three obvious examples, together have graduated precisely two—repeat, two—young men, in the whole course of the war, who were drafted and killed in action in Vietnam. The kind of men who volunteer for dangerous jobs—the Walter Mittys, if you will—still fortunately exist. Yale has had 34 such volunteering types killed in Vietnam, Harvard thirteen, and Princeton thirteen, including civilians. But the only draftees were one Army corporal (Yale) and one private first class (Harvard).

Unless they are Walter Mittys, the small minority of college men who do end up in uniform rarely see any fighting. The Army has adopted a more or less explicit policy of encouraging well-qualified and intelligent young men to "volunteer" for noncombat supply and administrative jobs, to avoid being drafted into the infantry. This system explains why the Army is so reluctant to respond to the urgings of the President and Secretary Laird to set a date after which no draftees will be sent to Vietnam. Without the threat of drafting men into the infantry, the Army fears that its whole system of attracting volunteers by promising them noncombat jobs will break down.

It is a bit strange, surely, when an army recruiting system is squarely based on promising recruits they won't have to hear a bullet fired in anger. In fact, the American Government's message to young men is something like this: "If you are smart, and go to college, you will have a good chance to avoid the draft entirely. If not, you can at least avoid getting shot at by opting for a noncombat job. Leave the fighting to the peasants and the Walter Mittys."

This is not a very inspiring message for the idealistic young. Yet the message is heeded, for entirely understandable reasons. After all, what sensible young man wants to spend two years of his life being shouted at or shot at? The young men who do end up getting shouted at or shot at are of a very different sort from the college radicals.

Their faces appeared in eleven heartrending pages of pictures in Life magazine last year. The pictures, with names and hometowns, were of 242 men who had been killed in Vietnam in one week. It was only necessary to look at those young men, peering innocently out from beyond the grave, to know what kind of young men they were.

They were not the kind of young men to whom it would have occurred to get a teaching job or to go to divinity school in order to avoid the draft, or to get a logistical or noncombat intelligence job to avoid combat. The great majority of them were obviously fresh out of high school, or off the farm or the production line. Most of them came from small towns— Poquonock, Conn., or La Farge, Wis., or Nickerson, Neb., or Morganton, N.C., or the like.

There were a scattering of marines, and three Navy men, probably volunteers for the Navy's dangerous Vietnam river patrols. The rest had been drafted and assigned to the Army specialty known as Eleven Bravo. Eleven Bravo is the infantry. Hardly anyone volunteers for Eleven Bravo, for that is where people get killed.

The United States, according to the radical young, operates under a corrupt system. They are entirely correct. The system is indeed corrupt, in two absolutely fundamental ways.

There are two things the American Government can take away from the American citizen. It can take his money, in taxes. And it can take his body, for services in the armed forces—which can mean taking his life. The taxing power is exercised in such a way that a rich man who uses money to make money, can avoid paying anything like his fair share of taxes. To cite a single example, at current rates on tax-free bonds, a rich man can enjoy an income of $18,000 on $300,000 of capital, without paying a cent of income tax, or even filing a return. A man, with a wife and two children to support, who earned that much with his brains or his muscles, would have to pay the government $3,200, if he did not want to go to jail.

There are many other ways, of course, for a rich man to avoid paying taxes a wage earner has to pay. This blatant class discrimination corrupts the democratic process. The democratic process is even more fatally corrupted when the government's power of military recruitment is also based on class discrimination.

This second corruption of power has unquestionably contributed to the radicalization of the universities. A young man who exploits the system to duck the draft or avoid combat is only being sensible. But he can never quite shake off the knowledge that others are being shouted at or shot at in his place. In such circumstances, it is not really hard to see why many young men feel a psychic need to believe that America's role in Vietnam is wholly "obscene," and to believe also that the whole American system is rotten and corrupt. And in at least two ways, it is.

Newsweek, June 29, 1970

Vietnamese Alienate Cambodians in Fight Against Mutual Enemy

by Peter R. Kann

KOMPONG SPEU, Cambodia—It's open to debate whether American forays into Communist sanctuaries will prove to have had a significant effect on the war in South Vietnam, depriving the Communists of vital supplies and disrupting their logistics for months to come.

But it already seems clear the U.S. forces, which were withdrawn earlier this week, have had little impact on the widening war within Cambodia.

Saigon has been far more frank than Washington in publicly recognizing that no matter how many arms caches may have been uncovered along the border, a crucial issue now is the very survival of Lon Nol's anti-Communist regime in Phnom Penh. Saigon says what Washington knows: The fall of Lon Nol, and consequent return of Prince Sihanouk as a North Vietnamese puppet, would turn all Cambodia into a vast enemy sanctuary and staging area for attacks on South Vietnam.

In an effort to avert this development, the South Vietnamese Army (ARVN) has been dashing about much of Cambodia, operating as a mobile strike force to attack Communist troop concentrations and to blast them out of occupied Cambodian towns and cities.

Even long-time critics concede that ARVN has been operating efficiently and effectively—at least by its own standards of operation within South Vietnam. Regiments that rarely ventured out on anything more taxing than a two-day operation in South Vietnam have been constantly on the move and in contact with enemy forces for six to eight weeks in Cambodia.

South Vietnamese operations in Cambodia are all the more impressive in that many have been conducted beyond the range of American logistical and firepower support.

Not that ARVN is winning the war in Cambodia. It hasn't been able to prevent the Communists from opening a new river supply route down into Cambodia from southern Laos, from carving out giant new jungle sanctuaries in northeast Cambodia or from making all major Cambodian roads insecure. Nor has ARVN stopped the Reds from attacking Cambodian population centers or—perhaps most important—from extending Communist influence into the Cambodian countryside.

Moreover, it remains to be seen for how long and in what strength ARVN can continue to operate in Cambodia now that all direct American support has ended. The monsoon weather is becoming more and more inhospitable to tanks and trucks. And the South Vietnamese have ample military problems to deal with back home.

Nevertheless, if anything is going to keep the Lon Nol regime afloat it probably will have to be ARVN. And yet, ironically, ARVN is a savior that most Cambodians, regardless of their politics, don't really seem to want.

To an American, watching South Vietnam try to save Cambodia seems in many ways like a parody of the U.S. role in South Vietnam. There's the concept of "saving" a people at their own considerable expense. ARVN's patronizing attitude toward the Cambodian Army, whirlwind Cambodian visits of Vietnamese VIPs and official statements from Saigon about the need to develop a pacification program for the Cambodian population.

But if the American-Vietnamese alliance has often been strained, it's a perfect marriage compared with the Vietnamese-Cambodian partnership. There have been centuries of racial enmity and military hostility between the Vietnamese and Cambodian people. Vietnamese and Cambodians are as different as Germans and Frenchmen. They have little in common beyond eating rice. The years during which Vietnam was being racked by war while Cambodia slumbered in serenity have further accentuated national differences.

From the Vietnamese point of view, Cambodians are racial inferiors, an indolent and ignorant people who for years, whether actively or tacitly, have aided the Vietnamese Communists. Worst of all, in the first few weeks after the fall of

Sihanouk, the Cambodians—with a mindless kind of cruelty —massacred hundreds of innocent Vietnamese civilians living in Cambodia. Horror stories of these massacres, and the visible plight of tens of thousands of Vietnamese refugees streaming into South Vietnam from Cambodia, have fueled anti-Cambodian feeling among South Vietnamese, ARVN troops included. This goes a long way toward explaining why ARVN behavior in Cambodia is often less than gracious.

From the Cambodian point of view, Vietnamese of any sort are arrogant interlopers. The South Vietnamese soldiers are just another wave of Vietnamese aggressors, trampling across Cambodian soil, ostensibly to kill other equally noxious Vietnamese. In the process ARVN has ravaged and looted its way through Cambodian villages, producing a host of horror stories for Cambodian consumption. And Vietnamese arrogance in dealings with Cambodian military and civilian officials has created tensions even at the governmental level.

The strains between these two sudden allies point up what may be the inherent weakness of President Nixon's much-ballyhooed Guam Doctrine—that Asians shall help other Asians. The fact is that most Asians don't much like other Asians.

Several days spent with ARVN units operating well inside Cambodia offer some insights into the shakiness of the Vietnamese-Cambodian alliance.

Consider, for example, the recent battle for Kompong Speu, a Cambodian provincial capital 40 kilometers west of Phnom Penh that had been partially occupied by the Vietcong before it was liberated by ARVN armor and ground troops.

The 16th Regiment of the ARVN's 9th Division is headquartered here in a school yard. Under a tree are the ubiquitous maps, overlays and charts with box scores of captured weapons and dead Vietcong. The ARVN regimental commander describes the fight for Kompong Speu—how the enemy had moved into the administrative sector of the city, how the Cambodian Army had retreated to defend its own military compound, how ARVN units had swept into town killing 148 enemy troops and capturing 4,025 weapons. The weapons, he proudly reports, had been turned over to the Cambodian Army in a ceremony the day before.

Kompong Speu is battered but for the most part still intact. Fighting was largely confined to the administrative sector. There the damage is heavy. The hospital is a charred ruin, recognizable only by a row of blackened and twisted bedsprings. Nearby, Cambodian families are picking through the rubble that once was a row of houses. One woman is staring at the vaguely recognizable remains of a Singer sewing machine. Amid the rubble are several blackened and bloated bodies that could be Vietcong—or anyone.

But in the commercial center of the city, and in most of the residential areas, damage is slight. Few Vietcong had entered these parts of the city, and the South Vietnamese had not used heavy firepower to rout them out. Indeed, in a departure from frequent American and Vietnamese tactics, ARVN hadn't called in air strikes on Kompong Speu. "We have no control over the Vietnamese Air Force. They would have dropped bombs and napalm on everything and burned down the city," says Col. Vong Kim Sinh, Deputy Commander of the 9th Division.

If most of Kompong Speu's civilian population are alive and uninjured, they are far from happy with their Vietnamese "liberators." "Robbers, robbers," screams a middle-aged woman, yanking a suckling baby off her breast and dragging a stranger into her house. The interior is chaos. Cabinets are smashed, clothing is strewn about, drawers are yanked out and shelves and cupboards are broken and bare. "I am a poor woman all alone and these Vietnamese bandits, these pigs looted my house. They broke down my door. They came through the windows. They stole everything. Everything."

The story is the same throughout the town. Having liberated Kompong Speu, Vietnamese soldiers went on a wild looting spree, stealing nearly everything that could be carried away and smashing much that could not be.

Outside the woman's house is a Cambodian battalion commander, Commandant Soeung Kim Sea. "The Vietcong came but left with nothing. The South Vietnamese came and took everything. Our people have more fear of the South Vietnamese than of the Vietcong," he says.

Why didn't the Cambodian Army protect Cambodian homes against ARVN looters? he is asked.

The commandant is puzzled by the question. "But they would have shot us," he replies.

The commandant is proud of a unit of Functionaire Commandos (literally functionary commandos). These are civil servants, teachers and students who had been given a week of military indoctrination and five bullets to shoot before being sent out to fight under his command. The commandos had seen little action against the Vietcong, but the previous day they had ambushed an ARVN convoy piled high with loot from Kompong Speu. The commandos had shot out the tires of several trucks, forcing the South Vietnamese to abandon some of the booty. "It was most courageous," says the commandant.

A few kilometers outside town is the headquarters of Gen. Southenne Fernandez, commander of Cambodia's Second Military Region and the nation's closest thing to a Wellington. He derives his un-Cambodian name from a Filipino grandfather, a musician, who married into the Cambodian royal family.

The general seems to share the views of the housewife and the commandant regarding the ARVN liberation. "They ravaged the city, it is regrettable, no? The population is very discouraged with our South Vietnamese allies. I am also discouraged."

At this point an ARVN helicopter flies over his compound. The general gazes up and says wistfully: "Ah, all the Vietnamese generals have helicopters. Vietnamese generals can go everywhere, can control everything. But a poor Cambodian general must walk."

Gen. Fernandez is not optimistic about the war. "We have control in the administrative centers, but we have no means to control the people in the countryside. The Vietcong operate among them with propaganda and terror. What can I do?" he asks.

Just outside the general's compound is a large bonfire being fed with rifles. Why is the Cambodian Army, so short of weapons, burning rifles? "Frankly," says the general, "these are the 4,025 rifles presented to me yesterday by the South Vietnamese."

The guns, says the general, were not in fact captured from

the Vietcong. South Vietnamese troops actually had taken a Cambodian arms warehouse. The warehouse contained 4,025 ancient weapons. Many were shotguns and hunting rifles dating back to before World War I, and no ammunition was available for any of the weapons. "It is all most unfortunate," says Gen. Fernandez.

The general had graciously attended the Vietnamese ceremony the previous day and had accepted the gift of "captured Vietcong weapons" with profuse thanks. "I let the Vietnamese make their propaganda. I understand such things," he says.

But the South Vietnamese had publicized their largess, and news of it had spread to Phnom Penh. "This morning Lon Nol sent a message demanding some of the 4,025 captured weapons for the defense of Phnom Penh," says Gen. Fernandez. "I tried to explain that they were our guns to begin with, and that they do not shoot, but perhaps Lon Nol did not believe me."

What's more, says the general, "Perhaps the Americans will hear of all the weapons we have been given and will think Cambodia needs no American aid."

"So I burn all the rifles. Otherwise they cause me more trouble," he says decisively.

Back at South Vietnamese regimental headquarters, a truck pulls in carrying, under guard, a dozen Cambodian soldiers, their 1919 Lee Enfield rifles lying at their feet. These Cambodians had been found by an ARVN patrol on a riverbank a few miles away.

A discussion ensues. Are they Khmer Rouge (Cambodian Communists)? Deserters? Were they hiding? Or just sleeping? The 12 men are now squatting on the ground, occasionally grinning at the South Vietnamese officers. One explains, in pidgin French, that they are Cambodian home guards who were assigned to defend a village and who had been rounded up by the ARVN patrol while they were taking a siesta.

A Cambodian liaison officer finally shuffles over. Are the 12 men perhaps Khmer Rouge? he is asked.

"Ah no, no, they are only ordinary Cambodians," he replies.

The liaison officer, a 50-year-old sergeant who wears battle ribbons from the French Indochina army, is sadly watching two drunk ARVN soldiers weave around a clearing in a jeep occasionally colliding with coconut trees. "My jeep," says the sergeant. He explains that the Vietnamese soldiers had relieved him of his jeep the night before and replaced its Cambodian insignia with a Vietnamese marking.

At six o'clock the next morning the South Vietnamese break camp and move out in a long convoy of trucks and jeeps. Even as the vehicles pull out, Cambodian soldiers begin drifting in to scavenge among the piles of empty ammo boxes, shell cannisters, tin cans, bent bicycle frames, spilled rice bags and chicken bones. The same scene had been enacted a hundred times before in South Vietnam, with ARVN soldiers scrounging in American refuse piles. But the pickings are better at American bases.

The ARVN convoy rolls slowly down Highway No. 4 toward Phnom Penh, then swings south toward the province capital of Takeo. The roads are largely deserted. Several small towns along the route are badly damaged. Others seem intact but boarded up and abandoned.

However, the countryside is still populated, and every half mile or so the convoy passes a cluster of Cambodian men standing along the roadside. The Cambodians show absolutely no emotion, no smiles, no waves, only blank or sullen stares. At one village near Phnom Penh a portly Cambodian officer begins to applaud as the convoy rolls past. All the other onlookers remain totally impassive, and his applause dies away.

The Wall Street Journal, July 2, 1970

Scraps of Paper from Vietnam

by James Sterba

SECURITY
From an Army report:

> # CONFIDENTIAL
> ## This is a cover sheet.
> (This cover sheet is unclassified when separated from classified documents.)
> # CONFIDENTIAL
> ## Previous editions of this label are obsolete.
> # CONFIDENTIAL
> The security classification affixed to this report has been determined to be necessary to the national security interests of the United States even though no classified material was used and all information was derived from unclassified sources.

INTRODUCTIONS

Gentlemen, welcome to Vietnam and welcome to the 90th Replacement Battalion. Gentlemen, here, you will complete your in-country processing . . . Gentlemen, it is very hot today, and I know you will all want to complete your in-country processing as soon as possible, and therefore you will pay attention at all times . . .

And you will refrain from talking . . . Gentlemen, there is a snack bar and ice-cream shop next to the Finance Building.

129

Gentlemen, these facilities are off-limits to you until you have completed your processing . . . Now, I must have your complete attention, is that clear? Hey, you two, forget about that swimming pool—did you HEAR ME? . . . Gentlemen, there is no smoking allowed in this building. You will complete this portion of your processing in 25 to 30 minutes if you keep your mouths shut. There will be absolutely no talking.

Now, most of your special problems and questions have been anticipated. I want you now to prepare yourself to process. The pencil we are handing to you should be placed in front of you on top of your 201 File. Your health, dental and finance records you will not need. I want you now to put them under your chair. Gentlemen . . . Gentlemen, the card I have in my hand is your PX-ration card. I want you to put the last two digits of the number on that card next to your name on the sheet that is being passed to you. When you receive the sheet you will pass it directly to the man in back of you. You will not pass the sheet back and forth across the aisle . . . Gentlemen, the manila envelope you have been given is very important. I want you to treat it as though it was your 201 File . . .

There are a number of materials in the packet you have received which you should read after you have completed your processing . . .

READY REFERENCE FACTS

The enemy—is Communist NVN, and as its Southern arm, the Vietcong . . . The National Liberation Front, controlled by Hanoi, is the politico-military organization in SVN which claims that it is fighting "to liberate" the people. But this "arm of liberation" remains only a tool of Hanoi designed to achieve a Communist takeover in the South.

. . . Gentlemen, when you have finished your processing I want you all to write a letter to your parents and tell them you have arrived safely in Vietnam. You can tell them that you are 22 miles northeast of Saigon—and, of course, tell them that you are having a wonderful time.

Now, Gentlemen, you are in a combat zone. If a siren goes off, you can assume we are under attack—either incoming rockets or a ground attack. In the event of such an attack, do not try to help—you will only hinder. Are there any questions?

"Will we have a chance to use the swimming pool?"

Laughter.

"What the hell is this dental orientation bull—?"

They are going to teach you how to brush your teeth. . . . Gentlemen, we are now going to police up the area. This is your first mission in the Vietnam combat theater. Now do it right, Gentlemen—because if you f— it up, you will have to do it again. Look at the ground. Gentlemen, look at the ground.

THE LEARNING PROCESS
Robert V. Craig, director, New Life Development, IV Corps:

So somebody said, "Gee, why didn't that one win the hearts and minds of the people?" Then, in 1969, we reinstated the idea of village government, of letting the villages decide what the government should provide—not that the G.V.N. [Government of Vietnam] is the Red Cross of the Orient.

INGENUITY
A conversation in a bunker at the Tayninh base camp:

Tomorrow we get the beds. Two of them. We're going to put a curtain between them. Got 'em from Cuchi. They're coming up on a truck. We gave the guy who's bringing them up a membership. That's how we got the refrigerator. It was in Laikhe. Bought it for $20. We got two pilots from the 187th to fly over and pick it up—gave them memberships, too.

There's an air conditioner still over there, and I think we can get it if we can steal that chopper again for an hour. Actually, we scrounged most everything in this whole damn bunker. Except the fan. I already had that. Got the bar for six cases of C's and two cases of Lurps [rations]. And we got the mamasan who cleans up around here to bring in her two daughters the other day. Nice stuff, 15 and 18. We're gonna charge five bucks a throw to members. Three goes to the mamasan—she's gonna get rich—and we keep two for the bar. Guys in our unit get freebees when they come out of the boonies. We figure on gettin' the girls about three times a week. You know, Tim, the medic over at Charlie Med, he's gonna check out the girls once a week. We made him a member. . .

FARM ADVICE
An American agriculture adviser:

We've been getting in a lot of New Hampshires. That's a strong bird. Operating on a 21-day cycle, we've been getting 1,000 to 1,200 chicks per week. But we have a lot of problems. Vietnamese farmers have just let their chickens run around loose, but you gotta put these chicks in good pens. You gotta buy feed. You gotta vaccinate them. So we set up some mobile advisory vaccination teams to show them how. And the farmers are starting to accept that, especially when they start seeing the results in cash. These grow up to be big, solid chickens. They're tough. Strong. And if you keep them in pens, they'll start pecking each other to death. See, we teach the Vietnamese to keep their chickens in pens. Then they find out they gotta buy feed. Then they find out they gotta get 'em vaccinated. Then they find out the chickens are killing each other and they don't know what to do. The answer is simple: debeaking. You gotta debeak the chickens—blunt their beaks so they don't hurt each other. Except the Vietnamese—some of them—think that's bad. So we gotta set up some mobile advisory chicken debeaking teams. . .

SAVINGS

The withdrawal of American troops from Vietnam has led to a reduction thus far of from 144,000 to 105,000 in the number of cans of creamed-style corn consumed by troops in the war zone each day. There are other savings: The Army's bump-and-paint slush fund for taking dents out of the 13,000-odd sedans and pickup trucks in Vietnam will probably drop substantially from the fiscal 1970 figure of $180,000. The Army's office-machine repair bill—for fixing typewriters, duplicating machines and such—is also expected to drop from the fiscal 1970 total of $597,000.

WAR BOOTY

Members of the 11th Armored Cavalry Regiment on the radio in Cambodia:

"Hey, E Troop has just found a whole bunch of sh—."

"Alright, let's get a sitrep [situation report]."

"Whatdaya got?"

"Roger. We got *beaucoup* documents. Pictures of Ho Chi Minh's funeral and stuff like that, it looks like. Coupla comics. About 30 bicycles.

"Also got approximately eight pigs—blew away a couple, though. Chickens. And we got 35 pounds of peanuts."

"How many peanuts?"

"About 35 pounds. Repeat three-five pounds."

"Roger the peanuts, and thank you much."

MARINES

Sign in the First Marine Division Information Office:

> For those who have fought for it, life
> has a special flavor the protected
> will never know.

News Release from the First Marine Division Information Office:

Danang, Vietnam--Thanks to the efforts of their cooks and messmen, the Leathernecks of Headquarters Battalion, First Marine Division, are now able to enjoy that great American institution--the coffee break--here in the Republic of Vietnam . . .

A battalion snack bar was formally opened by Maj. Gen. Charles F. Widdecke, commanding general, First Marine Division . . .

THE OTHER WARRIORS
A grunt on adversaries:

I have only one thing to say for the people in the States, man: The termites rule the jungle. Spent many a night standing up, man, 'cause I couldn't get back in my hootch 'cause the termites were in there carryin' away all my sh—. Chomp. They'll bite the hell outaya. They're bad motherf—s. You can hear 'em comin' up on you. They travel in small herds—like about 20,000. And ants. We got ants. They got their own army, man. First they call in their air strikes—mosquitoes. You get a B-52 in every now and then—big flies. Then they call in the infantry—damn red ants crawlin' all over your body. Then APC's [armored personnel carriers] come out, f—in' termites. Then the big boys—tanks. When you get bit by a big boy, you been bit, man. Those motherf—in' scorpions really do a job on you.

INNOCENCE
Specialist 4 David D. Williams, 21, with the 25th Infantry Division in Cambodia:

They tried to be friendly. They just didn't know any better. One night a trip flare went off and we opened up on them. Killed one of them. It really tore me up. The Vietnamese know not to walk around at night like that. The Cambodians don't yet.

PROCEDURE
A MACV Joint Messageform:

UNCLASSIFIED
INSTRUCTIONS FOR THE MEDICAL AND AGRICULTURAL TREATMENT AND PROCESSING OF RETROGRADE MATERIAL:

. . . c. The basic theory of rat and flea control (plague control) in cargo and equipment is a three-phased operation: 1. Enclosing or trapping the rodent in an area free of food; 2. Providing food in the form of a rodent-bait block to kill the rodent; 3. Treat the area with insecticides, 2% Diazinon dust or vapona pest strip, to kill the fleas on the rat, or when they leave the dead rat.

MANUAL

From a leaders' guide for operations in Southeast Asia:

> *. . . Evasion: First, get as far away as possible. Sometimes this may mean several miles; at other times, just a few yards. Plan your escape, do not run blindly. Use your head—there is no substitute for common sense. As soon as possible, sit down, think out your problem, recall what you learned in training.*

BATTALION NEWSPAPER

From The Gimlet News, 3/21st Inf., 196th Inf. Brigade:

Gimlet Scoreboard
Totals for the Month

Enemy Killed. **39**
Chieu Hois. **3**
P.O.W.'s. **2**

News From the Companies

Annihilators

Congratulations are extended to SSG Schroder and SGT Balliett for receiving the Bronze Star for Service and the Army Commendation Medal for Achievement. . .

Black Death

Black Death wishes to welcome its new CO CPT Gary Gauthier to its family and to announce that 1LT Grant will be leaving the position of CO to become XO. . .

THE BOYS IN THE BAND
An interview with a trumpet player:

"What's its official name?"

"It's called the First Air Cavalry Division Skytrooper Band, Airmobile. Right now, we've got two flutes, ten clarinets, seven trumpets, four saxophones, one baritone, three French horns, one bassoon, three trombones and three drummers. Mostly we just play around the division area at Phuocvinh—ceremonies and stuff. But we get out in the boonies, too—to firebases. The grunts really appreciate us. We play light stuff, mostly, like Herb Alpert."

"How do you get to the firebases?"

"Chinook. We just fly over the jungle like everybody else, the whole band in one chopper. It's kind of a hassle, sometimes. We gotta carry our M-16's, you know, along with our instruments and music. But it's worth it, I guess. The guys in the boonies really believe you care about them when you go out there and play for them."

"Really?"

"Yeah. Except one time we went out to this base—it was way out there. And we set up and started playin' and the V.C. must of heard us 'cause they started pumpin' in mortars. We all scattered. Dove for the bunkers. Took five or six rounds, I guess, 'fore they stopped. A clarinet player and a trumpet man got hit. Nothing serious. But they both got Purple Hearts."

FORESTRY
From an Army news release:

> LAND CLEARERS REACH MILESTONE
>   By Capt. David Berkman
> Banmethuot (864th Engr Bn)--A
> land clearing company located
> here has reached a milestone
> for removing tropical jungle
> from the Republic of Vietnam to
> deny sanctuaries to the Viet-
> cong and North Vietnamese Army.
>   The 687th Engineer Company
> of the 864th Engineer Bat-

talion; 18th Engineer Brigade,
has cleared more than 30,000
acres since beginning such operations Feb. 13, 1969, near
Baoloc. The 30,000th acre was
cleared recently near Highway
TL-1 northwest of Ban-
methuot. . . .

OPINION

Two Marine grunts in the Queson Valley:

"As far as I'm concerned, the dinks can have this whole sonofa—in' place."

"There it is."

SONGS

A Marine major:

I guess they don't have the kinds of songs in this war that we had in Korea—good drinking songs. Oh, we had some dandies. One was "Those Mortar Shells are Breaking Up That Old Gang of Mine." The kids now are a lot different. They can get pretty irreverent now.

An irreverent song of unknown origin:

> *Spray the town and kill the people,*
> *   Drop your napalm in the square;*
> *Take off early in the morning,*
> *   Get them while they're still at prayer.*
>
> *Drop some candy to the orphans,*
> *   Watch them as they gather round;*
> *Use your 20 millimeter,*
> *   Mow the little b—s down.*
>
> *Spray the town and kill the people,*
> *   Get them with your poison gas;*
> *Watch them throwing up their breakfasts,*
> *   As you make your second pass.*
>
> *See them line up in the market,*
> *   Waiting for their pound of rice,*
> *Hungry, skinny, starving people,*
> *   Isn't killing harvests nice?*

ENTERTAINMENT
An invitation:

STAY ARMY
A Stars and Stripes news article, 1969:

> Longbinh, Vietnam—   Re-enlistments among U.S. Army troops in Vietnam during the past three months have exceeded goals set by the Department of the Army. . .
>
> Of those soldiers serving in the first enlistment in Vietnam during July, August and September, 42 per cent have 're-upped' for another hitch, said Sgt. Maj. William J. Roche of Atlanta, Ga., career counselor supervisor at USARV headquarters. . .

An Army memorandum, 1970:

> CONFIDENTIAL
>   Subject: Enlisted Personnel Shortages and Assignment Policies.
>
>   . . . Personnel with infantry MOS will be particularly critical in July and August. While Department of the Army is attempting to increase replacement flow, available sources are limited and significant improvement is not expected. . .
>
>   . . . Reenlistment out of MOS 11, 12, and 13 series (infantry, engineers and artillery specialties) which will result in removing enlisted men from assignments in these MOS's during their Vietnam tour are suspended until further notice from this headquarters. . .

A clerk-typist Phubai, 1970:

Ain't you heard, man? You can't re-up to get out of the field anymore. They changed the rule. 'Cause they were really hurtin' for grunts, I heard. So if you're out there humpin' now, you're gonna stay out there humpin' the whole damn time. The only way you can get out now is with a profile [medical record]. And you gotta be in a whole world of hurt 'fore they'll give you a profile now.

ANOTHER INVITATION
> *The Flower People—Saigon, Tet notwithstanding, invite you to see the light at the end of the tunnel, AGAIN, New Year's Eve. . .*

QUOTE
Col. Robert Rheault, former commander, Fifth Special Forces Group:

War is a difficult and dangerous business. People get killed in war.

GRAFFITI
In the men's room of a Saigon bar:

Who's Afraid of
Ellsworth Bunker?

JOB TRAINING
An Army news release:

> Several weeks ago Le Thi Nang, an 18-year-old girl from Bengat, was a janitor in a contractor's office at the Laikhe base camp.
> Today Miss Nang and six other members of her graduating

class are fully qualified
bulldozer operators. The nimble
Miss Nang can also handle with
ease a giant road leveler, but
according to her instructor,
Enrique Garcia, she is better
with the bulldozer.

OPTIMISM
Specialist 4 Stanley Morgan, 21, of White Plains, N.Y.:

That Man up there, He's got a long list, and I figure I'm
about a thousand names down. And my time ain't come up
yet.

COMPANIONSHIP
An article in Stars and Stripes:

> "We had moved to cordon and search a vil-
> lage early in the morning when I came
> across the mongoose," said Pfc. George
> Melici of Arlington, Mass. "He was only a
> few days old and still very weak."
>
> Melici placed the animal in a basket,
> which he kept tied to his rucksack. Soon the
> mongoose, growing stronger, left his basket
> to ride through the bush on the top of the
> rucksack.
>
> "I named him Ralph and made him my
> assistant machine gunner. At night Ralph of-
> ten wanders over to visit other members of
> the company, but he never fails to return to
> sleep near the gun."
>
> Ralph earned his Combat Infantryman's
> Badge his first day with the company when
> the unit encountered sniper fire. He showed
> his loyalty by staying with Melici through-
> out the action. . . .

AIR STRIKE

A forward air control pilot, "Sider Two Two," talking to an
F-100 pilot, "Litter Three":

"Hello, Sider Two Two, this Mission six five two inbound, two eight five at three niner from two three."

"Roger, Litter Three. Copy you two eight five. O.K., we've got good weather and you'll have 100 per cent visibility this afternoon. Can you give me your line-up?"

"O.K., Sider Two Two. Fox One here with eight napes, eight MK-82's, single fuse high drag and 1,280 rounds of 20 mikemike."

"Roger. O.K., the target is a K.E.L. [known enemy location]. It's in a single and double canopy area south of the trap about 200 meters at 180 west of circular rome plow cut we call the onion. I got friendlies about 3,000 meters to the whisky, so no problem there. You got a nice clean shot. The T.L. [target elevation] is zero zero niner zero . . . Give me your 82's [bombs] in pairs."

"Roger that, Sider, I'm in tight, rock wings."

"O.K., here goes."

"O.K., fine, Sider, got you spotted."

"Right, Litter. O.K., let's make it a run in echo-whisky [east-west] with a left pull. I'll be inside your pattern . . . O.K., arm 'em up . . . I'm in the mark."

"Roger, Sider, I have your smoke."

"O.K., let's see. Put it in 15 meters at 5 o'clock . . . You're cleared hot, Litter."

". . . Two away."

"Roger, Litter, good hit, right on the money . . . Make the next one 10 meters at 10 o'clock."

"Roger that, Sider . . . you're cleared hot."

"Litter Three, another good one. Right down the pipe . . . O.K., Litter Three, start your mikemike [strafing] 50 meters at 6 o'clock . . . You're cleared hot on the mikes . . . Oh-kay, Litter Three, real fine . . . Ready for the B.D.A. [bomb damage assessment]."

"Roger, Sider Two Two, give it to me."

"Roger, Litter Three. I've got 100 over 100, 50 per cent in 10 [half the bombs within 10 meters of the target] and 100 within 50. I had you in contact at 1523 and off at 1528. I have four bunkers destroyed and two sustained fires. That's about it."

"Roger, Sider Two Two. Is that all? Those were good runs. You see anything else?"

"Litter Three. I'll make another pass. Visibility's pretty poor through the canopy. Let's see . . . It was a fine pattern . . . Well . . . Let's make it five bunkers and . . . oh . . . well . . . one hootch . . . And I'll throw in 40 meters of trench line."

"Roger, Sider Two Two. Thank you much."

"That's O.K., Litter Three. Thank you. I really enjoyed working with you this afternoon."

"Roger that, Sider Two Two. It's been a real pleasure, and I'll see you another time."

"Roger, Litter Three, and out."

AIR STRIKE TOTALS
From an Air Force weekly summary, Sept. 18, 1970:

> U.S. Air Force fighter-bomber pilots and crews flew 1,039 tactical air strikes during the week of Sept. 10-16, providing close air support for allied ground forces and bombing and strafing enemy troop concentrations, base camps, fortifications, bunkers, sup-ply and staging areas, weapons positions and other military targets.
>
> Pilots and crews were credited by forward air con-trollers and allied forces making ground sweeps with killing 20 enemy soldiers and with destroying or damaging

383 bunkers and 181 fortifications. They touched off 59
secondary explosions and ignited 82 sustained fires.

AN OBSERVATION

Capt. Charles S. Hunt, 23, of Lafe, Ark., an F-4 fighter-bomber weapons man, after an air strike:

There were a large number of thunderstorms and light rain in the area. We had to weave our way in to avoid the storms to reach the target.

To the east of us were thunderstorms with a great deal of lightning, and to the west the sun was shining, creating a bright red background.

The result of all these conditions was revealed when we pulled off the target; there was a full-circle rainbow following us around. I heard the comment more than once over the radio that it was a heck of a place to have a war because it was just so incredibly beautiful.

RECREATION

An Army news release:

The recreation for soldiers
confined to fire-support bases
is often limited, and anything
beyond a volleyball net and a
couple of horseshoe pits is
unusual. But the men of the
First Infantry Division's
Second Battalion, 16th
Infantry, have devised a
competitive event at their
firebase which rivals "Wres-
tling at the Olympic" for
excitement.
    Each morning soldiers can
be seen walking around with

entrenching tools, recruiting
potential contenders. En-
trenching tools? Of course.
What else would you dig for
tarantulas with? Because these
big furry spiders are the
contestants in the "Rhode Island Bucket Fights."

Each spider is kept by his
owner in a C-ration can until
it's time for a match. Two of
the combatants are placed in a
bucket, where they visciously
battle it out until one or the
other loses a limb.

OTHER LIMBS
*Capt. Arthur J. Draper, chief medical officer aboard the
Hospital Ship Repose, March, 1970:*

The bulk of the injuries we are getting now are mines and
boobytraps, whereas in the past incidents of grenade and rifle
fire represented the bulk. In the past four or five months,
there appears to have been a four- or fivefold increase in multiple amputees.

I hope this is all incredible some day. Right now, it's all too
damn credible.

BLOOD
44th Medical Brigade news release:

Most of the blood trans-
fused in Vietnam is obtained
from donors at various military installations in CONUS
(Continental U.S.) . . . Following donation, the blood
from CONUS arrives in Vietnam
at the USARV Central Blood

Bank in Camranh Bay. Fixed-
wing aircraft distribute the
blood to the seven sub depots,
which are located in Danang,
Chulai, Pleiku, Quinhon, Nhatrang, Longbinh and Saigon.
These depots supply all types
of blood and fresh frozen
plasma to the surgical, field
and evacuation hospitals as it
is needed.

The equipment of the USARV
Blood Bank includes an 1,800
cubic-foot refrigerator for
storage of blood, six ice-
making machines and two
freezers for fresh frozen
plasma. Blood from 21 to 31
days old is saved for use in a
mass casualty situation. After
31 days the blood is de-
stroyed.

In Vietnam, 13,500 to
18,500 units (pints) of blood
a month are transfused to
2,500 to 4,500 patients. Patients that are transfused
received on the average of
four to five units of blood,
and some patients received as
many as 100 units. No one has
ever failed to receive blood
because there was not enough.

A military-hospital lab technician:
   "We use just about all the blood we get. We're in sort of a
slump now—not much action—so we got quite a bit on
hand."

"What do you do with it when it gets too old?"
"Give it to the gook hospitals."

ORDERS
Lieut. Col. Grail Brookshire of Stone Mountain, Ga.,
commander of the Second Squadron, 11th Armored Cavalry
Regiment:
Now caution your people to stay off that airstrip to the side.
I want to try to preserve it if at all possible. We might be able
to get 123's [supply planes] in there. When we get there, four-
six and three-six will break out and start down this way. And
I don't think that going down the red ball [highway] is necessarily the way we want to go. Work your way through the
rubber [trees]. One-six, you'll start here and move on up into
the town. Get a lema off into the rubber. Move on up the
road and start workin' your way slowly up there. Now, if you
take fire, return it. If you take heavy fire and you look like
you got prepared positions, back 'em out. Shoot like a son-
ofab— and back 'em out. Get 'em back out, and then we're
just gonna have to start preppin' it [bringing in air strikes] or
else we're gonna have to bypass it. We'll have a FAC [forward
air controller] overhead. We'll have a pink team [helicopter
gunship and scoutship] up helpin' us out. Now the pink team
took fire here at about 537342 or 3. Fifteen individuals with
A.K.'s.

This is a reconnaissance in force to find out what's in there
and also, if possible, to take the town—without destroying it.
I just want everybody up tight—weapons and flak jackets, steel
helmets on. And when you take fire, SHOOT. Try to avoid
shooting into crowds of civilians. In other words, if you're
taking light fire and there are civilians in the area, try to return
the fire without losing all the f—in' civilians.

Now, if we can get around these f—ers, we might have
them bottled up down in this end of the rubber. They figure
us to come right up Highway 7. Villagers between here and
there told intel they have broken the highway, and they undoubtedly have. We'll try to find a way around it. We can
always come up through the rubber through this draw. If you
have to start knockin' down rubber trees, they go down easy.

Intelligence:

"The villagers around here are hiding 'cause they're afraid of the V.C. and they're afraid of the battle that's gonna take place. They say there were about 1,000 to 2,000 Cambodian civilians in the town of Snoul. Don't know how many are still there. They say about 1,000 to 3,000 N.V.A. [North Vietnamese Army soldiers] are in there."

"One to three THOUSAND?"

"That's a roge."

BATTLE

The voices of a dozen soldiers in contact:

RRRRrrruuuuuuhhhhrrrr. CHEWCHEWCHEWCHEW-chewchew. TTTttthhhuuumm. . . Two-six has got contact . . . Four six, the loach has got two caliber 51's [machine guns] to your echo about 50 meters . . . RRRhhhrrrrrr . . . Get your asses over there . . . Roge . . . Get that Kit Carson [Vietnamese scout] . . . Hold your fire. HOLD YOUR FIRE! . . . Sir, they got 51's dug in all over the God— place, it looks like . . . They can prep the edges . . . We'll get these two f—ers . . . The Kit Carson's talkin' that sonofa— out . . . WATCH OUT FOR THAT GUN . . . O.K., O.K., he's got 'em . . . Will you look at that little f—er? Four-six, don't get bottled up . . . Spread 'em out . . . Give me some more 50 ammo . . . Don't give me any bull— . . . Hey, HEY GET YOUR GOD— ASSES AWAY FROM THAT GOD— HOLE! Get outa there . . . WHHHhhhooommmm . . . Jesus . . . Oh, my God . . . The major, the major's hit . . . Get down. There's another one in there . . . THE COLONEL'S HIT . . . What'd he throw? . . . Grenade . . . Is that sonofa— still in there? Yeah . . . GET A FRAG . . . Get a God— frag. We'll blow that b— outa there . . .

. . . Hey, man, you caught a piece of shrapnel . . . You gotta hole in you. You're bleedin' . . . I do? I don't feel anything. Well, f— me . . . He's still in there, watch . . . Yeah, I saw that c—er come outa there . . . One-six has got contact, heavy sh— . . . Oh, it's just a lot of blood. It's not too bad . . . Alright, let's blow that sonofa— outta there . . . Hasn't anyone got a f—in' grenade? . . . Where's that other f—er? I'll kill that b— . . . No, don't kill 'em . . . God—, it hurts

. . . Shhhhh, you're gonna be O.K. . . . You're all right . . . Man, the major's really f—ed up. How's the colonel? . . . Multiple frags, lots of blood, not bad—surface stuff . . . How many got hit? . . . Six . . . The major's the worst . . . MED-IVAC ON THE WAY . . . Hey, TURN THOSE GOD—TRACKS AROUND. Turn 'em around . . . Back out, you dumb b—s . . . Don't get bunched up. You know better than that . . . Watch out for that dud round . . . Oh, Jesus . . . Hasn't anybody got one God— grenade? . . .

ANOTHER PLACE, THE MORNING AFTER
Pfc. Floyd Schwalm, 20, of St. Paul, Minn.:
   Then all of a sudden they hit us. Ambush. They had A.K.'s, 60's [machine guns], and they were shootin' at us and it was just like the movies. I drops down and grabs my 60 and jumps up and shoots a six-round burst and my damn 60 jams. I throw it back—it was bad sh—. Really bad. They had 51's dug into the woodline. They had our track zeroed in, man. ZZZzzzzboom. One hits right alongside. One on the other side, ZZZZzzzzboom. I thought it was all over, and then we got a dud round right on top of our track and there wasn't no way I was gonna stand up and take that dud round off there. No way. Not EVER. Then one of the grenades caught the front of our track. It set off our C.S. [gas] grenades. Only time we're supposed to use the C.S. is when the gooks are in the perimeter. A lot of horse sh—. We had maybe half a dozen C.S. grenades on our turret. And they went off—SSSSSssss. I didn't think the C.S. was gonna be that bad. But I was coughin' and pukin' up. I grabbed a pair of overalls. Couldn't find a gas mask. And all around guys are screamin' and yellin', "I'm hit, I'm hit." And the shootin' was keepin' up. Bad. The lieutenant put me in for a Bronze Star. I don't see where I deserve it. I ain't going back out there, man. NO WAY . . .
   . . . Boy, if there was any way I didn't have to go back . . . Hey, Doc, you gotta look at my gums, Doc. I'm in a world of hurt. Doc. I don't even want to go back out. Man, them gooks had their sh— together. I mean, they were as good as we were. No way, Doc. Listen, Doc, my gums, they're hurtin'. I'm sick. Maybe I can catch a good stiff case of the clap . . . Ain't no way . . . Doc. Not EVER going back out there . . .

PROFESSIONAL DISSENT
*Capt. Arthur Moseley of Panama City, Fla., West Point, class
of '66, at Longbinh a year ago:*

When I came over here, of course, I was offered a company
'cause I was a West Point graduate. I needed the command
time for my career. But I just turned it down. I said I don't
want it. I'm not prepared to do those things a company commander has to do . . . I've been through the training. And I
think some of the techniques and the attitudes that come
through in the training could lead to what happened in
Sonmy . . . It's like cowboys and Indians—sort of glorified.
One of the first things at West Point was we started having
bayonet training. All these skinny plebes formed up, bracing
and scared to death. And the football team conducted bayonet
training. And they came out there and had these white
T-shirts with bayonets painted on them with blood drippin'
down off the bayonet . . . Over and over and over again, you
got that attitude: the spirit of the bayonet is to kill. If I've
said that one time I've said it a hundred times in my life. An
upperclassman comes up and says, "What's the spirit of the
bayonet?" "To kill, Sir." Over and over again. And when
you're that young, you're pretty impressionable. And after a
while, you begin to believe it. You think the thought, you talk
the talk. And then, you walk the walk . . .

If you graduate in the upper 5 per cent of your class, you
can choose your first assignment in graduate school. I went
to Harvard Business School, which gave me a chance to reflect
on a lot of things that had been grabbing me. I got a whole
different set of assumptions. All of a sudden not only was
killing not glorious, but it was vile. And that made sense to
me. It was just more logical. These new assumptions made
more sense to me than ones I had been subjected to . . .

I see my classmates now. Guys who really threw themselves
into it, and I guess I could be just like them. I was a good
cadet. I was a company commander, and the reason was because I was popular. We had peer ratings, and I was just a
good sh——. But seeing my classmates now—you know, I feel
sorry for them. I envied a guy, a classmate, for two years. He
was a good guy. A good man. He went to Ranger school and

he went to Airborne school and he went to Vietnam and he was just a John Wayne over here. He got a Silver Star, a bunch of Bronze Stars and Purple Hearts. And he came back to the States to learn Vietnamese and go back again. I met him then at Bragg. I asked him about the war, and he said, "You want me to tell you about the war." He said, "I wouldn't mind going back to Vietnam if they gave me a machine gun and just let me have South Vietnamese out in front of me." That's the way he felt about Vietnam. The gooks. That was the first thing he said. He didn't say anything about the V.C. or the N.V.A. . . . It's a good-old-boy concept, I guess. It is like a sporting game. There's a chance of getting killed, and maybe that just adds to it . . .

When we were seniors at the Academy, the generals or the heads of all the Army schools came in. They'd say, "I really envy you guys. When I graduated, there wasn't a war going on, but you guys have got a great chance. You're about to embark on the greatest adventures of your lives. And we're going to do everything we can to see that every one of you gets over there. We're going to do everything we can to see that as many young officers as possible get over there and get that GOOD TRAINING."

THE PRODUCT

Voices in a forward surgical hospital—patients, doctors, nurses and medics, all talking together:

Stand by. Stand by, we got six patients, three litter, three ambulatory. The medivac is five minutes out . . . Stand by for three U.S. litters, multiple frags . . . It's gonna be a long night . . . They said traumatic surgery was good training. Well, they can take this good training and shove it right up their—. . . All right, put him over there . . . Put him on this side. Hurry up, damn it . . . Aawwwwhhh, awwhh . . . Hey, now you're gonna be alright, you're gonna be fine . . . Get the I.V.'s going . . . Hey, hey, can you hear me, what's your name? . . . Ahh, Larry . . . Awwwhhhh, it hurts . . . O.K., Larry, now can you wiggle your toes? . . . I don't know . . . Try, try and do it . . . Ohhh, ohhh God . . . Listen, wiggle your toes . . . Talk to me, wiggle your toes . . . Can you feel this? . . . No, no, God no . . . Larry, take it easy, you're gonna be fine . . . Doc, it hurts, Doc . . . Is it just the right side? . . . He's got some in the shoulder, too, down here, one through the back, pretty deep . . .

Mike, how are you, boy? . . . I don't know . . . All right, I want his right knee X-rayed. Both knees X-rayed. Let's X-ray that hand . . . Mike, what's your unit? . . . Blackhorse Seven, 11th A.C.R. . . . Did you get a shot out there? . . . Did the medic give you a shot, some morphine, Mike? . . . Do you know, Mike? . . . No . . .

Oh, Jesus Christ . . . Shh, Larry, you're gonna be alright . . . O.K., let's go with him. Get him down to Op. . . . Mike, are you allergic to anything? Are you allergic to any medicine? . . . No . . . Hey, Mike, you still movin'? Good boy . . . You're not bad . . . OH NOOOO. OH NOOO, right through my God—arm. Oh God . . . Cover that arm . . . Oh Jesus Christ . . . Mike, does your side hurt? . . . Can you feel me touch your side? . . . Yes . . . Let me have a short form . . . You feel cold . . . I gotta talk to my parents. My parents . . . Mike, can you spell your last name for me? . . . One more thing, Mike, can you remember your Social Security number? . . .

The New York Times Magazine, October 18, 1970

AN ARMY OF RELUCTANT DRAFTEES:
OCTOBER 1970

You Can't Just Hand Out Orders

by John Saar

FOR 17 DAYS at a time through monsoon rains and tropical heat, the men of Alpha Company, First Battalion, 8th Cavalry, 1st Air Cavalry Airmobile hunt NVA soldiers and supply caches close to the Cambodian border. Stealthing through the bamboo-thicketed hills, they have the same air of acquired professionalism as drafted GIs of past wars. They look the same, even smell the same: a drab green centipede of men in soiled fatigues with the same boy-man faces under the bobbing steel helmet brims.

In reality, the 118 men of Alpha are quite different. They are a microcosm of an Army in evolution, an Army trying to adjust to the winding-down war in Vietnam. Old ideas of dress, behavior, discipline and rank no longer apply. Virtually no draftee wants to be fighting in Vietnam anyway, and in return for his reluctant participation he demands, and gets, personal freedoms that would have driven a MacArthur or a Patton apoplectic. It is an Army in which all questions—including "Why?"—are permissible. Alpha Company seethes with problems, but it has not fallen into chaos. Much of the reason is that a special kind of relationship, new in the Army, exists between the "grunts"—liberated, educated, aware young draftees—and their youthful commander, Captain Brian Utermahlen, West Point class of 1968.

Captain Utermahlen lets it be known in Alpha that he came close to quitting West Point eight separate times. He still rings the bells to which youth responds: honesty, independence, resistance to authority. These are shared attitudes which give him an instinctive rapport with his men, despite his Germanic name, bearing, blond good looks and his obvious devotion to the Army.

Utermahlen's continuing problem is to find an effective

153

compromise between his own professional dedication and his draftees' frank disinterest in anything that might cost an American life. Nothing could suit them better than President Nixon's recent proposal for a cease-fire in place, for Alpha Company has no desire to go on fighting. Grunt logic argues that since the U.S. has decided not to go out and win the war, there's no sense in being the last one to die. Followed to its conclusion and multiplied by every infantry company in Vietnam, this sort of logic—and the new permissiveness—has unquestionably affected the whole Army's combat efficiency. It is no longer the pliant and instantly responsive instrument of the past. Many officers frankly doubt that they could get their men to fight another costly battle such as the 1969 assault on Hamburger Hill that took 84 lives.

"The colonel wants to make contact with the enemy and so do I," says Utermahlen, "but the men flat don't. It's frustrating, but I understand how they feel." Including himself, there are only five career soldiers in the company—"lifers," the draftees call them.

Joe Curry, aged 25, is not one of them. He wears beads and a peace medallion and is one of Utermahlen's platoon sergeants. He was drafted out of an executive job and a prosperous home in Greenwich, Conn. "The object," Curry says, "is to spend your year without getting shot at, or if you do, to get the fewest people hurt. We don't try to frustrate the captain's attempts to kill gooks, but we don't put our hearts in it. If we did we could kill a lot more. Supposedly the mission comes first. I put the welfare of the men first." Pfc. Steve Wright says succinctly: "Two of them want to kill gooks, and the rest of us never want to see any again."

Curry's view finds a partial echo up the line. "We could kill a lot more enemy than we do," says Lt. Colonel Jack Galvin, CO of the battalion of which Alpha is a part, "but we'd have to pay for it, and I won't sacrifice anybody. I won't allow my companies to charge into a bunker area. I'd rather take some criticism." Utermahlen, for the most part, sees eye to eye with the colonel. "Charging up hills," he says happily, "has gone right out of fashion."

When Alpha takes to the jungle on its 17-day missions,

Utermahlen is scarcely recognizable as a traditional Army officer. He runs his company with a "hands-off" technique that develops a subtle community self-discipline. "That way I don't have to be too much of a bad guy," he says. "They police one another." The two black bars on his lapels are superfluous. If the job went up for vote, he would be elected—probably unanimously. "These guys are no longer blindly following puppets," he says. "They're thinkers and they want intelligent leadership. It's not a democracy, but they want to have a say. If I ran this company like an old-time tyrant, I'd have a bunch of rebels. There are people in the company with more experience than I have, and if they think I'm doing something grossly wrong, I'm ready to listen."

Utermahlen has not always had Alpha's support. He relieved a very popular commanding officer. When he took over, he was half prepared for a vengeance grenade attack from his own men—a "fragging." "They told me horror stories about how bad the company was," Utermahlen remembers, "and there were signs around saying the colonel wasn't welcome. I thought, my God, I'm going to be fragged."

He gingerly settled in, but found his position threatened from above by the colonel (Galvin's predecessor) and from below by the grunts. "The colonel told me every time we had contact, we would report at least two confirmed kills. I said, 'I can't do that, sir.' It went against everything I believed in. Only a change of command saved me."

The death of three of his men when they blundered into an ambush that had been set by other GIs was a crushing blow to Utermahlen, and it almost led to a no-confidence strike by the grunts. "I still think of it as my fault," he says, "and I fully expected to be relieved."

A member of the company remembers, "Everybody I knew was pretty sore at him. The platoon the guys were from discussed not going back to the field." Utermahlen survived the immediate crisis. Gradual vindication turned to acceptance and admiration when Utermahlen outfoxed an NVA mortar crew that Alpha was chasing. When night fell, the Communists were still up ahead somewhere, and Utermahlen guessed that they might have his position pinpointed. He ordered his angry company to mount up in the darkness and crabbed them off to a flank. The NVA shells screeched into the vacated spot and exploded harmlessly.

Since the death of a favorite radio operator, Utermahlen has often voiced his hate for the NVA. "Dammit," he will say, pounding his knee, "it's nice to kill gooks." Few if any of his draftee soldiers can work up such a depth of feeling. Says Platoon Sergeant Curry, "I don't understand what makes him dislike gooks so bad he wants to kill them. He once said he had a desire to strangle a gook, and that sickened me."

Pfc. Wayne Johnson, aged 21, from Kissimmee, Fla., has asked for a transfer out of infantry: "I don't like to kill. I hate the thing they believe in, but not the people themselves. Our business is killing, but my heart's not in it."

Perhaps half of Alpha's 21 blacks agree with the alienated view of Pfc. John Munn, a tall, somber soul brother. "I have my life to preserve," says Munn, "but I have nothing against that little man out there. They're fighting for what they believe in, and you can't knock that. I lie on my air mattress at night and I say what am I doing here? I can imagine a war back in the world that I'd fight and wouldn't mind dying in—to keep your people free." Utermahlen quashed a court-martial charge against Munn after witnessing his bravery under fire. He agrees that blacks generally do not get their share of promotions.

During a meal break two grunts were calmly discussing the theory and practice of fragging NCOs:

"If you keep hassling people, tension builds and it has to bring a release."

"A can of tear gas is like a first warning . . ."

Midway through a mission the spindle-legged figure of Pfc. Duane Sedler approaches Utermahlen. Sedler has already won a Bronze Star, but now he politely announces he must refuse an order to go on night ambush. Without rancor Utermahlen tells him he will probably be court-martialed. Sedler, a California college dropout with gentle deep-set eyes and sucked-in cheeks, is obviously distressed: "Those small ambushes with people who don't know what they're doing are dangerous. It's my life and I'd like to try to keep it."

Sedler's friends are sympathetic. "Nobody owns anyone around here," says Pfc. Eugene Dillon. "If he doesn't want to go, it's up to him." Sedler stays with the company, is eventually said to have "shaped up," and the court-martial is quietly forgotten. Disciplinary action in the field is disastrous for morale—and ineffective besides. Military justice has no answer to the grunt's ironic question: "What can they do to me: send me to Vietnam?"

One episode that got under Utermahlen's skin was an odd disagreement with Pfc. Bill Johnson, who twice turned down the Bronze Star. "He's obviously sincere about not wanting any of the Army's medals, and the more I think about it, I may be the one that's screwed up. I told him, 'Don't expect any favors.' Johnson kept his cool and said, 'That's fine with me.' He made me feel," says Utermahlen, his finger and thumb an inch apart, "about that big."

One of Alpha's veteran second-tour soldiers is Sgt. Chris Manis, owner of a tigerish smile, and a special favorite of Utermahlen for his skill and aggression. Manis saw heavy fighting in 1967–68: "We make a lot less contact now, and guys are a lot more afraid. I don't know why." For a time Manis led an elite recon squad popularly known as the "Crazy Eight," until draftee members balked at the discomfort and danger. The unit dissolved.

Marty Hyland is another man who has earned a special relationship with Utermahlen. Hyland is a draftee, a high school graduate, a wearer of beads, peace symbols and generally unbarbered hair. He is also quick, intelligent, quite irreverent and cool enough to pick up, in the field, the skills of an artillery spotter. "He's come through all the problems smelling like a rose," says Utermahlen. The forward observer job is generally held by a lieutenant. Hyland is still a Pfc. The two meet easily, as equals. Utermahlen pretends not to hear when Hyland talks wistfully of civilian days: "Man, did you ever get to hear Janis Joplin at the Fillmore? Outasight. Those were the days of wine and weed."

After 17 days in the bush the company waits to be taken out. The achievements are not very exciting: hospitalization of a Vietnamese couple who surrendered to get medicine for their child; capture of an ancient NVA helmet; claim of two

enemy dead, which Utermahlen himself doubts. Success depends on the conscientious execution of patrols; many of the
patrols are squad-size, and all nine of the squad leaders are
draftees. Sgt. Jim Sgambati is a Silver Star holder: "They screw
up the old man. They go out on a patrol and avoid the enemy." And yet compared with other units in Vietnam, Alpha
is an exceptionally good company.

As the fleet of Hueys dragonflies in to take them back to
Firebase Betty, various men evaluate their recent mission. SP4
Dave Clark, radio operator: "It was all right. Main thing was
we got through without getting anyone hurt. We didn't get
anything done, but I don't care." SP4 Earl Rucker, medic:
"I'm real pleased. No contact and no one got hurt." Captain
Brian Utermahlen, company commander: "I'm not pleased.
It's fine that we didn't get anybody hurt, but we didn't ac-
complish anything. Professionally I'm still hungry."

After the jungle, firebase defense is like garrison duty, and
the men relish it. Alpha splits into two roughly equal groups
for the evening parties: the "juicers" lay in supplies of cold
beer, while the "smokers" roll their joints and pack their pipe
bowls with strong Vietnamese marijuana. Estimates on marijuana users within Alpha vary from Utermahlen's low of 7%
up to the senior pothead in the company's enthusiastic 85%.
"We pass the pipe around," says a squad leader, "and we ask
what the hell are we doing here?"

Among the grunts there is a general taboo against smoking
grass in the field, although some do: "We had one guy who
was on grass all the time, and he won the Silver Star. He had
it down to an exact science. He'd feel the breeze blowing
away from the lifers, and he'd say, 'Hey, the wind's right. Let's
get nice.'"

Utermahlen is resolutely opposed to marijuana. "It has no
place in the field where you rely on quick thought and re-
flexes. I know the people who smoke it, but I can never catch
them." Marijuana smoking is so extensive that anything more
than token enforcement would antagonize a dangerously high
percentage of the company. No commander as perceptive as
Utermahlen cares to risk confrontations of that nature in Vietnam just now. So downwind from Firebase Betty at night, it
sometimes smells as though a large haystack were burning.

Utermahlen's views on military appearance are also relaxed. "What they wear or look like out in the field is very low on my list of priorities. It's one of the compromises I make. As long as a man does his job, I don't care if he wears peace beads or symbols or if he shaves."

The sudden appearance of Neanderthal man would hardly have caused a greater stir than the arrival, in the middle of the mission, of the company's new first sergeant—a 44-year-old, six-foot-two, big bellied, 257-pound giant with a bikinied girl tattooed over 12 inches of forearm. The draftees instantly read about his 25 years of Army service in his seamed face, and they avoided him like an alien being. Captain Utermahlen was uneasy, unwelcoming. It was a sad and unequal contest from the start: a high school dropout asked to administer and discipline a young company where 50% of the GIs have college time.

The first sergeant had served with the same battalion in 1965–66, until he was wounded, but the Army since then had altered beyond his comprehension. "Things have changed. Before, everyone was gung ho and wanted to mix it with Charlie. Now it seems everyone's trying to avoid him." He paused to mop the sweat from his brow with the tattooed girl. "I'm still out to kill gooks; that is what I get paid for. The only thing you can do is force men into contact, but with their attitude now, I don't think we can go on like this for long." Back at the firebase, he announced his dislike of the casual way soldiers responded to some of Utermahlen's less urgent orders. The litter of abandoned ammunition at the firebase also annoyed him. Loose talk about fragging incensed him. He finally reached an insupportable level of frustration. Twice when his patience gave out he drew and leveled his pistol to enforce orders. The second time, the young soldier he had been arguing with about garbage called his bluff and ran off to get his M16 rifle. As the two readied for an incredible high-noon showdown in the middle of the firebase, other soldiers intervened. There was no shooting but, at Captain Utermahlen's request, the first sergeant was reassigned to the States.

On occasion Utermahlen has declined to comply with Colonel Galvin's suggestions. Once, when requested to leave an ambush patrol in his rear, Utermahlen said his men were not well enough trained. The request was pressed, and Utermahlen's jaw dropped into a mulish set as he once again refused. It is this sort of blunt frankness that prompts the grunts to award Utermahlen the supreme accolade of being "a good dude."

In contrast to his men, Captain Utermahlen will probably never be happier or more fulfilled in the service of the United States Army than he is as Alpha's commander. Against the personal exultation of doing the job for which he has been educated, trained and equipped, other factors are relatively insignificant. In the jungle, where his resources, instincts and intelligence are tested to the utmost, he feels no crisis of conscience about the morality of the war. Yet Utermahlen is incapable of divorcing himself from his generation, and ahead lies the certainty of strained relations with the Army. Removed from the simplicity of the jungle, his thoughts move in new directions: "Is there such a thing as a moral war? I don't know. I think about it, and the doubt has been raised in my mind by the protest in the U.S.

"I believe 100% in the U.S. Army," he says, "but I'm not ready to compromise my principles: being honest with people and doing the best job possible for people under and over me. If that hurts my career, then it's just part of the ball game. The job I have comes before any moral judgment on the war, but if I thought it was wrong I definitely would not be fighting here. If I were given an unlawful order, I wouldn't be able to do it. I'd rather suffer the consequences. I've told my wife not to be surprised if I have to leave the Army."

Utermahlen and other officers of his caliber have the flexibility to accommodate the changing generation of soldiers. The question is whether the tradition-steeped hierarchy can in turn meet the demands that officers like Utermahlen are sure to have.

Life, October 23, 1970

from
Who Was *Lyndon Baines Johnson?*

by Doris Kearns

Guns, butter, and prophecy

LBJ was great in domestic affairs, elder statesman Averell Harriman once observed. "Harry Truman had programs but none got through. Kennedy had no technique. FDR talked simply during the crisis but didn't act enough later. Johnson went back past the New Frontier all the way to the New Deal. He loved FDR and it was fantastic what he did. If it hadn't been for . . . Vietnam he'd have been the greatest President ever. Even so he'll still be remembered as great."

If it hadn't been for Vietnam . . . How many times this phrase has been spoken in conversations assessing Johnson's place in history. For it is impossible to disconnect Johnson from that war, and undeniable that the fighting abroad halted progress toward the Great Society. Indeed, Johnson claimed he himself foresaw and weighed the devastating consequences of war on domestic reform, but felt he had no choice but to escalate the war.

"I knew from the start," Johnson told me in 1970, describing the early weeks of 1965, "that I was bound to be crucified either way I moved. If I left the woman I really loved—the Great Society—in order to get involved with that bitch of a war on the other side of the world, then I would lose everything at home. All my programs. All my hopes to feed the hungry and shelter the homeless. All my dreams to provide education and medical care to the browns and the blacks and the lame and the poor. But if I left that war and let the Communists take over South Vietnam, then I would be seen as a coward and my nation would be seen as an appeaser and we would both find it impossible to accomplish anything for anybody anywhere on the entire globe.

"Oh, I could see it coming all right; history provided too

many cases where the sound of the bugle put an immediate end to the hopes and dreams of the best reformers: the Spanish American War drowned the populist spirit, World War I ended Woodrow Wilson's New Freedom, World War II brought the New Deal to a close. Once the war began, then all those conservatives in the Congress would use it as a weapon against the Great Society. You see, they'd never wanted to help the poor or the Negroes in the first place. But they were having a hard time figuring out how to make their opposition sound noble in a time of great prosperity. But the war. Oh, they'd use it to say they were against my programs, not because they were against the poor—why they were as generous and as charitable as the best of Americans—but because the war had to come first. First we had to beat those godless Communists, and then we could worry about the homeless Americans. And the generals. Oh, they'd love the war too. It's hard to be a military hero without a war. Heroes need battles and bombs and bullets in order to be heroic. That's why I am suspicious of the military. They're always so narrow in their appraisal of everything. They see everything in military terms. Oh, I could see it coming. And I didn't like the smell of it. I didn't like anything about it, but I think the situation in South Vietnam bothered me most. They never seemed able to get themselves together down there. Always fighting with one another. Bad. Bad.

"Yet everything I knew about history told me that if I got out of Vietnam and let Ho Chi Minh run through the streets of Saigon, then I'd be doing exactly what Chamberlain did in World War II. I'd be giving a big fat reward to aggression. And I knew that if we let Communist aggression succeed in taking over South Vietnam, there would follow in this country an endless national debate—a mean and destructive debate—that would shatter my presidency, kill my Administration, and damage our democracy. I knew that Harry Truman and Dean Acheson had lost their effectiveness from the day that the Communists took over in China. I believed that the loss of China had played a large role in the rise of Joe McCarthy. And I knew that all these problems, taken together, were chickenshit compared with what might happen if we lost Vietnam.

"For this time there would be Robert Kennedy out in front leading the fight against me, telling everyone that I had betrayed John Kennedy's commitment to South Vietnam. That I had let a democracy fall into the hands of the Communists. That I was a coward. An unmanly man. A man without a spine. Oh, I could see it coming all right. Every night when I fell asleep I would see myself tied to the ground in the middle of a long, open space. In the distance, I could hear the voices of thousands of people. They were all shouting at me and running toward me: Coward! Traitor! Weakling! They kept coming closer. They began throwing stones. At exactly that moment I would generally wake up . . . terribly shaken. But there was more. You see, I was as sure as any man could be that once we showed how weak we were, Moscow and Peking would move in a flash to exploit our weakness. They might move independently or they might move together. But move they would—whether through nuclear blackmail, through subversion, with regular armed forces, or in some other manner. As nearly as anyone can be certain of anything, I knew they couldn't resist the opportunity to expand their control over the vacuum of power we would leave behind us. And so would begin World War III. So you see, I was bound to be crucified either way I moved."

Did Lyndon Johnson believe all this? Yes . . . some of the time. Was it true? Some of it; and the rest was not simply pure illusion. For even Johnson's most grotesque exaggerations were always constructed on some fragment of reality, so that they could never be totally disproven by factual evidence or unanswerable logic alone, only by rejecting his judgment for one more reasonable, more consonant with the known facts.

Johnson's description of the nature of the challenge in Vietnam was, of course, a product of his unique personal qualities. But it is important to remember that many others shared this view, although they would not have expressed it with such color or hyperbole. And they, like Johnson, derived their convictions from historical experience.

Johnson's most trusted advisers on Vietnam, Robert McNamara and McGeorge Bundy, contended that step-by-step escalation would allow continuous monitoring of the reactions of China and Russia; it would emphasize America's limited objective; it might press Hanoi to negotiate in order to prevent the terrible damage which large-scale bombing would inflict. Johnson chose gradual escalation. It was a predictable choice, based, as it was, on the type of approach he found most congenial: limited bombing represented the moderate path between the competing extremes of widespread destruction and total withdrawal. Of course sometimes, as every automobile driver knows, the middle of the road is the most dangerous place to be.

In Johnson's view, limited bombing was "seduction," not "rape," and seduction was controllable, even reversible. "I saw our bombs as my political resources for negotiating a peace. On the one hand, our planes and our bombs could be used as carrots for the South, strengthening the morale of the South Vietnamese and pushing them to clean up their corrupt house by demonstrating the depth of our commitment to the war. On the other hand, our bombs could be used as sticks against the North, pressuring North Vietnam to stop its aggression against the South. By keeping a lid on all the designated targets, I knew I could keep the control of the war in my own hands. If China reacted to our slow escalation by threatening to retaliate, we'd have plenty of time to ease off the bombing. But this control—so essential for preventing World War III—would be lost the moment we unleashed a total assault on the North, for that would be rape rather than seduction, and then there would be no turning back. The Chinese reaction would be instant and total."

Johnson's metaphor suggests an effort to force the contest in Vietnam into a pattern drawn from the politics he knew so well. As long as he could use force as a means of bargaining, he could moderate his anxiety about the difficulties and unknowable dangers of this strange war in an unfamiliar land.

In the White House Situation Room—the illusion of control

JOHNSON needed to believe that the Vietnamese experience could be assimilated into his own framework; he needed to interpret everything on his own terms. This master practitioner of bargaining and negotiation was also a man who perceived the fragility of that process. He preached rationality and compromise, but continually feared and imagined the emergence of unreasoning passions and unyielding ideologies. His conduct and words expressed a will to believe, a fear of his own doubts. Johnson was always afraid that he himself might give way to irrational emotions; control came to appear a requirement of survival of the self. By treating the struggle in Vietnam as an exercise in bargaining, he sought to deny that it might exist somewhere beyond the healthy bounds of reasonable negotiations. Thus, the purpose of the bombs was not to hurt or destroy; that was a by-product. They were all means of bargaining without words. Since Johnson, if not an expert on warfare, was a master bargainer, he would retain final control over when and where to bomb so that his knowledge of detail could be both used and increased. The same attention to the minutiae of power that had characterized his relations with the Congress would now characterize his conduct of the war.

Long hours of discussion preceded the choice of each bombing target. Tracing his fingers across the map of Vietnam, the President would point to various potential targets —railroad bridges, army barracks, oil storage depots, airfields, armored truck convoys, factories—demanding to know the costs and benefits of attacking each one. "How many tons of bombs will it take to destroy this?" he would ask, while waving a photograph of a railroad bridge twenty miles from Da Nang. "How important is that [a petroleum storage depot] to the North Vietnamese? If we choose these army barracks fifteen miles from Haiphong, how can we be certain of the accuracy of our aim?" So it went: one by one. In developing his list of permissible targets, Johnson operated on the fundamental premise that he could only bomb up to a certain point. To move beyond that point—for example, to mine Haiphong Harbor or bomb the Red River dikes—might risk war with Russia or China. Suspicious that the North Vietnamese had entered into secret treaties with the Communist superpowers, Johnson lived in constant fear of triggering some imaginary provision of some imaginary treaty.

This belief was linked to, became part of, his continued magnification of the stakes. Vietnam was no longer just a "test case for wars of national liberation," a "lesson for aggressors," a necessity to "prevent the fall of Southeast Asia," or part of the "containment of China." America fought in Vietnam to prevent the otherwise inevitable onset of World War III. It was an aspect of Johnson's own dimension, the size of his personal needs and his huge ambitions to satisfy the needs of all others, that only the largest cause of all—to forestall world-wide destruction—could justify actions which were now so threatening to the public's admiration, his life as a public man, and his capacity to lead others, in their own interest, to accept his grandly benevolent intention.

"I never knew," Johnson later said, "as I sat there in the afternoon, approving targets one, two, and three, whether one of those three might just be the one to set off the provisions of those secret treaties. In the dark at night, I would lie awake picturing my boys flying around North Vietnam, asking myself an endless series of questions. What if one of those targets you picked today triggers off Russia or China? What happens then? Or suppose one of my boys misses his mark when he's flying around Haiphong? Suppose one of his bombs falls on one of those Russian ships in the harbor? What happens then? Or suppose the fog is too thick or the clouds are too high or the target too small and the bomb drops by mistake within the thirty-mile radius of Hanoi?" The more questions he asked, the more agitated he became. "I would then begin to picture myself lying on the battlefield in Da Nang. I could see an American plane circling above me in the sky. I felt safe. Then I heard a long, loud shot. The plane began to fall faster, faster, faster. I saw it hit the ground, and as soon as it burst into flames, I couldn't stand it anymore. I knew that one of my boys must have been killed that night. I jumped out of bed, put on my robe, took my flashlight, and went into the Situation Room."

After hours of being alone, he felt so weary that he sought the world of action. At 3 A.M. the Situation Room was the perfect escape. There, at any time of day or night, he could find what he needed: people, light, and talk. Around the table in the middle of the room sat five or six men on loan from the Pentagon and the CIA, responsible for receiving messages from Saigon and Da Nang. As the pilots completed their bombing missions, they would report the results over their radios to American headquarters at Saigon: mission accomplished, bridge destroyed. The message would then be transmitted to the White House in the form of a summary telegram. With these Telex reports before them, the Situation Room staff would make the appropriate markings on a giant map, indicating which strikes had destroyed what targets.

As it turned out, the classified wires and reports were endowing illusion with the appearance of precision. Johnson had reason to worry about whether the bombs were actually hitting their targets, but it was not the reason he thought. The real concern was not that a mistaken strike might provoke China or Russia, but that the bombers, flying over hundreds of hamlets and hillocks and villages, could not even begin to separate enemies and innocents, soldiers and civilians.

As the military increased its involvement and responsibility, errors in reporting became standard operating procedure. Exaggerated descriptions of American success were matched by diluted reports of North Vietnam's strength. The estimates of progress improved with each step of the journey from Army headquarters in Vietnam to the Situation Room in the White House. Soon it became almost impossible for anyone in Washington to know what was really going on in Vietnam. But Lyndon Johnson was not about to question a process of reporting that provided him with what he wanted to hear. If the enemy body count seemed inordinately high, that was to be expected when poorly trained men without photo equipment or spotting devices were engaged in battle with the most technologically accomplished civilization in the history of the world. How could America possibly fail to force the North Vietnamese into bargaining? Lyndon Johnson wanted one thing from his nightly visit—the feeling that he was still in control—and that was the only thing that the maps and the men and the messages were able to provide.

A full-scale public commitment to Vietnam would have required Johnson to accept the fact that he could not secure all of the goals he desired. It would have required him to admit that even this leader must make choices and accept limits. It would have meant defining priorities and settling the conflicts

among them. But here, as always, Johnson attempted to compromise conflict instead of choosing sides, manipulating and
orchestrating the political process in order to shape a formula
that would satisfy every competing claim.

How could Johnson have imagined that he could conduct
a major war in virtual secrecy while simultaneously summon-
ing the American people toward a Great Society? In early positions of leadership Johnson found that he could move in
contradictory directions, so long as he compartmentalized his
leadership, and kept his dealings with one group a secret from
the next. Even in the search for votes, the process of campaigning permits, indeed requires, stressing some facts and
minimizing others. The politician's talent, as Johnson interpreted it, was the ability to embrace and enter into the habits
and ways of life of many different men. This required control
over information. Johnson could not allow his immediate
audience access to contradictory information about the particular "self" he was playing to them, permit a person who
had seen him in the "right" role happen upon him in the
"wrong" role. And when his leadership proved effective,
Johnson had been praised by the very Senate on which he had
practiced his deceptions. The country, then, would also reward the President for "pulling off," as he described it, "both
the war in Vietnam and the Great Society at home," even if
he hadn't told them everything at the time.

The public, Johnson reasoned, would only hurt itself by
knowing too much. Democracy demanded good results for
the people, not big debates. But the most important thing
about a democratic regime is what questions it refers to the
public for decision or guidance, how it refers them to the
public, how the alternatives are defined, and how it respects
the limitations of the public. Above all, the people are powerless if the political enterprise is able to take them to war
without their consent. The business of war involves the se-
verest sacrifices falling on the ordinary men and women in the
country. Here more than anywhere else, the people must have
an opportunity to make a choice. For in the end, no statesman
can pursue a policy of war unless he knows for what goals,
and for how long, his people are prepared to fight.

Lyndon Johnson had wanted to surpass Franklin Roosevelt;

and Roosevelt, after all, had not only won the reforms John-son envied, he had waged a war. But there was a critical difference: Roosevelt did not attempt the New Deal and World War II at the same time. Only Johnson among the Presidents sought to be simultaneously first in peace and first in war; and even Johnson was bound to fail.

"I figured when my legislative program passed the Con-gress," Johnson said in 1971, "that the Great Society had a real chance to grow into a beautiful woman. And I figured her growth and development would be as natural and inevi-table as any small child's. In the first year, as we got the laws on the books, she'd begin to crawl. Then in the second year, as we got more laws on the books, she'd begin to walk, and the year after that, she'd be off and running, all the time growing bigger and healthier and fatter. And when she grew up, I figured she'd be so big and beautiful that the American people couldn't help but fall in love with her, and once they did, they'd want to keep her around forever, making her a permanent part of American life, more permanent even than the New Deal.

"But now Nixon has come along and everything I've worked for is ruined. There's a story in the paper every day about him slashing another one of my Great Society pro-grams. I can just see him waking up in the morning, making that victory sign of his and deciding which program to kill. It's a terrible thing for me to sit by and watch someone else starve my Great Society to death. She's getting thinner and thinner and uglier and uglier all the time; now her bones are beginning to stick out and her wrinkles are beginning to show. Soon she'll be so ugly that the American people will refuse to look at her; they'll stick her in a closet to hide her away and there she'll die. And when she dies, I too will die."

The professors and the protesters

IN THE BEGINNING, Johnson had feared his country would become obsessed with failure if Vietnam were lost. As the war went on, the obsession he feared for his country became his own. Indeed, as the Great Society disintegrated, the lower the President's popularity fell, the more Johnson *had* to see his decision to escalate as the only decision he could have made. He had committed everything he had to Vietnam. Regardless of all evidence, he simply had to be right. To think otherwise, to entertain even the slightest doubt, was to open himself to the pain of reliving old decisions, options, and possibilities long since discarded. "No, no, no," Johnson shouted at me one afternoon, as I tried to discuss earlier opportunities for peace. "I will *not* let you take me backwards in time on Vietnam. Fifty thousand American boys are dead. Nothing we say can change that fact. Your idea that I could have chosen otherwise rests upon complete ignorance. For if I had chosen otherwise, I would have been responsible for starting World War III."

In the heady days of the Great Society and at the start of the escalation, Johnson was confident that he could deal rationally and successfully with the small, scattered strands of criticism on the war. At that time, he was able to maintain a bantering, almost friendly tone—so long as those critics remained few in number and confined their critiques to private conversations.

"Well, Bill [Fulbright]," one conversation began in 1965, "what have you been doing today to damage the Republic? You say you've got a bad stomach. Well, that's because you've been so anti-Johnson lately. I told you that it's bad for you to take after me. Now you tell your wife I love her and I am sorry you're so damned cranky and grouchy all the time." But as the opposition proliferated and surfaced in the public forums, and as support for the Administration's policies plummeted in the polls, Johnson no longer debated or discussed the substance of the critics' charges. Increasingly, he endeavored to dismiss the content by discrediting the source.

Strangely, however, he was probably least harsh toward the protesting young, although he heard each taunt and chant, and they wounded him deeply. But they were not, he believed, motivated by self-interest or personal animosity; their dissent sprang from the ignorance of their youth. "Why should I listen to all those student peaceniks marching up and down the streets? They were barely in their cradles in the dark days of World War II; they never experienced the ravages of Adolf Hitler; they were only in nursery school during the fall of

China; they were sitting in grammar school during the Korean War; they wouldn't know a Communist if they tripped over one. They simply don't understand the world the way I do." And how else could he deal with the young? Certainly not as enemies. They were, after all, the future for which he had hoped to build, and for which, he believed, he was now fighting. If they marched against him because of what they did not know, then there was a chance that someday they would understand.

But Johnson could be unsparing of the professors who had failed to guide their students. All his life he had maintained a distinction between the doers and the thinkers, as if membership in one category walled off the other. Now, his mounting stress served to reinforce that wall. The thinkers were the critics, a negative chorus jealously intent upon the destruction of all he had built. "The professors believe you can get peace by being soft and acting nice. But everything I know about history proves this absolutely wrong. It was our lack of strength and failure to show stamina, our hesitancy, vacillation, and love of peace being paraded so much, that caused all our problems before World War I, World War II, and Korea. And now we're really up for grabs. We're the richest nation in the world. And the minute we look soft, the would-be aggressors will go wild. We'll lose all of Asia and then Europe, and we'll be an island all by ourselves. And when all that comes to pass I'd sure hate to have to depend on the Galbraiths and that Harvard crowd to protect my property or lead me to the Burnet Cave."

Suspicion of motive became his chief instrument in discrediting critics on the Hill. "Fulbright's problem," Johnson told himself, "is that he's never found any President who would appoint him secretary of state. He is frustrated up there on the Hill. And he takes out his frustration by making all those noises about Vietnam. He wants the nation to stand up and take notice of Bill Fulbright, and he knows the best way to get that attention is to put himself in the role of critic. He would have taken that role whichever way I moved on Vietnam. And then beside Fulbright there were all those liberals on the Hill squawking at me about Vietnam. Why? Because I never went to Harvard. That's why. Because I wasn't John F.

Kennedy. Because I wasn't friends with all their friends. Because I was keeping the throne from Bobby Kennedy. Because
the Great Society was accomplishing more than the New
Frontier. You see they had to find some issue on which to
turn against me, and they found it in Vietnam. Even though
they were the very people who developed the concept of limited war in the first place.

"And then," Johnson continued, "there were the columnists. They turned against me on Vietnam because it was in
their self-interest to do so, because they knew that no one
receives a Pulitzer Prize these days by simply supporting the
President and the Administration. You win by digging up contrary information, by making a big splash. Truth no longer
counts so long as a big sensation can be produced. Every story
is always slanted to win the favor of someone who sits higher
up. The Washington press are like a wolf pack when it comes
to attacking public officials, but they're like a bunch of sheep
in their own profession, and they will always follow the bell-
wether sheep, the leaders of their profession, Lippman and
Reston. As long as those two stayed with me, I was okay. But
once they left me in pursuit of their fancy prizes, everyone
else left me as well. But the more they screamed and
squawked, the more determined I was to stick it out."

Conspiracy theorist

AS UNPLEASANT as it was for him to feel "done in" by his
opponents, he was not accepting blame. Indeed, his ensuing
feeling of martyrdom brought a temporary rise in self-esteem.
That his polls were down meant only that the conspirators
had been successful in creating a false image. It was one thing
to look for unworthy motives, however unfairly or inaccurately described. But to believe oneself the target of a giant
conspiracy was such a leap into unreason that it could only
mean some disintegration of Johnson's thought, that the bar-
riers separating reason from irrational thought and delusion
were crumbling.

"No matter what anyone said," Johnson once argued, "I
knew that the people out there loved me a great deal. All that
talk about my lack of charisma was a lot of crap. There is no

such thing as charisma. It's just the creation of the press and the pollsters. Deep down I knew—I simply knew—that the American people loved me. After all that I'd done for them and given to them, how could they help but love me? And I knew that it was only a very small percentage that had given up, who had lost faith. We had more than three million young people serving in uniform. I heard from 100 of them every day. They didn't get the attention the TV people gave the exhibitionists. They didn't have anyone to make signs for them and parade around for them. They were just there, from daylight to dark, fighting for freedom and willing to die for it.

"The problem is that I was sabotaged. Look what happened whenever I went to make a speech about the war. The week before my speech, the St. Louis *Post-Dispatch* or the Boston *Globe* or CBS News would get on me over and over, talking about what a terrible speaker I was and about how awful the bombing was, and pretty soon the people began to wonder, they began to think that I really must be uninspiring if the papers and the TV said so. They began to think that I might be wrong about the war. And gradually they stopped coming to my speeches. And then the press gleefully reported a small crowd and an uninspiring speech. Why it's just as if you were making a tour of the nation and I was an advance man going into every town ahead of you, telling people you were a prostitute, a mean woman, out to cheat them of their hard-earned money. Well, at first the people might still come to see you, dismissing all that talk as nasty rumors. But after a while, some of it would have to sink in. And then more and more. And then there would be absolutely nothing you could do to stop the tide."

Johnson's critics did in fact have a reinforcing effect upon each other. The eastern media did exaggerate the sentiments of the people. There were those in the Kennedy crowd out to get Johnson. But in the past Johnson had displayed a fine sense of discrimination about his political opponents, recognizing that his enemies today might be his allies tomorrow. Now he became unrestrained and reckless, creating a fantasy world of heroes and villains. Members of the White House staff who had listened to the President's violent name-calling were frightened by what seemed to them signs of paranoia. Suddenly, in the middle of a conversation, the President's voice would become intense and low-keyed. He would laugh inappropriately and his thoughts would assume a random, almost incoherent quality as he began to spin a vast web of accusations.

"Two or three intellectuals started it all, you know. They produced all the doubt, they and the columnists in the Washington *Post*, the New York *Times*, *Newsweek*, and *Life*. And it spread and it spread until it appeared as if the people were against the war. Then Bobby began taking it up as his cause, and with Martin Luther King on his payroll he went around stirring up the Negroes and telling them that if they came out into the streets they'd get more. Then the Communists stepped in. They control the three networks, you know, and the forty major outlets of communication. It's all in the FBI reports. They prove everything. Not just about the reporters but about the professors too.

"The Communists' desire to dominate the world is just like the lawyer's desire to be the ultimate judge on the Supreme Court or the politician's desire to be President. You see the Communists want to rule the world, and if we don't stand up to them, they will do it. And we'll be slaves. Now I'm not one of those folks seeing Communists under every bed. But I do know about the principles of power, and when one side is weak, the other steps in. And that's just what the Communists did when they realized the soft spots in the American liberal community.

"You see, the way it worked, the opponents of the war went on jags which pretty much originated in the Communist world and eventually found their way to the American critics. One jag was that we were killing civilians. The next was that we needed a bombing pause. The first bombing pause came after a Communist diplomat talked to some influential Americans. Bobby Kennedy sat with me and told me that he knew that if we ordered a pause something would happen. So I ordered a pause. We delivered a letter to North Vietnam and they threw it back the next day. Later, Senator Morse came in and told me the Soviet ambassador said that such and such would happen if we stopped the bombing. They were telling the same thing to Fulbright, Clark, Mansfield, Church, and others. Then McGeorge Bundy had lunch with Dobrynin, and suddenly he became an ardent advocate for peace. Fortas was against the pause. So was Rusk, and Clifford. I also thought it was wrong, that it would make us look like a weak sister. But I hated to see history record that I stood in the way of peace. So again I ordered a pause and again nothing happened. Isn't it funny that I always received a piece of advice from my top advisers right after each of them had been in contact with someone in the Communist world? And isn't it funny that you could always find Dobrynin's car in front of Reston's house the night before Reston delivered a blast on Vietnam?"

Sometimes it seemed as if Johnson himself did not believe what he was saying, as if all the surmises were a bizarre recreation, a way to relax. But at other times, his voice carried so much conviction that his words produced an almost hypnotic effect. Conversations with Cabinet members would begin with the question, Why aren't you out there fighting against my enemies? Don't you realize that if they destroy me, they'll destroy you as well? Discussions on legislation would be interrupted by diatribes against "the critics." Private luncheons and dinners would be dominated by complaints about "the traitors."

In 1967, Secretary of Defense Robert McNamara began to move away from the President's policy of escalation. As McNamara now saw the situation in Vietnam, the war was going badly and should be capped. But as McNamara's pessimism grew, his access to the President diminished. Johnson did not want to hear other people's doubts. He needed loyalty and support. So, in November 1967, the President suddenly announced that McNamara was leaving the DOD to accept the directorship of the World Bank. Here again Johnson conjured an explanation which precluded the necessity for dealing directly with the content of McNamara's doubts.

"McNamara's problem," Johnson later said, "was that he began to feel a division in his loyalties. He had always loved and admired the Kennedys; he was more their cup of tea, but he also admired and respected the presidency. Then, when he came to work for me, I believe he developed a deep affection for me as well, not so deep as the one he held for the Kennedys, but deep enough, combined with his feelings about the office itself, to keep him completely loyal for three long years. Then he got surrounded by [Assistant and Deputy Assistant Secretaries of Defense] Paul Warnke, Adam Yarmolinsky, and Alain Enthoven; they excited him with their brilliance, all the same cup of tea, all came to the same conclusion after old man Galbraith. Then the Kennedys began pushing him harder and harder. Every day Bobby would call up McNamara, telling him that the war was terrible and immoral and that he had to leave. Two months before he left he felt he was a murderer, and didn't know how to extricate himself. I never felt like a murderer; that's the difference. Someone had to call Hitler and someone had to call Ho. We can't let the Kennedys be peacemakers and us warmakers simply because they came from the Charles River.

"After a while, the pressure got so great that Bob couldn't sleep at night. I was afraid he might have a nervous breakdown. I loved him and I didn't want to let him go, but he was just short of cracking and I felt it'd be a damn unfair thing to force him to stay. When he told me in November that the only job he really wanted then was the World Bank, I told him any job he wanted in the Administration he could have. Now the man who deserved that bank job all along was Henry Fowler; he'd been waiting for it all the way through. When I told him McNamara was going to get it, tears came to his eyes. But at that point, I had no choice."

LBJ's reasons why

THE DEPTH of Johnson's feelings about Vietnam, and the distance between his view and that of those who opposed the war, were brought home to me in a long conversation with him during the summer of 1970. In the course of the conversation, I expressed a feeling that, too often, the debate about Vietnam was confined to tactical questions, focusing on the means of war—the effectiveness of bombing, the viability of strategic enclaves, the success or failure of pacification—at the expense of understanding the rightness or wrongness of the ends. After I finished, Johnson talked uninterruptedly for nearly three hours.

"How in the world can you and your friends say that South Vietnam is not a separate country with a traditionally recognized boundary? That boundary was created and internationally recognized by the Geneva Accords. Fifty nations recognized it; the Communist states recognized Hanoi's regime as a sovereign entity. The final decision specified two zones. That's that. Oh, sure, there were some Koreans in both North and South Korea who believed their country was one country; yet was there any doubt that North Korean aggression took place? And does the belief of some within a country determine the legality of the boundaries? . . . It's just perverted history to claim that it's civil war, just pure bad history manufactured by the Harvards and the Galbraiths. No understanding of the thirty years before. There was no insurrection before the Communists decided to take part. Ho was a Communist all his adult life. He was trained in Moscow Communist headquarters. He was the founding father of the Communist party in Indochina. After the Geneva Accords thousands of guerrillas moved from North to South, waiting word from Ho. All under Communist discipline, directly under Ho's command. The myth these professors have that it's a nice family fight, papa and mamma and children, is pure crap. Why, the decision to renew the fight was made in Hanoi in 1959. The NLF was organized by the central committee of the Communist party in Hanoi, and announced from Hanoi. Sure, there's some free movement, but look at who controls it, who determines its direction. It is Hanoi, loud and clear.

"As for the argument that it was our aggression, not the North's aggression, against the people's will, well, that's just nonsense and naïveté. What better proof do you want of 'the people's' will than the elections in September, 1967? What better proof of the existence of a large fraction of dedicated anti-Communists in the South than their struggle in this war? And when you and your friends speak of the peasants physically suffering at the hands of the South Vietnamese government, just compare that with the suffering at the hands of the Vietcong—where every village chief, teacher, and doctor is killed to destroy the infrastructure.

"And when you all speak of a consensus among well-informed writers that the pro-Vietcong element is larger, just recognize the stake that Lacouture, a Frenchman, has in seeing it that way, and the academics and journalists make money and sell papers not by agreeing with government policy but by disagreeing with it. And you people read their history. While we read the security and intelligence reports of the CIA, the State Department, the DOD—men whose interest it is to find out what's really happening over there. You see, we just read different histories, that's all.

"You see, I deeply believe we *are* quarantining aggressors over there, just like the smallpox. Just like FDR and Hitler, just like Wilson and the Kaiser. You've simply got to see this thing in historical perspective. What I learned as a boy in my teens and in college about World War I was that it was our lack of strength and failure to show stamina that got us into that war. I was taught that the Kaiser never would have made his moves if he hadn't been able to count Uncle Sam out because he believed we'd never come in. Then I was taught in Congress and in committees on defense preparedness and by FDR that we in Congress were constantly telegraphing the wrong messages to Hitler and the Japanese—that the Wheelers, the Lindberghs, the LaFollettes, and the America Firsters were letting Hitler know he could move without worrying about Uncle Sam.

"So I knew that if the aggression succeeded in South Vietnam, then the aggressors would simply keep on going until all of Southeast Asia fell into their hands, slowly or quickly, but inevitably at least down to Singapore, and almost certainly to Djakarta.

"Oh, sure, I recognize your argument about the diversity of communism and your claim that nationalism is strong as well as communism, but the question is, which is stronger? And I believe that the Communists—in terms of resources, skill, leadership, and training—have the upper hand in every battle against nationalist uprisings. I wish it were otherwise. It would certainly make the world a safer place. But look at Czechoslovakia. Now there you had a deep and strong, solid nationalist faith, but in the crunch of Soviet tanks how did that faith hold up? 'Spirit' cannot stand up to superior force. You've got to understand the facts of power.

"And then you all speak of a united Vietnam as the best bulwark against Communist aggression, and you talk approvingly of social revolution as a base for popular government. Well, you tell me when was the last major social revolution that came out successfully while a country was carved up in a war? Well, that's something for your sociologists. And don't give me the Bolshevik Revolution, that's a lot different. And to talk about Vietnam as a bulwark against Communist China—that's sheer Fulbright nonsense. Only slightly less nonsense than Dulles' claim that Laos was a bulwark of democracy. Vietnam ain't a bulwark of anything right now. It's in the midst of a struggle against communism. And if you think it is, it's just because you don't understand the country. You don't understand the way in which the Communists control the resources over there. You simply see a different country than I do. First, we've got to get the Communists out, and *then* begin the process of building South Vietnam as a stronghold.

"But the most unfair part of all is your constant screeching about the bombing, like I wanted to bomb civilians. There is nothing I wanted less, which is why I made sure that I had more control over the generals than any other civilian President in history. I insisted on that. I knew what the generals wanted. To saturate the whole area. To bomb the hell out of the North. Look at what's happening under Nixon. He's already dropped more bombs than I did in all my years. I spent ten hours a day worrying about all this, picking the targets one by one, making sure we didn't go over the limits.

"As for your criticism of our pacification, you are right that war is devastating. But we were doing everything we could to limit that. We rebuilt as we went along. That was our Mekong River Delta project. Hospitals, schools, technology. We wanted to modernize Vietnam society. You talk of land enclosure as a good thing. Well, I see it as an enclosure of spirit and mind. The promise of America has always been freedom from narrow boundaries. The frontier. The future. And technology is essential for that freedom and that future. Sure, the

Vietnamese will never be the same again, but they've had a whole world opened to them. More choices. Freedom from superstition. The freedom of alternative lives. You can't talk about the quality of life until food and basic minimums are provided. We *will* get those things there. As soon as this conflict is peaceably settled. America will do it. You'll see. We've got in our history a tradition of benevolence. It will show up here too. I am as certain of that as I am of anything in my life."

Atlantic Monthly, July 1976

A Frantic Night on the
Edge of Laos

by John Saar

LATE AFTERNOON, 6 February 1971. I first hear the distant whistle of a plane as Larry Burrows and I stand chatting at the roadside headquarters of Task Force 11 just three kilometers from the Laos border. Tomorrow, or maybe the day after, this amalgam of elite South Vietnamese army units will pull its armored track carriers back on to dusty Route 9 and head into Laos. We plan to ride with them.

The U.S. advisers are relaxed and pleasant and Task Force 11's commander, Lt. Colonel Bui The Dung, returns our greeting with a warm smile. Everyone knows that across the border in Laos there will be hard battles, but today the mood is light-hearted, almost festive. Chattering and joking, the paratroops are settling in, gouging out slit trenches, stringing tents. Rice savored with onions and vegetables bubbles over dozens of fires, scalding tea in blue-and-white china bowls passes delicately from one hand to the next.

Like a horn on New York's Fifth Avenue, the rising whine of a jet fighter is simply a background noise in Vietnam. I hear it, think "jet on a strike run" and ignore it. Why not? Every so often someone will say, "Hey, look at that jet roll out," and you watch—detached, safe, vaguely sympathetic to the recipients of the ton of high explosive or tanks of napalm. To the allied armies and the press who travel with them, our air power is as innocuous and reliable as home electricity. Only this time the jet was rolling in on us.

In the fading light the diving plane is hardly visible. But two men, a Vietnamese officer and his American adviser, see it, and the three bombs tumbling toward them. They go headlong into a trench. Alabama-born Staff Sergeant Bob Logan later spoke of it as "high diving without a pool."

Burrows is talking about film shipments. Two bangs snatch

my attention—close, but safe. Then explosions are on us, in us, among us. The world is one terrible *kkerrussh* of sound and blast—and the brain lurches with the impact. For a frozen microsecond I read incredulity and horror on the faces around me, then we are all down and scrabbling for cover.

A shallow cooking trench. Two big fires, two simmering pots inches away. Christ, I'm going to roast to death. But my head is saying, don't move, mortars, mortars, another salvo any moment. I carry that helmet everywhere, where is it? I look around. One man is moving—fast, decisive—toward the impact area: Larry Burrows. In a thought vacuum I follow. The sunset is still pale gold on the mountaintops. Now there is a stronger, wickeder yellow: flames are licking from the turret of a burning track. We run on and Burrows goes prone to frame the scene. We are the first ones here, and the brain can't accept the visual evidence as real. People bleeding, tattered, broken people strewn everywhere by the steel cyclone. Nightmarishly outlined in the half light, dust-gray apparitions already showing ominously dark, spreading blotches rise to an elbow and extend a pleading arm. From all sides comes the elemental moan of men beseeching help.

Pandemonium. Two officers are already on the radio, calling for Medevac helicopters, but most are momentarily shocked into inactivity. And pandemonium in my head. Again it is Burrows who gives me the lead. "Come and help me bring that chap in," he says. No stretchers. Awkwardly, we pick him up by legs and arms. God, this is not only macabre, it's difficult and tiring as well. We stumble across the broken ground. My hands are slick with the man's blood and I feel its seeping wetness in my clothes. He is hard hit to the chest and stomach, now I know he must be hit in the head as well. From the depths of him comes a groan of unspeakable pain. It wrings from Burrows an answering groan of commiseration.

We bring in two more badly wounded and lay them at the edge of a bomb crater where a dressing station is hubbubbing into action. Excited voices gabbling into radios, figures blundering into one another. A wide-eyed medic arrives running barefoot with a "panic bag" in hand. A roar of exploding ammunition from a burning armored personnel carrier adds to the confusion.

Now the wounded are coming in thick and fast, very few walking. The talk is not of NVA rockets or mortars but of something called CBU dropped accidentally by a friendly plane. These cluster bomb units leave the plane as a single bomb, then explode apart into numbers of oval grenades, which in turn explode individually to create a blizzard of steel. If one plane on one run can inflict such savage hurt, I think, what unimaginable suffering has been inflicted by thousands of planes on thousands of runs?

For perhaps 10 minutes Task Force 11 has been overwhelmed by shock. Now paralysis passes and the pressure of emergency reveals personality. Most assertive is Major Todd, Georgian, senior adviser to the paratroops, who bellows orders in a mixture of pidgin English and bastard French which reduces everything to stark essentials. When the first helicopter is coming in, we hear him yell, "Only the man. No stretchers. 'Cause so beaucoup many."

Major Bill Aiken, senior adviser to the cavalry squadron, is on his second tour, but he has seen nothing like this. He sits, head sunk, shoulders hunched, and when one of his team tells him that "So-and-so is badly shaken up," Aiken replies, "He ain't the only one." But later, when there is work to do, he is on hand.

In his command center, neat in a long great-coat, Colonel Dung coordinates the recovery of the wounded and alerts his outer defenses. He is outwardly calm, but his emotions are suppressed, not absent, and in the morning he allows himself a single telling comment: "It is sad to lose men in this way."

One of two wounded officers is paratrooper Major Nguyen Son Ha. A chirpy man of exquisite manners and delightfully deplorable English, he declines to be Medevaced until 12 hours later. By that time his broken arm is grossly swollen and his face is blanched with pain.

After 30 minutes the wounded are still coming in. Among the last is a man with a broken leg who staggers in unaided. How many are there? Thirty, forty, Christ, at least fifty. Two medics were killed outright and even at full strength there is no way the aid teams could cope with these numbers. As I watch, it becomes plain that the two doctors have been forced to leave some of the worst casualties untended in order to

save those with a better chance. Two of the men Burrows and
I brought in are dying where we left them. Some of the band-
aging has been too hasty. One man squelches in a pool of his
own blood as he rocks to and fro with pain. Three medics
come over and replace the blood-soaked field dressings. The
man is still contorted with pain and rams his head into the
side of a corpse alongside.

The moon glides from behind clouds and lights the small
slope. It is littered with wounded, blood stains showing starkly
against the gleaming white bandages. The medics and the
other unwounded figures who scurry about are impossible to
distinguish as American or Vietnamese. One man, whose left
leg is nothing but bone and shredded flesh, raises his head to
see while the medics are scissoring away the cloth. He sees
and falls back soundlessly. The thought of what he sees chills
me inside. Another man lying on the ground in the crucifix
position moves inch by inch to the man next to him. He
gropes for the man's hand and clasps it tight. The wounded
are talking to one another. I can't imagine, nor do I want to
know, what they say.

The Vietnamese follow the Chinese philosophy: pain must
be borne with minimum display, and to a Westerner the sto-
icism is awesome. Men in terrible fear and pain are murmuring
for the aid of their Creator and whimpering gently. I yearn
for someone to scream so that I too may cry. No one does.
But there is no unobtrusive exit for men who are 20 years old
and want to live. They fight for breath until you long for them
to die. Chest heaving with the effort, one man emits a rasping,
almost metallic rattle as he sucks air through a blood-filled
throat. At last he dies, chest expanded, as though that last
effort stopped his heart. The man whose blood stained my
trousers is also dead. One of the two doctors working with
frenzied speed is 29-year-old Dr. Phan Van Chuong, who
joined the army only six weeks ago. He is appalled by the
number and severity of the casualties. In the morning, close
to tears, he will say, "It was impossible, impossible."

The first American Medevac helicopter circles cautiously
down through the cloud cover and clacks in to land, then pulls
away.

"What's the problem?"

"He can't see to land." Route 9 is ankle-deep in dust, and the blades throw up a cloud which drowns the bright landing light.

"Throw water to damp the dust."

The helicopter lands and there is another obscene drama half-seen through the dust. There are too many casualties, no place for stretchers. Little groups of half-real, half-glimpsed figures run out with the worst wounded in their arms. The blinking red lights on the chopper glow eerily on their helmets and seem to pulse HURRY, HURRY, HURRY. Forced to treat their comrades like so many carcasses, the paratroops shove wounded on top of one another until the cabin is a surreal slaughterhouse. Then the chopper sets off on its dangerous return flight.

The airlift goes on for three hours. The accidental bombing by an American aircraft, probably Navy, cost seven dead and 54 wounded. Several of the wounded were expected to die. But slowly Task Force 11 recovers its confidence, turns its face away from the grave of personal calamity and back to the war. After two hours the first quiet laugh is heard. Clunking shovels heap fresh soil on the blood-stained ground, the dead are packaged in ponchos, tied with bandages, packs and weapons of the missing men are heaped for removal. An American voice suggests that the helicopter pilots should be called in to back-haul the bodies tonight without being told they are running risks for the dead. Fortunately, Major Todd will have none of that nonsense. The bodies stay. Before they are taken away in the morning, a Vietnamese trooper looks for, finds and removes a pair of boots which are apparently his size.

But now there are still more wounded to move. "How many to go?" a paratrooper asks.

"Three, I think." And then to me, "Is that one dead?"

I stoop over a man whose face is shrouded from the dust by a towel. My hand is on his chest and I feel a slight movement. "No, he's alive."

"Okay, make it four."

Life, February 19, 1971

At Border Crossing Into Laos, the Litter of Troops and History

by Gloria Emerson

ON ROUTE 9, near the Laotian border, Feb. 15—Now there is only the garbage of war. Empty C-ration cans of fruit cocktail and turkey loaf, an empty Pall Mall cigarette package, a single khaki sock and two mounds of sandbags are strewn about at the border crossing into Laos on Route 9.

A week ago it was here that thousands of South Vietnamese troops, supported by American planes and artillery, marched into Laos, leaving the litter behind.

It hardly looks like a place where the history of Indochina has been dramatically changed.

No man stands guard. Stretched across the road are two long bamboo poles tied together with string to show where Laos begins and American soldiers must not go.

The sign "Warning! No U.S. Personnel Beyond This Point" has dozens of names scrawled on it. On the back, facing Laos, is a faintly scrawled message to the North Vietnamese Army: "Warning! No N.V.A. Beyond This Point."

There are no American trucks in this section of Route 9. A long, narrow roller coaster of a road, whose rising dust is white, then orange, sometimes dark brown, it cuts through elephant grass, bamboo trees and nine-foot stalks topped by ostrichlike plumes and is just wide enough for one truck to squeeze by another.

No supplies are moving into Laos on the road, for the South Vietnamese troops are being supplied by air. It is a lonely road and a bad one to walk on. There are snipers, there are North Vietnamese rockets coming in from positions in Laos as well as here in Vietnam. There is a silence even at noon that makes men with M-16 rifles uneasy.

The American soldiers are 300 yards from the border on a

lump of a hill where seven tanks and armored personnel carriers form the defense perimeter of a miniature fire base. The men are soldiers from the Americal Division and from an infantry battalion of the First Brigade of the Fifth Infantry Division (Mechanized).

"Christ, we're defenseless here!" said Pvt. George Miller, a 22-year-old Newark man. "They could fire pot shots at us all day and all night long if they wanted to."

The Americans' job is to secure the road, search the area and stay alive.

On the unnamed hill are a mixture of tankers—the men who drive the machines—the grunts, or infantryman, and the mortar squads. There is friendly friction, a tribal competitiveness, that provides their only entertainment.

Many of the Americans here, their faces sore from the dust and grime, their bodies covered with the small open boils that infest unwashed Westerners fighting in Vietnam, wish they could have gone into Laos.

"I'd love to go into Laos. If we did, we'd get everything organized right, see," Specialist 4 Anthony Hockman of Battletown, Ky., said.

Few of the men here think the South Vietnamese can seal off the Ho Chi Minh Trail network. There is still a deep suspicion that they will not do as well as Americans would; it is a conviction the G.I.'s like to voice.

"I saw them fight in Kontum—they got into contact and they ran out, they bugged out, and left two wounded behind," said Specialist 4 Harold Dingus of South Shore, Ky.

There are some men who feel that it is not doing any good to be here, who say they are outnumbered by the North Vietnamese in the surrounding highlands.

"You might say it's a case of the unwilling helping the ungrateful to kill the unwanted," Sgt. Kirk Coles said.

Less than a mile down from the border are South Vietnamese troops from the 11th Airborne Battalion. The paratroopers, who often trade their packages of precooked rice for C-rations, are not so sure that the Ho Chi Minh Trail can ever be cut.

Cpl. Le Ngu said in Vietnamese: "Do you think the N.V.A. are all fools? I can tell you the Ho Chi Minh Trail is very complicated—you attack here, you attack there, but they will get through in other places."

"When do we have peace, heh?" a Vietnamese paratrooper asked as he ate his lunch of rice and duck, using chopsticks made of bamboo.

Another soldier snorted. "Write a letter to Mr. Thieu and ask him," he said, referring to Nguyen Van Thieu, President of South Vietnam. Corporal Ngu shook his head, shoveled more rice into his mouth and replied: "Goddammit, Thieu never knows, Nixon never knows!"

Yesterday the South Vietnamese here suffered 20 wounded when two mortar rounds hit their camp, where there are nearly 150 men.

The Americans, who are closer to the border, were hit by a North Vietnamese rocket today. Every man jammed on his steel helmet.

Sitting on the sandbags around one of the two 81-mm. mortars, Pvt. Richard Ferguson of Columbus, Ohio, told why he did not get married last year before he was drafted and sent to Vietnam.

"You read about all these guys getting shot up," he said. "I thought it was as bad as what it's getting to be." That struck half a dozen men as very witty.

None of the G.I.'s here look upon the North Vietnamese forces as being on their last legs or as a ragtag army that has nothing to fight with and lacks the spirit to win.

"They are hard to kill—I once put six bullets in a gook and still he don't die," Specialist 4 Manuel R. Navarro of San Antonio, Tex., said. "He looked about 17."

At a few minutes before 2 P.M., an infantry platoon "got in real trouble," as one G.I. put it. The radio operator of the platoon, which believed it was surrounded, had the voice of a man trying hard to sound steady.

"Most of us had to retreat," he said. "I'll give you further word when I figure out what's going on around here."

No one seemed sleepy then. The small talk about favorite movies and much-loved cars, about girls with long, blond hair and perfect legs, stopped.

Half a dozen men clustered around the field radio listening to the pilot of a gunship find his target, to the pilot of a helicopter removing wounded men through the triple canopy of jungle.

An hour later the site where the platoon had taken fire was mashed by 8-inch howitzer shells and burned by white phosphorus and blasted by 6,000 bullets a minute from the air.

"Goddam good show, and probably all for nothing, too," a soldier said. "The dinks have gone underground or scattered."

Specialist 4 Harry Crane of Steubenville, Ohio, began to cook dinner, as he does every night, in two steel helmets over an open fire.

"I use the same two pots for cooking every night," he said. "I just mix together a lot of C's and some rice and noodles that the Vietnamese trade us for cigarettes. You have to put in lots of hot sauce and garlic salt."

The New York Times, February 18, 1971

The Meo of Laos

by John E. Woodruff

CIA Alliance Brings Ruin to Proud Race

BAN SON, Laos—A decade of feeding men into the only aggressive pro-government army in Laos has made totally dependent refugees of the hundreds of thousands of once fiercely independent hill tribesmen now gathered about this malaria-infested valley.

"I don't know why we carry on with these people," an Air America pilot shouted over the whine of his helicopter high above a cloud bank somewhere over northern Laos. "They won't fight any more, but we just go on dropping rice and medicine to them, just like in the old days."

In Vientiane, a top American official discusses the relationship with the Meo and other hillmen who make up the Central Intelligence Agency's clandestine army:

"Look, they came to us for help [in 1960] and we have given them plenty of help."

He then hastens to assure his questioner that the United States can accept it philosophically if rank-and-file Meo finally make the uncomfortable accommodation with the North Vietnamese that he feels sure must inevitably come some day.

The accommodation is one that some Americans insist the tribesmen would have made several years and tens of thousands of lives ago had the Americans not armed them and exhorted them to keep fighting.

Until 1960, the Meo of Laos lived much as their grandfathers did—in primitive freedom and disease, on hilltops seldom lower than 3,500 feet, in villages of no more than 20 or 30 thatch houses.

Since the mid-1800's, when they came from Yunnan province of China, where most Meo still live, they had often carried their flintlocks and crossbows down to the valleys to defend their independence against their Lao and other neighbors. The fights earned them a reputation as aggressive, cruel attackers.

The alliance with the Americans radically changed their way of fighting—and their way of living.

It turned the Meo into a far more modern and potent army than they could have imagined in 1945—long before the Americans came—when they added a few European rifles left over from World War II to their own primitive arsenal and won their first fight with the North Vietnamese.

For the Americans, it also provided the badly needed military punch that officials readily acknowledge was the main strength of all United States policy in Laos for the last 10 years.

But to many who have long watched the war in Laos, the new strength provided by the Americans seems, in ironic retrospect, to have been the tribesmen's downfall: it made them, these observers say, a force the North Vietnamese had to crush in order to maintain the Laotian Communist control of the "liberated zones" of the country.

Today, a fourth of the Meo, maybe more, are dead—thousands of soldiers from combat and tens of thousands of civilians from exhaustion or illness as they walked for weeks on end to escape the enemy they have fought for 10 years as allies of the United States.

More than half the Meo mountain tribesmen of Laos are gathered here now, and it is virtually impossible to find anyone here who has not lost at least one close relative to the long war.

Semi-official estimates—based on recorded death benefit payments—list 10,000 Meo, Lao Thung, Yao and Thai Dam tribesmen killed in combat, from an army that has probably never numbered more than 15,000 men at any one time.

But by far the greater death toll has been exacted by long walks forced upon entire villages in recent years since the Lao Peoples' Revolutionary Army and North Vietnamese troops began systematically removing both the CIA army and the Meo population from traditional Communist territory.

Some villages have walked for as long as three weeks with little rest and scant food to escape enemy pressure. Some have had to move as many as six times in a single year as one out-post after another fell to the Communists.

A few village leaders tell gory tales of reprisal massacres in which, they say, North Vietnamese soldiers methodically slaughtered the women, children and old men who make up most of the refugees.

But these incidents seem to have been the exception. The most efficient killer has been the sheer torture of the long marches.

Weakened by exposure to hot sun or monsoon rains, ex-hausted by days or weeks of walking with only nominal rest stops, sometimes hungry for days on end until pilots with the United States Agency for International Development can find their trail and drop rice to them, the refugees soon fall victim to the chronic malaria which their bodies have learned to resist under normal conditions.

The very young and the very old tend to die on the trail. So do mothers weakened by pregnancy or recent child-birth—and their number is far larger than in the West, for many Meo women bear children almost annually.

Many of those who survive the walk soon fall victim to the new strains of malaria or dysentery in their new home—or to the tuberculosis, pneumonia and dozens of other diseases to which the malaria and dysentery leave them susceptible. American refugee workers say that whenever they take a cen-sus at the end of a major move, between 10 and 15 per cent of the population is dead a year later.

Edgar L. Buell, a retired Indiana farmer who has worked with the Meo hill people since 1960, believes that the Meo and other hill tribes have lost a fourth of their population in refugee moves and combat.

A combination of his estimate with the aid agency's figures showing about 200,000 tribal refugees now under American care suggests that more than 65,000 tribesmen have died—the vast majority of them Meo civilians forced to leave their villages. A few officials give lower estimates; most run far higher.

The Meo of Southeast Asia—there there may be as many as 4 million of them altogether, scattered in tiny hilltop villages across northern Thailand, Burma's Shan plateau, northern Indochina and eastern Yunnan and western Kwei-chow provinces in China—are traditionally among the richest of the many hill tribes that complicate the region's teeming ethnic divisions and subdivisions.

In Laos, their most famous source of wealth was the poppy, from which they took the opium sap by processes their ancestors brought from China when they came to Laos just over 100 years ago.

The opium of Sam Neua province, now the Communist "capital" of Laos, is known to all the world's smuggling rings as some of the best there is.

The $100 or so a Meo farmer was able to get for his annual crop enabled some men eventually to adorn their wives with as many as five or six of the heavy, ornate silver necklaces Meo women use to dress up their traditional black shirts and long pants. Even infant daughters—and sometimes sons—commonly wore two or three lighter necklaces, and sometimes a bracelet.

By primitive tribal standards, the Meo also were skilled at raising livestock and fruits, and their herbs and orchards were measures of prestige as well as wealth.

All of that is lost now to the Meo of the CIA army.

The poppy fields and the orchards, if they are still being farmed, are well inside the Lao Communists' territory. The livestock gradually has been left behind in the chaotic mass escapes of the last three years.

Even most of the silver jewelry has been sold off for money. All that is left is American aid.

American officials in Vientiane are quick to point out the spectacular Western-style efforts that the Agency for International Development has made to help the Meo.

Heroic pilots of Air America and Continental Air Services, they point out, have braved tiny mountain passes, incredible weather problems and Communist gunfire to drop rice and medicines to hilltop villages.

Men like Mr. Buell—whom the Meo call Tan Pop, which translates roughly as Mr. Sent-From-Above—have risked all manner of hardship and disease to live in Meo villages and bring them schools, train village medics and improve their farm tools, the Americans say.

Days in Meo refugee villages and interviews with Meo and American refugee officials fill in the details of some of these claims.

The rice distribution program to Meo villages is years old now, but refugee officials in Vientiane acknowledge that it was only under intense pressure from doctors working with the tribesmen that the Agency for International Development finally started last spring a $1 million-a-year program of distributing meats and other protein supplements.

That program, they say, is calculated to provide for about one refugee in every five now under the agency's care. It goes to tribesmen chosen by doctors according to their illnesses or their degree of malnutrition.

Some officials who work with the program acknowledge that the food the aid agency provides is calculated to fend off starvation but not to replace even the simple diet the Meo had before their constant moves cost them their livestock and farms. Every medical worker interviewed said that malnutrition is now extremely widespread among the Meo, even by primitive tribal standards.

The American-sponsored village health program has brought small, thatched-roof dispensaries and trained medics to most Meo communities.

But the refugee subcommittee of the Senate Judiciary Committee, headed by Senator Edward M. Kennedy (D., Mass.), has documented the need to which this program was the American response: It was undertaken when it became clear that the CIA army's wounded were getting virtually no care except that of the traditional Meo witch doctors, whose ancient ritual of shrieks, gongs, charms and dances quickly proved unequal to the effects of modern grenades and automatic rifles.

Pop Buell estimates that 100 of the medics trained for this ostensibly civilian public-health program have died on the battlefield. That, he says, is about one in every five.

Even the small, thatched schoolrooms Pop Buell encouraged the Meo to build have sometimes been turned to benefit the CIA-sponsored war effort, according to some U.S. aid workers.

"I was in a village one day when the neighboring village was attacked," one aid worker says. "A naikong (village leader) came to the classroom and rounded up all the boys over 10 years old, handed them guns and flintlocks and started giving them instructions just outside the school—it was an instant recruiting pool."

But the schools also have brought the Meo arithmetic, reading, writing, which no government ever tried to give them before, and has taught them the language of the lowland Lao, the language of government in Laos. In so doing, the schools have greatly strengthened their ability to deal with the Lao, Chinese, Indian and Vietnamese merchants who have traditionally exploited their simplicity.

Baltimore Sun, February 21, 1971

U.S. Finances Victor-to-Refugee Transit

VIENTIANE, Laos—On September 25, 1945, Toubhy Lyfong received a letter from Gen. Le Thiep Hong, then Viet Minh commander of the Vinh region of North Vietnam.

It is from this letter that Mr. Lyfong, who soon afterward would be dubbed "King of the Meo" by French journalists, dates the chain of events that eventually brought his people to their current state of total dependence on United States aid.

Mr. Lyfong says the letter notified him that Viet Minh troops planned to cross into Laos through Xieng Khouang province, where he was the French-appointed chief of Meo hill tribesmen. It asked him to let them pass so they could start organizing resistance to the expected return of the French after World War II.

He refused—largely, he says, out of loyalty to the French, who had given him eight years of schooling, the most ever permitted a Meo. Two weeks later, Viet Minh troops and a few of their Lao allies fought Mr. Lyfong's Meo mountain tribesmen at an outpost near Nong Het, just inside Laos.

The fight was a chaos of aged French and British colonial weapons, Meo crossbows and flintlocks and a few Japanese and American rifles scrounged during World War II; history seems to have overlooked it, although it may well have been the seminal battle of the tragi-comic struggle that still sputters backward and forward across Laos today.

That day, according to Toubhy Lyfong's memory, the Meo were the winners.

Mr. Lyfong organized loosely run Meo guerrilla forces for the French from then until 1954, when the Viet Minh scored their spectacular victory at Dienbienphu and drove the French from Indochina.

When Mr. Lyfong went to France to retire after the war, though, his loyalty was scarcely rewarded; refused permission to transfer his $250,000 fortune to Paris from the colonial bank, he relates, he had to return to Indochina after only two weeks.

By 1960, his continued presence in Laos was to prove helpful to new foreigners: the Americans, who were starting to organize an army of hill tribesmen to supplement the pathetically ineffective Royal Lao Army they tried to build for the Vientiane government in the late 1950's.

It was in that year that Toubhy Lyfong says he cemented an alliance with the right-wing Gen. Phoumi Nosavan and Prince Boun Oum—and thus with the United States Army and Central Intelligence Agency, which then were financing and supplying the Phoumist army in southern Laos.

Throughout 1960, Mr. Lyfong lent his prestige—as well as the many local officials he had appointed while province chief and his remaining friendships from the days as a guerrilla organizer—to a little-known army major named Vang Pao.

Maj. Vang Pao, the highest-ranking Meo in the Lao Army, twice had been refused an overdue promotion to lieutenant colonel by Lao officers who could not accept the idea of a hill tribesman as their equal, according to Mr. Lyfong.

Promised better treatment by General Phoumi and Prince Boun Oum—and promised money and arms by the Americans—Vang Pao set out to build a hill-tribe army. For General Phoumi and Boun Oum, the alliance offered at last the prospect of a friendly force in parts of northern Laos that long had been largely the preserve of neutralist and pro-Communist forces with whom they frequently had quarreled.

By early 1961, as minister of social welfare under a short-lived government headed by Prince Boun Oum, Mr. Lyfong was able to give Vang Pao's infant army more tangible help. He diverted Lao and American refugee goods to the Meo of the Plain of Jars region, whom Vang Pao had regrouped according to a prearranged plan when neutralist troops took over the plain as they retreated before a drive on Vientiane by General Phoumi's men.

Soon afterward, Vang Pao became commander of Military Region II, Xieng Khouang and Sam Neua provinces, the toughest Communist-held territory in northern Laos.

Vang Pao's regroupment of the Meo onto seven strategically located hilltops surrounding the plain radically altered the course of the war in northern Laos, for it welded a large group of rugged Meo mountaineers into the beginnings of what gradually became the Vientiane government's most effective single fighting force.

It also radically altered the lives of the Meo by separating them from their tiny hilltop villages of no more than 20 or 30 houses each.

Now Vang Pao's Meo followers were gathered into settlements that soon proved too crowded for their way of farming, which consists of cutting and burning trees and brush from the sunny side of a mountain, planting rice and corn for two or three years until the soil is depleted and then starting over again on a different hillside.

The refugee supplies sent from Vientiane by Mr. Lyfong —largely rice bought in Thailand with American money—thus became the first step in the Meo's decade-long walk to total dependence on United States aid.

It is fashionable among high American officials in Vientiane today to point out that the Meo already had had some fights with the Communists before the Americans organized them and to insist that the Meo "came to us."

"Look, these people came to us for help, and we have given them plenty of help," one top-level diplomat says.

An anonymous memorandum of the Vientiane office of the agency that preceded the United States Agency for International Development presents a more complex picture.

Arguing in favor of giving the Meo help that was soon to

be justified publicly as humanitarian refugee aid, the 1960 memorandum said, in part:

"Toughened by their hard work in the high mountains, accustomed from childhood to firearms and to hunting in groups, used to traveling long distances on foot from one village to another, they become excellent fighters with a minimum of training.

"For many months now, ever since the Communists seized control of the Plain of Jars, the Meo, working together with officers and soldiers from the Lao armed forces, have been formed into regular [Laotian Army] military units. They have defended their homes and given great assistance to their brothers in arms elsewhere in Laos by harassing the enemy's convoys and military columns."

Some lower-level Americans who work with the Meo argue that the relationship established in 1960 was by nature unequal, even if it had been a simple case of responding to a Meo request for aid.

One says: "It's no help to your case if you tell the judge the 12-year-old girl invited you into her bedroom.

"The Meo were primitive people who thought for a long time that we were generously helping them defend their little hilltops and thatched huts. They know now that they are being used in something bigger, of course, but now it's too late.

"We saw the thing in terms of geopolitics—or the struggle against communism, or whatever you want to call it—from the beginning, and we were only too relieved to find some effective warriors in Laos who were willing to take on an enemy much bigger than they could ever have understood."

Whatever the precise relationship was at first, the uses to which the Meo army soon was put give little support to the "they-came-to-us" view.

By 1962, Meo units were stiffened by the presence of "white star" teams of the Green Berets and had spread the American-paid army deep into Sam Neua province, the regroupment area granted to the pro-Communists Pathet Lao by the 1954 Geneva agreements.

Edgar L. Buell, now head of the United States AID program for hill-tribe refugees, talks of this achievement by his beloved Meo with considerable pride: "When I came here in

[1960, as a $65-a-month International Voluntary Service worker], we couldn't set foot inside Sam Neua province. Within a couple of years, we were able to work the whole province."

Then the 1962 Geneva conference on Laos called for an end to the confused fighting and prohibited foreign troops on Lao soil.

But its chief effect on the American-backed Meo army was to shift it from Green Beret to CIA sponsorship.

By this time, Vang Pao's army had become a force the Communists would not ignore, and soon after the cease-fire Pathet Lao and North Vietnamese forces attacked Meo positions near the Plain of Jars, arguing that the Meo and their American advisers had been parachuted into the mountains after the cease-fire.

Baltimore Sun, February 22, 1971

A War-Exhausted People Seek a Way Out

VIENTIANE, Laos—Edgar L. (Pop) Buell believes that many Meo hill tribesmen are starting—gradually and in small groups—to make a painful peace with the Lao and Vietnamese Communists they have fought on and off for 25 years.

"I've lost about 75,000 people, Meo and others, in the last 18 months," says Mr. Buell, a retired Indiana farmer who has worked with the Meo as a civilian adviser since 1960. "Of course, some of them are dead from the war and the long walks. But most of them, I'm convinced, are Meo, and a few from other tribes, who have finally either found their way back into their old places in Communist areas or else decided the last time the Communists came that they just were not going to run any more."

Many Americans here believe that Pop Buell's figures are extravagant, but few question his sense for the trend of Meo affairs. One top military official says, "The Meo are terrifically worn down as fighters.

"Their morale is shot, and they are slow to engage in battle. If you are going to have a guerrilla Army, you have to make your move fast and clear out fast. That is what the Meo used to do best; now they just don't do it."

Another top-level official says, "If the fight goes on, and the North Vietnamese really decide to turn on the pressure, the Meo will be crushed.

"What else can they do? They are going to have to find some way to get out of the way of the battle sooner or later, and if the worst comes, many of the leaders like Vang Pao [leader of the Meo Clandestine Army] will have to come here to Vientiane or maybe even leave the country."

No one is proclaiming it as a policy, but this tacit assumption that most Meo eventually will end their decade of fighting and running under U.S. sponsorship by finding a way to co-exist with their old enemies is the stated expectation even at the very top of the U.S. mission here.

Mr. Buell is convinced that such an accommodation is possible, although it will by no means be pleasant.

"The Communists know their limits with the Meo—they know they can tax them so far, and they can get so much forced labor, and they can go just so far with the political ideas, and then they stop.

"And this isn't going to be any overnight thing—it's going to go on like it is now, a few hundred or a few thousand here and there.

"And I don't hardly expect the Meo are going to fight for the other side after all, for the Communists. It would be a big thing to just get the Meo the hell out of the war."

Many critics of American policy insist that the kind of accommodation Mr. Buell describes is what the Meo would have had to do 10 years ago—before losing their health, their wealth and much of their population—had the United States not provided the massive backing that enabled them to become a fighting force too important for the Communists to shrug off.

That argument was outlined at length last May 7 by Ronald J. Rickenbach, who served for several years as a U.S. Agency for International Development Worker at Sam Thong.

In testimony before the refugee subcommittee of the Senate Judiciary Committee, headed by Senator Edward M. Kennedy (D., Mass.), Mr. Rickenbach argued that when the North Vietnamese moved into Laos, the choices open to the Meo were to "accommodate themselves, fight or flee."

"They could not very well fight without arms and assistance; they could flee, but to nowhere as suitable to their way of life than where they already were, or they could accommodate themselves in some peaceful, subservient way to the Vietnamese presence, and thereby allow something of a local political balance to be effected in cognizance with the realities of the time."

When the Americans came on the scene with unlimited arms and extensive food supplies, he said, the Meo yielded to the temptation to fight. A primitive tribe thus "became unwitting pawns of the United States."

American officials in Vientiane generally reject this argument.

Even the Americans who now readily accept the probability that the Meo one day will have to make their peace with the Communists insist that could not have happened in 1960, pointing out that the Meo were already fighting the Communists under the French before 1954.

More recently, an intensive American effort has often been needed to keep the Meo in the fight, and that effort is invariably made, even by Americans who personally feel strongly that the Meo are a depleted and exhausted people and that their Army has a severe case of combat fatigue.

Americans at several levels are known to have visited Gen. Vang Pao many times to dissuade him from a plan he often mentions to move the Meo en masse into Sayaboury province of western Laos, where there has been little fighting. Ambassador G. McMurtrie Godley, himself is known to have made more than one such visit to General Vang Pao since becoming ambassador a year and a half ago.

One key U.S. official says: "Hell, what else could the old man have done—it's still true that without the Meo, there would just be no such thing as American policy in Laos; we just wouldn't have any force to back it up with."

The ambassador is known not to take the Sayaboury idea seriously and to regard his visits with the general as efforts to bolster the morale of a highly mercurial man who is temporarily "down in the dumps."

Americans who work with Vang Pao say that the Sayaboury move is only one of a collection of half-formulated ideas he often mentions as means of retiring the Meo from the war.

But the inability of a man who grew up a primitive tribes-man to formulate a plan fully does not, they insist, mean that he does not take the problem seriously.

"It's a deep and constant preoccupation," one American says.

"Sometimes, it's as if he were the only Meo leader with the foresight to understand how important it is to their people."

Some time ago, they had an annual "meeting at Long Cheng. He spent half the day with the civilian politicians—we call them the Meo Mafia—and the other half with the top Army officers. He told them the time had come to get out, and that place was where they would go, and they should start getting ready.

"When he finished, they just sat there—both the morning group and the afternoon group—just silence, no questions, no interest, no response.

"That's how it's been a lot of times—no action until the fighting actually starts. The Meo are just that way."

Others confirm the story but insist that the Meo are not "just that way."

"They've moved so damn many times, and every time it was just this once more," one says. "How can we expect them to move again when there isn't really even a plan to follow?"

The absence of plans—or the profusion of half-coherent and conflicting plans—is as striking among the Americans as it is among the Meo.

Various responsible Americans mention at least five different parts of Laos, including Sayaboury province, as places where they expect the main body of Meo to go to escape the war.

How the Meo will get there, where they will get food and supplies to tide them over the year it will take to harvest their first crops, what will become of their weapons—all of these and other equally fundamental questions go unanswered.

The absence of planning has provoked bitterness among a few Americans who care deeply about the Meo.

"We always had plenty of plans for how they should defend our gear at Phou Pha Thi, and for scouting missions, and for how they could disrupt the North Vietnamese for us," one says. "It's only now that we seem to be running out of plans."

This bitterness is not shared by most Americans, however. Most argue that if what the Meo must do is make peace with the Communists, then too much American intervention can only poison prospects that are already bleak from a decade of bitter warfare.

Meanwhile, even the location of the Meo refugee camps is becoming controversial among the Americans, some of whom contend that the long, oval-shaped gathering of camps east of Ban Son was planned deliberately to keep the Meo in the line of Communist advance toward Vientiane.

"I don't buy that idea," one experienced American says. "If the Communists want to take Vientiane, they can skirt the Meo and come right up the Mekong."

Talks with Americans who work with the refugees suggest that most of the hill-tribe villages east of Ban Son got there mainly because the people there came from eastern Laos and simply stopped walking when they got to relatively secure territory.

However the refugees got where they are, the Communist pattern of recent years has not suggested that any direct attack on Vientiane is in their plans.

Instead, they have sought to move the battlefield from place to place north of Vientiane—and the royal capital of Luang Prabang—in a manner that creates an impression of growing pressure on the two capitals.

The areas where this tactic can be most effective are approximately the ones where the Meo are concentrated, and the increasing presence of North Vietnamese troops around Long Cheng and Sam Thong suggest that the Meo are not yet out of the way.

"I'm not going to say they're through yet," Pop Buell says. "God knows nobody thought they could make it this long—it was always just hold out for six more months, and then six more and six more."

Baltimore Sun, February 23, 1971

Copters Return from Laos with the Dead

by Gloria Emerson

KHESANH, South Vietnam, Feb. 27—The dead began to come into the emergency field hospital here today after 1 P.M.

The first South Vietnamese soldier, killed yesterday in Laos, was wrapped tightly in an American Army poncho held by bandage strips used as string. All that could be seen were his small, bare feet—dark with dust—hanging over the stretcher's edge.

He lay on the reddish earth while a Vietnamese officer of the hospital at the airborne division's forward command post looked at a large tag and wrote down one more name and unit.

Fifteen minutes later—raising a furious blizzard of dust that stings the eyes and whips the face—another United States medical evacuation helicopter landed. Two more dead, then 10 more dead.

By 3 P.M. there were 30 dead and over 200 wounded.

A small despairing scene, it is being repeated every day in the face of mounting Communist resistance to the South Vietnamese drive into Laos. This week the South Vietnamese command reported a total of 320 dead, 1,000 wounded and 99 missing in action since the operation began on Feb. 8. It is suspected that the figures are unrealistically small.

At this hospital, an emergency station with a few tents and an underground surgical bunker with only stretchers for the critically wounded, the Vietnamese orderlies stand in groups near a small helicopter pad.

They seemed uncertain of how to remove the dead and the wounded most quickly from the choppers, which are flown by American crews.

One young orderly kept rushing toward the craft holding a stretcher in front of him as a shield against the dirt, but then he dropped it as he came closer and did not seem to know what to do next.

Other orderlies did not bother with the stretchers. Some carried the wounded in a stumbling file of piggyback rides. Those Vietnamese who were wounded but could somehow walk made the few hundred yards by themselves, weaving a little in the scorching sun.

In one tent, where the day's wounded lie on American cots waiting for Vietnamese medics or Dr. Tran Qui Tram, who is 21 years old, to help them, there were more than a dozen men in the stifling heat. Some closed their eyes and were silent but others would not restrain their groans.

The most seriously wounded man, a North Vietnamese, Third Lieut. Mac Thang Nong, a member of the 35th North Vietnamese Commando Battalion, a demolition outfit, was on a wooden table as the medics dressed his wounds. They did not give him an anesthetic—no one had that.

"I was on a reconnaissance mission with three others," he said, whispering slowly in Vietnamese. "We were near Hill 30 when I was hit by fire from the hilltop. I considered myself as already dead. From now on I do not worry about anything."

He was captured by the South Vietnamese on the hill, where heavy fighting has been going on this week.

Lieutenant Nong, who said he left North Vietnam only a month ago, declined to talk about his family and closed his eyes.

The South Vietnamese wounded paid no attention to the enemy officer. They were too busy with their own thoughts and their own pain.

Pvt. Nguyen Huu Thanh, a combat engineer supporting South Vietnamese airborne troops in Laos, does not know the name of the place where he was hit by rocket fragments. The tears rolled down his face as he muttered in Vietnamese.

"Do you know whether they will amputate my arm?" he pleaded. "I am afraid they will cut off my arm here."

But he could not bring himself to put the question to the medics. When they bent his arm in a splint—no one knew whether it was fractured or only full of steel splinters—he cried out. There was no one to soothe him and no one to give him water.

Pvt. Tran Van Gu, a Ranger with the 21st Battalion, which fought on Hill 30, was wounded by North Vietnamese recoilless-rifle fire. "The North Vietnamese are frightening," he said. It was hard to hear him because of the bandage around his face.

"The North Vietnamese were hit by three waves of B-52 bombers last night, but still they survived and they shelled us early this morning," he related.

"Many of the Rangers wish that they would be ordered to withdraw," he continued, "because all of us are surrounded and cannot figure out a way to fight back against the North Vietnamese. They don't fear air strikes or artillery. I am convinced that we cannot fight them in Laos."

An infantryman with the First Division fighting at Hotel 2, where the North Vietnamese have attacked ground forces 18 miles southwest of Laobao, told of the assault.

"They fired on us day and night with rockets, mortars and recoilless rifles," Pvt. Tran Van Ngo said, sighing. "At 4 P.M. yesterday I was wounded. So were seven others. The choppers couldn't land all day to get us out because of the enemy fire."

The soldier said he was 49 years old though his papers say he is 40. "A long long time ago my father changed the age on my papers from 28 to 19 to keep me from being drafted by the French to fight the Germans," he said. "I am far too old to be in the army now as a private, with all the hardship that comes to a man. I dodged one war only to be caught finally in another."

The New York Times, March 3, 1971

Spirit of Saigon's Army Shaken in Laos

by Gloria Emerson

KHESANH, South Vietnam, March 27—The morale of many soldiers in South Vietnam's finest military units, who fought the North Vietnamese in Laos, is shattered.

Men in the crack First Infantry Division, in the marines and in the Airborne Division say that the Laos invasion was a nightmare for them and for other soldiers.

Through an interpreter they spoke of how the North Vietnamese outnumbered them and advanced in wave after wave, running over the bodies of comrades and never stopping.

In low, strained voices, the South Vietnamese spoke of what they termed the enemy's ability to survive American air strikes and B-52 bombings, which they themselves feared so much.

While these men did not say that they spoke for all the 20,000 South Vietnamese soldiers who took part in the Laos campaign, they asserted that the morale of their fellow soldiers was low. Those interviewed were in the state of dejected fatigue that is common to men coming out of a long retreat under heavy enemy fire, and perhaps their views will be less gloomy after some rest.

In Saigon, for example, a paratroop lieutenant who was wounded early in the campaign said that for the next six months his men would prefer to desert and risk jail rather than go into such a battle again, but that later, perhaps, they would be ready to face the enemy once more.

For many of the South Vietnamese soldiers, most of whom are in their twenties, the Laos campaign was their first fierce encounter with North Vietnamese ground forces; not for years has there been major fighting in South Vietnam to compare with the operation against enemy supply trails in Laos.

It was a test, and now most South Vietnamese veterans frankly admit that their forces failed. They had no chance, these men say.

Although it is not known whether the effects of the Laos operation will be permanent, some experienced South Vietnamese noncommissioned officers are wondering if their units will be able to fight well again and respect their officers.

What has dramatically demoralized many of the South Vietnamese troops is the large number of their own wounded who were left behind, begging for their friends to shoot them or to leave hand grenades so they could commit suicide before the North Vietnamese or the B-52 raids killed them.

Some soldiers who had been in the drive into Cambodia last year said they had never dreamed that the Laos operation would not be as simple. Since there was no significant fighting in Cambodia, these South Vietnamese felt that the enemy was no longer a threat. They learned differently in Laos and they will not soon forget it.

"The best units were sent in and the best units got the worst beating in combat," Sgt. Nguyen Van Lac said. "Now you see the North Vietnamese chasing us out. We lost 59 artillery pieces—105-mm. and 155-mm. howitzers—or the equivalent of three artillery battalions."

The sergeant is an artillery liaison man at the forward command post here of an American unit, the First Brigade of the Fifth Infantry Division (Mechanized).

More chilling accounts of the Laos fighting came from the men who lived through it, the tired and shaken men who said they were not prepared for what had happened.

In American helicopters they came out of Laos this week without their combat packs, their rations or their steel helmets—and sometimes without their weapons. Nothing mattered, they said, except getting out.

One of them was a 22-year-old marine who came back to South Vietnam on Wednesday after walking through the jungle for two nights and a day before the airlift.

His version of the fighting near a fire base called Delta on Hill 547, about eight miles inside Laos, told how the South Vietnamese troops ran for their lives, each man struggling for himself only.

"The last attack came at about 8 P.M.," Private Moc, the marine, said in Vietnamese. "They shelled us first and then came the tanks moving up into our positions. The whole brigade ran down the hill like ants. We jumped on each other to get out of that place. No man had time to look for his commanding officer. It was quick, quick, quick or we would die. Oh, God, now I know for sure that I am really still alive."

Private Moc asked, as did other men, that his full name and unit be withheld for he was afraid that he would be punished for telling what happened to him.

"When I was far from the hill, with about 20 other marines, there was a first lieutenant with us," he continued. "We moved like ghosts, terrified of being ambushed by the North Vietnamese. We stopped many times when there was firing —not daring to breathe. How terrible those minutes were."

Private Moc came back to South Vietnam with the legs of his pants ripped off, and his thigh showing through the tatters. A small thin man, he had only his M-16 rifle left of his equipment. He continued his account of the action in Laos:

"Only last Tuesday our group bumped into a North Vietnamese unit, and we ran again like ants. And the Lieutenant, he whispered to us 'Disperse, disperse, don't stick together or we will all be killed.' After each firing, there were fewer and fewer of us. Nobody cared for anybody else at all."

What made his blood run cold, Private Moc said, was how the North Vietnamese kept coming and coming, running over the bodies of their own men, and not stopping.

"They were everywhere and they were so daring," he said. "Their firepower was so enormous, and their shelling was so accurate, that what could we do except run for our lives."

Hearing the assault shout of the North Vietnamese, remembering how they screamed "Xung phong!" will long haunt one man, Sgt. Nguyen Minh. He fought with Brigade A of the Second Marine Artillery Battalion.

The entire brigade ran away, he said.

Its position in Laos was south of Route 9, the east-west axis of the drive, about seven miles inside the border. The brigade arrived there March 5 and stayed for two weeks before it retreated.

"For days," he related, "we had been made desperate by their constant shellings and assaults, by their strange attitude of ignoring death and always moving closer and closer to us.

Never were the marines in such trouble, and we were never so afraid.

"They knew everything about us. They shouted to us, 'We know that you are Company One of Battalion Two. Surrender, brothers. We have hot meals and hot tea for you out here!'

"And, then, hearing them shout for assault, knowing they were all around us, our fear was so great."

An infantry platoon leader who has been in the army for 18 years also discussed the terror he felt in Laos.

Sergeant Co, 38, is now AWOL. He does not care.

"All that counts is surviving the Laos operation," he said. "Being absent for a few days, getting some punishment, that is nothing to me."

There was no room on the American helicopters that came to pick up his battalion in Laos on March 6, so Sergeant Co clung to the skids of one craft.

"Each helicopter could have been the last one, so what choice was there for me?" he asked. "Only the madmen would stay and politely wait for the next helicopter."

During the last three days his battalion was in Laos, he said, 30 of the men were killed and 20 wounded. "Only about 100 men were still okay at the end out of 400," Sergeant Co said. "The North Vietnamese could have killed us all if they had wanted to do it."

A corporal in the marines who fought on Hill 547 in Laos on the night of March 22 said that many of his friends had killed themselves because they were wounded. No American helicopters could extract them because of heavy antiaircraft fire.

"The papers and the radio in Saigon kept on saying there was a Laos victory, I have learned now, but what a joke," Corporal Ti said. "We ran out like wounded dogs."

"The most heartbreaking thing," he continued, "was that we left behind our wounded friends. They lay there, crying, knowing the B-52 bombs would fall on them. They asked buddies to shoot them but none of us could bring himself to do that. So the wounded cried out for grenades, first one man, then another, then more."

"I could not bear it," he said. "We ran out at 8 P.M. and

about midnight we heard the bombs explode behind us. No more bodies! They all became dust. Some men who were wounded in the legs or arms tried to run out with us, but they could not make it."

As for the effect these experiences will have on the soldiers, a 38-year-old sergeant major who has seen combat with the infantry many times in the last 11 years is worried.

"I am afraid that we will have a lot of deserters," said the sergeant, who did not want to give his name. "When many of the men get back to the rear, and think back on what they have been through, and hear the other soldiers talk, then their fear will get worse.

"It can happen. I know this kind of thing all too well."

The New York Times, March 28, 1971

The Homecoming of Chris Mead

by Karl Fleming

CHRIS MEAD sat halfway back in the bus, staring vacantly out the mud-streaked window at the wintry Michigan country-side. The trees were black and bare. A patchy snow covered the ground. The only sounds were the whack-whack of the windshield wipers and the drowsy whine of the tires on wet pavement. Mead was wearing a brand-new Army uniform, with Sp/4 insignia on the sleeves. But the war was over for him now, and he was going home.

Mead is one of the more than 2 million U.S. military men who have served in Vietnam and returned, and, like many of them, he came back discouraged by what he had seen of war and uncertain of what he will make of peace. He had been discharged only the day before at Oakland, Calif. It took all day before he got to the last steel cage and drew $524 in discharge pay. "Is that it? Am I out now?" he asked. "That's it," the paymaster said. Mead started out, past a huge wall painting of Uncle Sam in tears. I'LL MISS YOU, it said. Mead gave the poster the finger.

That was his farewell. He had joined the Army with six classmates from Ovid-Elsie Consolidated High School near Owosso, Mich.; three are still in, two got medical discharges, one was killed in action. Mead himself took a lot of gun-fire—"I was dead for sure a couple of times." He saw trucks blown up, kids maimed, women killed, buddies bleeding and dying. Once he saw a Viet Cong running away on the stumps of his shot-away legs. And now he was out, and no one said good-by or good luck. There was just the "Certificate of Appreciation" with President Nixon's facsimile signature. "I extend to you my personal thanks and the sincere appreciation of a grateful nation," it said. "You have helped maintain the security of the nation during a critical time in its history."

Only coming home, you'd never know it. Elsie, Mich., is just the sort of Middle American town that used to welcome its boys noisily home from the wars. But when Mead's bus pulled into the dingy Indian Trails Bus Depot in nearby Owosso in a light snow, the only one there to meet him was his kid brother Greg, 19. They bear-hugged. "You've gotten so big, man," Chris said. "You're bigger than I am."

They got into the family car, a green 1967 Chrysler. Mead drove, out of town and across the tracks and past big red barns and herds of Holsteins and crossroads stores with Smith-Douglass Fertilizer signs. They didn't talk about the war at all. "Check it out: I'm 21 now," Mead said; he had turned 21 three days before his discharge. He asked about his bedroom, his record collection, his clothes. And girls. "I've got to scope me out a really neat chick. One I can rap with, not one who just wants to have babies. How's the girl situation?" Greg grinned and said, "They're still around."

And then they were home. A sign on the side of the barn said Orlo Mead & Sons, and an electric Christmas star glowed on top. "Mom turned on the light to let the neighbors know you're home," Greg said.

Mead pulled into the icy driveway. The whole family tumbled out the side door to greet him: his parents and Vicki, 14, Neil, 11, and Brad, 7. Mrs. Mead was having a new $300 linoleum-tile floor put down in the kitchen and was apologetic about the homecoming dinner. She had managed pork chops and gravy, mashed potatoes, green peas and pumpkin pie and a store-bought birthday cake. But Mead's ulcer was bothering him. "Wow, I wish I could eat," he said. "I'm not even interested in food any more."

They sat around the table and exchanged news, and finally they had to talk about the war. It came up because Mrs. Mead was worried about what Greg should do when he has to go into the service. "Join the Navy," Mead said flatly. "If you go to 'Nam you'll be a grunt for sure. If you can get out of it, don't go. You don't want to go over there and get yourself blown away. All of it is bad and scary. One minute you're talking to a buddy and the next you're out policing him up."

"We could have cleaned up this mess a long time ago," his

dad said, "if we would go all-out. I don't understand fighting and not going all-out to win. It's nothing but a big political war."

"It's not worth anybody getting killed for," said Mead. "It's for nothing. The people over there don't care. They're ingrates to the max. The Arvins on the Red Ball Highway sit on their asses on the bridges and the GI's have to go in and get theirs blown away," Mead said. "All the people are interested in is money. Little kids were selling us our own soda pop for 90 cents a bottle. I know what I was fighting for: nothing."

They talked some more, the children gawking saucer-eyed at Mead, till finally he blinked and exclaimed: "Goddam! I can hardly believe it. I'm really home. It seems like it was a long, bad dream." The kids drifted upstairs to bed, and Mead got out his suitcase. His combat boots were tied to the handle. He opened the bag and started taking out his souvenirs.

One was a water pipe, ornately carved in brass and wood. His father and mother looked at each other.

"Is that for smoking marijuana?" Mrs. Mead asked.

There was a long pause. Then Mead said, "Yeah."

"I don't believe in that," his dad said.

Mead took the suitcase upstairs. There was a homemade "Welcome Home, Chris" sign with a peace symbol on his door. Stuck on the bedroom walls were old Steppenwolf and Beatles album covers and a flower he'd drawn as a child. His longbow was standing in the corner beside the ancient TV set.

Kid stuff. Mead had gone away a boy and come back a man, and now he had to start thinking about work in an economy grown suddenly inhospitable to its homecoming young. The Meads have 160 acres and used to be dairy farmers. But the profit went out of it, so they sold the cows, and now Mead's father commutes 40 miles to Flint every day to work as an electrician. Mead thought of working there too, and when he came back downstairs he asked about the chances of getting a job. But his father shook his head. "It doesn't look good at all."

Mead didn't want to worry about it—not right away. He asked for the car.

"Sure," his father grinned. "Where you going? Terrorizing?"

"A lot of girls have been asking about you," his mother said.

He and Greg drove to the outskirts of Owosso, had a couple of coffees at the Tri-Ami Bowl, then moved on and parked at the Elias Big Boy coffeeshop. Local kids kept circling the block in cars. "Hey, what's happening?" they yelled at each other. Nothing was happening, and the Meads went home to bed.

He slept late next morning, then headed back into Owosso to buy some clothes. He handled the car easily—he drove a water truck and sometimes an amphibious "duck" in Vietnam—and on the way he said, "Man, I can't wait to get some wheels. Everybody's born with something they can do well. I like to drive." But his $524 coming-out pay wasn't enough. He spent $84 of it on clothes at the Yankee Giant Plaza and $291 on a Panasonic eight-track stereo-radio and a dozen cartridges—the Grand Funk Railroad, Jethro Tull, Paul McCartney, The Who, The Moody Blues. "Goddam," he said. "Now I'll have to go to work right away to get some wheels. But I have to have music to get my head back where it was. I want some peace of mind. No hassles, no responsibilities. I'm tired of thinking about 'Nam."

That afternoon, Mead drove back to Elsie (population: 1,045). Main Street was dead, and he didn't know whether he could settle in again. "I hate to put it this way," he said, "but I want to be some place where there's a chance I might get into trouble—know what I mean?" There isn't much trouble to get into in Elsie. He bought a bottle of Cold Duck wine for $3.11; then he bumped into a couple of old school pals and they talked awhile. One of them, Phillip Saxton, had a job at Vaughn Seed Co. Mead asked about work there. Saxton didn't think they were hiring. So Mead said maybe he would try applying at the Elsie Door and Specialty. And do something about the war. "*Something's* got to be done, man. You just can't sit around with all this stuff going on."

Next day—the third day back—he just hung around home. His mother, at his request, hadn't told anybody except family that he was back. "I don't want nobody making a big deal out of it," he said. "The people who would notice me are the ones I don't want to have anything to do with—the gung-ho types who're for the war. Anyway, I'm not proud of what I did over there. I'm sorry. I don't even want anybody to know I was there. It's lousy and there's no sense in it. I wish I hadn't even gone. Maybe I should have gone to Canada or broke a leg or something."

Newsweek, March 29, 1971

Who Wants To Be the Last American Killed in Vietnam?

by Donald Kirk

MILITARY REGION ONE.
South Vietnam.
IF THERE is any war, that is, an American war, involving American troops and costing American lives, it is mainly here in Military Region One, once known as "I Corps," whose mountains and rice fields have absorbed more American blood in the past six years than South Vietnam's other three regions combined.

"We lost 18 men in our company last month to booby traps," says a platoon sergeant encamped on one of the outcroppings of Charlie Ridge, a forbidding dark rise on the skyline some 10 miles west of here. "All we get out of it was killing two dinks in an ambush." Just two nights before I spoke with the sergeant, down the same ridge, he and his men heard the whine of Soviet-made 122-millimeter rockets whistling overhead—aimed not at them but at a South Vietnamese firebase in the lowlands. "They was shootin' from the rocket belt behind us," says one of the G.I.'s, pulling out his canteen during a break on a patrol through thick underbrush toward a small stream hidden at the base of the slope. "There was nothin' we could do but call in artillery. That was some hilarious fight, listening to them rounds goin' back and forth above us."

The morning after the rocket attack half a dozen of the G.I.'s were sitting around an old shellhole eating C-rations when one of them tripped a hidden wire, setting off a booby trap concealed in the hole. Three men were wounded—two of them partially blinded, one with possible brain damage. "There all night and nothing happens," says a rifleman, recounting the incident as we pause by the stream. "Sit here

217

and watch a buddy get blown away. The whole thing's point-less. We'll never win."

It is, in reality, a desultory kind of struggle, punctuated by occasional explosions and tragedy, for the last Americans in combat in Vietnam. It is a limbo between victory and defeat, a period of lull before the North Vietnamese again seriously challenge allied control over the coastal plain, as they did for the last time in the Tet, May and September offensives of 1968. For the average "grunt," or infantryman, the war is not so much a test of strength under pressure, as it often was a few years ago, as a daily hassle to avoid patrols, avoid the enemy, avoid contact—keep out of trouble and not be "the last American killed in Vietnam."

"I mean, what does it accomplish—what does it gain," asks our forward observer, a captain who attended Officer Candidates' School after having graduated from the University of Southern California in Los Angeles. "Even if we kill 500 dinks, to me it's not worth it." The F.O. calls in artillery strikes on suspected targets in the nearby hills, but he does so with notable lack of relish. "I just saw three dinks down in that rice field," he says. "One of them was carrying a shiny tube. They were probably V.C., but maybe they were civilians with an old shell. I don't think it's right to look for some excuse for shooting at them." Although the F.O. is a captain, he articulates the views of the G.I.'s with whom I go on patrol down the ridge.

"The dinks are just playin' with us, waitin' for us to go home, then they'll beat the —— out of the ARVN [Army of the Republic of Vietnam]," says the rifleman in front of me, reiterating a view held by many of his superiors. "It's a lifer's playground, a chance for the generals to test their strategies," the G.I. enlarges, in thick Georgian tones, as we scramble up from the stream bed—only to stop again a minute later so our "pigman" can test-fire his machine-gun. "Git them cows down there," another G.I. yells, grinning while the M-60 spews a torrent of bullets into the bushes in front of us. The cows, grazing on a rise half a mile away, amble off at the urging of a boy who hears the shots. A couple of the grunts idly curse all the "lifers"—the C.O., the N.C.O.'s, anyone vaguely responsible for issuing them orders and threats. "If the lifers don't get you," says one, explaining why we don't radio a false location and rest instead of walk, "then the V.C. will."

Their chatter is hardly unique. In a month visiting units in the field and rear areas around Military Region One, I found literally no young G.I.'s in favor of the war, none who didn't think we should "get out," few who didn't hate the "lifers" almost as much as the "dinks"—a term sometimes used to describe ARVN as well as enemy forces. For all the complaints, though, cases of refusal to fight or go to the field are quite rare—perhaps an average of two or three per battalion per month. Virtually every G.I. in the bush theoretically yearns for a softer job somewhere else, but almost all of them admit that time slips by faster here, that "lifers don't hassle you so much" over petty matters of haircut and dress, that drugs are less available and duty not so dull as in the rear.

Nor are there more than slim odds these days that a combat G.I. will die despite the danger of mines set and re-set daily by V.C. sympathizers—often farmers or small boys selling PX cokes by the road at 50 cents a can. Casualty figures in July receded to the lowest ebb in six years, 11 killed one week, 29 another, about 70 for the month—the first since 1965 in which the number of American "K.I.A.'s" (killed in action) was below 100. (The U.S. command now emphasizes low American casualties with the same enthusiasm that it once accorded such statistics as enemy "body counts." At a briefing in the middle of August, for instance, a military spokesman proudly disclosed a weekly average of 19 American K.I.A.'s for the previous two and a half months, "exactly half the average of 38 K.I.A.'s for the year to date." These figures, he noted happily, compared with an average of 81 killed each week of last year.) Specifically ordered to hold down casualties, commanders rarely invade traditional enemy base areas among shadowy crags and valleys to the west—and carefully disengage from battles in the lowlands if heavy losses seem inevitable or even conceivable.

Only occasional incidents or intelligence reports still remind G.I.'s—and commanders—that "a war's going on here, y'know." On the "Arizona Territory," a shell-pocked stretch of abandoned rice fields southwest of Danang, Vietcong guerrillas intermittently fire on armored personnel carriers and tanks rumbling through land that Marines failed to secure in six years before the last of them pulled out of here several months ago. One night at the end of August, for instance, the V.C. killed five and wounded seven G.I.'s sitting behind their vehicles in a circular night defensive position. Commanders put all 70,000 U.S. troops remaining in Military Region One on special alert in anticipation of small-scale attacks by North Vietnamese regulars and local terrorists bent on exploiting Vietnam's unending political problems.

But the American military posture remains basically defensive and low-keyed. No more than 8,000 U.S. troops are "beating the bush" in Military Region One these days—and they rarely pursue the enemy beyond the first few ridgelines.

"There's no longer that intense aggressiveness," laments Lieut. Col. Lee Roberts, who enlisted in 1948 at the age of 19, attended O.C.S. after having been turned down for West Point—and now commands a battalion from a mountain firebase 20 miles southwest of Danang. "Instead of going on lengthy sweeps, our companies set up defensive positions from which they send out patrols," he explains, sipping coffee from a paper cup in front of his sandbagged command bunker, overlooking an undulating velvet-green valley. "If they get into contact," he says, surveying his A.O.—area of operations—through baleful, slate-gray eyes, "they back off and call in air and artillery."

"What we're performing is defense-in-depth," summarizes the information officer at the headquarters of the Americal division, which totals some 20,000 troops south and west of Danang, including those patrolling Charlie Ridge and the Arizona territory. "We're interdicting enemy supply routes and infiltration of troops to the lowlands." Off-duty, in the officers' club behind the headquarters, built on rolling sand dunes at Chulai, for which marines fought bunker to bunker in 1965, a couple of R.O.T.C. lieutenants joke about the Americal's notorious past. First there was exposure of the massacres at Mylai, a few miles to the south, followed by the case of a former brigade commander charged with mowing down civilians from his helicopter and, late last year, revelation of the use of a chemical defoliant capable of inducing cancer. Then, in June, the commanding general was relieved in the aftermath of an attack on a firebase in which 33 G.I.'s were killed.

"I'm afraid to tell anyone back in the world I'm with the Americal," says one of the lieutenants, laughing sardonically. "No one has much pride in the division. That's one reason morale is so bad."

Despite the image, however, the mission of the Americal—and the attitude of its men—is no different from those of the only other full-strength U.S. division in Vietnam, the 101st Airborne, based at Camp Eagle, midway between Danang and the DMZ. Just as the Americal defends Danang and the coast to the south, so the 101st patrols the lowlands and hills beyond the one-time imperial capital of Hue, for political and cultural reasons South Vietnam's most important city after Saigon. Once regarded as the toughest of U.S. divisions, the 101st now appears as wary of combat, as reluctant to fight, as lax in discipline, as the Americal. Commanders proudly evoke its traditional nickname "Screaming Eagles," but G.I.'s these days prefer to call it, not without a certain touch of reverse pride, "the one-oh-*worst*."

"I have seen the Screaming Eagles in action—in the jungles and air and assisting the people of northern Military Region One—and can testify that the outstanding reputation enjoyed by the 101st is completely justified," brags the division commander, Maj. Gen. Thomas M. Tarpley, somewhat defensively, perhaps, in a letter on the inside front cover of the division's slick-paper color magazine, Rendezvous With Destiny. The cover itself, however, testifies to the war-weariness of the men whom Tarpley tries to praise. In a water-color sketch of defoliated trees etched against glowering gray clouds, three G.I.'s are standing on a truck, reaching toward a crane helicopter hovering above them. Black peace symbols adorn drab army-green cannisters containing 155-millimeter artillery shells, and the twisted limbs of three leafless trees form the initials F.T.A., —— the Army.

Already a legend around the 101st, the cover evokes the mood of the grunts whom I accompany on a couple of patrols by a stream along which the V.C. slip men and supplies into the lowlands. The platoon leader is a gung-ho career soldier, a first lieutenant out of O.C.S., airborne, ranger and jungle schools, who inwardly regrets he's arrived in Vietnam a couple of years too late for "the real war." He has been here only three weeks, and he wants to play by the rules. Maybe, if he succeeds, there's still enough time for him to get a regular—as opposed to a reserve—commission, a promotion to captain and command of a company in the field, if not exactly in full-fledged combat.

"Shoot to capture, not to kill," the lieutenant, an athletic, lifeguard type with close-cropped hair and finely chiseled features that remind me of a carving of a Roman centurion, earnestly abjures his troops, in an upstate New York twang. The men, saddled up for a RIF (reconnaissance in force) through abandoned rice fields and one-time hamlets, erased except for occasional cement foundations by air and artillery strikes, grin and snicker. "I shoot for K.I.A.'s, not P.O.W.'s," retorts Specialist 4 Robert Latchaw, a wiry Pole from South River, N.J., laughing at the lieutenant's naiveté. "Whaddya want us to do, shoot an ear off?" jibes Doc, the medic. The lieutenant, unfazed, insists he's following policy set down by "higher higher" headquarters. "We're not after body counts anymore," he says. "We'd prefer information. K.I.A.'s don't talk." With that, we sally forth through tall grass toward a stream near which our platoon sergeant, remaining behind with a squad, swears he saw "two dinks running that way."

It is clear to everyone but the lieutenant, though, that we're not seriously pursuing "the dinks," who were fleeing a fight with some South Vietnamese near the ruins of an old French fort, first booby-trapped by the V.C. and then leveled by American bombs, dropped to set off the booby traps. "Just walkin' around don't accomplish nothin'," says Latchaw, a church-going Catholic with a wife "back in the world" who sends him weekly packages of "world food," good canned stuff to supplement the boring, bland diet of C-rations. "I been here nine months, and I ain't been in no firefight yet. Most I did was spend 100 days in the mountains during the monsoon without changing my clothes once." We are, by this time, beside the stream, filling canteens, after an hour-long stroll broken by frequent halts for rest and talk. If there are any V.C. in the area, they are as eager to keep out of our way as we are to keep out of theirs.

All of us, that is, except for the lieutenant: next morning, around 10, he leads another RIF toward the stream, this time aiming for the "draw," the ravine down which the water tumbles from the last ridgeline into the lowlands. It seems like another easy walk in the sun before we begin, but our point man is still hacking away with his machete several hours later. (Murmurs from the grunts behind me: "I want to be back in Kentucky rabbit-huntin'." "When I get back to the world I don't even care if I see another forest. I'm stayin' in the city.") The lieutenant sends a couple of riflemen—a bull-necked Chicano named Quito and the Kentuckian—into the bush in hopes of finding an easier route. They return a few minutes later. "Gettin' too theek," says Quito. "Might see some dinks we don't want to see." We plunge straight ahead, find a trickle of flowing water, fill canteens, keep going another hour until we stumble on the same stream we reached, lower down, on yesterday's patrol. Some of the men flop in, lying on their backs in the fast-running water, cleansing bodies, fatigues and socks. We would be easy marks for an ambush. No one is standing guard.

Across the stream we see clear signs of V.C. movement—little footpaths leading across open clearings. For the first time we spread apart, a routine precaution. Behind us rises the slope of the ridgeline, burned off by a fire ignited by one of the Delta Tangos—"Defensive Target" artillery rounds—called in by the lieutenant a couple of nights ago. We follow the path along the stream, wade in the water for a while, then emerge about where we'd been the day before. A couple of hundred yards from the bank a neat path cuts a straight line through the bush—the kind of trail along which guerrilla soldiers could run full-speed if necessary, dropping for cover at the sound of approaching helicopters.

"We're going to work this area really well," the lieutenant advises his men, who remain sullenly silent. "We're gonna set up ambush positions in here and set out a couple of claymore mines—get them as they fall back from fighting the ARVN." As soon as we return to our original position, the lieutenant announces his plan to our platoon sergeant, a hard-talking Midwesterner who's been with the unit only a couple of days, but knows how to handle eager young officers.

The sergeant reminds the lieutenant a resupply helicopter is about to arrive, that it'll take a while sorting out the stuff, burning off the waste. He says he's found a "beautiful N.D.P."—night defensive position—"over there by the trees." The lieutenant hesitates, wavers. He senses that his men, from the new sergeant on down, are against him. "We don't have enough men for an ambush," the sergeant argues. "We get into a fight, we'll get waxed." The lieutenant finally settles for setting a single claymore on the trail this side of the stream.

That night we hear the crackle of small arms from over near the ARVN positions, a mile or so away. Helicopters circle overhead, muttering machinegun fire, and artillery and mortar rounds thud across the fields. Next morning, the lieutenant is beside himself with anger and frustration. "Should have sent out that goddam ambush," he says, not looking at the sergeant. "Could have gotten them running away. Godammit, we gotta get moving. It's late already. This happens again, I'm gettin' everyone up at 5 o'clock."

It is 10:30 before the men are ready. Then the lieutenant gets more bad news, this time over the radio. The battalion commander, on a firebase a couple of miles away, is ordering the entire company in to guard the base perimeter. "Just routine rotation." In vain the lieutenant pleads that he needs "a couple more days to work the area by the stream." His men curse him silently. "Godammit, if no one was looking, I'd frag the sonuvabitch," says one of them.

The threat of a fragging—explosion of a fragmentation or hand grenade—in this case is probably not serious. The G.I. who makes it not only walked point the morning before but willingly went on patrol again in the evening to plant the mine. An Iowa farm boy, he criticizes the war on the grounds that "we're not fightin' it like we should." Since we failed to invade North Vietnam, H-bomb Hanoi and Haiphong and declare "free fire zones" of V.C. hamlets, he says "we oughta quit wastin' time and go home." Like most of the grunts in the field, he may lack motivation but he's not really bored—an intrinsic factor in turning casual threats into deeds.

It is mainly in the rear, among the troops whom the grunts disdainfully call the REMF's for Rear Echelon Mother ——, that talk of fragging, of hard drugs, of racial conflict, seems bitter, desperate, often dangerous. At the combat base at Quangtri, the last provincial capital below the DMZ, I walk into a dimly lit single-story barracks one afternoon hoping to find perhaps a couple of G.I.'s with whom I can talk—and count 16 of them reclined in the shadows of a lounge shielded by blankets and curtains hanging from the windows. "Welcome to the head hootch," says a thin, hollow-cheeked private first class of 18 or 20, waving me to a spot on the couch after I convince him I'm a reporter, not a criminal investigator. The G.I.'s proudly explain that their hootch is a meeting place for potheads from all over the base, but I don't smell any marijuana in the air. "How many of you smoke scag [heroin]," I ask. They all raise their hands.

Who are the heads in the hootch—and why have they "graduated" from pot to heroin? They are, for the most part, white, with 10 to 12 years of education, a few with records of juvenile delinquency or petty crime in civilian life. While some might not perform well under any circumstances, all of them seem hopelessly demoralized both by the war and by their immediate surroundings. "I was supposed to be a heavy-equipment operator but all I do is pick up beer cans," says one. "They haven't got anything for us to do," says another. "They just want to keep us busy." Several are aimless drifters, too strung out for work, awaiting courts-martial or undesirable discharges, demotions and restrictions. Many, if they report for duty at all, put in only a few hours a day before finding some excuse to return to the hootch—or else they just go back with no excuse at all.

It's far from clear whether the men are more at odds with their commanders and sergeants or the war in general. "They tell you to do something, then they yell at you for doing it," says the equipment operator. "They harass you about haircuts and beards and burn you for sleeping on guard when you've been working all day." Most of the complaints are petty, often unjustified, but they also suffer from the same sense of futility, of pointlessness, that affects thousands of other G.I.'s in the midst of withdrawal of American troops. "The gooks are winning this war," says one. "The ARVN are afraid to fight. They run away. The gooks can have the place when we leave."

While we are talking one of the heads slowly stirs a plate of "hard times," all but powerless marijuana seeds and stems. "It's what I got left," he says. "It's gettin' so hard to score marijuana around here, guys have to turn to scag"—which doesn't smell, comes in much smaller quantities and is easier to hide. Another G.I. idly tells a story, verified by his friends, of ordering more than 300 vials of heroin at $2 a vial from a Vietnamese "cowboy" on a motorcycle by the gate of the base. "I gave him $200 for a hundred and robbed the rest and ran," says the G.I. "He drove away grinning, and I knew I was the one that was ripped off. It was all salt and sodium acid." The next day the G.I. armed with his M-16, bought 200 vials from a trusted pusher in a nearby village. "I sell it here for $5 a vial," says the G.I., a personable, fair-haired Midwesterner who served six months of a five-year term "back in the world" before enlisting in the Army.

That night a couple of the G.I.'s—a black and a Chicano—invite me to a pot party at a helicopter hangar on the other side of the runway. The air in the little room in the back of the hangar is heavy with the sweet smell of "dew." A helicopter pilot tells me he's been "stoned ever since getting to Vietnam"—that he performs better that way but is "scared —— of scag." Beside him is a doctor, an army captain, silently smoking pot in a corncob pipe. Some of the helicopter crewmen pass freshly rolled cigarettes around. A couple of other G.I.'s stand lookout, glancing from time to time over the walls to see if M.P.'s are coming. One of the chopper pilots argues convincingly for legalization of pot—says it's not habit-forming, is no more harmful than beer. He doesn't know it, but several of the enlisted men in the room have laced their marijuana with heroin. Some of them plan to go to "the party after the party"—an all-night get-together in one of the perimeter bunkers for speed freaks, pill-poppers who get the pills by mail from home or buy them on the local market, often at ordinary pharmacies.

It is difficult to quantify the use of drugs in the rear. It is obvious though, that a relatively high proportion of the REMF's, perhaps 20 per cent, is on the hard stuff as opposed merely to marijuana, while only a marginal few indulge in the bush. ("We see a guy using it out here, we take care of him, or the C.O. sends him back to the rear," one of the men on Charlie Ridge tells me. "Otherwise he'll be high some time when we're under attack. You can't hardly walk if you're high all the time.") The use of drugs in base camps accounts for widespread thefts—and also is a major factor in fraggings. G.I.'s on drugs will steal almost anything, ranging from stereo sets to food from the mess hall, to sell in exchange for heroin, peddled by small boys and women, cowboys on Hondas, even South Vietnamese soldiers operating near Americans.

Addicts resort to fraggings—or threats and intimidation— whenever commanders order shakedown searches, restrict them to quarters or otherwise attempt seriously to cut down the flow. At each camp I visit there are tales of incidents in which G.I.'s have blown up orderly rooms, sometimes wounding or killing the wrong man, or have merely exploded grenades outside windows for shock effect. One of the favorite techniques is to set off a tear-gas cannister—a harmless antic that creates momentary chaos and serves a warning of more violence later. At the rear headquarters of one of the battalions of the 196th Brigade, on a road leading to Freedom Hill out- side Danang, the battalion's new executive officer, in the midst of a crusade against drugs, walks into his quarters one day and finds a grenade pin on his pillow—a symbol of what may happen to him if he keeps up his campaign.

"It's like war: you take chances," says the exec, Maj. John O'Brien, a bluff, outspoken man with a strong Massachusetts edge to his voice, who served 10 years in the enlisted ranks before attending O.C.S. The major, on his second tour in Vietnam, arrived here in June totally unprepared for the new mood among G.I.'s in the rear. He found heroin vials, empty, discarded around battalion headquarters, in the latrines, under barracks. At least 20 of more than 100 men assigned to his battalion "rear" were perpetually too high and too weak to perform. At the same time, a number of others were not only opposed to the use of drugs but willing to work with him to prevent it. "We had a couple of meetings just brain- storming," says O'Brien, who, unlike many career officers, seems capable of talking with young G.I.'s on an informal basis. "We were receptive to any ideas anyone wanted to offer. The situation was so desperate, we had to be open to everything." The result was a well-balanced combination of force and propaganda.

"As of this date I'm declaring war on drug abuse in this battalion," begins the mimeographed "Open Letter to All Drug Users," posted on bulletin boards around the battalion area. "I will seek out and find every drug user and pusher" in the battalion. The letter recounts what many of the G.I.'s already know—that the major, assisted by a special "drug squad" of half a dozen men, has already confiscated more than 100 vials filled with heroin. "Things are going to get a hell of a lot tighter before the problem is satisfactorily resolved," the letter promises. "There will be more shakedowns and inspections. The flow of traffic in and out of the compound is going to be dramatically reduced. My officers and senior N.C.O.'s are now authorized to conduct unannounced search of any man on this compound." The letter invites addicts to turn themselves in voluntarily to the army's amnesty program, under which they can spend several days in a special ward getting over the immediate physical effects of the habit—or else face prosecution and court-martial.

Major O'Brien has no real illusions, however, about the long-range efficacy of his program. He thinks he's drastically reduced the use of heroin in his own compound but points out a couple of cases in which addicts went through amnesty withdrawal, only to pick up the habit again a few days later. He doesn't like to talk about the grenade pin left on his pillow—fears that publicity might encourage a fragging—but points with a grin at a copy of his "open letter," scrawled with defiant notations. "Happiness is a Vial of Smack," says one of them. "Major O'Brien is a Smack Freak," says another. "Stay A Head." Perhaps over-optimistically, the major views the comments as a good sign. "It shows they're worried," he says. "At least I'm getting a response."

Major O'Brien's program, I discover, is the exception, not the rule. By far the majority of the commanders and executive officers whom I meet are simply not aware of the scope of the problem in their own units. They tend, in many cases, to rely on the word of their N.C.O.'s—most of whom are so conservative, not to mention so hooked on alcohol, as to distort their whole attitude toward the drug problem. Another complication is that officers and N.C.O.'s also must cope with racial conflict—protests against authority by young blacks who claim the army discriminates against them. Racial tension, like drugs, is of secondary importance in the field, but it threatens to explode in base camps where blacks have time to form their own Panther or antiwar "liberation" organizations—and chafe under petty harassment by lifers who often, in fact, do reveal instinctive, subconscious, if not explicit, forms of prejudice.

The racial question is so sensitive at Camp Baxter, on a road lined with military installations and Vietnamese refugee shanties near Marble Mountain, just south of Danang, that military officers don't want me on the base. Finally the camp commander, Col. Joseph Otto Meerboth, a graying West Pointer, agrees to let me talk to G.I.'s—but asks me to "come back tomorrow" when I show up for my appointment. As I am escorted toward the gate, he orders military policemen to seal off the post to intruders and search the barracks for half a dozen blacks, whom he's convinced are plotting a major racial disturbance. The next day, Colonel Meerboth explains that the blacks transferred four days ago to another base, returned without warning to pick up their possessions—and that one of them, at least, is "extremely dangerous."

"He's organized an extralegal confederacy," says the colonel, who admits having had little experience with either drug or racial problems before his assignment to Camp Baxter last fall. "The traditional method for rendering extralegal confederacies ineffective is to dismember them. Last night I brought in three of these men one by one, talked to them and told them they had to leave. They have been escorted elsewhere." Colonel Meerboth's decision, however, has not necessarily conquered the problem, characterized by intermittent demonstrations, a couple of killings, secret meetings and threats, spread over the past 8 or 10 months. At the service club, where he reluctantly permits me to interview G.I.'s, both blacks and whites criticize the transfer of troublemakers—and claim the one singled out by the colonel as the "ringleader" was actually instrumental in keeping the blacks from staging an armed, open revolt.

"A white man just don't understand the problem," says

Sgt. Clarence Chisholm, a graduate of the Tuskegee Institute who was drafted into the Army and works as a communications specialist. "Whenever you try to explain what's happening, you're branded as a 'militant.'" Chisholm, due to rotate home from Vietnam in a couple of days, charges the white officers and N.C.O.'s with practicing *de facto* segregation by recommending transfers mainly for blacks and leaving the camp, once 20 per cent black, almost entirely white. Some of the whites whom I meet agree with Chisholm's interpretation. "Our sergeant told me it's 'open season on blacks,'" says one of them. "The thing is this Colonel Meerboth cannot control this compound," says another, shouting excitedly in the middle of a circle of white soldiers who rush to the service club to talk to me when word gets around "there's a reporter there."

The G.I.'s charge all the "undesirables"—Black Panthers, drug addicts, whatever—were transferred to three or four nearby units reputed as dumping grounds for those not wanted elsewhere. The black "ringleader," I learn, has gone to Chulai, where he's now on permanent guard duty with the 277th Supply and Service Battalion. "I'm scared to go there," says another G.I., a Chicano, who's also been transferred to the 277th but has returned to Camp Baxter to pick up his stuff—and has somehow escaped the colonel's notice. "I hear they're *all* scag freaks down there." Intrigued, I go to Chulai the next day to meet the colonel's nemesis, Specialist 4 Loyle Green Jr., a tall, polite one-time student at Malcolm X University in Chicago, who once had visions of attending O.C.S. and making a career in the Army but has since decided "to help the brothers back in the world."

"They gave us five hours to pack our bags and leave after they notified us to our transfers," says Green, whom I meet in battalion headquarters. "We started to protest, but there was nothing we could do. We were railroaded to Chulai. The majority of the transfers were from minority groups—blacks, Spanish, Indians." Green attributes his transfer to his role in leading a sit-in outside Colonel Meerboth's headquarters in protest against the pretrial confinement of a black G.I. charged with assaulting a white. "It was so tense that a lot of blacks had gotten weapons," Green recalls, "but it was going to be a peaceful protest." The blacks, he notes with pride, simply turned their backs, got up and left when Colonel Meerboth emerged to order them to disperse. "Then there was the plan to destroy the entire compound," large enough for several thousand men, says Green. "I talked to a couple of the blacks and told them there was no way. We were already infiltrated by informants. We had the weapons, grenades to do it, but we would have lost in the end."

Green, acknowledged by Colonel Meerboth as a "persuasive speaker" and a "natural leader," appears less than militant in his outlook. Rather, he displays a sensitive judgment of power realities, an understanding of the limits to which the blacks can go—and determined, passive defiance of white authority. One factor that may have cast him as a sinister figure, in Meerboth's mind, was the funeral service in March for a black killed by a white in a brawl in the middle of the camp. "The blacks didn't want the chaplain to speak," says Green. "We had 200 or 300 there. We just turned our backs to the chaplain while he kept rattling on. We chanted, 'Black Power!' and put up a liberation flag—it had a black fist in the middle with the words 'Black Unity' in black letters on top, with a red background. The colonel stood there shaking his head. I told him we didn't want any American flag there. No blacks are American. I don't consider myself an American. I consider myself a black."

Green, like many of the black G.I.'s, wears the black-power band, made of black shoelaces, around his wrist. A black-power ring, in the form of a clenched fist, gleams from the index finger of his right hand. In defiance of authority, he is growing a full-scale beard, in addition to the regulation mustache. Ironically, in view of his antiwhite, antiwar outlook, he has never been disciplined, court-martialed or reduced in rank. He does not refuse to work, as do many blacks, particularly those on drugs. "I was a clerk-typist and a driver," he says. "It was challenging at first, but there wasn't enough to do"—an explanation, combined with opposition to the war, that may account for most of the Army's problems in the rear.

Unlike Green, however, black G.I.'s whom I meet at the 277th headquarters in Chulai seem not only depressed but openly, dangerously rebellious, possibly on the verge of armed revolt. One of them, interviewed in the presence of the battalion executive officer, tells me the blacks have a "secret arms cache" and plan to start using it "if things don't let up around here." The exec, Maj. Robert De Biasio, who has been trying to work with the blacks to find the causes of their problems, listens without interrupting. Later he tells me he doesn't think the black is kidding. "We've searched those barracks time and again and found nothing much," he says. "I think they have the arms underground somewhere. The only way we could find them would be to order everyone out of the barracks early in the morning, keep them under guard and go over the whole area with a mine detector."

Major De Biasio may face a tougher problem than does Major O'Brien at Freedom Hill. At the 661st, one of four companies in his battalion, G.I.'s estimate that 20 per cent of more than 100 troops don't work at all. The company commander, a pleasant, open man with eight years' enlisted time behind him before he went to O.C.S., may be afraid to impose tight discipline. He arrived several months ago—after the fragging of the quarters of his predecessor, who escaped unharmed but severely shaken. "We have some outstanding young men here," the C.O. blandly observes, venturing that only a dozen men in the entire battalion "use drugs on a somewhat irregular basis." In view of the C.O.'s easygoing tolerance, if not essential blindness to reality, it is not surprising that many of the troops whom I meet at the 661st focus their complaints on their sergeants rather than on the officers. Ironically, the most feared of the N.C.O.'s is a black, a 33-year-old Georgian known for his skill as a boxer and judo expert and nicknamed, as a token of both respect and dislike, "Karate Joe."

Karate is sipping beer with another N.C.O., a white sergeant from Tennessee, when I see him in his hootch. He's afraid to go to the enlisted men's club—doesn't want the men thinking he's trying to harass them off-duty. He's stopped counting the times he's found grenade pins on his pillow or been threatened verbally. "It doesn't even bother me any more," he says, but it is clear he is intensely unhappy. "My first tour here, we were all together," he says. "We worked as a team. I was doing the same thing then, running the ammo supply point, humping ammo into helicopters to take to the field. I never had no problems with the men. This time they don't really care no more."

Karate shouts and curses at the troops to get them to work, but he's beginning to feel he's engaged in a lost cause. "You discipline them so much and eventually the C.O. gets started on getting them 212's"—discharges on grounds of unsuitability or unfitness for service. "I just don't know what the answer is," he says, clenching his beer can. "It's not the same Army any more."

The only real answer, as far as *this* war is concerned, may be to keep withdrawing the men on an accelerated timetable and send only volunteers over here for the remaining advisory and rear-area jobs. Wherever I go in the northern provinces, whether in the field or in rear areas, I find the problem of motivation so overwhelming as to defy rational "solutions" and "programs" other than withdrawal. Below Charlie Ridge, on the Arizona Territory, I talk with a young captain on his first tour. He is a West Point graduate, in command of a troop of armored personnel carriers—an ideal position for a career-minded military man. He has been here only one week, but already he is filled with doubts and questions.

"They train you, send you to schools," says the captain, as we begin a bumpy ride through fields planted with mines and booby traps, "but nobody's prepared to see a guy killed or wounded. I had the most sobering experience of my life yesterday—I saw one of my men wounded with shrapnel. He's the first guy I've ever seen wounded. Once we've decided to get out, and then keep fighting, it seems kind of worthless. Nobody wants to be the last guy to die in Vietnam." That night, after the A.P.C.'s—or "tracks"—have formed a defensive circle by a small river, a lone guerrilla fires an AK-47 rifle from a couple hundred meters in front of us, sending bright red tracers over our position. The G.I.'s leap onto the tracks, answering with machine guns and M-16's. Helicopter gunships arrive, spraying the bushes with bullets. It is an eerie late show, played against the black backdrop of the sky and mountains, and it lasts for an hour.

"They got some nerve opening up against all our firepower like that," says one of the G.I.'s as the guns fall silent and we stretch out to sleep on cots unfolded behind our track. "Far as I'm concerned, they can have this whole country. There ain't no reason for us bein' here. We was fightin' to win, that'd be one thing, but we're just wastin' time." It is a typical G.I. commentary—one I hear countless times around Military Region One—at the butt end of a bad war.

The New York Times Magazine, September 19, 1971

Portrait of an Aging Despot

by Tom Buckley

"TAKE a case of beer with you," said the man who arranged the appointment. "He'll appreciate it." I thought I was being kidded, but I climbed the stairs to the third floor of the Defense Ministry with a case of Budweiser—$2.40 at the Post Exchange—on my shoulder. As I set it down in his office, Maj. Gen. Nguyen Ngoc Loan rose awkwardly on his braced leg to shake hands. He looked at me closely. At last he said, "I remember you," with a note of triumph in his voice. His eyes rolled away from me. It was only ten-thirty in the morning, but on his desk, which was clear otherwise, there was an empty bottle of Vietnamese "33" beer (so he would appreciate the Budweiser after all) and an empty glass. It was a small office at the end of a corridor, undecorated and barely furnished. Instead of a combination-lock filing cabinet for classified documents, there was a small refrigerator, in which an orderly stacked the Budweiser to chill.

Loan (say "low-ahn") had been promoted to permanent two-star rank only a few days earlier. He shrugged off my congratulations. "It is a joke," he said. "I have no troops and no duties. I am in charge of long-range planning, maybe for the next war. I ask to retire but they do not permit me to retire, so they give me two stars and a few more piasters. I can live on my salary, my wife does not complain, but I could get a good job in business. I could earn twice as much. After all, I took a management course at MIT." He pulled on his cigarette, and his laugh—almost a giggle—was broken up by a hacking cough.

It had been different the last time I had seen him, in March 1968. Loan was then the commander of the national police. From behind the walls of his headquarters compound, a sinister place that few Vietnamese approached if they could avoid it, he commanded 70,000 men—the police, the special branch, the paramilitary battalions of the Police Field Force, an army of spies and informers. His powers were those of life and death, and at his command tens of thousands of persons were imprisoned in the tiger cages of Conson Island and elsewhere; tortured in the dreaded provincial interrogation centers; were assassinated, executed, or simply not heard from again.

But even then, two of the three events that were to lead to his fall from power had already taken place. His friend and fellow Air Force pilot, Nguyen Cao Ky, had been induced to relinquish the premiership and run for the Vice-Presidency while Gen. Nguyen Van Thieu ran for the Presidency. Then in February 1968, during the Tet fighting, Loan had the misfortune to be photographed shooting a bound and helpless Vietcong prisoner in the head with his revolver. Loan might conceivably have escaped the consequences of these two events, but that May, when Saigon was attacked for the second time, he became, as far as I can tell, the only South Vietnamese general to be wounded in ground combat. His right leg was shattered by machine-gun bullets as he led an attack against a guerrilla unit. Thieu took the opportunity to replace him with one of his own men.

Loan was sent to Australia for treatment, but the photographs and television films of the shooting had made him notorious. He seemed to epitomize all that was vicious and cowardly about the war in general and the South Vietnamese forces in particular, and the public outcry forced him to leave. He was taken to the Walter Reed Army Hospital in Washington. The leg was saved, finally, but it was little more than a stick. Long after his recuperation, while Thieu consolidated his power, Loan and his family lived in virtual exile, in a house in Alexandria, Virginia, closely watched by the Central Intelligence Agency. When at last he received permission to return to Saigon, it was to a meaningless assignment and an empty office.

I first met Loan during the summer of 1967. The occasion was the graduation of a class of police recruits at Loan's headquarters. I had been invited to attend by the senior American public-safety adviser. He was a retired captain of the New York

State Police, an amiable enough fellow, particularly in comparison with some of his subordinates, among whom were old-time members of colonial police forces in Malaya, Burma, the Dutch East Indies, and a large number of agate-eyed former Deep South sheriffs and deputies, but his talents clearly would have been better employed as a supervisor of bank guards.

Loan was seated not far from me under a canopy made from an orange-and-white cargo parachute. He was not prepossessing. His forehead sloped and so did his chin, he was losing his hair, his eyes goggled, his teeth were bad, and he was skinny and stoop-shouldered. Senior officers, both Vietnamese and American, invariably wore immaculately starched combat fatigues and mirror-polished boots, no matter how deskbound they were, and set their faces in chin-back frowns to disguise the vast echoing hollows under their caps. Loan, by contrast, wore flopping sandals and the short-sleeved white shirt and baggy gray cotton trousers of the ordinary policeman. His homely face was alive with intelligence. Throughout the long ceremony he drank cognac and soda and joked with his subordinates, laughing so hard on occasion that his feet beat a tattoo on the ground as a reflex of his spasms. It was as though Loan were commenting on something everyone knew, that Vietnamese families paid heavily to have their sons accepted as police recruits, since it was generally a much safer job than the infantry and in time the opportunities were considerable for augmenting the small salary with all sorts of graft, notably heavy bribes from draft dodgers.

When the last medal for marksmanship and interrogation technique had been distributed, a buffet was served. The American press crowded around Loan. He seemed to enjoy the verbal sparring and he spoke English well, although he slurred his words—not just because of his drinking, I think, but because he didn't relish the taste of English vowels and consonants on his tongue. For the most part he dodged the questions, but at one point he said something rather elegant, although not, as things worked out, very accurate. "As long as Ky remains in power I will remain in power," he said, "and as long as I remain in power Ky will remain in power."

Between the election and the heavy skirmishing along the

demilitarized zone it was a busy summer. I did not see Loan again until early October. The committee on elections of the National Assembly had recommended that because of widespread cheating, the victory of Thieu and Ky should be invalidated. While the full Assembly was voting on the question, Loan slouched in a chair in a box overlooking the stage of the old opera house in Saigon where the Assembly met, his cap pushed back on his head, drinking beer and absentmindedly spinning the chambers of his revolver, a snub-nosed .38-caliber Smith & Wesson "Airweight." The committee's recommendation was rejected.

After weeks of trying I was able to arrange an appointment with Loan in early December of 1967. It was a time when American optimism about the course of the war was reaching a zenith of fatuity. General Westmoreland had gone to Washington to inform Congress that the other side was no longer capable of launching major offensive operations. Army units were pursuing the guerrillas near the Cambodian border, and the Marines had just reoccupied Khesanh in force. On New Year's Eve a group of bright young attachés at the American Embassy, calling themselves collectively "the Flower People," a term that was fresh and bright then, gave a "Light at the End of the Tunnel" costume party.

With its ten-foot concrete walls, guard towers, rusting rolls of concertina barbed wire and death's-head signs warning of mines, the exterior of Loan's compound proved to be more fearsome than the inside. At least there were no gibbets, whipping posts, or freshly dug graves. His office was on the second floor of a yellow stucco house shaded by trees that probably had been the residence of the commander when it was a regimental garrison for the French cavalry. When I entered the office, through padded double doors, Loan was reading dossiers. For fifteen minutes he did not look up. When at last he signaled me to sit on the chair in front of his desk, and ordered drinks, I asked him to tell me something about his early life. He said he had been born in Hué, the old imperial capital, in 1930, one of a family of eleven children. His father, he said, had been an engineer on the highways and railroads. It occurred to me that his status was probably sub-professional, since the French seldom permitted a Vietnamese to go higher. Nevertheless, the family must have been relatively well off as part of the small middle class created by the French, but distinct from and socially inferior to the traditional mandarin and landowning classes.

In 1951, while Loan was studying pharmacy at the University of Hué, the French became belatedly convinced after five years of war that victory or even the avoidance of eventual defeat was impossible without the formation of a Vietnamese national army. Until then the French force had been dominantly composed of troops from metropolitan France, the Foreign Legion, and colonial units from North Africa and Senegal. The 70,000 Vietnamese volunteers were formed in separate battalions, officered by Frenchmen, and were assigned mainly to defensive operations, as they were to be fifteen years later by the Americans.

Conscription was introduced, and for the first time more than a token number of Vietnamese were trained as officers. It was at this point that Loan, whose sympathies were dictated by his family's status, volunteered for officer training. Others of his generation made a different decision, fleeing into the jungle to join the Vietminh. Like many other senior Vietnamese officers I have spoken to, Loan told me that he had served briefly with the guerrillas while still a schoolboy but quit when he learned that they were Communists and not just simple nationalists fighting for Vietnamese freedom. It's a story I'm dubious about.

"At that time they didn't say a word about it," Loan said. "I was a Vietminh cadre from the time I am fourteen until nineteen, but all they say is just to fight against the Japanese, the Chinese, the French imperialists."

Loan was graduated at the top of his class, which included Ky, served briefly in the Delta, and was sent to what was then French Morocco for flight training. He also studied for a while at St. Cyr, the West Point of France. By the time he returned home, in 1955, the jungle was closing in over the wreckage of Dienbienphu, the French had signed the Geneva accords, and the new rump government of South Vietnam, headed by Ngo Dinh Diem, was being established by the United States.

The national army numbered 300,000 men at the time of
the French collapse, but never became an effective fighting
force. In *Vietnam: A Dragon Embattled*, Joseph Buttinger
states, quite accurately, "They were poorly trained and
equipped, but the major deficiency then and for a long time
to come was a lack of competent officers: The best elements
of the Vietnamese educated middle class had no desire to
serve in an army created to fight, still under French overall
direction, for a regime they despised and against people who,
even if led by Communists, were still known to be fighting
primarily for national independence."

It was these officers who formed the nucleus of Diem's
armed forces and hold all the senior positions today, and the
handicaps they began with have never been overcome. They
were recruited reluctantly, trained indifferently, patronized
and snubbed first by the French and then by the Americans
and throughout by the social and intellectual elite of their own
country, who reflected the traditional view in the Orient that
military men are down near the last rung on the social ladder.
And in the eleven years of the second Indochina war little has
happened to improve their sense of self-esteem.

The Vietnamese Air Force probably did not have so pronounced an inferiority complex as the other services, mainly
because the Vietcong did not have any airplanes—nothing
more, in fact, until recently, than a few machine guns to challenge the old propeller-driven Skyraiders supplied by the
United States. As Loan rose slowly in rank—he was promoted
to major only after the fall of Diem—he did less flying and
more staff work. He was sent to the United States for further
training and gradually emerged as an intelligence and security
specialist.

A Vietnamese who knew Loan in those days describes a
figure less flamboyant than the style set by Ky, a withdrawn,
seemingly rather timid young man who drank sparingly, did
not have a mistress, and whose only vice was a fondness for
the poker games played in an upstairs room over Brodard's
Café.

The Vietnamese Air Force had a brief moment of glory in
the spring of 1965. It flew the first two bombing raids against

North Vietnam. Ky, the commander of the Air Force, led the attack and Loan flew as his wingman. The raids were mainly symbolic. The Skyraiders didn't go very far north of the Benhai River; and because they were clearly no match for North Vietnamese missiles, radar-directed heavy flak guns, and MiG interceptors, they were restricted to operations in South Vietnam thereafter. It was not until 1968 that the Vietnamese Air Force received even a token number of jets, and these were not suitable for operations against the North either.

("You tied our hands," Loan said when I went back to see him. "You wanted to win the war all by yourselves." What else could he say? Moreover, it seems incontestably true that until it was too late the American command *had* decided to win the war with American troops and let the Vietnamese pick up the pieces.)

In June 1965, only a few months after the raids, Ky emerged as the leader of the military junta after two years of revolving-door governments. His elevation to power occurred just as American combat troops were beginning to arrive, and their presence provided an essentially false sense of stability. Older generals were shuffled off into exile or retirement. Loan was promoted to colonel and appointed director of military intelligence and security. A year later he was given command of the national police. He was Ky's most trusted confidant and, according to many observers, second only to him in power.

The Tet attacks began in the north and center of Vietnam early in the morning of January 30, 1968. Saigon and the Delta were hit twenty-four hours later. In the absence of Thieu, who was spending the holidays at his villa in Mytho, his wife's home city, Ky and Loan took charge of the defenses of the capital.

On the afternoon of February 1 there was a skirmish in the vicinity of the Anquang Pagoda, the headquarters of the "militant" wing of the Buddhist church, which was agitating for a negotiated peace with the Vietcong. During the course of the fighting a captive was brought to Loan, who stood with his aides perhaps a half block away. Without a word, Loan snapped away his cigarette and drew his revolver. He took a marksman's stance, his right arm extended, and, at a distance of perhaps three feet, put a single bullet into the side of the prisoner's head.

In the heat of his rage, Loan had ignored the fact that Eddie Adams, the ace photographer of the Associated Press, and an NBC camera crew were focused on him. He glared at them after the shooting and it seemed certain he would order their film seized, but, inexplicably, he did not. Within hours Adams' picture sequence was being transmitted around the world. The next night the film was shown on the Huntley-Brinkley television news.

The two minutes of air time swept by, the battle receded, but the image remains. Loan, booted, armored with a flak vest, is a symbol of implacable savagery. The prisoner, smaller, frail, helpless, his hands invisible, wired together behind his back, wears only a ragged shirt and shorts. His face is distorted, pushed to one side by the impact of the bullet in his brain, his hair stands up, his mouth opens in what might be a final cry.

That was, I think, the turning point, the moment when the American public turned against the war. The Tet offensive destroyed confidence in the judgment of the men who were directing it; the murder committed by Loan sealed its moral bankruptcy. At the same time there rose to the surface a grudging admiration for the courage of an enemy that had fought for so long without a single airplane, helicopter, tank, or artillery piece against the most powerful nation in the world and mercenaries hired from all over Asia.

There was a fine irony in all this. The prisoner was identified, accurately probably, as the commander of a Vietcong sapper unit. He was said to have had a revolver in his possession when he was captured and to have used it to kill a policeman. Unlike the main force battalions that invaded Saigon, which wore khaki uniforms, and the sappers who penetrated the United States Embassy, who wore red armbands, the prisoner had no similar identification. As a practical matter, his end was probably merciful, since he escaped the gruesome torture that would have almost certainly been a prelude to his death in captivity.

The killing that so shocked the United States had no similar impact in Vietnam. Few Vietnamese were even aware of it, and if they were, they could understand a certain appropriateness in Loan's action. The Vietcong frequently assassinated government officials, although giving these murders at least a semblance of legality by first convicting the victim of a capital crime in absentia in a revolutionary court and leaving a death warrant with the body. From time to time the Vietcong have carried out multiple murders. One I recall was inflicted on a village of Montagnards who had been working for the government. In Hué during the Tet fighting many hundreds of government officials, sympathizers, and members of their families were massacred. By and large, though, I think far more murders and atrocities were committed by the Allied side. For one thing, they had the firepower and mobility to strike at Vietcong villages. For another, they had the more pressing need for information about the enemy, which inevitably leads to torture and worse.

I next saw Loan a month or so after the killing, when I arranged to go on a night patrol of the city with him. The Vietcong offensive had receded but skirmishes still took place on the outskirts of the city. A "second wave" attack was anticipated, however, and Saigon remained under a strict curfew from 7:00 P.M. until dawn. A police jeep picked me up at my apartment building at 10:00 P.M. and took me to the compound, where he was waiting for me. I sat beside him as we rolled through the deserted, eerily quiet streets, one of a convoy of three jeeps.

He said that at least as far as he was concerned the assault on Saigon had come as no surprise. "We knew in advance they were going to attack," he said. "For three days before, I had meetings, meetings, meetings. On the night it happened Ky called me. 'How about you and your wife coming over?' he said. I said, 'No, thanks. I'm on combat alert.' But he insisted. So I went over for a few minutes. Ky looked at me. 'You carry a revolver in my house on the first day of the New Year?' he said. 'You know it's bad luck.'

"I only stayed for a few minutes," Loan said. "I stayed on the streets, riding around like we are doing now, until 2:00 A.M. I am just lying down on my cot at my headquarters when

I get the news. The VC are attacking all over. Ky calls me to say that Tansonhut is under attack. He says he is being advised to leave there. 'No,' I say, 'stay with the Air Force.' General Khanh, the Third Corps commander, calls me to tell me to take command in the city. I have very few troops. I send my last two armored companies to help Tansonhut. Then I round up a platoon of PFFs [the Police Field Force] and two armored cars, and we race to the radio station, which the Communists have overrun. We take it back and the man right next to me is shot dead and falls on top of me.''

Loan took a pull on a highball that was mixed for him by his orderly. The ingredients were kept in a small portable bar in the rear of the jeep. Sensing that he was in an amiable mood, I asked him to explain why he had shot the prisoner. ''I am not a politician,'' he replied. ''I am not a chief of police. I am just a soldier. When you see a man in civilian clothes with a revolver killing your people . . . when many of your people have already been killed, then what are you supposed to do? We knew who this man was. His name was Nguyen Tan Dat, alias Han Son. He was the commander of a sapper unit. He killed a policeman. He spit in the face of the men who captured him. What do you want us to do? Put him in jail for two or three years and then let him go back to the enemy?

''People in the United States do not know the things we know here,'' he said. ''I respect the Vietcong in uniform. They are fighting men like me. People know that when they are wounded I take care of them. I see they get to the hospital. But when they are not in uniform they are criminals and the rule of war is death.''

We had rolled over the high-backed bridge into the port district. Behind the warehouses and storage yards was a warren of shacks and tiny truck-gardening plots that even in the best of times was highly insecure. We turned off the main road and rolled slowly into a rutted alley for 100 yards and stopped. Loan's driver pulled a dashboard switch, and a floodlight on the jeep illuminated the featureless dwellings on both sides of us. He flashed the light quickly twice more. Another 100 yards away another jeep flashed a signal in reply. We started forward again, turned two or three times and emerged in a small square in front of a police post.

Scores of police materialized out of the shadows. Groups of men and women were being led forward to stand before camp tables at which were seated members of the special branch, who carefully checked the identification cards that all Vietnamese above the age of sixteen must carry. Raids and roundups were being carried out all over Saigon during those weeks. Here, in the port, an area had been cordoned off, the houses searched, and the residents brought to this central point.

Off to one side, squatting in the shadows, was a closely guarded group of fifteen or twenty civilians. Loan slouched over. The police officer in charge of the roundup said something in Vietnamese and pointed to an extraordinarily handsome man—tall, clear eyes, a coppery sheen to his skin—who wore clean white pajamas. Loan gave a word of command and the man was brought before him. Loan turned the man's identification card over in his hands, not looking at it. He asked questions, gently, as though thinking of something else. The man replied in an equally calm tone of voice.

Then Loan stepped back. He reached into his trousers pocket. He held what looked like a small automatic. He pointed it at the man's head. I had a momentary sense of— what shall I say—of rushing time, of dreadful weight. The man's expression didn't change. Loan's finger tightened on the trigger. There was a spurt of flame. With his other hand Loan flipped a cigarette out of a pack, put it in his mouth, and turned the barrel of his funny cigarette lighter to its tip. He took a drag and put his head back and laughed. He coughed on the smoke and laughed again. A scratching, hawking giggle, a shriek. His aides laughed and the police laughed, and the man in the white pajamas stood there motionless and silent.

"When I was in Washington the photographer who took the picture came to see me," Loan was saying in his bare little office with the beer bottle on his desk. "He said that he was sorry that he had to take it. He say that he have given his prize money to some organization like the Red Cross. I tell him, 'I am finished now; my career is over, but that is all right. What is past is past. To be alive or dead, to be liked or not liked, it doesn't matter. Life belongs to Buddha, to God, whatever it is that is higher than me.' "

Harper's Magazine, April 1972

We Are All "Bui Doi"

by Gloria Emerson

NO ONE was really invited to room 53 in the Hotel Continental except for two soldiers in armies at war with each other. One was an American, the other was North Vietnamese. I did not want people in that room. It was a place to take account, to listen to yourself.

The ceiling seemed more than 18 feet high and an old French fan hung from it. You could make those blades turn *"vite"* or *"moins vite."* I turned the fan on sometimes despite the sickly air conditioner with its rumbling cough. The walls of the room were green stucco that did not yield to any nail. I had brought the yellow seersucker bedspreads with me to Saigon and 11 books I never had time to read. (Once, waking, I lit a cigarette and then stubbed it out on Sainteny's *Histoire d'une Paix Manquée.* I don't know why.)

There was a palm tree in the room that I had bought in a Saigon market. I watered it too much.

On many mornings in Vietnam—I had 730 of them—I woke up in places far from Saigon and the trembling air conditioner and the shuttered high windows that were taped to prevent the glass from breaking in case of rockets or mortars. But when I was there, a roomboy brought me *café au lait* and two *croissants.* I ate breakfast like a woman with a wired jaw, so much did I dread having to leave that room and face it all.

I always sat in a huge green armchair—the furniture of the French colonials—by a window. There was a German down the hall who twice called me up very late at night, pleading to let him into my room because he needed to talk to someone, he said. I never saw him leaving his room in the mornings.

Once I came back to room 53 with a man's blood all over

my shirt and skirt. The roomboys, lying on their mats in the
hall, said nothing, for they had seen it all before: the correspondents rushing out in the mornings, thick necklaces of
cameras and lenses over their chests, and coming back, much
later, filthy and silent and spent.

The stains on me were the blood of Mr. Loan, a Vietnamese
driver for a rented white car (an Oldsmobile?), who had been
hurt on an April night when we were ambushed on Route
One. It was not even eight P.M., but night in Vietnam began
at five. It was I who had insisted he keep driving and he knew
of no way to silence me. The big white car must have startled
the Viet Cong who were mining the side of the road. They
opened fire with B-40 rockets and AK-47s. We crawled out
of the car—I was slow, fumbling for my bag—and hid in a
slight gully by Route One. Mr. Loan and I lay very close
together, so his blood wet the pale-blue stuff of my dress. He
was almost on top of me. Perhaps he could feel my tremors
and hoped to comfort me. There had been no time earlier
that day to put on blue jeans and sneakers and push back my
hair with a scarf. The South Vietnamese had gone into Cambodia and we had followed them to Prasaut. Hours later I lay
on the earth of Vietnam and let its insects explore and punish
me. Sometimes when Mr. Loan lay too still, I thought the
arm across my back belonged to a man who was dead.

The next morning I reached the hotel and, unable to bear
those dark bloody blotches on me, I called the roomboys for
salt, quick, salt. *Sel.* You always need it to wash out blood. A
roomboy brought a bucket of ice instead. It was what the
Americans always seemed to want.

Blood. Sometimes GIs in the field would talk about it. The
enemy did not bleed enough and they almost complained
about it.

"The dinks don't bleed—why, I see more blood when I cut
myself shaving," a GI from North Carolina said. I did not
correct him.

There were two yellowy plastic flowers on my desk in room
53. A Vietnamese woman had given them to me. I could not
bear to throw them away. She was the wife of a middle-class
retired civil servant named Ba. Their three sons were in the
army.

Mr. Ba did not much like my questions. They were especially vexing for him in the evening when he wanted to watch *The Fugitive* or *Bonanza* on the AFVN (Armed Forces Vietnam Network) channel. His Japanese-made television set was put back into a large box when these programs were over.

Yes, yes, he said patiently, he and his wife were aware of protesters who demonstrated in America against the war.

"We think these must be worried mothers," Mr. Ba said.

I thought of him almost three years later, on Inauguration Day, when a crowd stood on Pennsylvania Avenue yelling, "Bullshit! Bullshit! Bullshit!" as the girls on the floats and the bands marched by. No worried mothers there.

No one else ever slept in room 53 until I lent it to a GI named Dennis, whom I had found at Tan Son Nhut airport in Saigon, where he was trying to sleep on a bench. There was a big rip in the canvas of one of his boots. He wanted a Coke, but you needed piasters in the airport restaurant. His flight was delayed for 36 hours. He was going home on leave and he wasn't sure he would ever want to live in the United States again, maybe Australia was the better place. I was quitting Saigon for a week, so I told him to use my room. I always felt like Mary Poppins among those huge, tired children in the U.S. Army and it was the country boys I liked the most. (But it did not always pay to be too nice, to show too much concern. I remember the GI who began to cry telling me why he wouldn't be sent on the line again, holding up the hand on which the tips of two fingers were gone. And even when they were much older, you had to be distant. There was the major who asked me to take off my scarf on a helicopter ride at night so my hair would blow.)

When I got back, Dennis' boots were there and a pile of his underwear and a copy of his travel orders. The roomboys had even washed his boots, not knowing that Americans were proud when their boots turned that reddish brown, for it showed, as nothing else could, what they had endured. He had not read the books by Giap or Bernard Fall or Jonathan Schell. There was a note on top of *The Strawberry Statement* and I kept it for a very long time. It was difficult to read. Punctuation confused Dennis.

I just want to thank you very much for helping me out. Also I like to say that just knowing theres people like you around to help the small guys has given me new faith in people. I still don't know how I feel about going back to the States. That book *The Strawberry Statement*. From what I read seem to be about the way most guys feel. I wish I was man enough to stand up and say what I feel. May be one of these days I will. Well I guess I better be going. Thank you. Dennis.

That was not all. On the book he had written in pencil, "Keep truckin'."

The roomboys could not say why he had left his boots behind and if he had left barefooted for the airport. They seemed eager to report that Dennis had brought a whore to room 53. But not a young and pretty one. It was that that made me flinch.

"Vieille. Pas bon," a roomboy, who was in his mid-50s, said. Old. No good.

In the last month of that endless year, nothing in the room spoke of any season at all, or of how many had died, or of anything I had seen. You knew it was Christmas because people sent you cards and there were fake Christmas trees selling in the streets for the foreigners to buy. There were always paintings of Jesus Christ on sale. But not as many of him as of women with preposterous breasts and shiny hair, because Americans liked these ladies very much.

It was surely the month of Christmas, because Archbishop Henri Lemaitre, apostolic delegate to Vietnam and Cambodia, visited the prisoner-of-war camp for the Vietnamese at Bien-Hoa, although nearly all the men cared nothing about the birth of Christ. They were Buddhists and Buddha's birthday was in May.

American reporters were allowed to witness his visit. I went there with Tom Fox, a young American who speaks fluent Vietnamese. A long time afterward I understood why it was a more sickening day for him than for me. It was his Church that shamed him.

There were large signs at the entrance to the Bien-Hoa camp. MAY THE CHARITY OF CHRIST BE EVERYWHERE (in French), FOREVER MAINTAIN THE HIGH HONOR OF THE

MILITARY (in Vietnamese) and BLESSED IS HE WHO COMES IN THE NAME OF THE LORD (in Latin).

We were warned.

Several hundred prisoners had been standing for more than two hours before a stage when the press corps arrived at mid-morning. We stared at them, photographed and filmed them. Interviews were a violation of the Geneva Accords, which were carefully observed, the Vietnamese officials said again and again.

The prisoners—you could not call them men, for there were children there, shifting from leg to leg in the hot sun—had been given new pajamas to wear, so new they had not been washed or creased. We gawked at them, those lines and lines of Viet Cong, but only the smallest turned their heads to gawk back. One boy with a scar on his neck could not help snickering at us. It made Fox and me feel a little better.

There were 4400 prisoners in the camp. Only the wounded or mutilated were North Vietnamese. One thousand nine hundred of the prisoners were 17 years old or younger. Major Ma Sanh Qui said the youngest were 13 but, perhaps remembering how sentimental some Americans can be about children, refused to say how many there were.

Twenty-seven women and ten men over the age of 60 were also prisoners. We were not allowed to see the women.

There were speeches. The prisoners did not look alert or interested or pleased when the archbishop spoke to them. But they solemnly followed instructions from officers. Applaud. Cheer. Bow. Salute. Applaud.

No prisoner who was handed a gift by the archbishop leaned over to kiss his ring. Perhaps they did not dare. Perhaps it was because there were only 133 Catholics in the camp. The prisoners received little plastic sacks—some cigarettes, a bit of soap, a cloth towel, a colored picture of the Pope and some loose crackers that had already crumbled.

Ah, what the archbishop and Fox and I saw that day. Two amputees, once men in the National Liberation Front, had been assigned to show off new wheelchairs that they had never used before that day. I watched one of them without legs and with a wrecked hand try to steer his wheelchair in small circles.

He kept bumping into the other man, who had two hands I could not watch for very long.

We saw the archbishop say Mass in the chapel and we toured a compound where the most ruined men were kept. As the archbishop entered these rooms, an officer snapped: "Attention!" The men looked up. It was the most they could do. The archbishop spoke to some prisoners through an interpreter. Fox looked angry and ill. I tried to pity the archbishop, whose pallor was strange and whose eyes seemed too pale.

There was a blind man whose sockets seemed empty even of their lids.

ARCHBISHOP: How long have you been here?

PRISONER: Three years. I can only move when someone takes me about.

ARCHBISHOP: Where are you from?

PRISONER: Thanh Hoa.

ARCHBISHOP: Have courage.

An aide kept asking if there were any Catholics in these wards, but the Vietnamese did not know. The aide looked displeased.

The archbishop spoke to a boy whose body ended just below the hips. "Do you want to go home?"

PRISONER: Yes. But the situation in Vietnam does not permit it. I have had no news from my family in Quang Tri. I studied in North Vietnam. . . .

ARCHBISHOP: Have courage, my son.

The sickest men lay on wooden beds and some turned their heads away when a television crew filmed them.

There were cold Coca-Colas and little cakes for the press, a little party when the tour was ended, perhaps to remind us of what a pleasant performance we had just seen. Vietnamese officers spoke baby-talk English to Americans who spoke Vietnamese. I wondered if the man in the wheelchair had been told he could stop.

I took Fox to the office, where there was a bottle of Martell cognac from the PX. I had never drunk cognac before. It seemed time to start.

The room was dim and cool. Fox said he had pressed an officer at the camp to explain the presence of a large group of young Vietnamese girls who were wandering around, giggling and keyed up. They were members of a Catholic youth organization.

"The major said, 'The girls come here as a matter of freedom. They come for the fun of it,'" Fox told me. "For the fun of it."

The North Vietnamese soldier—who must have weighed no more than 115 pounds—came to my room that December, for we could not meet in the office. Twice he came to the room and sat in the green armchair. At first he was suspicious of its fat arms and high back and its deepness, for in all his life he had known only benches or straight-backed wooden chairs.

His name was Tien. A Vietnamese man told me in English what he was saying. Tien had been captured in a "liberated" village in Quang Nam Province a few months earlier while he was convalescing from malaria. His recovery meant working in the rice fields with the villagers. His face was so round, so unlike the beautifully boned, sharper faces of the Northerners, that it may have been swollen from his illness. His hair looked very dry and stood from his scalp like the bristles of a used-up brush. He could have been 16. He was 21.

So ill had Tien been that he could not walk quickly up the stairs of the Continental.

It was his legs that startled me, not the illness that had almost killed him. From his feet to his knees there were scars from the ulcers and sores no man could avoid moving down the Ho Chi Minh Trail through the jungles of Laos. For three months, in a company of 115 men, he had made the long march south.

"We walked eleven hours a day and the longer we walked the more bored and morose we became," Tien said. "There were many things I missed. First, I wanted a real cigarette. Then, I wanted to see my mother, to be close to her. And then, what I wanted badly was a whole day of rest."

After his capture, he had been flown to Tam Ky in a *truc thang*, the Vietnamese term for helicopter. The words mean up and straight. Tien had felt a fear he could hardly describe.

"The first Americans that I had ever seen were the two pilots. They looked unbelievably tall. So very huge. But they

smiled down at me. I don't know why. Some of my panic
went away."

I could not imagine chopper pilots smiling at any prisoner,
but this is what he said. Then Tien asked if he could ever ride
again in a *truc thang*. I said it was not likely.

He had dreaded being beaten by the Vietnamese who in-
terrogated him at Tam Ky, but they were nonchalant. He was
even allowed to contact rich relatives in Saigon who had left
the North many years before and it was decided that he would
declare himself a *hoi chanh*, an enemy soldier who defects under the Open Arms program and is not treated as a prisoner
of war. Tien had not defected to anyone, of course; he had
simply been too weak to run away from a South Vietnamese
platoon.

The last time he had seen his parents was on a June day in
1968 in his village, all that he had ever known, which was 50
miles south of Hanoi.

"They gave a small feast for me the day I left home to go
into the army. My father, who is a farmer, was unable to speak.
There were no words in his throat. My mother could not help
weeping. And I wept, too. As I left, she said: 'You must go,
I know that, but try to come back.' "

In his village, there were no men who had come back.
There were no letters from any of them. Before 1968, men
going south had been granted 15-day leaves, but these were
canceled. No family knew, or wondered aloud, who had been
wounded or killed.

Tien spoke often of his mother, as no young American soldiers had ever done with me. They mentioned their parents
and I remember the doctor who told me of the words of a
GI who had lost both of his legs and part of an arm, who lay
on a litter and asked: "Will my parents treat me the same?"

Tien was telling us how he had dreamed on the Ho Chi
Minh Trail of being a small boy again, back in his village,
talking to his mother, when a roomboy came in with my laundry. Saigon was a city of informers, so I spoke to him harshly
in the pidgin Vietnamese of GIs. *Di di mau*. Get out. The
roomboy scuttled away, not looking at any of us.

Tien and a friend had walked two miles from their village
to the district town to report for duty. After four months of

basic training in Hoa Binh Province—the words mean peace in Vietnamese—the young soldiers were restless to start their war, nervous that it would be over too soon.

It took ten days for battalion 1071 to cross the Annamite mountain range to reach the border of Laos. They passed by tree trunks on which thousands of men before them had stopped to carve their names, their villages and the dates of going south. Even battalion and company commanders had carved their names, Tien said, and the sight of those trees warmed him and made him feel less alone. I tried to smile to show him, yes, I could understand that.

It was six A.M. when they finally reached the frontier. The soldiers crossed a rope bridge over a ravine. Go quickly, quickly, they were told, for the Americans often strafed and bombed here. Do not look back.

But Tien did look back, he had to, and all he could see of his Vietnam was a blurred mountain range in the mist. He was told to move faster.

It surprised Tien that the Ho Chi Minh Trail did not start as a wide road. It began as just a small lane winding through a bamboo forest in Laos. He had only two personal possessions: a diary and a walking stick made of North Vietnamese bamboo.

"That stick was precious to me," Tien said. "We all had one. It eased my exhaustion when I was walking and it helped me keep my balance. You could use it to measure the depth of a spring we had to cross. If you wanted to rest, you propped the stick up under your pack so it made the weight lighter. We called it our 'third leg.' There was even a song. I sang these lines many times."

And he did once more, in a high, small voice.

> "It trains the legs for the long march without
>   letting them get away.
> It trains the spirit to go forward only, never
>   backward. . . ."

When Tien was tired of talking, and when we could hear no more. I showed him my Phillips cassette player and we listened to Country Joe & the Fish.

> "Come on all of you big strong men
> Uncle Sam needs your help again
> He's got himself in a terrible jam
> Way down yonder in Vietnam
> So put down your books, pick up a gun
> We're gonna have a whole lot of fun."

I had a friend, a reporter named Sterba, who said that song was always running through his head in all the months he covered the war. But it is not a song you can explain to a North Vietnamese infantryman. Tien liked the cassette player, though. He found it a marvel.

On the tenth day his company was moving down the trail, the B-52s came. Other soldiers, stationed by the trail, had described them to the men.

"One man told me, 'You will never hear the approach of the B-52s, for suddenly there will be great undreamed-of noises around you but still you never see the planes and if you are in the middle of where the bomb lands you will die, and if you are close then you will be deaf for the rest of your life,'" Tien told us. "But this man also told me that the mountains and forests were so wide it was very hard for B-52s to hit men."

Tien's company survived three raids. He wished they could go into combat. Once, they passed a group of wounded Southerners—soldiers in the National Liberation Front—who teased them.

"Some of them told us, 'Go fast or the liberation will be finished before you get there,' and this worried us very much. One man told me that it was easy to fight the Americans. 'They have very weak eyes,' he said. 'If it is sunny they cannot see well.'"

Tien never did find out if the Americans were made helpless by the sun. He never fired an AK-47. His malarial attacks, which lasted two to three hours, were so intense that two men were assigned to hold him up as the company kept moving. When they entered South Vietnam, the sickest were separated and left behind.

In Saigon, for the first time in his life, he owned a wrist watch and a pen. He wore white shirts. What Tien really wanted was to have his diary and his walking stick again, and to talk with soldiers Hong and Ngoan, who had been with him on the trail.

Once he said wistfully he would like to find out where his unit was and rejoin it. But he knew it was not possible, he knew it very well. His relatives sent him to be an apprentice in a Honda repair shop, but he stayed listless and sad, a man of longing and few words.

There were times when, pretending that friendships were possible, I thought of inviting Vietnamese to my room, not just to ask them what were their losses and how deep was their pain but to try to have a nice time together. They would not have come. There was a painter named Ha Cam Tam, who taught drawing to children in five elementary schools for a monthly salary worth about $40. He made money by selling paintings to Americans. One of them showed three gaunt, tormented Vietnamese posing like the three monkeys who see no evil, hear no evil, speak no evil. He called the painting *Nothing About Anything.*

"Perhaps Americans buy my paintings because they are troubled," Tam said. "But if it was a war only between Vietnamese, as it should be, it would be different. We would not feel guilty, as you do, for both sides have their causes.

"The Vietnamese people must be deaf, dumb and blind to what goes on around them," Tam added. "It is required of us."

But sometimes they refused to be and could stand it no longer. When the United States Air Force handed over its helicopter base in Soc Trang to the South Vietnamese air force, Americans removed the pews, altar and altar rails from the chapel. They left behind a fluorescent-lit cross and piles of litter, including a handbook on survival and a sign that read: THINK THINK THINK.

Angry Vietnamese soldiers painted a sign of their own: U.S. ARMY—DON'T TAKE GOD AWAY.

Sometimes in room 53 the telephone rang very late at night or before dawn with a message from the *Times*'s foreign desk in New York. It would be read, with patience and valor, by a Vietnamese named Mr. Lee, who worked at the Reuter's office and did not speak English. It was Mr. Lee who called on a summer morning to read a cable that said my father had died. His accent was so distracting that I had to have him read it three times. I went back to sleep in relief. There was no problem with a story, no inserts, no new facts needed. It was only another death, and not an unfair one, not a Vietnamese ending.

And as I moved from interview to interview, questioning the victims and those they made victims, always asking, "How much does it hurt?" or "How great is your fear?" the men who made up the fat and lumpy perimeter around the war went on with their daily lives. It was as though they could not see the graves and were never told of the dead.

There was Richard Funkhouser, for example, who tried to organize a 1971 decathlon in Chinese chess and winetasting to make Vietnam a cozier, more cheerful combat zone. (U.S. dead in 1970: 6065. U.S. wounded: 30,643.)

The fatuity of Funkhouser was concentrated in a memorandum he wrote on December 2, 1970. The subject: "Esprit de CORDS." It was a pun on the name of the agency, Civil Operations and Rural Development Support, which directed a network of pacification programs. One of them was called Brighter Life for War Victims. Few Americans who worked for CORDS took it well if you told them a brighter life for war victims meant ending the war. It was that kind of comment that made them uneasy with reporters.

Funkhouser, whose greater glory had been in Gabon, where he was U.S. ambassador, headed CORDS in the third military region (Vietnam had four). I pasted his memorandum on the wall of the tiny, sick-smelling bathroom of room 53. It was where it belonged.

"It has been suggested that there should be more interplay between the CORDS headquarters in the four regions," he wrote.

"It sounds like a great idea to us," he burbled, "and therefore we challenge representatives of other military regions to a 1971 decathlon comprising, for example, bridge, tennis, gin rummy, volleyball, nautical sports, Chinese chess, winetasting, close harmony, etc."

Nautical sports. Close harmony.

Each of the teams would be made up of six men and two

women, with "one ringer of general rank" and one Viet-namese expert.

"It is always open house here at Bienhoa for competitors," Funkhouser wrote, in that playful spirit so many of us in Viet-nam really lacked.

In the second year the room could no longer comfort or calm me. In no other place where I have ever lived did I grow so ugly or feel so finished. It was a malignant city, Saigon, and you could never quite sort out the horrors fast enough.

There was only a street to cross and a few hundred yards to walk between the *New York Times* office on Tu-Do and the Continental, but even that little strip provided surprises after curfew, when you might have thought it would be calm.

Alvin Shuster, the bureau chief, and I were walking to the hotel one night when we saw a big American, in civilian clothes, arguing with a Vietnamese woman and looking through her handbag as she pleaded with him. You often saw her on the terrace of the Continental.

She was a hooker, an old one, with a PX wig, and I hoped that Dennis had done better. The American was being very rough.

"Don't get involved," Alvin said. I told the man to stop it, leave her alone, because—the words came out wrong—that was no way to treat a lady. His answer was very odd. It upset Alvin and me.

"That's no lady," the American said. "It's a man." He added that he had been robbed. Perhaps she was. Sometimes I would see her on the terrace—she would always smile and nod at me after that night—and worry that a young man like Dennis might not understand and take her for just another whore, and ruin his life. Stop worrying, Alvin said, don't get involved. She tells them.

There was a nice garden at the Continental with round wooden tables under big umbrellas where you could have breakfast or tea and remember Graham Greene and his Rue Catinat. But no nice corner of Saigon could ever keep its early promise, so the war came into the little garden as it had come to all places.

It was there that I tried to save Madame Ngo Ba Thanh from being arrested, but they took her away.

She was tiny and silly, brave and brilliant. I could never quote her in a story, for she rushed so, in any of four languages, that no sentence was ever finished. A lawyer, she had studied at the University of Paris and in Barcelona. Her master's degree in comparative law was from Columbia University. Madame Thanh knew all about prisons: She had spent 25 months in them during 1966 and 1967.

There was nothing left to be afraid of, she would say. But there was: prison again and for longer. Be careful, I would say, watching her demonstrate time and time again against the government of Nguyen Van Thieu and running from the police on Tu-Do in her high heels.

So I, who stood 11 inches taller than she, could not save her at all. There had been a demonstration—a bitter, mocking one—in front of the National Assembly by a handful of deputies opposed to the one-man presidential election in October 1971. The only candidate was President Thieu seeking re-election. The police used canisters of tear gas, made in Harrisburg, Pennsylvania, as the protesters stood grouped on the steps, holding high their banners in Vietnamese. Madame Thanh was there, of course. She was always everywhere.

I ran behind her when the police charged and we ran into the little garden. There were two American officers sitting at a table and I said quick, quick, sit with them and the police cannot interfere. What is shaming, you see, is that I still believed that American officers would protect her. This, after all I had learned and seen and been told.

Sit down, sit down, I hissed at her in schoolgirl French. One of the men—a colonel—spoke to us in beautiful, serious French, offering to share his *café au lait* if the waiter did not soon appear. The other man, his brother, said he was a pilot on a Cobra gunship based at Tuy Hoa. Madame Thanh—who knew as well as I did what Cobra gunships can do to a village and its people—received this information calmly. Neither officer seemed to sense that something unusual had just taken place. Both of us had been crying from the tear gas. Her hair was disheveled. My nose was running. She was breathing in hoarse little gulps. It was her asthma again.

The officers seemed gallant and correct, those two, as though they had once learned a good deal of poetry, and taken sea voyages, and knew more about life than the Army wishes a man ever to know. Then the pilot began to speak of the war, why we had not won it and how he would be the last man to leave, because he wanted it won.

She chewed a piece of *croissant* and kept looking at the entrance. The deputies who had been in the demonstration rushed in, so she rose to join them. It was no longer possible to stay where she was. Now, at a much later time, I remember her rising and thanking the colonel, who bowed slightly and said in French:

"Perhaps we shall meet in times that are less turbulent, *madame.*"

The police came and the officers rose and left. I joined the deputies and Madame Thanh at their table while a policeman stood in front of us, taking our pictures on an American video tape to be used as evidence. Treason. Traitors. The Vietnamese sat there, not turning away their faces, looking solemnly at the American machine, as though they no longer cared what their punishment might be.

The deputies had diplomatic immunity and Madame Thanh did not. I tried to hold on to her when the police surrounded her.

But they won, tugging and pushing and circling her. We were told that the police threw her into the back of a jeep. It is much more than a year now since she was sent to prison and there is nothing I can do. I saw a picture of her once— long after I had left Saigon. She was in court, lying on a stretcher and looking, suddenly, quite old and helpless.

There is one more thing to tell: It is about the children. Living in that huge, solemn room, where there were sheets and hot water at times, I often thought I could easily share it with a child. There were so many of them, working the streets, living in the markets, so small and so frail that the Vietnamese called them the *bui doi*, or dust of life. It seemed inhuman to refuse them help. Sometimes I would invite them into the office, where they could use the shower and, if we were lucky, there were new clothes they could wear. The mothers of friends sent bundles of them to me.

The child I wanted to help most was a very thin, trembling 11-year-old girl named Pham Thi Hoa. I met her in a prison compound in Danang, where the Vietnamese police chief let me interview two children so I could see how the Viet Cong recruited the very young and exposed them to risks. She had been arrested as a messenger for the Viet Cong; there was a letter in her pocket. She had been in the detention center for children for five months.

"I have no father. My mother lived in Saigon," the child said. The interpreter could barely hear her.

"My mother gave me to Mrs. Xuan when I was very small. When Uncle Xuan died, I lived with Uncle Chi. When Uncle Chi died, I lived with Uncle Hien."

She had said it so many times before to her interrogators. Dang Von Song, head of the Special Police Branch, said the "uncles"—a respectful term in Vietnamese—were high-ranking Viet Cong cadre, in Quang Nam Province.

Pham Thi Hoa looked at no one as she spoke. She could not keep her hands still. They quivered and moved in strange, urgent ways. Mr. Song smiled as she spoke.

"Only Uncle Hien loves me. My mother does not love me. She gave me to Mrs. Xuan. Uncle Hien asked me whether I wanted to go to school and I said no, and he said: 'You decide. If you want, I will send you to school. If you don't, stay here with me.' Uncle Hien and the other uncles loved me. I lived in a bunker under a bamboo bush with Uncle Hien and Uncle Vinh. There was only one girl of my age living nearby. That was Thoai, but she and her mother went to Danang and her mother let her work as a servant for somebody.

"In the evening Uncle Hien hung up a hammock for me to sleep in."

It tired her to tell us this and her little hands did not stop their twitching. While the police were out of the room, she whispered to my interpreter that she had been beaten in the interrogation center. There was no time to ask her questions, for they came back.

Dang Von Song complained that Pham Thi Hoa had not been at all cooperative.

"This girl is very stubborn. Very. But we have found her weak point. She is very afraid of having her hair cut off," Mr. Song said. "So we say we will cut her hair if she is not more helpful."

The little girl showed that she feared this very much. She drew back as I tried to comfort her.

Another police official shook his head.

"I have offered to adopt her and take her home with me," he said. He repeated the offer, smiling at Pham Thi Hoa.

"I prefer to be in prison," she said. "I like to be in prison." She was taken away.

Perhaps because I looked queer or because my eyes were not dry, Mr. Song gave me some advice.

"Now, don't write an antiwar story, write how the Viet Cong exploit children," he said, wagging his finger at me.

There are other stories I could tell, about the living and the dead, much more than I have told here, but so very much has already been written, and none of it ever made any difference at all.

Playboy, June 1973

"Don't Sell Your Soul"

by Zalin Grant

David Harker. In the jungle I was always worried that I might wake up one morning, my eyes dim with that distant light I'd seen in other eyes before they went out. I made myself work, stay busy, take cold baths, fearing that if I stopped for a day it would happen to me too. When we reached Hanoi perhaps I let up too soon, for I fell deathly ill the first week with a high-fever malaria which several of my group had picked up on the trail. For a while I managed to get outside to sit on top of the bomb shelters in the yard. But I quickly reached a point where I couldn't drag myself out of bed. I was vomiting at midnight when a doctor arrived. He started shooting me with sugar in the veins, using a 50-cc syringe.

The malaria and dysentery eased. Then one night my respiration shot up, my heart pounded in my chest, I gasped for breath. I had to get out of the cell. I banged on the door and screamed for the turnkey. Two men pulled me back. "They aren't going to let you out," said Kushner, "take it easy." I was frantic, ready to kill to get outside, away from the suffocating cell. The other prisoners walked me around and finally coaxed me into lying down. I was shaky for two days.

We began to adjust after several weeks. Our appetites increased. The Vietnamese gave us a little extra food. We put on some weight and began to do daily exercises. Lunch was usually soup and bread. The soup seemed to have two six-month seasons, divided between pumpkin and cabbage. Once a day we got a side dish of fried vegetables or a little canned meat. The food was hardly anything to sing about but it was certainly much better than we'd had in the jungle. Five shower stalls were at the other end of the compound and we were allowed to take a bath sometimes every day.

It wasn't long till we were called to a classroom for indoctrination, a lecture on Vietnamese history. It was nothing we hadn't heard a hundred times before. The course lasted a week, six sleepy hours a day. We listened to the professor, wondering if he'd ever studied English or Spanish or French history, if he knew anything besides the Trung sisters and Nguyen Hue.

At the course's conclusion the North Vietnamese brought us an appeal to sign. I was very reluctant. I put them off several times, but wound up signing like everyone else. On July 4 we were called over to the villa. We sat around with the Vietnamese for an hour drinking tea. When we returned to our cells we discovered that no one else had been allowed outside that day. The North Vietnamese thought we were progressive, based on the fact, I suppose, that we had written antiwar stuff in the jungle. Our records were brought with us to Hanoi.

We were operating from attitudes formed in the jungle, formed when we had little choice. And at first Kushner taped for the intracamp radio and Pfister typed news material. But as we regained our strength we started thinking about opposing the North Vietnamese. We were out of touch with the rest of the camp. We knew nothing about what the senior officer's policies might be or even if there was such a thing. Meanwhile, the North Vietnamese took advantage of our confusion to move the Peace Committee next to our two cells.

Guy. From talking to my roommate, Major Elliott, I found that the army did not put a great emphasis on training soldiers in resistance methods. A course in escape and evasion techniques was taught during infantry training but it was nothing like the survival school that air-force personnel had to attend. I realized that we had a problem in the camp, because the majority of the POWs were army. I appointed Elliott as my deputy and we started working out methods to communicate with other cells.

In May, 1971, two new POWs were moved into the cell next door to us, a warrant officer and a captain, both wounded, who had been captured at the DMZ. We established contact almost immediately by yelling out the door and passing notes in our defecation cans. The two-liter cans were painted black, had a handle and a top that never fit, and around the can's base was a metal ring that held the bottom half an inch off the floor to keep it from rusting out. We sometimes put notes inside the ring and occasionally just dropped them on the excrement where they were picked up.

The warrant officer and captain were eventually moved out to the other end of the compound and we lost contact with them. Our real breakthrough came in July when all POWs captured in Laos were moved back to the Plantation. Four pilots were put in our section, two of them next door. They were very die-hard gung-ho fellows. The North Vietnamese made a big mistake the next morning when they allowed the pilots to use the bathhouse on the other end of the camp. The pilots immediately got in touch with the Corncrib, which was about a hundred fifty meters north of us. Then more pilots were transferred to the Gun Shed.

We set up overt and covert committees. I appointed an awards-and-decorations officer to keep track of heroic acts and achievements of POWs so when we got back we could recommend them for medals, which we did. It took from May, when we first started, to October to get communications through the whole camp. We had to go through individual cells and many people were still afraid of what would happen if they were caught; some of them wouldn't answer.

But over the months we were able to establish commo with everybody except the Peace Committee and the new group from the south, which we code-named the "Dirty Dozen" because their number suggested the movie of the same name. We frequently saw them exercising in the yard. A pilot in the cell next to me yelled to them, "Resist!" The Dirty Dozen—or at least the six who were out that day—turned and looked toward our cells. Nobody said anything. Everybody was scared, scared to death. Next day the North Vietnamese plugged up our louvered windows so we couldn't see out.

I didn't try to hide what I'd done earlier. I told them through commo that I had made a tape. I said, "Yes, they got me to that point in 1970 when I was very low and under a lot of mental pressure. I thought I could get word out to my family if I made a tape. The promise was broken so I quit. I expect everybody in this camp has a different breaking point, depending on how long you've been captured and your mental attitude on any given day. Some days you will be called in for interrogation and won't be able to resist at all. Okay, make the damn tape. But don't do it every day. Next time make them take you to that point or further. As far as writing, if you can write your family, go ahead, but don't sell your soul to do it."

There was still some reluctance in the camp and I made another policy decision. We had a typical GI cross section—guys who were AWOL when they were captured, a couple of deserters, some who had openly collaborated with the enemy. My new policy, which I put out via note, said: "I fully realize everybody can make mistakes. But no one should make the same mistake twice. I cannot grant amnesty to anybody for what they have done in the past. However, if on receipt of this note you follow my policies and directives from this time onward, I will do everything I can, I will even go to the president of the United States, to get you relieved from any acts committed before this date."

In one week there was an amazing change in camp. I could see it through the cracks in my door the Vietnamese weren't able to plug. A lot of men were taping and writing. I told them to taper off gradually so as not to arouse the suspicions of the North Vietnamese. The next day seven of the nine POWs who were taping quit. They were in different buildings for the most part. Others stopped bowing and some started giving the Vietnamese the finger. I sat in my cell practically quivering. Even I would bow in certain situations. But some prisoners walked past the camp commander, looked him straight in the eye, and wouldn't lower their heads.

The North Vietnamese, of course, immediately realized we had established commo. The first thing they did was stop us from using the bathhouse at the other end. They built a new bathhouse in our section and screened in our area with black tar-paper fences. We had contingency plans for such a move; new drop points had already been set up.

On October 7 the NVA found a note. The camp commander called me in for interrogation. He knew all my policies. He said, "We will not punish you if you admit you are wrong."

I said, "Okay, I admit I am wrong."

"And you will not do it again?"

"I will not do it again."

McMillan. Me and Jose Anzaldua were sweeping out our cell. Five prisoners had moved into the room next door. We swept over toward their cell. The door was open. The big thing was to ask people where they were from back in the world, you know. So we asked these guys their home towns, real quietlike, because we weren't supposed to be talking to them. Riate was from L.A.; Chenoweth was from Oregon; and Kavanaugh was from Denver.

These guys had a debate going on. One dude says to the others, "If my kid was a Communist I'd respect his opinion."

Me and Jose popped up and said, "Not us. We're imperialists."

They got the face at us then and didn't make any reply.

Kushner and Harker and four others were in the cell next to us. We went back and called them up and said, "Hey, something funny's going on next door."

A few days later Cheese came by and told us there was a Peace Committee in camp and asked if we wanted to join it. He showed us a magazine they had put together and said, "They have many extra privileges. They can write home and receive letters. They get beer and candy."

We said, "Naw, man, we don't want no part of this Peace Committee. The Peace Committee is gonna get burnt."

Cheese said, "Ya, ya. Peace Committee very good."

I saw Cheese often because I was having a little trouble with the guards. At night we kicked up a lot of noise in our room. The guards would beat on our door and tell us to be quiet but we usually ignored them. They would be patrolling the compound singing their war songs, and we'd start howling like dogs at the moon. "Yiiii." It really made them mad. Next day someone would be jerked out and taken to Cheese's office.

Cheese would say, "Lon, you very stupid." (Lon was my Vietnamese name—every POW had one.) "The guard tell the chickens to go to bed. Go to bed! He tell the pigs. Go to bed! But he tell you to go to bed and you not go. You stupid, Lon. You crazy. I think I punish you."

I said, "Look, man, I won't do it no more. I'm sorry." Of course, soon as I got back to the cell I started it again. Cheese had it in his mind that he could influence me to join the Peace Committee. That's why he didn't treat me rougher. If it had been Harker or those guys he would've put them in shackles in a minute.

Cheese was as thin as a toothpick. He must have been the oldest first lieutenant in the North Vietnamese Army. I think he had bugs or something because he was all the time scratching.

After we rapped a lot he asked me one day why I was always happy.

I said, "I'm just like that, you know. All you are doing by keeping me here is making me rich. My money is piling up in the States. When I get back I will really be a capitalist then."

"Black man, you being treated like a slave in America. Why do not you protest against the war? You away from your family. Yet and still you do not think about them. You think about money."

"Yeah, I love money, man. You said I've been a slave all my life, right?"

"Yes. You slave. You slave now."

"Okay. I want to stay here a long time so when I go back I won't be a slave. Dig?"

He didn't say anything. He just stared at me. I knew I was messing up his mind.

One morning Ol' Cheese walked out of the villa and when he got in front of our cell he started mumbling to himself and began to pace back and forth with his hands behind his back. He turned and went toward the villa, then reversed himself and headed for our room again. He did this for about five minutes. We said, "This dude is crazy, man. We better leave him alone because he might have us executed."

Daly. My attitude began to change when I got to Hanoi. In South Viet Nam we had nothing to read except some out-dated propaganda newspapers and a *Life* clipping about My

Lai. But as soon as we got to Hanoi we were given a series called *Viet Nam Studies.* I think everybody in our group thought the war was wrong. But to say why it was wrong, other than on moral grounds, we couldn't. We had no facts to really get our teeth into. As I read the *Viet Nam Studies* I picked out things right away that I knew to be the truth. The more I read, the more doubts I had about U.S. involvement. It sounded very logical that we should be against the war.

After the history course they began to call us out one by one for interrogation. Each of us went to Cheese's office. Cheese seemed to concentrate on my cell, which had the four blacks, Jose Anzaldua, and Long. He wasn't as interested in Harker's room. I don't know whether I should use the term reactionary, but that's the best way to describe Harker. He had turned worse and worse against the Vietnamese.

Anyway, Cheese started off the session by asking about my health. I suffered a lot when I got to Hanoi. Compared to the other guys, I looked healthy because I hadn't lost much weight, so they were given the vitamin shots and I got very little. Cheese would have a newspaper article on the war from the States and he'd show it to me and we'd discuss it. Then he asked me how I felt about the war and I told him. He wanted me to write about the things I'd seen and disliked when I was soldier in South Viet Nam. (These sessions were stretched out over several months; he worked slowly.) We talked about why the Americans acted as they did in Viet Nam. At the end he asked if I did not want to do something to help end the killing.

The North Vietnamese also explained about colonialism. They told us about the British empire and pointed out the difference between the British method and the American method, which they called neocolonialism. "Much different," Cheese said. The British installed their own government in foreign countries, but the Americans supported independence and just put puppets in key positions of power, as in South Viet Nam. "A puppet can't act on his own," he said. "Must have someone to pull the strings." This made good sense to me. I remembered how when I was first captured I had seen men, women, and children carrying supplies for the Viet

Cong. Trails and trails full of them. They certainly weren't supporting the Saigon government.

Every prisoner who went to the Big House came back with the same story, no matter how long he was gone. "Oh, the North Vietnamese just gave me the usual news about how they are winning the war," everyone would say.

One day Cheese came to the cell and gave Jose some paper to write an antiwar letter. He returned after a while to pick it up. Cheese looked at the letter and scratched his head. He said, "I do not understand. When you come to my office you write very good letters. But now you write in your room—ah, I think very poor."

We laughed. After Cheese left we teased Jose. He and I got into a fight about it. I knew goodness well you didn't go to Cheese's office just for him to tell you how the NVA were winning the war and then return with the oranges and candy he had given you. But everybody tried to pretend that was the way it worked. Cheese asked us if we would like to join the Peace Committee. We agreed more or less because we didn't want to oppose him. He had us write a letter to the camp commander asking permission to join. We wrote it but I don't think the other prisoners in the room were sincere, and nothing came of it.

In early fall, '71, we heard about Colonel Guy for the first time. We discussed what could happen if we returned to the States and Colonel Guy turned us in. It wasn't that we were doing anything, but we heard through commo what the camp thought about the Peace Committee and some guys in my room were afraid we might be lumped together with them. Everybody got real shaky and decided to send a note to Guy to let him know we weren't turning into communists. Someone wrote at the end of the note, "Better dead than red."

Harker. We had been isolated from military discipline so long that news of Colonel Guy being our camp commander was very startling. I wasn't exactly a military lover, but it made me feel sort of gung ho to know that someone was passing out orders, that we had an organization and were joined together. Colonel Guy ordered us not to make tapes for the radio after New Year's, '72. He said he would try to cover for anybody who had done anything before that date. I thought his policy was fair enough.

We had already begun to resist before we got word from him. Kushner had stopped doing the radio and stopped writing unless forced. Although he never wrote anything about the war he didn't actually believe to be true, he got tired of the North Vietnamese using him. On July 4 they had given him a pair of glasses his wife had sent to Hanoi, but they wouldn't give him the letter she had written, and he was sure there was one, so he wasn't at all happy with them. In November they tried to make him write an antiwar letter to a radical peace group in the States. He refused. Next morning at 7:00 A.M. the guards opened our door and said, "Kushner and Anton, take your beds and move to another room!" We were astounded by the bluntness of it all. Gus tried to give them a hand but a guard pushed him away. Taking them from our room was like pulling our teeth. We felt the absence for weeks. If anything, it hardened our opposition to the Vietnamese.

Davis. I caught a glimpse of Colonel Guy in the yard. He was sort of short, maybe five foot eight, thin, with a lantern jaw and brown hair neatly combed and parted. He looked clean and lean. You always think of guys in the air force as soft. Colonel Guy was more like an officer in the marines or army. A real tough nut.

McMillan. All the POWs called Colonel Guy hard-core. And he was, he really was. I liked him though. If it wasn't for him a lot more prisoners would've joined the Peace Committee. The thing that got me was his policy about not going home. Quite a few peace delegations from the States were coming to Hanoi and Colonel Guy told us not to accept probation. I said to myself, "Man, you're crazy. If these people call me and tell me I can go home—I'm going home." Colonel Guy might have been dedicated, but there are limits to any normal man's dedication.

Anton. Kushner and I sent a reply through commo that we respected his opinion but not his judgment and if offered unconditional release we would take it. Out of eighty-two prisoners in the Plantation at that time, we were the only two to tell him this. The rest ostensibly agreed with his policy but behind his back many said they'd be gone if the North Vietnamese offered to free them.

Guy sent us another message: "I remind you this is an order, not a request."

We didn't reply.

When we learned Colonel Guy was our camp commander we felt that—it's hard to say how we felt. For four years we had had to make our own decisions and both of us sort of rebelled against someone telling us what to do through commo which was passed on and distorted by fifteen different people. And to be honest, the Vietnamese had us a little hung up, because they were talking to us about a release. They told us, "Maybe you will be released." We said, no, it can't be. Yet we had a feeling that maybe it was. They played us very cleverly.

One day a guard opened our door and asked if we wanted some ice cream. We found out two weeks later that we and the Peace Committee were the only ones in camp who got it. And, of course, everybody watched our end of the camp, several prisoners did nothing but look out cracks in their doors all day long. They saw the ice cream going into our cell and, oh, wow!

We received a message saying, "I don't know what you're doing but whatever it is, stop it."

We said to ourselves, "And who the hell are you?"

Actually we weren't doing that much, although the day we were removed from Harker's room and placed in a cell by ourselves, the North Vietnamese had begun to work on us. We hadn't been in the new cell two minutes when a fat, happy little Vietnamese came by and asked if we needed more blankets or anything, just like room service. We called him Mao, Chairman Mao. He told us he'd like to learn English better and asked us to write a selection of American slang. Then he asked us to write some poetry. Just before Christmas he asked if we'd like to write a letter home. There was just one catch. If we wanted to write our families, he said, we first had to show our appreciation by writing a letter to the American people about our opposition to the war.

When we reached Hanoi we heard a lot about the antiwar movement. It seemed that it was more or less a hippie thing. Not that we disliked hippies, but we thought for that reason it wouldn't be effective in ending the war. As time passed we realized the movement was more than a small radical protest, that a large percentage of Americans were definitely part of it, though we were never really able to grasp the atmosphere of the thing, it was a period of history that remains lost to us.

I was confused by people like Senators Mansfield, Church, and even George McGovern. We heard edited versions of their remarks over the camp radio. I really respected Mansfield. If he was against the war, how could opposing it be so bad? So both of us wrote a few times. We occasionally wondered if what we were doing would ruin our careers. We never thought that we'd be court-martialed for it. Later, when we got roommates, pilots shot down in mid-'72, they told us that according to Pentagon policy any antiwar appeals that could be justified wouldn't be held against POWs.

In January the North Vietnamese gave us an article from the *New York Times*, a Christmas story written by Kushner's wife Valerie, who was active in an organization of POW wives who were against the war. After reading it Kushner wanted very badly to write his wife. The North Vietnamese said, "You write something for us and we'll let you write home."

I was touched by the article too. I wrote an appeal to Senator Mansfield, told him I supported what he was doing, and asked that he please urge Congress to increase the pressure on Nixon.

I Cannot Rejoice

by Valerie M. Kushner

1962—We were such newlyweds we counted Christmas Day as our four-month anniversary. My husband had just begun medical school. We didn't buy a tree (saving money) until at ten that night. We made much of trimming, then admitted that we missed our big family celebrations. The sleet turned to snow. By early morning we were on our way to our parents' house.

1963—So wonderful. Our daughter born on Christmas Day. A month earlier, Jack Kennedy had died. Feeling my child stir within me that November afternoon, I feared for her.

1964—A glory brought to us by our child. From now on birthday cake became the dessert for our Christmas dinner.

1965—Our daughter at 2 still played with the boxes more than the toys. I became a full-time wife and mother. In a few months my husband would finish school, and enter his profession.

1966—We swam on Christmas Day. My husband was doing an internship at Tripler Army Hospital in Honolulu. My husband made his rounds that morning at the hospital—so many wounded men. The next month he volunteered for duty in Vietnam.

1967—Explain to a child on her fourth what missing in action means. She reminds me: "Daddy said he won't be home when I get four, but he promised to be back when I get five." I was carrying our second child.

1968—The waiting. Gratitude for sure knowledge that he was alive, constant fear for his survival. Our son at nine months could not walk. I said to the children, "Maybe next year we will be together again."

1969—An airplane flying to Paris, 96 children and 45 wives and mothers sent by Ross Perot to plead for our men. The North Vietnamese told us to tell our children that their fathers were criminals.

1970—Beginnings of disillusionment. Public concern ineffective. Congress apathetic. The Sontay raid brought me to a low point. Some troops were being withdrawn, but my husband was not home. His agony was being used to prolong the war.

1971—I have been married for ten Christmases. This is the fifth year of our separation. The words choke me. Our Christmas child does not make any predictions for her ninth birthday. Withdrawn. Winding down. Vietnamization. Meaningless phrases. Must have an end to this war. I see no end. I cannot rejoice in the birth of the son of God. My son has no father.

This Christmas Day we celebrate the birth of a son to Mary. This Christmas Day some other mother's son will die in Vietnam. That death takes away all that was taught by Christ's birth.

We were given a number of books to read, though they weren't passed around to everyone. *War and Peace*, Shakespeare, a series of French classics. The Vietnamese didn't offer us any books on communism, but we noticed they had several in their offices and we asked to read them. It was the first time I'd read the *Communist Manifesto*. The book that influenced me the most, however, was *The United States in Vietnam*, by George McTurnam Kahin and John Wilson Lewis, two American academics. I was surprised the Vietnamese let me read the book because it was a balanced account of U.S. actions in

Viet Nam until 1968 and included such things as charts showing Viet Cong atrocities in the south. Here was something we
knew was not propaganda. The truth of it was overwhelming.

The Vietnamese were extremely aware of what the American press was writing about the war. They had their own library and read all the major stateside newspapers and news
magazines.

One guard told us he looked at *Playboy* every month. "Very
dirty," he said.

"Why do you read it if it's dirty?" we asked.

"Oh, I just have to see," he said.

Although we could get away with such conversations with
the guards, we didn't dare try it with Skinny, who was our
main source of information. Skinny was a lieutenant and apparently one of Hanoi's bright young men who held a top
position. He spoke the most fluent English of any Vietnamese
we saw (and better than a lot of Americans) and dealt with all
POWs in Hanoi. He usually escorted visiting foreign dignitaries around, we saw him in a film with Jane Fonda; and his
wife, a doctor who spoke four languages, was a member of
the American-Vietnamese Friendship Committee.

Skinny argued the North Vietnamese line but did it in a
down-to-earth manner, almost like an American intellectual.
He quoted congressmen and senators who were against the
war. He always had the latest *Time* in his black attaché case.
He gave us a copy once and let us take it to our room. The
issue had a picture of Jackie Kennedy in a see-through blouse.
That caused the biggest debate on the cell-block for months.
Should Jackie wear a see-through? A lot of POWs were absolutely indignant.

The spurts of activity notwithstanding, most of the time we
did nothing. Nothing. We were completely and utterly bored.
Had we been specifically sentenced to ten years in jail, at least
then we would've known how long we had to wait. But for
us the end could come tomorrow—or never. The uncertainty
was agonizing.

After our release someone from my group told a reporter
that Hanoi, compared to our jungle camp, was like a Holiday
Inn. The statement angered pilots who were held much
longer in North Viet Nam. But in a physical sense it was true,

Hanoi was much easier for us, nobody starved, nobody had to work themselves to death.

Yet there was no adequate way to compare the two. Confinement in a small cell held its own special terrors. You underwent a constant fight to keep your sanity. Some of the pressures could be worked off by dealing with the guards about little things, like cigarettes. We got six cigarettes a day. (I didn't smoke but I got them too.) Sometimes it was difficult to get the guards to bring a light and the smokers really got upset about this.

The pressures of closed-in living caused a lot of spats, arguments petty in retrospect but major at the time. Kushner and I were by ourselves from November till April, '72. We got along fine at first. But I wasn't the type to give in to his arguments, not when I thought they were wrong, and he believed he was never wrong. In the jungle, arguments could be avoided by simply getting up and walking away. But in a small cell there was no place to go. So we lost the closeness we'd once had. He said things to me I could never forget. Some of it had to do with what had happened in the jungle. He thought I hadn't tried hard enough. In April, after we got four new roommates, we went two weeks with out speaking to each other.

Harker. I saw the Peace Committee for the first time one day when we were allowed outside to play basketball. Their door was open and covered by a curtain. The ball accidentally went inside on a rebound. I went to get it and we talked several minutes while they stood behind the curtain. I saw peanuts and candy and Birley's lemonade on their table.

I asked who the prisoners were in the cell further down.

Someone, I think it was Chenoweth, said, "They're just hard-core reactionary officers."

I said, "What the hell. What's reactionary?"

The PC said, "Well, they won't give in. All they think about is their pay."

I was startled to hear them making excuses for why other Americans were kept in solitary confinement and punished for no apparent reason.

Jose Anzaldua's room, which was next to the PCs, was

talking to them. Jose's attitude was let's strike up an acquaintance and not worry about the political side of it. I couldn't do it. The Vietnamese had beat them, had let their own people die, and now were using them against their country. I couldn't see it. It wasn't simply a matter of being for or against the war. We were all against it.

Cheese told us that Jose's room was going to have a special Christmas ceremony with the Peace Committee and asked if we wanted to join them. We said no.

Daly. We were thinking about two things when we agreed to have Christmas with the Peace Committee. First, we saw the big preparations being made and we figured the NVA might be planning to release someone. We knew that if anybody was released it would probably be the PCs. The North Vietnamese seemed to like us too, and we didn't want to make them angry by refusing to join the PCs for Christmas. Maybe we would also be freed. And second, Jose said, "Perhaps by talking to the PCs we can get them to stop what they are doing." But when we met, the PCs did most of the talking and we did the listening.

Young. We honestly wanted the group from the south to enjoy themselves for a change. I suppose at the same time the North Vietnamese were sort of using us, for they took pictures of us playing cards and talking together. A few days before Christmas the guards began to leave our cell door open from 9:00 A.M. till 6:00 P.M. We could play basketball if we wished, but that got old fast, and we usually just sat outside in the sun reading. We were given extra candy, beer, cigarettes, a thermos jug, a goldfish bowl with twelve goldfish. The extra stuff was Cheese's idea. We weren't opposing the war because of the benefits we were getting, but a lot of POWs took it that way and the whole camp turned against us.

A room was set aside for us in the villa. We decorated it with Christmas scenes copied from old French cards. On Christmas Eve we went over and Jose's room joined us. Harker's room refused to come. We were sorry but there was nothing we could do. Jose's room, we found, was opposed to the war. But they didn't have the nerve to go out on a limb as we did.

One of the blacks said, "Look, we're getting money when we get back, more than we'll ever have at one time in our lifetimes. We don't want to jeopardize it."

That was the major thing keeping the younger enlisted men and many of the officers from speaking out. True, they feared military recriminations when they returned home. But their biggest worry was for all the back pay they were going to get.

We toasted Christmas with wine. Riate and Chenoweth and myself made talks about the war. Jose read a beautiful poem. Then Davis or McMillan began the Lord's Prayer. We tried to join in. The moment was too emotional. Everyone started to cry. We returned to our cells. On Christmas Day we ate in the villa. Vietnamese cooks brought out turkey with all the trimmings. Jose's room broke down again, this time with joy and disbelief. It pleased us to see that they were so happy.

Daly. I joined the Peace Committee on December 28. I had listened to their talks at Christmas and I was impressed. They sounded very sincere. I was tired of the hypocrisy in my room. One minute the men with me would be speaking about how the Viet Cong had helped us in certain situations in the jungle, and then the next minute they were cursing and wishing that Nixon would bomb hell out of Viet Nam.

Still, I wasn't totally convinced what the Peace Committee was doing was right. I thought perhaps if I joined I could talk to them about religion. I found it impossible to speak about religion to the group I'd lived with in the jungle. Even before I was captured I'd learned what I had to do to get along with other soldiers—joke and cuss like they did, which was something I'd never done in my life. Once I did this, though, it became difficult for me to talk about my religion because they laughed at me and reminded me of things I'd said earlier when I was just trying to be one of the gang.

The Peace Committee didn't know me. I thought I could get a fresh start with them. However, it didn't turn out that way. The first week after I joined I had a big argument with one of them about the Bible. Then I had to make an agreement that I wouldn't speak about religion any more, because it caused dissension in the room.

Davis. Daly said, "I think I'll be able to save these guys."

I asked him about his mother and sister, what would happen to them.

He said, "They'll be all right. I'm not sweating going to jail."

I think he wanted to get out of our room. Ike McMillan and Jose teased him a lot. After he left he wouldn't look at us when we saw him outside.

Harker. Fred Elbert, whom we'd known as John Peter Johnson in the jungle, started making regular nightly visits to the villa after New Year's. He told us he was writing his autobiography, which he'd never done before. Soon we realized he was actually going over to talk to the PCs. One day we went to take a bath and the guard ordered him to remain in the room. We washed our clothes and returned to the cell. Elbert and his bedding had disappeared.

from *Survivors*, 1975

We Have Always Survived

by Robert Shaplen

OUTSIDE the restaurant in Cholon, the Chinese section of Saigon, where a group of us were having dinner a couple of months ago, there was a sudden howl of sirens. After years in this city, I had become used to sirens, whose throbbing *wow-wow-wow* is heard constantly, and at first we paid no attention and went on enjoying our fried crab. Within a few minutes, however, it became apparent that some emergency vehicles had come to a stop directly in front of the restaurant. I went out, to find the block cordoned off, while American and Vietnamese military police carried out a house-to-house search in the glow of rotating red-and-white searchlights flashing from the tops of jeeps. Getting out my press credentials, I approached a young American M.P. who was waving his M-16 rifle like a fishing rod. He couldn't have been more than nineteen years old, and he looked as if he might have arrived in Vietnam the day before. When I asked him what was going on, he replied only, "Sir, you'll have to go back into that restaurant." A Vietnamese M.P.—an older man—muttered something in broken English about "students" and "more riot." The Saigon University residential compound, Minh Mang, was only a block away, and for the past week the students had been, as they often are, demonstrating—this time against some new rules designed to prevent just such activity. Pointing to the roof of one of the buildings across the street, the Vietnamese policeman said something about "terrorists." I again tried the young American, who was now ducking in and out of doorways and pointing his gun at anyone still on the street. He was so jittery that I was afraid the weapon could go off at any moment, and it was obvious that he was in no mood to listen to further questions from me. "Sir," he finally spluttered, "have you got a disaster pass?"

I had never heard of a disaster pass—nor, as I subsequently

found out, was there such a thing (the young M.P. was probably referring to a special pass entitling a small number of
officials to go anywhere at any time)—but the phrase has
stayed with me, and I have since reflected that, in a manner
of speaking, I have had a disaster pass for Saigon for a quarter
of a century. Between the date of my first arrival, in June,
1946, and the present highly uncertain time, I have seen the
city undergo myriad changes, almost all of them for the
worse—particularly over the past decade, during which I have
spent approximately half my time in Vietnam. From a 1946
estimate of four hundred thousand, not counting French colonial troops, the population has grown to almost three million, and that of what is called the Saigon metropolitan area,
embracing parts of Gia Dinh Province, which surrounds the
city, is more than four million. Official projections—including
one made by C. A. Doxiadis, the famous Greek city planner,
whose firm did a study of Saigon in 1965—range as high as
nine million two hundred thousand for the metropolitan area
by the year 2000. Once a gracious city of quiet streets lined
with tamarind and flame trees, with plentiful gardens and play
areas, Saigon has become a monstrous urban sprawl, full of
ugly, squalid slums, in which crime abounds. Most of Saigon's
decline and degradation, of course, can be blamed on the war,
and much of it has occurred since 1965, when the Americans
began arriving in strength. The first Indo-China war, between
the Vietminh and the French, from the end of 1946 until the
middle of 1954, affected Saigon, but not nearly as much, because the major impact was felt in North Vietnam and in the
northern parts of South Vietnam. Moreover, the French, having ruled Indo-China for a hundred years, blended into the
scene; they and the Vietnamese had developed their own
peculiar love-hate relationship and were used to each other.
The Americans, though, were, as in so many other parts of
the world, out of place and ill at ease in Vietnam—something
that is even more apparent today, when they are leaving.

In the time of the French war, long before the booming
blasts of rockets, mortars, and artillery were regularly heard
and orange flares filled the sky at night, Saigon was at least as
dangerous as it has been since. This was chiefly because there
was much more random terrorism. One sat in one or another

of the cafés on the main thoroughfare, the Rue Catinat (which was named after one of the first French vessels to come to the area and has now been renamed Tu Do, or Freedom Street), and several times a week, usually around eleven in the morning or five in the afternoon, young men hired by the Vietminh would hurl grenades at the cafés from bicycles. Sometimes they missed or the grenades proved to be duds, but more often than not they killed or wounded members of the motley French Army—including blacks from Africa and Foreign Legionnaires—or civilians who were foolish enough to sit outside. After a time, most of the cafés put up protective metal screens. There were, in the beginning, none of the modern *plastique* explosive devices, which can rip apart whole buildings, but over the months the grenades took their steady toll. Even so, the war never had much visible effect on the easy way of life centering around the cafés and the two main clubs, the Cercle Sportif and the Cercle Hippique. The official American representatives in those days, whose number grew from about a score when I first arrived to several hundred by the time of Dien Bien Phu and the French surrender, shared the pleasant life of Saigon, whose charm was enhanced by the lovely, lithe Vietnamese women, in their native *ao dais*—the traditional long-sleeved dresses with their long skirts slit in two panels to show wide trousers underneath—and by lovely Frenchwomen, too. There was, moreover, a constant feeling of excitement, a genuine sense of adventure. One could arrange clandestine meetings with Vietminh agents in teahouses on the outskirts of town, to which one travelled by *cyclo*—pedicab—and where one sat and sipped tea and discussed the theory and practice of revolution. In Saigon in those days, which now seem impossibly far off, there was none of the tawdriness and none of the dementia that the city reveals today.

General D. used to be one of South Vietnam's leading generals. He was in charge of IV Corps, in the Mekong Delta; he took part in several of the coups after the one that overthrew President Ngo Dinh Diem in November, 1963; and he once tried to mount one of his own, which petered out before it reached Saigon. Eventually, he lost his commission and sank into the limbo that has swallowed up so many Vietnamese leaders in recent years. Nowadays, dressed in stained trousers and a shirt, D. can regularly be seen on Tu Do, gesticulating and shouting wild imprecations. He occasionally comes onto the veranda or into the lobby of the Hôtel Continental—a rambling, high-ceilinged, musty, comfortable remnant of French colonialism, at which I have always stayed while in Saigon. Once, he went behind the room clerk's counter and started handing out room keys to everyone who walked in. The manager—a good-natured man named Philippe Franchini, who is part French and part Vietnamese, and who inherited the hotel from his French father—let him alone, and in time D. grew tired of his game and went off, still shouting. He is a victim of paresis.

There are demented people all over Saigon—most of them simply victims of war. One crazy woman who usually wanders around Tu Do wears an American Indian headdress and is always giggling. No one knows who she is, but she has become a daily feature of the landscape. There are deranged war widows who rant and rave, like General D., but they tend to be more bitter, and they deliberately squat to relieve themselves in front of hotels where Americans stay. Then there is a woman who directs a group of deaf-and-dumb prostitutes—most of them fourteen and fifteen years old, some even younger. They cluster nightly at the corner of Tu Do nearest the Continental, usually just before the curfew hour, which is 1 A.M. At this time of night, there are prostitutes—among them some whom I have watched grow old and tight-faced in the last ten years—standing at street corners all over town, hoping to be picked up by late-cruising customers. At this hour, too, pimps haul their girls around on the backs of motorcycles and offer them at bargain prices. They are scarcely bargains, though; the venereal-disease rate among prostitutes in Saigon is now estimated to be sixty-five per cent.

More tragic than the prostitutes, to my mind, are the street boys of Saigon—wild, tough youngsters, many of them as young as nine or ten, and many of them orphans who have no homes other than the doorways they sleep in at night. Some who work part time as shoeshine boys are as pestiferous as flies and, if finally given in to, curse their customers unless they get what they consider enough piastres. Some sell news-papers, peanuts, pencils, or postcards, or do any momentary job offered them. Most of the time, though, there is nothing for them to do, and increasingly often they steal—from black-market sidewalk stalls, from the open-air stores, from the pockets of careless pedestrians. They spend much of their time smoking cigarettes—marijuana if they can get it—and playing cards for money in the alleyways. Many seem beyond re-demption; some actually want to be arrested and to live in prison, even under the worst of conditions. An American friend of mine carried out an experiment last year. For several months, he had watched one particular boy, who was about nine, and whose life on the streets had not yet totally oblit-erated a look that was almost angelic. Each afternoon, the boy was to be seen around Tu Do, wearing the same tattered shirt and short pants, doing occasional begging or sometimes sell-ing newspapers. My friend took him home, gave him a bath, fed him, and dressed him in some new clothes. The boy thanked him and then asked if he might leave. An hour later, he was back at his station on Tu Do, wearing the old, dirty clothes.

Beggars are all over Saigon, and they range in age from three to three score and ten. Some are the children of refu-gees, and wander about with infant sisters or brothers strapped to their backs, and some are native Saigonese who have made a profession of begging during all the years of the war. Many of them are crippled, either born so or maimed in battle, and they sit on street corners where Americans are most likely to pass by, holding out their hats or cups, smiling and bobbing their heads. They are profuse in their thanks if someone gives them ten or twenty piastres (from three to five cents), but if they are ignored, they, like the shoeshine boys, will hurl curses—which they can be pretty sure the Americans won't understand. Saigonese beggary has become more than an ex-pression of poverty and despair. There is a special quality of self-degradation to it—of self-hatred and hatred of the foreigner who has reduced the whole society to shame and dependence. There is occasionally, of course, actual self-immolation, carried out by young Buddhist monks and nuns who burn themselves to death by soaking their robes in gasoline and then igniting them. The beggars, too, sometimes perform horribly self-destructive acts. One day, while I was walking along Tu Do with a friend, I saw a middle-aged man who had just cut his arms and legs with a knife and lay bleeding on the sidewalk, still holding out his hat. I said, "Oh, my God—only in Vietnam!" My companion, an American who has been in and out of the country for as many years as I have and is married to a Vietnamese woman, rebuked me. "Have you ever seen a big American city late at night, with all its brutality and ugliness and violence?" he asked. He paused, and then added, "It's true, though, that both we and the Vietnamese have a strong feeling of having sinned—against each other and against ourselves. Poor Vietnam is the whore, America the pimp."

Now that the Americans are withdrawing, a sense of impending change is everywhere. My Vietnamese friends—even those who have been closest to us—are bewildered and worried. Most of them have been making good money, but they have not let themselves become part of what I call the American-privileged Vietnamese class, which has grown up over the past five or six years, and which differs noticeably from the privileged Vietnamese class that the French created. My friends have not been motivated primarily by the urge for profit, as have the contractors who have built apartment houses and villas and rented them to Americans at exorbitant prices, or as have those Vietnamese who have taken jobs at high salaries with American construction companies or the American bureaucracy—to say nothing of the thousands of prostitutes, taxi-drivers, and café operators, or the countless black marketeers selling goods pilfered from the docks or stolen from the post exchanges. My friends are people who have simply made the most of the opportunity given them by the huge American presence to earn five, ten, or twenty times as much as they had ever earned before or will ever earn again. Some of those I am speaking of, many of whom are journalists, have remained ardent nationalists; some are strict neutralists; and some accept, with a sense of transcendent fate, the prospect of a Communist victory—mainly because they are so disillusioned by the ineptitude of successive local governments. Disillusion, in the case of the Thieu government, has become contempt; they consider it "Diemist" without Diem's redeeming attributes, which were, in the beginning at least, those of a true nationalist and patriot. There is today a universal distrust of the Army, which runs the country—of the corruption it promotes and countenances, and, in particular, of the money that the wives of generals and other high officers are making from such activities as the disposal of scrap bullet and bomb casings and of Army steel and cement. Such business, of course, has always existed as an adjunct to war, but there is something especially sleazy about the way it is carried on here now, and about the naïve, even bland, acceptance of it by the Americans. A conservative estimate is that fifteen thousand Americans, in uniform or out, have been involved in this process of corruption. These Americans have encouraged the black-marketing of all sorts of goods, have encouraged pilferage for payoffs, have raked in huge profits from the smuggling of drugs and other goods, from the illicit trade in dollars, from the operation of night clubs, from the importation of American call girls, and so on. The prevalence of corruption has its comic as well as its depressing aspects. A few months ago, a group of fifty angry women marched to the National Assembly building and staged a brief, shrieking demonstration to protest the demolition of their black-market street stalls by the police. The police take such action sporadically—and the stalls always reappear as soon as the police disappear. Many of the women who run the stalls are the wives of Army officers, and although they have the protection of their husbands they do not necessarily have that of the police, who obey their own instructions or their own instincts. However, the anger of the women on the march to the Assembly was directed not at the police so much as at the Americans and, indirectly, at the American post exchanges. As long as the Americans permitted various goods to be sold, or stolen—so ran the argument of the women—why blame them for selling those same goods?

The cynicism that dominates Saigon today is notably exemplified by the role that the Vietnamese and American draft-dodgers and deserters play there. Most Vietnamese Army deserters return eventually to their own units or to other units, but some flee to the cities—most often to Saigon—where they hide in the slums or, in some cases, obtain work under assumed names and at unusually low wages in Vietnamese or American companies. Occasional roundups are conducted, but since the ranks of the police are filled with men who are also seeking to avoid military service, the deserters and draft-dodgers are not too assiduously pursued. In addition to the thousands of Vietnamese deserters, there have been hundreds of American deserters in and around Saigon; now, of course, their number has dwindled. Most of the American deserters hide out in the slums, including an infamous area known as Hundred-P. Alley (the "P." stands for "piastre"), which is near Tan Son Nhut Airport and derives its name from the ease with which one may procure anything there—a girl, opium, heroin—for a relatively small fee. The American and Vietnamese police conduct sporadic raids on the place, and seize guns, dope of various kinds, forged leave passes; blank flight authorizations to leave the country, and so forth, all stolen from American bases. It is a world unto itself, one of many such enclaves that survive no matter what action the police take.

There are other spots where, in the receding tide of the American presence, total permissiveness has set in. Among them are night clubs and bars on Plantation Road, near Tan Son Nhut. Late last year, one of the underground G.I. newspapers in Vietnam, *Grunt Free Press*, printed a story about life on Plantation Road headed "Happiness Is Acid Rock." It dealt mostly with one of the more popular rock-and-roll places where young Vietnamese and Americans gather nightly, noting, "There is an empathy between them found nowhere else in Vietnam." The story continued:

> The vibrations are there in the flashing lights and the cool music and the hot air and smoke and crowding. It's a warm scene, as warm as any found in Haight-Ashbury, Greenwich Village, Santa Monica, Des Moines, London, Paris, Berlin, Tokyo, and anywhere else where under-thirties groove together. . . . "You know, it's like this [one American soldier said]. Some G.I.s bitch and moan about Vietnam, but, man, it ain't so bad as all that. Gimme a place like this and it don't matter if I'm in Saigon or Sioux City. There's some good thing

going for us here, man, but you got to know where it's at. . . . It's
the vibrations. I dig the vibrations here. There's something mellow
about these people when I come in here. And I don't get it anywhere
else."

Nearby, in a restaurant on the upper floor of a run-down
tenement, other G.I.s sit and smoke opium or hashish or
marijuana while stereo tapes blare out the latest pop tunes.
Marijuana can be bought virtually anywhere, in phony cigarette packs. A popular brand just now is Park Lane; the names
tend to change as crackdowns increase. Another underground
G.I. paper, *Rolling Stone* (no relation to the domestic sheet
of the same name), last fall quoted a G.I. as saying, "They
couldn't *pay* me to leave here before my enlistment's up. This
place is a gold mine. Hell, scoring grass here is easier than
buying a loaf of bread."

Advertisements like these still appear every day in the Saigon *Post* or the *Vietnam Guardian*, the two main English-
language papers:

THE PIONEERS
OF PROGRESS:

gbs
THE PROFESSIONALS

**What You Need,
We've Got It!**

71 *Ngo Tung Chau*
Sg. Tel. 21922
★

Promptest completion at most competitive fee: Passport, Visa, Extension, Work Permit, Sponsorship,
Cohabitation, Marriage Cert. &
any other paper procedures...
Top   price   purchase   of   non-used   properties   &
various usable items, from vehicles to kitchen sinks!...

(Cohabitation papers allow a Vietnamese girl to live legally
with a man—usually an American—though they are un-
married.)

One of the first victims of Vietnamization may be said to
be Miss Lee. Until early in 1970, the main part of her business
consisted in finding suitable girl partners for American servicemen and other foreigners in town. She kept files on about
fifty women, including young widows, "companions," and
middle-aged women. Her advertisements promised "beautiful

ladies of charm and class, for company, conversation, or . . ."
For five hundred piastres—about two and a half dollars—a
customer had the right to look through her album of photographs. Another five hundred entitled him to meet a girl
and look her over at the office of the agency. For fifteen hundred, a date would be arranged. If a marriage ensued, Miss
Lee took a further cut of twenty-five hundred piastres. The
following advertisement shows what Miss Lee is reduced to
today in the way of offering services:

MISS LEE:

— Needs to buy AIR-
CONDITIONERS &
CARS Top prices paid.

—Has **CAR FOR RENT**

monthly,   weekly,
daily   with insurance:
TOYOTA,   MAZDA,
DATSUN, VOLKSWA-
GEN, JEEP, MICROBUS

Sedan, Pick-up, mic-
robus)—GOOD CONDI-
TION,   SEASONABLE
PRICES.

—SERVANTS, COOKS,
DRIVER LICENCE
—VILLAS   APART-
MENTS, HOUSES
FOR RENT

Please Ask for:

MISS LEE

12-Bis Chi-Lang
GIA-DINH
PTT: 23.637
Daily: 08.00 2·000
including Sundays
and Holidays

Inevitably, the departure of the Americans has also meant
the closing down of many bars, hotels, night clubs, and restaurants in the main sections of Saigon that have thrived on
G.I. patronage. Some of these places, hoping to attract the
Americans' young Vietnamese hangers-on, have changed their
names from such things as Tennessee Bar, Texas, or G.I. Dolly
to Vietnamese ones—street names or the names of local movie
heroes or heroines. One straitlaced Vietnamese I know, who
regards the presence of the G.I.s as a necessary evil but the

self-degradation of his young countrymen as an unnecessary one, said of this transformation, "The rats have taken over."

Welcome To Happy Room

413—415 Phan-Thanh-Gian St.
Saigon Tel.: 90305
Air Conditioned ✳ New Decoration

TURKISH BATH: NIGHT CLUB:

★ Excellent Service   ★ State side Music
✳ Pretty Girl Massager ★ Magicial & Sexy Show
★ Private Steam Tubs   ★ Experienced Band &
                         Beautiful Singer

Here reserved the foreigner only.
Open every day from 09.00 AM To 24.00 PM.

There is also literal truth in this statement. The rat population has increased tremendously in the last two years, despite improvements in the garbage-collection system. One sees rats by the hundreds, especially at night, even around the best restaurants and homes, scurrying across streets, chasing and jumping over each other. Owing to a sad lack of medical facilities—there are approximately five hundred registered M.D.s in Saigon, along with hundreds of Chinese practitioners—illnesses caused by filth and rats are a mounting problem. In 1968, the infant-mortality rate was one in twenty; today, of twenty thousand recorded deaths each month more than half are those of children under five. A large number of deaths, particularly those of infants, go unrecorded. (It recently was revealed, incidentally, that some Saigon surgeons, who had earlier been sent to the United States for training as Army doctors, were devoting much of their talent and time to cosmetic surgery on local women who wanted to look more Occidental.)

Despite all this, and beneath the unrest that one feels today in Saigon—only a fraction of which takes the form of overt demonstrations by students, veterans, and others—one senses something else: an intense determination to endure. Again and again, the Vietnamese reveal a capacity for surviving almost anything: poverty, disease, bombed-out homes, loss of members of the family. Everywhere, Americans bemoan our failures and condemn both the Vietnamese and themselves

either for becoming so deeply involved in the war to begin
with or for not having fought "the right kind of war." There
is a constantly growing awareness among the Americans in
Saigon of the policies that have led us to disaster—and the
publication of the Pentagon Papers, of course, added to this.
But the Vietnamese think differently; among the Vietnamese
in Saigon, the Pentagon Papers scarcely caused a ripple. They
tended to shrug the revelations off with typical fatalism and
cynicism. Whatever they now think of us, their attitude is expressed over and over again in the words "We will survive.
We have always survived."

Saigon may be the most heavily polluted city in the world,
not excluding New York or Los Angeles. There are approximately a million registered vehicles in the area, and probably
at least as many more come and go. In addition to private
cars, small Renault taxis, and buses, there are several thousand
three-wheeled motor scooters and many thousand three-
wheeled *pousse-pousses*—motorized versions of pedicabs. All
these smaller motor vehicles, as well as many of the larger
ones, use kerosene or low-grade gasoline for fuel, so the Saigon air is constantly full of smoke and fumes, and a haze never
leaves the sky. To make matters worse, there are now
thousands of motorcycles, almost all Japanese-made, which
swarm like locusts and make life more hazardous than ever
for pedestrians. A wild Jet Set of Honda-riding youths races
down Tu Do each night, or along the Bien Hoa Highway,
outside town, and then the young men pile their motorcycles
on the sidewalks while they go to cafés or movies. The city
now has a considerable number of traffic lights, but in many
places streams of vehicles still seem to come from all directions
at once, and the ability to maneuver across a busy street at
the height of the morning, noon, or evening rush hour is the
mark of a veteran resident.

From my window at the Continental, I am mesmerized by
the noise and variety of the traffic flow and pedestrian dash.
Roaring convoys of American-made trucks, driven either by
G.I.s or by Vietnamese, are likely to be followed by screaming
police cars escorting some high government official or rushing
to some new disaster. Amid all this, small blue taxis scuttle

about like water bugs, and motorcycles dart in and out. Vietnamese women seem to handle motorcycles more skillfully than men—or, at least, less dangerously. They sit straight and prim in the saddle, often wearing colorful little hats, and their natural grace is even enhanced by their adept control of the sputtering machines. The motorcycles serve as family jitneys, taking children to school and parents to work. Partly owing to the kerosene fumes—and to the fact that some of the kerosene containers were once used for defoliants—Saigon has lost many of its lovely old trees; others have been cut down to widen the streets. The fumes have also affected the normal bird population. A friend of mine bounced into my room one afternoon recently, exclaiming, "Guess what! I just saw a pigeon."

In the past few years, Saigon has acquired an elaborate hippie culture and language. The hippies are categorized by age groups. A *hippie choi choi* (*"choi"* means "play") is a very young hippie, a teenybopper; a *hippie xom xom* is a twenty-year-old boy or girl; and a *hippie lau lau* is an old-time hippie, in his or her late twenties. *"Bui doi,"* which literally means "dust of life," denotes a general hippie attitude, and also is used to describe street youngsters. *"Quan voi"* means "elephant pants"—bell-bottoms. *"Trong cay si,"* literally "to plant love trees," means that one is madly in love. *"Xai tien nhieu my"* means "to spend money like the Americans," to live lavishly, and is used to describe not only the American way of life in Saigon but the American conduct of the war—the indiscriminate use of artillery and planes to achieve a non-achievable objective. *"Bay buom"* means "to fly like a butterfly," as from girl to girl. *"Cao boi,"* the most common term, is a Vietnamese phoneticism of "cowboy," meaning a young hoodlum or tough. In the past two years, *cao bois* have become increasingly numerous, wandering the streets in gangs. They have encouraged much of the increasingly overt anti-Americanism, sometimes jumping American soldiers or civilians on the street and beating them up, for no apparent reason or because they have been hired by somebody holding a grudge against the victim. They are also responsible for other growing street crime, including robberies; many are good at

deftly snatching watches off the wrists of pedestrians. Most of
the hippies, however, are harmless. They meet in cafés and sit
and talk and drink Coca-Cola or beer, complaining about the
futility of life or bragging about how they can stay in school
and out of the Army for two more years because their parents
have lied about their age. Like hippies the world over, they
favor long hair, and the boys have a special fetish—expensive
shoes. These may cost as much as fifteen dollars a pair—a very
high price in Saigon. Last fall, during an anti-crime campaign
that lasted three months, the police arrested more than two
thousand hippies, along with four hundred young men described as *cao bois* and hooligans, but the hippies—arrested
ostensibly because they refused to cut their hair—were quickly
released. During that campaign, almost a quarter of a million
people were apprehended, about half of them for alleged traffic violations. In Saigon nowadays, when one is driving a car
it is commonplace to be stopped by the police for failing to
obey some sort of traffic sign in Vietnamese. Almost always,
a five-hundred-piastre note—worth a bit more than a dollar
at the new official rate—will spare you a trip to the police
station. This, of course, is one way the vastly underpaid policemen make ends meet. In last year's crackdown, the second-
largest group of those apprehended consisted of polluters and
litterers. Then came illegal residents, "military troublemakers" (for the most part, veterans who had engaged in anti-
government demonstrations), draft-dodgers, people with false
identification papers, gamblers, and deserters. The campaign
was launched as a result of a decree, issued late in 1970, that
gave Lieutenant General Nguyen Van Minh, the head of the
Capital Military District, the right to do almost anything to
maintain order in the city, but since most of those arrested or
questioned were released, nothing much came of it all. It was
like the sporadic anti-corruption campaigns in Saigon. Every
now and then, there is a hue and cry about corruption, and
a scapegoat—a Chinese merchant, a Vietnamese found stealing at the docks, or someone caught at the airport in the act
of smuggling heroin or black-market dollars in or out of the
country—is arrested and tried. Then the hullabaloo is over,
and everything continues as before.
    Whether they are hippies or not, virtually all of Saigon's

young people are deeply embittered by what the war has done to them and their country, but, except for a relatively small element of revolutionary activists, they hold their bitterness tightly to themselves. Among the activists, some have covertly established direct liaison with the Communists, and others have made indirect contacts. In the past year, the Communists have stressed the importance of trying to build up the youth movement in the city. Since there are plenty of urgent political, social, and economic issues to be concerned about, a considerable number of high-school and college students have been aroused by the activists. This has been particularly true at times when the government has moved high-handedly, as it often has, to arrest student leaders and subject them to imprisonment and torture. Largely because of their contempt for the Saigon government, a good number of young people still feel admiration for the late Ho Chi Minh, whom most of them respect as a nationalist who led the Vietnamese to victory over the French, rather than as a Communist.

Recently, I talked with a student at the Buddhist Van Hanh University who expressed such admiration. The youth, whom I will call Thanh, was a senior, studying politics. At first, he said that the only people he admired were his parents; his father was a contractor, he told me, and his mother was "in the trading business." Then he observed that the only "world personage" he admired was Ho. When asked why, he replied, "Ho Chi Minh spent his life for Vietnam. He freed Vietnam from world domination. History will judge his actions. But as a very young man, with empty hands, he went to France, worked so hard to get what he got. I admire him on this point. That is what today's youth should learn from him." Like many other young men, Thanh said he liked the Americans as a people but felt they had done his country more harm than good.

The most activist, or most curious, of the Saigon youths go out into the countryside during their summer vacations and during Tet (the New Year period) and join the Vietcong. Whether or not they become Communist operatives, their action is, as much as anything, an expression of their disgust at the degraded, profiteering way of life in Saigon—and, in many cases, at their own parents' participation in it. Similarly, some girls from good middle-class or lower-middle-class families whose incomes are inadequate because of inflation are sent to work in bars and restaurants, and they occasionally sleep with Americans they like while retaining their ties with their families and their Vietnamese boyfriends. Young men from good families, while deprecating their parents' profiteering, are glad to have those parents pay bribes to keep them out of the Army, and they make a point of adeptly juggling the amounts of time they devote to leisure and to attending overcrowded classes so they can avoid military service.

These youths are not to be confused with the rich hippies whose parents keep them out of the service through sheer pull, or with a minority of serious and deeply troubled young men who object to the war. On a number of occasions over the past two years, I have had dinner with a group of six or seven of these serious young people. All are college graduates in their late twenties, and most have done graduate work in law, engineering, education, or administration. One of them works in the Presidential Palace, for one of Thieu's aides. "I have long legs," he says, with a sad smile, implying that he is used primarily as a messenger boy. Another is a lieutenant commander in the Navy, holding down a dull desk job. None of them are doing anything like the work for which they are qualified by their education and ability, and this is part of the tragedy of Vietnam today. The bureaucracy is still French-oriented, immobilized, so although some younger people have been elected to the House of Representatives or to provincial and village councils, the appointive jobs are mostly held by older men. Thus, most of the considerable younger talent that exists is being wasted. "The generation gap is very bad," one of my young friends said. "We are the transitional ones. Those younger don't care or aren't ready for anything. Most of them feel abandoned, and that's why, though they are really disillusioned, they pretend to be full of bravado, like the hippies and *cao bois*. The older intellectuals are lying low or have given up. We have nowhere to turn except to politics, which remains corrupt. The French created their privileged Vietnamese class—the *doc phu su*, or mandarin element—but they left the peasants and the middle class untouched. And they used the civil servants they created as just that—servants. When I was

twenty-one, I had a sense of direction—of behavior and morality. Now anything goes. There is a loss of faith in Vietnamese historical traditions. We know what's wrong here, but
there's nothing we can do about it. No one lets us. At least,
the French allowed the Vietnamese culture to exist, in its own
way, but you Americans have made us a nation of operators.
We're in a void. We're empty."

I reflected afterward that although there has been plenty of
repression of political prisoners and censorship of the press in
Saigon over the past few years, there has also been a greater
degree of freedom of expression—certainly more than there
was in the days of Diem. In the early sixties before Diem's
overthrow, the sort of discussion I easily had on my own with
this group of young men was occasionally possible but had to
be arranged with the utmost care to safeguard the participants. Nowadays though newspapers are regularly banned,
they usually reappear after several days or a week, and continue their criticism of the Thieu government until they are
banned again, and the process repeats itself. It is a kind of
endless anarchy—neither freedom nor total repression. Much
of the published dissent is dissent for dissent's sake—what is
called in Saigon *nham nho*, a phrase translated for me by one
Vietnamese as "bold and brazen talk that's out of place." This
is not to say that some important issues have not been raised
in the press. Considerable attention was given two years ago
to the arrest, trial, and sentencing of the opposition deputy
Tran Ngoc Chau, for example, and to the more recent arrest
of his fellow-deputy Ngo Cong Duc. Duc is the owner of the
most popular opposition paper, *Tin Sang*, which has achieved
the distinction of having been banned most often. (Duc was
defeated for re-election in August, but he continues his broadsides against Thieu.) *"Nham nho"* is also widely used to describe the so-called new culture, which consists largely of
cheap novels and an increasing amount of pornography. This,
like everything else meretricious, is blamed on the influence
of the Americans—and with similar justification.

Lately, however, there has been an awakening of something
new, perhaps best defined as an awareness of anger. This was
apparent a few months ago in an exhibition of paintings,

drawings, poems, scrolls, and pamphlets by students at the
College of Arts and Letters of Saigon University. Most of the
paintings and sketches were naturally concerned with the war,
and many of them had a harsh, "Guernica"-like quality. One
large panel depicted Americans as eagles, hawks, and wolves
devouring the countryside. There were many paintings or
drawings of cemeteries and skulls, of bare bones in fields, of
people on the run. One poignant painting, called "Going
Back," showed a group of boys returning to an empty village
in the war-ravaged wilderness. Another, which showed shackled prisoners, was entitled "Victory of the U.S. Over Prisoners
of War," and a slogan in Vietnamese read "Hate calls for hate,
blood for blood, skull for skull." A Vietnamese friend I went
to the exhibition with remarked that it was a display of "the
weapons of the weak." Without guidance, sense of direction,
or much talent, the young artists and poets were venting their
wrath against the Americans because, as my friend said, "they
have no other way to say anything—they can't attack the government, but the government lets them attack the United
States." There have been more and more anti-American car-
toons in the newspapers recently. Still, it is surprising to me
that the anti-American sentiment has risen so slowly. In Saigon, the slowness can be explained partly by the fact that,
with rare exceptions (such as an American jeep leaving the
scene of an accident, or a few G.I.s getting into fights with
Vietnamese in bars), the American troops have behaved well,
and that over the past two years fewer and fewer G.I.s have
been allowed to come to the capital. (Several other big cities
have been declared off limits entirely.) The worst instances of
American brutality, epitomized by My Lai, have occurred in
the countryside; the number of smaller but similar incidents
will never be known but must run into the thousands. On the
other hand, one must say that the average American who has
served in Vietnam for a year or eighteen months, though he
may have failed to understand the Vietnamese, has generally
left them alone. In the earlier days of the war, some friendships
were established between Americans and Vietnamese, but they
were nearly always surface relationships. The Vietnamese are
not easy to know, and they like to emphasize their inscru-

tability to the Americans, who shuttle in and out of their lives so quickly. After my twenty-five years of contact with the country, I have perhaps a score of close Vietnamese friends, all of them in Saigon.

One reason that the Vietnamese are not easy to know is that there has been a deplorable slowness in instituting systematic Vietnamese-language training for our people here. Vietnamese is extremely hard to learn, because of its many tones—some words can be pronounced five or six different ways, tonally, and have five or six altogether different meanings. Matters could have been improved quite easily, however, if we had subsidized the widespread teaching of English to the Vietnamese instead of letting them acquire it in local, often rather expensive, fly-by-night schools. For those under forty, English, rather than French, is the second language in Saigon, but it is not spoken as well as French was, and still is. Indeed, one of our greatest failures in Vietnam has been in the field of education in general. We have built schools all over the country, yet there are not enough teachers, books, or equipment. Though the Vietnamese, like the Chinese, are hungry for education, attendance in four of eleven Saigon school districts is less than fifty per cent of those eligible. This is because the city now has slightly more than a thousand classrooms in public and private elementary schools, with an enrollment of two hundred and fifty-seven thousand. A third to a half of the classroom space is operated on three shifts a day, which means that many of the children who are able to attend school at all are there for only three hours. There are twenty-five hundred teachers, or one teacher for more than a hundred pupils. Not surprisingly, then, only fifty-eight per cent of the children who enter school finish even the elementary grades.

The situation in the universities is in some ways even worse. Saigon University—one of eight universities and colleges in the country—has about thirty-five thousand students and three hundred and fifty teachers, or one teacher for about seventy-seven students. Many, if not most, of the professors and instructors devote only three hours a week to their Saigon classes, because they have to travel the length and breadth of the country to teach at other universities scattered from Hué, in the north, to Can Tho, in the south. Lectures are ordinarily handed out in mimeographed form, and there is virtually no classroom discussion. Moreover, there is so little scientific equipment that twenty-two thousand of Saigon University's thirty-five thousand students are enrolled in either its College of Arts and Letters or its law school—this in a country that, if it is to survive at all, needs many more engineers and scientifically trained graduates than lawyers or students of literature. One consequence of the university's inadequacy is that sons and daughters of the wealthy go abroad to study, and stay away. My friend Ton That Thien, who is a social historian and is the dean of Van Hanh University, a private Buddhist institution with thirty-six hundred students, sympathizes with those who can afford to go abroad, even while he bemoans the effects of their absence on Vietnam. "Who wants to come back to a huge prison and get killed?" he asks.

One of the idols of the younger generation is a slim, bespectacled young man, born in Hué, named Trinh Cong Son, who, at thirty-two, is the composer of some haunting antiwar songs, which, though banned in 1968 and 1969, are still played in a few night clubs and distributed on pirated cassettes. A twenty-three-year-old North Vietnamese refugee girl named Khanh Ly, whose deep, melodious voice is as haunting as the songs themselves, has helped make them famous. Perhaps the most famous of the songs is "The Love Song of a Madwoman," which contains the names of memorable battles in the long war:

I had a lover who died in combat at Pleime.
I had a lover from Zone D who died in combat at Dong
   Xoai.
I had a lover who died at Hanoi.
I had a lover who died in a hurry somewhere along the
   borders.
I had a lover who was killed in the battle of Chuprong.
I had a lover whose cadaver was floating down a river. . . .

Another of Son's songs is called "A Lullaby of Sounds of Cannon Fire in the Middle of the Night." The first part goes:

Every night the sounds of cannon fire reverberate through
   the city.
A city sweeper stands still in the street, a broom in his
   hands.
The sounds of cannon fire wake a mother from her sleep,
Fill the heart of a baby with poignant sadness. . . .
Shelters are being destroyed, laid in lifeless ruins,
Yellow skin, yellow flesh, what a tragedy being blown to
   pieces.

Trinh Cong Son, who sometimes sits in night clubs to hear
Khanh Ly sing his songs, has gained fame but little money
from them, for he has no control over the cassette distribution. What money he does make comes from sheet-music sales
of love ballads he has written. The government has more or
less left him alone, because of his popularity, but he has little
faith or trust in politicians and little interest in politics. A year
or so ago, some friends in the Vietnamese Air Force offered
him a safe assignment as an enlisted man, but he turned it
down. His songs are extremely popular with members of the
armed forces, who go to the club on Tu Do where Khanh Ly
sings them and sit and applaud her wildly. Sometimes, one
veteran, who has lost an arm, a leg, and an eye in battle, gets
up and sings the songs in a husky voice, with the spotlight
playing on him, creating a grotesque shadow play.
   I spent an afternoon talking with Trinh Cong Son and listening to a few of his latest songs, which are somewhat in the
nostalgic vein of the revolutionary ballads of the Spanish Civil
War. Among the titles are "We Are Determined to Live," "We
Can Count Only on Ourselves," and "Vietnam, Rise Up."
Hearing them, I thought of the words of a Vietnamese Communist marching-and-indoctrination song I had recently read.
It was taken from the body of a North Vietnamese soldier,
and had none of the sadness of Trinh Cong Son's songs. In
contrast with it, even his latest ones sound anachronistic and
sentimental. Here is one verse:

   To feel a resentment when our hatred boils,
   Living is to endure misery and pain,
   To be haughty, to subdue the enemy,
   To roar when our people are suffering,

To be ashamed when we are defeated.
Living is to snarl in fury,
To feel a hatred when our people are in misery,
To keep away vile and shameless people.
To be proud is moving forward in combat.
Living is to put the enemy to death.

While Hanoi has always been a city with a strong identity, both political and intellectual, Saigon has never had such a well-defined role or character. A friend of mine says, "You hear people say, 'I'm a New Yorker,' or *'Ich bin ein Berliner,'* but you never hear anyone say, 'I am a Saigonese.'" Even the history of the city is ill-defined. There are a number of theories about its beginnings. The land on which it stands was once a watery waste of marshes and swamps, with a few clusters of trees and tall reeds among countless small streams. Tigers, leopards, monkeys, snakes, and crocodiles were the only inhabitants. The first human beings known to have lived there were called Phu Nam, which may mean "people from the swamps of the south," and their origin is obscure, but in recent decades archeologists have uncovered earthenware and jewelry that are believed to have been fashioned by Phu Nam. In the first century A.D., according to Vietnamese historians, ships sailing from Rome to China by way of India touched at South Vietnam, but whether any of the sailors ventured as far inland as Saigon is doubtful. The name Sai Gon was first heard by Europeans in 1675, as reported by both a British travel writer and a French travel writer of the period. An early account speaks of Tay Cong—*"tay"* from the Chinese word meaning "west" and *"cong"* meaning "tribute." The suggestion is that what is now Saigon was a small outpost paying tribute to various kings or warrior leaders, probably including Chinese, Vietnamese, Siamese, and Cambodians, since these peoples fought back and forth over the lower part of Indo-China until the French began to dominate the peninsula, in the nineteenth century. Whatever its history, Saigon was never considered a capital by the rival Vietnamese emperors based at Hanoi, the capital of Tonkin, and Hué, the capital of Annam, who fought each other for control of all of Vietnam between the sixteenth and nineteenth centuries. Instead,

Saigon recurrently served as a place of refuge—a temporary haven for an exiled or defeated ruler—or a place the ruling emperor could put in the charge of an underling.

It was not until the French formally took over the entire country, around 1880, that Saigon, as the principal city of what European explorers had christened, from an earlier Chinese name, Cochin China, gradually became one of two Indo-Chinese capitals, Hanoi being the other. Thereafter, the French governor-general divided his time between the two. Over the years, though, Saigon remained more of a commercial center than a capital city. It was a place where people went to make money. As Ton That Thien says, "People come to Saigon at the dictates of their heads, not their hearts, and they come to take, not to give." This was probably true of the first Yankee traders to complete transactions in the area—Salem sea captains named John Brown and John White, aboard the ships Marmion and Franklin, who in 1819, after considerable negotiation, sailed home with cargoes of sugar. (The Vietnamese name for Americans, Hoa Ky, stems from this visit, when the Stars and Stripes was interpreted by the local people as the "flower [*hoa*] flag [*ky*].") In 1823, White published a book on the voyage. In a passage that calls to mind today's Saigon, he describes the amount of bribery and finagling he and Brown had to use to get the sugar they wanted, through local officials and merchants. Conversely, he reminds us of anything but modern Saigon when he tells how zealously some of the womenfolk were guarded.

When the French took over the South—in 1862, twenty-three years before they gained control of the North with the ostensible purpose of using it as a springboard for the development of the China trade—Saigon and Cholon were just two scattered collections of small settlements built up along the mudbanks of small canals and the Saigon River. The settlements were connected by dirt roads and paths that ran along the canals. In the following decades, particularly after 1900, the French built their familiar stucco structures with red tile roofs that still dominate the city. Official buildings and private homes were all in the same style, with open verandas and large gardens, and they stood on wide boulevards and streets that the French planted with hundreds of trees. One thing to be

said for the French colonialists is that they knew how to plan
and create cities, and Saigon was probably their gem. As the
capital of Cochin China—which was a colony, whereas Annam
and Tonkin were protectorates—Saigon from the outset was
primarily a commercial center.

Even before the First World War, the French met with a
good deal of political resistance from Vietnamese nationalists,
and crushed them ruthlessly, driving them from the cities into
the countryside and then conducting campaigns in which
whole villages were often wiped out for harboring a cell of
resistance leaders. In furthering their economic objectives, the
French dealt largely not with the Vietnamese but with the
local Chinese, and Saigon was essentially a French-Chinese
city rather than a Vietnamese one. The Chinese traders
formed a comprador class, much like that employed by Europeans in China, and they were also used in administrative
roles, subordinate to the French *fonctionnaire* class. However,
the French did start a number of primary and secondary
schools to train Vietnamese as interpreters and petty *fonctionnaires*. Largely because of the University of Hanoi, which was
opened in 1917 as a branch of the University of Paris, Hanoi
became the cultural and political center of Indo-China. (Saigon University was set up some thirty years later, as a branch
of Hanoi University.) Saigon, for its part, was dominated by
Chinese rice mills in Cholon and by a handful of powerful
French trading and shipping companies, which had some
Vietnamese employees. Most of the interpreters originally
used by the French were Vietnamese students from the French
Catholic schools, who also had some knowledge of the Latin
alphabet and of Chinese characters. What Vietnamese intellectuals there were sought haven in the countryside among
the local Vietnamese landowners, who led a precarious existence, because they hesitated to claim their ancestral holdings
under French sponsorship for fear the French would one day
be thrown out by the Vietnamese nationalists, whereupon a
restored royal government would take reprisals against them
as collaborators. A lot of land in the Delta thus being officially
unclaimed, the French claimed it for themselves; some of it
went to the local French-run Catholic Church. The *doc phu
su* mandarin element were allowed to have some land, too.

During the twenties and thirties, Saigon grew and became
more cohesive. Physically and politically, it was still quite distinct from Cholon, but streetcar lines now connected the two
(they lasted until the mid-fifties, when they were replaced by
bus lines). The two cities were not joined politically under a
common administration until after the French departed, but
there was commingling of commerce through the conduits of
the French and Chinese comprador system. Also, in 1936 the
French completed the Trans-Indo-China Railway, which ran
between Hanoi and Saigon (the trip took forty hours, and a
fourth-class ticket cost only a few dollars), and this helped
promote commerce and trade throughout the country. By the
late thirties, the *doc phu su* had become chiefs of districts or,
in Saigon, subordinate officers in the French municipal bureaucracy. During the thirties, some sons of *doc phu su* went
to France to study, as did the sons of rich peasants, and even
a few sons of workers. Most of these foreign students returned
to become teachers, lawyers, doctors, or pharmacists, but others became members of a burgeoning revolutionary element.

In the twenties and thirties, too, the French were building
up rubber, coffee, and tea plantations in the south and central
parts of the country, and many of them maintained luxurious
villas both on their plantations and in Saigon. In town, a
Frenchman, dressed in white shorts and shirt, would work a
few hours a day and then retire to his home and, after a siesta,
go to a café for an apéritif, after which it would be time for
dinner and a visit to his club. And after rice-harvest time there
could also be seen in Saigon some of the few wealthy Vietnamese landowners, dressed in rich silk robes, who were in
town for a couple of weeks to shop for French luxuries and
Chinese delicacies. There was also a new element arriving—
the Corsicans. Some had come as servicemen and Legionnaires, others as employees of the police or customs services;
in time, tougher, Mafia-type Corsicans, with international
smuggling and racketeering connections, showed up. A number of Corsicans opened restaurants or ran them for French
bosses, and these places, which, unlike the earlier French restaurants, served not only French food but Chinese, gave Saigon the reputation of combining the two best cuisines in the
world. In general, life in Saigon and in all of Cochin China

was soft and easy, even for the peasants—in contrast to life in the north, where the climate was more rigorous and the soil less fertile. The peasant in what is now North Vietnam spent many hours a day tilling his fields or fishing, but the southerner could turn his soil over in a couple of hours, throw in his seeds, and just let the rice grow; when he went fishing in his sampan, at dawn or at dusk, he would take along a lantern and two pieces of wood, which, when he clapped them together, attracted fish. In half an hour, he would have all the fish he could use, and, like his new French master, he could go home and relax. As always, the people who worked hardest were the Chinese. Cholon was already a close-knit society of clans and family branches. One of the earliest heads of the Chinese community was a rich merchant, Ong Tich, who owned a fleet of boats that brought rice from the Delta to the city along the rivers and canals. It was his chief assistant, Ma Tuyen, who in 1963 hid the fugitive dictator Ngo Dinh Diem and his brother Ngo Dinh Nhu before they were found by Vietnamese officers and murdered.

Though the French took Vietnamese or Chinese mistresses, there was little intermarriage. The good Vietnamese families disapproved of such marriages, for the most part, and a girl who became the wife of a Frenchman was looked down upon and often ostracized from her own circle. There were more marriages between Chinese and Vietnamese. A Chinese man who came to Cholon from southern China to make money frequently left a wife behind him but took a Vietnamese wife, too, and raised a family there, perhaps returning to China after ten or twenty years, leaving his Vietnamese wife behind. Some of the Chinese who came remained, though they might revisit China every few years—and, like all good overseas Chinese, they regularly sent remittances to their families back home. A Vietnamese song of the time indicates how the Vietnamese felt toward the French and toward the Chinese. It tells of a French boss who is returning to France and advises his Vietnamese *co-ba*, or mistress, to marry his Vietnamese interpreter. The Vietnamese interpreters, however, were then regarded as having prostituted themselves to the French and were held in contempt. The song goes on, "They are not good for each other, the girl and the interpreter, even if they both have tens of hundreds of piastres." The song concludes with the words "It is better for the girl to marry a humble Chinese who has a pole and two baskets to feed his pigs."

Between the two world wars, the French prided themselves on having defeated the national resistance movements in Vietnam—a pride that went before one of history's biggest falls. During the mid-thirties, resistance cells managed to stay alive in the South, though the jails were full of political prisoners, and by the late thirties the revolutionaries had become openly active again in the Saigon area. In 1940, what was known as the Insurrection of Cochin China took place. The leading Southern revolutionary at the time was Le Hong Phong, the head of the Cochin China Committee of the Indo-China Communist Party, which Ho Chi Minh had by then welded together (although the Party had been outlawed in 1939 and about two hundred members arrested). Just after the defeat of France in Europe, the Insurrection was savagely suppressed, and Phong and his wife were caught and executed. By the time the Japanese invaded Indo-China, a short while afterward, the rebellion was over. The French, under an admiral named Jean Decoux, were permitted by the Japanese to maintain control of the country's administrative apparatus, but the Japanese actually took control. They kept most of the Vietnamese Communists in jail but sent a few nationalists to Japan, as part of a long-range plan for indoctrinating local leaders to help Japan build its "Greater East Asia Co-Prosperity Sphere."

Under combined Japanese and French control, Saigon became a city in a cocoon. Though the Japanese were clearly the masters, life generally continued for a time at its easy pace. Gradually, however, this gave way to a harsher discipline. With their shaved heads and samurai swords and boots, the Japanese were privately mocked by the Vietnamese and French alike—except for a small number of collaborators—but, by and large, the Japanese were accepted with Oriental fatalism by most Saigonese. There was no coal coming into Saigon from the North because the Japanese were using it for war purposes, so rice had to be burned as fuel, and by 1944 there was an acute rice shortage all over Vietnam. More than a million people in the North were starving. In Saigon and the rest of the South, the Vietnamese were not as badly off, but they suffered, too, and the suffering increased as time went on, for the Japanese reduced the amount of rice grown, by forcing the people in the countryside to raise pigs and hemp, which the Japanese needed for food and fibre. The upper-class French, though cut off from France, were able to make do, and the Chinese, too, managed to survive fairly well, but the Vietnamese poor suffered more and more as the war dragged on. In Indo-China, the Japanese committed few atrocities compared to what they were responsible for in other parts of Southeast Asia, but as the war continued, a Vietnamese underground was formed to pass military information to the Allies, and those of its members who were caught were summarily executed. By 1944, the news that the Japanese were losing the war had become pretty well known in Saigon. Vietnamese who worked for Japan's Domei News Agency and members of the French Secret Service, including some double agents, had spread the word. (There was also a small group of Gaullists, and they helped.) By this time, American B-29 bombers, called "black tunas" because they came in from the sea, had begun bombing the docks of Saigon and the railroad station, and air-raid sirens were regularly heard in the city. The Japanese became aware of a growing lack of coöperation among the French and also of a growing Vietnamese resistance movement, led by Ho Chi Minh as head of the Vietminh, and Tokyo decided to take the administration out of French hands almost entirely. This was done on March 9, 1945, and the five months before the war ended constituted a twilight period. Five thousand French troops were interned by the Japanese in Saigon, but a few *fonctionnaires* were allowed to remain free to keep things running. The Vietnamese and the Chinese mostly stayed in their homes, awaiting the war's outcome.

Of the many changes that Saigon has undergone in the course of its history, probably none was as great as that which occurred in August and September of 1945. The first British occupation troops—mostly Indians—arrived early in September, and were warmly welcomed by the Vietnamese, who, moving swiftly, had already taken control of the city. For the most part, the welcomers were members of the Vietminh People's Committee, directed by General Nguyen Binh. Ho Chi Minh had sent Binh south in 1945 to take over command of the underground from Tran Van Giau, who, in Ho's estimation, had failed to put up an effective resistance to the French and the Japanese. Binh had quickly set up separate and distinct zones for revolutionary operations and started a training center, and he had placed his men not only in Saigon but in many hamlets in the Delta and in the region north of Saigon. The British refused to deal with the Vietminh, even though the Vietminh offered to coöperate in disarming some seventy thousand Japanese who remained in the South. Instead, the British commander, Major General Douglas Gracey, declared martial law, armed the five thousand French soldiers who had earlier been interned, and ordered the disarmament of the Vietminh and the Vietnamese police. Some Japanese troops were even used to suppress the Vietnamese nationalist movement, and hundreds of ordinary Vietnamese citizens suspected of revolutionary activity were rounded up and imprisoned by the French. The Vietnamese retaliated by calling a general strike, which virtually crippled Saigon. Guerrilla fighting had already broken out in the suburbs and the surrounding countryside. Each night, there were assassinations, and the sky above Saigon was red with the flames of exploding ammunition or fuel dumps or of the homes of suspected collaborators. Toward the end of September, the French mounted a coup against the remaining Vietminh in the city, attacking their last sanctuaries—the Hôtel de Ville, the Post Office, and Sûreté headquarters. Scores of additional Vietnamese were seized and jailed; others fled to the countryside to hide and wait. The campaign of terror continued into 1946, as General Binh reorganized his forces, and in December, 1946, when the war against the French broke out in earnest, Binh had control of sizable parts of the Delta. Meanwhile, the terrorist attacks in Saigon increased month by month.

These attacks had become really serious by 1950, the year in which the Americans made their fateful decision to support the French economically and with large amounts of matériel—a decision based to a considerable extent on the fact that in Europe we were trying, through the Marshall Plan, to put

France back on its feet after the ravages of the Second World
War. Of course, the drain on France would have been more
easily alleviated if the French had granted the Vietnamese a
real measure of autonomy and thus eased the colonial conflict.
Their only step in this direction was to set up the Annamite
Emperor Bao Dai as Chief of State. Bao Dai, whom I met
several times, was far less of a playboy than he was reputed to
be, but his efforts to gain real concessions from the French
were frustrated, and the resistance intensified. As for the
Americans, during this critical period our officials, except for
a handful, thought we should stand behind the French, while
gently prodding them to give the Vietnamese a few more independent functions. This was the real beginning of the tragic
United States involvement.

Despite the atmosphere of tension, Saigon in the late forties
and early fifties retained many aspects of a typical French provincial city. Except for the hours spent around the pool at the
Cercle Sportif by day and at the restaurants, gambling parlors,
and brothels at night, money-making was a pastime that absorbed everyone. Paris was the nerve center of the game, and
vast fortunes were made by the French and their friends
among the Vietnamese and Chinese on the basis of a totally
unrealistic rate of exchange between the franc and the piastre.
The trick was to wheel and deal in Saigon and then transfer
your ill-gotten piastres to Paris by telegraph, but one had to
have permits for the transfers, and huge bribes were paid to
get them.

In 1954, the United States Legation became an Embassy,
which brought in more Americans. Though they mingled with
the French at the Cercle Sportif, they otherwise kept to themselves, leading the compound-ridden lives that official Americans—and many business people as well—lead abroad, going
to their places of work by day and retiring at night into
barbed-wire-protected apartment houses and villas. Long before the major war began, this barbed wire had become a
common sight in Saigon, and I well remember the first enclo-
sures behind which the Americans shielded themselves.

The stream of Saigonese life continued to flow along Rue
Catinat. Day after day, one could see the whole swarm of

colonial and Vietnamese society on the broad avenue, lined with cafés and elegant shops filled with the best French goods. Nearby, some thirty thousand French civilians—the chief money-makers—lived in sumptuous villas. Catinat was their meeting place, and the delicate social nuances of Saigon could be detected in the manner in which people greeted each other—in the nature of a handshake and in the quick flick of a smile, or the lack of one. French and Vietnamese women flowed by like shoals of multicolored tropical fish. Then, there were Algerians, Moroccans, Tunisians, and Senegalese from the French Colonial Army. And there were the Indians, who flocked to Saigon after the war and became merchants and moneylenders. Today, the Indians are the main money-changers—the black market is sometimes called the Bank of India —but a recent crackdown on illegal financial dealings and a revised exchange rate have somewhat diminished the trade in black-market dollars.

While the area around Catinat remained the social and commercial hub of Saigon, the spokes of the city's wheel, now stretching out for miles, made up the real Saigon. The city's population quadrupled between 1940 and 1950, and the ever-increasing swarm of people for the most part lived precariously, on the edge of poverty. On the fringes of the city were the shantytowns, huts made of straw and mud and pieces of tin, that were haunts of the poor and the displaced, the coolies and all those others who managed in some way to earn a few piastres a day. In the somewhat better areas, closer to the center of the city, there were whole blocks of what were called *compartiments*, which were narrow one-story, or occasionally two-story, structures of wood or tin about twenty feet deep; they usually contained a store of some sort in front and living quarters in back. This was lower-middle-class Saigon. Among these structures and behind them, in dank corners in an intricate maze of alleyways, were cubicles used for prostitution and abortion, or for smoking opium. There were holes leading from one *compartiment* and one alleyway to another, and these not only afforded escape routes for criminals but served as a spawning ground for Vietminh cells. It was here that General Binh's terrorists met to get their grenades and here that they hid after using them.

The main business of this labyrinthine part of Saigon—including sections of Cholon—was gambling. The poor gambled at least as much as the rich, and were victimized by racketeers, who ran the gambling syndicates, as they ran everything else, including the brothels. The most famous of the houses in the early fifties was the House of the Four Hundred, which the French built and protected primarily for the use of their own military, though Vietnamese, too, were eventually allowed in. Customers could buy tickets and then choose any one of approximately four hundred girls (who were medically inspected every week). According to a friend of mine, "It was more like a slaughterhouse than a bordello, and the noise was enough to drive a man crazy." The plushest gambling casino was the Grand Monde, which was situated on the border of Saigon and Cholon. Initially, the major gambling houses were controlled by Chinese or Macanese, but then the Binh Xuyên, a local gangster organization run by a Vietnamese named Bay Vien, moved in and took over almost all the casinos, including the Grand Monde. With the approval of Bao Dai, he also won control of the police, and in effect, with a further nod from the French, became the "boss" of Saigon. He moved around town with an entourage of fancily clad armed bodyguards, and at night at the Grand Monde he dispensed purple chips worth five thousand piastres to his friends and snubbed anyone he didn't trust or who was of no use to him. At his headquarters, he had a private zoo, including tigers and poisonous snakes, and beneath it was a tunnel where he kept a large cache of guns and opium. Bay Vien's power did not wane until after the French defeat in 1954 and the assumption of power by Ngo Dinh Diem, who was appointed Premier by Bao Dai. After a number of bitter battles in the streets and in the marshes around the city, where the Binh Xuyên had hideouts, the organization was finally destroyed in 1955, and Bay Vien fled to France (where Bao Dai, deposed as Emperor by Diem, also settled in comfortable exile). I saw Bay Vien in Paris three years ago. He was acting the role of a benign old man, but the earlier soul of the gangster chief was still betrayed in his sharp, flickering smile and his small, darting eyes.

After the French defeat in 1954 and Ho Chi Minh's full

takeover in North Vietnam, there was a vast exodus of nearly a million people from North to South. The influence of these Northerners, many of them Catholics, on the Saigonese and the other Southerners has been a lasting one. Initially, Diem's idea was to place the majority of the refugees in a sort of *cordon sanitaire* around Saigon, in the hope that they would serve as a protective screen against the Vietminh, but most of the newcomers wanted to be in Saigon. They had come South with very little in the way of money and possessions, so they had to scramble to make a living, and the best place to scramble was in the city. Many of them were uprooted intellectuals and professional people who felt out of place in the commercial-minded Southern city, and their sense of isolation was enhanced first by the unrest and violence during Diem's early struggle to gain control and later by the fact that Diem himself, who came from central Vietnam, tended to rely strongly on his own small group of intimates and on Southerners he felt he could trust. Also, against the background of political intrigue in the South, the Northerners seemed more rational and tough-minded, whereas the Southerners were less sure of themselves, more given to subterfuge, and less sophisticated. Ultimately, however, the two groups began to mingle, and the process, which continues, was both a subtle and a useful one. In many respects, it was the Southerners who succumbed to the influence of the Northerners, or, to put it differently, the Southern way of life was absorbed into the Northern framework. Many, if not most, of Saigon's newspapers, for example, were taken over by Northerners, who made them more politically aggressive and also more comprehensive. The Northerners, who as a rule were better educated, had an enlivening influence on writing and poetry—to which, in time, the Southerners responded both by adapting to the cultural change and by mass-producing lower-quality material. Novels of romance and adventure began running in the papers as serials and appearing in bookstores and on sidewalk stands; once again making money counted for more than the quality of what was sold.

As for business in general, with the French influence diminished (though by no means eliminated, since the French kept rubber plantations and shipping and trading interests) the Southern and Northern Vietnamese competed to take over what had been dominated by French and Chinese. Because the Northerners were better competitors, they often won out, but the competition was healthy and served to heighten the spirit and temper of the city. The Northerners also led the Southerners to adopt more elaborate dress and more careful and precise manners, adding further variety and zest to the city's life. And yet, despite the slow and useful interplay, the two cultures remained basically separate. As time went on, the Diem regime, especially as it came to be dominated by Diem's brother Ngo Dinh Nhu and Mme. Nhu, became more and more authoritarian. Life in Saigon became increasingly tense. The Southerners withdrew more into themselves, while the Northerners alerted themselves more. By the time I returned to the city early in 1962, after an absence of a number of years, the mounting resistance to the Diem regime could be felt in the atmosphere, and it was apparent that it was only a matter of time before there would be an explosion. It was not too difficult to arrange clandestine meetings with those opposed to Diem, in the back rooms of private homes or tiny restaurants. Finally, when the explosion came, in November, 1963, and Diem and Nhu were overthrown with American help, Saigon seemed to breathe one vast sigh of relief.

Saigon is now officially one of eleven autonomous cities in the country—that is, cities independent of provincial authorities—but its mayor, Do Kien Nhieu, is responsible militarily to General Nguyen Van Minh, for he is chief not only of the Capital Military District but also of the III Corps area, which surrounds Saigon and stretches away to the north, northeast, and northwest. Ultimately, though, President Nguyen Van Thieu is the man who runs Saigon, by means of a tightly organized palace entourage, which controls the security forces throughout the city and determines all policy matters, such as how much freedom of speech and assembly the Buddhists and the students may be allowed at any given time. Whenever there is a crackdown on demonstrations, or a roundup of students or other dissident elements, or the arrest of an opposition political leader, one can be sure that the order for it came directly from the palace.

All the complex problems and violent conflicts besetting the city are compounded by tremendous overcrowding. By 1963, the population of the Saigon metropolitan area had reached two million two hundred thousand, and it has leaped upward each year since, owing to the influx of refugees from the countryside. Since 1965, three and a half million people are estimated to have become refugees, and of these two million have moved into the cities. The population of South Vietnam, approaching nineteen million, is now almost half urbanized, whereas before the war it was eighty per cent rural. Estimates are that perhaps a third of the present urban population will move back to the countryside after the war; the rest, however difficult life is in the city, will want to stay there, because of job opportunities and the sheer excitement of cosmopolitan as compared to rural life. Saigon's population density averages about seventy-five thousand per square mile, but there are some blocks where nearly two thousand people are crowded into three or four acres. An American official who has acted as an adviser to the Vietnamese on municipal problems for several years has estimated that ten per cent of the city's population live in splendor and comfort, forty per cent live a lower-middle-class life of survival, and fifty per cent live in abject squalor. Compared to Calcutta and some other cities in India, Saigon may not be so badly off, but there is no doubt that the war has created a grave situation and that very little is being done to correct it. On a number of occasions, I have flown back and forth across the city in a helicopter at just above housetop level and observed the growing patches of slums in most of the districts. From the air, too, one can see the pattern of destruction wrought by the war—mostly by the 1968 Tet offensive. Several thousand large re-settlement blocks have been erected, the majority of them on the fringes of the city, but they are not nearly enough to meet the demands for veterans' housing, let alone low-cost housing for civil servants and the general displaced public. As the city has expanded, the number of districts has grown in the past twenty years from five to sixteen, incorporating large parts of neighboring

Gia Dinh Province. Saigon, in its municipal housing program, has not yet discovered, as Singapore has, for example, the uses of high-rise housing—"high" here meaning four or five stories. There are, of course, a few Saigon hotels that rise to ten or eleven stories, and some office buildings that have as many as eight floors. But by and large the city is still flat and dotted—a mass of one- or two-story structures filling every available inch of space. Two-thirds of the population still occupy dwellings that lack the basic utilities, including water, which is drawn from neighborhood wells. Such dwellings—huts or shacks, usually made of a combination of mud, thatch, flattened-out beer cans, and American-donated sheets of tin—are classified by the government as unauthorized housing, and during the student and veteran demonstrations of the past two years some have been torn down by the police. In general, though, because there is no cohesive building program and no established procedure for assisting masses of the impoverished, the police and other officials turn their backs on the slum conditions—when they don't make money out of them through extortion. The city has a total of eleven public hospitals, with fewer than five thousand beds, and thirty-nine public dispensaries, and there were cholera epidemics in 1964 and 1966; it is thanks only to a mass inoculation program, mostly against cholera, that health conditions are not worse than they are, but both cholera and plague remain real threats. To collect eighty-five thousand tons of garbage and other refuse a month, the city has only a hundred and thirty modern trucks. While these have improved the sanitary situation, particularly in middle-class sections, it is still bad in the poorer areas, where there is no room for the vehicles to operate.

Facing the street on a typical slum block, or combination of blocks, in Saigon there are likely to be *compartiment*-type dwelling-workshops of a story or two, which look relatively clean and neat. In most of these, a narrow lane may lead from the street partway into the block, but it will soon dwindle into a series of narrower passageways—so narrow that it is difficult for even one person to walk through them. Packed tightly around these passageways are scores of ill-made huts, most often consisting of just one room, in which a whole family of six or seven—the average number—lives. Water is drawn from a community well, which may be several passageways distant from a family's hut, though sometimes rusty pipes carry water to communal faucets. Most likely, there will be no electricity at all, and cooking will be done over charcoal stoves. For toilets, there are nearby canals or a ditch in back of the huts. During the day and in the early evening, wandering salesmen, including venders of noodle soup, hot food, raw fish, and fruit, move in and out of this maze. Everything is crowded so close together that, except for a few square yards of open space here and there, no light enters from above, and the whole scene has an underground appearance. Children and grownups scurry about like moles.

A Vietnamese friend of mine, Nguyen Hung Vuong, who has been my assistant in Vietnam for the past decade, has lived during this time in a more middle-class lane complex, and he has given me some understanding of what life there is like and how it has changed. His house, a small one, faces a crowded lane about fifty yards long in the Third District, in the central part of Saigon. Vuong's immediate area is called Ban Co, which means "chessboard," after the manner in which the lanes are laid out. When Vuong first rented the house, in 1961—for a thousand piastres a month, plus a three-thousand-piastre down payment and another thousand to the person who arranged the deal—his lane was about six yards wide. It is less than half that now, because so many houses have been built there since, and because illegal extensions have been built on older ones. In contrast with the poorer sections of the city, Ban Co has electricity and running water, and some of the lanes, including Vuong's, have been covered with asphalt, so they seldom get flooded in heavy rains—something that happens routinely elsewhere—but to reach his home by car he has to weave his way in and out of an increasingly complex system of large and small lanes. The Vietnamese have a saying, *"Gan nha, xa ngo,"* which means, roughly, "My house is close to your house, but my lane is far from your lane."

All residents of Saigon except foreigners have to go through an elaborate identification procedure when they move into a new dwelling, and they are subject to constant checks and

rechecks by the police. Each family must have a census certificate, approved by the chief of the *lien gia*, or group of
families. The paper must then be certified by the head of
the *khom*—that is, a series of lanes or blocks, making up
something like a ward. Then the chief of the *phuong*, or sub-
district boss, has to give *his* approval. The *lien gia* system in
Saigon was adopted by the government in the mid-fifties.
(The Vietminh had used it before that, but its real origins date
back two thousand years to imperial China; it is said to have
been invented by a prime minister at the court of one of the
Eastern Chu emperors. When the minister fell out of favor
and tried to go into hiding, he was quickly discovered through
his own system and beheaded.) There are sixteen families in
Vuong's lane, and they make up one *lien gia*—an unusually
large one, the average being five or six families. Though the
head of a *lien gia* gets no salary, his position can make him
rich through the favors he is able to hand out. In Vuong's
area, an illiterate petty tradesman took the job a number of
years ago; bit by bit, he got rich, and moved from a house
without beds to one of the best houses in Ban Co, where he
serves fine meals and drinks. Vuong's guess is that he has been
involved, like so many other minor officials, in such activities
as smuggling, prostitution, handling stolen goods, or the lottery racket.

In the ten years that Vuong has been living in Ban Co, it
has increased in more than just population and size. There are
now several four- and five-story buildings in the area, and a
house near Vuong's that cost eighty thousand piastres in 1961
is now worth two million, while some multi-story ones are
selling for fifteen and twenty million. Pharmacies, which have
always been abundant in Saigon, are multiplying in Ban Co,
as elsewhere, at such a rate that registered pharmacists now
rent or sell the use of their degree to fake pharmacists, who
sell only packaged medicines—or, sometimes, dope. New restaurants, snack bars, and ordinary bars have proliferated, too,
despite the diminishing number of Americans. With the advent of new-style Western clothing, especially miniskirts, tailors and dressmakers have been doing good business in the
lanes and streets of Ban Co. Barbershops are thriving, as always, for they are centers of rumor and gossip, and some of

them are used by the police and by gangsters for gathering or passing information, or are used as rendezvous points by the Vietcong. The barbershops also pass out newspapers; most people in Vuong's lane and others like it don't buy papers or magazines but rent them from the barbershops or from the stands for an hour or so. Vuong's lane is fortunate in having a school, a hospital, and a police station nearby—though the last is something of a mixed blessing, for police stations are prime targets of Vietcong terrorists. When Secretary of State William Rogers was here in the spring of 1969, a band of terrorists was discovered in the school building, preparing to launch some 60-mm. mortar shells on sites in downtown Saigon and then to attack the police station with grenades. The year before, during the Tet offensive, there was fighting within several hundred yards of Vuong's lane, and a number of his neighbors fled. One of the more noteworthy manifestations of Saigon life is the camaraderie that exists among the people of a lane. After a death, for instance, even neighbors who have not been particularly friendly contribute money to the bereaved family and gather to mourn and to discuss the life of the lane and of the whole city beyond, which is so much a part of their daily existence and yet is in many ways so far removed.

A middle-class lane such as Vuong's is also fortunate in that it has fewer deserters, pimps, *cao bois*, petty gangsters, and other troublemakers than the poorer lanes have. Vietnamese are cliquish and clannish by nature, and sometimes snobbish, too; snobbery is ingrained in them, and, especially in the South, it was encouraged by the French. The Vietnamese also tend to be xenophobic. For example, Vuong, a well-educated man and an intellectual, remarked to me once, "Luckily, though we are overcrowded where I live, there are almost no foreigners—I mean Americans, Koreans, Filipinos, Thais, and so on. The Chinese are all right. They have adapted themselves to the Vietnamese way of life. But for us Vietnamese the foreigners are quite a nuisance—especially the Koreans, Filipinos, and Thais, because they are concerned only with their own security and with making money. It is the Americans who are responsible for bringing them here. The African soldiers that the French brought caused us less trouble."

Despite Vuong's desire not to be bothered by foreigners, Saigon will probably never again be a city of separate national identities, as it was under the French. With the coming of the Americans, there are few areas that have not suffered in social and demographic as well as psychological ways. The effects of the many changes wrought by the war are bound to be lasting, no matter what happens politically, and even if the Communists take over. A Franco-Vietnamese professor of urban affairs at Saigon University remarked to me recently, "Inevitably, there will be a flattening out of classes, and the Occidental influence will remain. There is a new and probably lasting amalgamation of elements—an in-touchness that, for better or worse, will be permanent. It's a matter not only of foreign influences but of what has happened to the Vietnamese themselves. There has been a complete breakdown of traditional images. Civil servants now live in close proximity to *cyclo-* and taxi-drivers who make three or four times what they make. There may be no real contact between them now, but in time it will become unavoidable. A rich undertaker—undertakers have become rich during this terrible war—may build a five-story house on top of the one-story hut he once lived in. For the moment, he may not have any association with the poor people in the lane alongside him, but sooner or later he will. But the rich will still be rich, the poor poor, though they will be living side by side, and the taller houses will overshadow the huts and shacks. We don't know how many will stay rich, or what the impact will be of, for instance, the newly arriving Japanese businessmen, who, although they are Orientals themselves, in many respects lead a Western life. There may emerge a whole new middle class, or there may be no middle class—just well-off people and poor people."

These comments seem especially pertinent as applied in Gia Dinh Province, part of which already blends into Saigon. It has a population of roughly a million and a third, consisting primarily of people who have had to leave Saigon for economic or other reasons and refugees who have come in from farther out and have settled there instead of in the city proper, though they may work in Saigon. A Vietnamese friend recently told me, "The outskirts in Gia Dinh are like boils on Saigon's skin. In the parts of the province that are closest to the city, you have a whole new classless society. It includes small shopkeepers and a large floating element, among them many criminals and hoodlums. The Communists try to infiltrate these floating groups, because deserters, gamblers, and gangsters are hard for the government to control. Farther out of town, in the areas that are somewhat more secure, well-off people have built new brick houses with high surrounding walls. They hire guards or else pay protection to both the government police and the Communists. There is no census, no way of knowing who is moving where or what effect the bombing of the countryside has had on driving people to the suburbs or the cities. No such thing as social mobility, in the traditional sense, any longer obtains."

If there is another large-scale Communist attack on Saigon, like the one in 1968, it will undoubtedly have its genesis in Gia Dinh, throughout which the Communists are establishing new cells. Much of the drug traffic and a good many other illicit activities have shifted from the city to the suburbs as police pressure has increased in Saigon, and this move will help the Communists. Partly for those reasons, Saigon and national officials want to bring large chunks of Gia Dinh under the direct control of Saigon municipal authorities. If the plan is followed, it will mean that some thirty-four hundred hamlets of Gia Dinh will be given over to Saigon, while the remainder of the province will either survive separately or be incorporated into adjacent provinces.

The one part of Saigon that has retained its identity is Cholon, for not even the long, abysmal war has had much of an effect there. The community demonstrates once again the Chinese capacity for remaining Chinese no matter where and no matter who rules China, and the fact that the Chinese in Vietnam have survived all but intact under the French, under the Vietnamese, and throughout the American invasion merely emphasizes the point. In the case of the million and a quarter or more Chinese in Vietnam—the largest group of them in Cholon—this "Chineseness" is doubly significant because in the early days of the Diem regime they were forced to become Vietnamese citizens. Moreover, their young men have been drafted to fight for a cause that most of them do

not believe in, though this is not to say that they are pro-
Communist. They were further humiliated, in 1967, by a government requirement that all Chinese establishments—shops,
hotels, and so on—identify themselves with Vietnamese names
painted above their Chinese names in Chinese characters.

A walk through Cholon, whether by night or by day, is
vastly different from a walk through Vietnamese Saigon. For
one thing, one sees fewer Americans or other white-skinned
foreigners, if one sees any at all. There are fewer vestiges of
colonialism, in the form of the stucco buildings that the
French built elsewhere in the city. Instead, there are rows
upon rows of neat, spick-and-span shops, stacked high with
Chinese and Western goods, including many one can't find
anywhere in the rest of Saigon. Indoor and outdoor restaurants abound, serving an infinite and marvellous variety of
Chinese food. The predominant smell is one of soy sauce,
whereas among the outdoor food stands of Vietnamese Saigon
the usual smell is that of *nuoc mam*, a strong fermented fish
sauce that the Vietnamese like. There are many more Buddhist
temples than there are in Saigon proper, and there is a playground next to each. (In the Vietnamese city, there is scarcely
any room left for children to play.) Chinese music fills the
air—lilting, high-toned instrumental variations on a few similar themes—whereas elsewhere in Saigon nowadays one
seldom hears Vietnamese music, which is more melodic and
sentimental than its Chinese counterpart; instead, there is only
the blare of rock and roll. The one big change in Cholon over
the years has been that the younger generation has adopted
Western clothes—for girls, skirts and blouses instead of the
long gowns called *cheongsams*, and, for boys, tight trousers
and shirts. Some of the older people—the old men, especially—still wear long Chinese robes.

It is said that the Chinese control three-quarters of the
economy of Vietnamese Saigon, and it is probably true. Even
the wealthy Vietnamese are tied into the Chinese financial
community one way or another. The Chinese dominate the
rice trade, they pull the strings of the money markets, and
they set prices for basic commodities like fish, vegetables,
pork, cement, and textiles. The illicit traffic in gold and opium
is under Chinese control, though the Vietnamese take part in

it. Most of the Chinese look down on the Vietnamese, and have either opposed or contemned the whole long series of governments that has followed the regime of Diem—whom, though he cracked down on the Chinese, they respected, because his birth and education gave him mandarin credentials.

A significant aspect of life in Cholon is a generation gap that is in many cases much deeper culturally than the similar manifestation among the Vietnamese. The younger generation of Chinese, who are better educated than Vietnamese youngsters, because the Chinese schools are better run and there are more of them, fall into three basic groups: the Maoists; the fence-sitters, who are fuzzily pro-Kuomintang; and the so-called "Western-trippers," who increasingly prefer American and European movies, for instance, to Chinese ones depicting ancient swordsmen killing scores of enemies with a single stroke. The number of Maoists is small—probably no more than five thousand—but they are hard-core believers in the new China, and they have organized themselves into Red Guard units. During the Tet offensive in 1968, these groups harbored the Vietcong terrorist and sapper squads, and their members took part in street demonstrations in Cholon when, for periods of hours, and even days, the Communists controlled certain blocks of the area and hoisted the Vietcong flag.

Since the overseas Chinese are great accommodators, and since they have even less faith in the future of the present Saigon government than the Vietnamese have, it is probable that if a poll could be taken many people in Cholon would be found to favor Hanoi, chiefly because they feel that under its government contact with the homeland would be easier. This pro-Hanoi sentiment is also in part a product of what is, perhaps unfairly and inaccurately, called "Chinese chauvinism," and it may prove unrealistic, for it is highly unlikely that if Hanoi eventually establishes its own rule over Saigon the Chinese will be allowed to continue playing the economic role they have played for so many years.

As for attitudes toward China among the Vietnamese, all of them, North and South, fear the Chinese and would prefer to remain independent of them. After all, most of Vietnam was occupied by the Chinese for more than a thousand years, and its people are proud that their ancestors finally drove off the northern conquerors and established their independence. Moreover, the most recent Chinese "occupation" of Vietnam—in 1945 and 1946, when some of Chiang Kai-shek's Kuomintang troops were sent in by the British-American Southeast Asia Command to occupy the northern part of the country temporarily while the British occupied the south—has not been forgotten; the occupying troops plundered the area and made fortunes from opium and other illegal traffic. (Indeed, remnants of these troops are still engaged in such activities in the wild border areas of Laos and Burma.) Although the Chinese Communists are regarded as friends by Hanoi, there is little doubt that the North Vietnamese want to maintain their tenuous balance between Moscow and Peking, which Ho Chi Minh managed so well for so long. It is likely that the Cholon Chinese similarly hope to go on hedging their bets.

When it comes to movies, more of the young in Vietnamese Saigon have broken sharply with tradition than have done so in Cholon. Late last year, a Vietnamese film entitled "Chan Troi Tim," or "Purple Horizon," for the first time showed a Vietnamese hero and heroine kissing each other on the lips. While essentially innocuous compared to many contemporary productions from the West, the film nevertheless contained what for the Vietnamese were touches of neorealism, including a scene that displayed a bare bosom. There were also scenes of bar girls, deserters, and other by-products of the war, and scenes of napalming and bombing by Vietnamese pilots in American planes. The film received a lot of favorable comment from the younger generation but some severe criticism from older Vietnamese. It was a box-office success.

The Vietnamese have taken to television avidly; even some of the poorest families have sets. There are two channels, one run by the United States Army and the other run by the Saigon government, and the American one is by far the more popular among the Vietnamese, who, even if they don't understand the dialogue, enjoy the action of such shows as "Mission: Impossible," "Wild, Wild West," and "Batman." The favorite Vietnamese TV show, "Cai Luong," is a dramatic series told in classical opera form, though the story line is modern; one episode dealt with a young woman who was forced to leave home and go to work as a bar girl. The Americans show a considerable number of propaganda films but, on or off TV, have made scant effort to improve Saigon's cultural life. One exception was the presentation last year, with the financial backing of about half the sixty members of the American Chamber of Commerce, of the German opera "Hansel and Gretel," of all things. It cost seven thousand dollars to put on five performances, and considerable criticism was voiced in the American community about the amount of money spent on something so seemingly irrelevant when the same sum could far better have been used to help refugees or orphans.

With some exceptions, the only regular contact between Americans and Vietnamese is at the G.I. level, where the motivation is for the most part sexual, would-be sexual, or at best superficial. There have, however, been several thousand marriages between Vietnamese girls and American soldiers, despite the fact that they are difficult to arrange—having been purposely made so by both sides. Many of the marriages have broken up once the couple has gone off to America, where the girl has very often found herself the only Oriental in a small American community. Some Americans have also adopted Vietnamese war orphans, with the help of a number of private and public organizations sponsored by Americans and Europeans, but the number of adoptions is infinitesimal in relation to the thousands of orphans who either will have to be reared in government institutions or will remain homeless and destitute.

Something that has not altered through the long years of the war is the importance in Saigon of fortune-telling. Virtually all Vietnamese, no matter how well educated, are firm believers in soothsayers of one kind or another, and depend on them for guidance in all sorts of decisions. President Thieu, former Vice-President Ky, and all the other people I know in the hierarchy of power have made many decisions only after seeking the advice of a favorite seer—and this may be one reason American advice hasn't been taken as often as many

people at home think it has. Even the most Western-minded
Vietnamese, who pretend to laugh at the way some of their
friends depend on fortune-tellers, secretly go to fortune-tellers
themselves and cling to traditional beliefs, such as the significance of who enters their houses in the first moments of the
new year. I know a number of Americans who have visited
Vietnamese friends on the eve of the new year and have politely been asked to leave at the last moment of the old year,
because "a good Vietnamese friend of mine is coming in a
few moments and it would be unlucky if you were here." The
most popular forms of fortune-telling are astrology, phrenol-
ogy, palmistry, the reading of playing cards, and scrying in
crystal balls. Over the past years, in which one disastrous series
of events has followed another, the timing of coups and
attempted coups has invariably been determined by what fortune-tellers told the generals involved. My friends—journalists, businessmen and others—have regularly told me whether
their luck at a given time would be good or bad, and, oddly,
they have been right more often than not.

Numerology plays a vital part in these predictions, with emphasis on the basic numbers three and five. Three is lucky, and
five is unlucky; the fifth, the fourteenth, and the twenty-third
days of the lunar month are always considered unlucky. (In
the second and third of these dates, the digits—one and four,
two and three—add up to five, accounting for the presumed
ill omens.) Finally, and most important, there is the twelve-
year Vietnamese calendar cycle, similar to the Chinese cycle,
with each of twelve successive years identified by a spirit in
the form of an animal figure, and each of these being considered lucky or unlucky for each man in certain years. The year
1971 was the Year of the Hog, and in February, 1972, the whole
cycle began again, with the Year of the Mouse, or Rat. Each
year, at the start of Tet, the family home is brightly lighted to
welcome not only the first visitor but the new spirit. Tables
are laden with food, flowers are placed everywhere, and at
dawn the family honors its ancestors by sitting down to the
first banquet of the Tet period, which lasts between seven
and ten days. When the meal is over, each member of the
family dresses in his best clothes to greet relatives, especially
grandparents. Each child receives a small sum of money in a

traditional red envelope, and foreign as well as Vietnamese employers are expected to give the Vietnamese who work for them, and even hotel managers and hotel servants, Tet gifts—if not a month's salary, then a few hundred or a few thousand piastres, depending on the importance of the relationship.

Some years ago, an American friend of mine undertook a study of the significance of fortune-telling and other forms of soothsaying, and came up with some interesting results. The sites of all buildings, including the Presidential Palace (currently considered to be in a bad spot), are thought to be lucky or unlucky according to their access to light, water, and space. The fortunes of the American Embassy in Saigon definitely seemed to change from good to poor when it was moved from its site downtown, on Ham Nghi Boulevard, facing away from the Saigon River and Vo Di Nguy Street, to its present site, on Thong Nhut Boulevard. A prominent geomancer has pointed out that President Thieu was born in the Year of the Mouse, and this means that 1972 doesn't look good for him. No one knows how much faith the Communists in North Vietnam place in all this, but certainly those of my Saigon friends who are from the North believe in the whole system implicitly.

Despite Saigon's wartime transfigurations, the Vietnamese remain a ritualistic people, and one of their fundamental rituals remains the transmission, after careful evaluation, of rumor and gossip. Ever since 1960, when the first coup against Diem occurred, the chief rumor-and-gossip mill has been called Radio Catinat, and the old name has stuck. Around 1962, its headquarters were at a restaurant called La Pagode, toward the upper end of the Rue Catinat. After the fall of Diem, the veranda of the Hôtel Continental and, subsequently, the bar of the Caravelle Hotel were part of the network, but its true center since Diem's overthrow has been a small restaurant and pastry shop called Givral, across the street from the Continental. (La Pagode, a block away, is now frequented by "phantom troops"—officers and noncoms whose families are rich enough to keep them in Saigon.) Much of the talk one hears at Givral is of questionable value, for people who frequent the restaurant often plant information on each other for a purpose. Among the clientele are National Assemblymen (the Assembly building is only fifty yards away), public officials, secret police, journalists, and businessmen. It is not uncommon to see an opposition deputy and a secret-police agent sitting together and fencing verbally. Everyone who comes to Givral does so not only to exchange information but to play the subtle conversational games the Vietnamese play so much better than Americans can—testing each other, putting each other on, trying to humor somebody and to denigrate somebody else. Cabinet ministers drop by from time to time, as do other high civilian and military officials; President Thieu used to, when he was still an Army officer. Businessmen not only listen to journalists and others here but use the place to test their own agents, one against another, for veracity or the ability to plant false rumors. There are three daily "broadcast times" at Givral—one around ten in the morning, one in midafternoon, and one between five and seven, after the daily press briefings are held at the National Press Center, across the way. The morning period is concerned mostly with business rumors and reports, and the two afternoon sessions with political and military matters.

If Radio Catinat is the most central and most public place for the dissemination of information, true and false, there are other places, not far off, which are also important, each in its own way. For several mornings, I accompanied a friend of mine, Pham Xuan An, who is employed by an American news magazine and is probably the hardest-working and most highly respected Vietnamese journalist in town, on his rounds of these spots. An, who loves animals and birds—he has eight birds, four dogs, and one fish—took me first to the Ham Nghi animal-and-bird market, near the old American Embassy building. The market, which stretches for about half a block, sells monkeys, civets, ocelots, rabbits, guinea pigs, and all sorts of dogs, cats, fish, and birds—among the last being cuckoos from Africa, pigeons from France and Mozambique, owls, myna birds, parrots, skylarks, pheasants, and canaries. For those who favor ancient folk remedies, bats are available; a well-regarded cure for tuberculosis involves cutting the throat of a bat and drinking its blood mixed with rice wine. Adjacent to Ham Nghi is a street called Nguyen Cong Tru, where each morning at about ten o'clock Chinese businessmen or their Vietnamese agents meet in two or three cafés to determine collectively what the day's black-market piastre rate will be and also to set the prices of rice, pork, and other basic commodities. Within half an hour after their decisions are made, the word goes out to the two main commodity markets in Saigon and Cholon and to the dollar black market. This Chinese-dominated strip dates back to the days of the French, who operated out of the same places through their Chinese compradors. In the same block, and extending along part of Ham Nghi, is the center of the sidewalk black-market traffic in American goods. Here, despite occasional crackdowns by the police, one can buy anything available at the American post exchanges and a wide range of other foreign products as well, including Japanese cameras and hi-fi sets. Because police roundups have been more frequent in the past year or so, the more expensive items are no longer displayed, but they can be bought on a C.O.D. basis; that is, a Vietnamese woman running a stall will ask a customer whether he wants such-and-such a camera, and if he is interested he will give her his address and she will come around the next morning, camera in hand, and bargain. Almost all the goods are perfectly genuine—except the whiskey, which is usually diluted with rice wine. The markup on black-market goods ranges from forty to five hundred per cent, but some things remain cheaper at the black-market-dollar rate (now about four hundred and fifty piastres to the dollar) than they are at the post exchanges. It all depends on the subtle process of supply and demand, and on one's ability to bargain. Some of what is sold has been pilfered from the docks on its way to the post exchanges, and then the price is ordinarily kept low, but usually something like a case of beer, which sells for three dollars at the PX, will cost six or eight dollars on the black market. A carton of American cigarettes, which costs a dollar-seventy at the PX, will cost four dollars on the black market.

In the same vicinity are a number of restaurants, each catering to a different clientele, and to these An took me in his search for tidbits of information. The Victory, a spacious place

on Ham Nghi specializing in Chinese food, has much the
same atmosphere in the morning that Givral has in the afternoon, but is not so crowded. Politicians, journalists, and
important businessmen exchange information there every
morning over tea or Chinese soup. The nearby Do Thanh is
more of a middle-class place, for officials of sub-Cabinet rank,
field-grade officers, and the second-rung diplomatic set. An,
being a journalist who, though he works for the Americans,
is also trusted by the Vietnamese, makes a point of visiting at
least five such places each morning before he heads for Givral;
then, after lunch, he goes to the official American and Vietnamese briefings and back to Givral. "It takes a long time to
build up your sources," he says. "You have to be frank and
sincere, and you have to protect your sources. You must also
do them favors—tell them things they want to know, buy
them lunches and dinners, give them Tet gifts. Saigon operates in this pattern of social circles. If you're not qualified for
one particular circle, you won't be accepted in its restaurant.
The people there will just ignore you. Journalists—the good
ones—are the most useful informants, because they are in a
position to hear things from so many different sources. The
whole thing is like a school. You can graduate from one circle
to another, just as you would from one class to another, once
you've passed your tests."

If rumors remain a large part of the daily life in Saigon,
hard facts are what the police deal with. Whether or not their
efforts are appreciated by the populace, the police have undoubtedly become more efficient in the past two years. This
is chiefly thanks to the efforts of Trang Si Tan, who was appointed police chief in January, 1971. Tan, a former prosecutor,
magistrate, and president judge of the Saigon Municipal
Court, is in charge of about twenty thousand men, including
the uniformed police, who handle traffic, administrative
work, and other routine functions; the Maritime Police; the
Field Force Police, who are engaged primarily in keeping
order and quelling disturbances; and, finally, the Special Police, who are in charge of security. There is considerable rivalry
and jealousy among the police, the Military Security Service,
the Vietnamese Central Intelligence Organization, and Viet-

namese Army Intelligence, just as there is among their American equivalents, yet Tan—who reports, through the National Police Chief, Colonel Nguyen Khac Binh, to Prime Minister Tran Thien Khiem (who is also Minister of the Interior)—is widely respected by all his colleagues. A quiet, soft-spoken man with the mien of a judge, he is a tough administrator, and he operates his force with more discipline and order than it has had for a long time. A while ago, I took two trips around Saigon with him and watched him in action.

Tan's Special Police are in charge of what is called "population control and classification." The population is divided into four categories—A, B, C, and D—and each household is given a rating that supposedly reflects its loyalty to the government. Tan and I visited one of five police stations, for example, in District Six, which embraces part of Cholon and is considered one of the least secure districts in the city, and I discovered that the almost twenty-five thousand households in the substation area were rated as follows: 16,007 were A, or pro-government; 7,944 were B, or uncommitted; none were C, or openly anti-government but non-Communist nationalist; and 277 were D, or pro-Vietcong (or suspected of being so). A file is kept on each member of each household, and each must have an identity card. The A houses in District Six are mostly those of government civil servants, members of the armed forces, or the People's Self-Defense Forces—the locally recruited "home guards." The uncommitted households, which are the majority in many areas, are most difficult for the police to identify. These households consist of people who maintain that their sole interest is in earning a living, and that they are neither for nor against the government—simply not interested in politics. While Tan's Special Police and their penetration agents—that is, men out of uniform who have penetrated pro-Communist or suspected pro-Communist groups and neighborhoods—keep a constant check on these houses, no one can tell for certain that the Communists have not planted some of their workers among them. Another thing the police are anxious to know is whether members of these households would, if they were given the chance, vote for a neutralist or a Communist candidate in an open election contest. The reason there were no C households in the area we visited—and there are very few anywhere—is, of course, that hardly anyone wants to be identified as being against the government.

When I asked Tan whether all this didn't really amount to total police control, he replied that it was not unlike what the Communists had always done, and that since the 1968 Tet attack it had become the only way to determine what the Communists were up to. Tan and his American advisers readily admit that in the most sensitive areas—particularly in Cholon and some of the newer districts of the city—the system is far from fully effective. Even so, incidents of terrorism, sabotage, and other forms of Communist activity have diminished considerably since it was put into effect. Throughout the city in 1969, according to police statistics, there were a total of three hundred and seven incidents of all kinds—bombings, mortar barrages, killings of policemen, and so on. In 1971, the total number of incidents was only about sixty-five. Tan says he believes there are now probably between two hundred and five hundred Communist Party members in the city, and perhaps fifteen thousand active sympathizers. It is undoubtedly much harder for them to move about than it used to be; they do maintain a courier system, though, and they are believed to have five secret mobile radio stations in Saigon. As a result of a tighter system of checkpoints that Tan's men have established on the outskirts of Saigon, he says, it is also harder for the Communists to move people into the city.

We visited one of these checkpoints, where all vehicles were stopped and searched by both uniformed police and plain-clothesmen. Former Vietcong members who were regarded as trusted returnees acted as spotters. At this particular checkpoint, Tan told me, twenty-five thousand people passed back and forth each day, and out of every five hundred perhaps ten were held for questioning. Though Tan said he did not believe that the Communists could conduct a large-scale assault on the city, he admitted that they could still conduct propaganda campaigns and carry on political activity almost anywhere, and that they were undergoing a thorough reorganization to improve their apparatus for another major attack. "As always, they will exploit the democratic process," Tan says, "and when that process is weakened by lack of authority, by lack of decent living standards, by lack of any useful long-range plans for making the city livable, the danger will remain, no matter how many checkpoints we set up or how much population control we maintain."

Although ten city plans have been drawn up for Saigon in the past ten years, almost nothing has been done to carry any of them out. After the Tet offensive of 1968, there was a brief period when the Americans and the Vietnamese got together on projects for repairing the worst damage—caused mostly by American planes bombing entrenched Communist attackers—but there has been little coördinated or long-range action since then to alleviate the overcrowding or to improve the dire condition of the slums, and the administrative organizations that were formed at the time have been allowed to die, mostly for lack of funds (though, according to Frank R. Pavich, who is one of a handful of American urban experts here, there are few Vietnamese with any real background in urban planning). A survey has been made of each block in Saigon to determine how the land is being used—for residential, commercial, or other purposes—but nothing has been done to identify the worst slum areas, to get fundamental economic-aid programs started, or to plan the construction of higher buildings as at least a temporary solution. What has happened is a considerable amount of indiscriminate, haphazard new building in various parts of the city, indicating, if nothing else, some degree of hope for the future of a non-Communist Saigon. However, there are few signs of any long-range outlook on the part of the central or municipal government. Pavich and others believe that the earlier plans, made by such experts as the Doxiadis group, to expand the city northward toward Bien Hoa, where the Americans have had their biggest airbase, are still valid, but that putting them into effect would require further detailed and constructive planning, and a lot more money. James P. Bogle, another American expert, who made a study of Saigon's growth problems a few years ago, concluded that, where urbanization was concerned, the government was facing problems familiar to all less developed countries, and that it was "extremely questionable" whether it would be able to cope with them. Unlike the North Vietnamese, who have continued to rebuild as the war has gone on, the South Vietnamese, except for the short period after the Tet offensive, have done very little to improve any of their cities.

Important as the rebuilding process is, social reconstruction and moral regeneration are more important. "We have fostered a whole new generation of drifters, who have lost all their Confucian values," one older Vietnamese in Saigon told me. "All they think of is dodging the draft, having fun, riding their Hondas." There is no doubt that the Americans have altered the entire fabric of Saigon life, and one feels that a new breakdown is inevitable unless something drastic is done. What we have done is to create a social spectrum with a *nouveau riche* class at one end, a new class of poor people, largely refugees, at the other, and in the middle a classless majority, who have lived off the American presence.

Another Vietnamese friend told me, "You Americans think you have given the Vietnamese a better material life, but it's not true. Most of the equipment you poured in here will end up as scrap. Perhaps the situation will have to disintegrate still further before something new can be built. The only hope is that a new younger group, with ideas of its own, will emerge, and that these young people will understand that both the old prewar society and the American superimposed one are finished. If we don't go Communist, it may take twenty years, or even longer, to bring about a new synthesis, but it will happen. First, though, we must undo the damage you have done. The Vietnamese like to raise monkeys. You have seen them in the animal market, in homes, in the parks. What you have done here in Saigon is create a monkey climate. The only Vietnamese you really know—the ones you have dealt with—are monkeys. Why don't you at least help us get rid of the monkeys before you go?"

The New Yorker, April 15, 1972

Report from the Inferno

by John Saar

THE LITTLE RADIO was hard to hear because 500 yards away the whole Laikhe ammo dump was erupting in gouts of fire and cataclysmic chain explosions. Through the shattering crumps and the shriek of errant metal came the urgent-voiced American Forces Radio newscast: giant B-52s were unloading high explosives on North Vietnam's port city of Haiphong. Awed and made puny by the monstrous destruction mush-rooming in front of us, we realized it was the simultaneous facsimile of another horror scene 660 miles north. Fireballs, leaping in the sky like crimson tumors, dwarfed the darting ambulances, and the men who bravely wheeled loaded mu-nitions trucks from the fiery base of a smoke column reach-ing 3,000 feet into the air were grimed, big-eyed and very frightened.

The message was impossible to deny—whether by a sapper's rocket in the South, or SAC's iron bombs in the North, Viet-nam was again springing into flames. The difference this time is that the mindless brutality of this quarter-century war has acquired a savage new sophistication. In the intransigence of the North Vietnamese grinding on through the blood of their youth and the Vietnamized forces of the South brought to parity by U.S. air power, one senses something close to a per-petual war formula. The most depressing aspect of this new offensive to end all offensives is the patterned automatism of the bloodletting. The governments of North and South yoke their people to unyielding conflict, and the great power em-inences are there at their shoulders to heap them with yet more efficient tools of destruction. The costs of the war for both North and South are now so grossly disproportionate to the size or importance of Vietnam that there can be none but Pyrrhic victories.

The early action was in the north and a civilian Air Vietnam

335

flight let us out into the blazing sunlight of Hué's Phubai
airfield where a group of wounded South Vietnamese marines
were awaiting Medevac. Nearby, a group of home-going GIs
lolled against a wall, staring through their shades and nodding
absently to a Joplin tape. The music floated over the sorry
group of South Vietnamese, heads and newly amputated limbs
wrapped in grubby bandages: "Freedom's just another word
for nothing left to lose. . . ." Vietnamization means the GIs
go home but the Vietnamese stay, to fight on indefinitely.

The Ranger-trained adviser, brush-cut and aripple with repressed energy, is quick to defend the Vietnamese soldiers
who abandoned 14 fire bases in the first retreat from the
DMZ: "Hell, the Japs might have stayed under the kind of
fire they were taking, Americans wouldn't. The way that
130-mm was coming in even the Russians would have *chieu
hoied.*" The logic makes perfect sense—why should the ARVN
fight from fixed positions in bad terrain and under constant
bombardment?

The road north to Dongha—the road, rail and river town
where the North Vietnamese advance was eventually
halted—is a gradual passage from a peaceful countryside of
buffalo boys and rice harvest to the haunted desolation of a
recent battlefield. Down the road toward us, tripping barefoot
quick, quick, quick, came a straggle of refugees Indian-file—
women, children, old men and a few dogs idling alongside.
Faces scared and strained with effort—fugitive people not *going* anywhere, but fleeing *from.* The war is a beast that leaves
a spoor of havoc—mounds of cartridge brass, motorcycles and
bikes flattened as neatly as pressed flowers by passing tanks,
ditches a confusion of hasty army litter, dried bloodstains in
the brown dust, bloated corpses of dogs, buffalo and Communist soldiers. Dongha is dying in a carnival of destruction
at the hands of the soldiers—from every quarter come shouts,
laughter, random shots, the splintering of glass and the breaking of doors. In the darkness of a general store we find a
Vietnamese marine swinging at cartons with a sugar-cane cut-
ter. "VC," he says, thumbing at the wreckage. The contents
of the shops and houses lie in the muddy streets like a knee-
deep snowfall; the stuff and identity of people's lives is a thor-

oughfare for proliferating rats and flies. And eddying heavily over the town is the revolting odor of rotting flesh—a smell you recognize instantly but thankfully never quite remember afterward. Mouth trembling between anger and tears, Le Thi Tin, 45-year-old mother of 14, picks through the looted disorder of her home for pots and pans and the minimal wherewithal of survival for her new-old life as a refugee. Incoming Communist shells whistle overhead and in a surge of panic she sweeps her two sons and herself into a bunker. Whitefaced and pathetically fearful, she says she stayed in Dongha because she was born and raised there. Will she ever come back to her home? "If peace comes." She does not sound hopeful, says the interpreter. Requiem for Dongha—once a town of 30,000 people—shelled and rocketed by Communists, sacked by ARVN.

There is a new desperate tenacity to this NVA offensive. We are seeing more Communist bodies than ever before because conventional warfare requires them to stand and fight more often. On the outskirts of Quangtri one such squad fought and died to a man. Now they lie strewn over the edges of their foxholes like the petals of a spent bloom, heads blown open like eggshells. Every inch of the schoolhouse wall behind them is pitted with fire. They might as well have been stood up against it for all the chance they had.

In a busload of refugees is an old man from the Eden-like valley of Camlo, captured and held by the Communists. He has the wispy goatee of venerated age and his eyes are like faded stained glass. "I left my home and belongings and have just these clothes," he says. "Many people are being killed by VC rockets and by bombing. Many compatriots were suffering and starving when we left. I saw a human hand in a tree and parts of human beings blown apart." The bus leaves.

With the withdrawal of the American ground troops whose own tactics in other times were said to have accidentally taken the lives of thousands of Vietnamese civilians, there has been extra compensatory use of air power. B-52s and tac air are plainly less discriminatory weapons than the GI with a rifle. Thuyen is a short, swarthy soldier in ARVN's Third Division. His left leg is bandaged and his eyes are dazed. "The planes dropped bombs on Camlo city and killed two of my children and severely injured my wife. Two of my brothers were also killed." A doctor with the rank of captain stops the interview and ejects us from the hospital. Why? we ask. "Because the soldiers do not tell the truth. They will only give you propaganda."

The quotient of loss and suffering is so high in South Vietnam that wherever you go, whomever you talk to, you stumble from one dismal personal tragedy to another. After decades of incipient disaster, the adjustment and return to apparent normality is rapid, but scratch the patina and you find the unhealed wounds. Death is so casual and commonplace that people husband their sorrow for their families only. In the barren moorland country off national Route 1 a handful of white-clad druidic figures are holding a service. A girl red-eyed with grief and clutching an offering of bananas and water climbs into a bus with two priests and drives off. Crumpled at the roadside is the jeep in which her father and six others were killed when it ran over a mine. The Vietcong set the mine; the killing was as random as the Camlo bombs.

The mud-stained truck grinding through the streets of Hué was a dirty brown. The officer in the back who asked for directions was wearing his olive-drab mac. The yellow-and-red flag draped over the coffin in the back seemed glaringly bright. As the truck meandered slowly through the maze of back streets, onlookers, stricken and glum, stared and pointed. Lt. Le Van Hoan, a gravely good-looking armor officer, was bringing home the body of his friend Minh, killed at Kontum with three of his men when their vehicle detonated a mine. The truck halted finally outside a trim whitewashed villa and Minh's family surged out. Streaming tears, the dead boy's sister threw herself over the coffin while two of his brothers, also weeping, tried to comfort her. Lieutenant Hoan nervously sucked his cigarette and blew out the smoke without taking it down.

Minh's father, a 60-year-old public servant, says he was terribly upset over his son's death, but glad Minh died fighting for his country—"besides, there are so many families who have had their sons killed in battle." Swinging round in his chair he points, "Over here a family, over here a family. . . ."

Minh, the 21-year-old who used to write poetry and play the Vietnamese guitar, was drafted into the army when he dropped out of high school. The family will remember him with the flag he came home under and a picture on the family altar of a slightly out-of-focus Vietnamese boy wearing an out-size U.S. Army steel helmet. Two of Minh's brothers are in ARVN and Thang will go next: "I think the young men in the North are like the men in the South. They are obliged to go in the army but in their hearts they want peace. If I have to go it is my duty, but I don't think my death would help my country."

Out in the reed flats south of Hué a U.S. helicopter dances like a dragonfly just feet off the water in search of Vietcong. Periodically there is small-arms fire. An ARVN officer tells us that a militia force has killed five VC. He claims only one friendly dead but the interpreter clearly hears the figure eight given over the radio. A sampan glides into the bank and government soldiers heave two VC bodies quivering onto the ground. They wear threadbare shorts and shirts and Ho Chi Minh sandals cut from old auto tires. In their drenched equipment bags are patched ponchos, plastic explosive, vials of Romanian penicillin. Like the two men, the can in which they kept fried pork to supplement their rice was torn and riddled with M-16 fire.

Colonel Bo, who can sometimes speak English and sometimes not, is officially an ARVN information officer. But foreign journalists agree that his province is closer to psychological warfare. At his invitation, we interviewed NVA Lt. Nguyen Khac Soan, aged 29, captured after escaping and evading for eight days. The prisoner is hollow-cheeked and faint from hunger and has eventually to be carried out. The interview is generally worthless and a Vietnamese colleague says, "Colonel Bo twists all the questions and answers."

Vietnam is a totally mobilized country and at around the age of 18 a young man has to decide whether he wants to kill for the government or for the VC. For reasons we could not find out as he was marched, arms bound, along Route 1 with his B-40 rocket-launcher hung around his neck, 23-year-old Le Hong Sinh chose to join the VC in 1968. The mud and blood freshly crusted on his face did not hide a ruddy flow of health, and his legs were thick with muscle. He was frightened but not cowed. The interpreter said, "I wished him luck. He's going to need it, he'll have a very rough time." A well-informed Vietnamese source later confirmed that prisoners were sometimes tortured or killed: "It is necessary to get information quickly or to make the others talk." Do the North Vietnamese torture their prisoners? "I'm sure they do. They're human too."

In the air-conditioned calm of the senior adviser's comfortable quarters the war seems very distant. The M-16 is hung on the wall, the helmet with the eagle of the full colonel by the door. The requisite paperback library on guerrilla warfare is on the bedside table. On the door is the adviser's poem:

> Mine is not to run this train;
> The whistle I can't blow.
> Mine is not to say
> How far this train can go.
> I'm not allowed to blow off steam
> Or even ring the bell.
> But let this train run off the track
> And see who catches hell.

The colonel has no such apprehensions. In fact, he's cock-ahoop: "They shot their wad and it didn't work out. Now, like they always do, they're stubbornly hanging on instead of pulling back to regroup and they're losing their asses every day." Already on this offensive, reporters have learned to be wary—an unprecedented amount of misinformation (optimistic, of course) is adrift. A trip to a fire base southwest of Hué puts the colonel's rose-tinted views in another perspective. On a fire base called Bastogne, a battalion of ARVN have had their guns knocked out, cannot evacuate their dead and wounded and are short food, water and ammunition.

"Excuse me, colonel, but as accredited MACV correspondents we are entitled to talk to these soldiers."

The colonel blocked the way. "Well, I'm not going to let you talk to them." He was as good as his word. The trucks carrying a company of the U.S. 196th Infantry rolled away moments later. In a conversation over a concertina-wire fence, other soldiers explained there had indeed been a misunderstanding and a temporary refusal by a company to go into the field. The soldiers are reasonable and rational, and after a two-hour appeal by their commanding officer they all agree to go. But the soldiers make it plain they feel no obligation to fight for Vietnam and will accept only such action as is necessary to protect themselves and other Americans.

A junior U.S. adviser, after a swift glance over his shoulder, gives his version of Anloc: "Things are getting worse and worse and the Vietnamese just aren't doing anything. The smell inside the town got so bad they bulldozed a mass grave for 300 dead ARVN. The NVA shelled the hospital and destroyed it with captured 155s and killed 61. Now they don't have a hospital or enough medical supplies and there are 500 to 600 ARVN wounded they can't get out."

At noon, Laikhe, headquarters for ARVN's Route 13 battle, was at a standstill for a two-hour lunch. No rushing trucks with badly needed ammo, no bustling staff officers with pressing plans—just the broiling 100° heat of the open, and the gentle swinging of hammocks in the beguiling shade of the rubber trees. Then a mortar round zonked into the road close to a chopper park. In the days of the U.S. war, crews would have materialized immediately to fly their birds from an insecure coop. Today the heat shimmers off the asphalt. No one appears and there are no more mortars—this time. You remember a Vietnamese friend saying, "At night the NVA run, they never walk, always they run. . . ."

The week's reporting ended with a ride back to Saigon in a U.S. Medevac helicopter. As we climbed away, black coils of smoke were rising from Laikhe's ammunition dump. It was, I imagined, pretty much like the scene over Haiphong's blazing harbor. For these people, peace seemed to be no closer than it was years ago when we, and the other side, first decided to help them with their war.

Life, April 28, 1972

The South Vietnamese Retreat

by Sydney H. Schanberg

HUE, South Vietnam, May 2—Thousands of panicking South Vietnamese soldiers—most of whom did not appear to have made much contact with the advancing North Vietnamese— fled in confusion from Quangtri Province today, streaming south down Route 1 like a rabble out of control.

Commandeering civilian vehicles at rifle point, feigning nonexistent injuries, carrying away C rations but not their ammunition, and hurling rocks at Western news photographers taking pictures of their flight, the Government troops of the Third Infantry Division ran from the fighting in one of the biggest retreats of the war.

No one tried to stop them: their officers were running too.

The battlefront north of Hue was thus left solely to a brigade of a few thousand South Vietnamese marines.

The Third Division had fallen back before, at the beginning of the enemy offensive a month ago, but the commander, Brig. Gen. Vu Van Giai, had managed to scrape it together again and put it back on the line around Quangtri until yesterday.

But today, according to American advisers, virtually the entire division—about 10,000 infantrymen plus 1,000 rangers —was in rout, not even stopping at the checkpoints where military policemen were supposed to halt runaways and turn them around.

It was the force that was supposed to have defended the city of Quangtri, which was abandoned yesterday and which had been the northernmost town held by the Government.

There does not seem to be much now between the North Vietnamese and their next and more important objective, the city of Hue, whose residents are already packing up and fleeing farther south in large numbers.

Many of the retreating troops are not even stopping in Hue, which is about 40 miles south of Quangtri, but are continuing on, taking their rifles, artillery pieces, tanks and armored cars with them.

The province chief went on the radio tonight, appealing to the people of Hue not to panic and flee and promising that the Government would defend them. As he spoke American advisers in Hue were calling Saigon to ask for every available aircraft to evacuate the thousands of refugees from the north who have flooded the city.

Bowling down Route 1 from Quangtri, the Government soldiers, their guns bristling at anyone who tried to interfere with them, clung to the sides and roofs and hoods and trunks of every available vehicle.

With horns blaring and headlights glowing in the midday sun, they raced down the center of the road, pushing other vehicles out of the way. They used trucks and tanks and they took over big buses and three-wheeled minibuses. They stole motorcycles, riding as many as four to the bike. There were also many on foot, particularly walking wounded.

Their anger at those who watched them running seemed born of their shame. Until the Third Division can be pulled together again, it hardly exists as a fighting force.

The South Vietnamese marines, the only units that have fought well on the northern front, are still holding three bridges on Route 1 between Quangtri and Hue. They are trying to slow the enemy advance, the first bridge being about 30 miles north of Hue and the last only 20 miles away.

No one expects that they can hold the positions very long. After those the only major defense before Hue is a large military base known as Camp Evans, or Hoa My, about 17 miles from the city. The new headquarters of the Third Division, it is packed with artillery pieces, which are constantly firing.

At the southernmost of the bridges, at a village called Photrach, the South Vietnamese marines watched with pained faces as the army men fled. They would not talk about it, but their embarrassment was plain.

Their American advisers were not so inclined to silence. "This is really sickening," a Marine lance corporal said.

"It's unbelievable," said an American Marine major, Robert

Sheridan, as he leaned on a jeep at the side of the road. "It's hard to comprehend. To stand here and watch this when you've seen the same people in your own units fight well because they have different leadership.

"You see the troops," he went on, waving his hand at the road. "But I don't blame them. Where are their officers? There's no one to tell them 'stop' and to pull them together."

The major said the Vietnamese marines in his unit were "very sad and very angry" at the army retreat. "They are embarrassed because I am standing here watching it," he added.

The marines stopped a thousand fleeing rangers last night as they tried to cross the northernmost bridge, he related. The reason for blocking their flight, he said, was that "we couldn't tell if they were enemy." At daylight they were allowed to pass because the marines had no authority to stop them.

The marines fought "a hell of a battle" at the forward bridge this morning, the major said, knocking out 18 tanks with the help of artillery and air strikes.

The major said that last night, when the Communists started moving in the area, he wanted to call in naval gunfire from American vessels standing off the nearby coast, but that South Vietnamese officials held off the fire, apparently because they thought it might hit the retreating forces.

Many of those on foot had inexplicably thrown away their boots and were limping along barefoot. Some had bandaged their feet with rags. All were tattered and muddy. Even those who were riding had had to plod for 10 miles through the countryside during the night before they got to the first bridge held by the marines, where transport was available.

Whether riding or walking, the fleeing men had no time for anything but their own escape.

The body of a soldier lay on the road just outside Camp Evans under the baking sun, a victim, perhaps, of a road accident. His gear lay strewn about him. The troops passed without a glance.

As this correspondent turned back toward Hue today with three other correspondents, an interpreter and a driver in an old Citroën, South Vietnamese soldiers waving automatic rifles and pistols forced the car to halt. Fifteen pushed in and on, blanketing the roof, hood and trunks. All appeared panic-stricken.

One was a major, Nguyen Van Niem, 45, commander of an ordnance company that had fled Quangtri. Laughing with embarrassment, he said he had no idea where his company was.

Like many of the fleeing men, Major Niem said that when he left Quangtri last night he had not seen any enemy troops, nor had he seen Government troops exchanging fire with the enemy. That apparently means that the Government force fled before it was attacked on the ground, although Quangtri had been under intense shelling by heavy artillery for three days.

Major Niem said he was going to Danang, 50 miles south of Hue, to join his parent unit. He said of the retreat: "We do not feel ashamed. The enemy fought very strongly and we have to withdraw and form a new front."

As the Citroën went on toward Hue, the driver craning out the window because the windshield was blocked, the soldiers brandished their weapons and uttered threats to keep others along the way from climbing on.

The ordnance major, who pushed his way into the car with great vigor, had developed a severe limp by the time the car reached Hue. He explained that he had been wounded by a rocket, and when he stepped out of the car he hobbled a few paces and collapsed into the arms of a military policeman, who carried him off.

Another soldier had a small neck wound that appeared to be healing nicely. Just before he got off in Hue he unwrapped his first-aid field bandage and asked that it be tied around his neck. A wounded man has a better chance of escaping shipment back to the battlefield.

Some of the retreating troops reached Hue early enough this morning to find time for relaxation and refreshment. A mud-spattered armored personnel carrier clanked through the gate of the main hotel at 9 A.M. and parked on the grass. A dozen soldiers and their captain clambered out, smiling, climbed the three flights to the terrace restaurant overlooking the Huong River and ordered an ample breakfast of omelets and French coffee.

The New York Times, May 3, 1972

———

HUE, South Vietnam, May 3—The fabric of Hue is disintegrating today, with at least 150,000 panic-stricken people fleeing south on foot, by truck and in flotillas of leaking sampans as the North Vietnamese push ever closer.

The government of Thuathien Province, of which Hue is the capital, is in the process of collapsing, and signs of anarchy began to permeate the city today.

South Vietnamese Army runaways from the scattered Third Division, which abandoned the northern city of Quangtri to North Vietnamese forces on Monday without a fight, were roaming through Hue today like armed gangsters—looting, intimidating and firing on those who displeased them.

Sniper fire and bursts from automatic weapons crackled all day, as rival factions of Third Division deserters clashed with one another.

Neither the city police nor the military police were doing much to try to stem the rampage, for the soldiers, with their automatic rifles and grenades, are much more heavily armed.

"Right now, it's everyone for himself," said a despondent Hue student.

"We are trying desperately to dampen the panic," said an American adviser, "trying to get the local government to form an emergency committee to keep essential services going—police, health, feeding the refugees. I've got my fingers in the dike, but I've got more holes than dike."

Of the deserters, he said: "They ought to shoot them."

Last night, a group of the deserters, who apparently number in the thousands, set fire to the city's sprawling central market place during a wild and drunken gunfight with another military unit. One report said that the other unit consisted of South Vietnamese Marines, who are the only Government troops reported fighting well on the northern front and who are ashamed and angry over the headlong flight of the Third Division.

The Third Division runaways are also angry—at their officers, who they say abandoned them in Quangtri, about 32 miles above Hue, and left them to find their own way out of the enemy encirclement. Many were penniless and had not eaten for two days when they reached Hue yesterday, and they told friends that they had set the fire to express their rage at their officers.

At one point last night, some soldiers shouted: "Burn it all, let's burn the whole city." The arson got no further than the market.

The fire burned spectacularly all night—lighting both the sky and the adjacent Huong River as it gutted acres of small shops and buckled the main steel and concrete market building.

This morning, as the market smoldered and occasionally flickered into flame, scavengers and looters, both civilian and military, roamed through the ruins, which were littered with the brass of expended rifle shells.

An old woman, trying to resurrect her smashed vegetable stall, shouted bitterly at some looters nearby: "Why are you taking things that don't belong to you?" They just smiled sheepishly at her.

There was nothing sheepish, however, about most of the looters. A family of three was banging away with steel bars at a locked metal chest to try to get at what might be inside.

A dozen people calmly looted a rice shop, shoveling the grains into sacks and boxes, not at all bothered that someone was photographing the scene.

And a Government political indoctrination worker in a black uniform strolled off grinning with several sacks of food and clothing slung over his shoulder.

A lieutenant from a commando unit watched the scene, sitting on his parked Honda motorbike. Asked why the army did not stop the looting, he replied mildly, "It is not our job."

When it was pointed out that soldiers had started the fire, he said: "I was not here."

On the open second floor of the main market building, the naked body of an old woman lay in a corner of the large hall. She had apparently been raped and then shot.

The market place was crucial to the food supply of Hue.

No eggs or bread were available today at the rundown Huong Giang Hotel, the city's best, where most of the large group of foreign reporters here are staying. One of the hotel room men—anticipating that the North Vietnamese would open their attack on the city soon—was wearing a steel helmet today as he made beds.

It is impossible to tell when the attack will begin, but the North Vietnamese pushed a little closer today—perhaps consolidating their forces for a final drive on Hue.

One American Marine adviser, a major posted with the South Vietnamese Marines on the front above Hue, said: "We're holding here, but we don't know what we're supposed to do. Nobody has given us any instructions."

Another Marine adviser at the front growled, "I don't know any more whether I'm in northern South Vietnam or southern North Vietnam."

The people of Hue apparently think the city will soon be part of North Vietnam. Hue had a normal population of 200,000, which in the last month was swelled to 350,000 by refugees pouring in from the north as the Communists advanced.

More than half of the people now have packed up frantically and pulled out of Hue—most of them in the last 24 hours—moving south toward Danang 50 miles away. The city is fast becoming deserted.

The roads out of the city today were choked with people, furniture, animals and vehicles. Most were going toward Danang. But thousands headed to the Tanmy naval base outside Hue in hopes of getting on one of the seagoing landing craft that bring ammunition to Hue and then return to Danang for more. And still others were leaving in fleets of sampans from the banks of the Huong River.

Almost all the shops in Hue are shuttered and locked. Many of the merchants have left, but some have boarded up their stores simply because of the looting.

Some basic government services continued to function, such as electricity, water and telephones. But large numbers of civil servants have fled. At the province headquarters, for example, 75 percent of the staff have gone.

And 90 percent of the staff have fled from Hue's central hospital, which is overflowing with hundreds of wounded refugees.

On one of the main street corners in the city today, an army psychological warfare truck with a loudspeaker blared out the following message from the northern command: "All soldiers who have lost contact with their units are directed to report to Phu Van Lau Square by tomorrow. After tomorrow, you will be considered deserters and will be tried before a military court."

Deserters in uniform and carrying their weapons, strolled by the truck, paying no attention.

The New York Times, May 4, 1972

A Record of Sheer Endurance

by Rudolph Rauch

THERE ARE perhaps six buildings left in the town, none with a solid roof. There is no running water or electricity. Every street is shattered by artillery craters and littered with the detritus of a battle that saw a bit of every kind of war. Everywhere you walk you hear the crackle of shifting shell fragments when you put your foot down. There are not more than half a dozen vehicles left that still function, and when I arrived, only one of those, a Jeep, had all four tires. All the others move fast enough, given the condition of the streets, on their wheel rims, and it is a common sight to see seven or eight Vietnamese lurching through the town in a Jeep without tires.

There were 30,000 civilians in An Loc two months ago. Now there are 2,000. Except for an estimated 1,000 who were killed by the Communist shelling, all the others have left. Thousands of refugees have fled down Highway 13, braving enemy mortar fire. Those who remain are huddled under a ridge to the east of the city in a village called Phu Duc. There are no gun positions in Phu Duc, no targets of military significance. Yet since fighting died down in the city itself at the beginning of June, an increasing percentage of the artillery shells poured into the city have been aimed at Phu Duc.

The provincial hospital was evacuated May 8, after it was mortared, perhaps accidentally, and 30 civilians who had crowded into it for sanctuary were killed. Since then, wounded civilians have been cared for in a pagoda in Phu Duc. There are no beds and few mats; most patients lie on the dirt floor or on bundles of rags. A child died of lock jaw because of a shortage of tetanus serum. Her body lies twisted like a snake under a shroud of rags. Two feet away an old woman is dying of malnutrition. She had stayed in her bunker for well over a month, switching from boiled rice to rice soup as her reserves dwindled, then to anything edible. She is the color of fine porcelain, and the flies are all over her face.

The province chief, Colonel Tran Van Nhut, has managed to set up a system of rice rationing. Bags of rice are handed across a wire fence to those who can come to get them. When a wizened man with a stump of a leg hobbles up, he cannot quite negotiate his crutch and his rice. He collapses in a heap, trying to figure out some way of fastening his ration to his loincloth.

The military casualties are, if possible, even more pitiful than the civilians. Their primary hospital is now a bunker. Some men have been there for as long as a month, with more lightly wounded comrades cooking for them over smoky wood fires on the bunker steps. There is no sterilization for instruments, and there is a shortage of cat-gut. Dr. Nguyen Van Quy, who performed 200 operations in two months, has taken to using thread from sandbags for sutures.

An Loc has withstood a battering given to no other city in this war. The worst day was May 11, when an estimated 7,000 rounds of artillery, mortar and rocket fire hit an area that can easily be walked across in ten minutes. Said one U.S. adviser: "Those were days when healthy men were taking antidiarrhea tablets to keep from having to go outside. Nature's calls seemed a lot easier to resist."

American and Vietnamese aircraft kept up a continuous bombardment throughout the three days I was in An Loc. Every sort of aerial weaponry was used: Gatling guns, CBU attacks, conventional bombs and finally, two hours before sunset on Thursday, a B-52 strike 900 meters to the northwest against a Communist tank concentration. But the guns keep moving, and rounds keep coming in. Right now, the situation in An Loc is considered calm, despite the unnerving intrusion of an average of 200 rounds a day.

The Vietnamese airmen whose job it is to fly out the wounded are remarkably unwilling to come into the stretch of Highway 13 that now serves as a landing strip. To confuse enemy gunners who have the strip zeroed in, chopper pilots can land almost anywhere in a stretch of road two kilometers long. In theory, the landing zone for each mission should be selected so as to allow the wounded to be on hand near by. But that never happens. Instead, the Vietnamese choppers come streaking in low along the highway, and hover two or three feet above the ground while any soldiers aboard jump off; only the less seriously wounded have a chance to jump on. Time after time, litter patients who have waited for hours in a sun of close to 100° are hoisted to the shoulders of their buddies. But then the chopper will zoom down, hover for ten seconds, and take off again, leaving the wounded with a new layer of the red Binh Long dirt in their wounds and another two hours to wait.

Had it fallen, An Loc would have been an important victory for the North Vietnamese. That it did not fall is a tribute to American airpower and to the fierce determination of its Vietnamese defenders and their American advisers. It is no credit at all to the ARVN column that remained pinned down for two months on Highway 13 by vastly smaller enemy forces—or to the South Vietnamese units within the city that engaged in open firefights in order to capture airdropped rations from each other. The important fact is that the city held. "The only way to approach the battle of An Loc is to remember that the ARVN are there and the North Vietnamese aren't," says an American adviser. "To view it any other way is to do an injustice to the Vietnamese people."

But for the foreseeable future, An Loc is dead—as dead as the hundreds of North Vietnamese who were caught in the city's northern edge by U.S. bombing, and whose putrefaction makes breathing in An Loc so difficult when the afternoon breeze comes up. Perhaps the best that can be said is that the city died bravely, and that—in a year that included the fall of Quang Tri and Tan Canh—is no small achievement.

Time, June 26, 1972

The South Vietnamese Army

by Peter Braestrup

Quangtri: Anything But Easy

SAIGON—As border outposts and outlying towns fell in April and May to Hanoi's troops, President Thieu faced a harsh reality: Many of the generals he had rewarded for political loyalty had brought on near disaster as field commanders.

Thieu redeployed Saigon's forces with surprising boldness to meet battlefield crises—at Anloc, at Kontum, at Hue, he issued stronger mobilization decrees to provide 70,000 replacements for South Vietnamese losses. He flew to the forward command posts to talk with his senior officers and pin medals on the brave.

But essentially, Hanoi's initial successes—and the command weaknesses they laid bare—did not lead Thieu to change South Vietnam's military-political "system."

Instead, he has as usual tried to balance "political security" against military necessity as he reshuffles commanders amid public outcry.

In American official eyes, and those of Thieu's domestic critics, the offensive has left the 46-year-old ex-general no real choice: As U.S. support dwindles, the army leadership cannot survive and remain mostly "political" and part "professional."

Under the pressure of events, Thieu has fired two of the country's four regional commanders, replaced three of its 13 division commanders, reshuffled perhaps a dozen of his 44 military province chiefs.

The net result overall, in U.S. eyes, is "modest improvement."

The most striking change—and possibly the most difficult politically for Thieu—has occurred in the north, where potential military catastrophe in May threatened the former imperial capital of Hue.

353

Here, the perils of South Vietnam's military politics-as-usual became most obvious. The general in charge of Military Region I, which embraces the northern five provinces, was Lt. Gen. Hoang Xuan Lam, 44, an amiable, round-faced officer who favored a swagger stick and a tanker's black beret. The shock of the offensive was just too much for him, as for others.

This April, when the North Vietnamese came across the Demilitarized Zone (DMZ), Lam did not establish a tactical headquarters at Hue. Nor did he often visit forward regimental command posts. Instead, he commuted daily 60 miles to Hue from his Danang headquarters by (American-piloted) helicopter, returning in time for lunch or dinner.

"The situation is serious, but not critical," he told newsmen.

For a month, Lam left the battlefield coordination of mutually antagonistic armor, rangers, infantry and marine units to a deputy at Hue, but delegated no authority. A junior U.S. adviser at the Hue citadel dubbed Lam the "absentee warlord."

Many reasons have been advanced for the subsequent May 1 rout of Saigon's forces at Quangtri City—the inexperience of the under-strength 3d Division; the apparent breakdown of its highly regarded commander, Brig. Gen. Vu Van Giai; poor coordination and the shock of enemy artillery fire. Most authoritative sources ultimately blame Lam's failure to face reality and grab hold.

But Thieu did not shift Lam to a desk job in Saigon until after the Quangtri debacle. He was grateful to Lam for his political loyalty as shown in 1967, when the generals met to decide whether Thieu or Air Vice Marshal Nguyen Cao Ky would head the government ticket in the fall elections. Lam then supported Thieu, ripping off his general's stars and throwing them on the table and saying he would quit if Thieu got the second spot. Thieu got the nod.

Thereafter Lam, with close ties to the locally-influential Dai Viet Party, was Thieu's trusted political-military boss for the northern region. Lam did not fire able non-political officers, but he did bring in his protege, Maj. Gen. Nguyen Van Toan, as commander of the 2d Division, south of Danang.

In U.S. eyes, Toan was an able commander; he was also

known, briefly, in 1968, as the "Cinnamon King," for his alleged use of army trucks in a Quangngai cinnamon venture with Lam's wife.

Moreover, like his colleagues, Lam's tactical abilities as a corps commander were seldom put to the test. The U.S. battalions were handling the big-unit war shielding the frontiers at Khesanh, on the DMZ, in the Ashau Valley. For the most part, Lam could focus on his role as Thieu's regional administrative boss.

This in itself is no small burden, even for the most energetic commander. As in many other Third World countries, the officer corps not only runs the army, but also plays the dominant role in local administration. This spreads the talent pretty thin.

With a guerrilla threat present everywhere, the 44 province chiefs, 220 district chiefs and six big-city mayors under South Vietnam's centralized French-style system have long been military men. They have overall responsibility both for leading the militia in combat and for running the civil bureaucracy.

This has, willy-nilly, involved army colonels and majors as well as generals in politics. And especially during the lavish U.S. build-up, many found opportunities to boost low official incomes through collusion with Vietnamese contractors, diversion of U.S. aid, or "taxes" on local commerce.

Not all money-minded province chiefs have been incompetents or cowards; for example, Brig. Gen. Ly Tong Ba, now commander of the 23d Division at Kontum, coupled high living on a low salary with great bravery in leading his militia in Binhduong Province during the 1968 Tet offensive.

Not all officials had to be crooks to get by, but reformers—in Vietnam as in Chicago—arouse hostility.

In June, for example, local politicians in Binhdinh Province succeeded in getting Thieu to remove Col. Nguyen Van Chuc, who was not only brave, but an outspoken foe of local corruption.

Chuc's leadership is credited by his American advisers with saving southern Binhdinh Province from the North Vietnamese in May, after the regular South Vietnamese army 40th Regiment, led by an incompetent, lost three northern districts in April.

But Chuc rocked the boat, antagonizing regular army unit

leaders and local businessmen alike. He also irritated his new superior, Gen. Toan, the ex-Cinnamon King, whom Thieu has just named as regional commander.

Thieu does not admire boat-rockers. To stay in office, like many another Third World leader, he has had to maintain a kind of "politburo" consensus among key army leaders. Of necessity, he has also operated since 1967 a kind of military patronage system, easing out allies of possible rivals (E.G., Ky), repaying past favors, rewarding loyalty above all else.

Given South Vietnam's past history of military coups, counter-coups and factional jealousies, Thieu has presumably felt that he could take no chances.

In any event, first the U.S. "shield" and then the lack of any overriding military threat prior to March 30, 1972, allowed Thieu, in army matters, to put political security foremost. Thus, Gen. Lam stayed on, along with others less competent.

To replace his friend Lam in early May, Thieu rushed in Lt. Gen. Ngo Quang Truong, 43, a thin, small officer who was widely known as Thieu's best general, a "clean" military professional.

To Thieu's credit, Truong had also been promoted rapidly: from brigadier commanding the 1st Division at Hue in 1968 to lieutenant general commanding the 16-province Mekong Delta region in 1970.

By all accounts, Truong did not get promoted by bucking the system, but by leaving politics and business to others and winning battles, notably at Hue in 1968.

According to one South Vietnamese colonel, both Truong and the fellow paratrooper who succeeded him as 1st Division commander, Maj. Gen. Phan Van Phu, "learned the right things from the Americans."

Truong, alone of all Vietnam's draftee division commanders, insisted on periodic retraining for his battalions. He developed a good staff and good subordinate commanders, and insisted on joining U.S. troops in big-unit operations.

And, important to the palace, he avoided publicity and obeyed Thieu's orders.

Truong returned to Hue—where he set up forward headquarters—and his decisive leadership, together with Thieu's dispatch of airborne reinforcements, warded off catastrophe.

Yet, Thieu elsewhere did not discard political caution.

For example, as far back as 1968, Gen. Creighton W. Abrams repeatedly urged that the three lackluster divisions (5th, 18th and 25th) around Saigon be headed by stronger men, with more qualifications than simple loyalty.

Thieu demurred, then and later. These three units were crucial to any military coup in the capital.

Prior to March 30, he changed two of the three division commanders; both new men were loyal, able former province chiefs, not necessarily a qualification for high military command. One of them has turned out to be brave, while the other has already found running a 12,000-man division in a big war too much to handle. The three divisions remain below par.

Thieu's sensitivity to Saigon's political security remains acute. For example, in April he appointed a Navy vice-admiral, Chung Tan Cang, with no past exposure to ground combat, as commander of the Capital Military District, charged with the defense of the city and surrounding Giadinh Province.

Cang's appointment engendered little public enthusiasm, and some apprehension, but Cang was a Thieu loyalist, if only out of gratitude.

Early in 1965, Cang was sacked as head of the navy by Dr. Phan Huy Quat's short-lived government, after he allegedly profiteered off government-run coastal shipping.

Later that year, when the military took over (again), Thieu rehabilitated Cang, possibly as a gesture to Cang's navy friends. He gave Cang a political staff job. Five years later, the admiral was assigned to the office of Gen. Tran Thien Khiem, the prime minister (and minister of defense and interior), as chief of an anti-corruption drive urged by the U.S. mission.

Cang is close to Thieu, and according to U.S. advisers, extremely energetic in organizing the capital's defenses.

But during the first few weeks of his tenure South Vietnamese sources said Thieu's personal staff kept tabs on Cang's whereabouts and associations. Even now, he is frequently summoned to the presidential palace for detailed instructions. When it comes to Saigon, Thieu keeps a tight rein.

Thieu's right-hand man in all this is Lt. Gen. Dang Van Quang, presidential "assistant for military security." Some

South Vietnamese politicians regard Quang, without affection, as the most powerful man in Vietnam—a kind of
J. Edgar Hoover, Carmine De Sapio and Robert S. McNamara
combined.

A classmate of Thieu's in the 1948 class at Dalat Military
Academy, Quang seldom makes speeches; but he keeps an eye
on intelligence matters, the police, province chiefs, the non-
Communist opposition, promotions and demotions, and all
things military.

It is he who telephones the corps commanders and other
senior officers, speaking in Thieu's name, to check on compliance with Thieu's orders.

This leaves Gen. Cao Van Vien, 53, the widely respected
head of the Joint General Staff since 1966, something of a
"broker between warlords" on many issues, notably personnel. A lean former paratrooper, wounded in action, Vien is
regarded as Thieu's man for the "professional" side of the
military.

By all accounts, Vien is apolitical, obeys Thieu's orders as
best he can, deals with the American military and works within
the system.

Last winter, tired, ailing and frustrated, Vien was ready to
retire; but after some rest he returned to duty in time to organize the South Vietnamese army's troop shifts in response
to the North Vietnamese spring attacks.

Thieu's political security considerations aside, Vien's task is
not easy.

The South Vietnamese military is not a national army in the
sense that its forces are accustomed to fighting and living anywhere in the country. Only the Saigon-based airborne and
marine divisions—the strategic reserve force—do that.

The officers change, but most regular infantry divisions are
regionally based and recruited. The men of the 7th Division,
for example, have been in the Mekong Delta at Mytho, with
wives and children, for 10 years.

And until March 30, most regular South Vietnamese division commanders had little cause to stretch their military talents—after 1969, most of the North Vietnamese army moved
back to Laos and Cambodia.

The battalions sweated and bled, along with the militia, to

expand the government presence and tamp down the Viet-
congs in the countryside. They largely succeeded.

But there was little strain at the sprawling division headquarters inherited from the departing Americans, and the
staffs knocked off for two-hour lunches. The idea was to avoid
mistakes, risks and excessive losses. It was a long war.

"It is one thing to fly around in a chopper to see how a
couple of your battalions are doing on a three-day sweep on
familiar ground in Haunghia," observed an experienced U.S.
Vietnam hand. "It's something else fending off a North Vietnamese division, shifting battalions, coordinating with other
units, getting the choppers, the artillery, the airstrikes, with
Saigon on your neck 24 hours a day."

Thus, the South Vietnamese army command structure—the
highly centralized leadership and the relatively passive
staffs—was ill-prepared for the ordeals of 1972. Despite their
U.S. equipment and U.S.-style briefings, complete with map
and pointer, the South Vietnamese military—like every
army—reflected their own national culture and their own experience.

Moreover, besides being a largely territorial force regionally
recruited and based—the South Vietnamese armed forces are
also a collection of military clans, reflecting a similar factionalism among the middle class civilian politicians.

As one U.S. senior officer has noted, some of the inter-
service rivalries in South Vietnam spring from "germs" left
by U.S. Air Force, Navy, Army and Marine advisers over the
years, as well as from past political feuds within South Vietnam
itself.

"It's not easy to command airborne or Marines temporarily
attached to your division," said a senior South Vietnamese
colonel. "They feel free to ignore the orders of a regimental
or division commander during an operation, especially when
they don't admire him."

Indeed, during one sweep, he said, "the airborne did not
turn on their radios, and we shouted for hours trying to get
answers. Another time, they turned on the radios only to complain and criticize us."

One problem is that the commanders of the Marines, the
Airborne, the Rangers and armored battalions do not depend

on corps commanders for promotions, but on their own home headquarters, for example, the armor command in Saigon.

"When a complaint by infantry about a particular Ranger unit goes to the Ranger command" in Saigon, an infantry officer said, "it will be torn up." Over and over again this spring, U.S. advisers would find that to avoid friction, South Vietnamese armored and infantry units had not been placed under a single commander but instead told to "cooperate" —an invitation to disarray.

"The big question," said a U.S. adviser in Haunghia, "is always: who's in charge?"

In U.S. eyes, perhaps the most damaging schism is that between helicopter crews and the infantry. In the U.S. Army, the division commander controls his own army helicopters. But partly because the first South Vietnamese helicopter pilots were former air force fighter-bomber pilots, the South Vietnamese air force got all the helicopters. Their crews have nothing to fear from a division commander if they ignore his orders. He's Army and they're Air Force.

"Personal relations are very important," observed a South Vietnamese staff officer in Saigon. "If the relations [between a helicopter flight leader and a ground commander] are not good, difficulties come in the evacuation of wounded or in resupply. The helicopter pilots have many excuses—weather, engine trouble, fuel is low, ground fire is too heavy." At Anloc and Quangtri, South Vietnamese helicopters' performance ranged from fair to awful.

Some of these "command and control" weaknesses as well as political side effects came to light—at least inside the military—long before Hanoi launched its offensive at the end of May. There were hesitations and foulups in Cambodia in 1970–71.

The big snarl came during "Lam Son 719"—the three-month foray in early 1971 against the Ho Chi Minh Trail complex in southern Laos. It was Saigon's big-war operation: the marine division, the airborne, the 1st Division plus armor and rangers. Despite the press photographs of fleeing South Vietnamese GIs hanging on sides of U.S. helicopters, the basic trouble in Lam Son 719 was leadership and staff work, not the troops' willingness to fight.

Who was nominally in charge? Lt. Gen. Lam, the amiable regional political boss. There were personal rivalries: Lt. Gen. Le Nguyen Khang, the marine commander, refused to talk to Lam.

Lacking faith in their own air force, the South Vietnamese ground commanders relied heavily on U.S. air support and helicopters.

But in contrast to this year's big war, there were no U.S. advisers on the ground in Laos with the units, to report on the real situation, to guide the air strikes and talk to the U.S. helicopter pilots.

According to U.S. after-action reports, South Vietnamese army staffs "were reluctant to press for current information unless first requested by senior commanders . . . The information [reaching headquarters] was often inaccurate and usually incomplete . . . Coordination of artillery fires between units was 'difficult . . .' As the operation went on, 'political directives' (from Thieu) were frequent. South Vietnamese commanders became 'unable to assess the situation.'" The planned withdrawal from Laos in March and April of 1971 became, at best, a costly retreat—in places a rout.

According to unpublished official records, South Vietnam lost heavily of its best troops—1,550 killed, 5,500 wounded, 650 missing—along with a division's worth of U.S. equipment: 54 tanks, 300 vehicles and 96 artillery pieces.

In Laos, the North Vietnamese were slow to react and suffered heavy losses, but they showed that they could marshal tanks, artillery and hard-charging infantry even under heavy U.S. airstrikes.

The lessons of Lam Son 719 were apparently lost on Thieu. No reshuffle of commanders resulted.

The 1971 election season was on, according to some South Vietnamese sources, and Thieu was preoccupied with political problems (E.G., Ky, Big Minh), not the seemingly remote prospect of a major conventional military test.

The surprising aspect of the 1972 offensive, so far, is that the South Vietnamese high command—for all its chronic weaknesses—survived the initial surprise and shock.

They were saved by the resilience of the average "binh chi," (GI), the presence of enough good units and adequate leaders at Anloc and other key places, the massive weight of U.S. airpower, and Hanoi's crucial failure to exploit its initial gains.

Moreover, Thieu has kept logistics on the home front going: Vigorous roundups of draft-dodgers and new mobilization decrees have kept up the strength of Saigon's forces in numbers, if not in quality. The training camps are full, and the AWOL rate is about what it was last year—12,000 to 14,000 a month.

But Thieu and his advisers also made some key military decisions: For the first time in the war, they shifted ordinary draftee outfits from their home turf to fight elsewhere; the 21st Division and part of the 9th from the Mekong Delta to Highway 13 and Anloc, north of Saigon; part of the 2d Division from south of Danang to Hue.

Thieu eventually committed his entire elite strategic reserve of marines and airborne to Hue, the most vulnerable target, relying on militia and draftees to defend Saigon.

And after the collapse of the 22nd Division and its commander north of Kontum, Thieu took advantage of North Vietnamese foot-dragging to rush a fresh division—the 23d—into place, to meet the enemy thrusts.

Thieu and Vien boldly stripped large areas of regular troops and left them for the provincial Regional Forces and district Popular Forces to defend. In marked contrast to Tet 1968, these militia, by and large, have filled the gap, notably in pitched battles in Haunghia, Tayninh, Quangtri and southern Binhdinh provinces.

But the old weaknesses have cropped up even during Saigon forces' efforts to retake lost ground.

One airborne brigade commander north of Hue swore that he would put a paratrooper with a pistol on every tank to make sure the attached armored cavalry unit didn't run off. Similar coordination troubles and over-reliance on air strikes have plagued Saigon's two-month-old effort to open Highway 13 to encircled Anloc.

Except for Truong's forces around Hue, regular South Vietnamese regimental commanders have followed low-risk, go-slow tactics—which ironically has often led to higher casualties from enemy mortars. "There are plenty of weak regiments," said a senior U.S. official.

In short, despite a certain current euphoria among the presidential staff, Thieu has only gained a respite on the battlefield. He and his countrymen have survived one more crisis in a long series of crises—at great cost.

Thieu has problems.

Even if he wanted to, he could not suddenly discard the military-political system he has partly inherited, partly created. No other organized political structure exists—or can be rapidly created—to replace the armed Forces' hierarchy and the civil administration it controls.

Yet, by all estimates, Thieu can ill afford militarily to continue the old ways.

Hanoi has not given up. Key territory must be regained. The South Vietnamese army's slim resources in trained combat-worthy units leave little margin for incompetence, or even mediocrity, among combat leaders.

As never before, the U.S. mission is pressing Thieu to shed some of his political caution and put more fighters, like Truong and Phu, in key command jobs.

As these sources see it—but Thieu may not—there is little other choice if Saigon is to survive.

The Washington Post, July 9, 1972

Viet Soldier Serves Officer, Not Nation

SAIGON—"Maybe the war will die out in the next few months because the Communists can't keep it up," said Pvt. Nguyen Van Lon.

"Where I was, they fired a thousand rounds of mortar and artillery a day at the start. Now they only shoot a few hundred."

A skinny, 20-year-old draftee, Lon was convalescing from a chest wound suffered May 11 during the South Vietnamese forces' seemingly interminable ARVN struggle to open Highway 13 to encircled Anloc, 60 miles north of Saigon.

As U.S. field advisers like to point out, it was not American airpower alone, but the resilience of the South Vietnamese army's ordinary "grunts" like Lon which ultimately slowed Hanoi's massive March 30 offensive.

Wearing a white sports shirt, dark slacks and sandals, Lon

sat in an open-sided cafe near the army recuperation center in
Saigon. He had let his fingernails grow long—a sign of ele-
gance among Saigon youth—but his hair was cut short, army
style. Puffing a Vietnamese Capstan brand cigarette, he talked
about himself, his outfit and the war with a mixture of pride,
resignation and hope.

"I never had a taste of the war until I was drafted," he said.
"I saw planes and helicopters overhead sometimes. But no
Communist troops ever came to the village, not even during
the 1968 Tet offensive."

"All I knew about the Communists was that people said
they were very harsh. They forced the people to pay taxes and
to go to indoctrination courses."

To Lon, as to many another young rural Vietnamese, such
notions as "the nation," "Communism" and "the government" were remote abstractions. Lon grew up in a hamlet in
the prosperous Phukhuong district near Tayninh City, site of
the "Holy See" of the Cao Dai sect, 75 miles northwest of
Saigon.

A nominal Cao Dai, Lon was the son of a small shopkeeper
who died when Lon was eight years old. His mother kept the
family alive by selling fish and vegetables from a stall in the
local market. Lon got a fourth-grade education in the village
school—standard Vietnam—and then went to work, helping
his mother and other relatives working in shops.

His older sister married a South Vietnamese ranger sergeant; his younger sister runs a flower stall at the airborne
division base in Saigon.

Lon had a girl friend; she has moved to Nhatrang on the
central coast and writes him every month. He had a lot of
teen-age cronies; most of them dodged the draft until the
police scooped them up.

"It was not a bad life," Lon said.

But at 18 he chose to be drafted into the regular army, rather
than join the local Regional Forces or Popular Forces.

"I wanted to travel around the country and see new
things," he said. "It was a mistake. I miss my family all the
time."

In 1970, Lon was shipped off to the big Quangtrung Recruit Training Center (output: 30,000 men a year) where he

got 10 weeks of basic training. After the easygoing life of the village, army discipline was a shock. He wound up in a 500-man battalion of the 25th Division, near Trangbang northwest of Saigon.

In 1970 and '71, it was not a rigorous war for Lon's unit: The allied invasion of the Cambodian sanctuaries had pushed most North Vietnamese regular battalions out of striking distance.

"Our battalion commander was easy on us, but not so brave," Lon recalled. "We did not do much hard fighting."

In those days, privates like Lon got four days' leave a month—and in some units, it is said, one could get one's leave extended, for a price.

Many of his comrades stayed longer. "They wanted to help their families, or just missed their families," Lon said.

When the errant trooper returned he wound up in a bamboo "Tiger cage," or (in the airborne) got a public beating or, in the worst cases, got sent to a penal battalion.

Since the March 30 offensive began, as Lon noted, desertions have continued. According to official sources, they now run at the rate of 12,000 a month—about the same level as last year—and the police have been fairly zealous about rounding them up.

Deserters in Vietnam do not normally defect to the Communists: They hide out with relatives or re-enlist in militia closer to home, or join the roving but Saigon-based elite marines or airborne.

Lon did not say whether he had ever gone AWOL, although his home village was only a 40-mile bus ride from Trangbang. "I often visited Saigon, with my friends," he said. He would spend a day's pay (70 cents) on a ticket to a Vietnamese movie, strong on passion and romance.

In any event, the army decided that Lon was needed further afield. He was transferred last December to the 21st Division's 31st Regiment, which was conducting a more arduous war in the swamps and canals of the Uminh forest in the Mekong Delta.

His new outfit was "better," Lon said. Why? The battalion commander, he allowed, was "not so easy on us. But he was brave and always with the troops."

With this remark, Lon touched on a theme common to all conversations in which South Vietnamese officers and U.S. advisers comment on the South Vietnamese army's fighting capacity: the extreme dependence of troops on personal leadership, in the absence of ideology, tradition or a coherent nationalism.

Indeed, another soldier, a Saigon-educated private from the 3rd Division, which was routed at Quangtri in May and now being rebuilt, said: "In the ARVN (South Vietnamese army), you are not serving the nation or the army. You are working for an individual. If he steals the rice, or mistreats the men, the unit is lousy. If he is good, the unit is good."

"In Vietnam," said a veteran U.S. adviser, "everybody looks up for direction, for inspiration. This culture puts a hell of a burden even on the good battalion commander. He's elder brother and big daddy to everybody. He decides everything. If he gets wounded or killed, the whole battalion of 500 men may fall apart."

This has caused Saigon's forces some grave losses during the current offensive. For example, the 20th Armor Battalion, newly equipped with 56 American M-48 tanks, reportedly fought well around Quangtri City in April until its commander was wounded. Then it fell apart. "The deputy who took over just didn't have the same charisma," said a U.S. adviser.

Lon's immediate superiors, by his account, were "brave" and "knew soldiering."

Most notably, his platoon leader was not a dandyish 19-year-old second lieutenant fresh out of Thu Duc Officer School —which until last year virtually guaranteed a commission to any middle-class youth who had passed his French-style baccalaureate (or university entrance exam). Nobody washed out of Thu Duc for lack of leadership qualities.

Lon's platoon was headed by a veteran sergeant first class, Danh Khuon. His company commander was a rarity in Saigon's forces, a first lieutenant promoted up from the enlisted ranks. He had been with the battalion for six years.

Lon himself became a squad leader, through seniority and the attrition of corporals and sergeants. He had only six men in his squad, instead of 10: two had been wounded, two others had been detailed to other jobs in the company.

"We get along well," he said. "We take turns cooking the rice (two meals a day) and getting the water." No senior officer, he said, levied a "tax" on the troops' $ -a-month ration allowance.

In April, Lon's division was shifted north from the Mekong Delta to the Highway 13 "front" north of Saigon. "At least we were out of the swamps," Lon said. "It was hot and flat, but it was dry."

At 9 A.M. on May 11, already tested by enemy fire, Lon's battalion joined yet another Saigon effort to open the road to Anloc. On that day, although Lon and his fellow troopers did not know it, the North Vietnamese army had begun a major assault on the battered town, coupled with a day-long barrage of some 6,000 rounds.

Lon's squad was, as usual, not briefed on the overall battalion plan, which was essentially a simple frontal push against North Vietnamese forces dug in on scrubby open terrain in deep bunkers.

The Saigon troops, then as later, had no heavy "direct fire" weapons of their own, such as 90 mm. recoilless rifles, to knock out the North Vietnamese bunkers. They had M-16s and grenades.

They had no special unit training in attacking fortified positions; Saigon's planners apparently hoped that air strikes and artillery shells, however imprecise, would do the job.

As the artillery burst over the treelines ahead, Lon said, Sgt. Khuon "pointed in the right direction, ordered us to advance, and everybody got up out of their foxholes and started moving ahead."

Seven crablike armored personnel carriers covered the advance, firing their .50-calibre machine guns.

Lon's company ran into a North Vietnamese listening post. "We had no foxholes to take cover in. We assaulted it from 30 meters away. We killed seven enemy and picked up four AK-47s," Lon said, with a touch of pride.

But the firefight alerted the enemy. The South Vietnamese skirmish line began to draw heavy fire from the main bunker line—which the bombs had once more failed to destroy.

Then 82 mm. mortar rounds began to explode among the exposed South Vietnamese infantrymen. The attack stalled.

The men went to ground. Their leaders felt that it was enough for one day in a long war.

"At noon, we pulled back to our old foxhole line and began digging deeper. The Communists kept shelling us with mortars. I got hit along with four others in the company," Lon said.

For lack of resources, Saigon's medical evacuation is a good deal less luxurious and speedy than the U.S. system. Lon was hastily bandaged and taken on a stretcher to the highway at Chonthanh.

A jolting truck ride to Laikhe got him to a division aid station where he got emergency treatment and a pain-killing shot of morphine. Only then was he lifted by helicopter, to Conghoa Hospital in Saigon.

"After 10 days in hospital," he said, "I felt better."

What's in prospect for Lon? "I'm hoping for a 30-day leave to go home," he said. "But they say only 15 days."

What after that?

"I'll go back to the unit. But maybe the war will end soon. I do not know."

The Washington Post, July 10, 1972

"WE HAVE BEEN FIGHTING ELEVEN CENTURIES":
NORTH VIETNAM, JULY 1972

Letter from Hanoi

by Joseph Kraft

AUGUST 1ST

MORE than any other capital in the world, probably—and maybe in history as well—Hanoi has grown accustomed to living with war. The city takes its lumps less in the heroic style of London during the blitz than in the spirit of New York at rush hour. Life is unpleasant, and there is an evident need to subordinate self to a larger interest. Still, the misery wears a familiar aspect. It comes in short bursts, and people act in the certain conviction that the trouble will somehow be surmounted.

One reason trouble seems routine is that the American bombing is routine. Almost every day around noon, for instance, a pilotless reconnaissance plane flies in to photograph Hanoi. It moves so rapidly that there is no warning of its approach, and there is small chance for hits by either anti-aircraft guns or the surface-to-air missiles, known as SAMs, that the North Vietnamese have received from the Russians. Only the noise of the drone's breaking through the sound barrier announces its advent. It is a startling noise—like a sudden clap of thunder—but after almost four months of bombing hardly anybody in Hanoi bothers to look up. The drone is dismissed with a shrug as "the noon plane."

Even serious air raids—the raids of June 27th, July 4th, and July 22nd—have a regular pattern. Danger is first signalled by a pre-alert, broadcast through loudspeakers all over town, which announces that American planes have been sighted approaching Hanoi, usually from the southwest, at a distance of more than fifty kilometres—about thirty miles. A second pre-alert, soon afterward, announces that the planes are within the fifty-kilometre radius. Then, within a few minutes, the alert itself sounds—a long, wailing siren note that rises, dips,

369

and then rises again. Minutes later, the planes come into sight—fighter-bombers, floating lazily and then diving on targets to drop bombs, which can be heard as they explode though not seen as they fall. As soon as the planes are visible, the racket of the anti-aircraft guns begins. Almost simultaneously, the SAMs can be seen, powered upward by rocket engines that give off a faint red glow. During the raid of July 4th, it was possible to follow the glow of a missile until a plane was struck and sent spinning to earth, trailing a cloud of black smoke. More often, the SAMs miss the planes, enter the upper atmosphere, and explode in a puff of white vapor. Then, suddenly, the planes are gone, and the siren is sounded on a steady note, signalling the all-clear. Several of the embassies here record the raids, both on film and on tape. The diplomats play the films and tapes over and over, and there has developed among them a kind of connoisseurs' taste in raids. One Canadian representative, before playing his recordings of the July 4th raid, remarked to me, "Visually, June 27th was a better raid, but sonically July 4th was superior." Listening to the recording, I had a chance to clock the raid; from first pre-alert to all-clear, it lasted twenty-seven minutes.

Short though the attacks are, they dominate life in Hanoi. A considerable part (some say forty per cent, some say twenty per cent) of the city's population has been removed to places of safety, in the mountains fifty miles northwest of Hanoi and elsewhere. Most of the government leaders seem to have left, apparently for a mountain hideout. Large numbers of young children have been evacuated, and the streets of Hanoi seem, by Asian standards, empty of boys and girls; when I went to change money recently at the state bank (a formidable pile that in French colonial days housed a main office of the Banque de l'Indochine), one of the women tellers had with her her little girl, who had come in from an evacuation camp for a couple of days.

As a further safety measure, virtually all public gatherings have been stopped. No films are being shown. The theatres are shut down, as are all museums. Boating on the Little Lake, a chief recreation spot in downtown Hanoi, has been suspended. The International Club, which has a pool where diplomats used to seek relief from the terrible hundred-degree

heat of summer days, has been closed. Sunday Mass at the
Cathedral is now said at four-thirty in the morning. The central markets have regulations to discourage shoppers from
dawdling over their purchases, and an effort has been made
to put decentralized, travelling markets in all neighborhoods.

The extent of the damage done by the bombing is hard to
determine, especially for foreigners. We are restricted in our
movements, and since even the driving of cars is forbidden,
correspondents and diplomats must rely on government-
assigned chauffeurs to get around. The general impression
among Western diplomats is that, for reasons of morale, the
government understates bombing losses. In trips I took outside Hanoi, I saw evidence of considerable destruction and
death. The two main bridges leading east from Hanoi to the
port of Haiphong have been bombed out, and the port itself
is in ruins. All the major bridges on the road leading south
to the Demilitarized Zone and the front lines have also been
destroyed. The textile town of Nam Dinh, about forty-five
miles southeast of Hanoi, has been badly battered, and presumably all towns farther south have been even more badly
battered. South of Hanoi, I saw two spots where American
bombs had seriously damaged the network of dikes that prevents the Red River from flooding in the rainy season (from
mid-May through September): near Phu Ly, I saw a sluice
gate that had been smashed; south of Nam Dinh, I saw a dike
badly cracked and pitted by bomb craters. The hits were probably accidental, since both sites were close to more likely targets—roads and a railroad. But they did take place, and, in a
sense—given the extent of the dikes (twenty-seven hundred
miles), the number of bombing sorties daily over North Vietnam (about three hundred), and the probable error made by
the pilots (quite substantial, in my judgment)—they were
bound to take place. If the hitting of the dikes was not deliberate, it was surely predictable.

On the morning of July 8th, I visited a town thirty-six miles
east of Hanoi—a trading center called Hung Wen, with a population of about twenty thousand—within twenty-four hours
after it had been struck by American planes. The bombs had
hit an area about a thousand yards long and five hundred yards

wide in the middle of town. According to the local authorities, eighteen blast bombs had been dropped, along with four anti-personnel bombs; each of the latter contains 192,500 steel pellets, which are hurled through the air when the bomb explodes. Seventeen persons were killed and twenty-five wounded. Forty-three houses were destroyed, thirty-six by fire and seven by the force of concussion. One of the houses destroyed belonged to Vo Nguyen Dam. He and two of his children were killed; his wife and three other children survived. In the rubble of their home, I met one of the survivors, a married daughter. She had been burned in the attack, and was poking about in a dazed way. Bits of a body—a charred jawbone, a hank of hair, what looked like a leg—were lying around, and she was trying to assemble them. She kept muttering, "My brother and sister were innocent."

Another destroyed home belonged to Nguyen Van Lam, a seventy-two-year-old grandfather. He said that he was a Catholic and that his family had been saying prayers when the attack came. His wife, his only son, and his grandson had all been killed. He stood in the rubble, a toothless old man dressed in brownish-red pajamas, and raised his fists to the heavens. "I feel deep hatred against the Americans!" he shouted. "As long as I live, I will have hatred in my heart!"

All sixteen beds in the emergency ward of the local hospital were filled. As I entered, I saw a five-year-old boy, his body covered with burns. There was a thirteen-year-old girl whose left leg had been severed just above the knee. There were two children whose bodies were full of steel pellets from the anti-personnel bombs. The doctor who took me around said as we emerged from the ward, "You Americans say you do not mean to kill people. Why, then, do you use anti-personnel bombs?"

Some sections of Hanoi proper have been bombed. I was shown three public-housing projects, comprising about five hundred apartments, that had been destroyed in the raids of June 27th and July 4th. The authorities claim that the raid of July 22nd knocked out a water-purifying plant. I was told that hospitals and schools had been hit in raids during the spring. The industrial power plant for the city has been destroyed, and the electric current that emanates from the remaining

Malcolm W. Browne, 1963. *(AP/Wide World Photos.)*

George Esper, 1966. *(Courtesy George Esper.)*

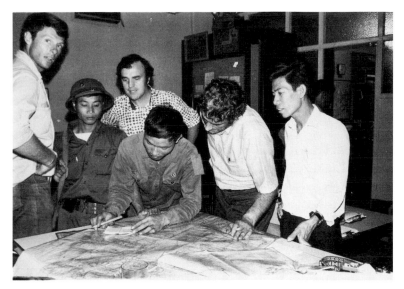

North Vietnamese soldiers in the Saigon office of the Associated Press, April 30, 1975. AP staff *(l. to r.)*: Matt Franjola, Peter Arnett, and George Esper. *(Courtesy George Esper.)*

Peter Arnett *(r.)* and Horst Faas, AP Office, Saigon. *(AP/Wide World Photos.)*

Gloria Emerson. *(Photo: John Harnett, courtesy Gloria Emerson.)*

Donald Kirk with South Vietnamese Regional Forces, Cam Lo, South Vietnam, March, 1968. *(Courtesy Donald Kirk.)*

Gloria Emerson with soldier of the Americal Division. *(Photo: Nancy Moran, courtesy Gloria Emerson.)*

Malcolm Browne, 1964. *(AP/Wide World Photos.)*

Stewart Alsop, 1973.
(AP/Wide World Photos.)

Joseph Kraft, 1972.
(AP/Wide World Photos.)

Sydney Schanberg in Neak Luong, Cambodia, during the last weeks of the war, 1975. *(Photo: Dith Pran, courtesy Sydney Schanberg.)*

Zalin Grant in Cambodia, 1970. *(Courtesy Pythia Press.)*

James P. Sterba with captured weapon, Cambodia, May 1970. *(Photo: Ray Cranbourne, courtesy James P. Sterba.)*

Peter Braestrup *(c.)* and Kevin Buckley *(r.)* near Tay Ninh, South Vietnam, 1968. *(Photo: François Sully, courtesy Archives and Special Collections, Healy Library, University of Massachusetts at Boston.)*

Bernard Weinraub, January 1968. *(New York Times Pictures.)*

Doris Kearns, 1971. *(AP/Wide World Photos.)*

Seymour M. Hersh after being awarded the Pulitzer Prize in 1970.
(AP/Wide World Photos.)

Francine du Plessix Gray.
*(Photo: Alexander Liberman,
courtesy Francine du Plessix
Gray.)*

H.D.S. Greenway on ferry
crossing the Mekong.
(Photo: Tim Page.)

Flora Lewis interviewing Xuan Thuy, North Vietnamese delegate to Paris peace talks, 1972. *(Photo: ©Marc Riboud/Magnum Photos.)*

Frances FitzGerald and Tran Ba Loc, 1971. *(Photo: Kevin Buckley, courtesy Frances FitzGerald.)*

John Saar, 1972. *(Photo: David Kennerly, courtesy Life.)*

Peter Arnett. *(AP/Wide World Photos.)*

John S. McCain III with wife and son in March 1973, after release from North Vietnam. *(AP/Wide World Photos.)*

James Michener in 1957. *(AP/Wide World Photos.)*

John Woodruff, Saigon, July, 1972. *(Photo: Neal Ulevitch.)*

Bob Tamarkin, Saigon, January 1975. *(Photo: Neal Ulevitch.)*

Michael Kinsley, 1972. *(Harvard Yearbook Photo.)*

(L. to r.) Robert Shaplen, Keyes Beech, George McArthur, and Bud Merrick aboard U.S.S. *Okinawa* after the evacuation of Saigon, May, 1975. *(Photo: Neal Ulevitch.)*

T. D. Allman with Laotian Prime Minister Souvannah Phouma, Vietiane, 1969. *(Courtesy T. D. Allman.)*

Hunter S. Thompson, 1977. *(AP/Wide World Photos.)*

Sydney Schanberg crossing the Mekong River near Neak Luong, Cambodia, late 1973. *(Photo: Sarah Webb Barrell, courtesy Sydney Schanberg.)*

Sydney H. Schanberg near Hue during the 1972 Easter Offensive. *(Photo: Nguyen Ngoc Luong, courtesy New York Times Pictures.)*

Sydney Schanberg *(standing left)* in the French Embassy after the fall of Phnom Penh to the Khmer Rouge *(Photo: Ennio Iacobucci, courtesy Sydney Schanberg.)*

Rudolph S. Rauch. *(Courtesy Rudolph S. Rauch.)*

Michael Herr at Tan Son Nhut airbase, South Vietnam. *(Photo: Tim Page.)*

Peter Kann at Long Hui, South Vietnam. *(Photo: Tim Page.)*

Michael Herr on the roof of the Caravelle Hotel, Saigon. *(Photo: Tim Page.)*

John Saar in War Zone D, South Vietnam. *(Photo: Tim Page.)*

Arnold Isaacs, 1972. *(Courtesy Arnold Isaacs.)*

power plant is feeble and subject to repeated failure. But otherwise Hanoi is remarkably intact. It bears the aspect of a nineteenth-century French provincial capital, very clean and rather drab, with broad, tree-lined avenues and airy public buildings of reddish or mustard-colored concrete. The working day starts around dawn, breaks at eleven for four hours, and resumes at three in the afternoon for another four hours. At the beginning and end of every break, the streets are filled with men and women going to and from offices, shops, and factories. The men wear sandals, cotton trousers, and short-sleeved sports shirts, usually white and open at the neck. The women are dressed in the traditional *ao dai*, and they all seem to have the lissome beauty made so familiar to Americans by the women of South Vietnam. Compared with Saigon, where the streets are messy with beggars, prostitutes, peddlers, and families cooking on the sidewalks, Hanoi has almost no street life. The police and the military, both highly visible in Saigon, are rarely seen in Hanoi; even their manning of checkpoints at the city gates—by soldiers in little huts, which they rarely leave—is discreet.

Most shopping is done in the early morning, and the closest thing to a crowd in Hanoi is the collection of housewives bustling about the central market just after dawn. By making huge purchases of food, both abroad and from peasants at home, and by rationing such goods as rice and cloth, the government keeps the prices of necessities within the reach of a consuming public whose earnings average ninety dong, or thirty dollars, a month. Rationed rice (under a system that allots thirty-three pounds a month to a worker, nineteen to a child, and thirty to a government minister) costs about six and a half cents a pound. When I visited the market, beef was going for about forty-five cents a pound, fresh carp for thirty-five cents a pound, fish sauce for twenty cents a pound, and fresh eggs for a dollar a dozen. Pineapples cost twenty cents apiece, tomatoes thirty-five cents a pound. Ducks were being sold, live, at thirty cents a pound.

Goods other than food are bought at government-controlled department or specialty stores. At one department store, I priced soap at twenty cents a bar for a Russian-made brand and forty cents a bar for a luxury item from East

Germany, conical hats at eighty cents apiece, plastic raincoats at a dollar apiece, and sleeping mats at forty cents. Sandals cost four dollars a pair, and shoes were on special sale, reduced from eight dollars a pair to six dollars. A short-wave radio cost three hundred and fifty dollars, a Russian-made camera five hundred dollars. Next to the department store was a tailor shop, and there I found shirts selling for three dollars and fifteen cents apiece, and trousers for four dollars and seventy-five cents a pair. Next to the tailor shop was a Western restaurant—the Restaurant of European Dishes. Its menu, which was displayed, in the Continental style, outside the entrance, included a beef dish for thirty cents, an omelette for thirty cents, and stuffed crab for sixty cents. I had some of the crab, and it was very good.

The availability of fresh seafood in a Hanoi restaurant bears on one of the never-ending American arguments about Vietnam. Despite the mining of the harbors since mid-May, and the intensive bombing of all internal transportation lines, North Vietnam is plainly not paralyzed. Large quantities of goods move at a fairly rapid clip all the time. Trucks provide the chief means of transport, and downtown Hanoi, where the bombing is relatively sporadic, has become a kind of national parking lot. The railways have been cut at all the major rivers, but at night I saw several trains being pulled by steam locomotives on the lines between bridges. One foreign ambassador told me that on a nighttime trip to Haiphong he had counted seven moving freight trains. I myself have no evidence that a way around the mining has been found, but the Swedish Embassy here recently received a consignment of tonic water sent by sea, and curtains sent by ship to the British mission arrived the other day. Rumors persist that the North Vietnamese are unloading freighter cargoes at sea onto landing craft and other shallow-draft wooden vessels, which pass over the mines without activating them.

Laborious individual effort, systematically organized and repeated over and over again, is required to keep transport moving. Pontoon bridges have been set up to replace most of the bombed-out road bridges. Traffic moves in one-way bursts of half an hour each; at fixed times sections of the pontoon bridges are removed to allow passage of river traffic. To supplement the pontoon bridges, ferries—usually barges pushed by river steamers—have been set up at most major crossings. Sections of the railways are constantly being demolished by bombing and are constantly being replaced. Pontoon bridges cannot replace the destroyed railway bridges, but the North Vietnamese move merchandise by rail between bridges, then load it on trucks for the river crossing, and then back on freight cars. The trucks come from all corners of the Communist world—Russia, China, Czechoslovakia, East Germany —and they have been painted brown, numbered, and incorporated into a national fleet. They move mainly by night, with headlights hooded. During the day, they line the streets of Hanoi, parked in the shadow of buildings or trees and often camouflaged with leafy branches.

Underlying this laborious effort is a furious concentration on the war and its object—reunification with South Vietnam. The foremost official expression of this well-nigh obsessive focus is the last will and testament of President Ho Chi Minh, written in May of 1969 and published at his death, on September 3rd of that year. "Even though our people's struggle against U.S. aggression, for national salvation, may have to go through more hardships and sacrifices, we are bound to win total victory," the testament begins. A subsequent passage asserts:

The war of resistance against U.S. aggression may drag on. Our people may have to face new sacrifices of life and property. Whatever happens, we must keep firm our resolve to fight the U.S. aggressors till total victory.

> Our mountains will always be, our rivers will always be,
>   our people will always be;
> The American invaders defeated, we will rebuild our land
>   ten times more beautiful.

No matter what difficulties and hardships lie ahead, our people are sure of total victory. The U.S. imperialists will certainly have to quit. Our fatherland will certainly be reunified. Our fellow-countrymen in the South and in the North will certainly be reunited under the same roof. We, a small nation, will have earned the signal honor of defeating, through heroic struggle, two big imperialisms—the French and the American—and of making a worthy contribution to the world national-liberation movement.

The six leading officials of North Vietnam—Le Duan, the First Secretary of the Workers', or Communist, Party; Truong Chinh, the President of the National Assembly; Vo Nguyen Giap, the Defense Minister; Pham Van Dong, the Prime Minister; Nguyen Duy Trinh, a Deputy Prime Minister and Foreign Minister; and Le Duc Tho, the Politburo member who sits on the North Vietnamese delegation to the Paris peace talks—have all sworn allegiance to Ho's testament. Parts of the testament are reprinted under pictures of Ho in markets, offices, and other public places. A placard bearing the line "No matter what difficulties and hardships lie ahead, our people are sure of total victory" is situated at a particularly lovely spot on the shore of the Little Lake in Hanoi. When I remarked to my interpreter that that seemed a queer place to put a call to arms, he replied that, on the contrary, it was entirely appropriate. The Little Lake, he told me, was also known as the Lake of the Restored Sword. In the early fifteenth century, at a time when Vietnam was being invaded by the Chinese from the north, the Emperor Le Loi was out boating, and a tortoise surfaced and gave the Emperor a sword. With that sword, the Emperor beat the Chinese. He then went back to the lake and returned the sword to the tortoise. "The lake," my interpreter said, "is the symbol of our will to be a nation."

Another sign of the intense national commitment to the struggle is the Vietnamese radio. The Voice of Vietnam, as the radio is called, is the principal national medium. Among the twenty-one million residents of North Vietnam, there are five hundred thousand private radios and six hundred thousand loudspeaker units to relay broadcasts to the villages and hamlets. "Our main subject is the fight against U.S. aggression," Tran Lam, the director of the Voice of Vietnam, told me. "Our whole program has as its central theme the strength of our people versus U.S. aggression." On one typical morning, broadcasting began at five with a fifteen-minute program for the peasants. The subject, according to Mr. Lam, was "how to achieve high yield in rice cultivation despite the bombing." At five-fifteen, there was a two-part news bulletin. The first part announced "victories achieved in the past twenty-four hours in North and South Vietnam." The second part dealt with "threats to the dikes by U.S. imperialists and the condemnation of their action by the world public." At five-thirty-five, an announcer read the day's lead editorial in *Nhan Dan*, the official newspaper of the Workers' Party; it dealt with an anti-aircraft unit and the techniques used against low-flying American planes. At five-forty-five, there was a children's program on the subject of "how young people in the country should receive city children who are being evacuated." So it went for the rest of the day. The last program, at eleven o'clock at night, was a study of "crimes committed by the U.S. and the lackey Thieu [as President Nguyen Van Thieu is always called here] in terrorizing the students of South Vietnam." The sign-off, at eleven-thirty, was an announcement of the number of American planes shot down —with a separate figure for hits on B-52s—since the war began.

This ceaseless concentration on a war waged against heavy odds has caused some Vietnamese, particularly in the leadership circles, to see themselves at the center of world history—a nation anointed to carry the torch of revolution. In a speech published on February 3rd, which is now deemed important as an expression of Hanoi's decision to launch the March 30th offensive in South Vietnam, Truong Chinh, the Assembly President, called Vietnam "the focus of the basic contradictions of human society." Nguyen Khac Vien, the French-educated editor of the scholarly publication *Vietnamese Studies*, with whom I had one of my rare unsupervised interviews, expounded on the theme without any evident self-consciousness. "Vietnam has become the focus of the three conflicts central to the present age," he said, as though he were stating a known fact apparent to the meanest intelligence. "It is the front line in the fight between colonialists and anti-colonialists. It is the front line in the fight between capitalists and Socialists. It is the front line in the international class struggle between the rich and the people."

Hong Chuong, an editor of the Communist monthly

theoretical journal *Hoc Tap*, made the same point with what seemed to me melodramatic self-importance. I met him in the *Hoc Tap* offices, which are in a pleasant tower-shaped building overlooking a pond. The reception room was decorated with cases full of historical mementoes, including a first edition of *Pravda*, some medals depicting Lenin and Ho Chi Minh, and some fragments of American bombs. The ashtrays in the reception room were made from bomb casings. I opened the conversation by asking for a few biographical details, and Mr. Chuong told me, "We don't speak about ourselves, because we consider each individual a drop of water in the ocean of the people. But I can tell you that I am a journalist about fifty years old."

I asked Mr. Chuong whether he was born in North or South Vietnam. He said, "We don't make that distinction. Our President, our Prime Minister, and the First Secretary of our Party were born in the South. Our country is one. The problem of partition is a problem that has been made by you American imperialists."

I asked him to tell me about the Vietnamese approach to Marxism and how it differs from the Russian and Chinese approaches. He said, "Our tradition is one of fighting, and we put it in the framework of Leninism. It is not enough to say that we have been fighting for thirty years. We have been fighting for much longer than that. We have made a contribution to Socialism in military thinking. Let me take as an example our national hero Tran Huong Dao. He rose up against the Mongol invasions two centuries before Columbus. These were the same Mongols who took China and India and Europe. They were defeated in Vietnam. Not once but three times we defeated them. And each time, I may say, we took prisoners and released them—fifty thousand each time. I once read an article by an American comparing Tran Huong Dao with Clausewitz. I think that underestimates Tran Huong Dao. Clausewitz existed in the eighteenth century; Tran Huong Dao was five centuries before him. Moreover, Tran Huong Dao was not only a great military writer, as was Clausewitz. He was also a great general of armies. I think Tran Huong Dao is a head taller than Clausewitz.

"But you asked about the originality of Vietnamese Social-

ism. Here is an example. In Russia, Lenin replaced Kerensky
and the Czar. Lenin represented the proletariat, and Kerensky
and the Czar represented the bourgeoisie and the nobles. But
they were all Russians. In China, Mao Tse-tung replaced
Chiang Kai-shek. Mao represented the peasants, and Chiang
was a representative of the warlords. But they were both Chinese. In Vietnam, however, Ho Chi Minh replaced the Japanese Fascists and the French colonialists. President Ho was
Vietnamese. They were foreigners. Our contribution to Marxism is not a question of doctrine. We have creative minds, and
we are not stuck on any formula. One mistake that the Americans always make is to think that we will do what the Russians
did or the Chinese did. In that sense, you are dogmatists. But
we follow our own ways, and that is why you are being defeated. If there is a single piece of advice I would give to
Kissinger, the adviser of Nixon, it would be: Abandon dog-
matism. For instance, in chess you can imagine a board full
of pieces where the right move will win. You can also imagine
a board where most of the pieces are gone and where the right
move will also win. We have used both tactics against the
Americans."

I said that I was not sure I followed his argument, and he
said, "A baby of two cannot understand an adult of forty, but
an adult of forty can understand a baby of two. The United
States will be two hundred years old in four years. Vietnam is
now four thousand years old. Vietnam can understand the
two-hundred-year-old United States. But the United States
cannot understand the four-thousand-year-old Vietnam.
Nixon said recently that the war had lasted eleven years and
had been hard and long. For us, it has not been long enough.
We have been fighting eleven centuries, not eleven years. We
fought eighty years against the French. When we came to
understand that we would have to fight against the United
States, we were sure it would take longer. We thought it
would take a century, and we are ready to fight for a century.
But Nixon has only two cards to play now. He can destroy
Hanoi. That is one. He can destroy the dikes. That is the
other. But we are not afraid. Let him play them. After that,
he will be defeated."

After that interview, I told Ngo Dien, the official of the

North Vietnamese Foreign Office who had finally approved
my application for a visa to Hanoi, that some of his countrymen seemed to me positively fanatical in their single-minded
attention to Vietnam and the war. He said, "We are not fanatics. If we were fanatics, we would lynch the pilots when
they were shot down, not treat them correctly in prison
camps. If we were fanatics, you would not be here." He went
on to point out that immoderate boasting was one response
of a small and backward country caught up in a war with a
great power, and that another response was to show the special modesty personified by Ho Chi Minh. "The example of
our President," he said, "has had a great impact on the Vietnamese people."

Perhaps by accident, perhaps by prearrangement, in everything that happened to me thereafter in Hanoi the softer side
of the Vietnamese character emerged. A curious instance occurred at a dinner given for me by the Vietnamese press association. Among the guests was Colonel Ha Van Lau, the
officer who negotiated the military cease-fire with the French
back in 1954, and a former member of the North Vietnamese
delegation to the Paris peace talks—a man whom I had come
to know as the toughest of the tough. Colonel Lau is now in
charge of the office that investigates what the North Vietnamese call American war crimes. In an earlier encounter during my visit to Hanoi, Colonel Lau had described American
depredations against his country in the harshest terms. He had
flung out his words contemptuously, the way a Spaniard spits.
But at dinner he was another person. We talked about President Nixon's visit to China and his trip to the Great Wall. I
said that the President's comments had not been distinguished
but that it was hard to know how an American President
should respond to the sight of the Great Wall. Someone suggested that he should have written a poem. "Better a song,"
Colonel Lau put in. He said that songs were particularly suitable to memorable places. He said there was one song that
always reminded him of Paris. It was sung by an American,
Josephine Baker. Did I know it? And suddenly the severe military man, who sometimes, in the fury of his nationalism,

affected not to speak French, began to sing, in a voice that wasn't at all bad:

> *"J'ai deux amours*
> *Mon pays et Paris. . . ."*

The next day, an interview was arranged with Nguyen Dinh Thi, a writer, whose work ranges from a critique of Aristotle to a song that the national radio uses as its theme. One of his novels, "The Dike That Exploded," was a best-seller. As secretary of the Writers' Union, he has been in touch with literary figures the world over. Yevtushenko had been his guest during a visit to Vietnam. "I liked him very much," Thi said. "But he is an actor. I told him, 'You are the Don Quixote of world literature.' " Thi told me that "by tradition and wisdom and the teachings of Ho Chi Minh, the Vietnamese people have developed a spirit of bitter intransigence in a fight." He went on, "Our people are performing now as the victims of barbarism. I regret that you haven't seen another side of us. We are poor. We are used to a hard life. We have typhoons every year. We do the back-breaking work of cultivating rice. Our tradition is that everybody helps everybody else. We respect literature more than war in our country, and there has never been a military caste here, as there was in Japan. An expression we use all the time is '*Tinh thuong,*' which means a combination of pity, compassion, and love. We know that we live on the edges of the great powers. We see that we have to be prudent and modest. We have a great sense of humanity, a sense of the pity of humanity."

At a reception the day after that, I met Ton That Tung, a distinguished surgeon and a relative of the former emperor Bao Dai. Among other things, Dr. Tung has translated into French the works of To Huu, a leading contemporary poet, who works in the Secretariat of the Workers' Party. I told Dr. Tung that some of his countrymen seemed peculiarly harsh to me—as if fighting were the only way they knew of to achieve things. I asked him if there was anything that he found unique in the Vietnamese personality. He said, "You should notice that when we entertain we never lord it over people—we put them wholly at ease. And we don't have religious disputes;

except when foreigners were involved, we had toleration for all religions."

He asked me what other impressions I had of North Vietnam. I said something about the need to end the war. Feeling that to be banal, I added that the two sides seemed so far apart and that there was so little mutual trust that I was pessimistic about a settlement. Dr. Tung was not so pessimistic. He said, "I know your people are tired of the war. Do you think our people want to go on fighting forever?"

I found that leaving Hanoi was almost as hard as getting there. Only four regular planes a week come to Hanoi: two small Chinese planes with chancy connections through Nanning to Canton and Hong Kong; an Ilyushin 18, run by Aeroflot, which goes out through Laos; and a converted Second World War Stratoliner, which is run by the International Control Commission set up at the Geneva Conference of 1954, and which also goes out through Laos. Bad weather forced two cancellations, but finally I left aboard the Russian airliner. My chauffeur, my interpreter, and a woman guide from the Foreign Ministry who had supervised my entire trip all came out to the Gia Lam airport to escort me through customs and wait for the plane to take off. As we sipped beer and lemonade in the departure lounge, a good cross-section of the foreign diplomats and journalists stationed in Hanoi passed in review. They are cut off from normal Vietnamese life by the language barrier and various restrictions, including the prohibition against driving cars. Much as settlers in the West used to arrange their lives around the pony express, the foreign colony in Hanoi orders its life around the planes from the outside world. Among those I saw were an Arab diplomat, who assured me that a particularly tough statement put out the night before by the North Vietnamese Foreign Ministry was done for "domestic consumption," and an East European diplomat, who said the statement showed that revisionism was finally taking hold in Hanoi. A military attaché observed that he had recently been counting the number of anti-aircraft guns parked along the road from Hanoi to Gia Lam; it was down from ninety-six a week ago to sixty-two—a probable sign that the guns had been moved south, toward the front. A West European diplomat observed that though the Paris peace negotiations had resumed, they would probably not get anywhere, because the North Vietnamese did not feel for Nixon the kind of trust they felt for Pierre Mendès-France, who negotiated the Geneva settlement back in 1954. I also saw a Russian diplomat, with whom I shared a bomb shelter at the Foreign Ministry during an air-raid alert, and a Soviet journalist—one of two indistinguishable heavies representing *Pravda* and *Izvestia*, who were known to the speakers of English in Hanoi as Mutt and Jeff. As each of these passing acquaintances talked, my guide drew for me on a napkin the ideograms used to denote their countries. I asked her to draw the characters for America. She did, and then she said, "Literally, the characters mean 'beautiful country.' I wish you Americans would stop behaving in a way that is— I won't say it. I wish you would start behaving again in a way that is beautiful."

The New Yorker, August 12, 1972

from *Fear and Loathing on the Campaign Trail '72*

by Hunter S. Thompson

Dozen Protestors Do About-Face

Sgt. Roy Gates, an Army recruiter in Miami Beach, looked out his carpeted and paneled office at a sign in the window saying, "Non-delegates—Help Wanted."

In what must rank as one of the Army's finest recruiting efforts, Gates thought he had convinced 13 non-delegates during the conventions to enlist in the military.

Nine of the protesters, however, failed to pass the Army's intelligence tests.

"Their low education surprised me—around the eighth grade and wanting to change the world," he said. "They said they didn't want to go along with the hard core radicals. It's amazing the different types you find." —Miami *News*, Friday, August 25

On Tuesday afternoon my car disappeared. I left it on the street in front of the hotel while I went in to pick up my swimming trunks, and when I came back out, it was gone.

To hell with it, I thought, it was time to get out of Miami.

I went up to my room and thought for a while, sitting with my back to the typewriter and staring out the window at the big ocean-going yachts and luxury houseboats tied up across the street, at the piers along Indian Creek. Last week they'd been crawling with people, and cocktail parties. Every time the Fontainebleau lobby started buzzing with rumors about another crowd of demonstrators bearing down on the hotel from the direction of Flamingo Park, the boats across Collins Avenue would fill up with laughing Republican delegates wearing striped blazers and cocktail dresses. There was no better place, they said, for watching the street action. As the demonstrators approached the front entrance to the hotel, they found themselves walking a gauntlet of riot-equipped police on one side, and martini-sipping GOP delegates on the other.

One yacht—the Wild Rose, out of Houston—rumbled back and forth, just offshore, at every demonstration. From the middle of Collins Avenue, you could see the guests lounging in deck chairs, observing the action through high-powered field glasses, and reaching around from time to time to accept a fresh drink from crewmen wearing white serving jackets with gold epaulets.

The scene on the foredeck of the Wild Rose was so gross, so flagrantly decadent, that it was hard to avoid comparing it with the kind of bloodthirsty arrogance normally associated with the last days of the Roman Empire: Here was a crowd of rich Texans, floating around on a $100,000 yacht in front of a palatial Miami Beach hotel, giggling with excitement at the prospect of watching their hired gladiators brutalize a mob of howling, half-naked Christians. I half-expected them to start whooping for blood and giving the Thumbs Down signal.

Nobody who was out there on the street with the demonstrators would be naive enough to compare them to "helpless Christians." With the lone exception of the Vietnam Veterans Against the War, the demonstrators in Miami were a useless mob of ignorant, chicken-shit ego-junkies whose only accomplishment was to embarrass the whole tradition of public protest. They were hopelessly disorganized, they had no real purpose in being there, and about half of them were so wasted on grass, wine, and downers that they couldn't say for sure whether they were raising hell in Miami or San Diego.

Five weeks earlier, these same people had been sitting in the lobby of the Doral, calling George McGovern a "lying pig" and a "warmonger." Their target-hotel this time was the Fontainebleau, headquarters for the national press and many TV cameras. If the Rolling Stones came to Miami for a free concert, these assholes would build their own fence around the bandstand—just so they could have something to tear down and then "crash the gates."

The drug action in Flamingo Park, the official campground

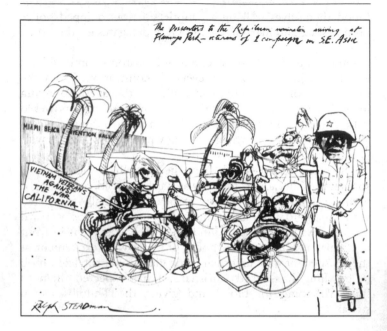

for "non-delegates" and other would-be "protesters," was so bottom-heavy with downers that it was known as "Quaalude Alley."

Quaalude is a mild sleeping pill, but—consumed in large quantities, along with wine, grass, and adrenaline—it produces the same kind of stupid, mean-drunk effect as Seconal ("Reds"). The Quaalude effect was so obvious in Flamingo Park that the "Last Patrol" caravan of Vietnam Vets—who came here in motorcades from all parts of the country—refused to even set up camp with the other demonstrators. They had serious business in Miami, they explained, and the last thing they needed was a public alliance with a mob of stoned street crazies and screaming teenyboppers.

The Vets made their camp in a far corner of the Park, then sealed it off with a network of perimeter guards and checkpoints that made it virtually impossible to enter that area unless you knew somebody inside. There was an ominous sense of dignity about everything the VVAW did in Miami. They rarely even hinted at violence, but their very presence was menacing—on a level that the Yippies, Zippies, and SDS street crazies never even approached, despite all their yelling and trashing.*

The most impressive single performance in Miami during the three days of the GOP convention was the VVAW march on the Fontainebleau on Tuesday afternoon. Most of the press and TV people were either down at the Convention Hall,

---

*Earlier that week, Lucian Truscott from the *Village Voice* and I tried to arrange a brief chat between John "Duke" Wayne and about two dozen Vets from the vanguard of the Last Patrol. They had just arrived in Miami and when they heard Wayne was holding an "open" press conference at Nixon headquarters in the Doral they decided to stop by and pick up on it.

But the GOP security guards wouldn't let them in—so they moved about a half block down Collins Avenue to a public parking lot on the edge of the ocean—where they were quickly surrounded, at a discreet distance, by a cordon of Florida state troopers.

"Say, man," a vet in a wheelchair called out to me after I'd used my press credentials to penetrate the cop-cordon, "Can you get that asshole Wayne out here to talk to us?"

"Why not?" I said. "He's tough as nails, they say. He'd probably *enjoy* coming out here in the sun and abusing you dope-addled communist dupes for a while."

"The Duke fears nothing," Lucian added. "We'll bring him out right after his press conference."

But John Wayne was not eager that day for a chat with the Last Patrol. "What the hell do they want to talk about?" he asked.

"Yeah, *what?*" said his drinking buddy, Glenn Ford. They were standing on the front steps of the Doral waiting for a cab.

"They just want to shoot the bull," said Lucian. "You know, maybe talk about the war . . ."

"*What* war?" Ford snapped.

"The one in Vietnam," Lucian replied. "These guys all fought over there—a lot of them are crippled."

The Duke seemed agitated; he was scanning the street for a cab. Finally, without looking at us, he said: "Naw, not today. I can't see the point in it."

"Why not?" Lucian asked. "They just want to *talk*. They're not looking for trouble. Hell, the place is crawling with cops."

Wayne hesitated, then shook his head again as he suddenly spotted a cab. "So they just want to *talk*, eh?" he said with a thin smile.

I nodded. "Why not. It won't take long."

"Bullshit," Wayne replied. "If they got somethin' to say to me, tell 'em to put it in writing."

Then he waved us away and eased off across the driveway to the waiting cab. "Playboy Plaza," he barked. "Jesus, I need a *drink*."

covering the "liberals vs. conservatives" floor-fight over rules
for seating delegates in 1976—or standing around in the boil-
ing mid-afternoon sun at Miami International Airport, waiting
for Nixon to come swooping out of the sky in Air Force One.

My own plan for that afternoon was to drive far out to the
end of Key Biscayne and find an empty part of the beach
where I could swim by myself in the ocean, and not have to
talk to anybody for a while. I didn't give a fuck about watching the rules fight, a doomed charade that the Nixon brain-
trust had already settled in favor of the conservatives . . . and
I saw no point in going out to the airport to watch three
thousand well-rehearsed "Nixon Youth" robots "welcome
the President."

Given these two depressing options, I figured Tuesday was
as good a day as any to get away from politics and act like a
human being for a change—or better still, like an animal. Just
get off by myself and drift around naked in the sea for a few
hours. . . .

But as I drove toward Key Biscayne with the top down,
squinting into the sun, I saw the Vets. . . . They were moving up Collins Avenue in dead silence; twelve hundred of
them dressed in battle fatigues, helmets, combat boots . . .
a few carried full-size plastic M-16s, many peace symbols,
girlfriends walking beside vets being pushed along the street
in slow-moving wheelchairs, others walking jerkily on
crutches. . . . But nobody spoke; all the "stop, start," "fast,
slow," "left, right" commands came from "platoon leaders"
walking slightly off to the side of the main column and using
hand signals.

One look at that eerie procession killed my plan to go swimming that afternoon. I left my car at a parking meter in front
of the Cadillac Hotel and joined the march. . . . No,
"joined" is the wrong word; that was not the kind of procession you just walked up and "joined." Not without paying
some very heavy dues: an arm gone here, a leg there, paralysis,
a face full of lumpy scar tissue . . . all staring straight ahead
as the long silent column moved between rows of hotel
porches full of tight-lipped Senior Citizens, through the heart
of Miami Beach.

The silence of the march was contagious, almost threatening. There were hundreds of spectators, but nobody said a word. I walked beside the column for ten blocks, and the only sounds I remember hearing were the soft thump of boot leather on hot asphalt and the occasional rattling of an open canteen top.

The Fontainebleau was already walled off from the street by five hundred heavily armed cops when the front ranks of the Last Patrol arrived, still marching in total silence. Several hours earlier, a noisy mob of Yippie/Zippie/SDS "non-delegates" had shown up in front of the Fontainebleau and been met with jeers and curses from GOP delegates and other partisan spectators, massed behind the police lines. . . . But now there was no jeering. Even the cops seemed deflated. They watched nervously from behind their face-shields as the VVAW platoon leaders, still using hand signals, funneled the column into a tight semicircle that blocked all three north-bound lanes of Collins Avenue. During earlier demonstrations—at least six in the past three days—the police had poked people with riot sticks to make sure at least one lane of the street stayed open for local traffic, and on the one occasion when mere prodding didn't work, they had charged the demonstrators and cleared the street completely.

But not now. For the first and only time during the whole convention, the cops were clearly off balance. The Vets could have closed all six lanes of Collins Avenue if they'd wanted to, and nobody would have argued. I have been covering anti-war demonstrations with depressing regularity since the winter of 1964, in cities all over the country, and I have never seen cops so intimidated by demonstrators as they were in front of the Fontainebleau Hotel on that hot Tuesday afternoon in Miami Beach.

There was an awful tension in that silence. Not even that pack of rich sybarites out there on the foredeck of the Wild Rose of Houston could stay in their seats for this show. They were standing up at the rail, looking worried, getting very bad vibrations from whatever was happening over there in the street. Was something *wrong* with their gladiators? Were they spooked? And why was there no noise?

After five more minutes of harsh silence, one of the VVAW platoon leaders suddenly picked up a bullhorn and said: "We want to come inside."

Nobody answered, but an almost visible shudder ran through the crowd. "O my God!" a man standing next to me muttered. I felt a strange tightness coming over me, and I reacted instinctively—for the first time in a long, long while—by slipping my notebook into my belt and reaching down to take off my watch. The first thing to go in a street fight is always your watch, and once you've lost a few, you develop a certain instinct that lets you know when it's time to get the thing off your wrist and into a safe pocket.

I can't say for sure what I would have done if the Last Patrol had tried to crack the police line and seize control of the Fontainebleau—but I have a fair idea, based on instinct and rude experience, so the unexpected appearance of Congressman Pete McCloskey on that scene calmed my nerves considerably. He shoved his way through the police line and talked with a handful of the VVAW spokesmen long enough to convince them, apparently, that a frontal assault on the hotel would be suicidal.

One of the platoon leaders smiled faintly and assured McCloskey that they'd never had any intention of attacking the Fontainebleau. They didn't even *want* to go in. The only reason they asked was to see if the Republicans would turn them away in front of network TV cameras—which they did, but very few cameras were on hand that afternoon to record it. All the network floor crews were down at the Convention Hall, and the ones who would normally have been on standby alert at the Fontainebleau were out at the airport filming Nixon's arrival.

No doubt there were backup crews around somewhere—but I suspect they were up on the roof, using very long lenses; because in those first few moments when the Vets began massing in front of the police line there was no mistaking the potential for real violence . . . and it was easy enough to see, by scanning the faces behind those clear plastic riot masks, that the cream of the Florida State Highway Patrol had no appetite at all for a public crunch with twelve hundred angry Vietnam Veterans.

Whatever the outcome, it was a guaranteed nightmare situation for the police. Defeat would be bad enough, but victory would be intolerable. Every TV screen in the nation would show a small army of heavily armed Florida cops clubbing unarmed veterans—some on crutches and others in wheelchairs—whose only crime was trying to enter Republican convention headquarters in Miami Beach. How could Nixon explain a thing like that? Could he slither out from under it?

Never in hell, I thought—and all it would take to make a thing like that happen, right now, would be for one or two Vets to lose control of themselves and try to crash through the police line; just enough violence to make *one* cop use his riot stick. The rest would take care of itself.

Ah, nightmares, nightmares. . . . Not even Sammy Davis Jr. could stomach that kind of outrage. He would flee the Nixon family compound on Key Biscayne within moments after the first news bulletin, rejecting his newfound soul brother like a suckfish cutting loose from a mortally wounded shark . . . and the next day's Washington *Post* would report that Sammy Davis Jr. had spent most of the previous night trying to ooze through the keyhole of George McGovern's front door in Washington, D.C.

Right . . . but none of this happened. McCloskey's appearance seemed to soothe both the crowd and the cops. The only violent act of the afternoon occurred moments later when a foul-mouthed twenty-year-old blonde girl named Debby Marshal tried to ram her way through the crowd on a 125 Honda. "Get out of my way!" she kept shouting. "This is ridiculous! These people should go back where they belong!"

The Vets ignored her, but about halfway through the crowd she ran into a nest of press photographers, and that was as far as she went. An hour later she was still sitting there, biting her lips and whining about how "ridiculous" it all was. I was tempted to lean over and set her hair on fire with my Zippo, but by that time the confrontation had settled down to a series

of bullhorn speeches by various Vets. Not much of what was said could be heard more than fifteen feet from the bullhorn, however, because of two Army helicopters that suddenly appeared overhead and filled the whole street with their noise. The only Vet speaker who managed to make himself plainly understood above the chopper noise was an ex-Marine Sergeant from San Diego named Ron Kovic, who spoke from a wheelchair because his legs are permanently paralyzed.

I would like to have a transcript or at least a tape of what Kovic said that day, because his words lashed the crowd like a wire whip. If Kovic had been allowed to speak from the convention hall podium, in front of network TV cameras, Nixon wouldn't have had the balls to show up and accept the nomination.

No . . . I suspect that's wishful thinking. Nothing in the realm of human possibility could have prevented Richard Nixon from accepting that nomination. If God himself had showed up in Miami and denounced Nixon from the podium, hired gunsels from the Committee for the Re-Election of the President would have quickly had him arrested for disturbing the peace.

Vietnam veterans like Ron Kovic are not welcome in Nixon's White House. They tried to get in last year, but they could only get close enough to throw their war medals over the fence. That was perhaps the most eloquent anti-war statement ever made in this country, and that Silent March on the Fontainebleau on August 22 had the same ugly sting to it.

There is no anti-war or even anti-establishment group in America today with the psychic leverage of the VVAW. Not even those decadent swine on the foredeck of the Wild Rose can ignore the dues Ron Kovic and his buddies have paid. They are golems, come back to haunt us all—even Richard Nixon, who campaigned for the presidency in 1968 with a promise that he had "a secret plan" to end the war in Vietnam.

Which was true, as it turns out. The plan was to end the war just in time to get himself re-elected in 1972. Four more years.

from Fear and Loathing on the Campaign Trail, '72, 1973;
illustrations by Ralph Steadman

The Saigon Follies, or, Trying to Head Them Off at Credibility Gap

by Sydney H. Schanberg

SAIGON: Not long ago a key officer in the military office of information told a newsman that his previous job in Washington—he had come from a high information post at the Pentagon—had been much harder. In Washington, he explained, there were continual "leaks" from Capitol Hill that had to be reacted to and denied quickly so as to get the denials into the next morning's newspapers, whereas in Vietnam things were simpler because "there's no competing line."

Before this officer arrived in Saigon a few months ago, one of his franker colleagues-to-be was asked what kind of man he was. "He's got a reputation," the man said wryly, "as a leading graduate of the Pentagon school of escape and evasion." Escape and evasion about sum up the attitude that most American officials in Vietnam have taken toward newsmen most of the time—an attitude that, notwithstanding areas of guarded coexistence, generally consists of suspicion, distrust and sometimes outright animosity.

Recently, when two reporters from the same American publication arrived for an interview, a high embassy official physically pushed one of them out of his office on the ground that he was hostile to the story the embassy was then marketing. Usually the relationship between the American Establishment in Vietnam and the press has been more civil than this, at times even cordial, but the outcome has been the same: very little information has been dispensed. The Establishment has been "nothing but a huge fact-suppression machine," says one seasoned American newsman.

There is absolutely no reason to believe that obfuscations and falsehoods would suddenly cease with a cease-fire. On the contrary, there is every reason to believe that until love and brotherhoood break out in epidemic form all over Indochina there will be no public frankness about what is going on here.

I am not an old hand in Vietnam—my reporting here consists of a brief 10-day stint in 1970 during the American incursion into Cambodia and most recently a four-and-a-half month tour to cover the North Vietnamese offensive—so I cannot personally compare what it was like to cover the war in, say, the nineteen-sixties to what it is like today. Yet from all accounts—though the American Establishment has always tried to suppress unhappy facts—it would seem that with more of the American involvement becoming hidden from the press (such as the air bases in Thailand that are usually closed to newsmen), American officials in Saigon have been more secretive and more obstructive.

News stories from Saigon almost never use the word "lie" about American press releases and reports—perhaps because of the need for coexistence and because softer words will get the idea across. But there is really no other word for some of the stories the Americans put out. For example, when the number of bombing raids against North Vietnam increased markedly in the period from Nov. 8, 1971, to March 8, 1972, the American command explained it by saying the weather had improved. It later turned out that this explanation concealed the fact that the Seventh Air Force commander, Gen. John D. Lavelle, frustrated by the restrictions on bombing of North Vietnam, had ordered unauthorized raids on military targets in the North and called them "protective reaction" attacks. The raids suddenly stopped from March 8 until March 30, the day the current North Vietnamese invasion of South Vietnam began. The command said the weather had closed in again.

What had happened had nothing to do with the weather. General Lavelle's activities had been exposed by the Air Force intelligence specialist who wrote to his Senator about the unauthorized raids—and all missions over the North had then been halted while an investigation was under way. General Lavelle was recalled to Washington, demoted and relieved of command.

This is but one of almost daily instances of distortions and omissions of facts—a practice which stems more from official embarrassment over the course of events than from reasons of military security. The South Vietnamese information apparatus is even less truthful—their briefers occasionally announce victories that simply have not occurred and often omit all mention of defeats—but foreign newsmen do not generally expect Vietnamese officials to tell the truth about how the war is going. It is appreciated that, unlike the Americans, they have more at stake than failure of a foreign policy.

The idea of the press as an adversary to government is certainly not new. All governments try to control the news, especially in crises. But I for one have never been in a reporting situation quite as frustrating as the one in Vietnam. Reporters can, from time to time, obtain interviews with all the top American officials—with Ambassador Ellsworth Bunker and also the commanding generals—but none will speak for the record. No names can be used. No one accepts personal responsibility for what he says. What this means is that these men can get things in print as the official American view— sometimes outrageous things—and never have to answer for them personally if events prove their analyses totally wrong. How many times did we "turn the corner" in Vietnam or sight that famous light at the end of the tunnel? Usually, these officials do not assume this cloak of anonymity out of venality but rather out of fear, and presumably because of instructions from Washington. Toward the end of April, when Brig. Gen. Thomas W. Bowen spoke frankly and on the record to reporters in Hue about the deteriorating situation on the northern front, he was admonished and silenced by his superiors in Saigon, who had apparently got the word from Washington.

Few of the reporters I know in Vietnam, though they often get frustrated, ever get truly angry at being treated hostilely or with suspicion by American generals or embassy officials. They accept that this hostility is born of the failure of American policy here and of the inability of those whose careers have become so entwined with Vietnam to admit it. Some of these men have been in Vietnam for a decade. They know virtually no other life but the one of trying to make American policy come out right. To admit defeat would be to throw away the linchpin of their existence. But the press has reported their failures for them, and under such circumstances, no one can be surprised at their distrust and dislike of newsmen.

Typical of such men was the American general advising on the northern front who agreed to talk off the record with a half-dozen Western reporters one day. He immediately made it clear that he considered us unpatriotic, because he assumed, correctly, that we had been writing stories saying the war was not going well for the allied side.

"I want you to get something straight," he said, pointing an accusing finger. "You're talking to a hawk. You know that. The only solution possible is a military solution. It's going to take a military victory to end it. We've got to prove to the North Vietnamese that they can't invade and take over." The general then said that the North Vietnamese high command does not put the same value on life as Americans and South Vietnamese do. "They've already determined they can expend 100,000 men this year on the offensive and they don't care if they come back or not. A North Vietnamese officer has the power of life and death over his men. They shoot a man if he refuses to go on attack." Saying these things seemed to console the general.

He then repeated what had become a standard allied briefing note—"The North Vietnamese are chained inside their tanks. They are also chained together in their bunkers." But he acknowledged that he had never seen this himself nor did he know anyone who had. There were no pictures, either, of such forced military service among the Communists. If this had been a popular war, perhaps the relationship between the generals and the press would have been a more salutary one, as it was in World War II. But most of the generals blamed the press largely for the war's unpopularity and this made *détente* impossible.

For a reporter, talking with the generals can be an unsettling experience, for there is often no communication, as if two people from different planets had just met. Naturally each believes the other is not addressing reality. Actually both are wrong: They are simply dealing in different realities. Many of the military men still cannot grasp why the rules of war have been changed for them between World War II and Vietnam. They have not understood the seriousness of the social stresses triggered by this war on the people back home. They cannot cope with the fact that Air Force aces are no longer welcomed as dashing young heroes when they go home these days but as shadowy, questionable figures whose bombs may have killed or maimed civilians. In short, these men are bitter.

"We wiped out whole cities, whole cities, in World War II," an Air Force general fumed in a recent interview, "and there wasn't a single protest. Now one bomb falls outside the target area and they scream in righteous moral indignation. It's all baloney." This general, another anonymous member of the American hierarchy, became greatly exercised during the interview, frequently pounding his desk and raising his voice in exasperation. I rather doubt whether anything I said was responsible, for I said very little—the interview was largely a monologue. It was just that his frustration was terrible and he needed someone to rail at, and I was a newsman and per se a culprit.

"The thing that's played up is the alleged wrongs of the military, the bombing of the dikes, when it's not being done," he said. "It's the big lie. We haven't done any of these things you read about. That's why we introduced 'smart bombs.' I look at every photo like a hawk. This thing is on my desk at all times [waving a large magnifying glass]. I've never seen a picture of a hospital hit. I have a hard time finding any misses. I think you'd be hard-pressed to find 3 per cent of the bombs outside the target area. And then they're not very far out." He refused to talk about civilian casualties. Or to discuss the war in human terms at all. At one point I said that his press releases used a jargonized form of language that made the bombing sound like a clean surgical operation instead of the mess and horror that war actually is. He was polite but in his next sentence he talked of bombing "on a surgical precision basis." We were discussing two different realities.

In criticizing the American Establishment for being less than frank, I am not suggesting that the press corps in Saigon has no warts. Some reporters suffer from the same malaise that seems to grip their readers—a sense of weary *déjà vu* about Vietnam and maybe a hardening of viewpoint. Judging from the readers' letters received by me and my reporter friends, and from the reactions reported by other newsmen who have returned from home leaves in the States, most Americans seemed to have made up their minds and taken sides on the war long ago and haven't wanted to read or hear anything that might interfere with their point of view. It's not hard to understand this, but it is difficult to write for an already locked-in audience and even more difficult to read their letters.

Consider a letter from a young antiwar activist in Maine who wanted to help a wounded and orphaned 3-year-old girl I had written about. He wrote "as an American whose Government is the prime mover" behind the war and behind this particular incident, ignoring what I had clearly written in my story—that this little girl had been wounded and her mother killed by North Vietnamese troops who had fired deliberately on civilians trying to flee south out of embattled Quangtri province. Or consider the letter from a doctor in New Jersey who began his epistle, "Dear S——berg" and then went on to accuse me of working for the Communists.

I think some reporters do come to Vietnam with their opinions, like the letter writers', already formed, but I would contend that these are a small minority. The press corps in Saigon, as in Washington or any capital, is hardly a corps at all in the sense that its members think or act in a uniform manner. Many reporters, if not most, have spent a lot of time in the field, seeing the fighting and its consequences for themselves. If the bulk of reporting from Vietnam over the past decade has suggested the existence of a chasm between optimistic official pronouncements and actual events in the field, it is because reporters, separately, have personally observed that chasm, not because they sat in bars in Saigon and cooked it up to be perverse.

One myth fostered by supporters of United States policy in Vietnam is that the Saigon press corps is a monolithic body whose members, to a man, are antiwar ideologues who spend their days searching sedulously for negative things to write about. These people would be pleased to learn that there are prominent reporters in Saigon who have been sympathetic to American policy—and they are the only ideologues this reporter met while in Vietnam.

Item: A British correspondent, who has earned a reputation

as a hawk, not only writes for a leading London newspaper but also prepares reports for Sir Robert Thompson, the guerrilla warfare specialist who receives huge fees for advising the United States Government. Sir Robert's reports have generally told the Americans the light-at-the-end-of-the-tunnel things they wanted to hear, and the one report I saw done by the British correspondent for Sir Robert did much the same thing. Presumably it was passed on to the Nixon Administration as expert analysis. That correspondent almost never moves out of Saigon and his report was based on developments in combat theaters he had never been to. He asked my opinion of the report and I pointed out several major errors of fact about battles I had covered—errors which made his conclusions ridiculous. But I got the impression that he had no intention of changing a word.

Item: The acting bureau chief of a major American publication, whose sympathies with the American Embassy and the Saigon Government are well-known, first allowed one of the bureau reporters to prepare a story on the torture of political prisoners by the Government and then successfully killed the story by telling his editors in New York that the subject was old hat and had been well covered before. But he acknowledged to the reporter later that the real reason he had scotched the piece was that "this is a sensitive time for [President Nguyen Van] Thieu and I don't think we should add to his troubles."

At the moment, there are more than 350 newsmen in Vietnam accredited by the South Vietnamese Government and the American command, known as MACV (Military Assistance Command, Vietnam). This includes both freelancers and full-time salaried correspondents. Of the total, about 150 are Americans and the rest are about evenly divided between third-country nationals and Vietnamese newsmen working for foreign news agencies. The press corps was larger in the early weeks of the Communist offensive that began last spring. It reached 490 in late May. The record was set during the Communist Tet offensive of 1968, when the number reached 647.

It goes without saying that not all stories written from Vietnam are prize-winners. There cannot be a reporter in Vietnam who doesn't cringe at the memory of some of the stories he wrote in the innocence of his early days in the country or on the basis of information that looked absolutely solid at the time. I would give a lot to be able to redo a story I wrote in late July reporting that South Vietnamese units were making progress in clearing Communist troops off Route 13 between Saigon and Anloc—which was true at the time. But the story also suggested that the road might be opened up soon—which never happened. Route 13 has been cut since early April and it remains so.

Newsmen also suffer occasionally, from real and imagined pressures. There is the pressure of competition, felt most keenly by the international wire services, each of which has had to put out a combat story every day and then face a rating system by its editors according to the play the story received around the world. And some newsmen feel a compulsion, when they haven't written a story for several days, to sit down at the typewriter just "to get something in the paper." Right or wrong, reporters often feel their editors are grading them, at least partly, on quantity.

And then there are the pressures from melodramatic editors. A correspondent for a popular British paper received the following cable from his home office last April 25: "In view of rapidly worsening Vietnam situation, editor wants you to give top priority to big piece on the plight of Saigon. He sees it as Berlin-type situation with Red forces closing in from all sides. The city built up on American money, where one could get anything from a missile to a beautiful girl. Now the whole infrastructure likely to be dismantled. David wants good hard, color-packed copy which would make spread. Repeat, must be serious but perhaps cynical to match mood of nation facing defeat and mood of Nixon in almost hopeless dilemma." This cable would be laughable if it were not so professionally disgraceful. At no time in the North Vietnamese offensive has the city of Saigon been directly threatened. I do not know if the reporter wrote a story along the lines suggested.

There was also an Italian correspondent who received this cable on Aug. 23: *"Mandaci un pezzo sull'offensiva di Giap e l'assedio che stringe Saigon."*—"Send a piece on Giap's offensive and the siege that squeezes Saigon."

These reports are extreme cases, and fairly rare, but moderately misguided cables from editors are common. It is up to the reporter, who is not always willing to risk a fight with his desk, to resist writing such poorly conceived stories. However, as often as not the clinkers about Vietnam have been the result of something doled out in a press release or briefing by the American or South Vietnamese commands. For instance, one wire service, United Press International, went along with the Government claims in reporting the recapture of Quangtri Citadel in early July, and did not back off the story for nearly a week. The citadel was finally retaken, but not until September. Such episodes underscore one of the basic difficulties with coverage of Vietnam and one of the caveats the reader of Vietnam news should be apprised of: The core of the combat story that many American newspapers run as a daily staple comes from an afternoon briefing in downtown Saigon that bears about as much relation to reality as a trip through a funhouse at an amusement park.

The briefing, which has become known as "the Follies," begins at 4:15 P.M. in a sweltering unair-conditioned auditorium that is part of a euphemistic operation known as the Press Center. Press releases are passed out beforehand—one from MACV, a separate one from the American Navy that expands on items already in the MACV release (the Air Force also puts out a separate one but distributes it in news-agency mail boxes), and one from the South Vietnamese armed forces, prepared by their Political Warfare Department. Political warfare is perhaps as good a way as any to describe what the American and South Vietnamese officers do at the briefing, which lasts anywhere from five minutes to half an hour. The Vietnamese military briefer steps to the lectern first, adding late developments to the press release, if there are any, and then accepting questions. The MACV briefer who follows conducts a similar performance.

Their releases and answers are notable primarily for their omissions. Entire battles have gone unreported. In early September, an Associated Press correspondent, through other sources, had learned of and written about a major two-day clash that had taken place less than 40 miles north of Saigon in which 180 North Vietnamese were killed and about 200

South Vietnamese were killed or wounded. When the battle had gone unmentioned at the briefing for two days, the correspondent asked the reason for the omission.

The South Vietnamese briefer went shuffling through the mound of papers on his clipboard and finally announced: "Between noon and early evening on Friday, Sept. 1, ARVN [Army of the Republic of Vietnam] elements engaged an undetermined-sized enemy force 12 kilometers north of Laikhe; 83 enemy were killed. On the ARVN side, 76 were wounded." On the face of it, this report was preposterous—it would take a miracle to produce a battle in which 76 men get wounded and not a single one dies. ARVN was simply covering up its losses again. These lies and omissions have tended to increase whenever battle losses have.

The American briefers, who smile knowingly about ARVN's doctoring of battle statistics, have not been much more forthcoming themselves with the facts of war. Their language, which has no connection with everyday English, has been designed to sanitize the war. Planes do not drop bombs, they "deliver ordnance." Napalm is a forbidden word and when an American information officer is forced under direct questioning to discuss it, he calls it "soft ordnance." In the press releases and the answers to newsmen's questions, there is never any sense, not even implicit, of people being killed, homes being destroyed, thousands of refugees fleeing.

What has made the briefers' job of obfuscation easier is that nearly all the American involvement in the war was gradually moved out of the sight of newsmen. With ground combat troops phased out, the air offensive became virtually the only American combat function left, aside from advisers in the field, and most of the air offensive has been conducted in secrecy. In mid-October, an estimated 800 to 900 jet fighter-bombers were involved in the air war and as many as 200 B-52 eight-engine heavy-load bombers. But of this armada of more than 1,000 planes, fewer than 50 were left in South Vietnam. Some of the B-52's were based on Guam, but all the rest of our planes flew either from seven bases in Thailand or from carriers off the Vietnam coast. Visits by newsmen to carriers could be arranged, but they were carefully controlled. And

the Thai bases have been virtually closed to newsmen. After
years of press appeals to the American command in Thailand
and the Thai Government (which has paper jurisdiction over
the bases), a one-day tour of two of the Thai bases was finally
arranged for a group of reporters on Aug. 29. But it turned
out to be even more controlled and deodorized than the carrier visits. A few selected American airmen were produced for
interviews, but newsmen were not allowed to talk to any
others.

"The main difference between then and now," Malcolm W.
Browne, a Times correspondent in Saigon who won a Pulitzer
Prize for his coverage of Vietnam for The Associated Press in
1964, said recently, "is that then they tried to persuade us.
Now they don't bother. They just freeze us out." In short,
newsmen have known little more about the air war than what
they were told by official releases and briefers, and there is
strong evidence that much has been left out. For example,
Pentagon sources in Washington disclosed to a Times correspondent that, from the start of the North Vietnamese offensive March 30, fighter-bombers on occasion attacked railroad
targets in North Vietnam within 25 miles of the Chinese border—that is, inside the 25-mile buffer zone in which American
planes were forbidden to strike without special permission
from Washington. In two or three instances, these officers
said, planes strayed very close to Chinese air space before being warned back by radar controllers, and on at least one of
these occasions, Chinese jets were scrambled, but there was
no shooting.

None of these raids were ever reported by the American
information machine in Saigon. The operation was, in a sense,
denied, in one recent four-month period, on every occasion
when the vague geographical description of a strike in the
press releases suggested that it might possibly have been inside
the 25-mile buffer zone. The New York Times bureau in Saigon asked the command information office if this was the
case, and the office flatly said no. When the story broke from
Washington in late August, I called the information office and
asked one of the briefers why the raids had not been reported
and, rhetorically, I asked him if he didn't agree that this sort
of thing seriously damaged MACV's credibility. He expressed

regret and helplessness and finally said: "What can we do? Sometimes they just don't tell us things."

The credibility gap in Saigon makes other such gaps look like hairline fractures. Perhaps every story based on the official communiqués—such as those about the bombing of the North—should be preceded by a paragraph in italics telling the reader that since the allies' track record on facts has been so poor, we have no way of knowing whether they are telling the truth and therefore cannot advise him on how credible the following story is.

Of course, the North Vietnamese and Vietcong propaganda apparatus, broadcasting and publishing from Hanoi, can hardly be considered reliable either. And since the Communists have refused to allow foreign newsmen to cover the war from their side of the fighting lines in South Vietnam, a large piece is, unavoidably, missing from the coverage. This press blackout obviously suits Hanoi's purposes—the mystery about the Communists' military operations has tended to cast an aura of invincibility around them. This is reinforced by the fact that without air support of their own, the Communists, indeed, kept coming despite the awesome American bombing. In any case, the Hanoi broadcasts and press releases are not treated in the American press with the respectability given to the American command's communiqués. They are treated as propaganda, as they should be, and buried in a paragraph or two at the bottom of other stories.

All the obstructionism notwithstanding, it was never really difficult to find out how the war was going. All it took was traveling to the field. It is there that reporters, often at great personal risk, have used their eyes and ears and common sense to paint an accurate picture of Vietnam over the years. In any journalistic situation, no single story is ever the whole truth. But after the fallible reporter has written 50 or 100 stories on the same subject, a true pattern emerges and the reader, if he has been patient, will have been enlightened. This is what has happened in Vietnam. There is no place for sham in the field, where the possibility of death is always so near, and this is why the story gets "trued up" there.

"I don't kid myself," says a weary American Marine adviser

whom I met on a recent visit to the northern front. "Our mission was to bring democratic representative government to South Vietnam. The fact is, we lost. The fact is, they're not going to get democratic government." South Vietnamese artillery batteries are pounding a Communist-held village less than a mile away, but the exhausted soldiers around this command post—knowing how precious are their minutes away from the fighting—have learned to sleep through it. Some are awake, however, writing letters home, playing Chinese checkers. In a makeshift lean-to, a private with a guitar sings a ballad for his buddies in which a South Vietnamese girl laments her lover's departure for the front: "I ask you, I ask you when will you come back. Please tell me, please tell me, that tomorrow or the day after you will return."

A few days later, a blond Marine major, James Dyer, orders a drink at an American canteen in Hue and tries to behave normally, but can't keep up the façade. His face twists in pain, as he fights back the tears. "Worst day in my life," he blurts to a complete stranger next to him. "My buddy got it. Dan Kingman. His chopper got hit. Oh, damn. Damn. Damn. They shot him out of the sky." His head drops to his chest. "Nothing's worth Dan Kingman," he says, almost in a whisper. "Nothing. He was a soldier. A soldier. That's all you've got to know."

The reporter returns to Saigon to sit through an interview with an embassy official, anonymous as usual, who tells him, in response to allegations of widespread torture of political prisoners in South Vietnam's prisons, that although there are 150 American "public safety" advisers working with the Vietnamese on police and prison matters, the embassy has no information one way or the other. Because he knows this sounds incredible, he adds that "all kinds of deplorable things may well be going on," but he quickly tacks on, in amelioration of this torture the embassy knows nothing about, that some of the people arrested are known anti-Government activists involved in terrorist activities—"and who aren't exactly the nice college kids next door."

Perhaps this official's peculiar morality touches the crux of the problem for reporters in Vietnam. As long as the Governments involved continue to portray the issue as a struggle between good and evil, then the conflict between the press and these Governments will continue. For there are no good guys or bad guys in Vietnam. There are only victims.

The New York Times Magazine, November 12, 1972

Who Was This Enemy?

by Fox Butterfield

When the war has ended and the road is open again,
the same stars will course through the heavens.
Then will I weep for the white bones heaped together in
  desolate graves
of those who sought military honors for their leaders.
                                        —From a diary of an unknown
                                        North Vietnamese soldier, 1965.

SAIGON. One afternoon many years ago when the Vietnam war was still new to Americans, an eager young U.S. Special Forces officer lay watching a branch of the Ho Chi Minh trail in the jungle of southern Laos. It was raining hard, and as he and his three companions waited uncomfortably under their camouflaged ponchos, a silent column of North Vietnamese soldiers suddenly materialized on the path in front of them.

"They were marching in perfect discipline, like nothing I'd ever seen before," the American officer recalled recently. "They didn't talk, shout or horse around, like G.I.'s or South Vietnamese troops; and they kept the proper distance between one another. For two hours they kept filing past; there must have been a couple thousand of them."

What particularly surprised the officer was that intelligence reports from prisoners and captured documents showed that the Communist troops on the trail were badly short of food, exhausted and homesick. " 'How could they maintain discipline like that if they were in such bad shape,' I asked myself."

It is a mystery that has confounded a generation of C.I.A. agents, Pentagon planners and White House advisers. And it is precisely the problem that has made President Nguyen Van Thieu nervous about the peace settlement—for under the accord more than 100,000 North Vietnamese soldiers will be permitted to stay on in the South, men who were well-disciplined enough to march down the trail even while thinking that for the vast majority of them it would be a one-way street. They were men who subsisted for weeks at a time on little better than a handful of rice and some roasted salt. They were bombed by B-52's that fly so high they could neither see nor hear them until the bombs exploded. Once in the South they were not able to send or receive mail; and if they died, their families were not notified for years afterward, if ever.

Of the 700,000 to 800,000 North Vietnamese soldiers who have come down the trail since 1965—about 100,000 men a year—virtually none except for high-ranking officers ever got back to North Vietnam before 1968, American intelligence officials believe. Soldiers who had been sent south simply fought on until they were killed or were too badly wounded to continue, in which case they were taken to rest camps and hospitals nearby in Laos and Cambodia. After the Tet offensive of 1968, however, there was a gradually increasing flow of wounded and disabled troops back to North Vietnam, perhaps 200,000 in all. But there was little rotation of active units back to the North.

Fortunately, many North Vietnamese infantrymen kept a record of their experiences—diaries, poems, notebooks of comments by comrades, even some letters that they carried with them for months, unposted. At night, or during rests on the march, when their officers weren't listening, they read their diaries and poems aloud to entertain one another. Though usually laconic, and though often studded with what to us seem Communist clichés, they tell a poignant tale of ordinary men, with ordinary frailties, facing unremitting hardship. But judging by their accounts, even ordinary men can, at times, be transformed by a subtle chemistry of patriotism, skillful political control and sheer force of circumstances.

Date to remember forever—2:30 P.M., Jan. 4, received notice to report for induction into the army on Jan. 10.

Thus Bui Quang Vinh, a country boy from a village north of Hanoi, began his diary. Like many North Vietnamese, Vinh appears torn between patriotism and his foreboding of doom, for no one from his village had ever returned from the war in the South. Of all the events he goes on to record, he dwells longest on these last few days at home before departing for

the army. But there is no mention of a farewell ceremony or
parting words from his family; North Vietnamese prisoners
have testified that parents often cannot bring themselves to
speak when their sons leave.

*Tomorrow, in a few days, I go. Go forever, with no return.
Oh, let me go and get it over with. What is the use in looking
back? I am only a plain soldier. I will have only superiors.*

*Now the cocks are crowing for the first time tonight. It is very
late, why don't I sleep? It is because I am going away. Whatever
hardships, whatever difficulties, I will never forget moments like
this.*

*Why, for what reason, do they think that way? Why do they
say, "He is going away, he is very happy"?*

In one of the few references to his family he allows himself,
Vinh thinks wistfully of his sister:

> *I have a younger sister named Thi Huong,*
> *her hair streaming like sunrays and her eyes like a mirror.*
> *She is 18 this year*
> *and many a young man in the village finds himself*
>   *wondering.*

A friend writes in his diary to encourage him:

> *At noon on a cold winter day*
> *you are leaving when I am on the way home from school.*
> *We meet on the road*
> *for the last time in our native place.*
> *Getting down from my bicycle I shake your hands,*
> *to say good-by and wish that*
> *while I study hard at home,*
> *you achieve many victories.*

And more prosaically, another friend adds:

*Answering the call of the country, Vinh, step up with no hes-
itation. Facing difficulty, don't be a coward. Vinh, be fully confident and optimistic. Someday the sunshine will be thousands
of times more beautiful when the American pirates are submerged in the black mud.*

Cheered, Vinh copies a patriotic poem:

Death
Though death is feared nobody can avoid it,
but a man's death must have its reason.
How to die without blackening your name—
to die of illness is an ordinary death
to die of old age is a natural death
to die of frustrated love is a shameful death
to die for the people on the battlefront,
oh, what a sacred and beautiful death!
Death comes in a second but your name is
  remembered for thousands of years.
This death makes everybody salute.

Many of the diaries of the North's troops, like Vinh's, were kept in tiny, pocket-sized, plastic-covered notebooks distributed by the soldiers' regiments. They bear the imprimatur "Gift of the Regiment," and the slogan, "Study and Practice the Will of the Great Uncle Ho." Inside the front cover, some of the diaries have brief texts of the most recent Central Committee resolutions, lists of important Vietnamese historical battles and distances of provinces from Saigon.

Last October Vinh's diary was found on his body by South Vietnamese paratroopers near the ruins of Quang Tri city. He had come south in August as a replacement for the 308th North Vietnamese Division but apparently dozens of his comrades deserted under the pressure of incessant artillery bombardment and air strikes. Torn to the end between duty and self, Vinh wrote in his last entry:

Today is Oct. 6 and we must again fight this war. We stay in the bunker all day, eat, sleep and relieve ourselves in the bunker. The enemy shelling is all around us. Only nine of us remain [probably out of his company of more than a hundred]. *The rest of them left in groups for the North. I do not know how to decide. In many ways I wanted to go back with them; but thinking of the honor of my family, my own honor, and the country, I had to stay.*

I don't know what my fate will be. Life and death are already too close to each other. The more I think, the more I miss my father, mother, family and friends. I wish one day that I could see my family again. But, that is too luxurious a wish. If I die,

I only regret that I have left my country, my northern land, and could never get back to it. Farewell, fatherland.

If anyone, any comrade, any friend happens to read this note, please have understanding for me. I have been so long in the war.

Of all the experiences recorded by North Vietnamese soldiers, invariably the most traumatic is the march south. The Ho Chi Minh Trail, or as the Vietnamese themselves call it, the Truong Son Route (after the range of mountains it crosses), has been highly developed since its primitive beginnings in the late nineteen-fifties. Now an intricate web of surprisingly well-built roads and paths, it has its own system of way stations—every four or five miles—hospitals with up to 200 beds and detention camps for deserters. But even for the few select groups who got to ride down it on trucks—high-ranking officers, medical units, army motion-picture teams—it was often fatal.

Luong Trong Tan, an ordinary infantryman in the 320th North Vietnamese Division, began his march south to Kon Tum Province in the Central Highlands on a chill, rainy day in December, 1971. He was 23 years old and had already been in the army and away from his family for nearly two years:

Dec. 6—I attended a political indoctrination session on the heroic example of a heroic unit in the morning and received military clothing in the afternoon. My request for home leave was disapproved again, and I felt very homesick when the regiment departed at 4 A.M.

Dec. 20—We arrived at Way Station 13 after dark and had to dig our own trenches. There was no water, so we had to fetch it from the stream and carry it up to the top of the mountain. I felt exhausted to the point where I thought the tiredness would even stop my breathing.

Dec. 25—We had to begin our march at 3 A.M. because we were going to cross a river [they were afraid of U.S. warplanes spotting them if they crossed in daylight]. *It was a tricky route in the darkness, and I felt unhappy. My feet already hurt from the earlier days' marching.*

Dec. 30—At 7:30 A.M. we arrived at Station 42. There I participated in constructing tunnels. I felt exhausted, but I had to accept the situation because I had no other choice.

Jan. 8—We climbed high slopes on the Truong Son range. I felt very tired because of the heavy load on my back, and because the road had been destroyed by B-52's. My life is getting more miserable. We have only rice, salt and water; for nearly one month I have not eaten any vegetables. I read my wife's old letter again. I miss her very much but I have no way to send mail to her. Please understand my situation. Tonight I trembled with malaria.

A poem recited by members of Luong Trong Tan's unit:

Who forced me to climb slopes and wade streams,
Who urged me to travel across jungles?
I have become a human wreck because of that,
And a deep sorrow I feel as I remember my native place.

Jan. 12—During the meal my platoon became sick from eating poisonous cassava.

Jan. 14—I have not taken a bath for 15 days. No water has been available.

Jan. 26—Upon arrival at Station 75, I dug trenches and then was given soup of taro leaves. How delicious it was, after so long without vegetables.

Feb. 5—We were shown a film on heroic soldiers. I enjoyed it very much, since I had not seen a movie for two months.

Feb. 7—The battalion gathered to listen to an orientation briefing by a cadre from the political staff. I felt a distaste for life. Probably everybody at home now is busy making preparations for Tet [the Vietnamese New Year and the biggest holiday of the year]. *Instead, we are getting ready for combat. Tomorrow I will offer my youth to the revolution. Tomorrow our country will be unified and I will enjoy a peaceful spring.*

Feb. 25—The early morning rain made the trenches wet. I felt very sad and an extreme hatred toward the war. All comrades were ravenous but could find nothing to eat. For a week we have had nothing but some bowls of rice gruel.

March 1—During the night enemy B-52's continuously bombed around the hill where we are camped, and I couldn't sleep all night.

March 8—At 9 A.M. my unit received the order for withdrawal and to destroy trenches before we left. Oh, what a dread-

ful thing for me. As I was destroying trenches, a helicopter flew in so low that I thought it was going to land on the hill. But it circled the area twice and then flew away. As I was lying flat on the ground, I could clearly see an American in the helicopter looking down at the hill; how panic-stricken I was at that moment.

March 10—I stayed in the trench all day. How miserable I was; I was very hungry and did not have enough to eat. All I could do was to lie down or sit with my head on my knees. How pitiful it was for those whose rice was stolen. They had nothing left to eat. That this critical shortage resulted from theft was a surprise to me. If I had concealed food in another place it might not have been lost. How I detest war.

March 18—The unit received orders to make preparations for a major attack. I felt very worried writing down this note.

It was his last entry.

Whatever the North Vietnamese soldiers' own troubles and shortcomings, their Southern cousins have always held them in awe, ascribing to the Northerners all the martial virtues they themselves are not disposed toward: discipline, courage, abstention from drunkenness and looting.

Awareness of the differences proved helpful to a Government officer, Col. Ton That Hung, last spring when troops of the 320th North Vietnamese Division overran the Government base at Tan Canh. The South Vietnamese there gave themselves little hope of escape. Colonel Hung, after hiding for a week in a deserted mountain village, finally thought he would be captured when he heard voices approaching early one morning before sunrise. But suddenly Colonel Hung jumped up from his hiding place, and though he still couldn't make out the uniforms of the newcomers embraced them— they were Government Rangers. He knew they were not the enemy, Colonel Hung said later, because they were cursing and shouting, and certainly no North Vietnamese soldiers would do that on patrol.

Nguyen Van Nang, a former Vietcong lieutenant colonel, now in a center for defectors in Saigon:

"The thing that makes the Communist army work is the political officer—everything depends on him. The troops may not like their political officer, they call him 'Mr. Argument,' but they respect him. And he is always there to watch them."

Pham Minh Phat, a company political officer, now in prison:

"What does the political officer do? He makes sure the soldiers get their rations, he calls meetings to indoctrinate them in the party line, he leads them in criticism sessions. In theory the military officer of a unit is its commander, but in fact the political officer of a unit is more powerful—he reports to higher echelons on the military officer."

A lean, ascetic-looking man with a high forehead, Phat spent 11 years in the army, and his narrow, darting eyes suggest someone constantly on the lookout for signs of trouble. He does not smile often. Asked if he could recall any jokes his men told about life in the army, he replied: "No, there were no jokes in my company. Everyone was satisfied, for discipline was strict and evenly applied to all ranks. So why would they make jokes?

"Political officers are carefully recruited on the basis of class background and ability," Phat explained. "They must be party members, be from worker or peasant families, and must be able to endure hardship better than anyone else in their unit. They can never display any lack of faith in the leadership of the party."

Pausing to light another of the cigarettes that he smokes down to the very tip, Phat continued: "It is simple, really. We indoctrinate the soldiers to realize they are struggling to liberate the nation and gain human rights for themselves. They are usually very young, and they are flattered to think that they are fighting for something great, something superhuman. Since soldiers may be killed at any moment and must ignore material comforts, they must have something to fight for more than their pay.

"There were other techniques that were useful too," Phat recalled, his deep, penetrating voice growing louder as he warmed to the subject. "We held competitions in the battalion, emulation campaigns, to see which company best followed the model of heroic units. And before a battle I always called the troops together, listing the crimes of the enemy unit against the people to make the men angry.

"Of course, sometimes there were problems. For example, when we went out on an operation, a comrade might get thirsty and climb a peasant's coconut tree to steal the fruit. But the other soldiers would accuse him later in a criticism session and force him to confess. A soldier with a high degree of political consciousness would confess even without being criticized."

Notes kept by a company political officer, Mai Tan Lam, of a regimental party committee meeting, Kon Tum Province, April, 1972, shortly before the spring offensive:

Comrades, we are facing a great opportunity for the party, and the people of the South are waiting for our army to liberate them. We have made much progress in preparing for the coming combat mission, but the majority of our cadre and soldiers are still new and inexperienced. Some are passive and wait to be assigned tasks. Some do not dig enough trenches and practice proper camouflage procedures; they leave their clothes to dry in open areas and fail to use care in dissipating smoke from cooking fires, so that enemy airplanes can locate our positions. A few comrades are afraid of violent combat—

Therefore, political cadre must classify soldiers into categories, progressive and backward, in order to facilitate indoctrination and control their thought. Each unit must control the thought of all soldiers and eliminate all illusions of peace, fear of sacrifice and liberalism. If indoctrination courses are frequently held, soldiers should have peaceful minds when going into battle—

Soldiers should be encouraged to emulate heroic units and to carry out the last will of Uncle Ho—

Before departing for the combat mission, do not disclose to personnel the schedule of movement, the participating units or the direction of movement.

Long live the People's Democratic Republic of Vietnam.

Since the Tet offensive of 1968, with a gradual return of as many as 200,000 wounded and disabled North Vietnamese back up the Ho Chi Minh trail to the North, veterans have become an increasing headache for Hanoi. On paper the Government has instituted a careful program of veterans' benefits: factories and cooperative farms must rehire all previous employes no matter what their injury; all veterans are entitled to complete their education at state expense; pensions for the disabled are to be strictly paid. But as the candid North Vietnamese press often admits, many men without arms and legs have had trouble finding jobs and acceptance in civilian society. In a lengthy article on the veterans' problem last year, the official party journal Hoc Tap decried the lack of public sympathy for wounded soldiers and the families of the dead. "Many party members do not properly understand the policy toward wounded combatants and the war dead," Hoc Tap said, "and this has adversely affected the feelings of the invalids, the families of the dead and the soldiers."

Unlike the American Government and military in Vietnam, with their light-at-the-end-of-the-tunnel philosophy, which insisted that every report show progress, the Vietnamese Communists tended to look for problems. Identify the trouble and then solve it, seemed to be the method in many captured Communist documents and newspaper articles. The resulting frequent admissions of food shortages, low morale and poor leadership often led hopeful American officials to conclude that the North Vietnamese were finished.

Perhaps the most common problem was the simplest one—most veterans had been away for at least two years and their families had little or no word of their fate.

A letter to the editor of Tien Phong, the Hanoi party youth newspaper, from a veteran, Duong Ngan:

Dear Comrade:

Previously my wife and I were in love and treated each other equally. Because of the anti-U.S. task I had to go far away. Recently I was able to return home and found that my wife had had a child by another man and that the child was already 4 years old. I was very hurt.

Some of the neighbors advised me to forgive her and make up, but others advised me to cut it off. I am a young party member and don't know what to do to sort things out. I hope you can give me some advice.

The published reply:
Dear Comrade Duong Ngan:
We have never before been faced with such a difficult question.
We can see that the solution is not simple. Only a very deep love
can help you overcome your heartache and forgive your wife.
You should listen to the voice of your own heart. If you do not
love her, then everything is lost and you will not live happily
together. We hope, however, that there is love in the heart of a
young party member. A generous husband will triumph.

To prepare for their major 1972 spring offensive, Hanoi's leaders in 1971 drastically revised North Vietnam's draft law, expanding the age limits from 18–32 to 17–40 and abolishing exemptions for young men with critical skills, such as teachers, skilled workers and administrative cadre on farms and factories. For the first time, Catholics—whom the Government has always distrusted—and even some women were called up for front-line service. In some small villages where all eligible youths had already been drafted, 15- and 16-year-olds were inducted, and many boys were called out of school in the middle of semesters. In the rush to get as many troops as possible to the South for the series of large-scale conventional attacks, the usual rigorous nine-month training period was cut to three months.

One result of the new draft policies, as occurred in the U.S. Army after 1968, was a large influx of relatively well-educated and already well-established young men, especially teachers, who were not as unquestioning of authority as boys fresh off the farm. The Communists' usually small desertion rate is said to have been affected, and occasionally a new, more philosophical attitude is reflected in the soldiers' diaries.

Nguyen Van Minh, apparently a schoolteacher in civilian life, wrote a letter to his girl friend, Hoa, on July 10 last year. It was found, unposted, in September by South Vietnamese militia in Binh Duong Province near Saigon:
Dearest Hoa,
It is already summer at home, the sweet jasmine must be in
bloom again and your younger brothers and sisters are playing
in the garden, I imagine. Everything is so peaceful there—
You are finished teaching, now that summer is here, and your

classes are over. I am always afraid that you are seeing Hai, the mathematics teacher—the way you used to look at him. He is so handsome, even with his arrogant manner and loud voice. Now you can wait for him every day at the gate after school. Probably your parents have already approved the match. Do you tell him you love him the way you told me, lying there under the trees by the river, do you remember, Hoa? Your long hair brushed my face, my golden summer butterfly.

Maybe you should get married. The enemy here is very barbarous and many comrades have been killed and lain down to sleep forever. Last week three members of our squad were buried by the Americans' B-52's. We did not know they were above us until the bombs burst around us; I was lucky to crawl into my bunker in time and only suffered a bloody nose from the concussion. My right ear still rings from the noise. Now I feel death very near whenever I see an airplane coming through the clouds.

This terrible war makes so many strange thoughts race through my head. I would like to jump straight up for thousands of miles to get away from here, from this killing. Before, I did not know what it was to kill a man; now that I have seen it, I don't want to do it any more.

But it is the duty of a soldier to die for his country, me for our fatherland, the enemy for his. There is no choice.

The New York Times Magazine, February 4, 1973

Vietnam Peace Pacts Signed; America's Longest War Halts

by Flora Lewis

PARIS, Jan. 27—The Vietnam cease-fire agreement was signed here today in eerie silence, without a word or a gesture to express the world's relief that the years of war were officially ending.

The accord was effective at 7 P.M. Eastern standard time.

Secretary of State William P. Rogers wrote his name 62 times on the documents providing—after 12 years—a settlement of the longest, most divisive foreign war in America's history.

The official title of the text was "Agreement on Ending the War and Restoring Peace in Vietnam." But the cold, almost gloomy atmosphere at two separate signing ceremonies reflected the uncertainties of whether peace is now assured.

The conflict, which has raged in one way or another for over a quarter of a century, had been inconclusive, without clear victory or defeat for either side.

After a gradually increasing involvement that began even before France left Indochina in 1954, the United States entered into a full-scale combat role in 1965. The United States considers Jan. 1, 1961, as the war's starting date and casualties are counted from then.

By 1968, when the build-up was stopped and then reversed, there were 529,000 Americans fighting in Vietnam. United States dead passed 45,000 by the end of the war.

The peace agreements were as ambiguous as the conflict, which many of America's friends first saw as generous aid to a weak and threatened ally, but which many came to consider an exercise of brute power against a tiny nation.

The peace agreements signed today were built of compromises that permit the two Vietnamese sides to give them contradictory meanings and, they clearly hope, to continue their unfinished struggle in the political arena without continuing the slaughter.

The signing took place in two ceremonies. In the morning, the participants were the United States, North Vietnam, South Vietnam and the Vietcong. Because the Saigon Government does not wish to imply recognition of the Vietcong's Provisional Revolutionary Government, all references to that government were confined to a second set of documents. That set was signed in the afternoon, and by only the United States and North Vietnam.

At the last moment, it was found that two copies in English of the texts, which were to have been signed by Mr. Rogers and North Vietnam's Foreign Minister, Nguyen Duy Trinh, in the afternoon ceremony, were missing.

The plan had been to give a signed copy in each language to each of the four delegations. The United States prepared the English documents and had given the two copies to the South Vietnamese to inspect. They were not returned, leaving a total of six instead of eight sets of documents to be signed by the United States and North Vietnam.

These texts began by saying that North Vietnam "with the concurrence of the Provisional Revolutionary Government of the Republic of South Vietnam" and the United States "with the concurrence of the Government of the Republic of Vietnam" had reached agreement.

South Vietnam's foreign minister, Tran Van Lam, indicated that he did not want to accept signed copies of this text, because Saigon objects to mention of the revolutionary government by that name.

Asked whether the South Vietnamese action might weaken or undermine the degree of Saigon's "concurrence," American officials said, "No, no. They have concurred."

Each of the other delegations wound up with four sets of signed agreements. Saigon took only two, the English and Vietnamese versions mentioning only "parties" to the conference.

In the morning ceremony, all four parties signed identical agreements, except for one protocol, or annexed document, in which the United States agreed to remove the mines it had planted in the waters of North Vietnam.

The preamble on the four-party documents mentioned no government by name and referred only to the "parties participating in the Paris conference on Vietnam."

That was the formula that had broken the final deadlock.

Almost immediately after the morning session involving four foreign ministers, military delegations of the Vietcong and the North Vietnamese flew off on their way to Saigon.

They, with American and South Vietnamese officers, will form a joint military commission that is to carry out the cease-fire. Their departure for the South Vietnamese capital gave a touch of reality to the strangely emotionless way in which the rite of peace was performed in Paris.

After the morning ceremony, which lasted 18 minutes, the four foreign ministers, their aides and guests filed wordlessly through separate doors into a curtained foyer.

There, participants said, they clinked champagne glasses, toasted "peace and friendship" and shook hands all around. But such amiability was concealed from observers and above all from the cameras that might have recorded a scene of the Vietnamese enemies in social contact.

A similar 15 minutes of cordiality followed the 11-minute afternoon ceremony, attended only by the American and North Vietnamese delegations.

The agreement was signed at the gigantic round table, covered with a prairie of green baize, where the four parties to the Paris conference have been speechifying at each other, and often vilifying each other, almost weekly for four years.

The great ballroom of the former Hotel Majestic, where the table stands, is crammed with crystal and gilt chandeliers, lush tapestries and ornate gilt moldings. But the scene was as glum as the drizzly, gray Paris sky outside. The men all wore dark suits.

The touches of human color were few. Mrs. Nguyen Thi Binh, Foreign Minister of the Vietcong Provisional Revolutionary Government, wore an amber ao dai with embroidery on the bodice, an unusual ornament for her.

Mrs. Rogers wore a dress with a red top and navy skirt. In the afternoon, when there were only two delegations and thus more room for guests, all the American secretaries who had been involved were brought in and they brightened the room.

The texts of the agreements were bound in different colored leather—red for the North Vietnamese, blue for the United States, brown for South Vietnam and green for the Vietcong. French ushers solemnly passed them around on each signature. Mrs. Binh overlooked one place to sign and had to be given an album back for completion.

Mr. Rogers and Mr. Trinh used a large number of the black pens and then handed them to delegation members as souvenirs. William J. Porter, the new Deputy Undersecretary of State who had been the United States delegate to the semi-public talks until this month, flew to Paris with Mr. Rogers and sat at the table with him.

Heywood Isham, acting head of the United States delegation, Marshall Green, Assistant Secretary of State for East Asian and Pacific Affairs, and William H. Sullivan, Mr. Green's deputy, who has been leading technical talks with the North Vietnamese here, completed the American group at the table.

Two rectangular tables, carefully placed alongside the main table to symbolize the separation of the four delegations into two warring sides at the start of the conference in 1969, were reserved for the ambassadors of Canada, Hungary, Indonesia and Poland.

Their countries are contributing troops to an international commission that is to supervise the cease-fire.

Mr. Rogers and his Washington-based aides flew home immediately after the ceremony. Unexpectedly, Mr. Lam went with them.

Mr. Sullivan remained in Paris to receive the list of American prisoners from Hanoi and to hold further technical meetings on the many unsettled details of how arrangements are to be carried out.

At the airport before leaving, Mr. Rogers made his only comments on the event so long awaited with spurts of hope and bitter despair.

"It's a great day," he said.

He said President Nixon had devoted himself to building a structure of peace and continued: "The events in Paris today are a milestone in achieving that peace."

"I hope there'll be a cease-fire soon in all of Indochina," he added.

The New York Times, January 28, 1973

War Lingers in Hamlets as Cease-Fire Hour Passes

by Arnold R. Isaacs

TUONG HON, South Vietnam—Fleeing a war that was officially over, the villagers of Tuong Hoa began trudging away from the gunfire at 9 A.M. yesterday, when the Vietnam cease-fire was exactly one hour old.

At the head of the column, a woman jogged clumsily with a wailing child, bleeding from shrapnel wounds, clinging to her back. Behind her the rest filed by with frozen faces— "Vietnamese are used to suffering," a sergeant had remarked in the last village—except for one girl of 10 or 11, who wept hysterically. An old man trying to comfort her indicated with gestures that someone, possibly her mother, had been shot.

In the hamlet, the shells whirred in rhythmically, exploding every 10 seconds with the characteristic dull, metallic slams that sound as if they were landing in rain barrels. Close by but out of sight, rifles and machine guns sputtered among the houses.

At 9.05 A.M., an hour and five minutes after the war ended, two infantrymen carried a dead or badly wounded soldier out of the hamlet. They were followed shortly by an entire infantry company, apparently abandoning the hamlet to the Communists.

Before anyone could ask if all the South Vietnamese were pulling out, a flurry of rifle shots snapped the air overhead. It was clearly time to leave, and there was no way for any of us to report the result of the fight.

Tuong Hoa, about 22 miles north of Saigon, was one of scores of hamlets where the Communists had attacked in hope of being able to hold them when the cease-fire came.

Many of them, like Tuong Hoa, were the scene of bitter fighting hours after the 8 A.M. deadline—fighting that could have been merely the last spasms of a generation old war or the beginnings of a continued wave of violence.

Yesterday, Tuong Hoa was also the midpoint on a journey through the first hours of a "peace" that may have been hailed in the rest of the world but was greeted in Vietnam with wary uncertainty.

At 7 A.M., with an hour to go before the cease-fire was scheduled to take effect, the People's Self Defense Force patrols, South Vietnam's home guard, were returning to their homes after a night on guard.

Teen-agers and leather-faced old men, carrying antiquated arms and wearing only bits of uniforms, reflected the extent to which war has enveloped the entire South Vietnamese population.

Overhead, three luminous white contrails across the lavender dawn sky marked the soundless passage of a flight of B-52 bombers—certainly the last trip for those crews, maybe one of the last for any American airmen over Vietnam.

In the hamlet Chanh Hiep, the distant thumping of artillery seemed to come from all directions. A machine gun was firing just off the road; a soldier explained that the fighting had been going on since 3 A.M., when the Viet Cong approached the hamlet and called to government soldiers over loudspeakers, urging them to lay down their arms rather than fight in the last hours before a cease-fire.

Most of the people were standing in front of their homes, listening to the firing and glancing frequently at their watches, wondering if it really would stop on time.

At 8 A.M., the hour of the cease-fire, on the main street a group of soldiers—actually cadets from the Army Engineering School who were assigned to hamlet security for the expected heavy attacks during the last night—heard the time signal on a portable radio, and then President Nguyen Van Thieu began to speak, urging his countrymen to remain "vigilant" against possible Communist violations. The nearby automatic weapons fire and the distant artillery did not even slow down, and there was no emotion, neither elation nor surprise nor shock, on the faces of the villagers.

"The president can say anything, but this war will never end," a sergeant remarked bitterly.

Across the street, Duong Ba Trang was quivering with news of a more personal sort. He had come from Saigon for his usual Sunday visit with his 18-year-old son and arrived just at 8 A.M., only to be told his son had been captured by Viet Cong or North Vietnamese troops earlier in the week during savage fighting at the Michelin rubber plantation to the west.

"He is lost now," Mr. Trang said despairingly over the drone of President Thieu's voice from the radio. "There is one chance in a million of finding him. If the Viet Cong have him I will never see him again."

At each burst of firing, the soldiers looked at their watches, breaking into nervous chuckles as the time moved on to 8.15 A.M. By 8.30 A.M. there was still no halt to the shooting.

9.35 A.M.: The war had been over for 1 hour and 35 minutes. After Tuong Hoa we drove through Phu Cuong, the capital of Binh Duong province, to head back to Saigon, but beyond the city two armored cars stood on the road and there was more firing just ahead.

As we turned around, Huong, our interpreter, lighted a cigarette, and I expressed surprise. The bitterness in her voice was like ripping cloth: "It's not every day I celebrate a cease-fire."

The other road back to Saigon passes a military hospital, and two jeeps raced by with casualties. Artillery was still firing all around and alongside the road people from Communist occupied hamlets waited to see if government troops would move back in.

11 A.M.: The war had been over for three hours. On the portable radio the Armed Forces Vietnam network's news announcer was describing President Nixon's prayer of thanksgiving "for the end of the combat"—and on that very word, the car stopped suddenly at a road block just at the entrance to Long Thanh, east of Saigon.

A few hundred yards away smoke was rising from a fire set by a Communist mortar shell and there was heavy fighting at the other end of the town.

An old man argued desperately with the policeman, trying to get through the roadblock to find his wife, who was wounded two hours ago (when the war had only been over an hour) and taken away. There were no Communist troops around, and he thought it was a South Vietnamese shell that had hit his wife.

"I don't believe in anybody or anything anymore," he said bitterly.

4.15 P.M.: At the daily press briefing the U.S. military communique began: "All offensive military operations by U.S. forces in the Republic of Vietnam ended at 0800 today." For the Americans, it was the last daily communique and the last day of the "5 o'clock follies," the name by which the daily command briefings are still called though they have long since been starting at 4.15 P.M.

The follies ran for 8 years and 28 days—"The longest running show in town," Maj. Jere K. Forbus, the briefing officer, commented as he left his last performance.

Although one American was listed as killed yesterday—the fourth since the cease-fire was announced—and four pilots missing, the United States is on its way out of the war.

But the Vietnamese are not so sure they will not have a war to keep talking about. Lt. Col. Le Trung Hien, the Vietnamese Army spokesman, announced there were 53 Communist cease-fire violations yesterday—and he would be back at the press center tomorrow.

Baltimore Sun, January 29, 1973

A Night with the Vietcong

by H. D. S. Greenway

LONGMY, South Vietnam—At night in the Mekong River Delta, pale lights bob and flicker like fireflies through the banana trees and over the rice paddies, dry in the harvest now and white in the moonlight.

The lights are dimmed U.S. Army flashlights, but they belong to the Vietcong who move through the countryside, as they have always done, long after the government troops have locked themselves up in their mud forts for the night.

There is the sound of artillery in the distance, for the war in this contested province of Chuongthien still goes on much as it has for the last 10 years. What has changed, in this cease-fire that is not a cease-fire, is that the Vietcong, or the Provisional Revolutionary Government as they prefer to call themselves, now welcome foreign visitors to the zones they control.

For Americans, walking with these former enemies where one dared not tread before is a strange and unsettling experience. If one has seen armed Vietcong before, it had been a fleeting glimpse in a flash of gunfire or clay-colored corpses in the morning after an attack.

But now, with the Americans withdrawing, the PRG is anxious to legitimize its areas, and as a top political cadre said when we were brought to his jungle camp: "We welcome you and it does not matter if you are journalists or CIA because we have won the war."

Through all the conversation, rhetoric and repetition of one long night there emerged a pattern of men absolutely convinced that they had won a great victory over the Americans and that the American withdrawal proved it. There was still a struggle with Thieu to follow, they said, but they would certainly win that struggle because Thieu could not last without the Americans.

We met in a small village at the edge of the forest in the

no-man's land that separates the government's control from the PRG. It was afternoon and the villagers had been watching a silver South Vietnamese jet bombing PRG territory about five miles to the east. They stood silently as clouds of black smoke rose in the sky preceding the sound.

We had sent a small boy across the fields to the forest and soon armed men began to emerge from the tall grass.

Three of them marched across the paddy dikes and, giving us a snappy salute, shook hands. As we were escorted to the edge of the forest a dozen more appeared—most of them uniformed in dark green jackets and hats and black pants, but some of them in the traditional black pajamas of the Delta.

Only a few carried the Soviet designed AK-47, the standard assault rifle of the North Vietnamese. Most were armed with captured American M-16 rifles and grenade launchers. They had American field radios and communications between units seemed surprisingly good. In contrast to their battle-ready appearance, most of them wore dressy Seiko watches with expansion wrist bands such as one finds in the better shops of Saigon.

Once in the tree line, however, we found that this was not to be the escorted tour of a happy Vietcong village with flags flying that is available in provinces further to the north. This was a Vietcong battalion, probably the Longmy local force, holding on to a contested area where most of the houses had been destroyed.

For half an hour there seemed to be some question as to whether we were guests or prisoners, with hard looks from some of the cadre and talk about searching us.

But eventually a girl cadre appeared with the red-blue-and-yellow flag of the PRG and the tension broke. We were accepted.

The sound of a helicopter in the sky, once so comforting, became a sound of terror and our small column vanished in the grass and under the banana leaves.

At dusk, the three of us were given a meal of fish and rice, and as the word of our coming spread, a small crowd gathered, including about 30 children. They seemed anxious to prove that they had enough to eat and could protect the population under their control from government attack.

They spoke of the bombing and of the chemicals dropped from planes to kill the rice. They said these chemicals caused infection, sores, swollen eyes and dysentery—especially among the children.

After a few hours we were led through the darkness to another location where the local commander wanted to give us yet another meal. There, with small oil lamps lighting the faces of the gathered cadre, we were given again a litany of cease-fire violations committed by the government side.

Just before midnight we were told that high PRG officials would see us now and we left again, this time by boat, riding through the darkness farther into the interior with our boatmen singing revolutionary songs for our benefit. We managed a weak-voiced "We Shall Overcome" for their benefit and tried to explain its meaning in America.

After an hour on the river we were brought ashore blinking into a little open-sided hut with a Coleman lantern and several men sitting in chairs before a table. There was a picture of Ho Chi Minh on the wall.

Their leader, an impressive man whose conversation ran from battle to classical Vietnamese poetry, had been wounded nine times. Once, he said, they had put coconut milk in his veins instead of intravenous fluid—one of the many tricks Vietcong doctors had for saving lives despite a shortage of modern medicines.

The evening went on and on and although our heads began to nod there was no sign that we were to be allowed to sleep.

Shortly before four in the morning, another meal appeared and we felt like Sheherazade working on her 900th tale. "It isn't every day you meet with high officials of the PRG," our host said. "You can do without sleep."

Everyone spoke of the victory over the American imperialists, and the importance of the Paris agreement to them was that the Americans had admitted their defeat. "The history of Vietnam shows that we always win against aggressors," they said, and the Americans were merely going the way of the "Mongols, the Japanese and the French."

The Americans now admitted, they said, that there was "only one Vietnam from the Chinese border to Camau." Although everyone we met but one was a southerner, they did not hide the presence of North Vietnamese Troops. There was only one Vietnam, they said, and Hanoi was its capital. They said if northerners came down to help their brothers in the South, who could call them aggressors in their own country?

The anti-foreign nature of their struggle seemed extremely important to them, and now that American troops were leaving it was equally important to brand Thieu as a tool of the Americans.

"Thieu is like a corpse being held up by the Americans," they said. "If the Americans should let him go he would collapse." That the Americans were not letting Thieu go aggrieved them.

"The Vietnamese issue must be settled by the Vietnamese themselves," they said, "and the commitment the United States made was to admit that the problem should be solved by the Vietnamese themselves."

They said they had received orders from "high up" not to violate the cease-fire unless the people under their control came under government attack. They said that all the fighting in this region had been caused by attempts to grab PRG territory.

There is ample evidence that the PRG has been responsible for its own share of cease-fire violations, but the Vietcong of Longmy district gave the impression that they would rather have seen the struggle switch from all-out war to an armed political struggle and they blame the United States for not forcing Thieu to allow this to happen.

But there was not the slightest suggestion that the cease-fire, even if observed by Thieu, would mean an end to the struggle. Thieu was a traitor, they said, and could never be trusted. The PRG could rely only on their own strength and the rightness of their cause.

The PRG was willing to pursue a policy of reconciliation and concord, they said, but the very thought of it frightened Thieu and "caused him to tremble."

They said there was not much hope in elections solving anything because Thieu would "force people to vote for him."

But if Thieu was frightened to engage in a political struggle, the PRG could handle him, they said—soon, if the Americans would stop holding him up, but eventually in any case.

"If Thieu does not apply the agreement strictly there will be some real activities and you will see later," one leader said.

"Today you see us in the forest but tomorrow you will see us in the cities," said another.

They said that we had seen Thieu violating the cease-fire with our own eyes, and the increasing violence was only a sign that Thieu was getting weaker and more desperate.

Peace was their ultimate goal, they said—peace in which "everyone has enough to eat, a house and enough clothes to wear but not the profits from bribes."

To the PRG of Longmy it seemed that peace with honor meant nothing less than the completion of the Vietnamese revolution started so long ago by Ho Chi Minh and that the American withdrawal and the cease-fire agreement were significant victories but by no means the last step along that road.

The Washington Post, March 15, 1973

How the POW's Fought Back

by John S. McCain III,
Lieut. Commander, U.S. Navy

THE DATE was Oct. 26, 1967. I was on my 23rd mission, flying right over the heart of Hanoi in a dive at about 4,500 feet, when a Russian missile the size of a telephone pole came up—the sky was full of them—and blew the right wing off my Skyhawk dive bomber. It went into an inverted, almost straight-down spin.

I pulled the ejection handle, and was knocked unconscious by the force of the ejection—the air speed was about 500 knots. I didn't realize it at the moment, but I had broken my right leg around the knee, my right arm in three places, and my left arm. I regained consciousness just before I landed by parachute in a lake right in the center of Hanoi, one they called the Western Lake. My helmet and my oxygen mask had been blown off.

I hit the water and sank to the bottom. I think the lake is about 15 feet deep, maybe 20. I kicked off the bottom. I did not feel any pain at the time, and was able to rise to the surface. I took a breath of air and started sinking again. Of course, I was wearing 50 pounds, at least, of equipment and gear. I went down and managed to kick up to the surface once more. I couldn't understand why I couldn't use my right leg or my arm. I was in a dazed condition. I went up to the top again and sank back down. This time I couldn't get back to the surface. I was wearing an inflatable life-preserver-type thing that looked like water wings. I reached down with my mouth and got the toggle between my teeth and inflated the preserver and finally floated to the top.

Some North Vietnamese swam out and pulled me to the side of the lake and immediately started stripping me, which is their standard procedure. Of course, this being in the center of town, a huge crowd of people gathered, and they were all hollering and screaming and cursing and spitting and kicking at me.

When they had most of my clothes off, I felt a twinge in my right knee. I sat up and looked at it, and my right foot was resting next to my left knee, just in a 90-degree position. I said, "My God—my leg!" That seemed to enrage them—I don't know why. One of them slammed a rifle butt down on my shoulder, and smashed it pretty badly. Another stuck a bayonet in my foot. The mob was really getting up-tight.

About this time, a guy came up and started yelling at the crowd to leave me alone. A woman came over and propped me up and held a cup of tea to my lips, and some photographers took some pictures. This quieted the crowd down quite a bit. Pretty soon, they put me on a stretcher, lifted it onto a truck, and took me to Hanoi's main prison. I was taken into a cell and put on the floor. I was still on the stretcher, dressed only in my skivvies, with a blanket over me.

For the next three or four days, I lapsed from consciousness to unconsciousness. During this time, I was taken out to interrogation—which we called a "quiz"—several times. That's when I was hit with all sorts of war-criminal charges. This started on the first day. I refused to give them anything except my name, rank, serial number and date of birth. They beat me around a little bit. I was in such bad shape that when they hit me it would knock me unconscious. They kept saying, "You will not receive any medical treatment until you talk."

I didn't believe this. I thought that if I just held out, that they'd take me to the hospital. I was fed small amounts of food by the guard and also allowed to drink some water. I was able to hold the water down, but I kept vomiting the food.

They wanted military rather than political information at this time. Every time they asked me something, I'd just give my name, rank and serial number and date of birth.

I think it was on the fourth day that two guards came in, instead of one. One of them pulled back the blanket to show the other guard my injury. I looked at my knee. It was about the size, shape and color of a football. I remembered that when I was a flying instructor a fellow had ejected from his plane and broken his thigh. He had gone into shock, the blood had pooled in his leg, and he died, which came as quite a surprise to us—a man dying of a broken leg. Then I realized that a very similar thing was happening to me.

When I saw it, I said to the guard, "O.K., get the officer." An officer came in after a few minutes. It was the man that we came to know very well as "The Bug." He was a psychotic torturer, one of the worst fiends that we had to deal with. I said, "O.K., I'll give you military information if you will take me to the hospital." He left and came back with a doctor, a guy that we called "Zorba," who was completely incompetent. He squatted down, took my pulse. He did not speak English, but shook his head and jabbered to "The Bug." I asked, "Are you going to take me to the hospital?" "The Bug" replied, "It's too late." I said, "If you take me to the hospital, I'll get well."

"Zorba" took my pulse again, and repeated, "It's too late." They got up and left, and I lapsed into unconsciousness.

Sometime later, "The Bug" came rushing into the room, shouting, "Your father is a big admiral; now we take you to the hospital."

I tell the story to make this point: There were hardly any amputees among the prisoners who came back because the North Vietnamese just would not give medical treatment to someone who was badly injured—they weren't going to waste their time. For one thing, in the transition from the kind of life we lead in America to the filth and dirt and infection, it would be very difficult for a guy to live anyway. In fact, my treatment in the hospital almost killed me.

I woke up a couple of times in the next three or four days. Plasma and blood were being put into me. I became fairly lucid. I was in a room which was not particularly small—about 15 by 15 feet—but it was filthy dirty and at a lower level, so that every time it rained, there'd be about a half inch to an inch of water on the floor. I was not washed once while I was in the hospital. I almost never saw a doctor or a nurse. Doctors came in a couple of times to look at me. They spoke French, not English.

For a guard, I was assigned a 16-year-old kid—right out of the rice fields. His favorite pastime was to sit by my bed and read a book that had a picture in it of an old man with a rifle in his hand sitting on a fuselage of an F-105 which had been shot down. He would point to himself, and slap me and hit me. He had a lot of fun that way. He fed me because both my arms were broken. He would come in with a cup that had noodles and some gristle in it, and fill a spoon and put it in my mouth. The gristle was very hard to chew. I'd get my mouth full after three or four spoonfuls, and I'd be chewing away on it. I couldn't take any more in my mouth, so he'd just eat the rest himself. I was getting about three or four spoonfuls of food twice a day. It got so that I kind of didn't give a damn—even though I tried as hard as I could to get enough to eat.

After I had been there about 10 days, a "gook"—which is what we called the North Vietnamese—came in one morning. This man spoke English very well. He asked me how I was, and said, "We have a Frenchman who is here in Hanoi visiting, and he would like to take a message back to your family." Being a little naïve at the time—you get smarter as you go along with these people—I figured this wasn't a bad deal at all, if this guy would come to see me and go back and tell my family that I was alive.

I didn't know at the time that my name had been released in a rather big propaganda splash by the North Vietnamese, and that they were very happy to have captured me. They told a number of my friends when I was captured, "We have the crown prince," which was somewhat amusing to me.

They told me that the Frenchman would visit me that evening. About noon, I was put in a rolling stretcher and taken to a treatment room where they tried to put a cast on my right arm. They had great difficulty putting the bones together, because my arm was broken in three places and there were two floating bones. I watched the guy try to manipulate it for about an hour and a half trying to get all the bones lined up. This was without benefit of Novocain. It was an extremely painful experience, and I passed out a number of times. He finally just gave up and slapped a chest cast on me. This experience was very fatiguing, and was the reason why later, when some TV film was taken, it looked to many people as if I had been drugged.

When this was over, they took me into a big room with a nice white bed. I thought, "Boy, things are really looking up." My guard said, "Now you're going to be in your new room."

About an hour later in came a guy called "The Cat." I found out later that he was the man who up until late 1969 was in charge of all the POW camps in Hanoi. He was a rather dapper sort, one of the petty intelligentsia that run North Vietnam. He was from the political bureau of the Vietnamese Workers Party.

The first thing he did was show me Col. John Flynn's identification card—now Gen. John Flynn—who was our senior officer. He was shot down the same day I was. "The Cat" said—through an interpreter, as he was not speaking English at this time—"The French television man is coming." I said, "Well, I don't think I want to be filmed," whereupon he announced, "You need two operations, and if you don't talk to him, then we will take your chest cast off and you won't get any operations." He said, "You will say that you're grateful to the Vietnamese people, and that you're sorry for your crimes." I told him I wouldn't do that.

Finally, the Frenchman came in, a man named Chalais—a Communist, as I found out later—with two photographers. He asked me about my treatment and I told him it was satisfactory. "The Cat" and "Chihuahua," another interrogator, were in the background telling me to say that I was grateful for lenient and humane treatment. I refused, and when they pressed me, Chalais said, "I think what he told me is sufficient."

Then he asked if I had a message for my family. I told him to assure my wife and others of my family that I was getting well and that I loved them. Again, in the background, "The Cat" insisted that I add something about hoping that the war would be over soon so that I could go home. Chalais shut him up very firmly by saying that he was satisfied with my answer. He helped me out of a difficult spot.

Chalais was from Paris. My wife later went to see him and he gave her a copy of the film, which was shown on CBS television in the U.S.

As soon as he left, they put me on the cart and took me back to my old dirty room.

After that, many visitors came to talk to me. Not all of it was for interrogation. Once a famous North Vietnamese writer—an old man with a Ho Chi Minh beard—came to my room, wanting to know all about Ernest Hemingway. I told him that Ernest Hemingway was violently anti-Communist. It gave him something to think about.

Others came in to find out about life in the United States. They figured because my father had such high military rank that I was of the royalty or the governing circle. They have no idea of the way our democracy functions.

One of the men who came to see me, whose picture I recognized later, was Gen. Vo Nguyen Giap, the hero of Dienbienphu. He came to see what I looked like, saying nothing. He is the Minister of Defense, and also on North Vietnam's ruling Central Committee.

After about two weeks, I was given an operation on my leg which was filmed. They never did anything for my broken left arm. It healed by itself. They said I needed two operations on my leg, but because I had a "bad attitude" they wouldn't give me another one. What kind of job they did on my leg, I do not know. Now that I'm back, an orthopedic surgeon is going to cut in and see. He has already told me that they made the incision wrong and cut all the ligaments on one side.

I was in the hospital about six weeks, then was taken to a camp in Hanoi that we called "The Plantation." This was in late December, 1967. I was put in a cell with two other men, George Day and Norris Overly, both Air Force majors. I was on a stretcher, my leg was stiff and I was still in a chest cast that I kept for about two months. I was down to about 100 pounds from my normal weight of 155.

I was told later on by Major Day that they didn't expect me to live a week. I was unable to sit up. I was sleeping about 18 hours, 20 hours a day. They had to do everything for me. They were allowed to get a bucket of water and wash me off occasionally. They fed me and took fine care of me, and I recovered very rapidly.

We moved to another room just after Christmas. In early February, 1968, Overly was taken out of our room and released, along with David Matheny and John Black. They were the first three POW's to be released by the North Vietnamese. I understand they had instructions, once home, to say nothing about treatment, so as not to jeopardize those of us still in captivity.

That left Day and me alone together. He was rather bunged up himself—a bad right arm, which he still has. He had escaped after he had been captured down South and was shot when they recaptured him. As soon as I was able to walk, which was in March of 1968, Day was moved out.

I remained in solitary confinement from that time on for more than two years. I was not allowed to see or talk to or communicate with any of my fellow prisoners. My room was fairly decent-sized—I'd say it was about 10 by 10. The door was solid. There were no windows. The only ventilation came from two small holes at the top in the ceiling, about 6 inches by 4 inches. The roof was tin and it got hot as hell in there. The room was kind of dim—night and day—but they always kept on a small light bulb, so they could observe me. I was in that place for two years.

As far as this business of solitary confinement goes—the most important thing for survival is communication with someone, even if it's only a wave or a wink, a tap on the wall, or to have a guy put his thumb up. It makes all the difference.

It's vital to keep your mind occupied, and we all worked on that. Some guys were interested in mathematics, so they worked out complex formulas in their heads—we were never allowed to have writing materials. Others would build a whole house, from basement on up. I have more of a philosophical bent. I had read a lot of history. I spent days on end going back over those history books in my mind, figuring out where this country or that country went wrong, what the U.S. should do in the area of foreign affairs. I thought a lot about the meaning of life.

It was easy to lapse into fantasies. I used to write books and plays in my mind, but I doubt that any of them would have been above the level of the cheapest dime novel.

People have asked me how we could remember detailed things like the tap code, numbers, names, all sorts of things.

The fact is, when you don't have anything else to think about, no outside distractions, it's easy. Since I've been back, it's very hard for me to remember simple things, like the name of someone I've just met.

During one period while I was in solitary, I memorized the names of all 335 of the men who were then prisoners of war in North Vietnam. I can still remember them.

One thing you have to fight is worry. It's easy to get up-tight about your physical condition. One time I had a hell of a hemorrhoid and I stewed about it for about three days. Finally, I said, "Look, McCain, you've never known of a single guy who died of a hemorrhoid." So I just ignored it as best I could, and after a few months it went away.

The story of Ernie Brace illustrates how vital communication was to us. While I was in the prison we called "The Plantation" in October, 1968, there was a room behind me. I heard some noise in there so I started tapping on the wall. Our call-up sign was the old "shave and a haircut," and then the other guy would come back with the two taps, "six bits."

For two weeks I got no answer, but finally, back came the two taps. I started tapping out the alphabet—one tap for "a," two for "b," and so on. Then I said, "Put your ear to the wall." I finally got him up on the wall and by putting my cup against it, I could talk through it and make him hear me. I gave him the tap code and other information. He gave me his name—Ernie Brace. About that time, the guard came around and I told Ernie, "O.K., I'll call you tomorrow."

It took me several days to get him back up on the wall again. When I finally did, all he could say was, "I'm Ernie Brace," and then he'd start sobbing. After about two days he was able to control his emotions, and within a week this guy was tapping and communicating and dropping notes, and from then on he did a truly outstanding job.

Ernie was a civilian pilot who was shot down over Laos. He had just come from 3½ years' living in a bamboo cage in the jungle with his feet in stocks, and an iron collar around his neck with a rope tied to it. He had nearly lost use of his legs. He escaped three times, and after the third time he was buried in the ground up to his neck.

In those days—still in 1968—we were allowed to bathe

every other day, supposedly. But in this camp they had a water problem, and sometimes we'd go for two or three weeks, a month without a bath. I had a real rat for a turnkey who usually would take me out last. The bath was a sort of a stall-like affair that had a concrete tub. After everyone else had bathed, there usually was no water left. So I'd stand there for my allotted five minutes and then he'd take me back to my room.

For toilet facilities, I had a bucket with a lid that didn't fit. It was emptied daily; they'd have somebody else carry it, because I walked so badly.

From the time that Overly and Day left me—Overly left in February of 1968, Day left in March—my treatment was basically good. I would get caught communicating, talking to guys through the wall, tapping—that kind of stuff, and they'd just say, "Tsk, tsk; no, no." Really, I thought things were not too bad.

Then, about June 15, 1968, I was taken up one night to the interrogation room. "The Cat" and another man that we called "The Rabbit" were there. "The Rabbit" spoke very good English.

"The Cat" was the commander of all the camps at that time. He was making believe he didn't speak English, although it was obvious to me, after some conversation, that he did, because he was asking questions or talking before "The Rabbit" translated what I had said.

The Oriental, as you may know, likes to beat around the bush quite a bit. The first night we sat there and "The Cat" talked to me for about two hours. I didn't know what he was driving at. He told me that he had run the French POW camps in the early 1950s and that he had released a couple of guys, and that he had seen them just recently and they had thanked him for his kindness. He said that Overly had gone home "with honor."

I really didn't know what to think, because I had been having these other interrogations in which I had refused to co-operate. It was not hard because they were not torturing me at this time. They just told me I'd never go home and I was going to be tried as a war criminal. That was their constant theme for many months.

Suddenly "The Cat" said to me, "Do you want to go home?"

I was astonished, and I tell you frankly that I said that I would have to think about it. I went back to my room, and I thought about it for a long time. At this time I did not have communication with the camp senior ranking officer, so I could get no advice. I was worried whether I could stay alive or not, because I was in rather bad condition. I had been hit with a severe case of dysentery, which kept on for about a year and a half. I was losing weight again.

But I knew that the Code of Conduct says, "You will not accept parole or amnesty," and that "you will not accept special favors." For somebody to go home earlier is a special favor. There's no other way you can cut it.

I went back to him three nights later. He asked me again, "Do you want to go home?" I told him "No." He wanted to know why, and I told him the reason. I said that Alvarez [first American captured] should go first, then enlisted men and that kind of stuff.

"The Cat" told me that President Lyndon Johnson had ordered me home. He handed me a letter from my wife, in which she had said, "I wished that you had been one of those three who got to come home." Of course, she had no way to understand the ramifications of this. "The Cat" said that the doctors had told him that I could not live unless I got medical treatment in the United States.

We went through this routine and still I told him "No." Three nights later we went through it all over again. On the morning of the Fourth of July, 1968, which happened to be the same day that my father took over as commander in chief of U.S. Forces in the Pacific, I was led into another quiz room.

"The Rabbit" and "The Cat" were sitting there. I walked in and sat down, and "The Rabbit" said, "Our senior officer wants to know your final answer."

"My final answer is the same. It's 'No.'"

"That is your final answer?"

"That is my final answer."

With this "The Cat," who was sitting there with a pile of papers in front of him and a pen in his hand, broke the pen in two. Ink spurted all over. He stood up, kicked the chair over behind him, and said, "They taught you too well. They taught you too well"—in perfect English, I might add. He turned, went out and slammed the door, leaving "The Rabbit" and me sitting there. "The Rabbit" said, "Now, McCain, it will be very bad for you. Go back to your room."

What they wanted, of course, was to send me home at the same time that my father took over as commander in chief in the Pacific. This would have made them look very humane in releasing the injured son of a top U.S. officer. It would also have given them a great lever against my fellow prisoners, because the North Vietnamese were always putting this "class" business on us. They could have said to the others, "Look, you poor devils, the son of the man who is running the war has gone home and left you here. No one cares about you ordinary fellows." I was determined at all times to prevent any exploitation of my father and my family.

There was another consideration for me. Even though I was told I would not have to sign any statements or confessions before I went home, I didn't believe them. They would have got me right up to that airplane and said, "Now just sign this little statement." At that point, I doubt that I could have resisted, even though I felt very strong at the time.

But the primary thing I considered was that I had no right to go ahead of men like Alvarez, who had been there three years before I "got killed"—that's what we used to say instead of "before I got shot down," because in a way becoming a prisoner in North Vietnam was like being killed.

About a month and a half later, when the three men who were selected for release had reached America, I was set up for some very severe treatment which lasted for the next year and a half.

One night the guards came to my room and said, "The camp commander wants to see you." This man was a particularly idiotic individual. We called him "Slopehead."

One thing I should mention here: The camps were set up very similar to their Army. They had a camp commander, who was a military man, basically in charge of the maintenance of the camp, the food, etc. Then they had what they called a staff officer—actually a political officer—who was in charge of the interrogations, and provided the propaganda heard on the radio.

We also had a guy in our camp whom we named "The Soft-Soap Fairy." He was from an important family in North Vietnam. He wore a fancy uniform and was a real sharp cookie, with a dominant position in this camp. "The Soft-Soap Fairy," who was somewhat effeminate, was the nice guy, and the camp commander—"Slopehead"—was the bad guy. Old "Soft-Soap" would always come in whenever anything went wrong and say, "Oh, I didn't know they did this to you. All you had to do was co-operate and everything would have been O.K."

To get back to the story: They took me out of my room to "Slopehead," who said, "You have violated all the camp regulations. You're a black criminal. You must confess your crimes." I said that I wouldn't do that, and he asked, "Why are you so disrespectful of guards?" I answered, "Because the guards treat me like an animal."

When I said that, the guards, who were all in the room—about 10 of them—really laid into me. They bounced me from pillar to post, kicking and laughing and scratching. After a few hours of that, ropes were put on me and I sat that night bound with ropes. Then I was taken to a small room. For punishment they would almost always take you to another room where you didn't have a mosquito net or a bed or any clothes. For the next four days, I was beaten every two to three hours by different guards. My left arm was broken again and my ribs were cracked.

They wanted a statement saying that I was sorry for the crimes that I had committed against North Vietnamese people and that I was grateful for the treatment that I had received from them. This was the paradox—so many guys were so mistreated to get them to say they were grateful. But this is the Communist way.

I held out for four days. Finally, I reached the lowest point of my 5½ years in North Vietnam. I was at the point of suicide, because I saw that I was reaching the end of my rope.

I said, O.K., I'll write for them.

They took me up into one of the interrogation rooms, and for the next 12 hours we wrote and rewrote. The North Vietnamese interrogator, who was pretty stupid, wrote the final confession, and I signed it. It was in their language, and spoke about black crimes, and other generalities. It was unacceptable to them. But I felt just terrible about it. I kept saying to myself, "Oh, God, I really didn't have any choice." I had learned what we all learned over there: Every man has his breaking point. I had reached mine.

Then the "gooks" made a very serious mistake, because they let me go back and rest for a couple of weeks. They usually didn't do that with guys when they had them really busted. I think it concerned them that my arm was broken, and they had messed up my leg. I had been reduced to an animal during this period of beating and torture. My arm was so painful I couldn't get up off the floor. With the dysentery, it was a very unpleasant time.

Thank God they let me rest for a couple of weeks. Then they called me up again and wanted something else. I don't remember what it was now—it was some kind of statement. This time I was able to resist. I was able to carry on. They couldn't "bust" me again.

I was finding that prayer helped. It wasn't a question of asking for superhuman strength or for God to strike the North Vietnamese dead. It was asking for moral and physical courage, for guidance and wisdom to do the right thing. I asked for comfort when I was in pain, and sometimes I received relief. I was sustained in many times of trial.

When the pressure was on, you seemed to go one way or the other. Either it was easier for them to break you the next time, or it was harder. In other words, if you are going to make it, you get tougher as time goes by. Part of it is just a transition from our way of life to that way of life. But you get to hate them so bad that it gives you strength.

Now I don't hate them any more—not these particular guys. I hate and detest the leaders. Some guards would just come in and do their job. When they were told to beat you they would come in and do it. Some seemed to get a big bang out of it. A lot of them were homosexual, although never toward us. Some, who were pretty damned sadistic, seemed to get a big thrill out of the beatings.

From that time on it was one round of rough treatment followed by another. Sometimes I got it three or four times a week. Sometimes I'd be off the hook for a few weeks. A lot of it was my own doing, because they realized far better than we did at first the value of communicating with our fellow Americans. When they caught us communicating, they'd take severe reprisals. I was caught a lot of times. One reason was because I'm not too smart, and the other reason was because I lived alone. If you live with somebody else you have somebody helping you out, helping you survive.

But I was never going to stop. Communication with your fellow prisoners was of the utmost value—the difference between being able to resist and not being able to resist. You may get some argument from other prisoners on that. A lot depends on the individual. Some men are much more self-sufficient than others.

Communication primarily served to keep up morale. We would risk getting beat up just to tell a man that one of his friends had gotten a letter from home. But it was also valuable to establish a chain of command in our camps, so our senior officers could give us advice and guidance.

So this was a period of repeated, severe treatment. It lasted until around October of '69. They wanted me to see delegations. There were antiwar groups coming into Hanoi, a lot of foreigners—Cubans, Russians. I don't think we had too many American "peaceniks" that early, although within the next year it got much greater. I refused to see any of them. The propaganda value to them would have been too great, with my dad as commander in the Pacific.

David Dellinger came over. Tom Hayden came over. Three groups of released prisoners, in fact, were let out in custody of the "peace groups." The first ones released went home with one of the Berrigan brothers. The next peace group was a whole crew. One of them was James Johnson, one of the Fort Hood Three. The wife of the "Ramparts" magazine editor and Rennie Davis were along. Altogether, I think about eight or nine of them were in that outfit. Then a third group followed.

The North Vietnamese wanted me to meet with all of them, but I was able to avoid it. A lot of times you couldn't face them down, so you had to try to get around them. "Face" is a big thing with these people, you know, and if you could get around them so that they could save face, then it was a lot easier.

For example, they would beat the hell out of me and say I was going to see a delegation. I'd respond that, O.K., I'd see a delegation, but I would not say anything against my country and I would not say anything about my treatment, and if asked, I'd tell them the truth about the condition I was kept under. They went back and conferred on that, and then would say, "You have agreed to see a delegation, so we will take you." But they never took me, you see.

One time, they wanted me to write a message to my fellow prisoners at Christmas. I wrote down:

"To my friends in the camp who I have not been allowed to see or speak to, I hope that your families are well and happy, and I hope that you will be able to write and receive letters in accordance with the Geneva Convention of 1949 which has not been allowed to you by our captors. And may God bless you."

They took it but, of course, it was never published. In other words, sometimes it was better to write something that was laudatory to your Government or against them than say, "I won't write at all"—because a lot of times it had to go up through channels, and sometimes you could buy time this way.

At this point I want to tell you the story of Capt. Dick Stratton. He was shot down in May of 1967, when the American peace groups were claiming that the United States was bombing Hanoi. We were not at that time.

Dick was shot down well outside of Hanoi, but they wanted a confession at the time an American reporter was over there. That was in the spring and summer of '67—remember those stories that came back, very sensational stories about the American bomb damage?

"The Rabbit" and the others worked on Dick Stratton very hard. He's got huge rope scars on his arms where they were infected. They really wrung him out, because they were going to get a confession that he had bombed Hanoi—this was to be living proof. They also peeled his thumbnails back and burned him with cigarettes.

Dick reached the point where he couldn't say "No." But when they got him to the press conference, he pulled this bowing act on them—he bowed 90 degrees in this direction, he bowed 90 degrees in that direction—four quadrants. This was not too wild to the "gooks," because they're used to the bowing thing. But any American who sees a picture of another American bowing to the waist every turn for 90 degrees knows that there's something wrong with the guy, that something has happened to him. That's why Dick did what he did. After that they continued to keep pressure on him to say he wasn't tortured. They tortured him to say that he wasn't tortured. It gets to be a bad merry-go-round to be on.

Dick made some very strong statements at his press conference here in the States a few weeks ago. He said he wanted the North Vietnamese charged with war crimes. He's a fine man. He and I were at "The Plantation" together for a long time, and he did a very fine job there. He's an outstanding naval officer, a very dedicated American, and a deeply religious man.

I think a great deal of Dick Stratton. He just was very, very unfortunate in getting the worst that the "gooks" could dish out.

We had a particularly bad spring and summer in 1969 because there had been an escape at one of the other camps. Our guys carried out a well-prepared plan but were caught. They were Ed Atterberry and John Dramesi. Atterberry was beaten to death after the escape.

There's no question about it: Dramesi saw Atterberry taken into a room and heard the beating start. Atterberry never came out. Dramesi, if he wasn't such a tough cookie, would probably have been killed, too. He's probably one of the toughest guys I've ever met—from south Philly. His old man was a pro boxer, and he was a wrestler in college.

The reprisals took place all through the other camps. They started torturing us for our escape plans. The food got worse. The room inspections became very severe. You couldn't have anything in your room—nothing. For example, they used to give us, once in a while, a little vial of iodine because many of us had boils. Now they wouldn't let us have it because Dramesi and Atterberry had used iodine to darken their skin before they tried to escape, so they would look like Vietnamese.

That summer, from May to about September at our camp, twice a day for six days a week, all we had was pumpkin soup and bread. That's a pretty rough diet—first, because you get awfully damn tired of pumpkin soup, but also because it doesn't have any real nutritional value. The only thing that could keep any weight on you was the bread, which was full of lumps of soggy flour.

On Sunday we got what we called sweet bean soup. They would take some small beans and throw them in a pot with a lot of sugar and cook it up, with no meat whatsoever. A lot of us became thin and emaciated.

I had the singular misfortune to get caught communicating four times in the month of May of 1969. They had a punishment room right across the courtyard from my cell, and I ended up spending a lot of time over there.

It was also in May, 1969, that they wanted me to write—as I remember—a letter to U.S. pilots who were flying over North Vietnam asking them not to do it. I was being forced to stand up continuously—sometimes they'd make you stand up or sit on a stool for a long period of time. I'd stood up for a couple of days, with a respite only because one of the guards—the only real human being that I ever met over there—let me lie down for a couple of hours while he was on watch the middle of one night.

One of the strategies we worked out was not to let them make you break yourself. If you get tired of standing, just sit down—make them force you up. So I sat down, and this little guard who was a particularly hateful man came in and jumped up and down on my knee. After this I had to go back on a crutch for the next year and a half.

That was a long, difficult summer. Then suddenly, in October, 1969, there were drastic changes around the camp. The torture stopped. "The Soft-Soap Fairy" came to my room one day and told me that I would get a roommate. The food improved greatly and we started getting extra rations. The guards seemed almost friendly. For example, I had a turnkey who used to just bash me around for drill. The door would open—and he'd come in and start slugging me. They stopped that kind of thing. I attribute all this directly to the propaganda effort that was directed by the Administration and the people in the United States in 1969.

My younger brother, Joe, was very active in the National League of Families of American Prisoners of War and Missing in Action in Southeast Asia. That was the umbrella for all the POW family groups. So he has filled me in on why the North Vietnamese attitude toward the American prisoners changed, and given me this information:

As the bombing of the North picked up in 1965, 1966, Hanoi made its first propaganda display by parading beaten, subjugated American pilots through the streets. To their surprise, the press reaction around the world was generally negative.

Next, the North Vietnamese tried the tactic of forcing Cdr. Dick Stratton to appear and apologize for war crimes. But he had obviously been mistreated, and was doing this only under extreme duress. That backfired, too. They followed this by releasing two groups of three POW's in February and October, 1968. These men had been there less than six months and had suffered no significant weight loss and were in pretty good shape.

Until the Nixon Administration came to office in 1969, the Government back home had taken the attitude: "Don't talk about the prisoner-of-war situation lest you hurt the Americans still over there." Secretary of Defense Melvin Laird, early in 1969, went over to the peace talks with the North Vietnamese and Viet Cong in Paris. [Talks had begun under President Johnson late in 1968.] Laird took pictures of severely beaten men, such as Frishman, Stratton, Hegdahl—all of whom had suffered extreme weight loss. He got the photos through foreign news services. He told the North Vietnamese: "The Geneva Convention says that you shall release all sick and wounded prisoners. These men are sick and wounded. Why aren't they released?"

In August, 1969, Hanoi let Frishman come home. He had no elbow—just a limp rubbery arm—and he had lost 65 pounds. Hegdahl came out and had lost 75 pounds. Also released was Wes Rumbull, who was in a body cast because of a broken back.

Frishman was allowed to hold a press conference and spilled out the details of torture and maltreatment. Headlines appeared all over the world, and from then on, starting in the fall of 1969, the treatment began to improve. We think this was directly attributable to the fact that Frishman was living proof of the mistreatment of Americans.

I'm proud of the part Joe and my wife, Carol, played here at home. The temptation for the wives, as the years went by, was to say, "God, I want them home under any circumstances." When Carol was pressed to take this line, her answer was, "Just to get him home is not enough for me, and it's not enough for John—I want him to come home standing up."

I received very few letters from Carol. I got three in the first four months after I was shot down. The "gooks" let me have only one during the last four years I was there. I received my first package in May of 1969. After that, they let me have approximately one a year.

The reason I got so little mail was that Carol insisted on using the channels provided by the Geneva Convention for treatment of prisoners of war. She refused to send things through the Committee for Liaison with Families run by the antiwar groups.

This brings me to something that I want to discuss in more detail:

As you may know, back in 1954, the North Vietnamese had a big hand in toppling the French Government in Paris because the French voters had no more stomach for the Vietnam war their Government was waging at the time. That was the way the North Vietnamese won in 1954—they didn't win in Vietnam.

The French agreed to pull out of Indo-China with no questions asked when they signed the agreement. As a result, they got back just one third of their POW's.

I'm convinced that Hanoi hoped to win in our case by undermining morale among the people at home in America. They had to marshal world opinion on their side. I remember in 1968 or '69 [North Vietnam Premier] Pham Van Dong's speech to the National Assembly, because we were blasted with these things on the loud-speakers. The title of his address was, "The Whole World Supports Us," not, "We Have Defeated the U.S. Aggressors," or anything like that.

In 1969, after the three guys who were released went back to the U.S. and told about the brutality in the POW camps, President Nixon gave the green light to publicizing this fact. It brought a drastic change in our treatment. And I thank God for it, because if it hadn't been for that a lot of us would never have returned.

Just one small example of the way things improved: Over my door were some bars, covered by a wooden board to keep me from seeing out, and to block ventilation. One night, around the end of September, 1969, "Slopehead," the camp commander himself, came around and pulled this thing off, so that I could have some ventilation. I couldn't believe it. Every night from then on they pulled that transom so I could get some ventilation. We started bathing more often. It was all very amazing.

In December of 1969 I was moved from "The Pentagon" over to "Las Vegas." "Las Vegas" was a small area of Hoala Prison which was built by the French in 1945. It was known as the "Hanoi Hilton" to Americans. "Heartbreak Hotel" is also there—that's the first place that people were usually taken for their initial interrogations and then funneled out to other camps.

This whole prison is an area of about two city blocks. At "Las Vegas," I was put in a small building of just three rooms called the "Gold Nugget." We named the buildings after the hotels in Vegas—there was the "Thunderbird," "Stardust," "Riviera," "Gold Nugget" and the "Desert Inn."

I was moved into the "Gold Nugget," and immediately I was able to establish communications with the men around the camp, because the bath area was right out my window, and I could see through cracks in the doors of the bath and we would communicate that way. I stayed in that one, in solitary confinement, until March of 1970.

There was pressure to see American antiwar delegations, which seemed to increase as the time went on. But there wasn't any torture. In January of 1970, I was taken to a quiz with "The Cat." He told me that he wanted me to see a foreign guest. I told him what I had always told him before: that I would see the visitor, but I would not say anything against my country, and if I was asked about my treatment I would tell them how harsh it was. Much to my shock and surprise he said, "Fine, you don't have to say anything." I told him I'd have to think about it. I went back to my room and I asked the senior American officer in our area what his opinion was, and he said he thought that I should go ahead.

So I went to see this visitor who said he was from Spain, but who I later heard was from Cuba. He never asked me any questions about controversial subjects or my treatment or my feelings about the war. I told him I had no remorse about what I did, and that I would do it over again if the same opportunity presented itself. That seemed to make him angry, because he was a sympathizer of the North Vietnamese.

At the time this happened, a photographer came in and took a couple of pictures. I had told "The Cat" that I didn't want any such publicity. So when I came back—the interview lasted about 15, 20 minutes—I told him I wasn't going to see another visitor because he had broken his word. Also at that time Capt. Jeremiah Denton, who was running our camp at that time, established a policy that we should not see any delegations.

In March, I got a roommate, Col. John Finley, Air Force. He and I lived together for approximately two months. A month after he moved in, "The Cat" told me I was going to see another delegation. I refused and was forced to sit on a stool in the "Heartbreak" courtyard area for three days and nights. Then I was sent back to my room.

The pressure continued on us to see antiwar delegations. By early in June I was moved away from Colonel Finley to a room that they called "Calcutta," about 50 yards away from the nearest prisoners. It was 6 feet by 2 feet with no ventilation in it, and it was very, very hot. During the summer I suffered from heat prostration a couple or three times, and dysentery. I was very ill. Washing facilities were nonexistent. My food was cut down to about half rations. Sometimes I'd go for a day or so without eating.

All during this time I was taken out to interrogation and pressured to see the antiwar people. I refused.

Finally I moved in September to another room which was back in the camp but separated from everything else. That was what we called "the Riviera." I stayed in there until December, 1970. I had good communications, because there was a door facing the outside and a kind of louvered window above it. I used to stand up on my bucket and was able to take my toothbrush and flash the code to other prisoners, and they would flash back to me.

In December I moved into "Thunderbird," one of the big buildings with about 15 rooms in it. The communication here was very good. We would tap between rooms. I learned a lot about acoustics. You can tap—if you get the right spot on the wall—and hear a guy four or five rooms away.

Late in December, 1970—about the twentieth, I guess—I was allowed to go out during the day with four other men. On Christmas night we were taken out of our room and moved into the "Camp Unity" area, which was another part of Hoala. We had a big room, where there were about 45 of us, mostly from "Vegas."

There were seven large rooms, usually with a concrete pedestal in the center, where we slept with 45 or 50 guys in each room. We had a total of 335 prisoners at that time. There were four or five guys who were not in good shape that they kept separated from us. The Colonels Flynn, Wynn, Bean and Gaddis also were kept separate. They did not move in with us at that time.

Our "den mother" was "The Bug" again, much to our displeasure. He made life very difficult for us. He wouldn't let us have meetings of more than three people at one time. They were afraid we were going to set up political indoctrination. They wouldn't let us have church service. "The Bug" would not recognize our senior officer's rank. This is one thing that they did right up until the end, till the day we left. If they had worked through our seniors, they would have gotten co-operation out of us. This was a big source of irritation all the time.

In March of 1971 the senior officers decided that we would have a showdown over church. This was an important issue for us. It also was a good one to fight them on. We went ahead and held church. The men that were conducting the service were taken out of the room immediately. We began to sing hymns in loud voices and "The Star-Spangled Banner."

The "gooks" thought it was a riot situation. They brought in the ropes and were practicing judo holds and that kind of stuff. After about a week or two they started taking the senior officers out of our room and putting them over in another building.

Later in March they came in and took three or four of us out of every one of the seven rooms until they got 36 of us out. We were put in a camp we called "Skid Row," a punishment camp. We stayed there from March until August, when we came back for about four weeks because of flooding conditions around Hanoi, and then we went back out again until November.

They didn't treat us badly there. The guards had permission to knock us around if we were unruly. However, they did not have permission to start torturing us for propaganda statements. The rooms were very small, about 6 feet by 4 feet, and we were in solitary again. The most unpleasant thing about it was thinking of all our friends living in a big room together. But compared with '69 and before, it was a piece of cake.

The great advantage to living in a big room is that way only a couple or three guys out of the group have to deal with the "gooks." When you're living by yourself, then you've got to deal with them all the time. You always have some fight with them. Maybe you're allowed 15 minutes to bathe, and the "gook" will say in five minutes you've got to go back. So you have an argument with him, and he locks you in your room so you don't get to bathe for a week. But when you're in a big room with others, you can stay out of contact with them and it's a lot more pleasant.

All through this period, the "gooks" were bombarding us with antiwar quotes from people in high places back in Washington. This was the most effective propaganda they had to use against us—speeches and statements by men who were generally respected in the United States.

They used Senator Fulbright a great deal, and Senator Brooke. Ted Kennedy was quoted again and again, as was Averell Harriman. Clark Clifford was another favorite, right after he had been Secretary of Defense under President Johnson.

When Ramsey Clark came over they thought that was a great coup for their cause.

The big furor over release of the Pentagon papers was a tremendous boost for Hanoi. It was advanced as proof of the "black imperialist schemes" that they had been talking about all those years.

In November of 1971 we came back from "Skid Row," and they put us in one of the big rooms again in the main Hoala Prison area. This was "Camp Unity." From that time on we pretty much stayed as a group with some other people who were brought in later. We ended up with about 40 men in there.

In May, 1972, when the U.S. bombing started again in earnest, they moved almost all the junior officers up to a camp near the China border, leaving the senior officers and our group behind. That was when President Nixon announced the resumption of the bombing of North Vietnam and the mining of the ports.

"Dogpatch" was the name of the camp near the border. I think they were afraid that Hanoi would be hit, and with all of us together in one camp one bomb could have wiped us out. At this time, the "gooks" got a little bit rougher. They once took a guy out of our room and beat him up very badly. This man had made a flag on the back of another man's shirt. He was a fine young man by the name of Mike Christian. They just pounded the hell out of him right outside of our room and then carried him a few feet and then pounded him again and pounded him all the way across the courtyard, busted one of his eardrums and busted his ribs. It was to be a lesson for us all.

Aside from bad situations now and then, 1971 and 1972 was a sort of coasting period. The reason why you see our men in such good condition today is that the food and everything generally improved. For example, in late '69 I was down to 105, 110 pounds, boils all over me, suffering dysentery. We started getting packages with vitamins in them—about one package a year. We were able to exercise quite a bit in our rooms and managed to get back in a lot better health.

My health has improved radically. In fact, I think I'm in better physical shape than I was when I got shot down. I can do 45 push-ups and a couple hundred sit-ups. Another beautiful thing about exercise: It makes you tired and you can sleep, and when you're asleep you're not there, you know. I used to try to exercise all the time.

Finally came the day I'll never forget—the eighteenth of December, 1972. The whole place exploded when the Christmas bombing ordered by President Nixon began. They hit Hanoi right off the bat.

It was the most spectacular show I'll ever see. By then we had large windows in our rooms. These had been covered with bamboo mats, but in October, 1972, they took them down. We had about a 120-degree view of the sky, and, of course, at night you can see all the flashes. The bombs were dropping so close that the building would shake. The SAM's [surface-to-air missiles] were flying all over and the sirens were whining—it was really a wild scene. When a B-52 would get hit—they're up at more than 30,000 feet—it would light up the whole sky. There would be a red glow that almost made it like daylight, and it would last for a long time, because they'd fall a long way.

We knew at that time that unless something very forceful was done that we were never going to get out of there. We had sat there for 3½ years with no bombing going on—November of '68 to May of '72. We were fully aware that the only way that we were ever going to get out was for our Government to turn the screws on Hanoi.

So we were very happy. We were cheering and hollering. The "gooks" didn't like that at all, but we didn't give a damn about that. It was obvious to us that negotiation was not going to settle the problem. The only reason why the North Vietnamese began negotiating in October, 1972, was because they could read the polls as well as you and I can, and they knew that Nixon was going to have an overwhelming victory in his re-election bid. So they wanted to negotiate a cease-fire before the elections.

I admire President Nixon's courage. There may be criticism of him in certain areas—Watergate, for example. But he had to take the most unpopular decisions that I could imagine—the mining, the blockade, the bombing. I know it was very, very difficult for him to do that, but that was the thing that ended the war. I think the reason he understood this is that he has a long background in dealing with these people. He knows how to use the carrot and the stick. Obviously, his trip to China and the Strategic Arms Limitation Treaty with Russia were based on the fact that we're stronger than the Communists, so they were willing to negotiate. Force is what they understand. And that's why it is difficult for me to understand now, when everybody knows that the bombing finally got a cease-fire agreement, why people are still criticizing his foreign policy—for example, the bombing in Cambodia.

Right after the Communist *Tet* offensive in 1968, the North Vietnamese were riding high. They knew President Johnson was going to stop the bombing before the 1968 elections. "The Soft-Soap Fairy" told me a month before those elections that Johnson was going to stop the bombing.

In May of 1968 I was interviewed by two North Vietnamese generals at separate times. Both of them said to me, in almost these words:

"After we liberate South Vietnam we're going to liberate Cambodia. And after Cambodia we're going to liberate Laos, and after we liberate Laos we're going to liberate Thailand. And after we liberate Thailand we're going to liberate Malaysia, and then Burma. We're going to liberate all of Southeast Asia."

They left no doubt in my mind that it was not a question of South Vietnam alone. Some people's favorite game is to refute the "domino theory," but the North Vietnamese themselves never tried to refute it. They believe it. Ho Chi Minh said many, many times, "We are proud to be in the front line of armed struggle between the socialist camp and the U.S. imperialist aggressors." Now, this doesn't mean fighting for nationalism. It doesn't mean fighting for an independent South Vietnam. It means what he said. This is what Communism is all about—armed struggle to overthrow the capitalist countries.

I read a lot of their history. They gave us propaganda books. I learned that Ho Chi Minh was a Stalinist. When Khrushchev denounced Stalin in the late 1950s, Ho Chi Minh did not go along with it. He was not a "peaceful coexistence" Communist.

At this particular juncture, after *Tet* in 1968, they thought they had the war won. They had gotten General Westmoreland [commander of U.S. forces in South Vietnam] fired. They were convinced that they had wrecked Johnson's chances for re-election. And they thought that they had the majority of the American people on their side. That's why these guys were speaking very freely as to what their ambitions were. They were speaking prematurely, because they just misjudged the caliber of President Nixon.

To go back to the December bombing: Initially, the North Vietnamese had a hell of a lot of SAM's on hand. I soon saw a lessening in the SAM activities, meaning they may have tied them up. Also, the B-52 bombings, which were mainly right around Hanoi in the first few days, spread out away from the city because, I think, they destroyed all the military targets around Hanoi.

I don't know the number of B-52 crewmen shot down then, because they only took the injured Americans to our camp. The attitude of our men was good. I talked to them the day before we moved out, preparing to go home, when they knew the agreements were going to be signed. I asked one young pilot—class of '70 at West Point—"How did your outfit feel when you were told that the B-52s were going to bomb Hanoi?" He said, "Our morale skyrocketed."

I have heard there was one B-52 pilot who refused to fly the missions during the Christmas bombing. You always run into that kind. When the going gets tough, they find out their conscience is bothering them. I want to say this to anybody in the military: If you don't know what your country is doing, find out. And if you find you don't like what your country is doing, get out before the chips are down.

Once you become a prisoner of war, then you do not have the right to dissent, because what you do will be harming your country. You are no longer speaking as an individual, you are speaking as a member of the armed forces of the United States, and you owe loyalty to the Commander in Chief, not to your own conscience. Some of my fellow prisoners sang a different tune, but they were a very small minority. I ask myself if they should be prosecuted, and I don't find that easy to answer. It might destroy the very fine image that the great majority of us have brought back from that hellhole. Remember, a handful of turncoats after the Korean War made a great majority of Americans think that most of the POW's in that conflict were traitors.

If these men are tried, it should not be because they took an antiwar stance, but because they collaborated with the Vietnamese to an extent, and that was harmful to the other American POW's. And there is this to consider: America will have other wars to fight until the Communists give up their doctrine of violent overthrow of our way of life. These men should bear some censure so that in future wars there won't be a precedent for conduct that hurts this country.

By late January of this year, we knew the end of the war was near. I was moved then to the "Plantation." We were put together in groups by the period when we were shot down. They were getting us ready to return by groups.

By the way—a very interesting thing—after I got back, Henry Kissinger told me that when he was in Hanoi to sign the final agreements, the North Vietnamese offered him one man that he could take back to Washington with him, and that was me. He, of course, refused, and I thanked him very much for that, because I did not want to go out of order. Most guys were betting that I'd be the last guy out—but you never can fathom the "gooks."

It was January 20 when we were moved to the "Plantation." From then on it was very easy—they hardly bothered us. We were allowed out all day in the courtyard. But, typical of them, we had real bad food for about two weeks before we left. Then they gave us a great big meal the night before we went home.

There was no special ceremony when we left the camp. The

International Control Commission came in and were permitted to look around the camp. There were a lot of photographers around, but nothing formal. Then we got on the buses
and went to Gia Lam Airport. My old friend "The Rabbit"
was there. He stood out front and said to us, "When I read
your name off, you get on the plane and go home."

That was March 15. Up to that moment, I wouldn't allow
myself more than a feeling of cautious hope. We had been
peaked up so many times before that I had decided that I
wouldn't get excited until I shook hands with an American in
uniform. That happened at Gia Lam, and then I knew it was
over. There is no way I can describe how I felt as I walked
toward that U.S. Air Force plane.

Now that I'm back, I find a lot of hand-wringing about this
country. I don't buy that. I think America today is a better
country than the one I left nearly six years ago.

The North Vietnamese gave us very little except bad news
about the U.S. We didn't find out about the first successful
moon shot [in 1969] until it was mentioned in a speech by
George McGovern saying that Nixon could put a man on the
moon, but he couldn't put an end to the Vietnam war.

They bombarded us with the news of Martin Luther King's
death and the riots that followed. Information like that
poured continuously out of the loud-speakers.

I think America is a better country now because we have
been through a sort of purging process, a re-evaluation of
ourselves. Now I see more of an appreciation of our way of
life. There is more patriotism. The flag is all over the place. I
hear new values being stressed—the concern for environment
is a case in point.

I've received scores of letters from young people, and many
of them sent me POW bracelets with my name on it, which
they had been wearing. Some were not too sure about the
war, but they are strongly patriotic, their values are good, and
I think we will find that they are going to grow up to be
better Americans than many of us.

This outpouring on behalf of us who were prisoners of war
is staggering, and a little embarrassing because basically we
feel that we are just average American Navy, Marine and Air

Force pilots who got shot down. Anybody else in our place would have performed just as well.

My own plans for the future are to remain in the Navy, if I am able to return to flying status. That depends upon whether the corrective surgery on my arms and my leg is successful. If I have to leave the Navy, I hope to serve the Government in some capacity, preferably in Foreign Service for the State Department.

I had a lot of time to think over there, and came to the conclusion that one of the most important things in life—along with a man's family—is to make some contribution to his country.

U.S. News & World Report, May 14, 1973

Last GIs Leave South Vietnam

by H. D. S. Greenway

SAIGON, March 29—The last plane load of American troops left Vietnam from Saigon's Tansonnhut airport today, in the heat of a late afternoon sun—bound for Clark Field in the Philippines, Honolulu and home.

The last contingent, consisting of 68 Army, Navy and Air Force personnel who had been responsible for processing the day's withdrawal, boarded a silver C-141 Air Force jet shortly after 5 p.m.

Members of the four-party Joint Military Commission were on the runway to check the manifest and a North Vietnamese officer with a movie camera recorded the last departure on film.

Lt. Col. Bui Tin, who has often acted as the North Vietnamese delegation spokesman, was on hand in his Russian-style officer's cap and green uniform with a little red Ho Chi Minh button.

Bui Tin had a small bamboo scroll painting of a Hanoi pagoda and a pack of Ho Chi Minh post cards to give the last American soldier to leave Vietnam.

"This is an historic day," he said. "It is the first time in 100 years that there are no foreign troops on the soil of Vietnam."

As it was, Bui Tin gave the scroll and the pictures to an embarrassed master sergeant, Oax Beilke from Alexandria, Minn. But in fact the last two to board the plane were Tansonnhut base commander, Col. David Odell, and his chief master sergeant, Vincent R. Jacobucci.

Odell and Jacobucci had brought a bottle of champagne out to the plane for a ceremonial swallow.

The Communist members of the Joint Military Commission were full of smiles for peace and friendship and the Americans responded gracefully. Only one, Col. Einar Himma, seemed to mind and he ground his teeth as he passed the North Vietnamese and Vietcong on the way to the plane.

The South Vietnamese members of the JMC were put off by the amount of attention Bui Tin was receiving from the press and one of them pointed to a row of 21 flag-draped coffins about 100 yards away.

They contained the bodies of South Vietnamese soldiers killed during the last few days up North and flown to Saigon from Danang. There were a few Vietnamese civilians there, oblivious to the last departure of American troops, and one woman knelt and tried to straighten the flag that had slipped from a corner of a wooden coffin.

The last plane out was more symbolic than realistic. There are still more than 800 American military men connected with the JMC who will be leaving Friday and Saturday. After that, except for a 14-man graves commission, the only American military in Vietnam will be about 50 military attaches and the 159-man embassy Marine guard.

A few hours earlier, as the American soldiers were being processed at Tansonnhut's Camp Alpha, an ugly scene took place. A couple of hundred Vietnamese civilians forced their way through the wire fence, broke into the mess hall and looted the larder.

In minutes they had dragged out tables, chairs, fans, canned goods, "everything that wasn't bolted down," as one American put it. According to Capt. George Parrott, commander of the 178th Replacement Company, the Vietnamese military policeman on duty helped move the loot out through the wire.

When the Americans arrived on the scene, the Vietnamese fled and the mess hall lay in shambles. Eggs, flour, mustard, catsup, cold cereal and ice cream lay together on the floor in one gorgeous omelet.

The mess hall was supposed to be turned over to the U.S. embassy, Capt. Parrott said. He was annoyed, but he took it philosophically and said: "I don't think they are trying to belittle us or anything. They were just trying to get what they can while they can."

Elsewhere, there were heaps of abandoned helmets, fatigues, combat boots, and other military paraphernalia which the departing GI's had abandoned outside their barracks. Vietnamese who helped around the base were free to try on boots and take what they wanted.

Most of the GI's being processed inside did not know or care what was going on outside. Most were happy to be leaving, but some were a little sad.

"It's kind of a mixed feeling," said Sp. 4 Harold O. Wells of Dover, Del. "You make a lot of friends over here."

Wells was bound for home and 30 days leave, but a good number of today's contingent were Air Force personnel bound for bases in Thailand.

Some of them will be involved in war again, for the Thai-based B-52 bombers are not yet still and they are bombing Cambodia more heavily than ever before. One staff sergeant in the Air Force security police said that he was bound for Laos where he would join a group of American military men manning a radar station at a place called Kho Khoa.

When asked if he knew that American troops were not supposed to be deployed in Laos, his buddies quickly said: "You don't really think you are going to get us to talk about that, do you?"

[Pentagon sources say it is possible that the Royal Laotian government has a radar station at a place called Khao Khoual, about 75 miles north of Udorn and 30 miles inside Laos. A 2,200-foot mountain peak and an old airstrip are at that location, which makes it a favorable spot for radar surveillance. But Pentagon sources claim there are no U.S. Air Force radar installations or servicemen inside Laos.]

The day's event began at 1 p.m. with a dreary little ceremony to deactivate the Military Assistance Command-Vietnam, better known as MACV. It was first brought into being in February 1962.

Commanding Gen. Frederick C. Weyand stood at attention in the sun-baked parking lot of MACV with Ambassador Ellsworth Bunker at his side. A recording of the Star Spangled Banner was played and a message from Defense Secretary Elliot Richardson, saying that MACV had accomplished its mission, was read aloud.

The Chairman of the Joint Chiefs of Staff, Adm. Thomas Moorer sent a message saying that although the U.S. military in Vietnam had not "enjoyed the full measure of public support it deserved," it nevertheless had "recorded a crucial and unforgettable chapter in the history of the U.S. armed forces."

Weyand said that MACV's mission had been to "prevent an all-out attempt by an aggressor to impose its will through raw military force."

"That mission has been accomplished," he said, "and the rights of the people of the Republic of Vietnam to shape their own destiny and to provide for their self-defense have been upheld."

The blue flag with the white sword in a red and yellow MACV emblem was carefully rolled and bagged by the color guard and MACV, which had once commanded more than a half a million men, was no more.

Inside the sprawling yellow building that came to be known as the "Pentagon East," there were soldiers dragging out large bags of classified material to be burned. The building, which is now a little tatty with rust around the windows and boils in the paint, is to be turned over to the military attaches.

Weyand and Bunker were among the few there this afternoon who remembered the day six years ago when the "Pentagon East" first opened or the days when Gen. William C. Westmoreland used to greet visitors in his immaculate fatigues to explain his war of attrition in the far reaches of the country.

Few remembered the battles—the Iadrang, the Iron Triangle, the Ashau Valley or Dak to where the airborne, badly mangled in the mountains of the Central Highlands, ate turkey dinners atop Hill 875 on Thanksgiving Day six years ago while the woods still reeked with the unburied dead.

Or the bases—Khesanh, the Rockpile, Dongha, Giolinh or Conthien.

So many of these places where Americans fought are now deep behind North Vietnamese and Vietcong lines, and if there are monuments to the dead there now they are not to Americans.

In the midafternoon the government of South Vietnam staged a more elaborate good-bye ceremony for Weyand outside the VIP lounge of Tansonnhut airport. A Vietnamese honor guard and a brass band were drawn up in front of a reviewing stand and a big red banner read, "Bon Voyage to the American Soldiers."

American and Vietnamese flags snapped in the breeze and a statement from President Thieu was read to the assembled American, Vietnamese and foreign dignitaries.

President Thieu thanked the Americans and said that they had, by their participation "at our side in this historic struggle," brought time for the republic to "develop and strengthen adequate defense forces, and at the same time to build a solid infrastructure for economic development."

Weyand read a short speech in Vietnamese, in which he said, "today my command terminates its presence on Vietnamese soil . . ." But the armed forces of South Vietnam had "clearly proven their ability on the battlefield," he said.

"Our mission has been accomplished," he said. "I depart with a strong feeling of pride in what we have achieved and what our achievement represents . . . it is our sincere hope that the peace with honor that has been our goal will last forever," said Weyand.

Vietnamese Wacs then placed garlands of flowers around the necks of Weyand and his staff, and as the Vietnamese band played "Auld Lang Syne," Weyand walked to his waiting plane, gave a thumbs-up gesture and a little wave and flew away.

All of these ceremonies took place in or near Tansonnhut airbase, away from the center of Saigon, and the symbolic passing of American forces caused not a ruffle on the noisy surface of this city. In a sense the final departing was an anticlimax.

Seventeen years ago the French expeditionary force departed Saigon forever. On April 10, 1956, a last farewell was held and wreathes were laid in front of the monument for the French dead in Chiensi Place.

There is an account of it to be found in the yellowing back issues of a French language newspaper here.

"We were struck by the gentillese—there is no other word—of the Vietnamese public and even more by the often visible sympathy," the paper said.

After the ceremony, five French detachments and one Vietnamese detachment marched down Tudo Street, the city's main street.

The French had called it Rue Catinat in earlier years and during the last parade, the paper said, the street became Rue Catinat again, if only for a few minutes as the French colors passed.

The dissolution of the French High Commission for Indochina occurred on April 28, 1956, when the commander of all French forces in Indochina, Gen. Pierre Jaquot, sailed down the Saigon River bound for France on the liner S.S. Canaboge.

The French monument to those who died for France was, in later years torn down and in place today there stands a sculpture incorporating the likeness of a giant turtle—a Vietnamese symbol of longevity.

The Washington Post, March 30, 1973

Bomb Error Leaves Havoc in Neak Luong

by Sydney H. Schanberg

NEAK LUONG, Cambodia, Aug. 8—The destruction in this town from the accidental bombing on Monday is extensive.

Big chunks of the center of town have been demolished, including two-story concrete buildings reinforced with steel. Clusters of wood and thatch huts where soldiers lived with their families have been erased, so that the compounds where they once stood look like empty fields strewn with rubbish.

On Monday evening the United States Embassy described the damage as "minimal."

"I saw one stick of bombs through the town, but it was no great disaster," said Col. David H. E. Opfer, the air attaché at the embassy, who briefed the press then. "The destruction was minimal."

[A United States Embassy spokesman in Phnom Penh said Wednesday that American aircraft, in their third bombing error in three days, hit a village on the Phnom Penh–Saigon highway, Reuters reported. In Washington, the Pentagon denied the report.]

The nearly 400 casualties from Monday's bombing, which the Americans say was carried out by a lone B-52 with a 20-ton-plus load, make it the worst accidental bombing of the Indochina war. Official figures show 137 killed and 268 wounded, most of them soldiers and their families. The Americans originally put total casualties at around 150 but have since acknowledged their error.

However, the toll could be somewhat higher because the count does not include minor wounds. Moreover, some townspeople say they believe a few bodies remain in the wreckage. The smell of decaying flesh is still prevalent in parts of town.

The atmosphere in Neak Luong, on the east bank of the

Mekong River 38 miles southeast of Phnom Penh, is silent and sad—and bewildered at being bombed by an ally. Everyone has lost either relatives or friends; in some cases entire large families were wiped out.

Yesterday afternoon a soldier could be seen sobbing uncontrollably on the riverbank. "All my family is dead!" he cried, beating his hand on the wooden bench where he had collapsed. "All my family is dead! Take my picture, take my picture! Let the Americans see me!"

His name is Keo Chan and his wife and 10 of his children were killed. All he has left is the youngest—an 8-month-old son. The 48-year-old soldier escaped death because he was on sentry duty a few miles away when the bombs fell.

The bombs went right down the middle of the town from north to south as it lay sleeping shortly after 4:30 A.M. Over 30 craters can be seen on a line nearly a mile long, and people reported others in jungle areas outside the town that this correspondent could not reach.

Some witnesses said the bombs exploded above the ground, indicating that they might have been antipersonnel devices.

A large part of the market area in the center of town is smashed flat and many of the two-story concrete shops and apartment buildings on either side are shattered and uninhabitable, with walls and roofs reduced to rubble. Other buildings still usable have large holes.

A third of the hospital is demolished, with the rest badly damaged and unusable until major repairs are made. Several patients were wounded and some are believed killed. A bomb fell on the northeast corner of the hospital, blowing some walls down and scattering concrete, beds and cabinets.

At his press briefing Colonel Opfer, who visited Neak Luong within a few hours of the bombing, said that there was "a little bit of damage to the northeast corner of the hospital" and talked about some "structural cracks" in a wall.

The bombs also hit a compound for marines, which had a large field full of flimsy shacks in the back. The shacks were leveled and the main building, a two-story concrete structure, was turned into a stark shell, with only some walls left standing, and those badly cracked and tilted. The shacks, of thatch and wood and corrugated metal, where the marines lived with their families, is a rubbish heap crisscrossed with fallen coconut trees.

Ammunition also exploded in this compound and many people died. A woman's scalp sways on a clump of tall grass. A bloody pillow here, a shred of a sarong caught on barbed wire there. A large bloodstain on the brown earth. A pair of infant's rubber sandals among some unexploded artillery shells.

Colonel Opfer referred to the soldiers' shacks as "hootches" suggesting that not much of value had been destroyed. The attaché said further that the bombing "took place in what is essentially a small village." Actually, by Cambodian standards it is a big town; about 10,000 people live in and around Neak Luong, half of them in the town proper.

Asked the reaction of the people when he walked through Neak Luong, Colonel Opfer said, "They were sad, but they understand that this is war and that in war these things happen."

"I do not understand why it happened," said Chea Salan, a 21-year-old soldier who lost relatives and army buddies. "Before, every time we saw the planes coming we were happy because we knew the planes came to help us. Now I have lost heart."

Another soldier asked, "Did the Government capture the pilot yet."

"Why did this happen to us?" said Keo Sakhoun Tha, also a soldier. "I want world opinion to judge what happened here." He added, almost as an afterthought, "I am frightened at night now when the planes come."

"At first, after the bombing, I thought it must be a North Vietnamese plane," still another soldier commented. "I did not believe it could be an American plane. Now I believe it."

Though several soldiers and residents said they were angry, their tone carried no anger, and little anti-American reaction was discernible. Rather the people were confused, hurt and bewildered that such a disaster should befall them, and especially that it could be caused by an ally.

"I am simply desolated," said a naval ensign, Phiboun Doutch, "but we must continue the struggle against the enemy."

Local people, in their confusion over the bombing, continually stressed that there had been no enemy activity in the vicinity.

The bombs struck a fuel and ammunition dump. Trees for acres around are stripped of leaves and charred, with sheets of tin from soldiers' huts hanging from some of the high branches. A magic necklace, specially blessed by a Buddhist priest to ward off harm and misfortune, lay broken.

There is one unexploded bomb buried in the main street near the central market. The people are jittery about it. "When are you Americans going to take it away," a man called to a visitor.

The New York Times, August 9, 1973

Scars of Delta Savagery

by Philip A. McCombs

OLAM, South Vietnam—Capt. Chau Reaps, proud, soldierly but chinless, his face twisted grotesquely from a wound, smokes a Philip Morris and gazes across the sunsplashed plains toward the rocky, glinting hills. A scene of peace.

Four years ago, I first met Chau Reaps in this isolated corner of South Vietnam, near the Cambodian border 120 miles west of Saigon. Olam was then a crazy, savage world.

A small team of American advisers lived in a mud fort here and worked with Chau Reaps and his 188th Regional Force company of ethnic Cambodian troops, which he still commands.

The Americans are gone now, but the story of what happened here tells something about America's role in Vietnam then and now and about what is presently happening in the rice-rich Mekong Delta, economically the most important part of South Vietnam and the home of about half its 20 million people.

You could get to this place only by helicopter four years ago, the chopper sweeping low across the plains toward a rocky hill called Coto Mountain, barreling in at 120 knots, the skids only a few feet above the rice, then slamming to a hovering halt with a pounding flapping of rotor blades as the chatter of a North Vietnamese army .51-cal. machine gun came from the hill a few hundred yards away.

Then Chau Reaps, shirtless in the blazing heat, and the sweating, grim-faced young Americans, jumped into their mortar pits. The pop-pop-pop of the tubes pumping rounds into Coto Mountain sounded above the roar of the chopper making its getaway.

They were happy then, having just repulsed a North Vietnamese dawn assault, killing 20 or more North Vietnamese troops. Recalling the fight, his first major combat, one of the

Americans said, his voice dropping to a whisper, "When dawn came, you know, I looked out across the perimeter and there were the bodies hanging in the wire. Jesus . . ."

Now Chau Reaps recalls how they carved the livers out of those corpses and ate them in a symbolic act of hatred and revenge, the Cambodians instigating it, the Americans joining in for the sake of camaraderie.

"We ate their livers because we hated them so much," recalled Chau Reaps, speaking Vietnamese with a heavy Cambodian accent. "It made us braver, too."

Across the plain about a mile away at the far end of Coto Mountain is a rocky knoll that the Americans called "Million Dollar Knoll" because they had pumped that many mortar rounds and dropped that many bombs on it.

Now, although there is still a company or so of North Vietnamese soldiers somewhere on Coto Mountain, the knoll is free of them and, my little white Volkswagen chugs safely past it.

The local people look up in surprise at the Western visitor as I bump past the little dirt fort, still intact in the same place and still occupied by soldiers.

Farther on is another bigger, newer dirt fort. Chau Reaps emerges from it, lean, ramrod-straight, his green fatigues starched stiff, the clean-scrubbed smell of talcum powder coming from him.

He remembers, and we embrace.

The area is secure now, he says. There has not been a fight in months.

That is important, because Coto Mountain is one of the "Seven Mountains," the Rocky Hills that stand isolated on the vast Mekong rice plain, one of the few natural hiding places in the Delta and, when I was last here, a key North Vietnamese infiltration route from Cambodia into South Vietnam.

Now, for unknown reasons, the North Vietnamese army is no longer using this route heavily.

It may have something to do with the strained relations between the North Vietnamese and Cambodian insurgent troops just across the border.

In the four years since I was last here, the war in Cambodia has been raging, and in that time relations between the Communist allies there have worsened so that the North Vietnamese no longer have the free run of Communist zones there.

According to intelligence reports available in Saigon, there is more infiltration into the Delta by sea and in areas far to the northeast of here and closer to Saigon.

The last major fighting in this area, according to Chau Reaps, came just after the January 1973, cease-fire when Vietnamese Communist units attacked several villages near here and were driven back after three days of heavy fighting.

Except for the lack of fighting, this area seems very much the same as it did four years ago. There never was here, nor in most other parts of the Delta, any overwhelming presence of American combat troops.

Mostly the American presence was felt in small advisory teams, like the one that was here, when I was, in the tactical air support that the Americans made available, in the B-52 strikes that pummelled the mountains, and in the generous supply of war material.

The bulk of the fighting then was done by Chau Reaps's troops, ethnic Cambodians of Vietnamese citizenship serving in the South Vietnamese army in this border country where they were born and raised.

"Before, when I got support from the U.S. advisers it was a lot easier to do our job here," says Chau Reaps, adjusting his large, horn-rimmed glasses. "Now I lack material. You can look around here and see that the defense system isn't as good as it could be."

To the untrained eye it seems fine—row after row of barbed wire around the perimeter, mortar shells neatly stacked in small bunkers near their tubes. The command fort is immaculate, the packed dirt swept clean with brooms, all metal polished, everything neatly in place, troops saluting snappily.

But Chau Reaps says he needs more barbed wire and that his ammunition supplies are minimal despite continued American military aid to South Vietnam.

"The U.S. advisers were helpful because they could call in air strikes, artillery, choppers," says Chau Reaps. "They were always pleasant with the people, too. Now it's difficult to get that kind of help. If I need to be resupplied, I've got to call in by radio two or three days in advance. I've got enough mortar shells now for defense but not for mounting attacks."

Four years ago, the Americans had blasted Coto Mountain much of the night I stayed there with "harassment and interdiction" fire not aimed at specific targets, an expensive luxury. There is none of that now.

After a tour of his fort, Chau Reaps took me down the road to his native hamlet where a feast had been laid on for a wedding.

We parked the car among the straw houses under the trees. Mats were on the ground, and we all danced around with the prospective bride, to the exotic wheezing sawing of a Cambodian string orchestra, drank from quart-sized bottles of Saigon-made Larue beer, and feasted from heaping, fly-infested platters of pork and beef.

Chau Reaps, 33, said he was born here. He met his wife in nearby Triton. He went to school in Triton and Phnom Penh, 70 miles north of here, then became a Buddhist monk.

In the early 1960s, Chau Reaps became a soldier, living as an outlaw in the rocky caves of the mountains, fighting against both the Vietnamese Communists and the troops of the Ngo Dinh Diem government.

The bands of outlaw Cambodian troops were persuaded to join the government side after Diem's death. It was his repressive measures against ethnic Cambodians that they opposed, Chau Reaps says.

He advanced quickly in the South Vietnamese army, becoming the commander of his all-Cambodian unit here in the late 1960s.

On the night of Aug. 12, 1969, Chau Reaps was leading a patrol up the side of Coto Mountain not far from here when a North Vietnamese B-40 rocket blew off his chin.

He spent six months in American hospitals, and his chin was partially rebuilt. It was just after his return here, in early 1970, that I first met him.

He had an offer at that time to go to a U.S. hospital in Japan for further work on his chin, but he turned it down because action was hot and he wanted to stay with his men. The chance slipped by and was lost.

Now things are quiet and he would like to go. He asks me if it is still possible.

"Perhaps some officer in the U.S. Army will help me to go," he said.

The Washington Post, March 26, 1974

Viet Vets: A Sad Reminder

by William Greider

THE OLD ANGER, the old pain came back briefly to haunt the nation's capital yesterday, a melancholy reminder of Vietnam, the war everyone wants to forget.

The day was meant to be a straightforward, if belated, tribute to all the millions of Vietnam veterans, but somehow the event evoked, not so much glory, but the grief that still lingers in some sectors of American life.

On Capitol Hill, there were hundreds of young men, maimed and whole, packed together in a Senate hearing room, choking on their bitterness. Dressed in olive drab motley from their battlefield days, they shouted down U.S. senators and hooted skeptically at new promises of government assistance.

Downtown at one of the big hotels, a more sedate scene expressed the crippled patriotism of the war. The earnest ladies who arranged a big star-spangled luncheon to honor the vets, who hoped to touch the nation's conscience, looked out at a half-empty banquet hall. The VIP list which was read became inadvertently an honor roll of the missing in action—all the senators and congressmen and Cabinet members who didn't come.

And the day also revived the poisoned politics associated with the war. Angry antiwar vets, ignoring their brethren's pleas to cool it, shouted for amnesty, while downtown Sen. Strom Thurmond (R-S.C.) raised conservative thunder about draft dodgers slinking off to Canada.

Everyone, from the senators who used to be known as "doves" to the flag-waving conservatives, is for the vets. The "doves" ran the Senate hearing. The conservatives dominated the luncheon. But that doesn't extinguish their old differences about the war.

President Nixon found relatively safe ground in between

the two events—a military ceremony at Ft. McNair where a small gathering of military and civilian leaders plus hospitalized war veterans heard him predict that someday America will be proud of its role in Vietnam.

The soldiers and airmen who served there, he said, can be proud that the "American effort . . . was in good conscience, honorably undertaken and honorably ended." That judgment, he added, is "quite different from the instant analysis we see and hear."

Whether most American veterans of Vietnam share that perspective is not known. But it was clearly at odds with the angry tone expressed at the Senate veterans hearing, where the mention of Mr. Nixon's name elicited cat-calls, where three officials from the Veterans Administration manfully weathered a storm of ad-lib complaints.

Sen. Vance Hartke (D-Ind.), chairman of the Veterans Affairs Subcommittee, fed the packed crowd of vets some raw-meat rhetoric and they responded lustily, as the television cameras rolled. Hartke held up a bumper sticker proclaiming the "Honor Vietnam Veterans" sentiment—a bumper sticker issued by the luncheon's conservative sponsors, The National Honor Vietnam Veterans Committee.

"A bumper sticker won't pay the tuition," said Hartke archly. "It also won't put any food on the table. You can't eat bumper stickers, can you?" The vets roared.

The man on Hartke's griddle was Odell W. Vaughn, the VA's director of benefits, who happens to be a disabled vet himself from World War II. "The records show," Vaughn said quietly, "that a greater percentage of Vietnam-era vets are taking advantage of benefits than after World War II."

"No, no!" they shouted. "Not so!"

Hartke argued that the educational stakes are higher today, both the cost and the necessity of going to college. "Amen," someone shouted. "Money, man, money," said another angry voice. A black vet from Massachusetts held aloft a sign that said: "Brother, can you spare a dime?"

Hartke turned to other aggravations, like the late checks that leave veterans and their families without living expenses, not to mention their tuition. It touched another nerve.

"We take these people," the senator said, "and move them

6,000 miles across the ocean and put them in the jungle with a gun in their hands and tell them to fight and we do that efficiently and ably. Yet we can't get a VA check out on time." The room thundered with applause and shouting.

Odell Vaughn smiled gamely. When he tried to explain another VA program, one that pays full college tuition for seriously disabled men who can study anywhere, a veteran taunted him: "Why do you have to get shot to go to Harvard?"

As Smith and his aides departed, a shaggy vet from Texas, wearing a John Dean T-shirt, threw a handful of pills at them. "You can have them back," he snarled, "pill-head!"

A panel of veterans got their turn at the witness tables, and Warren Nagle from New York read a GI bill of rights that laid out the problems, from inadequate cash to the less-than-honorable discharges that blight the future for hundreds of thousands of veterans.

And the senator from Indiana discovered that, once the guys from the VA had departed, the crowd turned to him as the next best target for their wrath. When Hartke tried to close the show, the vets let him have it. He promised more hearings in April.

"April?" shouted one of them. "We don't want more hearings, goddammit!"

"Starvation with honor!" another hollered. Hartke suggested they should take their message downtown to the VA headquarters. They booed louder.

"Lies, lies, lies," said someone at the microphone. Hartke gaveled adjournment. A white vet and a black vet grabbed the mike at the witness table.

"They walked out on us," the white vet exclaimed. "They don't want to hear what we're saying."

"That's American justice, brother, that's American justice," said his companion. Hartke smiled gamely and the hearing ended in noisy discontent.

Some of the veterans there were disappointed that emotions outshouted the hard facts of their case. "I told these guys to cool down and stop alienating people," complained Paul Camacho from Boston College. "Right now we're down here to talk about money."

At the White House, as Mr. Nixon was departing for a weekend in Florida, a group of five disgruntled veterans tried to get an audience with him. They did get in for a brief meeting with presidential assistant James Cavanaugh, who promised a prompt response to their inventory of grievances.

Ron Kovic, the group's wheelchair-bound leader from Delray, Calif., said afterwards: "We left the White House today with the idea that somebody is going to take some positive action. But if the administration doesn't respond, they're going to see a veterans' protest like nothing they've ever seen."

The luncheon at the Washington Hilton was something else—martial music from the Army Band, spring chicken tarragon, a heavy speech against communism by Strom Thurmond, a general theme of proud patriotism. Roughly half of the 700 seats were empty, so was the third tier of VIP seats on the dais.

If Gay Pitcairn Pendleton, a gray-haired lady with a jeweled flag pin on her suit-coat, was disappointed by the response, she concealed it nicely. She is a wealthy Philadelphian—from the Pittsburgh Plate Glass family—who put together the affair.

Her own speech was brief and touching and, unlike Thurmond's, attempted to put aside the old political arguments about Vietnam in favor of doing something now for the veterans.

"The end of our involvement in Vietnam was a day of rejoicing for the millions of families who had waited so long for their sons, husbands and brothers to come home," she said. "But it was also a dark day for America. It was the first time in our history when Americans, who had fought on foreign soil, as a result of answering their country's call to duty, returned without flag-waving, ticker-tape parades and public acclaim."

She warned her audience of civic leaders, political figures, veterans officials, that the debt is still owed to those 2.5 million men.

"Because we set aside this day to honor those men does not excuse this nation from the responsibility of righting the wrongs that have been done," she said. "This should be not only a day to honor our Vietnam veterans, but it should and must be a day to make restitution."

Her special day also provided a platform for a few of the vets to explain some of the things that continue to plague them. Carl McCardin, a black Army major from New York, said he felt uneasy at the banquet table when so many vets were unemployed or without adequate cash.

"Yet," he said, "it is hard for me to come down hard on the people in this room because you apparently care. I can feel that."

The Washington Post, March 30, 1974

A KHMER ROUGE EXECUTION: JULY 1974

"I watched them saw him 3 days"

by Donald Kirk

TUOL SAMPEOU, Cambodia—Twenty-five-year-old Sanguon Preap had been serving in the Khmer Rouge for only three months when he witnessed a display of ruthlessness that led him to flee to the sanctuary of this refugee village some eight miles southwest of Phnom Penh.

"I was very frightened when I saw the Khmer Rouge saw off the neck of a civilian with the sharp edge of sugar palm leaves," said Preap, standing amid a cluster of refugees beside a row of flimsy huts.

"They spent three days cutting his head off," said Preap. "They sawed a little one morning, and then in the evening, and finally the following day in the morning and then in the evening, and finally the following day in the morning and night.

"They made the victim stand up while they were cutting in front of hundreds of people living in the Khmer Rouge area. Then they held him up when he could stand no longer."

The episode was not just an isolated case but one of many I heard during visits to refugee camps. Khmer Rouge soldiers also have used the knife-like edges of sugar palm leaves to lop off the heads of Cambodian officers captured while overrunning nearby towns and military installations.

"They want the victims to suffer more and to serve as examples for people," said one informant. "They denounce them as traitors before the crowd."

"I had to join the Khmer Rouge army or they would have killed me," said Preap. "Those who refuse to serve they send to their deaths. They walk thru villages telling the people to follow them, and the people must obey."

Another refugee, who fled here with his wife and nine children from an area some 50 miles to the east, said that he had never personally witnessed any executions.

484

"They tied up people by putting both hands behind their backs and telling them they were sending them to the high command," said the refugee Lach Pech. "Whenever they did that, then we knew the man would be sent to his death in the forests. It was a secret why they killed people, and nobody dared ask why."

Lach Pech said that in his village Buddhist monks were forced to dig up the roots of large trees—and then throw bodies into the ground where roots had been.

"There is no real security around here," said one village leader. "There are government soldiers somewhere, but there are not enough of them. We worry the enemy will come back again, and we will be in danger. They are only a mile away."

Chicago Tribune, July 14, 1974

In a Besieged Cambodian City

by Sydney H. Schanberg

NEAK LUONG, Cambodia, Jan. 14—Every 15 minutes or so a shell screams down and explodes in this besieged town and another half-dozen people are killed or wounded. It goes on day and night.

The tile floors of the military infirmary and civilian hospital are slippery with blood. They have long since run out of pain-killing drugs. Bodies are everywhere—some people half conscious crying out in pain, some with gaping wounds who will not live. Some are already dead and, in the chaos, just lie there with no one to cover them or take them away.

Fifty yards away, behind a wall, another shell bursts. Those who are conscious jump involuntarily. The seriously wounded are too weak to react.

Inside the infirmary a 7-year-old girl, a filthy bandage over the wound in her stomach, lies on a wooden table. The only doctor in the town feels her pulse. It is failing.

Suddenly her father appears, a soldier. He has come from the spot where another of his children, a 5-year-old girl, has just been killed by a mortar shell. His wife was killed three years ago by shelling in another town.

He picks up his daughter in his shaking arms; his face, bathed in a cold sweat, contorts as he tries to hold back the tears that come anyway.

"I love all my children," is all he says as he walks away with the dying child—heading for the helicopters that are too few to carry all the wounded to Phnom Penh.

There is deep hunger in Neak Luong, too. The soldiers here are getting by, for American and Cambodian transport planes are dropping some food by parachute for them—but there is none for the civilians.

By today, the 30,000 or more refugees who have fled to Neak Luong from outlying areas as the Communist-led insurgents have advanced toward the town have been reduced to subsistence on the thinnest of rice gruel. Every day it becomes thinner. Many are living in the open and it rains almost every night.

Yesterday the Catholic Relief Services, whose dogged Cambodian staff has stayed in Neak Luong to run gruel kitchens, tried to send a barge with 25 tons of rice down the Mekong River the 38 miles from Phnom Penh to the isolated town. But at the last minute the barge was ordered to stay in Phnom Penh. The Cambodian military said the situation was too dangerous and the barge would probably be sunk if it tried to run the insurgents' gantlet.

"They're going to have to airdrop more food," said one disheartened relief worker. "That's all there is to it. Otherwise people will starve."

Already, as one walks around the shell-marked town one hears everywhere the sound of children whimpering.

The military situation here, though grave, does not seem to be deteriorating. Government reinforcements continue to pour in by helicopter and, while the Cambodian insurgents are right across the Mekong from Neak Luong, on the western bank of the river and also very close on most sides of the town itself, it does not appear likely at this point that they can overrun the town.

Yet until the Government troops do more than just hold on—that is, until they push the insurgents back far enough to take the town out of shelling range—the human misery here, with shells raining in indiscriminately, will continue.

The Government's determination to save Neak Luong stems from the town's importance as virtually the last Government position on the lower Mekong. If it fell, the Government would lose all hope of getting supplies into Phnom Penh by way of the Mekong.

With all other surface routes cut long ago in this five-year war, the American-backed Government is now dependent on the Mekong for 80 per cent or more of its supplies from the outside world.

Even now, the Mekong is temporarily blockaded. The rebels, in the annual dry season offensive that began New Year's Day, have seized control of so much of the river and its parallel road, Route 1, that the Americans have been forced to post-pone indefinitely all the supply convoys—which come up from Thailand and South Vietnam.

As people went about their tasks today, many hardly seemed to hear mortars exploding, sometimes only 50 yards away, or the machine-gun fire sputtering around the edges of town, or the rockets whooshing into enemy positions from helicopter gunships overhead.

Amid all this, there was at times a preposterous normality.

In the market, where a few Chinese-run shops were open for those who still had money, a colonel who had just flown in with his fresh troops was examining a bottle of French cologne with a discriminating air. His boots were highly polished, his uniform starched, his neck scarf just so. He squeezed the atomizer, sniffed the spray, then put it back and walked away disdainfully.

Last night the insurgents began increasing their shelling—with mortars, recoilless cannon and rockets. Through the night, the casualties rose.

At dawn, with the explosions heaviest in the southern sector of town, where most of the refugees had been huddled in the streets, a pagoda and a primary school, the refugees began fleeing with their sackfuls of belongings to the northern fringe of Neak Luong, which was not safe but at least safer.

There was squalor, fear and bedlam. But there was also the traditional Buddhist fatalism of the Cambodian people. Some of this trapped population, which totals at least 250,000 counting the refugees, seemed almost to accept that being caught here is simply their lot.

The colonel was an incongruity in Neak Luong today. The norm was blood-soaked stretchers, the smashed bodies of infants attached to plasma bottles, wounded soldiers being dragged or dragging themselves from every lane, and a meadow on the northern edge of town where the wounded who still had a chance were carried to await the evacuation helicopters.

The New York Times, January 16, 1975

A Highlands Mother Escapes, but Pays a Terrible Toll

by Bernard Weinraub

SAIGON, South Vietnam, March 18—Her face swollen with grief, Ly Thi Van stands beside a half-open door near the Saigon docks clutching her infant son and staring vacantly at scooters and buses speeding past.

She has lost three children in the recent surge by North Vietnamese troops across the Central Highlands—a surge that resulted in the Government's decision to abandon most of the highlands and that has stirred terror among tens of thousands of South Vietnamese.

Ly Thi Van seems in shock. "Whenever we ask her a question she starts to cry," says her sister, Ly Thi Tinh, also a refugee from the Central Highlands town of Ban Me Thuot. "We don't talk about—" and she stopped and bit her lip and turned away.

The sisters are widows. Ly Thi Van's husband, a 34-year-old master sergeant named Bui Duc Hoan, died last year on a patrol in the highlands.

The husband of Ly Thi Tinh, also an enlisted man, was killed in the highlands in 1966. The 33-year-old woman has a son of 10. The two women, carrying bundles of clothes, pots and photographs came to Saigon the other morning to stay briefly with an uncle.

Both women have lived for years in Ban Me Thuot, a pleasant town of Vietnamese and Chinese shopkeepers, of farmers, montagnard tribesmen, Italian and French coffee planters and American missionaries. They lived next to each other in thatch-roofed homes near the sector command post, working as rice venders and collecting widows' pensions of about $80 every three months.

Last week the North Vietnamese began their fierce rocket

and tank attack on the sleepy town, an attack that was part of the Communist advance across the highlands.

"We didn't know what to do," said Ly Thi Tinh in Vietnamese. "We picked up everything in bags and ran to the neighbor's home. Everyone was crying. What to do? What to do?

"We ran to the airstrip where there were helicopters. We closed our eyes. We did not want to open them. Everywhere there were bodies, there were shells flying all over. I knew I would die."

At a crossroads leading to the airstrip the fighting was so intense that the women and their children turned back, ran through alleyways and hid on a rubber plantation with hundreds of other refugees. Their fears were compounded because many were widows and families of South Vietnamese soldiers, and others were refugees from North Vietnam who came south in 1954. "Everyone was sure we would die," she repeated.

In the confusion and panic that followed, the two sisters and their family split up. Ly Thi Van and her five children—ranging in age from 18 months to 15 years—began their flight from Ban Me Thuot with hundreds of others, dashing east along a road crammed with refugees.

About three miles out, the family boarded a packed bus bound for Phuoc An, 30 miles east, on Route 21. Somewhere along the route—Ly Thi Van can barely speak about the incident—the bus and trucks were halted at a roadblock set up by the Vietcong.

Speaking in a murmur, she said: "We saw other buses stop, too. There were three VC on the road and many hidden in the jungle, many, many VC. All of a sudden we heard planes overhead. The VC became panicky. Everybody became panicky. One VC in the jungle yelled, 'Open fire.' Another VC near the buses said 'No, don't fire, everyone's a civilian.'

"There was a mistake, I don't know what happened," said the 36-year-old woman. "There were explosions all around, the bus exploded. People began firing at us." Her voice trailed off.

In the moments that followed, she saw the charred body of her 5-year-old son beside the bus. Clutching her infant, Ly

Thi Van saw her groaning 9-year-old son on the ground. She picked up the boy and began running.

"All the way he was crying," she said. "All the way he said that his chest was burning. Oh my God! What could I do? Then he stopped crying. I looked at him. His lips were getting darker and darker and darker, and he died."

A third child, a teen-age boy, is missing and presumed dead. The woman buried the 9-year-old with the help of montagnard tribesmen who fed her and the infant and took them to the district capital of Phuoc An. There the sisters were reunited. Ly Thi Tinh, her child and a wounded uncle spent about three days walking the 30 miles from Ban Me Thuot to Phuoc An.

"It was a miracle," she said. "We stayed at the airfield in Phuoc An and we met a helicopter pilot, a friend of my husband from Ban Me Thuot. He took us to Nha Trang by helicopter."

From Nha Trang, a city on the South China Sea 200 miles northeast of Saigon, the women and their children flew to Saigon. "We asked for money, we begged for money and people helped us," said Ly Thi Tinh. "You sometimes meet good people."

The women lost their savings, their jewelry, the documents enabling them to collect war-widow pensions. "Everything went up in smoke, everything," said Ly Thi Tinh. Her sister, gripping the infant, trembled and groaned and began to weep.

The New York Times, March 19, 1975

A Flight Into Hell

by Paul Vogle

DA NANG, March 29 (UPI)—Only the fastest, the strongest, and the meanest of a huge mob got a ride on the last plane from Da Nang Saturday.

People died trying to get aboard and others died when they fell thousands of feet into the sea because even desperation could no longer keep their fingers welded to the undercarriage.

It was a flight into hell, and only a good tough American pilot and a lot of prayers got us back to Tan Son Nhut air base alive—with the Boeing 727 flaps jammed and the wheels fully extended.

It all started simply enough. I asked World Airways Vice President, Charles Patterson, if he had anything going to Da Nang. He said, "Get on that truck and you've got yourself a ride."

It was a ride I'll never forget.

World Airways President Ed Daly was aboard. He was angry and tired. Daly said he had been up all night arguing with American and Vietnamese officials for permission to fly into besieged Da Nang to get some more refugees out.

Daly finally said to hell with paperwork, clearances, and caution, and we were on our way.

It seemed peaceful enough as we touched down at the airport 370 miles northeast of Saigon.

Over a thousand people had been waiting around a quonset hut several hundred yards away from where we touched down.

Suddenly it was a mob in motion. They roared across the tarmac on motorbikes, Jeeps, Lambretta scooters, and on legs speeded by sheer desperation and panic.

Ed Daly and I stood near the bottom of the 727's tail ramp. Daly held out his arms while I shouted in Vietnamese, "One at a time, one at a time. There's room for everybody."

There wasn't room for everybody and everybody knew damn well there wasn't.

Daly and I were knocked aside and backward.

If Ed Daly thought he'd get some women and children out of Da Nang, he was wrong. The plane was jammed in an instant with troops of the 1st Division's meanest unit, the Hac Bao (Black Panthers).

They literally ripped the clothes right off Daly along with some of his skin. I saw one of them kick an old woman in the face to get aboard.

In the movies somebody would have shot the bastard and helped the old lady on the plane. This was no movie. The bastard flew and the old lady was tumbling down the tarmac, her fingers clawing toward a plane that was already rolling.

A British television cameraman who flew up with us made the mistake of getting off the plane when we landed, to shoot the loading.

He could not get back aboard in the pandemonium. In the very best tradition of the business he threw his camera with its precious film into the closing door and stood there and watched the plane take off.

We heard later that an Air America helicopter picked him up and carried him to safety.

As we started rolling, insanity gripped those who had missed the last chance. Government troops opened fire on us. Somebody lobbed a hand grenade towards the wing. The explosion jammed the flaps full open and the undercarriage in full extension.

Communist rockets began exploding at a distance.

Our pilot, Ken Healy, 52, of Oakland, Calif., slammed the throttles open and lurched into the air from the taxiway. There was no way we could have survived the gunfire and got onto the main runway.

A backup 727 had flown behind us but had been ordered not to land when the panic broke out. He radioed that he could see the legs of people hanging down from the undercarriage of our plane.

UPI photographer Lien Huong, who was in the cockpit of that backup plane, saw at least one person lose his grip on life and plummet into the South China Sea below.

There were 268 or more people jammed into the cabin of the little 727 limping down the coast.

Only two women and one baby among them. The rest were soldiers, toughest of the tough, meanest of the mean. They proved it today. They were out. They said nothing. They didn't talk to each other or us. They looked at the floor.

I saw one of them had a clip of ammunition and asked him to give it to me. He handed it over. As I walked up the aisle with the clip, other soldiers started loading my arms with clips of ammunition, pistols, hand grenades. They didn't need them anymore. In the cockpit we wrapped the weapons and ammo in electrical tape.

There was no more fight left in the Black Panthers this day.

They had gone from humans to animals and now they were vegetables.

We flew down the coast, the backup plane behind us all the way. Healy circled Phan Rang air base 165 miles northeast of Saigon, hoping to put down for an emergency landing.

On the backup plane Lien Huong served as interpreter, radioing Phan Rang control tower that the Boeing had to land there in an emergency. The reply came back that there was no fire fighting equipment at Phan Rang so Healy aimed the plane for Tan Son Nhut.

I heard Healy on the radio, telling Tan Son Nhut, "I've got control problems." The backup plane was shepherding us in.

Huong, in the cockpit of the backup plane, told me later when we touched down safe the pilot and cabin crew on his plane pulled off their headphones, some of them crossed themselves, and all thanked God for a small miracle delivered this Easter weekend.

When we touched down the troops who had stormed us were offloaded and put under arrest. They deserved it.

A mangled body of one soldier, M16 rifle still strapped to his shoulder, was retrieved from the undercarriage. He got his ride to Saigon, but being dead in Saigon is just the same as being dead in Da Nang.

Over a score of others came out of the baggage compartment, cold but alive. Somebody told me that four others crawled out of the wheel wells alive. One died.

The last plane from Da Nang was one hell of a ride. For me. For Ed Daly. For Ken Healy. For the Black Panthers. And for two women and a baby.

But the face that remains is that of the old woman lying flat on the tarmac seeing hope, seeing life itself, just off the end of her fingertips and rolling the other way.

UPI dispatch, March 29, 1975

For Those Who Flee, Life Is "Hell on Earth"

by Le Kim Dinh

SAIGON, South Vietnam, April 1—Cam Ranh Bay, one of the most picturesquely beautiful places on the South China Sea, has become a hell on earth for the hundred thousand or more refugees who have arrived there from Da Nang and also from the whole central part of the country.

Today, they are scarcely safer than when they fled; they are starving and gasping from thirst.

Cam Ranh Bay, one of the best deep-water ports in Asia, was the main United States logistical base in Vietnam.

Some of the refugees had paid as much as $1,200 to get to Cam Ranh from the dying city of Da Nang.

At Cam Ranh, I found, money does not matter. Fortunes are stolen by some, and these are robbed by others. Piasters, gold, diamonds, bits of priceless family treasure—none of it means anything in comparison with the need to survive.

At Cam Ranh, the suffering of the civilians was far and away the worst, with babies dying on ships or ashore, with the body of an old man lying ignored all day at a pier. But the ragged remnants of the South Vietnamese forces there have their ordeal, too.

The general morale has not been buoyed by the fact that many senior officials of Military Region II have left Cam Ranh for Saigon.

The chaotic situation was alleviated somewhat by the arrival from Saigon of some shock troops, whose specialty is combat reconnaissance. They were sent in to protect the Vietnamese naval training center, the headquarters of Military Region II and the main airport.

But there were clashes between these troops and many marines and rangers who came here from Da Nang. Many of those men became bandits after they discarded rifles, equipment, ammunition and even their uniforms to swim out to the barges and other boats off the dying city.

For the last day or so there have been pitched battles between the shock troops and the men from Da Nang. All through the night last night shots rang out in Cam Ranh, some from the military men, some from looters shooting their way into buildings.

The marines scarcely seem to exist any longer as a military force.

The shock troops themselves have been doing some stealing. They have been seizing loot from the "renegades," as they call the men from the north, as they find it. Bags of money, radios, gold and other valuables taken from the bandits have been piled up near the gate of the naval center and some of the loot has been stolen once more—by the shock troops.

On a street near Cam Ranh Bay today a major recognized a captain and shouted, "Do you know where the colonel is?"

The captain replied, "I think I saw him on a fishing boat. Maybe he made it."

A lieutenant colonel who had commanded an armored brigade said, "I am not sure how many tanks and armored personnel carriers we lost, and I am not sure how many of my men succeeded in getting aboard.

"Let's not talk about it," he added. "I am exhausted and worried and I don't know where my wife is."

This morning there were 11 ships in Cam Ranh Bay waiting to unload their bedraggled cargoes of soldiers and civilians. They had been at sea two days or more.

Two small ships carried rich civilians who had paid one million piasters ($1,200) per person to come from Da Nang to Saigon, only to be told they would not be permitted to go beyond Cam Ranh Bay.

Most of them remained on the ships suffering terribly from hunger and thirst, rather than face the horrors on shore.

It was said that Saigon authorities were not willing to permit a flood of refugees into the capital, and had therefore ordered the navy to prevent the civilian ships from going farther. But some said it was just a question of money.

"When they are willing to pay another one million piasters per person, then those ships will set sail for Saigon," a military man said.

No one has any clear idea how many have died. Bodies eventually just disappear. One wealthy man is said to have been murdered on shipboard in front of his wife, and his body was thrown overboard. Four babies were reported trampled to death on another ship.

There are no Americans at Cam Ranh, and there is no help in the form of transport planes or helicopters.

For nearly everyone who traveled so far to get here, this appeared to be the end of the line—waiting and listening for the approaching rumble of North Vietnamese tanks.

The New York Times, April 2, 1975

The Battle of Xuan Loc

by Philip Caputo

One small act in a bloody drama—
S. Viet Rangers prove they can fight

Hung Loc, Viet Nam—If a trademark could be stamped on the five-week-old Communist offensive in Viet Nam, it would look something like the scene around this deserted village on Highway One, the main road to Saigon from the north.

It was the second day of a North Vietnamese army attack on Xuan Loc, a provincial capital eight miles away and the first large city in the Saigon area to feel the brunt of the North Vietnamese advance.

Dug into the slope of a hill, a South Vietnamese tank was pumping shells into the village, where a North Viet Nam commando unit had set up positions the night before in what seemed to be an attempt to cut the road and prevent supplies and reinforcements from reaching the government division at Xuan Loc.

As the Patton tank's 90 mms struck home, plumes of dirty, yellow smoke rose thru dense clumps of palm that concealed all but the red-tile roofs of the village huts.

Shells from a South Vietnamese artillery battery miles to the rear went overhead with a sound like ripping silk and slammed into a wooded hill where an antiaircraft gun was thought to be emplaced.

Behind the tank were a few armored personnel carriers, their radio antennae swaying in the hot breeze like steel reeds, and a platoon of South Vietnamese Rangers, green flak jackets over their camouflage uniforms. They were to assault the village when the shelling lifted.

"The North Vietnamese moved in last night and they're well dug in," one of the Rangers said. "We don't know how many, but they're in there in strength. If we don't dislodge them, they'll cut the road and nothing will be able to move up to Xuan Loc."

The sound of the battle for the provincial capital was audible—a hollow, menacing rumbling that sounded like an enormous oil drum rolling thru a tunnel. As the South and North Vietnamese heavy guns exchanged fire, jets of black smoke spouted from the ridgeline overlooking the city.

There, according to reports in Saigon, the South Vietnamese 18th Division had repelled armor and infantry assaults by the North Vietnamese 6th Division.

But the North Vietnamese had shelled the city remorselessly —2,000 rounds on Tuesday, another 1,000 early Wednesday—and they were said to be bringing up reinforcements. It was, therefore, still a question whether the 18th could hold, especially if North Vietnamese commandos like those here cut the division's supply and communications lines.

For the moment, tho, the South Vietnamese army appears to be pulling itself together after the catastrophic defeats of last month.

The Ranger platoon around Hung Loc even managed a few smiles and thumbs-up signs as the barrage lifted and their armored personnel carriers clattered forward.

The road ahead was empty. Shimmering in the heat, it wound the 500 yards down to the village like an asphalt river upon which floated old shell casings, fragments of barbed wire coils, empty canvas bandoliers—the junk of war.

This reporter and a British correspondent moved at a safe distance behind the personnel carriers, which turned into the undergrowth at the town's edge. Within moments a barrage of communist 82 mm mortars crashed around them.

The Rangers, apparently without casualties, dismounted and vanished into the trees. A brisk, running fight took place. Machine guns and rifles stuttered, punctuated by the crumps of the incoming mortars. Given the rout of South Vietnamese forces last month, we half-expected to see the Rangers come fleeing out. But they continued the attack.

Of course, too much should not be made out of the performance of a single platoon in a small-unit road-clearing operation. The North Vietnamese have yet to commit the full weight of their forces in the battle for Xuan Loc, and the commandos dug into this village showed the Communists usual ability to fight stubbornly and well under heavy fire.

If there has indeed been an improvement in the South Vietnamese army's fighting abilities, there is one feature of the current offensive's trademark which has not changed. On the road behind Hung Loc leading to Bien Hoa were thousands of new refugees from Xuan Loc.

They moved in ragged columns down the sticky macadam, women bent beneath shoulder poles with heavily laden baskets at each end, boys on motor bikes, mothers clutching infants to their breasts, old men whose seamed faces peered impassively from behind the brims of their cork sun-helmets, peasants wearing conical straw hats jammed into the backs of sputtering, smoke-belching Lambrettas.

The only difference from the March retreats was that these people moved without panic, tho soldiers sometimes had to fire their rifles as the refugees pressed, like a human stream, against the roadblocks that dammed their flight.

Chicago Tribune, April 11, 1975

S. Viets take skeleton of city

XUAN LOC, South Viet Nam—Col. Le Xuan Hieu, commander of the 40th Regiment of South Viet Nam's 18th Division and an officer whose slang reflects his American training, stood in what was left of his headquarters and told war correspondents Sunday that this devastated city was now fully in South Vietnamese hands.

"This morning they attacked," Hieu said while North Vietnamese shells were bursting not 500 yards away. "No sweat. We've chased the VC [Viet Cong] 2,000 meters away from here.

"This morning they attacked again with 12 tanks, but we drove them off, burned two tanks, and damaged several others, no sweat."

The colonel then took newsmen on a tour of the city to demonstrate that no North Vietnamese troops remained in it. Not much else remained, either.

In the last five days, this provincial capital—which can be

considered a gateway to Saigon—has been struck by 6,000 enemy shells, a bombardment of World War II proportions.

It is still under fire. As the newsmen approached its outskirts, a steady barrage of rockets and mortars was slamming into the marketplace, sending a pall of black smoke and red dust over the collapsed roofs of what once were the homes of thousands of people.

They are likely to consider the army's victory here—its first since the Communist offensive began six weeks ago—a dubious one. Almost every building has been damaged, and the town center reduced to rubble.

The streets are pocked with craters, gouged out of the asphalt by the 130-millimeter shells that come whistling in from the green, brooding hills to the north.

What once were houses are now heaps of pulverized stone and charred timbers. The market, its tin-roofed stalls twisted into weird shapes, looks like a junk yard, and the bus station, where the initial fighting took place, is recognizable as such only by the blackened skeletons of a few buses.

Even the Catholic church steeple has not escaped. Like the ruin of some ancient tower, it looks over the wreckage, over the flames licking at the walls of a house struck by a shell minutes before, and over the corpses, bloated and rotting in the sun, of North Vietnamese soldiers that lay here and there in the odd positions of death.

"It looks like a city from the Second World War," said one South Vietnamese soldier.

The physical destruction aside, the 18th division's successful action here since Wednesday has given the Saigon government a much-needed morale boost. During the several hours the correspondents spent in Xuan Loc, not a single round of Communist small arms fire was heard, demonstrating that the city and its immediate surrounding area were under government control.

Brig. Gen. Le Minh Dao, commander of the 18th division, told newsmen the equivalent of two North Vietnamese divisions are in the Xuan Loc area and three regiments have made six separate assaults on the city.

"But we repulsed them, we killed and captured many," Gen. Dao told newsmen at his field headquarters in a rubber plantation outside Xuan Loc. He said at least six Communist T-54 tanks have been destroyed and enemy armor can no longer approach the city.

"I will hold Long Khanh [the province of which Xuan Loc is capital]. Even if they bring three divisions here, it is no problem," the general said. "I will knock them down."

Gen. Dao revealed that the North Vietnamese have used long-range 130-millimeter guns in bombarding Xuan Loc. It was previously thought the Communists did not have heavy artillery in the region. With a range of 16 miles, the 130 could cause grave problems to Saigon if the Communists ever break thru the 18th.

Besides the obvious fighting qualities of the veteran 18th, one of the reasons for the North Vietnamese lack of success here appears to be the inexperience of the troops it sent into the battle.

Nguyen Dan Thanh, 19, one of the North Vietnamese prisoners being held at divisional headquarters, said he had not seen combat since his company came to South Viet Nam by truck a year ago.

Nevertheless, the South Vietnamese hold on the city remains tenuous. Highway 1 between Xuan Loc and Bein Hoa province is cut, preventing reinforcements and supplies by road, at least three more enemy regiments are in the wooded hills nearby, and it is possible they could be used in a concerted, divisional assault.

There also seems to be an underlying instability in the South Vietnamese army even in moments of success.

At the helicopter pad from which the newsmen were lifted out of the battle zone, a chaotic scene was enacted as soldiers and refugees scrambled to climb on board.

Severely wounded men were totally ignored. This correspondent had to help carry two of them to the choppers. As I lifted the stretcher, two rangers pushed against me in their desperation to get on and started to shove the casualty outside, apparently deaf to his groans.

I had to pull one of the rangers away and punch the other before we were able to evacuate the wounded man.

One wondered how such troops will behave should events at Xuan Loc take a turn for the worse.

The Fall of Phnom Penh

by Sydney H. Schanberg

Cambodia Reds Are Uprooting Millions as They Impose a 'Peasant Revolution'

BANGKOK, Thailand, May 8—The victorious Cambodian Communists, who marched into Phnom Penh on April 17 and ended five years of war in Cambodia, are carrying out a peasant revolution that has thrown the entire country into upheaval.

Perhaps as many as three or four million people, most of them on foot, have been forced out of the cities and sent on a mammoth and grueling exodus into areas deep in the countryside where, the Communists say, they will have to become peasants and till the soil.

No one has been excluded—even the very old, the very young, the sick and the wounded have been forced out onto the roads—and some will clearly not be strong enough to survive.

The old economy of the cities has been abandoned, and for the moment money means nothing and cannot be spent. Barter has replaced it.

All shops have either been looted by Communist soldiers for such things as watches and transistor radios, or their goods have been taken away in an organized manner to be stored as communal property.

Even the roads that radiate out of the capital and that carried the nation's commerce have been virtually abandoned, and the population living along the roads, as well as that in all cities and towns that remained under the control of the American-backed Government, has been pushed into the interior. Apparently the areas into which the evacuees are being herded are at least 65 miles from Phnom Penh.

In sum the new rulers—before their overwhelming victory they were known as the Khmer Rouge—appear to be remaking Cambodian society in the peasant image, casting aside everything that belonged to the old system, which was generally dominated by the cities and towns and by the élite and merchants who lived there.

Foreigners and foreign aid are not wanted—at least not for now. It is even unclear how much influence the Chinese and North Vietnamese will have, despite their considerable aid to the Cambodian insurgents against the Government of Marshal Lon Nol. The new authorities seem determined to do things themselves in their own way. Despite the propaganda terminology and other trappings, such as Mao caps and Ho Chi Minh rubber-tire sandals, which remind one of Peking and Hanoi, the Communists seem fiercely independent and very Cambodian.

Judging from their present actions, it seems possible that they may largely isolate their country of perhaps seven million people from the rest of the world for a considerable time—at least until the period of upheaval is over, the agrarian revolution takes concrete shape and they are ready to show their accomplishments to foreigners.

Some of the party officials in Phnom Penh also talked about changing the capital to a more traditional and rural town like Siem Reap, in the northwest.

For those foreigners, including this correspondent, who stayed behind to observe the take-over, the events were an astonishing spectacle.

In Phnom Penh two million people suddenly moved out of the city en masse in stunned silence—walking, bicycling, pushing cars that had run out of fuel, covering the roads like a human carpet, bent under sacks of belongings hastily thrown together when the heavily armed peasant soldiers came and told them to leave immediately, everyone dispirited and frightened by the unknown that awaited them and many plainly terrified because they were soft city people and were sure the trip would kill them.

Hospitals jammed with wounded were emptied, right down to the last patient. They went—limping, crawling, on crutches, carried on relatives' backs, wheeled on their hospital beds.

The Communists have few doctors and meager medical supplies, so many of these patients had little chance of surviving. On April 17, the day this happened, Phnom Penh's biggest hospital had over 2,000 patients and there were several thousand more in other hospitals; many of the wounded were dying for lack of care.

A once-throbbing city became an echo chamber of silent streets lined with abandoned cars and gaping, empty shops. Streetlights burned eerily for a population that was no longer there.

The end of the old and the start of the new began early in the morning of the 17th. At the cable office the line went dead for mechanical reasons at 6 A.M. On the previous day, amid heavy fighting, the Communist-led forces had taken the airport a few miles west of the city, and during the night they had pressed to the capital's edges, throwing in rockets and shells at will.

Thousands of new refugees and fleeing soldiers were filling the heart of the capital, wandering aimlessly, looking for shelter, as they awaited the city's imminent collapse.

Everyone—Cambodians and foreigners alike—thought this had to be Phnom Penh's most miserable hour after long days of fear and privation as the Communist forces drew closer. They looked ahead with hopeful relief to the collapse of the city, for they felt that when the Communists came and the war finally ended, at least the suffering would largely be over. All of us were wrong.

That view of the future of Cambodia—as a possibly flexible place even under Communism, where changes would not be extreme and ordinary folk would be left alone—turned out to be a myth.

American officials had described the Communists as indecisive and often ill-coordinated, but they turned out to be firm, determined, well-trained, tough and disciplined.

The Americans had also said that the rebel army was badly riddled by casualties, forced to fill its ranks by hastily impressing young recruits from the countryside and throwing them into the front lines with only a few days' training. The thousands of troops we saw both in the countryside and in Phnom Penh, while they included women soldiers and boy militia, some of whom seemed no more than 10 years old, looked healthy, well organized, heavily armed and well trained.

Another prediction made by the Americans was that the Communists would carry out a bloodbath once they took over—massacring as many as 20,000 high officials and intellectuals. There have been unconfirmed reports of executions of senior military and civilian officials, and no one who witnessed the take-over doubts that top people of the old regime will be or have been punished and perhaps killed or that a large number of people will die of the hardships on the march into the countryside. But none of this will apparently bear any resemblance to the mass executions that had been predicted by Westerners.

[In a news conference Tuesday President Ford reiterated reports—he termed them "hard intelligence"—that 80 to 90 Cambodian officials and their wives had been executed.]

On the first day, as the sun was rising, a short swing by automobile to the northern edge of the city showed soldiers and refugees pouring in. The northern defense line had obviously collapsed.

By the time I reached the Hotel Le Phnom and climbed the two flights of stairs to my room, the retreat could be clearly seen from my window and small-arms fire could be heard in the city. At 6:30 A.M. I wrote in my notebook: "The city is falling."

Over the next couple of hours there were periodic exchanges of fire as the Communists encountered pockets of resistance. But most Government soldiers were busy preparing to surrender and welcome the Communists, as were civilians. White flags suddenly sprouted from housetops and from armored personnel carriers, which resemble tanks.

Some soldiers were taking the clips out of their rifles; others were changing into civilian clothes. Some Government office workers were hastily donning the black pajama-like clothes worn by Indochinese Communists.

Shortly before 9 A.M. the first rebel troops approached the hotel, coming from the north down Monivong Boulevard. A crowd of soldiers and civilians, including newsmen, churned forth to greet them—cheering and applauding and embracing and linking arms to form a phalanx as they came along.

The next few hours saw quite a bit of this celebrating, though shooting continued here and there, some of it only a few hundred yards from the hotel. Civilians and Buddhist monks and troops on both sides rode around town—in jeeps, atop personnel carriers and in cars—shouting happily.

Most civilians stayed nervously indoors, however, not yet sure what was going on or who was who. What was the fighting inside the city all about? they wondered; was it between diehard Government troops and the Communists or between rival Communist factions fighting over the spoils? Or was it mostly exuberance?

Some of these questions, including the nature of the factionalism, have still not been answered satisfactorily, but on that first day such mysteries quickly became academic, for within a few hours, the mood changed.

The cheerful and pleasant troops we first encountered—we came to call them the soft troops, and we learned later that they were discredited and disarmed, with their leader declared a traitor; they may not even have been authentic—were swiftly displaced by battle-hardened soldiers.

While some of these were occasionally friendly, or at least not hostile, they were also all business. Dripping with arms like overladen fruit trees—grenades, pistols, rifles, rockets—they immediately began clearing the city of civilians.

Using loudspeakers, or simply shouting and brandishing weapons, they swept through the streets, ordering people out of their houses. At first we thought the order applied only to the rich in villas, but we quickly saw that it was for everyone as the streets became clogged with a sorrowful exodus.

Cars stalled or their tires went flat, and they were abandoned. People lost their sandals in the jostling and pushing, so they lay as a reminder of the throng that had passed.

In the days to follow, during the foreign colony's confinement in the French Embassy compound, we heard reports on international news broadcasts that the Communists had evacuated the city by telling people the United States was about to bomb it. However, all the departing civilians I talked with said they had been given no reason except that the city had to be reorganized. They were told they had to go far from Phnom Penh.

In almost every situation we encountered during the more than two weeks we were under Communist control, there was a sense of split vision—whether to look at events through Western eyes or through what we thought might be Cambodian revolutionary eyes.

Was this just cold brutality, a cruel and sadistic imposition of the law of the jungle, in which only the fittest will survive? Or is it possible that, seen through the eyes of the peasant soldiers and revolutionaries, the forced evacuation of the cities is a harsh necessity? Perhaps they are convinced that there is no way to build a new society for the benefit of the ordinary man, hitherto exploited, without literally starting from the beginning; in such an unbending view people who represent the old ways and those considered weak or unfit would be expendable and would be weeded out. Or was the policy both cruel and ideological?

A foreign doctor offered this explanation for the expulsion of the sick and wounded from the hospital: "They could not cope with all the patients—they do not have the doctors—so they apparently decided to throw them all out and blame any deaths on the old regime. That way they could start from scratch medically."

Some Western observers considered that the exodus approached genocide. One of them, watching from his refuge in the French Embassy compound, said: "They are crazy! This is pure and simple genocide. They will kill more people this way than if there had been hand-to-hand fighting in the city."

Another foreign doctor, who had been forced at gunpoint to abandon a seriously wounded patient in midoperation, added in a dark voice: "They have not got a humanitarian thought in their heads!"

Whatever the Communists' purpose, the exodus did not grow heavy until dusk, and even then onlookers were slow to realize that the people were being forcibly evacuated.

For my own part, I had a problem that preoccupied me that afternoon: I, with others, was held captive and threatened with execution.

After our release, we went to the Information Ministry because we had heard about a broadcast directing high officials of the old regime to report there. When we arrived, about 50 prisoners were standing outside the building, among them Lon Non, the younger brother of President Lon Nol, who went into exile on April 1, and Brig. Gen. Chim Chhuon, who was close to the former President. Other generals and Cabinet ministers were also there—very nervous but trying to appear untroubled.

Premier Long Boret, who the day before had made an offer of surrender with certain conditions only to have it immediately rejected, arrived at the ministry an hour later. He is one of the seven "traitors" the Communists had marked for execution. The others had fled except for Lieut. Gen. Sisowath Sirik Matak, a former Premier, who some days later was removed from the French Embassy, where he had taken refuge.

Mr. Long Boret's eyes were puffy and red, almost down to slits. He had probably been up all night and perhaps he had been weeping. His wife and two children were also still in the country; later they sought refuge at the French Embassy, only to be rejected as persons who might "compromise" the rest of the refugees.

Mr. Long Boret, who had talked volubly and articulately on the telephone the night before, had difficulty speaking coherently. He could only mumble yes, no and thank you, so conversation was impossible.

There is still no hard information on what has happened to him. Most people who have talked with the Communists believe it a certainty that he will be executed, if indeed the execution has not already taken place.

One of the Communist leaders at the Information Ministry that day—probably a general, though his uniform bore no markings and he declined to give his name—talked soothingly to the 50 prisoners. He assured them that there were only seven traitors and that other officials of the old regime would be dealt with equitably. "There will be no reprisals," he said. Their strained faces suggested that they would like to believe him but did not.

As he talked, a squad crouched in combat-ready positions around him, almost as if it was guarding him against harm.

The officer, who appeared no more than age 35, agreed to chat with foreign newsmen. His tone was polite and sometimes he smiled, but everything he said suggested that we, as foreigners, meant nothing to him and that our interests were alien to his.

Asked about the fate of the 20 or so foreign journalists missing in Cambodia since the early days of the war, he said he had heard nothing. Asked if we would be permitted to file from the cable office, he smiled sympathetically and said, "We will resolve all problems in their proper order."

Clearly an educated man, he almost certainly speaks French, the language of the nation that ruled Cambodia for nearly a century until the nineteen-fifties, but he gave no hint of this colonial vestige, speaking only in Khmer through an interpreter.

In the middle of the conversation he volunteered quite unexpectedly: "We would like you to give our thanks to the American people who have helped us and supported us from the beginning, and to all people of the world who love peace and justice. Please give this message to the world."

Noting that Congress had halted aid to the Phnom Penh Government, he said, "The purpose was to stop the war," but he quickly added: "Our struggle would not have stopped even if they had given more aid."

Attempts to find out more about who he was and about political and military organization led only to imprecision. The officer said: "I represent the armed forces. There are many divisions. I am one of the many."

Asked if there were factions, he said there was only one political organization and one government. Some top political and governmental leaders are not far from the city, he added, but they let the military enter first "to organize things."

Most military units, he said, are called "rumdos," which means "liberation forces." Neither this commander nor any of the soldiers we talked with ever called themselves Communists or Khmer Rouge (Red Cambodians). They always said they were liberation troops or nationalist troops and called one another brother or the Khmer equivalent of comrade.

The nomenclature at least is confusing, for Western intelligence had described the Khmer Rumdos as a faction loyal to Prince Norodom Sihanouk that was being downgraded by Hanoi-trained Cambodians and losing power.

The Communists named the Cambodian leader, who was deposed by Marshal Lon Nol in 1970 and has been living in exile in Peking, as their figurehead chief of state, but none of the soldiers we talked with brought up his name.

One over-all impression emerged from our talk with the commander at the Information Ministry: The military will be largely in charge of the early stages of the upheaval, carrying out the evacuation, organizing the new agrarian program, searching for hidden arms and resisters, repairing damaged bridges.

The politicians—or so it seemed from all the evidence during our stay—have for the moment taken a rear seat. No significant political or administrative apparatus was yet visible; it did not seem to be a government yet, but an army.

The radio announced April 28 that a special national congress attended by over 300 delegates was held in Phnom Penh from April 25 to 27. It was said to have been chaired by the Deputy Premier and military commander, Khieu Samphan, who has emerged—at least in public announcements—as the top leader. Despite that meeting the military still seemed to be running things as we emerged from Cambodia on Saturday.

One apparent reason is that politicians and bureaucrats are not equipped to do the dirty work and arduous tasks of the early phases of reorganization. Another is that the military, as indicated in conversations with Khmer-speaking foreigners they trusted somewhat, seemed worried that politicians or soft-living outsiders in their movement might steal the victory and dilute it. There could be severe power struggles ahead.

After leaving the prisoners and the military commander at the ministry, we headed for the Hotel Le Phnom, where another surprise was waiting. The day before, the Red Cross turned the hotel into a protected international zone and draped it with huge Red Cross flags. But the Communists were not interested.

At 4:55 P.M. troops waving guns and rockets had forced their way into the grounds and ordered the hotel emptied within 30 minutes. By the time we arrived 25 minutes had elapsed. The fastest packing job in history ensued. I even had time to "liberate" a typewriter someone had abandoned since the troops had "liberated" mine earlier.

We were the last ones out, running. The Red Cross had abandoned several vehicles in the yard after removing the keys, so several of us threw our gear on the back of a Red Cross Honda pickup truck and started pushing it up the boulevard toward the French Embassy.

Several days before, word was passed to those foreigners who stayed behind when the Americans pulled out on April 12 that, as a last resort, one could take refuge at the embassy. France had recognized the new government, and it was thought that the new Cambodian leaders would respect the embassy compound as a sanctuary.

As we plodded up the road, big fires were burning on the city's outskirts, sending smoke clouds into the evening sky like a giant funeral wreath encircling the capital.

The embassy was only several hundred yards away, but what was happening on the road made it seem much farther. All around us people were fleeing, for there was no refuge for them. And coming into the city from the other direction was a fresh battalion marching in single file. They looked curiously at us; we looked nervously at them.

In the 13 days of confinement that followed, until our evacuation by military truck to the Thai border, we had only a peephole onto what was going on outside, but there were still many things that could be seen and many clues to the revolution that was going on.

We could hear shooting, sometimes nearby but mostly in other parts of the city. Often it sounded like shooting in the air, but at other times it seemed like small battles. As on the day of the city's fall we were never able to piece together a satisfactory explanation of the shooting, which died down after about a week.

We could see smoke from the huge fires from time to time, and there were reports from foreigners who trickled into the embassy that certain quarters were badly burned and that the water-purification plant was heavily damaged.

The foreigners who for various reasons came in later carried stories, some of them eyewitness accounts, of such things as civilian bodies along the roads leading out of the city—people who had apparently died of illness or exhaustion on the march. But each witness got only a glimpse, and no reliable estimate of the toll was possible.

Reports from roads to the south and southeast of Phnom Penh said the Communists were breaking up families by dividing the refugees by sex and age. Such practices were not reported from other roads on which the refugees flooded out of the capital.

Reports also told of executions, but none were eyewitness accounts. One such report said high military officers were executed at a rubber plantation a couple of miles north of the city.

In the French Embassy compound foreign doctors and relief agency officials were pessimistic about the survival chances of many of the refugees. "There's no food in the countryside at this time of year," an international official said. "What will they eat from now until the rice harvest in November?"

The new Communist officials, in conversations with United Nations and other foreign representatives during our confinement and in statements since, have rejected the idea of foreign aid, "whether it is military, political, economic, social, diplomatic, or whether it takes on a so-called humanitarian form." Some foreign observers wondered whether this included China, for they speculated that the Communists would at least need seed to plant for the next harvest.

Whether the looting we observed before we entered the French compound continued is difficult to say. In any case, it is essential to understand who the Communist soldiers are to understand the behavior of some of them in disciplinary matters, particularly looting.

They are peasant boys, pure and simple—darker skinned than their city brethren, with gold in their front teeth. To them the city is a curiosity, an oddity, a carnival, where you visit but do not live. The city means next to nothing in their scheme of things.

When they looted jewelry shops, they kept only one watch for themselves and gave the rest to their colleagues or passers-by. Transistor radios, cameras and cars held the same toy-like fascination—something to play with, as children might, but not essential.

From my airline bag on the day I was seized and threatened with execution they took only some cigarettes, a pair of boxer underwear shorts and a handkerchief. They passed up a blue shirt and $9,000 in cash in a money belt.

The looting did not really contradict the Communist image of rigid discipline, for commanders apparently gave no orders against the sacking of shops, feeling, perhaps, that this was the least due their men after five years of jungle fighting.

Often they would climb into abandoned cars and find that they would not run, so they would bang on them with their rifles like frustrated children, or they would simply toot the horns for hours on end or keep turning the headlights on and off until the batteries died.

One night at the French Embassy, I chose to sleep on the grass outside; I was suddenly awakened by what sounded like a platoon trying to smash down the front gates with a battering ram that had bright lights and a loud claxon. It was only a bunch of soldiers playing with and smashing up the cars that had been left outside the gates.

Though these country soldiers broke into villas all over the city and took the curious things they wanted—one walked past the embassy beaming proudly in a crimson-colored wool overcoat that hung down to his Ho Chi Minh sandals—they never stayed in the villas. With big, soft beds empty, they slept in the courtyards or the streets.

Almost without exception foot soldiers I talked with, when asked what they wanted to do, replied that they only wanted to go home.

The New York Times, May 9, 1975

American's Brief Brush with Arrest and Death

BANGKOK, Thailand, May 8—Some of the foreigners who stayed behind after the American evacuation of Phnom Penh learned quickly and at first hand that the Communist-led forces were not the happy-go-lucky troops we had seen in the initial stage of the Communist take-over.

I had my first experience with the tough Khmer Rouge troops early in the afternoon of the first day of the take-over.

With Dith Pran, a local employe of The New York Times, Jon Swain of The Sunday Times of London, Alan Rockoff, a freelance American photographer, and our driver, Sarun, we had gone to look at conditions in the largest civilian hospital, Preah Keth Mealea. Doctors and surgeons, out of fear, had failed to come to work and the wounded were bleeding to death in the corridors.

As we emerged from the operating block at 1 P.M. and started driving toward the front gate, we were confronted by a band of heavily armed troops just then coming into the grounds. They put guns to our heads and, shouting angrily, threatened us with execution. They took everything—cameras, radio, money, typewriters, the car—and ordered us into an armored personnel carrier, slamming the hatch and rear door shut. We thought we were finished.

But Mr. Dith Pran saved our lives, first by getting into the personnel carrier with us and then by talking soothingly to our captors for two and a half hours and finally convincing them that we were not their enemy but merely foreign newsmen covering their victory.

We are still not clear why they were so angry, but we believe it might have been because they were entering the hospital at that time to remove the patients and were startled to find us, for they wanted no foreign witnesses.

At one point they asked if any of us were Americans, and we said no, speaking French all the time and letting Mr. Dith Pran translate into Khmer. But if they had looked into the bags they had confiscated, which they did not, they would have found my passport and Mr. Rockoff's.

We spent a very frightened half-hour sweating in the baking personnel carrier, during a journey on which two more prisoners were picked up—Cambodians in civilian clothes who were high military officers and who were, if that is possible, even more frightened than we.

Then followed two hours in the open under guard at the northern edge of town while Mr. Dith Pran pulled off his miracle negotiation with our captors as we watched giddy soldiers passing with truckloads of looted cloth, wine, liquor, cigarettes and soft drinks, scattering some of the booty to soldiers along the roadside.

We were finally released at 3:30 P.M., but the two Cambodian military men were held. One was praying softly.

The New York Times, May 9, 1975

Grief and Animosity in an Embassy Haven

BANGKOK, Thailand, May 8—For the 800 foreigners, including this correspondent, who spent two weeks in the French Embassy in Phnom Penh after the Communists took over, the time seemed like a chaotically compressed generation of life.

A baby was born, another died. A dozen marriages were performed—all marriages of convenience to enable Cambodians to get French passports so that they could escape the country and its peasant revolution.

There were days of deep sorrow. Cambodians without foreign papers had to go on the trek into the countryside. Friends were torn apart. Families broke up as Cambodian husbands were separated from their European wives. On those days sobbing could be heard in every corner of the compound.

And there were days when hopes rose, days when the rumors said that evacuation was imminent.

Heroes and knaves emerged—more of the latter than the former. There was no running water and food was limited, and out of this grew tensions and rivalries between groups.

Between French officials living well in the embassy and French civilians living in the driveways and gardens outside. Between the outside French and the French staff of Calmette Hospital, who were also living fairly well. And between the non-French foreigners, including the favorite targets—Americans and journalists—and everyone else.

There was more selfishness than sharing. A minor example: Put a pack of cigarettes on a table for 10 seconds and turn around, and it would be gone.

The first convoy of foreigners who had taken refuge in the embassy for 13 days, including this correspondent, arrived in Thailand Saturday after three and a half days on the road.

Hundreds of other refugees remained in the embassy even longer and arrived in Thailand today.

To describe what life was like in the compound is to describe sheer incongruity. A French doctor walked the hospital's pet sheep around the gardens. (The hospital's pet gibbon was taken by the Communists and led around the street outside in a pink dress.) Some of the Frenchmen in the compound fed their dogs better than other people were able to feed their children.

Our group of foreigners lived in the building that used to be the ambassador's residence, one of three buildings on the grounds; the others are a chancellery and a large cultural center. Eighteen of us, using sofa cushions and pillows as mattresses and linen tablecloths for blankets, slept on the floor of a large living room—surrounded by humming air-conditioners, an elegant upright piano, a crystal chandelier and some of the embassy's best silver, except for the silver teapots, which were used to boil water over wood fires outside.

For a few days it might have been fun—a curious experience to dine on when you got home. But as time wore on, nerves frayed more and more and hardly an hour went by without an argument somewhere in the compound, usually over something petty.

The water supply ended a few days after our arrival, after which we had to rely on water tapped from our air-conditioners and that delivered periodically in barrels by the new Government. There was never enough for bathing, and the odor of unwashed people was ripe.

With food limited and with no running water, sanitation deteriorated and there were scores of cases of diarrhea—the evidence of which filled every walkway and garden in the compound.

The compound was difficult at times, but never as difficult as was suggested by the radio news reports we kept listening to, which said our situation was "more and more precarious." Sometimes when we were hearing those bulletins we were swilling Scotch and smoking long cigars.

Though some people managed not to fare too badly, for most of those in the compound the situation was far more than a series of annoyances; there was nothing funny about it.

There was nothing funny for Mrs. Nha, an Air France employe who sat sobbing under a tree on the morning of April 19. Her mother and father were missing, and in two days she would be forced to take her young son and go into the countryside herself.

"I was an optimist," she said as the tears coursed down her cheeks. "Not only me. All Cambodians here thought that when the Khmer Rouge came it would be all welcomes and cheering and bravo and the war would be over and we would become normal again. Now we are stunned, stunned."

There was nothing funny for Mrs. Praet, a Belgian whose Cambodian husband was being forced to leave her and join the march. As she wept into her handkerchief he embraced her gently. "Courage, ma cherie. Courage, ma cherie," he whispered. She could not control herself and her small body shook with her weeping as their two little girls looked on uncomprehending.

Some Cambodian women, realizing that their infants could not survive the long trek, tearfully gave theirs to French families for foster care or adoption.

"My first baby, my only baby!" a mother in shock shrieked. "Save him! Save him! You can do it."

It was raining as the Cambodians left. The hospital's sheep, tethered to a truck, was bleating mournfully; no one paid any attention.

At one time, about 1,300 people were living in the attractively landscaped compound, which is 200 yards by 250 yards or so. Then the Communists ordered out all Cambodians without foreign passports or papers, which forced about 500 people to take to the road.

Family or not, we all lost someone close to us, and when the Cambodians trudged through the gate we foreigners stood in the front yard, weeping unashamedly.

The forced evacuation was part of an apparent campaign to make it clear to Jean Dyrac, the consul and senior French official at the embassy, and to everyone else in the compound that the new Government, not foreigners, was in charge—and under its own rules.

The first thing the Communists did was declare that they did not recognize the compound as an embassy, simply as a regroupment center for foreigners under their control. This shattered the possibility of asylum for high officials of the ousted regime who had sought sanctuary. On the afternoon of April 20, in a gloomy drizzle, Lieut. Gen. Sirik Matak, who was among those marked for execution, and a few other leading figures were taken away in the back of a sanitation truck.

Throughout our stay the Communists continued their campaign of proving their primacy—refusing to let a French plane land with food and medical supplies, refusing to allow us to be evacuated in comfort by air instead of by rutted road in the back of military trucks, and, finally, shutting down the embassy radio transmitter, our only contact with the outside world.

At the same time they did not physically harass or abuse us—the only time our baggage was searched was by Thai customs officials when we crossed the border—and they did eventually provide us with food and water. The food was usually live pigs, which we had to butcher.

Though the new rulers were obviously trying to inflict a certain amount of discomfort—they kept emphasizing that they had told us in radio broadcasts to get out of the city before the final assault and that by staying we had deliberately gone against their wishes—but there was another way to look at it. From their point of view we were being fed and housed much better than their foot soldiers were and should not complain.

But complain we did—about the food, about each other, about the fact that embassy officials were dining on chicken and white wine while we were eating plain rice and washing it down with heavily chlorinated water.

Among the embassy denizens, even in the midst of the tears and heartache, a search for the appearance of normalty went on.

A Frenchwoman picked orange-colored blossoms from a bush and twined them in her laughing child's hair.

Gosta Streijffert, a former Swedish Army officer from a patrician family who is a Red Cross official, sat erect in a straight-backed chair he had carried outside and read a British news magazine with his monocle fixed.

At a table nearby a United Nations official and a Scottish

Red Cross medical team played bridge and drank whisky; someone carped loudly about the way his partner conducted the bidding.

In the midst of all this an American airplane mechanic who did not leave Cambodia on the day the United States Embassy staff was evacuated because he was too drunk had an epileptic seizure. The Red Cross doctors carried him on the run to the building where the hospital staff was quartered with their equipment.

The American recovered slowly. His case interrupted the staff's dinner—steak. We were envious, and they seemed embarrassed and angry when journalists made notes about their full larder.

Why was there not more sharing, more of a community spirit? What made us into such acquisitive, self-protective beings?

Why did all the Asians live outside, in the heat and rain, while many of the Caucasians, like my group, lived inside, with air-conditioning? We explained it by saying the living arrangements were up to the embassy, but this was clearly not an answer. Was our behavior and our segregation a verdict on our way of life?

Amid the generally disappointing behavior of the Westerners there were exceptions—people who rose above the squabbling and managed to hold things together.

There was François Bizot, a Frenchman who worked for many years in the countryside restoring ancient temples and ruins. He lost his Cambodian wife and mother-in-law, who were forced on the march. Yet his relationship with the Communists was strong and they trusted him, for he had met some in his work in the interior and he speaks Khmer fluently.

It was Mr. Bizot who, in the early days of our confinement, was allowed to scout for food and water. And it was he who successfully argued the cases of some Asians whose papers were not in perfect order. A number of people who were in the compound probably owe their futures to him.

There were others who performed constructive roles, among them Douglas A. Sapper 3d, an American with a Special Forces background who was involved in a private airline company.

Sapper, as everyone calls him, organized our group's kitchen and food rationing to make sure supplies would last. His ranger training—and his colorful language, none of which can be reproduced here—kept us eating regularly and kept pilferers out of the larder.

These special people notwithstanding, the general level of behavior remained disappointing throughout our stay. We held constant group meetings and made endless lists of who was supposed to perform what chores, and we were constantly going through the movements of organizing, but we never really got organized.

Lassitude and depression set in as the days dragged on. People lay dozing on their makeshift beds throughout the day, waiting only for the next feeding. One journalist slipped into a torpor in which he had energy only to lift his aerosol insecticide can and spray away flies.

Occasionally, however, there was an occurrence dramatic enough to break this morphic aura—such as the sighting of a Chinese plane on April 24 coming in for a landing at the airport, possibly carrying high Cambodian and Chinese officials from Peking.

There was also the unexpected arrival the day before of the seven Russians who had been holding out at the Soviet Embassy. They had been desperately trying to make friendly contact with the new Cambodian leaders to counterbalance Chinese influence.

But it was the Chinese and not the Russians who had been supplying the Khmer Rouge with arms. The Cambodian Communists rebuffed the Soviet overtures, fired a rocket through the second floor of their embassy, looted the building and ordered the Russians to the French compound.

This phase came to an end for us in the early hours on April 30 when—after an evening of sipping champagne "borrowed" from embassy stocks and singing determinedly hardy traveling songs such as "It's a Long Way to Tipperary," we were awakened as scheduled, after a few hours' sleep, and told to board the trucks.

As we stepped into the pleasantly cool air with our sacks and suitcases, we could see in the night sky the lights of many planes coming from the direction of South Vietnam and heading west. Saigon was falling, and South Vietnamese pilots, carrying their families and other refugees, were making their own evacuation journey to Thailand.

The New York Times, May 9, 1975

Evacuation Convoy to Thailand: Arduous Trip Through the Secret Cambodia

BANGKOK, Thailand, May 8—The evacuation journey by truck to Thailand from Phnom Penh, where hundreds of foreigners had been confined in the French Embassy compound for nearly two weeks, gave a brief but revealing glimpse into the covert spy system and communally organized countryside of the Cambodian Communists—a glimpse that as far as is known no Westerners had ever had before.

We traveled on some of the well-defended dirt roads that had been built by hand and used as clandestine supply routes during the five years of the war that ended with the seizure of the Cambodian capital on April 17.

None of these roads show on maps of Cambodia, yet some were only half a mile or so from the main highways.

On the 250-mile trip we saw reservoirs, dikes, bridges—all built with hand tools. No machines or earth-moving equipment were visible.

We also saw boy militia units on patrol everywhere and male-female work crews repairing roads.

For those in the truck convoy the trip was arduous. It was especially difficult for the very young and the very old, and some fell ill. On our second day out, as we stopped in Kompong Chhnang for the night, a 9-month-old retarded child died in the bedlam of the governor's residence where we spent the night. French doctors who accompanied us said they knew before we started that the child could never survive such a trip. But the parents had no alternative—they could either take the child with them and pray for a miracle or leave him behind in Phnom Penh to die.

For the strong and healthy, the trip was tolerable. During rest stops we were able to forage for coconuts, mangoes and other fruit. And at every stop there were a few abandoned houses with big clay urns filled with rainwater, which we poured over our steaming heads.

The petty squabbling between various groups that often dominated our lives in the French Embassy compound followed us on the journey to the border. A group of Soviet diplomats refused to share their food with anyone. They even complained that they were not getting their proper convoy ration of rice.

At one point, in pique, the Russians threatened to expose stowaways on our truck. We in turn, advised them that if they persisted with their threats we would write a long story about their behavior, which, we suggested, would not go down very well in Moscow. They eased up a bit after that and offered us some vodka and tinned meat.

The French and the Vietnamese with French passports also continued to act like badly behaved zoo denizens, whenever the Communists brought us food.

If the Communists were looking for reasons to expel us as unfit and unsuited to live in a simple Asian society, we gave them ample demonstration on this journey.

The trip from the French Embassy began early on April 30 in virtually the same welter of chaos in which we had entered the embassy as refugees 13 days earlier.

In the darkness before dawn there was utter confusion in the embassy yard as more than 500 of us clambered into the 26 Soviet, Chinese and American-made military trucks for the journey.

There were supposed to be exactly 20 persons to each truck. But in the darkness and confusion some stowaways managed to sneak aboard. Five were on our truck—three Asian wives of Westerners whose papers were incomplete but who were fiercely determined to get out, a child of one of these women, and a German television correspondent.

The German sat upright, but the other stowaways slipped under our legs and we covered them with towels, bush hats and other oddments. Somehow, the officials who checked the convoy never noticed them.

At 6 A.M., with the sun just coming up, the convoy moved out. As it did, we saw a fresh battalion of troops marching single file into the city from the north.

Then the scenes changed and we met new images. The street lights burned, casting their artificial ray along the boulevards of a deserted city. Abandoned cars and assorted trash marked the trail of the departed population.

Every shop had been broken open and looted. Not a single civilian was visible—only the many soldiers camping in the shops and on the sidewalks.

We suddenly turned right—that is, west—down the road to the airport, and this was puzzling because we were supposed to be heading north and northwest toward Thailand.

We did not know it yet, but this was to be the detour that kept us from seeing that early stretch of Route 5 north of Phnom Penh that had been clogged with refugees forced out of Phnom Penh and may now be dotted with bodies.

Our convoy started southwest out of the capital down Route 4, then cut north along a rutted secondary road until we picked up Route 5 near Kompong Chhnang.

From there to the border, along Route 5, we encountered a wasteland of broken bridges, abandoned fields and forcibly evacuated highway towns.

The trip was a grueling one—with our trucks often lost or broken down for long hours either in the blistering sun or torrential downpours.

Some of these areas we passed through had been badly bombed by the United States Air Force in the early years of the war. Fields were gouged with bomb craters the size of swimming pools. But our American group and the other Westerners encountered almost no hostility from the local people.

While some sections we passed through were battered, others showed that they had been developed and organized over a long period of time and that they had remained untouched sanctuaries throughout the war.

The whole trip—with us jammed in the back of the bone-jarring military trucks—took more than three days. It was Saturday morning, after riding and bouncing all night, before we arrive at Poipet, the border town on the Cambodian side. Formalities took about an hour, but the Communist officials never searched our baggage or film or anything else we imagined they might be interested in.

Finally, at 11:20 A.M. I crossed over the rickety frontier bridge into Thailand. The first person to greet me was Chhay Born Lay, a Cambodian reporter for The Associated Press who left his country with his family on a press-evacuation flight.

As we walked forward to embrace each other, the back of my right hand caught on a roll of barbed wire marking the border and the scratch began to bleed. Lay instantly bent his head, grabbed the hand and began sucking the blood from the cut. I tried to pull my hand away, but he held tight.

This is what it is like to have a Cambodian friend. We both had left many Cambodian friends behind. We were both crying.

The New York Times, May 9, 1975

"Running Again—the Last Retreat"

by Philip Caputo

LONG BINH, South Viet Nam—This is a personal account of what must be one of the great tragedies of modern times.

What is happening here is an exodus of humanity of staggering magnitude, so staggering that no words of mine can capture anything but the smallest fraction of it.

I am writing this in a thatch hut on Highway 1, the long Vietnamese road which the French soldiers who fought in Indochina, dubbed la rue sans joie, the street without joy.

Today, Sunday, it is living up to that name. A hundred yards away, North Vietnamese mortar shells and rockets are slamming into government positions guarding the bridge over the Dong Hai River, whose brown waters meander with mocking indifference thru green rice fields and murky swamps.

[The Associated Press reported that early Monday Communist sappers had seized a section of Highway 1, cutting the refugee flow into the capital from the east.]

I am writing under the pressure of those bursting shells.

Pouring over the river bridge is another kind of stream, a stream of flesh and blood and bone, of exhausted, frightened faces, of crushed hopes and loss. The long, relentless column reaches forward and backward as far as the eye can see, for miles and miles and in places 50 feet across.

These are thousands upon thousands of Vietnamese refugees fleeing the fighting in Trang Bom, east of here, the shellings in Long Thanh, south of here, the attacks near Bien Hoa, north of here. They are jammed on the blacktop in crowds as thick as those pouring out of a football stadium, but this crowd is at least 20 miles long.

They are running from what looks like the Communist drive on Saigon and that's where they're trying to go. Many of them are refugees two and three times over—people who

527

ran from Xuan Loc, from Da Nang and Ham Tan and Qui Nhon.

Now they are running again, but this is their last retreat. This is the end of the road, for them, for South Viet Nam, and for a war that's gone on for over a generation.

They are filing past me on foot, their sandals scraping mournfully against the pavement, their heads hunched down against the driving monsoon rain that lashes them.

They are riding on motor scooters, in cars, in trucks, buses, oxcarts all piled up with crates and suitcases and ragged bundles of clothes. Sometimes the noise of the vehicles is deafening, but not so deafening as to drown out the wind-rushing sound of an incoming rocket that whips over their heads to burst in the paddylands beyond the river.

At other times, all you hear is that solemn, processional shuffling of sandled feet, bare feet, bloodied feet against the rainslick asphalt. You hear that and the chorusing of crying children.

A three-year-old boy, his face and hands covered with sores and insect bites, a toy-like sun helmet on his toy-like head, toddles thru the crowd, whimpering for his lost parents.

They find him finally and his whimpering stops as they prop him on their motor scooter.

Two enemy mortars have just exploded near the South Vietnamese bunkers and earthworks guarding the bridge. White and gray smoke is billowing upward, dissipating, wafting over the multitudes like some noxious cloud.

Some of the scenes here are almost Goyaesque in their horror. Vietnamese soldiers are picking thru slabs of meat which they will eat for supper. In the middle of the road a few yards away is the lower half of a man's leg swollen and rotting in the rain. The upper half is a mass of rended flesh indistinguishable from the meat the soldiers are preparing to cook.

An old woman with teeth turned blackish-red from chewing betel-nuts screams at a truck that seems to be slowing down to pick her up. She grabs her bundle of clothes, but it is almost as heavy as she is, and it breaks open, and as she tries to gather it up, the truck presses on.

A company of South Vietnamese soldiers and sailors stationed at the naval base on the river stumbles across the paddies into the village where the North Vietnamese mortars are emplaced.

They vanish into the trees. Soon shells are thudding in on top of them. Small arms fire crackles in between the punctuating thumps of the mortars. Then the soldiers come running out, fanning thru the sea of green rice like flushed rabbits.

A heavy shell whines in, explodes on the river bank with an ear-splitting crash.

"Ya, ya, eeyah," a farmer shouts at his herd of water buffalo as they plod across the bridge, fouling up the traffic even more, the great gray beasts tossing their horned heads and bellowing at the sound of man at war.

Mixed into the column are scores of retreating soldiers, some with their weapons, some without, all beaten.

The endless river of people flows on, part of it coming from further east on Highway 1, part from Highway 15 to the south, both parts meeting in a sorrowful confluence at this bridge.

A flight of South Vietnamese fighters screams overhead. Within minutes comes the hollow rumbling of bombs. A pillar of smoke, as if rising from an enormous funeral pyre, swirls into the leaden, sagging sky. The planes are strafing Communist tank columns rumbling up Route 15. They are only a few miles away.

A teen-age boy, behind the wheel of a rickety truck in which his parents and family sit amidst piles of belongings, looks at me and says:

"We come from Long Thanh. Many shells fall on us last night. Many VC [Viet Cong] in Long Thanh. Much fighting. Many die."

Meanwhile, all up and down the column, South Vietnamese soldiers are firing their rifles into the air in an attempt to stem the tide.

It is futile. The crowd seems to have a momentum all its own, and the sharp cracks of the soldiers' M-16s is not half as frightening as the Communist tanks that growl like armored monsters somewhere behind this procession.

A few have stopped to rest at the entrance to the National Military Cemetery. They flop down in the shadow of a statue of a South Vietnamese soldier.

He is sitting, his jaw slack with exhaustion, his helmet

pushed back on his head, his rifle lying across his knees. He is a symbol of the weariness and the pity of war.

At the base of the monument, mingled with refugees, a few living soldiers are sitting in almost the same position.

Like the statue, their pose seems to say that it is over. This is the end of the road, the end of a war. And the nearness of an end is all there is to mitigate the incalculable suffering of the Vietnamese who are making their last march down the street without joy.

Chicago Tribune, April 28, 1975

We Clawed for Our Lives!

by Keyes Beech

ABOARD THE USS HANCOCK—Tuesday morning I had breakfast on the ninth floor of the Caravelle Hotel in Saigon and
watched a column of ugly black smoke framed by the tall,
twin spires of the Catholic cathedral in Kennedy Square just
up the street.

Tan Son Nhut airport was burning; the streets were bare of
traffic, unnaturally but pleasantly quiet.

The waiters were nervous and the room boys said I couldn't
have my laundry back until "tomorrow."

What tomorrow?

Six hours later I was fighting for my life and wishing I had
never left the hotel. I nearly didn't make it out of Saigon.

My Daily News colleague, Bob Tamarkin, telephoned to say
the embassy had ordered a full-scale evacuation—immediately.
He said he hoped to see me later.

I joined others who were leaving and we went to a prearranged assembly point, a U.S. embassy building only a couple of blocks away.

Three buses were quickly filled with a mixed bag of correspondents and Vietnamese. Some of the more dignified
among us held back rather than scramble for seats and waited
for the fourth bus.

That was a mistake.

The first three buses made it inside Tan Son Nhut airbase
and their passengers flew out. Ours never made it inside, and
that accounts for one of the longest days of my life.

We heard the bad news over the driver's radio on the way
out: "Security conditions are out of control at Tan Son Nhut.
Do not go to Tan Son Nhut. Repeat, do not go to Tan Son
Nhut."

We went on anyway, the sound of explosions and the rattle
of automatic weapons growing louder by the second—in-

coming mixed with outgoing fire. South Vietnamese soldiers were firing wildly in the air for no apparent reason.

South Vietnamese sentries turned us back at the first checkpoint. For the thousandth time, I made mental note of the billboard legend that departing Americans see as they leave Saigon:

"The noble sacrifices of allied soldiers will never be forgotten."

We tried another approach to the airbase but were again waved back. No way, as the Vietnamese are fond of saying.

The evacuation had broken down.

It was 2 P.M. when we headed back to the city. Nobody on that bus will ever forget the next few hours. We cruised aimlessly about Saigon for at least three hours while our security escorts tried to figure out what to do with us.

We were a busload of fools piloted by a man who had never driven a bus and had to wire the ignition when it stalled because the Vietnamese driver had run away with the keys the night before.

"I'm doing the best I can," said Bill Austin of Miami, Okla., the man at the wheel, as we careened through narrow streets, knocking over sidewalk vendors, sideswiping passing vehicles and sending Vietnamese scattering like leaves in the wind.

When the back seat driving became too much, Austin, an auditor, stopped the bus and said: "If there is a bus driver aboard, I'll be glad to let him take the wheel."

There were no takers. By now we had been joined by two other buses and half a dozen cars packed with Vietnamese who figured that by staying with us they could get out of the country.

At every stop, Vietnamese beat on the doors and windows pleading to be let inside. We merely looked at them. We already had enough Vietnamese aboard. Every time we opened the door, we had to beat and kick them back.

For no reason, except that we were following another bus, we went to the Saigon port area, one of the toughest parts of the city, where the crowds were uglier than elsewhere. Police fired into the air to part the mob and let us through onto the dock.

I got off the bus and went over to John Moore, the embassy

security officer who was sitting in one of those sedans with the flashy blinker on top.

"Do you know why we are here and what you are going to do with us?" I asked him.

Moore shrugged helplessly. "There are ships," he said, gesturing toward sandbagged Vietnamese vessels lying alongside the dock.

I looked around at the gathering crowd. Small boys were snatching typewriters and bags of film. This, as the Chinese would say, looked like bad joss. I didn't know how or whether I was going to get out of Saigon, but I damned well knew I wasn't going to stay here.

I got back on the bus, which was both our prison and our fortress. And other correspondents including some of my closest friends—Wendell S. (Bud) Merick of U.S. News and World Report and Ed White of the AP—felt the same way. White's typewriter, his most precious possession at the moment, next to his life, was gone.

Again we had to fight off the Vietnamese. Ed Bradley of CBS, a giant of a man, was pushing, kicking, shoving, his face sad. I found myself pushing a middle-aged Vietnamese woman who had been sitting beside me on the bus and asked me to look after her because she worked for the Americans and the Viet Cong would cut her throat.

That's what they all said and maybe they are right. But she fought her way back to my side. "Why did you push me?" she asked. I had no answer.

Austin didn't know what to do with us so we drove to the American embassy. There the Vietnamese woman decided to get off.

"I have worked for the United States government for 10 years," she said, "but you do not trust me and I do not trust you. Even if we do get to Tan Son Nhut, they wouldn't let me on the plane." She was right, of course.

"I am going home and poison myself," she said. I didn't say anything because there was nothing to say.

For lack of anything better to do, Austin drove us to the embassy parking lot across the street. The embassy was besieged by the Vietnamese that we were abandoning. Every gate was closed. There was no way in.

I went to the parking lot telephone and called an embassy friend. Briefly, I stated the situation: "There are about 40 of us—Americans, British and two or three Japanese. We can't get in."

"Hold it," he said. A few minutes later, he came back on the phone with the following instructions:

"Take your people to the MacDinh Chi police station next to the embassy. They know you are coming. They will help you over the wall."

An uncertain Moses, I led my flock out of the parking lot, across the street and through the police barricades to the police station. They never heard of us. When we tried to talk to them, they told us to move on and fired into the air to make their point.

We dribbled around the corner to the rear of the embassy compound, where several hundred Vietnamese were pounding at the gate or trying to scale the wall. There was only one way inside: through the crowd and over the 10-foot wall.

Once we moved into that seething mass, we ceased to be correspondents. We were only men fighting for their lives, scratching, clawing, pushing ever closer to that wall. We were like animals.

Now, I thought, I know what it's like to be a Vietnamese. I am one of them. But if I could get over that wall I would be an American again.

My attache case accidentally struck a baby in its mother's arms and its father beat at me with his fists. I tried to apologize as he kept on beating me while his wife pleaded with me to take the baby.

Somebody grabbed my sleeve and wouldn't let go. I turned my head and looked into the face of a Vietnamese youth.

"You adopt me and take me with you and I'll help you," he screamed. "If you don't, you don't go."

I said I'd adopt him. I'd have said anything. Could this be happening to me?

Suddenly my arm was free and I edged closer to the wall. There were a pair of marines on the wall. They were trying to help us up and kick the Vietnamese down. One of them looked down at me.

"Help me," I pleaded. "Please help me."

That marine helped me. He reached down with his long, muscular arm and pulled me up as if I were a helpless child.

I lay on a tin roof gasping for breath like a landed fish, then dropped to the ground. God bless the marines. I was one myself in the last of the just wars.

One American offered me a cup of water and a doctor asked me if I wanted a tranquilizer. I accepted the water and declined the tranquilizer. "Are you sure you're all right?" the doctor said anxiously.

"Sure," I croaked. "I'm just fine. But my friends?"

I looked up and saw a yellow shirt coming over the wall. That was Bud Merick of U.S. News & World Report. Minutes later I saw the sweaty red face of big Ed White from the Associated Press come over.

I was very happy to see him. He is not only my friend. He was carrying my typewriter.

A tall, young embassy officer in a pink shirt looked at me and said, "Aren't you Keyes Beech?"

I admitted I was. His name is Brunson McKinley and I last saw him in Peking two years ago. We made our way through the crowd of Vietnamese evacuees gathered around the embassy swimming pool and through to the main embassy building and took the elevator to the sixth floor.

Our embassy friends seemed glad to see us and expressed awe that we had come over the embassy wall. I was pretty awed too, now that I think of it.

A retired American general who has been around here a long time, Charles Timmes, said he had been on the phone to "Big" Minh, the new president, urging him to ask the North Vietnamese for a cease-fire.

"He said he was trying but they wouldn't listen," Charlie said. "Anyway, they haven't shelled the embassy yet."

"That's nice of them," I said, slumping into a soft chair.

The man I really wanted to see was down on the third floor. His name is Graham Martin and he was our ambassador. In my view, he gambled with American lives, including mine, by dragging his heels on the evacuation.

A few minutes later I was on the embassy roof and inside a Marine helicopter and on my way to the carrier Hancock.

It was exactly 6:30 P.M.

My last view of Saigon was through the tail door of the helicopter. Tan Son Nhut was burning. So was Bien Hoa. Then the door closed—closed on the most humiliating chapter in American history.

I looked at the man next to me. He was a Vietnamese and I moved away from him. Forty-five minutes later we put down on the Hancock.

The salt sea air tasted good.

Chicago Daily News, May 1, 1975

Diary of S. Viet's Last Hours

by Bob Tamarkin

ABOARD THE USS OKINAWA—"They lied to us at the very end," said Capt. Stuart Herrington, the tears welling in his eyes. "They promised. They promised," he said, biting hard on his lip to hold the tears back.

Shirtless, he sat on the edge of the bunk, shaking his head. He continued:

"I have never received an order in my life to do something I was ashamed of. If I would have known how it was going to end, I would have refused the order."

He was speaking of the evacuation of the Americans and Vietnamese during the frantic day last Tuesday when the Americans pulled out of South Vietnam, leaving hundreds of Vietnamese in the embassy compound and thousands of others who had been promised evacuation working in Saigon and the rest of the country.

Lt. Col. H. G. Summers, a barrel-chested 250-pounder, sitting in the bunk next to Herrington, turned to me and said:

"I asked you to come here because you were the last newsman to see the end. Do you know what you saw? Do you really know what you saw?" he asked.

"I saw the evacuation of the U.S. Embassy—the last hours," I answered.

"No," Summers said, pausing. "You saw deceit. You saw how we let this country down to the very end."

Both men hadn't slept for more than 24 hours and both were emotionally drained.

The two had been assigned to the embassy to assist with the evacuation. For nearly 20 hours they organized groups of people, assuring them that they would be evacuated. They used Vietnamese firemen on standby to protect Americans should a helicopter accident occur.

In the end, even the firemen were left behind.

"We had arranged the people in groups of 70. We made them throw away their suitcases. They listened to us and believed us. They waited confidently in those rows, believing their friends would not let them down," Herrington said.

Until a few minutes before they themselves were flown out on the last choppers before the marines left, Herrington and Summers believed those 500 in the compound would be flown out. The two officers said they were told that Ambassador Graham Martin and his key aides would be leaving in the last helicopter, remaining until all evacuees were taken out. They left well before that.

"They didn't have the courtesy to tell us," Summers said. "We learned by accident the ambassador had left earlier. And we knew that those other people would not be going.

"They lied to us at the very end. One thing you don't do is lie to your own people."

There was no indication that the evacuation was going to stop until a security agent told them they would be taking the last chopper out, Summers said.

A total of 70,000 people were evacuated Tuesday. The operation employed 80 helicopters flying 495 sorties.

But as one senior diplomatic official put it:

"The big numbers are irrelevant. The rest of our lives we will be haunted by how we betrayed those people. It made me cry when I got here. There were lots of people who were crying when they got here."

On the second floor of a small annex building just behind the wall the marines had set up a 50-caliber machinegun ready to strafe the walls should the Vietnamese try storming it.

A three-foot space along the top of the wall, where the barbed wire had been pushed aside, was the only way into the massive embassy compound. The embassy was sealed.

I had gone to the embassy earlier in the day, at noon, about 90 minutes after the evacuation alert was sounded. I was late arriving at a pre-designated pickup point, from which I would have been taken by bus to the defense attache office at Tan Son Nhut Airport.

Four other Americans stood with me outside the gate, where only minutes before a portly man dressed in a blue suit had been allowed to enter. He was Gen. Dang Van Quang, the national securities affairs adviser to former President Nguyen Van Thieu.

I now stood with the other Americans, who were waving passports as proof of their citizenship. We were refused entrance.

John Hogan, the embassy press officer, whom I knew, assured me I could get in. But he gave no instructions. As I was walking away, he poked his finger at me from behind the gate and said: "Don't write one word about this evacuation." I returned to my hotel room and filed a story about the initial evacuation alert.

By the time I had returned to the entrance at 25 Hog Thap Tu St. I saw my 61-year-old colleague, Keyes Beech, scrambling to get through the three-foot space. As he was pulled up by the marines, he was pulled back by the Vietnamese clinging to him, hoping that somehow they would be pulled up with him. The Marines had orders to grab Americans first, then third-country nationals and then the Vietnamese.

The scene at the wall was brutal. Marines and other embassy personnel threw Vietnamese people off the wall. One official drew his revolver, stuck it point-blank in the face of a young Vietnamese boy and screamed: "Get down, you bastard, or I'll blow your head off. Get Down!"

The marines brought the butts of their rifles down on the fingers of those trying to climb the walls. Elderly women and children who were being pushed up by the sheer force of bodies beneath them became enmeshed in the barbed wire, their skin punctured with bloody wounds.

One official who had thrown a young girl from the wall three times finally gave in. "I couldn't take it anymore. I feel sorry for her," said Jeff Kibler, 24, an embassy accountant.

A bus pulled up to the gate jammed with people and with scores more clinging to the top. Under the threat of being machinegunned, the driver backed away.

One American woman, who had arrived from Honolulu on Saturday to get a family of seven out of the country, arrived at the gate, trailed by the family. She stopped, realizing the futility of the situation.

"I couldn't put them through that," she said, the tears welling in her eyes. She sent the family away and returned to go over the wall herself.

Most of those who were legitimately to be evacuated were ignored as the marines began pulling people up. In some cases, families were separated forever. They were hoisted up and over like sacks of potatoes, dumped wherever they landed. I got in that way.

As the only correspondent who stayed to cover the evacuation of the embassy through the departure of Ambassador Martin (I left 45 minutes after he had), I kept a diary of the events and people I met in those desperate hours.

Following is a chronology of America's last few hours in South Vietnam, as I witnessed them.

3 P.M.—The embassy was surrounded by Vietnamese who wanted to get out of the country. They were screaming, crying, trampling one another, and some clawed at the gates in their futile efforts to get inside the embassy compound.

5:39 P.M.—I was hauled through the gap in the barbed wire. It had taken me more than 1½ hours to inch through the bodies to the marines' grasp, just three yards away.

One marine was pulled off the fence by hands that grabbed his legs. At that point, the mood of the marines turned from bare tolerance into fitful rage. They began pushing back harder and screaming louder.

Security guards in the neighboring French embassy stood on walls of their compound casually watching the pandemonium. Many people ran up to them, waving their papers and cards. The French ignored them.

6 P.M.—The rampage started quietly, and then it snowballed.

A few youngsters wandered into an inconspicuous storeroom filled with 200 or so cases of soft drinks and grabbed a couple of bottles apiece. Within minutes hundreds were storming the storeroom carrying away several bottles at a time. Within minutes the storeroom had been cleaned out. The assault set the mood for what was to follow.

The fever spread into the embassy restaurant, where people began grabbing what they could. They devoured and drank anything they could get their hands on.

The binge spread to the food lockers, where frozen foods were kept. Slabs of ribs and frozen steaks and beef briskets were pounded with hammers and dull-edged knives to soften the meat to be cooked on the stoves and in the ovens, which were in control of the evacuees.

Then they found the store-room to the restaurant above the main embassy restaurant. Down they came. This time they carried off cases of canned goods, juices, boxes containing cartons of cigarets. Some were stopped by the marines, who began beating looters.

9:40 P.M.—A grim-faced Graham Martin, his hair perfectly combed, followed by four Marines, disappeared up a flight of stairs. He surveyed the pillage. The crowd did not recognize the ambassador. He came swiftly down the stairs minutes later, the marines still following closely. He disappeared through the gate that leads to the main embassy courtyard, where the helicopters land on the parking lot.

As the helicopters circled overhead, their red lights blinking off and on, orange flames and thick smoke poured out of the embassy's smoke stack. The remaining documents and papers, some collected since 1954, when the United States established its embassy in Saigon, were being burned in the incinerator.

10 P.M.—Only an hour earlier, a marine had threatened to blow the head off a young Vietnamese boy. He pointed his .45 automatic at the youth, forcing him to drop the carton of cigarets he had taken from the storehouse. Then the marines walked the same steps, stuffing cartons into their own knapsacks.

10:30 P.M.—A 30-year-old American woman named Marilyn (she would not give her last name) who came to Vietnam only a few days ago to be with a Vietnamese friend, decided she wanted to go back over the wall. She begged a marine guard to let her go. There were still thousands at every gate to the embassy, but they were quiet, sitting in the darkness, hoping they would be allowed in the next morning.

"In all good conscience, I can't let you go over the wall," the marine said. "You must get permission from the embassy officials in charge of the evacuation."

She was disappointed, but agreed.

The marines began rounding up the last few Americans in

the compound. It had been 12 hours since the evacuation began.

11:30 P.M.—The marines were ordered to round up the Americans and let them pass through to the landing pad door first. The Vietnamese sensed something might be wrong and began to stir. They began to advance toward the gate, but were stopped. The process of getting through the gate is slow. Fifty to 80 people at a time allowed to pass. A normal helicopter load is 50 people, but now they were jamming the copters with as many as 80 and 90. The sound of small-arms fire pierced the night along with the muffled sound of artillery.

MIDNIGHT—Some of the marines were edgy and a few turned sadistic. One stood before the hundreds of Vietnamese who stared blankly ahead, and said: "All right, now everybody sings." He began waving his hands through the air, conducting them. They didn't understand. He laughed loudly. They just stared in bewilderment, their faces blank. One young Vietnamese boy and a man tried to squeeze through the gate.

They were beaten, brutally.

The choppers began landing on the roof of the embassy and on the parking lot. The group I was with was led into the embassy to take off from the heliport.

1 A.M.—The inside of the embassy now appeared to have been ransacked. The marines and embassy security officials systematically went through every room tearing up, ripping out and destroying whatever might reveal anything to the enemy.

1:15 A.M.—Ambassador Martin was in the office of Conrad F. LaGeux, a special assistant. A senior diplomatic official, sipping a glass of champagne, was going over last-minute details with Henry Boudreau, counselor of administrative affairs. Martin, still in shirtsleeves, was calm. They were joined by Josiah W. Bennett, head of political affairs. Meanwhile, the deputy ambassador, Wolfgang J. Lemann, roamed throughout the embassy, walkie talkie in hand, monitoring the evacuation efforts.

2 A.M.—About 200 evacuees had been led to the stairwell of the top floor and were planted there to wait for another chopper to land. The door to the floor was locked. For more than two hours they waited, sealed in the well without water.

One man said that he had been at the embassy since 7 A.M. waiting to leave. An American who worked as a computer analyst heard on the radio at 8 P.M. that all the Americans had left. He was unaware of the evacuation.

At midnight a friend called to let him know the helicopters were still flying. He got to the embassy at 1 A.M. and was pulled over the fence.

3 A.M.—A security official said the evacuation was 12 hours behind schedule.

3:30 A.M.—Marines were stretched out sleeping on the floor of the embassy lobby, machineguns, M-16s, knapsacks, walkie talkies spread out everywhere. In a back room on the first floor was Major J. Keene, commander of the 140-man detail assigned to provide evacuation protection. He was grabbing a few minutes of sleep, his feet propped up on a desk. A young marine in a corridor gathered his gear, stuffing a paperback book into his knapsack. The book: "The Fall of Rome."

Amid the big plastic bags of shredded paper a flagless pole stood forlornly, and there were still plaques on the lobby wall. One plaque was in honor of four embassy personnel—an American woman and three Vietnamese—who were killed by a Viet Cong bomb while on duty at the embassy on March 30, 1965.

The other plaque read: "Embassy of the United States of America. Built in time of war. Dedicated to the cause of peace. In memory of those who have served their nation in Vietnam. Ellsworth Bunker Ambassador. September 1967."

4:15 A.M.—Ambassador Martin appeared in the lobby. He was wearing a light brown suit, and carried a small attache case and a folded clothes bag.

He first walked outside, but several minutes later he and top aides returned. Instead of leaving from the ground-level site, he was instructed to depart from the heliport atop of the embassy. He spoke to no one, but stood waiting for the elevator to the sixth floor for the last time. With him were special assistants, Thomas Polgar, LaGeux, and George Jacobson. An air of deep depression surrounded them as they walked into the elevator.

About 15 minutes later, a marine helicopter carried off the ambassador, his aides, two security guards, several personnel from the mission warden's office and a missionary couple, officially ending America's presence in South Vietnam.

They were on their way to the USS Blue Ridge, the flagship of the 7th Fleet.

As the Jolly Green Giant CH-53 lifted Martin and the others into the blackness, the lights of Saigon glimmered below and fires could be seen on the city's outskirts. They were from the fighting of the encroaching and overpowering North Vietnamese Army, tightening its grip for the kill. Lightning from monsoon rains in the distance lit up the sky periodically.

A stream of lights headed down from the direction of Bien Hoa, 15 miles north of Saigon, where the Communist tanks and troop trucks pushed toward the scared and panicked city. It was just a matter of time before 30 years of war would come to an end.

To the end, Martin maintained the somber aloofness that characterized him. Yet, he maintained a certain dignity.

5 A.M.—A sense of panic overtook even the marines. So far there was no actual fighting, just threats and shots fired into the air.

5:15 A.M.—The remaining American civilians—there were three of us—were instructed to go to the sixth floor. One civilian was the young woman who would not give her name. The other civilian was a portly man in his late 30s, who also refused to give his name or even his home in the States. He arrived in Saigon only on Monday to try to help some Vietnamese friends out. It was too late. Now he sulked, turned to an officer and said: "You know, I had ordered $100 worth of tailor-made clothing yesterday when I arrived, and I paid for it in advance." The soldier merely nodded.

The embassy security head appeared, a walkie talkie in hand. Martin Garrett turned to the group of army officers, marines and civilians and several other embassy security staff, and said:

"We just got orders from President Ford that the evacuation is to stop immediately. The pilots have been flying for 14 hours, and the President has ordered the commander of the 7th fleet to halt operations."

He carefully gave instructions to the marines to station themselves on the roof and to leave all their gear behind.

Those marines who were still on the embassy grounds were told to walk back into the embassy casually when the next chopper left, and secure the doors behind them. They, too, would be leaving from the heliport.

5:30 A.M.—The marines took their place on the roof. The helicopter landed, its massive propellers whooshing through the air, creating cyclonic winds, drowning out the sounds of the night.

My chopper lifted off, its red lights blinking, and headed toward the South China Sea. The passengers, including me, sat stoically in the dark, tired and numb. Some were dazed, finding it difficult to believe that the Americans were pulling out in this manner skulking away in the darkness.

Below in the courtyard, where the big choppers had been loading, the headlights from the cars and trucks surrounding the parking lot were still on to light the way for the choppers.

Hundreds of Vietnamese looked up, waiting for the next one.

It never came.

Chicago Daily News, May 6, 1975

Communists Enter Saigon

by George Esper

SAIGON, South Vietnam, April 30 (AP)—Communist troops of North Vietnam and the Provisional Revolutionary Government of South Vietnam poured into Saigon today as a century of Western influence came to an end.

Scores of North Vietnamese tanks, armored vehicles and camouflaged Chinese-built trucks rolled to the presidential palace.

The president of the former non-Communist government of South Vietnam, Gen. Duong Van Minh, who had gone on radio and television to announce his administration's surrender, was taken to a microphone later by North Vietnamese soldiers for another announcement. He appealed to all Saigon troops to lay down their arms and was taken by the North Vietnamese soldiers to an undisclosed destination.

[Soon after, the Saigon radio fell silent, normal telephone and telegraph communications ceased and The Associated Press said its wire link to the capital was lost at 7 P.M. Wednesday, Saigon time (7 A.M. Wednesday, New York time).

[In Paris, representatives of the Provisional Revolutionary Government announced that Saigon had been renamed Ho Chi Minh City in honor of the late president of North Vietnam. Other representatives said in a broadcast monitored in Thailand that former government forces in eight provinces south of the capital had not yet surrendered, but no fighting was mentioned.] The transfer of power was symbolized by the raising of the flag of the National Liberation Front over the presidential palace at 12:15 P.M. today, about two hours after Gen. Minh's surrender broadcast.

Hundreds of Saigon residents cheered and applauded as North Vietnamese military vehicles moved to the palace grounds from which the war against the Communists had been directed by President Nguyen Van Thieu, who resigned April 21, and by President Ngo Dinh Diem, who was killed in a coup in 1963. Broadcasting today in the early hours of the Communist takeover, the Provisional Revolutionary Government's representatives said: "We representatives of the liberation forces of Saigon formally proclaim that Saigon has been totally liberated. We accept the unconditional surrender of Gen. Duong Van Minh, president of the former government."

Meanwhile, many former soldiers sought to lose themselves in the populace. However, one police colonel walked up to an army memorial statue, saluted and shot himself. He died later in a hospital.

Shots rang out at one point around the City Hall. A North Vietnamese infantry platoon, dressed in olive-drab uniforms and black rubber sandals, took up defense positions in the square in front of the building. They exchanged shots with a few holdouts. Some people on motorbikes looked apprehensively to see where the firing was coming from. In a short while it subsided.

Between Gen. Minh's surrender broadcast and the entry of the Communist forces into the city, South Vietnamese soldiers and civilians jammed aboard several coastal freighters tied up along the Saigon River, hoping to escape. They dejectedly left the ships as the Communist troops drove along the waterfront in jeeps and trucks, waving National Liberation Front flags and cheering. As the Communist troops drove past, knots of civilians stood in doorways and watched without apparent emotion. Later, as more North Vietnamese troops poured into the city, many people began cheering.

Ky Nhan, a Vietnamese who had been submitting photographs to The Associated Press for three years, came to the agency's office with a Communist friend and two North Vietnamese soldiers and said, "I guarantee the safety of everybody here."

"I have been a revolutionary for 10 years," said Mr. Nhan. "My job in the Viet Cong was liaison with the international press." This correspondent served them Coca-Cola and some leftover cake. One of the soldiers, a 25-year-old sergeant named Binh Huan Lam, said he was from Hanoi and had been a soldier for 10 years. "I have not married because it was not necessary during the war," he said.

After smoking a cigarette, Tran Viet Ca, a 24-year-old private, told the Americans he had served seven years in the North Vietnamese army.

"Two days ago we attacked Bien Hoa," he said. "Today we drove down the highway past the United States Army base at Long Binh. Our forces were led by a brigade of tanks. There was a little resistance, but most Saigon soldiers had already run away. Then we drove into Saigon."

Loud explosions were heard in the late afternoon in Saigon. They were said to have taken place aboard an ammunition barge burning in the Saigon River, but no damage was reported in the city except at the United States Embassy and other American buildings, which Saigonese looted. At the embassy they took virtually everything, including the kitchen sinks and a machine to shred secret documents.

A bronze plaque with the names of five American servicemen who died in a 1968 attack by Communist guerrillas was torn from the lobby wall. An Associated Press correspondent retrieved it. Another memento from the embassy that was saved was a color portrait of former President Richard M. Nixon and his family, inscribed "To Ambassador and Mrs. Graham Martin with appreciation for their service to the nation. From Richard Nixon."

A French businessman who said he was taking refuge in the New Zealand Embassy grabbed the picture.

"I know the ambassador," he said. "I will personally deliver it to him in the United States some time in the future." Outside the embassy, Thong Nhut Boulevard was littered with burned cars.

AP wire copy, April 30, 1975

U.S. Embassy Looted

by Peter Arnett

SAIGON, South Vietnam, April 30 (AP)—The six-story United States Embassy in Saigon withstood a determined Viet Cong commando attack in 1968, and five Americans were killed defending it.

Today, without its armed guards, the embassy was no match for thousands of Saigonese getting their last American handout. They took everything, including the kitchen sinks and a machine to shred secret documents.

The bronze plaque with names of the five American servicemen killed in the embassy in 1968 was torn from the lobby wall. It lay amid piles of documents and furniture on the back lawn. We carried it back to The Associated Press office.

"It is our embassy now," said a laughing young Vietnamese soldier as he pranced gleefully along the littered hallway of the administrative building.

The handsome embassy building on Thong Nhut Boulevard was abandoned by a detachment of U.S. Marines at 7:50 Wednesday morning, Saigon time. They had remained behind after Ambassador Graham Martin had gone to prevent waiting Vietnamese from rushing the last helicopters.

As the Marines left, they threw tear-gas grenades into the elevator shaft. But after their helicopter lifted off the roof, the Vietnamese rushed in, ignoring the gas as they tore into filing cabinets and cupboards.

The Vietnamese had started at dawn on the embassy annex at the rear of the main building.

Eleven young people, some of them soldiers in uniform, tried to smash open a heavy safe they had turned on its face.

They looked at our white faces and cameras suspiciously, but when we claimed French citizenship, they laughed conspiratorially and invited us to share in the proceeds. We didn't stay for the opening.

Rolls and rolls of Bank of America embassy payroll checks were strewn across a concrete parking lot.

Smashed typewriters and overturned filing cabinets marked with red "secret" and "classified" stickers were in many rooms.

A group of Vietnamese were dragging a large shredder for destroying documents from a basement room. Five large drums marked "One each, Document Destroyer, drum type without igniter" were in a corner of the room. Piles of dust that probably had been secret papers the night before were on the floor.

In the back of the main building, automobiles had been smashed. Amid broken tables and broken pictures, what seemed like tons of documents floated about in the breeze.

About 50 Vietnamese men, women and children still perched on the helicopter pad on the roof. They beckoned to us to come up to them, apparently believing that if white people were there, the helicopters might come back.

We entered through the broken back door of the embassy and started up the stairs. The reek of tear gas was almost overwhelming. Every room we looked into appeared to have been hit with a battering ram.

The gas drove us back downstairs.

AP wire copy, April 30, 1975

Tenderness, Hatred and Grief Mark Saigon's Last Days

by Malcolm W. Browne

ABOARD THE U.S.S. MOBILE, in the South China Sea, May 3 —Like a failed marriage, the Vietnamese-American relationship of the last generation has ended in a mixture of hatred and suspicion, coupled with a strong remnant of tenderness and compassion on both sides.

It ended with an embittered Saigon policeman pistol-whipping an American reporter and with Government troops and policemen taking potshots at American cars and buses, or sometimes just at any "big nose"—non-Asian.

The parting was often a time of anxiety and grief, however, and both American and Vietnamese faces were lined with tears.

There were the Americans—private citizens now—who lived and worked in Vietnam years ago and who came back before the end to do what they could. They went into debt to buy air tickets, arriving within a few days of the surrender, in a desperate effort to find Vietnamese friends or the relatives of their Vietnamese wives. Most of them failed, but at least in trying they avoided the extra load of guilt they would have felt at doing nothing.

"At least during those final hours at the gate outside the airport trying to get my own people in," an American said. "I maybe helped one woman. She was Vietnamese, with an American passport, but of course without a big nose no one was getting through on their own. I had to leave my own behind, but at least I got her through."

The tens of thousands aboard the huge evacuation armada sailing away from Vietnam have told endless stories of heroism, loyalty and love in the last hours.

But for millions of Vietnamese and not a few Americans the dominant memory will be sorrow and betrayal and guilt.

There was scarcely an American in the final weeks who was not forced to share personally in that intense feeling of guilt. For each of them had what Vietnamese call a big nose—the only real passport to salvation. Caucasian features could do almost anything: cash checks, cut through the maddening bureaucratic impediments that had been erected both by Saigon and Washington and, most of all, get a few Vietnamese to safety.

Nonetheless, countless Vietnamese, knowing they would remain despite all, worked for their American friends to the last.

On the other hand, many an American organization, private and official, locked its doors and left without any effort to help Vietnamese employes and associates.

Some, like Northrop, the airplane builder, offered help to Vietnamese employes but not to their families; in most cases this amounted to leaving the employes behind.

The Saigon branches of American banks closed, sent their records and American employes home and left tens of thousands of Vietnamese depositors unpaid.

Many organizations had some access to the "black lift"—a semiclandestine airlift of selected Vietnamese and their families that operated for about a week like an underground railroad before the frantic final exodus under fire.

Details of how it worked will have to remain secret for a time to protect the Vietnamese and Americans involved, but a considerable number of Vietnamese found out about it.

Any American, including newsmen, suspected of having anything to do with it became the object of an endless procession of supplicants, some pleading, some offering bribes, some asking for marriage. Only a handful of places were available, so the Americans involved dissembled, comforted and lied.

There were Vietnamese who could have gone and chose not to—thoughtful, courageous men and women who made their decisions after agonizing reflection. Among them was one of the principal reporter-photographers on the staff of The New York Times, Nguyen Ngoc Luong.

One of them explained: "In the end the color of the skin counts for more than politics. Anyone who has lived in either the United States or Vietnam knows this, and I have done both. The Vietcong, like me, are yellow."

For an overwhelming majority desperation and panic prevailed. Some who knew from the first that they could not leave, however much they wanted to, tried to send out last precious parts of themselves—photographs, the ashes of ancestors, keepsakes and children.

On the last day, as frantic people took to the streets despite the thunder of rockets and the popping of rifles, someone spread a blanket on the sidewalk next to the Continental Hotel, in the heart of the downtown foreign quarter. On the blanket lay a sleeping baby, beside it a small plastic bag containing ragged clothing and toys. Clearly the hope was that someone would carry it away to America, but by then it was too late.

There was the maid who, believing she could not go herself and having no living relatives, wanted to send her cat, all she had. Both were evacuated.

The prospect of leaving, real or imagined, often led to bitterness. There were those Vietnamese who had been promised that they would be evacuated but who gave way to morose suspicion—to the widespread Vietnamese belief, carefully nurtured by the Communists, that even those Americans considered the closest of friends could not be trusted.

In the long decades of American involvement in Vietnam there were an appreciable number of Americans who learned to understand and love the country. Unfortunately, it seemed to some of them, the more Americans who came the greater was the number who preferred to avoid any real relationship with the Vietnamese.

Increasingly the Americans walled themselves into compounds, command posts and official buildings, which they furnished with air-conditioning, supermarkets, swimming pools and clubs—everything possible to keep the Vietnamese reality from penetrating the American one. For most the outside represented the threat of death, robbery, disease and the hatred presumed to be lurking behind the mask of an Asian face.

Of course there were just enough such evidence as Vietnamese units abandoning or betraying American advisers under fire to lend substances to many Americans' attitudes. Americans were ambushed in supposedly safe places and killed; they were robbed and cheated.

On the other hand, there were countless cases in which Americans short-changed or cheated Vietnamese—sometimes because of misunderstandings arising from the language barrier—and instances of brutal and overbearing behavior. Not least was the killing and wounding of people seemingly without reason.

The Communists were provided with ample evidence to support their denunciations of "American imperialism."

Despite the recriminations tenuous contact was maintained between Americans and Communists through an indirect telephone link. On the final day this correspondent telephoned the Vietcong delegation after a particularly heavy shelling of the Saigon airport by their side to ask about their safety, among other things.

"I cannot tell you how grateful we are for asking, especially considering the circumstances," was the reply. "We hope you all get through this somehow."

A few minutes before one of the last groups of distraught Americans rushed from their ravaged offices and hotel rooms to look for a bus to the airport, a Vietnamese friend arrived to say farewell. Some of the Americans were in tears, and the Vietnamese, seeking to comfort them, patted their shoulders and said:

"You may hear after you leave that some here have died, perhaps even at their own hand. You must not spend the rest of your lives with that guilt. It is just a part of Vietnam's black fate, in which you, all of you, became ensnared for a time. Fate is changeless and guiltless."

The New York Times, May 6, 1975

Dispatches

by Michael Herr

Breathing In

There was a map of Vietnam on the wall of my apartment in Saigon and some nights, coming back late to the city, I'd lie out on my bed and look at it, too tired to do anything more than just get my boots off. That map was a marvel, especially now that it wasn't real anymore. For one thing, it was very old. It had been left there years before by another tenant, probably a Frenchman, since the map had been made in Paris. The paper had buckled in its frame after years in the wet Saigon heat, laying a kind of veil over the countries it depicted. Vietnam was divided into its older territories of Tonkin, Annam and Cochin China, and to the west past Laos and Cambodge sat Siam, a kingdom. That's old, I'd tell visitors, that's a really old map.

If dead ground could come back and haunt you the way dead people do, they'd have been able to mark my map CURRENT *and burn the ones they'd been using since '64, but count on it, nothing like that was going to happen. It was late '67 now, even the most detailed maps didn't reveal much anymore; reading them was like trying to read the faces of the Vietnamese, and that was like trying to read the wind. We knew that the uses of most information were flexible, different pieces of ground told different stories to different people. We also knew that for years now there had been no country here but the war.*

The Mission was always telling us about VC units being engaged and wiped out and then reappearing a month later in full strength, there was nothing very spooky about that, but when we went up against his terrain we usually took it definitively, and even if we didn't keep it you could always see that we'd at least been there. At the end of my first week in-country I met an information officer in the headquarters of the 25th Division at Cu Chi who showed me on his map and then from his chopper

555

*what they'd done to the Ho Bo Woods, the vanished Ho Bo Woods,
taken off by giant Rome plows and chemicals and long, slow
fire, wasting hundreds of acres of cultivated plantation and wild
forest alike, "denying the enemy valuable resources and cover."*

*It had been part of his job for nearly a year now to tell people
about that operation; correspondents, touring congressmen,
movie stars, corporation presidents, staff officers from half the
armies in the world, and he still couldn't get over it. It seemed
to be keeping him young, his enthusiasm made you feel that even
the letters he wrote home to his wife were full of it, it really
showed what you could do if you had the know-how and the
hardware. And if in the months following that operation inci-
dences of enemy activity in the larger area of War Zone C had
increased "significantly," and American losses had doubled and
then doubled again, none of it was happening in any damn Ho
Bo Woods, you'd better believe it. . . .*

I

Going out at night the medics gave you pills, Dexedrine
breath like dead snakes kept too long in a jar. I never saw the
need for them myself, a little contact or anything that even
sounded like contact would give me more speed than I could
bear. Whenever I heard something outside of our clenched
little circle I'd practically flip, hoping to God that I wasn't the
only one who'd noticed it. A couple of rounds fired off in the
dark a kilometer away and the Elephant would be there kneeling on my chest, sending me down into my boots for a breath.
Once I thought I saw a light moving in the jungle and I
caught myself just under a whisper saying, "I'm not ready for
this, I'm not ready for this." That's when I decided to drop
it and do something else with my nights. And I wasn't going
out like the night ambushers did, or the Lurps, long-range
recon patrollers who did it night after night for weeks and
months, creeping up on VC base camps or around moving
columns of North Vietnamese. I was living too close to my
bones as it was, all I had to do was accept it. Anyway, I'd save
the pills for later, for Saigon and the awful depressions I always
had there.

I knew one 4th Division Lurp who took his pills by the

fistful, downs from the left pocket of his tiger suit and ups from the right, one to cut the trail for him and the other to send him down it. He told me that they cooled things out just right for him, that he could see that old jungle at night like he was looking at it through a starlight scope. "They sure give you the range," he said.

This was his third tour. In 1965 he'd been the only survivor in a platoon of the Cav wiped out going into the Ia Drang Valley. In '66 he'd come back with the Special Forces and one morning after an ambush he'd hidden under the bodies of his team while the VC walked all around them with knives, making sure. They stripped the bodies of their gear, the berets too, and finally went away, laughing. After that, there was nothing left for him in the war except the Lurps.

"I just can't hack it back in the World," he said. He told me that after he'd come back home the last time he would sit in his room all day, and sometimes he'd stick a hunting rifle out the window, leading people and cars as they passed his house until the only feeling he was aware of was all up in the tip of that one finger. "It used to put my folks real uptight," he said. But he put people uptight here too, even here.

"No man, I'm sorry, he's just too crazy for me," one of the men in his team said. "All's you got to do is look in his eyes, that's the whole fucking story right there."

"Yeah, but you better do it quick," someone else said. "I mean, you don't want to let him catch you at it."

But he always seemed to be watching for it, I think he slept with his eyes open, and I was afraid of him anyway. All I ever managed was one quick look in, and that was like looking at the floor of an ocean. He wore a gold earring and a headband torn from a piece of camouflage parachute material, and since nobody was about to tell him to get his hair cut it fell below his shoulders, covering a thick purple scar. Even at division he never went anywhere without at least a .45 and a knife, and he thought I was a freak because I wouldn't carry a weapon.

"Didn't you ever meet a reporter before?" I asked him.

"Tits on a bull," he said. "Nothing personal."

But what a story he told me, as one-pointed and resonant as any war story I ever heard, it took me a year to understand it:

"Patrol went up the mountain. One man came back. He died before he could tell us what happened."

I waited for the rest, but it seemed not to be that kind of story; when I asked him what had happened he just looked like he felt sorry for me, fucked if he'd waste time telling stories to anyone dumb as I was.

His face was all painted up for night walking now like a bad hallucination, not like the painted faces I'd seen in San Francisco only a few weeks before, the other extreme of the same theater. In the coming hours he'd stand as faceless and quiet in the jungle as a fallen tree, and God help his opposite numbers unless they had at least half a squad along, he was a good killer, one of our best. The rest of his team were gathered outside the tent, set a little apart from the other division units, with its own Lurp-designated latrine and its own exclusive freeze-dry rations, three-star war food, the same chop they sold at Abercrombie & Fitch. The regular division troops would almost shy off the path when they passed the area on their way to and from the mess tent. No matter how toughened up they became in the war, they still looked innocent compared to the Lurps. When the team had grouped they walked in a file down the hill to the lz across the strip to the perimeter and into the treeline.

I never spoke to him again, but I saw him. When they came back in the next morning he had a prisoner with him, blindfolded and with his elbows bound sharply behind him. The Lurp area would definitely be off limits during the interrogation, and anyway, I was already down at the strip waiting for a helicopter to come and take me out of there.

"Hey what're you guys, with the USO? Aw, we thought you was with the USO 'cause your hair's so long." Page took the kid's picture, I got the words down and Flynn laughed and told him we were the Rolling Stones. The three of us traveled around together for about a month that summer. At one lz the brigade chopper came in with a real foxtail hanging off the aerial, when the commander walked by us he almost took an infarction.

"Don't you men salute officers?"

"We're not men," Page said. "We're correspondents."

When the commander heard that, he wanted to throw a spontaneous operation for us, crank up his whole brigade and get some people killed. We had to get out on the next chopper to keep him from going ahead with it, amazing what some of them would do for a little ink. Page liked to augment his field gear with freak paraphernalia, scarves and beads, plus he was English, guys would stare at him like he'd just come down off a wall on Mars. Sean Flynn could look more incredibly beautiful than even his father, Errol, had thirty years before as Captain Blood, but sometimes he looked more like Artaud coming out of some heavy heart-of-darkness trip, overloaded on the information, the input! The input! He'd give off a bad sweat and sit for hours, combing his mustache through with the saw blade of his Swiss Army knife. We packed grass and tape: Have You Seen Your Mother Baby Standing in the Shadows, Best of the Animals, Strange Days, Purple Haze, Archie Bell and the Drells, "C'mon now everybody, do the Tighten Up. . . ." Once in a while we'd catch a chopper straight into one of the lower hells, but it was a quiet time in the war, mostly it was lz's and camps, grunts hanging around, faces, stories.

"Best way's to just keep moving," one of them told us. "Just keep moving, stay in motion, you know what I'm saying?"

We knew. He was a moving-target-survivor subscriber, a true child of the war, because except for the rare times when you were pinned or stranded the system was geared to keep you mobile, if that was what you thought you wanted. As a technique for staying alive it seemed to make as much sense as anything, given naturally that you were there to begin with and wanted to see it close; it started out sound and straight but it formed a cone as it progressed, because the more you moved the more you saw, the more you saw the more besides death and mutilation you risked, and the more you risked of that the more you would have to let go of one day as a "survivor." Some of us moved around the war like crazy people until we couldn't see which way the run was even taking us anymore, only the war all over its surface with occasional, unexpected penetration. As long as we could have choppers like taxis it took real exhaustion or depression near shock or a dozen pipes of opium to keep us even apparently quiet, we'd still be running around inside our skins like something was after us, ha ha, La Vida Loca.

In the months after I got back the hundreds of helicopters I'd flown in began to draw together until they'd formed a collective meta-chopper, and in my mind it was the sexiest thing going; saver-destroyer, provider-waster, right hand–left hand, nimble, fluent, canny and human; hot steel, grease, jungle-saturated canvas webbing, sweat cooling and warming up again, cassette rock and roll in one ear and door-gun fire in the other, fuel, heat, vitality and death, death itself, hardly an intruder. Men on the crews would say that once you'd carried a dead person he would always be there, riding with you. Like all combat people they were incredibly superstitious and invariably self-dramatic, but it was (I knew) unbearably true that close exposure to the dead sensitized you to the force of their presence and made for long reverberations; long. Some people were so delicate that one look was enough to wipe them away, but even bone-dumb grunts seemed to feel that something weird and extra was happening to them.

Helicopters and people jumping out of helicopters, people so in love they'd run to get on even when there wasn't any pressure. Choppers rising straight out of small cleared jungle spaces, wobbling down onto city rooftops, cartons of rations and ammunition thrown off, dead and wounded loaded on. Sometimes they were so plentiful and loose that you could touch down at five or six places in a day, look around, hear the talk, catch the next one out. There were installations as big as cities with 30,000 citizens, once we dropped in to feed supply to one man. God knows what kind of Lord Jim phoenix numbers he was doing in there, all he said to me was, "You didn't see a thing, right Chief? You weren't even here." There were posh fat air-conditioned camps like comfortable middle-class scenes with the violence tacit, "far away"; camps named for commanders' wives, LZ Thelma, LZ Betty Lou; number-named hilltops in trouble where I didn't want to stay; trail, paddy, swamp, deep hairy bush, scrub, swale, village, even city, where the ground couldn't drink up what the action spilled, it made you careful where you walked.

Sometimes the chopper you were riding in would top a hill and all the ground in front of you as far as the next hill would be charred and pitted and still smoking, and something between your chest and your stomach would turn over. Frail gray smoke where they'd burned off the rice fields around a free-strike zone, brilliant white smoke from phosphorus ("Willy Peter/Make you a buh liever"), deep black smoke from 'palm, they said that if you stood at the base of a column of napalm smoke it would suck the air right out of your lungs. Once we fanned over a little ville that had just been airstruck and the words of a song by Wingy Manone that I'd heard when I was a few years old snapped into my head, "Stop the War, These Cats Is Killing Themselves." Then we dropped, hovered, settled down into purple lz smoke, dozens of children broke from their hootches to run in toward the focus of our landing, the pilot laughing and saying, "Vietnam, man. Bomb 'em and feed 'em, bomb 'em and feed 'em."

Flying over jungle was almost pure pleasure, doing it on foot was nearly all pain. I never belonged in there. Maybe it really was what its people had always called it, Beyond; at the very least it was serious, I gave up things to it I probably never got back. ("Aw, jungle's okay. If you know her you can live in her real good, if you don't she'll take you down in an hour. Under.") Once in some thick jungle corner with some grunts standing around, a correspondent said, "Gee, you must really see some beautiful sunsets in here," and they almost pissed themselves laughing. But you could fly up and into hot tropic sunsets that would change the way you thought about light forever. You could also fly out of places that were so grim they turned to black and white in your head five minutes after you'd gone.

That could be the coldest one in the world, standing at the edge of a clearing watching the chopper you'd just come in on taking off again, leaving you there to think about what it was going to be for you now: if this was a bad place, the wrong place, maybe even the last place, and whether you'd made a terrible mistake this time.

There was a camp at Soc Trang where a man at the lz said,

"If you come looking for a story this is your lucky day, we got Condition Red here," and before the sound of the chopper had faded out, I knew I had it too.

"That's affirmative," the camp commander said, "we are *definitely* expecting rain. Glad to see you." He was a young captain, he was laughing and taping a bunch of sixteen clips together bottom to bottom for faster reloading, "grease." Everyone there was busy at it, cracking crates, squirreling away grenades, checking mortar pieces, piling rounds, clicking banana clips into automatic weapons that I'd never even seen before. They were wired into their listening posts out around the camp, into each other, into themselves, and when it got dark it got worse. The moon came up nasty and full, a fat moist piece of decadent fruit. It was soft and saffron-misted when you looked up at it, but its light over the sandbags and into the jungle was harsh and bright. We were all rubbing Army-issue nightfighter cosmetic under our eyes to cut the glare and the terrible things it made you see. (Around midnight, just for something to do, I crossed to the other perimeter and looked at the road running engineer-straight toward Route 4 like a yellow frozen ribbon out of sight and I saw it move, the whole road.) There were a few sharp arguments about who the light really favored, attackers or defenders, men were sitting around with Cinemascope eyes and jaws stuck out like they could shoot bullets, moving and antsing and shifting around inside their fatigues. "No sense us getting too relaxed, Charlie don't relax, just when you get good and comfortable is when he comes over and takes a giant shit on you." That was the level until morning, I smoked a pack an hour all night long, and nothing happened. Ten minutes after daybreak I was down at the lz asking about choppers.

A few days later Sean Flynn and I went up to a big firebase in the Americal TAOR that took it all the way over to another extreme, National Guard weekend. The colonel in command was so drunk that day that he could barely get his words out, and when he did, it was to say things like, "We aim to make good and goddammit sure that if *those guys* try *anything cute* they won't catch us with our pants down." The main mission there was to fire H&I, but one man told us that their record was the worst in the whole Corps, probably the whole country, they'd harassed and interdicted a lot of sleeping civilians and Korean Marines, even a couple of Americal patrols, but hardly any Viet Cong. (The colonel kept calling it "artillerary." The first time he said it Flynn and I looked away from each other, the second time we blew beer through our noses, but the colonel fell in laughing right away and more than covered us.) No sandbags, exposed shells, dirty pieces, guys going around giving us that look, "We're cool, how come you're not?" At the strip Sean was talking to the operator about it and the man got angry. "Oh *yeah*? Well fuck *you*, how tight do you think you want it? There ain't been any veecees around here in three months."

"So far so good," Sean said. "Hear anything on that chopper yet?"

But sometimes everything stopped, nothing flew, you couldn't even find out why. I got stuck for a chopper once in some lost patrol outpost in the Delta where the sergeant chain-ate candy bars and played country-and-western tapes twenty hours a day until I heard it in my sleep, some sleep, *Up on Wolverton Mountain* and *Lonesome as the bats and the bears in Miller's Cave* and *I fell into a burning ring of fire*, surrounded by strungout rednecks who weren't getting much sleep either because they couldn't trust one of their 400 mercenary troopers or their own hand-picked perimeter guards or anybody else except maybe Baby Ruth and Johnny Cash, they'd been waiting for it so long now they were afraid they wouldn't know it when they finally got it, *and it burns burns burns.* . . . Finally on the fourth day a helicopter came in to deliver meat and movies to the camp and I went out on it, so happy to get back to Saigon that I didn't crash for two days.

Airmobility, dig it, you weren't going anywhere. It made you feel safe, it made you feel Omni, but it was only a stunt, technology. Mobility was just mobility, it saved lives or took them all the time (saved mine I don't know how many times, maybe dozens, maybe none), what you really needed was a flexibility far greater than anything the technology could provide, some generous, spontaneous gift for accepting surprises, and I didn't have it. I got to hate surprises, control freak at the crossroads, if you were one of those people who always thought they had to know what was coming next, the war could cream you. It was the same with your ongoing attempts at getting used to the jungle or the blow-you-out climate or the saturating strangeness of the place which didn't lessen with exposure so often as it fattened and darkened in accumulating alienation. It was great if you could adapt, you had to try, but it wasn't the same as making a discipline, going into your own reserves and developing a real war metabolism, slow yourself down when your heart tried to punch its way through your chest, get swift when everything went to stop and all you could feel of your whole life was the entropy whipping through it. Unlovable terms.

The ground was always in play, always being swept. Under the ground was his, above it was ours. We had the air, we could get up in it but not disappear in *to* it, we could run but we couldn't hide, and he could do each so well that sometimes it looked like he was doing them both at once, while our finder just went limp. All the same, one place or another it was always going on, rock around the clock, we had the days and he had the nights. You could be in the most protected space in Vietnam and still know that your safety was provisional, that early death, blindness, loss of legs, arms or balls, major and lasting disfigurement—the whole rotten deal—could come in on the freakyfluky as easily as in the so-called expected ways, you heard so many of those stories it was a wonder anyone was left alive to die in firefights and mortar-rocket attacks. After a few weeks, when the nickel had jarred loose and dropped and I saw that everyone around me was carrying a gun, I also saw that any one of them could go off at any time, putting you where it wouldn't matter whether it had been an accident or not. The roads were mined, the trails booby-trapped, satchel charges and grenades blew up jeeps and movie theaters, the VC got work inside all the camps as shoeshine boys and laundresses and honey-dippers, they'd starch your fatigues and burn your shit and then go home and mortar your area. Saigon and Cholon and Danang held such hostile vibes that you felt you were being dry-sniped every time someone looked at you, and choppers fell out of the sky like fat poisoned birds a hundred times a day. After a while I couldn't get on one without thinking that I must be out of my fucking mind.

Fear and motion, fear and standstill, no preferred cut there, no way even to be clear about which was really worse, the wait or the delivery. Combat spared far more men than it wasted, but everyone suffered the time between contact, especially when they were going out every day looking for it; bad going on foot, terrible in trucks and APC's, awful in helicopters, the worst, traveling so fast toward something so frightening. I can remember times when I went half dead with my fear of the motion, the speed and direction already fixed and pointed one way. It was painful enough just flying "safe" hops between firebases and lz's; if you were ever on a helicopter that had been hit by ground fire your deep, perpetual chopper anxiety was guaranteed. At least actual contact when it was happening would draw long raggedy strands of energy out of you, it was juicy, fast and refining, and traveling toward it was hollow, dry, cold and steady, it never let you alone. All you could do was look around at the other people on board and see if they were as scared and numbed out as you were. If it looked like they weren't you thought they were insane, if it looked like they were it made you feel a lot worse.

I went through that thing a number of times and only got a fast return on my fear once, a too classic hot landing with the heat coming from the trees about 300 yards away, sweeping machine-gun fire that sent men head down into swampy water, running on their hands and knees toward the grass where it wasn't blown flat by the rotor blades, not much to be running for but better than nothing. The helicopter pulled up before we'd all gotten out, leaving the last few men to jump twenty feet down between the guns across the paddy and the gun on the chopper door. When we'd all reached the cover of the wall and the captain had made a check, we were amazed to see that no one had even been hurt, except for one man who'd sprained both his ankles jumping. Afterward, I remembered that I'd been down in the muck worrying about leeches. I guess you could say that I was refusing to accept the situation.

"Boy, you sure get offered some shitty choices," a Marine

once said to me, and I couldn't help but feel that what he really meant was that you didn't get offered any at all. Specifically, he was just talking about a couple of C-ration cans, "dinner," but considering his young life you couldn't blame him for thinking that if he knew one thing for sure, it was that there was no one anywhere who cared less about what *he* wanted. There wasn't anybody he wanted to thank for his food, but he was grateful that he was still alive to eat it, that the motherfucker hadn't scarfed him up first. He hadn't been anything but tired and scared for six months and he'd lost a lot, mostly people, and seen far too much, but he was breathing in and breathing out, some kind of choice all by itself.

He had one of those faces, I saw that face at least a thousand times at a hundred bases and camps, all the youth sucked out of the eyes, the color drawn from the skin, cold white lips, you knew he wouldn't wait for any of it to come back. Life had made him old, he'd live it out old. All those faces, sometimes it was like looking into faces at a rock concert, locked in, the event had them; or like students who were very heavily advanced, serious beyond what you'd call their years if you didn't know for yourself what the minutes and hours of those years were made up of. Not just like all the ones you saw who looked like they couldn't drag their asses through another day of it. (How do you feel when a nineteen-year-old kid tells you from the bottom of his heart that he's gotten too old for this kind of shit?) Not like the faces of the dead or wounded either, they could look more released than overtaken. These were the faces of boys whose whole lives seemed to have backed up on them, they'd be a few feet away but they'd be looking back at you over a distance you knew you'd never really cross. We'd talk, sometimes fly together, guys going out on R&R, guys escorting bodies, guys who'd flipped over into extremes of peace or violence. Once I flew with a kid who was going home, he looked back down once at the ground where he'd spent the year and spilled his whole load of tears. Sometimes you even flew with the dead.

Once I jumped on a chopper that was full of them. The kid in the op shack had said that there would be a body on board, but he'd been given some wrong information. "How bad do you want to get to Danang?" he'd asked me, and I'd said, "Bad."

When I saw what was happening I didn't want to get on, but they'd made a divert and a special landing for me, I had to go with the chopper I'd drawn, I was afraid of looking squeamish. (I remember, too, thinking that a chopper full of dead men was far less likely to get shot down than one full of living.) They weren't even in bags. They'd been on a truck near one of the firebases in the DMZ that was firing support for Khe Sanh, and the truck had hit a Command-detonated mine, then they'd been rocketed. The Marines were always running out of things, even food, ammo and medicine, it wasn't so strange that they'd run out of bags too. The men had been wrapped around in ponchos, some of them carelessly fastened with plastic straps, and loaded on board. There was a small space cleared for me between one of them and the door gunner, who looked pale and so tremendously furious that I thought he was angry with me and I couldn't look at him for a while. When we went up the wind blew through the ship and made the ponchos shake and tremble until the one next to me blew back in a fast brutal flap, uncovering the face. They hadn't even closed his eyes for him.

The gunner started hollering as loud as he could, "Fix it! Fix it!," maybe he thought the eyes were looking at him, but there wasn't anything I could do. My hand went there a couple of times and I couldn't, and then I did. I pulled the poncho tight, lifted his head carefully and tucked the poncho under it, and then I couldn't believe that I'd done it. All during the ride the gunner kept trying to smile, and when we landed at Dong Ha he thanked me and ran off to get a detail. The pilots jumped down and walked away without looking back once, like they'd never seen that chopper before in their lives. I flew the rest of the way to Danang in a general's plane.

II

You know how it is, you want to look and you don't want to look. I can remember the strange feelings I had when I was a kid looking at war photographs in *Life*, the ones that showed dead people or a lot of dead people lying close together in a field or a street, often touching, seeming to hold each other. Even when the picture was sharp and cleanly defined, something wasn't clear at all, something repressed that monitored the images and withheld their essential information. It may have legitimized my fascination, letting me look for as long as I wanted; I didn't have a language for it then, but I remember now the shame I felt, like looking at first porn, all the porn in the world. I could have looked until my lamps went out and I still wouldn't have accepted the connection between a detached leg and the rest of a body, or the poses and positions that always happened (one day I'd hear it called "response-to-impact"), bodies wrenched too fast and violently into unbelievable contortion. Or the total impersonality of group death, making them lie anywhere and any way it left them, hanging over barbed wire or thrown promiscuously on top of other dead, or up into the trees like terminal acrobats, *Look what I can do.*

Supposedly, you weren't going to have that kind of obscuration when you finally started seeing them on real ground in front of you, but you tended to manufacture it anyway because of how often and how badly you needed protection from what you were seeing, had actually come 30,000 miles to see. Once I looked at them strung from the perimeter to the treeline, most of them clumped together nearest the wire, then in smaller numbers but tighter groups midway, fanning out into lots of scattered points nearer the treeline, with one all by himself half into the bush and half out. "Close but no cigar," the captain said, and then a few of his men went out there and kicked them all in the head, thirty-seven of them. Then I heard an M-16 on full automatic starting to go through clips, a second to fire, three to plug in a fresh clip, and I saw a man out there, doing it. Every round was like a tiny concentration of high-velocity wind, making the bodies wince and shiver. When he finished he walked by us on the way back to his hootch, and I knew I hadn't seen anything until I saw his face. It was flushed and mottled and twisted like he had his face skin on inside out, a patch of green that was too dark, a streak of red running into bruise purple, a lot of sick gray white in between, he looked like he'd had a heart attack out there. His eyes were rolled up half into his head, his mouth was sprung open and his tongue was out, but he was smiling. Really a dude who'd shot his wad. The captain wasn't too pleased about my having seen that.

There wasn't a day when someone didn't ask me what I was doing there. Sometimes an especially smart grunt or another correspondent would even ask me what I was *really* doing there, as though I could say anything honest about it except "Blah blah blah cover the war" or "Blah blah blah write a book." Maybe we accepted each other's stories about why we were there at face value: the grunts who "had" to be there, the spooks and civilians whose corporate faith had led them there, the correspondents whose curiosity or ambition drew them over. But somewhere all the mythic tracks intersected, from the lowest John Wayne wetdream to the most aggravated soldier-poet fantasy, and where they did I believe that everyone knew everything about everyone else, every one of us there a true volunteer. Not that you didn't hear some over-ripe bullshit about it: Hearts and Minds, Peoples of the Republic, tumbling dominoes, maintaining the equilibrium of the Dingdong by containing the ever encroaching Doodah; you could also hear the other, some young soldier speaking in all bloody innocence, saying, "All that's just a *load*, man. We're here to kill gooks. Period." Which wasn't at all true of me. I was there to watch.

Talk about impersonating an identity, about locking into a role, about irony: I went to cover the war and the war covered me; an old story, unless of course you've never heard it. I went there behind the crude but serious belief that you had to be able to look at anything, serious because I acted on it and went, crude because I didn't know, it took the war to teach it, that you were as responsible for everything you saw as you were for everything you did. The problem was that you didn't always know what you were seeing until later, maybe years later, that a lot of it never made it in at all, it just stayed stored there in your eyes. Time and information, rock and roll, life itself, the information isn't frozen, you are.

Sometimes I didn't know if an action took a second or an hour or if I dreamed it or what. In war more than in other life you don't really know what you're doing most of the time, you're just behaving, and afterward you can make up any kind of bullshit you want to about it, say you felt good or bad, loved it or hated it, did this or that, the right thing or the wrong thing; still, what happened happened.

Coming back, telling stories, I'd say, "Oh man I was scared," and, "Oh God I thought it was all over," a long time before I knew how scared I was really supposed to be, or how clear and closed and beyond my control "all over" could become. I wasn't dumb but I sure was raw, certain connections are hard to make when you come from a place where they go around with war in their heads all the time.

"If you get hit," a medic told me, "we can chopper you back to base-camp hospital in like twenty minutes."

"If you get hit real bad," a corpsman said, "they'll get your case to Japan in twelve hours."

"If you get killed," a spec 4 from Graves promised, "we'll have you home in a week."

TIME IS ON MY SIDE, already written there across the first helmet I ever wore there. And underneath it, in smaller lettering that read more like a whispered prayer than an assertion, *No lie, GI*. The rear-hatch gunner on a Chinook threw it to me that first morning at the Kontum airstrip, a few hours after the Dak To fighting had ended, screaming at me through the rotor wind, "You *keep* that, we got *plenty*, good *luck*!" and then flying off. I was so glad to have the equipment that I didn't stop to think where it had to have come from. The sweatband inside was seasoned up black and greasy, it was more alive now than the man who'd worn it, when I got rid of it ten minutes later I didn't just leave it on the ground, I snuck away from it furtive and ashamed, afraid that someone would see it and call after me, "Hey numbnuts, you forgot something. . . ."

That morning when I tried to go out they sent me down the line from a colonel to a major to a captain to a sergeant, who took one look, called me Freshmeat, and told me to go find some other outfit to get myself killed with. I didn't know what was going on, I was so nervous I started to laugh. I told him that nothing was going to happen to me and he gave my shoulder a tender, menacing pat and said, "This ain't the fucking movies over here, you know." I laughed again and said that I knew, but he knew that I didn't.

Day one, if anything could have penetrated that first innocence I might have taken the next plane out. Out absolutely. It was like a walk through a colony of stroke victims, a thousand men on a cold rainy airfield after too much of something I'd never really know, "a way you'll never be," dirt and blood and torn fatigues, eyes that poured out a steady charge of wasted horror. I'd just missed the biggest battle of the war so far, I was telling myself that I was sorry, but it was right there all around me and I didn't even know it. I couldn't look at anyone for more than a second, I didn't want to be caught listening, some war correspondent, I didn't know what to say or do, I didn't like it already. When the rain stopped and the ponchos came off there was a smell that I thought was going to make me sick: rot, sump, tannery, open grave, dump-fire—awful, you'd walk into pockets of Old Spice that made it even worse. I wanted badly to find some place to sit alone and smoke a cigarette, to find a face that would cover my face the way my poncho covered my new fatigues. I'd worn them once before, yesterday morning in Saigon, bringing them out of the black market and back to the hotel, dressing up in front of the mirror, making faces and moves I'd never make again. And loving it. Now, nearby on the ground, there was a man sleeping with a poncho over his head and a radio in his arms, I heard Sam the Sham singing "Lil' Red Riding Hood."

I turned to walk some other way and there was a man standing in front of me. He didn't exactly block me, but he didn't move either. He tottered a little and blinked, he looked at me and through me, no one had ever looked at me like that before. I felt a cold fat drop of sweat start down the middle of my back like a spider, it seemed to take an hour to finish its run. The man lit a cigarette and then sort of slobbered it out, I couldn't imagine what I was seeing. He tried again with a fresh cigarette. I gave him the light for that one, there was a flicker of focus, acknowledgment, but after a few puffs it went out too, and he let it drop to the ground. "I couldn't

spit for a week up there," he said, "and now I can't fucking
stop."

*When the 173rd held services for their dead from Dak To the
boots of the dead men were arranged in formation on the
ground. It was an old paratrooper tradition, but knowing that
didn't reduce it or make it any less spooky, a company's worth
of jump boots standing empty in the dust taking benediction,
while the real substance of the ceremony was being bagged and
tagged and shipped back home through what they called the KIA
Travel Bureau. A lot of the people there that day accepted the
boots as solemn symbols and went into deep prayer. Others stood
around watching with grudging respect, others photographed it
and some just thought it was a lot of bitter bullshit. All they saw
out there was one more set of spare parts, and they wouldn't
have looked around for holy ghosts if some of those boots filled up
again and walked.*

*Dak To itself had only been the command point for a combat
without focus that tore a thirty-mile arc over the hills running
northeast to southwest of the small base and airfield there from
early November through Thanksgiving 1967, fighting that grew
in size and fame while it grew more vicious and out of control.
In October the small Dak To Special Forces compound had taken
some mortar and rocket fire, patrols went out, patrols collided,
companies splintered the action and spread it across the hills in
a sequence of small, isolated firefights that afterward were described as strategy; battalions were sucked into it, then divisions,
then reinforced divisions. Anyway, we knew for sure that we had
a reinforced division in it, the 4th plus, and we said that they
had one in it too, although a lot of people believed that a couple
of light flexible regiments could have done what the NVA did
up and down those hills for three weeks, leaving us to claim that
we'd driven him up 1338, up 943, up 875 and 876, while the opposing claims remained mostly unspoken and probably unnecessary. And then instead of really ending, the battle vanished.
The North Vietnamese collected up their gear and most of their
dead and "disappeared" during the night, leaving a few bodies
behind for our troops to kick and count.*

*"Just like goin' in against the Japs," one kid called it; the
heaviest fighting in Vietnam since the Ia Drang Valley two years*

before, and one of the only times after Ia Drang when ground fire was so intense that the medevacs couldn't land through it. Wounded backed up for hours and sometimes days, and a lot of men died who might have been saved. Resupply couldn't make it in either, and the early worry about running out of ammunition grew into a panic and beyond, it became real. At the worst, a battalion of Airborne assaulting 875 got caught in an ambush sprung from behind, where no NVA had been reported, and its three companies were pinned and cut off in the raking fire of that trap for two days. Afterward, when a correspondent asked one of the survivors what had happened he was told, "What the fuck do you think *happened? We got shot to pieces." The correspondent started to write that down and the paratrooper said, "Make that 'little pieces.' We were still shaking the trees for dog tags when we pulled back out of there."*

Even after the North had gone away, logistics and transport remained a problem. A big battle had to be dismantled piece by piece and man by man. It was raining hard every day now, the small strip at Dak To became overloaded and unworkable, and a lot of troops were shuttled down to the larger strip at Kontum. Some even ended up as far out of their way as Pleiku, fifty miles to the south, for sorting and transport back to their units around II Corps. The living, the wounded and the dead flew together in crowded Chinooks, and it was nothing for guys to walk on top of the half-covered corpses packed in the aisles to get to a seat, or to make jokes among themselves about how funny they all looked, the dumb dead fuckers.

There were men sitting in loose groups all around the strip at Kontum, hundreds of them arranged by unit waiting to be picked up again and flown out. Except for a small sandbagged ops shack and a medical tent, there was no shelter anywhere from the rain. Some of the men had rigged up mostly useless tents with their ponchos, a lot lay out sleeping in the rain with helmets or packs for pillows, most just sat or stood around waiting. Their faces were hidden deep inside the cover of their poncho hoods, white eye movement and silence, walking among them made you feel like you were being watched from hundreds of isolated caves. Every twenty minutes or so a helicopter would land, men would come out or be carried out, others would get on and the chopper would rear up on the strip and fly away, some toward Pleiku and the hospital, others back to the Dak To area and the mop-up operations there. The rotors of the Chinooks cut twin spaces out of the rain, forcing the spray in slanting jets for fifty yards around. Just knowing what was in those choppers gave the spray a bad taste, strong and briny. You didn't want to leave it on your face long enough to dry.

Back from the strip a fat, middle-aged man was screaming at some troops who were pissing on the ground. His poncho was pulled back away from the front of his helmet enough to show captain's bars, but nobody even turned around to look at him. He groped under his poncho and came up with a .45, pointed it into the rain and fired off a shot that made an empty faraway pop, like it had gone off under wet sand. The men finished, buttoned up and walked away laughing, leaving the captain alone shouting orders to police up the filth; thousands of empty and half-eaten ration cans, soggy clots of Stars and Stripes, an M-16 that someone had just left lying there and, worse, evidence of a carelessness unimaginable to the captain, it stank even in the cold rain, but it would police itself in an hour or two if the rain kept up.

The ground action had been over for nearly twenty-four hours now, but it was still going on in compulsive replay among the men who'd been there:

"A dead buddy is some tough shit, but bringing your own ass out alive can sure help you to get over it."

"We had this lieutenant, honest to Christ he was about the biggest dipshit fool of all time, all time. We called him Lieutenant Gladly 'cause he was always going like, 'Men . . . Men, I won't never ask you to do nothing I wouldn't do myself gladly,' what an asshole. We was on 1338 and he goes to me, 'Take a little run up to the ridge and report to me,' and I goes like, 'Never happen, Sir.' So he does, he goes up there himself and damned if the fucker didn't get zapped. He said we was gonna have a real serious talk when he come back, too. Sorry 'bout that."

"Kid here [not really here, "here" just a figure of speech] gets blown away ten feet in back of us. I swear to God, I thought I was looking at ten different guys when I turned around. . . ."

"You guys are so full of shit it's coming out of your fucking ears!" one man was saying. PRAY FOR WAR was written on the side of his helmet, and he was talking mostly to a man whose *helmet name was* SWINGING DICK. *"You were pissing up every-thing but your fucking toenails, Scudo, don't you tell me you weren't scared man, don't you fucking dare, 'cause I was right fucking there man, and I was scared shit! I was scared every fucking minute, and I'm no different from any body else!"*

"Well big deal, candy ass," Swinging Dick said. "You were scared."

"Damn straight! Damn straight! You're damn fucking straight I was scared! You're about the dumbest motherfucker I ever met, Scudo, but you're not that dumb. The Marines *aren't even that dumb man, I don't care, all that bullshit they've got in the Marine Corps about how Marines aren't ever afraid, oh wow, I'll fucking bet. . . . I'll bet the Marines are* just as scared*!"*

He started to get up but his knees gave under him. He made a quick grasping spasm out of control, like a misfire in the nervous system, and when he fell back he brought a stack of M-16's with him. They made a sharp clatter and everyone jerked and twitched out of the way, looking at each other as though they couldn't remember for a minute whether they needed to find cover or not.

"Hey baby, hey, watch where you're goin' there," a para-trooper said, but he was laughing, they were all laughing, and Pray For War was laughing harder than any of them, so hard that it filled suddenly with air and cracked over into high giggles. When he lifted his face again it was all tracked with tears.

"You gonna stand there, asshole?" he said to Swinging Dick. "Or are you gonna help me up on my fucking feet*?"*

Swinging Dick reached down and grabbed his wrists, locking them and pulling him up slowly until their faces were a couple of inches apart. For a second it looked like they were going to kiss.

"Looking good," Pray For War said. "Mmmm, Scudo, you are really looking good, man. It don't look to me like you were scared at all up there. You only look like about ten thousand miles of bad road."

What they say is totally true, it's funny the things you remember. Like a black paratrooper with the 101st who glided by and said, "I been *scaled* man, I'm *smooth* now," and went on, into my past and I hope his future, leaving me to wonder not what he meant (that was easy), but where he'd been to get his language. On a cold wet day in Hue our jeep turned into the soccer stadium where hundreds of North Vietnamese bodies had been collected, I saw them, but they don't have the force in my memory that a dog and a duck have who died together in a small terrorist explosion in Saigon. Once I ran into a soldier standing by himself in the middle of a small jungle clearing where I'd wandered off to take a leak. We said hello, but he seemed very uptight about my being there. He told me that the guys were all sick of sitting around waiting and that he'd come out to see if he could draw a little fire. What a look we gave each other. I backed out of there fast, I didn't want to bother him while he was working.

This is already a long time ago, I can remember the feelings but I can't still have them. A common prayer for the over-attached: You'll let it go sooner or later, why not do it now? Memory print, voices and faces, stories like filament through a piece of time, so attached to the experience that nothing moved and nothing went away.

"First letter I got from my old man was all about how proud he was that I'm here and how we have this *duty* to, you know, *I* don't fucking know, whatever . . . and it really made me feel great. Shit, my father hardly said good morning to me before. Well, I been here eight months now, and when I get home I'm gonna have all I can do to keep from killing that cocksucker. . . ."

Everywhere you went people said, "Well, I hope you get a story," and everywhere you went you did.

"Oh, it ain't so bad. My last tour was better though, not so much mickeymouse, Command gettin' in your way so you can't even do your job. Shit, last three patrols I was on we had fucking *orders* not to return fire going through the villages, that's what a fucked-up war it's gettin' to be anymore. My *last* tour we'd go through and that was it, we'd rip out the hedges and burn the hootches and blow all the wells and kill every chicken, pig and cow in the whole fucking ville. I mean, if we can't shoot these people, what the fuck are we doing here?"

Some journalists talked about no-story operations, but I never went on one. Even when an operation never got off the

ground, there was always the strip. Those were the same journalists who would ask us what the fuck we ever found to talk
to grunts about, who said they never heard a grunt talk about
anything except cars, football and chone. But they all had a
story, and in the war they were driven to tell it.

"We was getting killed and the Dinks was panicking, and
when the choppers come in to get us out, there wasn't enough
room for everybody. The Dinks was screaming and carrying
on, grabbing hold of the treads and grabbing hold of our legs
till we couldn't get the choppers up. So we just said smack it,
let these people get their own fucking choppers, and we
started shooting them. And even then they kept on coming,
oh man it was wild. I mean they could sure as shit believe
that Charlie was shooting them, but they couldn't believe that
we was doing it too. . . ."

That was a story from the A Shau Valley years before my
time there, an old story with the hair still growing on it.
Sometimes the stories were so fresh that the teller was in
shock, sometimes they were long and complex, sometimes the
whole thing was contained in a few words on a helmet or a
wall, and sometimes they were hardly stories at all but sounds
and gestures packed with so much urgency that they became
more dramatic than a novel, men talking in short violent
bursts as though they were afraid they might not get to finish,
or saying it almost out of a dream, innocent, offhand and
mighty direct, "Oh you know, it was just a firefight, we killed
some of them and they killed some of us." A lot of what you
heard, you heard all the time, men on tape, deceitful and
counterarticulate, and some of it was low enough, guys whose
range seemed to stop at "Git some, git some, harharhar!" But
once in a while you'd hear something fresh, and a couple of
times you'd even hear something high, like the corpsman at
Khe Sanh who said, "If it ain't the fucking incoming it's the
fucking outgoing. Only difference is who gets the fucking
grease, and that ain't no fucking difference at all."

The mix was so amazing; incipient saints and realized hom-
icidals, unconscious lyric poets and mean dumb motherfuckers
with their brains all down in their necks; and even though by
the time I left I knew where all the stories came from and
where they were going, I was never bored, never even unsur-

prised. Obviously, what they really wanted to tell you was how tired they were and how sick of it, how moved they'd been and how afraid. But maybe that was me, by then my posture was shot: "reporter." ("Must be pretty hard to stay detached," a man on the plane to San Francisco said, and I said, "Impossible.") After a year I felt so plugged in to all the stories and the images and the fear that even the dead started telling me stories, you'd hear them out of a remote but accessible space where there were no ideas, no emotions, no facts, no proper language, only clean information. However many times it happened, whether I'd known them or not, no matter what I'd felt about them or the way they'd died, their story was always there and it was always the same: it went, "Put yourself in my place."

One afternoon I mistook a bloody nose for a headwound, and I didn't have to wonder anymore how I'd behave if I ever got hit. We were walking out on a sweep north of Tay Ninh City, toward the Cambodian border, and a mortar round came in about thirty yards away. I had no sense of those distances then, even after six or seven weeks in Vietnam I still thought of that kind of information as a journalists' detail that could be picked up later, not something a survivor might have to know. When we fell down on the ground the kid in front of me put his boot into my face. I didn't feel the boot, it got lost in the tremendous concussion I made hitting the ground, but I felt a sharp pain in a line over my eyes. The kid turned around and started going into something insane right away, "Aw I'm sorry, shit I'm sorry, oh no man I'm *sorry*." Some hot stinking metal had been put into my mouth, I thought I tasted brains there sizzling on the end of my tongue, and the kid was fumbling for his canteen and looking really scared, pale, near tears, his voice shaking, "Shit I'm just a fucking oaf, I'm a fucking clod, you're okay, you're really okay," and somewhere in there I got the feeling that it was him, somehow he'd just killed me. I don't think I said anything, but I made a sound that I can remember now, a shrill blubbering pitched to carry more terror than I'd ever known existed, like the sounds they've recorded off of plants being burned, like an old woman going under for the last time. My hands went flying everywhere all over my head, I had to find it and touch it. There seemed to be no blood coming from the top, none from the forehead, none running out of my eyes, my *eyes*! In a moment of half-relief the pain became specific, I thought that just my nose had been blown off, or in, or apart, and the kid was still going into it for himself, "Oh man, I'm really fucking sorry."

Twenty yards in front of us men were running around totally out of their minds. One man was dead (they told me later it was only because he'd been walking forward with his flak jacket open, another real detail to get down and never fuck with again), one was on his hands and knees vomiting some evil pink substance, and one, quite near us, was propped up against a tree facing away from the direction of the round, making himself look at the incredible thing that had just happened to his leg, screwed around about once at some point below his knee like a goofy scarecrow leg. He looked away and then back again, looking at it for a few seconds longer each time, then he settled in for about a minute, shaking his head and smiling, until his face became serious and he passed out.

By then I'd found my nose and realized what had happened, all that had happened, not even broken, my glasses weren't even broken. I took the kid's canteen and soaked my sweat scarf, washing the blood off where it had caked on my lip and chin. He had stopped apologizing, and there was no pity in his face anymore. When I handed his canteen back to him, he was laughing at me.

I never told that story to anyone, and I never went back to that outfit again either.

III

In Saigon I always went to sleep stoned so I almost always lost my dreams, probably just as well, sock in deep and dim under that information and get whatever rest you could, wake up tapped of all images but the ones remembered from the day or the week before, with only the taste of a bad dream in your mouth like you'd been chewing on a roll of dirty old pennies in your sleep. I'd watched grunts asleep putting out the REM's like a firefight in the dark, I'm sure it was the same with me. They'd say (I'd ask) that they didn't remember their dreams either when they were in the zone, but on R&R or in the hospital their dreaming would be constant, open, violent and clear, like a man in the Pleiku hospital on the night I was there. It was three in the morning, scary and upsetting like hearing a language for the first time and somehow understanding every word, the voice loud and small at the same time, insistent, calling, "*Who? Who?* Who's in the next room?" There was a single shaded light over the desk at the end of the ward where I sat with the orderly. I could only see the first few beds, it felt like there were a thousand of them running out into the darkness, but actually there were only twenty in each row. After the man had repeated it a few times there was a change like the break in a fever, he sounded like a pleading little boy. I could see cigarettes being lighted at the far end of the ward, mumbles and groans, wounded men returning to consciousness, pain, but the man who'd been dreaming slept through it. . . . As for my own dreams, the ones I lost there would make it through later, I should have known, some things will just naturally follow until they take. The night would come when they'd be vivid and unremitting, that night the beginning of a long string, I'd remember then and wake up half believing that I'd never really been in any of those places.

Saigon *cafarde*, a bitch, nothing for it but some smoke and a little lie-down, waking in the late afternoon on damp pillows, feeling the emptiness of the bed behind you as you walked to the windows looking down at Tu Do. Or just lying there tracking the rotations of the ceiling fan, reaching for the fat roach that sat on my Zippo in a yellow disk of grass tar. There were mornings when I'd do it before my feet even hit the floor. Dear Mom, stoned again.

In the Highlands, where the Montagnards would trade you a pound of legendary grass for a carton of Salems, I got stoned with some infantry from the 4th. One of them had worked for months on his pipe, beautifully carved and painted with flowers and peace symbols. There was a reedy little man in the circle who grinned all the time but hardly spoke. He pulled a thick plastic bag out of his pack and handed it over to me. It was full of what looked like large pieces of dried fruit. I was stoned and hungry, I almost put my hand in there, but it had a bad weight to it. The other men were giving each other looks, some amused, some embarrassed and even angry. Someone had told me once, there were a lot more ears than heads in Vietnam; just information. When I handed it back he was still grinning, but he looked sadder than a monkey.

In Saigon and Danang we'd get stoned together and keep the common pool stocked and tended. It was bottomless and alive with Lurps, seals, recondos, Green-Beret bushmasters, redundant mutilators, heavy rapers, eye-shooters, widow-makers, nametakers, classic essential American types; point men, *isolatos* and outriders like they were programmed in their genes to do it, the first taste made them crazy for it, just like they knew it would. You thought you were separate and pro-tected, you could travel the war for a hundred years, a swim in that pool could still be worth a piece of your balance.

We'd all heard about the man in the Highlands who was "building his own gook," parts were the least of his troubles. In Chu Lai some Marines pointed a man out to me and swore to God they'd seen him bayonet a wounded NVA and then lick the bayonet clean. There was a famous story, some re-porters asked a door gunner, "How can you shoot women and children?" and he'd answered, "It's easy, you just don't lead 'em so much." Well, they said you needed a sense of humor, there you go, even the VC had one. Once after an ambush that killed a lot of Americans, they covered the field with copies of a photograph that showed one more young, dead American, with the punch line mimeographed on the back, "Your X-rays have just come back from the lab and we think we know what your problem is."

"I was sitting in a Chinook and this guy across from me had his sixteen loaded and it was pointing like ha-ha at my heart. I made signs for him to kind of put it up and he started laugh-ing. He said something to the guys next to him and they started laughing too. . . ."

"He probably said, 'Asshole here wants me to put my gun up,'" Dana said.

"Yeah, well, you know . . . sometimes I think one of them's

going to just do it, clear his weapon like bbbdddrrrpp, ya ha! I
got a reporter!"

"There's a colonel in the Seventh Marines who said he'd give
a three-day pass to any one of his men who killed a correspondent
for him," Flynn said. "A week if they get Dana."

"Well that's just bullshit," Dana said. "They fucking think
I'm God."

"Yeah, it's true," Sean said. "It's true, you little fucker, you're
just like they are."

Dana Stone had just come down from Danang for more
equipment, he'd fed all his cameras to the war again, they were
either in the shop or totaled. Flynn had come back the night
before from six weeks with the Special Forces in III Corps, he
hadn't said a word about what had gone on up there. "Spaced":
he was sitting on the floor by the air-conditioner with his back
against the wall trying to watch the sweat running down from
his hairline.

We were all in a room at the Continental Hotel that belonged
to Keith Kay, the CBS cameraman. It was early May and there
was a lot of heavy combat all around the city, a big offensive,
friends came in from there and went out again all week long.
Across the way, on the latticed porches of the Continental annex,
we could see the Indians shuffle back and forth in their underwear, bushed from another hard day of buying and selling
money. (Their mosque, near L'Amiral Restaurant, was called
the Bank of India. When the Saigon police, the White Mice,
raided it they found two million in cold green.) There were
trucks and jeeps and a thousand bikes moving in the street, and
a little girl with a withered leg darting back and forth on
wooden crutches faster than a dragonfly to sell her cigarettes. She
had a face like a child dakini, so beautiful that people who
needed to keep their edge blunt could hardly bear to look at her.
Her competition were street boys, "Changee money," "Boom-
boom picture," "Dinkydao cigarette," hustle and connection
ran like a current down Tu Do, from the cathedral to the river.
Rounding Le Loi there was a large group of correspondents coming back from the briefing, standard diurnal informational
freak-o-rama, Five O'Clock Follies, Jive at Five, war stories; at
the corner they broke formation and went to their offices to file,
we watched them, the wasted clocking the wasted.

A new correspondent came into the room to say hello, just arrived from New York, and he started asking Dana a lot of questions right away, sort of bullshit questions about the killing radius of various mortars and the penetration capability of rockets, the ranges of AK's and 16's, what shells did when they hit treetops, paddy and hard ground. He was in his late thirties and he was dressed in one of those jungle-hell leisure suits that the tailors on Tu Do were getting rich cranking out, with enough flaps and slots and cargo pockets to carry supply for a squad. Dana would answer one question and the man would ask two more, but that made sense since the man had never been out and Dana hardly ever came in. Oral transmission, those who knew and those who didn't, new people were always coming in with their own basic load of questions, energetic and hungry; someone had done it for you, it was a kind of blessing if you were in a position to answer some questions, if only to say that the questions couldn't be answered. This man's questions were something else, they seemed to be taking on hysteria as they went along.

"Is it exhilarating? Boy, I'll bet it's exhilarating."

"Aw you wouldn't believe it," Dana said.

Tim Page came in. He'd been out at the Y Bridge all day taking pictures of the fighting there and he'd gotten some CS in his eyes. He was rubbing them and weeping and bitching.

"Oh you're English," the new man said. "I was just there. What's CS?"

"It's a gas gas gas," Page said. "Gaaaaaa. Arrrrgggh!" and he did a soft version of raking his nails down his face, he used his fingertips but it left red marks anyway. "Blind Lemon Page," Flynn said, and laughed while Page took the record that was playing on the turntable off without asking anybody and put on Jimi Hendrix: long tense organic guitar line that made him shiver like frantic electric ecstasy was shooting up from the carpet through his spine straight to the old pleasure center in his cream-cheese brain, shaking his head so that his hair waved all around him, Have You Ever Been Experienced?

"What does it look like when a man gets hit in the balls?" the new man said, as though that was the question he'd really meant to ask all along, and it came as close as you could get to a breach of taste in that room; palpable embarrassment all around, Flynn

moved his eyes like he was following a butterfly up out of sight,
Page got sniffy and offended, but he was amused, too. Dana
just sat there putting out the still rays, taking snaps with his
eyes. "Oh I dunno," he said. "It all just goes sort of gooey."

We all started to laugh, everyone except Dana, because he'd
seen that, he was just telling the man. I didn't hear what the
man started to ask next, but Dana stopped him and said, "Only
thing I can tell you that might actually do you some good is to
go back up to your room and practice hitting the floor for a
while."

Beautiful for once and only once, just past dawn flying toward
the center of the city in a Loach, view from a bubble floating
at 800 feet. In that space, at that hour, you could see what
people had seen forty years before, Paris of the East, Pearl of
the Orient, long open avenues lined and bowered over by
trees running into spacious parks, precisioned scale, all under
the soft shell from a million breakfast fires, camphor smoke
rising and diffusing, covering Saigon and the shining veins of
the river with a warmth like the return of better times. Just a
projection, that was the thing about choppers, you had to
come down sometime, down to the moment, the street, if
you found a pearl down there you got to keep it.

By 7:30 it was beyond berserk with bikes, the air was like
L.A. on short plumbing, the subtle city war inside the war had
renewed itself for another day, relatively light on actual violence but intense with bad feeling: despair, impacted rage, impotent gnawing resentment; thousands of Vietnamese in the
service of a pyramid that wouldn't stand for five years, plug-
ging the feed tube into their own hearts, grasping and gorg-
ing; young Americans in from the boonies on TDY, charged
with hatred and grounded in fear of the Vietnamese;
thousands of Americans sitting in their offices crying in bored
chorus, "You can't get these people to do a fucking thing,
you can't get these people to do a fucking thing." And all the
others, theirs and ours, who just didn't want to play, it sickened them. That December the GVN Department of Labor
had announced that the refugee problem had been solved,
that "all refugees [had] been assimilated into the economy,"
but mostly they seemed to have assimilated themselves into

the city's roughest corners, alleyways, mud slides, under parked cars. Cardboard boxes that had carried air-conditioners and refrigerators housed up to ten children, most Americans and plenty of Vietnamese would cross the street to avoid trash heaps that fed whole families. And this was still months before Tet, "refugees up the gazops," a flood. I'd heard that the GVN Department of Labor had nine American advisors for every Vietnamese.

In Broddards and La Pagode and the pizzeria around the corner, the Cowboys and Vietnamese "students" would hang out all day, screaming obscure arguments at each other, cadging off Americans, stealing tips from the tables, reading Pléiade editions of Proust, Malraux, Camus. One of them talked to me a few times but we couldn't really communicate, all I understood was his obsessive comparison between Rome and Washington, and that he seemed to believe that Poe had been a French writer. In the late afternoon the Cowboys would leave the cafés and milk bars and ride down hard on Lam Son Square to pick the Allies. They could snap a Rolex off your wrist like a hawk hitting a field mouse; wallets, pens, cameras, eyeglasses, anything; if the war had gone on any longer they'd have found a way to whip the boots off your feet. They'd hardly leave their saddles and they never looked back. There was a soldier down from the 1st Division who was taking snapshots of his friends with some bar girls in front of the Vietnamese National Assembly. He'd gotten his shot focused and centered but before he pushed the button his camera was a block away, leaving him in the bike's backwash with a fresh pink welt on his throat where the cord had been torn and helpless amazement on his face, "Well I'll be dipped in shit!"; as a little boy raced across the square, zipped a piece of cardboard up the soldier's shirtfront and took off around the corner with his Paper Mate. The White Mice stood around giggling, but there were a lot of us watching from the Continental terrace, a kind of gasp went up from the tables, and later when he came up for a beer he said, "I'm goin' back to the war, man, this fucking Saigon is too much for me." There was a large group of civilian engineers there, the same men you'd see in the restaurants throwing food at each other, and one of them, a fat old boy, said, "You ever catch one of them li'l nigs just pinch 'em. Pinch 'em hard. Boy, they hate that.''

Five to seven were bleary low hours in Saigon, the city's energy ebbing at dusk, until it got dark and movement was replaced with apprehension. Saigon at night was still Vietnam at night, night was the war's truest medium; night was when it got really interesting in the villages, the TV crews couldn't film at night, the Phoenix was a night bird, it flew in and out of Saigon all the time.

Maybe you had to be pathological to find glamour in Saigon, maybe you just had to settle for very little, but Saigon had it for me, and danger activated it. The days of big, persistent terror in Saigon were over, but everyone felt that they could come back again any time, heavy like 1963–5, when they hit the old Brinks BOQ on Christmas Eve, when they blew up the My Canh floating restaurant, waited for it to be rebuilt and moved to another spot on the river, and then blew it up again, when they bombed the first U.S. embassy and changed the war forever from the intimate inside out. There were four known VC sapper battalions in the Saigon–Cholon area, dread sappers, guerrilla superstars, they didn't even have to do anything to put the fear out. Empty ambulances sat parked at all hours in front of the new embassy. Guards ran mirrors and "devices" under all vehicles entering all installations, BOQ's were fronted with sandbags, checkpoints and wire, high-gauge grilles filled our windows, but they still got through once in a while, random terror but real, even the supposedly terror-free safe spots worked out between the Corsican mob and the VC offered plenty of anxiety. Saigon just before Tet; guess, guess again.

Those nights there was a serious tiger lady going around on a Honda shooting American officers on the street with a .45. I think she'd killed over a dozen in three months; the Saigon papers described her as "beautiful," but I don't know how anybody knew that. The commander of one of the Saigon MP battalions said he thought it was a man dressed in an *ao dai* because a .45 was "an awful lot of gun for a itty bitty Vietnamese woman."

Saigon, the center, where every action in the bushes hundreds of miles away fed back into town on a karmic wire strung so tight that if you touched it in the early morning it would sing all day and all night. Nothing so horrible ever happened upcountry that it was beyond language fix and press relations, a squeeze fit into the computers would make the heaviest numbers jump up and dance. You'd either meet an optimism that no violence could unconvince or a cynicism that would eat itself empty every day and then turn, hungry and malignant, on whatever it could for a bite, friendly or hostile, it didn't matter. Those men called dead Vietnamese "believers," a lost American platoon was "a black eye," they talked as though killing a man was nothing more than depriving him of his vigor.

It seemed the least of the war's contradictions that to lose your worst sense of American shame you had to leave the Dial Soapers in Saigon and a hundred headquarters who spoke goodworks and killed nobody themselves, and go out to the grungy men in the jungle who talked bloody murder and killed people all the time. It was true that the grunts stripped belts and packs and weapons from their enemies; Saigon wasn't a flat market, these goods filtered down and in with the other spoils: Rolexes, cameras, snakeskin shoes from Taiwan, air-brush portraits of nude Vietnamese women with breasts like varnished beach balls, huge wooden carvings that they set on their desks to give you the finger when you walked into their offices. In Saigon it never mattered what they told you, even less when they actually seemed to believe it. Maps, charts, figures, projections, fly fantasies, names of places, of operations, of commanders, of weapons; memories, guesses, second guesses, experiences (new, old, real, imagined, stolen); histories, attitudes—you could let it go, let it all go. If you wanted some war news in Saigon you had to hear it in stories brought from the field by friends, see it in the lost watchful eyes of the Saigonese, or do it like Trashman, reading the cracks in the sidewalk.

Sitting in Saigon was like sitting inside the folded petals of a poisonous flower, the poison history, fucked in its root no matter how far back you wanted to run your trace. Saigon was the only place left with a continuity that someone as far outside as I was could recognize. Hue and Danang were like remote closed societies, mute and intractable. Villages, even large ones, were fragile, a village could disappear in an afternoon, and the countryside was either blasted over cold and dead or already back in Charles' hands. Saigon remained, the repository and the arena, it breathed history, expelled it like toxin, Shit Piss and Corruption. Paved swamp, hot mushy winds that never cleaned anything away, heavy thermal seal over diesel fuel, mildew, garbage, excrement, atmosphere. A five-block walk in that could take it out of you, you'd get back to the hotel with your head feeling like one of those chocolate apples, tap it sharply in the right spot and it falls apart in sections. Saigon, November 1967: "The animals are sick with love." Not much chance anymore for history to go on unselfconsciously.

You'd stand nailed there in your tracks sometimes, no bearings and none in sight, thinking, *Where the fuck am I?*, fallen into some unnatural East-West interface, a California corridor cut and bought and burned deep into Asia, and once we'd done it we couldn't remember what for. It was axiomatic that it was about ideological space, we were there to bring them the choice, bringing it to them like Sherman bringing the Jubilee through Georgia, clean through it, wall to wall with pacified indigenous and scorched earth. (In the Vietnamese sawmills they had to change the blades every five minutes, some of our lumber had gotten into some of theirs.) There was such a dense concentration of American energy there, American and essentially adolescent, if that energy could have been channeled into anything more than noise, waste and pain it would have lighted up Indochina for a thousand years.

The Mission and the motion: military arms and civilian arms, more combatant between themselves than together against the Cong. Gun arms, knife arms, pencil arms, head-and-stomach arms, hearts-and-minds arms, flying arms, creeping-peeping arms, information arms as tricky as the arms of Plastic Man. At the bottom was the shitface grunt, at the top a Command trinity: a blue-eyed, hero-faced general, a geriatrics-emergency ambassador and a hale, heartless CIA performer. (Robert "Blowtorch" Komer, chief of CORDS, spook anagram for Other War, pacification, another word for war. If

William Blake had "reported" to him that he'd seen angels in the trees, Komer would have tried to talk him out of it. Failing there, he'd have ordered defoliation.) All through the middle were the Vietnam War and the Vietnamese, not always exactly innocent bystanders, probably no accident that we'd found each other. If milk snakes could kill, you might compare the Mission and its arms to a big intertwined ball of baby milk snakes. Mostly they were that innocent, and about that conscious. And a lot, one way or the other, had some satisfaction. They believed that God was going to thank them for it.

Innocent; for the noncombatants stationed in Saigon or one of the giant bases, the war wasn't much more real than if they'd been getting it on TV back at Leonard Wood or Andrews. There was the common failure of feeling and imagination compounded by punishing boredom, an alienation beyond tolerance and a terrible, ongoing anxiety that it might one day, any day, come closer than it had so far. And operating inside of that fear was the half-hidden, half-vaunted jealousy of every grunt who ever went out there and killed himself a gook, furtive vicarious bloodthirsting behind 10,000 desks, a fantasy life rich with lurid war-comics adventure, a smudge of closet throatsticker on every morning report, requisition slip, pay voucher, medical profile, information handout and sermon in the entire system.

Prayers in the Delta, prayers in the Highlands, prayers in the Marine bunkers of the "frontier" facing the DMZ, and for every prayer there was a counter-prayer—it was hard to see who had the edge. In Dalat the emperor's mother sprinkled rice in her hair so the birds could fly around her and feed while she said her morning prayers. In wood-paneled, air-conditioned chapels in Saigon, MACV padres would fire one up to sweet muscular Jesus, blessing ammo dumps and 105's and officers' clubs. The best-armed patrols in history went out after services to feed smoke to people whose priests could let themselves burn down to consecrated ash on street corners. Deep in the alleys you could hear small Buddhist chimes ringing for peace, *hoa bien*; smell incense in the middle of the thickest Asian street funk; see groups of ARVN with their families waiting for transport huddled around a burning prayer strip. Sermonettes came over Armed Forces radio every couple of hours, once I heard a chaplain from the 9th Division starting up, "Oh Gawd, help us learn to live with Thee in a more dynamic way in these perilous times, that we may better serve Thee in the struggle against Thine enemies. . . ." Holy war, long-nose jihad like a face-off between one god who would hold the coonskin to the wall while we nailed it up, and another whose detachment would see the blood run out of ten generations, if that was how long it took for the wheel to go around.

And around. While the last falling-off contacts were still going on and the last casualties being dusted off, Command added Dak To to our victory list, a reflexive move supported by the Saigon press corps but never once or for a minute by reporters who'd seen it going on from meters or even inches away, and this latest media defection added more bitterness to an already rotten mix, leaving the commanding general of the 4th to wonder out loud and in my hearing whether we were or weren't all Americans in this thing together. I said I thought we were. For sure we were.

"*. . . Wow I love it in the movies when they say like, 'Okay Jim, where do you want it?'*"

"*Right! Right! Yeah, beautiful, I don't want it at all! Haw, shit . . . where do you fucking want it?*"

Mythopathic moment; *Fort Apache*, where Henry Fonda as the new colonel says to John Wayne, the old hand, "We saw some Apache as we neared the Fort," and John Wayne says, "If you saw them, sir, they weren't Apache." But this colonel is obsessed, brave like a maniac, not very bright, a West Point aristo wounded in his career and his pride, posted out to some Arizona shithole with only marginal consolation: he's a professional and this is a war, the only war we've got. So he gives the John Wayne information a pass and he and half his command get wiped out. More a war movie than a Western, Nam paradigm, Vietnam, not a movie, no jive cartoon either where the characters get smacked around and electrocuted and dropped from heights, flattened out and frizzed black and broken like a dish, then up again and whole and back in the game, "Nobody dies," as someone said in another war movie.

*

In the first week of December 1967 I turned on the radio and heard this over AFVN: "The Pentagon announced today that, compared to Korea, the Vietnam War will be an economy war, provided that it does not exceed the Korean War in length, which means that it will have to end *sometime* in 1968."

By the time that Westmoreland came home that fall to cheerlead and request-beg another quarter of a million men, with his light-at-the-end-of-the-tunnel collateral, there were people leaning so far out to hear good news that a lot of them slipped over the edge and said that they could see it too. (Outside of Tay Ninh City a man whose work kept him "up to fucking here" in tunnels, lobbing grenades into them, shooting his gun into them, popping CS smoke into them, crawling down into them himself to bring the bad guys out dead or alive, he almost smiled when he heard that one and said, "What does that asshole know about tunnels?")

A few months earlier there had been an attempt Higher to crank up the Home For Christmas rumor, but it wouldn't take, the troop consensus was too strong, it went, "Never happen." If a commander told you he thought he had it pretty well under control it was like talking to a pessimist. Most would say that they either had it wrapped up or wound down; "He's all pissed out, Charlie's all pissed out, booger's shot his whole wad," one of them promised me, while in Saigon it would be restructured for briefings, "He no longer maintains in our view capability to mount, execute or sustain a serious offensive action," and a reporter behind me, from *The New York Times* no less, laughed and said, "Mount this, Colonel." But in the boonies, where they were deprived of all information except what they'd gathered for themselves on either side of the treeline, they'd look around like someone was watching and say, "I dunno, Charlie's up to something. Slick, slick, that fucker's *so* slick. Watch!"

The summer before, thousands of Marines had gone humping across northern I Corps in multi-division sweeps, "Taking the D out of DMZ," but the North never really broke out into the open for it, hard to believe that anyone ever thought that they would. Mostly it was an invasion of a thousand operation-miles of high summer dry season stroke weather, six-canteen patrols that came back either contactless or chewed over by ambushes and quick, deft mortar-rocket attacks, some from other Marine outfits. By September they were "containing" at Con Thien, sitting there while the NVA killed them with artillery. In II Corps a month of random contact near the Laotian border had sharpened into the big war around Dak To. III Corps, outside of Saigon, was most confusing of all, the VC were running what was described in a month-end, sit/rep handout as "a series of half-hearted, unambitious ground attacks" from Tay Ninh through Loc Ninh to Bu Dop, border skirmishes that some reporters saw as purposely limited rather than half-hearted, patterned and extremely well coordinated, like someone was making practice runs for a major offensive. IV Corps was what it had always been, obscure isolated Delta war, authentic guerrilla action where betrayal was as much an increment as bullets. People close to Special Forces had heard upsetting stories about the A Camps down there, falling apart from inside, mercenary mutinies and triple cross, until only a few were still effective.

That fall, all that the Mission talked about was control: arms control, information control, resources control, psycho-political control, population control, control of the almost supernatural inflation, control of terrain through the Strategy of the Periphery. But when the talk had passed, the only thing left standing up that looked true was your sense of how out of control things really were. Year after year, season after season, wet and dry, using up options faster than rounds on a machine-gun belt, we called it right and righteous, viable and even almost won, and it still only went on the way it went on. When all the projections of intent and strategy twist and turn back on you, tracking team blood, "sorry" just won't cover it. There's nothing so embarrassing as when things go wrong in a war.

You couldn't find two people who agreed about when it began, how could you say when it began going off? Mission intellectuals like 1954 as the reference date; if you saw as far back as War II and the Japanese occupation you were practically a historical visionary. "Realists" said that it began for us in 1961, and the common run of Mission flack insisted on 1965, post-Tonkin Resolution, as though all the killing that had gone before wasn't really war. Anyway, you couldn't use standard methods to date the doom; might as well say that Vietnam was where the Trail of Tears was headed all along, the turnaround point where it would touch and come back to form a containing perimeter; might just as well lay it on the proto-Gringos who found the New England woods too raw and empty for their peace and filled them up with their own imported devils. Maybe it was already over for us in Indochina when Alden Pyle's body washed up under the bridge at Dakao, his lungs all full of mud; maybe it caved in with Dien Bien Phu. But the first happened in a novel, and while the second happened on the ground it happened to the French, and Washington gave it no more substance than if Graham Greene had made it up too. Straight history, auto-revised history, history without handles, for all the books and articles and white papers, all the talk and the miles of film, something wasn't answered, it wasn't even asked. We were backgrounded, deep, but when the background started sliding forward not a single life was saved by the information. The thing had transmitted too much energy, it heated up too hot, hiding low under the fact-figure crossfire there was a secret history, and not a lot of people felt like running in there to bring it out.

One day in 1963 Henry Cabot Lodge was walking around the Saigon Zoo with some reporters, and a tiger pissed on him through the bars of its cage. Lodge made a joke, something like, "He who wears the pee of the tiger is assured of success in the coming year." Maybe nothing's so unfunny as an omen read wrong.

Some people think 1963's a long time ago; when a dead American in the jungle was an event, a grim thrilling novelty. It was spookwar then, adventure; not exactly soldiers, not even advisors yet, but Irregulars, working in remote places under little direct authority, acting out their fantasies with more freedom than most men ever know. Years later, leftovers from that time would describe it, they'd bring in names like Gordon, Burton and Lawrence, elevated crazies of older adventures who'd burst from their tents and bungalows to rub up hard against the natives, hot on the sex-and-death trail, "lost to headquarters." There had been Ivy League spooks who'd gone bumbling and mucking around in jeeps and beat-up Citroëns, Swedish K's across their knees, literally picnicking along the Cambodian border, buying Chinese-made shirts and sandals and umbrellas. There'd been ethnologue spooks who loved with their brains and forced that passion on the locals, whom they'd imitate, squatting in black pajamas, jabbering in Vietnamese. There had been one man who "owned" Long An Province, a Duke of Nha Trang, hundreds of others whose authority was absolute in hamlets or hamlet complexes where they ran their ops until the wind changed and their ops got run back on them. There were spook deities, like Lou Conein, "Black Luigi," who (they said) ran it down the middle with the VC, the GVN, the Mission and the Corsican Maf; and Edward Lansdale himself, still there in '67, his villa a Saigon landmark where he poured tea and whiskey for second-generation spooks who adored him, even now that his batteries were dead. There were executive spooks who'd turn up at airstrips and jungle clearings sweating like a wheel of cheese in their white suits and neckties; bureau spooks who sat on dead asses in Dalat and Qui Nhon, or out jerking off in some New Life Village; Air America spooks who could take guns or junk or any kind of death at all and make it fly; Special Forces spooks running around in a fury of skill to ice Victor Charlie.

History's heavy attrition, tic and toc with teeth, the smarter ones saw it winding down for them on the day that Lodge first arrived in Saigon and commandeered the villa of the current CIA chief, a moment of history that seemed even sweeter when you knew that the villa had once been headquarters of the Deuxième Bureau. Officially, the complexion of the problem had changed (too many people were getting killed, for one thing), and the romance of spooking started to fall away like dead meat from a bone. As sure as heat rises, their time was over. The war passed along, this time into the hard hands of firepower freaks out to eat the country whole, and with no fine touches either, leaving the spooks on the beach.

They never became as dangerous as they'd wanted to be, they never knew how dangerous they really were. Their adventure became our war, then a war bogged down in time, so much time so badly accounted for that it finally became entrenched as an institution because there had never been room made for it to go anywhere else. The Irregulars either got out or became regular in a hurry. By 1967 all you saw was the impaired spook reflex, prim adventurers living too long on the bloodless fringes of the action, heartbroken and memory-ruptured, working alone together toward a classified universe. They seemed like the saddest casualties of the Sixties, all the promise of good service on the New Frontier either gone or surviving like the vaguest salvages of a dream, still in love with their dead leader, blown away in his prime and theirs; left now with the lonely gift they had of trusting no one, the crust of ice always forming over the eye, the jargon stream thinning and trickling out: *Frontier sealing, census grievance, black operations* (pretty good, for jargon), *revolutionary development, armed propaganda.* I asked a spook what that one meant and he just smiled. Surveillance, collecting and reporting, was like a carnival bear now, broken and dumb, an Intelligence beast, our own. And by late 1967, while it went humping and stalking all over Vietnam the Tet Offensive was already so much incoming.

IV

There were times during the night when all the jungle sounds would stop at once. There was no dwindling down or fading away, it was all gone in a single instant as though some signal had been transmitted out to the life: bats, birds, snakes, monkeys, insects, picking up on a frequency that a thousand years in the jungle might condition you to receive, but leaving you as it was to wonder what you weren't hearing now, straining for any sound, one piece of information. I had heard it before in other jungles, the Amazon and the Philippines, but those jungles were "secure," there wasn't much chance that hundreds of Viet Cong were coming and going, moving and waiting, living out there just to do you harm. The thought of that one could turn any sudden silence into a space that you'd fill with everything you thought was quiet in you, it could even put you on the approach to clairaudience. You thought you heard impossible things: damp roots breathing, fruit sweating, fervid bug action, the heartbeat of tiny animals.

You could sustain that sensitivity for a long time, either until the babbling and chittering and shrieking of the jungle had started up again, or until something familiar brought you out of it, a helicopter flying around above your canopy or the strangely reassuring sound next to you of one going into the chamber. Once we heard a really frightening thing blaring down from a Psyops soundship broadcasting the sound of a baby crying. You wouldn't have wanted to hear that during daylight, let alone at night when the volume and distortion came down through two or three layers of cover and froze us all in place for a moment. And there wasn't much release in the pitched hysteria of the message that followed, hyper-Vietnamese like an icepick in the ear, something like, "Friendly Baby, GVN Baby, Don't Let This Happen to *Your* Baby, Resist the Viet Cong Today!"

Sometimes you'd get so tired that you'd forget where you were and sleep the way you hadn't slept since you were a child. I know that a lot of people there never got up from that kind of sleep; some called them lucky (Never knew what hit him), some called them fucked (If he'd been on the stick . . .), but that was worse than academic, everyone's death got talked about, it was a way of constantly touching and turning the odds, and real sleep was at a premium. (I met a ranger-recondo who could go to sleep just like that, say, "Guess I'll get some," close his eyes and be there, day or night, sitting or lying down, sleeping through some things but not others; a loud radio or a 105 firing outside the tent wouldn't wake him, but a rustle in the bushes fifty feet away would, or a stopped generator.) Mostly what you had was on the agitated side of half-sleep, you thought you were sleeping but you were really just waiting. Night sweats, harsh functionings of con-sciousness, drifting in and out of your head, pinned to a can-vas cot somewhere, looking up at a strange ceiling or out through a tent flap at the glimmering night sky of a combat zone. Or dozing and waking under mosquito netting in a mess of slick sweat, gagging for air that wasn't 99 percent moisture, one clean breath to dry-sluice your anxiety and the backwater smell of your own body. But all you got and all there was were misty clots of air that corroded your appetite and burned your eyes and made your cigarettes taste like swollen insects rolled up and smoked alive, crackling and wet. There were spots in the jungle where you had to have a cigarette going all the time, whether you smoked or not, just to keep the mosquitoes from swarming into your mouth. War under water, swamp fever and instant involuntary weight control, malarias that could burn you out and cave you in, put you into twenty-three hours of sleep a day without giving you a minute of rest, leaving you there to listen to the trance music that they said came in with terminal brain funk. ("Take your pills, baby," a medic in Can Tho told me. "Big orange ones every week, little white ones every day, and don't miss a day whatever you do. They got strains over here that could waste a heavyset fella like you in a week.") Sometimes you couldn't live with the terms any longer and headed for air-conditioners in Danang and Saigon. And sometimes the only reason you didn't panic was that you didn't have the energy.

Every day people were dying there because of some small detail that they couldn't be bothered to observe. Imagine being too tired to snap a flak jacket closed, too tired to clean your rifle, too tired to guard a light, too tired to deal with the half-inch margins of safety that moving through the war often demanded, just too tired to give a fuck and then dying behind that exhaustion. There were times when the whole war itself seemed tapped of its vitality: epic enervation, the machine running half-assed and depressed, fueled on the watery residue of last year's war-making energy. Entire divisions would function in a bad dream state, acting out a weird set of moves without any connection to their source. Once I talked for maybe five minutes with a sergeant who had just brought his squad in from a long patrol before I realized that the dopey-dummy film over his eyes and the fly abstraction of his words were coming from deep sleep. He was standing there at the bar of the NCO club with his eyes open and a beer in his hand, responding to some dream conversation far inside his head. It really gave me the creeps—this was the second day of the Tet Offensive, our installation was more or less surrounded, the only secure road out of there was littered with dead Vietnamese, information was scarce and I was pretty touchy and tired myself—and for a second I imagined that I was talking to a dead man. When I told him about it later he just laughed and said, "Shit, that's nothing. I do that all the time."

One night I woke up and heard the sounds of a firefight going on kilometers away, a "skirmish" outside our perimeter, muffled by distance to sound like the noises we made playing guns as children, KSSSHH KSSSHH; we knew it was more authentic than BANG BANG, it enriched the game and this game was the same, only way out of hand at last, too rich for all but a few serious players. The rules now were tight and absolute, no arguing over who missed who and who was really dead; *No fair* was no good, *Why me?* the saddest question in the world.

Well, good luck, the Vietnam verbal tic, even Ocean Eyes, the third-tour Lurp, had remembered to at least say it to me that night before he went on the job. It came out dry and distant, I knew he didn't care one way or the other, maybe I admired his detachment. It was as though people couldn't stop themselves from saying it, even when they actually meant to express the opposite wish, like, "Die, motherfucker." Usually it was only an uninhabited passage of dead language, sometimes it came out five times in a sentence, like punctuation, often it was spoken flat side up to telegraph the belief that there wasn't any way out; tough shit, *sin loi,* smack it, good luck. Sometimes, though, it was said with such feeling and tenderness that it could crack your mask, that much love where there was so much war. Me too, every day, compulsively, good luck: to friends in the press corps going out on operations, to grunts I'd meet at firebases and airstrips, to the wounded, the dead and all the Vietnamese I ever saw getting fucked over by us and each other, less often but most passionately to myself, and though I meant it every time I said it, it was meaningless. It was like telling someone going out in a storm not to get any on him, it was the same as saying, "Gee, I hope you don't get killed or wounded or see anything that drives you insane." You could make all the ritual moves, carry your lucky piece, wear your magic jungle hat, kiss your thumb knuckle smooth as stones under running water, the

Inscrutable Immutable was still out there, and you kept on or not at its pitiless discretion. All you could say that wasn't fundamentally lame was something like, "He who bites it this day is safe from the next," and that was exactly what nobody wanted to hear.

After enough time passed and memory receded and settled, the name itself became a prayer, coded like all prayer to go past the extremes of petition and gratitude: Vietnam Vietnam Vietnam, say again, until the word lost all its old loads of pain, pleasure, horror, guilt, nostalgia. Then and there, everyone was just trying to get through it, existential crunch, no atheists in foxholes like you wouldn't believe. Even bitter refracted faith was better than none at all, like the black Marine I'd heard about during heavy shelling at Con Thien who said, "Don't worry, baby, God'll think of something."

Flip religion, it was so far out, you couldn't blame anybody for believing anything. Guys dressed up in Batman fetishes, I saw a whole squad like that, it gave them a kind of dumb esprit. Guys stuck the ace of spades in their helmet bands, they picked relics off of an enemy they'd killed, a little transfer of power; they carried around five-pound Bibles from home, crosses, St. Christophers, mezuzahs, locks of hair, girlfriends' underwear, snaps of their families, their wives, their dogs, their cows, their cars, pictures of John Kennedy, Lyndon Johnson, Martin Luther King, Huey Newton, the Pope, Che Guevara, the Beatles, Jimi Hendrix, wiggier than cargo cultists. One man was carrying an oatmeal cookie through his tour, wrapped up in foil and plastic and three pair of socks. He took a lot of shit about it ("When you go to sleep we're gonna eat your fucking cookie"), but his wife had baked it and mailed it to him, he wasn't kidding.

On operations you'd see men clustering around the charmed grunt that many outfits created who would take himself and whoever stayed close enough through a field of safety, at least until he rotated home or got blown away, and then the outfit would hand the charm to someone else. If a bullet creased your head or you'd stepped on a dud mine or a grenade rolled between your feet and just lay there, you were magic enough. If you had any kind of extra-sense capacity, if you could smell VC or their danger the way hunting guides smelled the coming weather, if you had special night vision, or great ears, you were magic too; anything bad that happened to you could leave the men in your outfit pretty depressed. I met a man in the Cav who'd been "fucking the duck" one afternoon, sound asleep in a huge tent with thirty cots inside, all empty but his, when some mortar rounds came in, tore the tent down to canvas slaw and put frags through every single cot but his, he was still high out of his mind from it, speedy, sure and lucky. The Soldier's Prayer came in two versions: Standard, printed on a plastic-coated card by the Defense Department, and Standard Revised, impossible to convey because it got translated outside of language, into chaos—screams, begging, promises, threats, sobs, repetitions of holy names until their throats were cracked and dry, until some men had bitten through their collar points and rifle straps and even their dog-tag chains.

Varieties of religious experience, good news and bad news; a lot of men found their compassion in the war, some found it and couldn't live with it, war-washed shutdown of feeling, like who gives a fuck. People retreated into positions of hard irony, cynicism, despair, some saw the action and declared for it, only heavy killing could make them feel so alive. And some just went insane, followed the black-light arrow around the bend and took possession of the madness that had been waiting there in trust for them for eighteen or twenty-five or fifty years. Every time there was combat you had a license to go maniac, everyone snapped over the line at least once there and nobody noticed, they hardly noticed if you forgot to snap back again.

One afternoon at Khe Sanh a Marine opened the door of a latrine and was killed by a grenade that had been rigged on the door. The Command tried to blame it on a North Vietnamese infiltrator, but the grunts knew what had happened: "Like a gook is really gonna tunnel all the way in here to booby-trap a shithouse, right? Some guy just flipped out is all." And it became another one of those stories that moved across the DMZ, making people laugh and shake their heads and look knowingly at each other, but shocking no one. They'd talk about physical wounds in one way and psychic wounds in another, each man in a squad would tell you how crazy everyone else in the squad was, everyone knew grunts who'd gone crazy in the middle of a firefight, gone crazy on patrol, gone crazy back at camp, gone crazy on R&R, gone crazy during their first month home. Going crazy was built into the tour, the best you could hope for was that it didn't happen around you, the kind of crazy that made men empty clips into strangers or fix grenades on latrine doors. That was *really* crazy; anything less was almost standard, as standard as the vague prolonged stares and involuntary smiles, common as ponchos or 16's or any other piece of war issue. If you wanted someone to know you'd gone insane you really had to sound off like you had a pair, "Scream a lot, and all the time."

Some people just wanted to blow it all to hell, animal vegetable and mineral. They wanted a Vietnam they could fit into their car ashtrays; the joke went, "What you do is, you load all the Friendlies onto ships and take them out to the South China Sea. Then you bomb the country flat. Then you sink the ships." A lot of people knew that the country could never be won, only destroyed, and they locked into that with breathtaking concentration, no quarter, laying down the seeds of the disease, roundeye fever, until it reached plague proportions, taking one from every family, a family from every hamlet, a hamlet from every province, until a million had died from it and millions more were left uncentered and lost in their flight from it.

Up on the roof of the Rex BOQ in Saigon I walked into a scene more bellicose than a firefight, at least 500 officers nailed to the bar in a hail of chits, shiny irradiant faces talking war, men drinking like they were going to the front, and maybe a few of them really were. The rest were already there, Saigon duty; coming through a year of that without becoming totally blown out indicated as much heart as you'd need to take a machine-gun position with your hands, you sure couldn't take one with your mouth. We'd watched a movie (*Nevada Smith*, Steve McQueen working through a hard-revenge scenario, riding away at the end burned clean but somehow empty and old too, like he'd lost his margin for regeneration through violence); now there was a live act, Tito and His Playgirls,

"Up up and awayeeyay in my beaudifoo balloooon," one of those Filipino combos that even the USO wouldn't touch, hollow beat, morbid rock and roll like steamed grease in the muggy air.

Roof of the Rex, ground zero, men who looked like they'd been suckled by wolves, they could die right there and their jaws would work for another half-hour. This is where they asked you, "Are you a Dove or a Hawk?" and "Would you rather fight them here or in Pasadena?" *Maybe we could beat them in Pasadena*, I'd think, but I wouldn't say it, especially not here where they knew that I knew that they really weren't fighting anybody anywhere anyway, it made them pretty touchy. That night I listened while a colonel explained the war in terms of protein. We were a nation of high-protein, meat-eating hunters, while the other guy just ate rice and a few grungy fish heads. We were going to club him to death with our meat; what could you say except, "Colonel, you're insane"? It was like turning up in the middle of some black looneytune where the Duck had all the lines. I only jumped in once, spontaneous as shock, during Tet when I heard a doctor bragging that he'd refused to allow wounded Vietnamese into his ward. "But Jesus Christ," I said, "didn't you take the Hippocratic Oath?" but he was ready for me. "Yeah," he said, "I took it in America." Doomsday celebs, technomaniac projectionists; chemicals, gases, lasers, sonic-electric ballbreakers that were still on the boards; and for back-up, deep in all their hearts, there were always the Nukes, they loved to remind you that we had some, "right here in-country." Once I met a colonel who had a plan to shorten the war by dropping piranha into the paddies of the North. He was talking fish but his dreamy eyes were full of mega-death.

"Come on," the captain said, "we'll take you out to play Cowboys and Indians." We walked out from Song Be in a long line, maybe a hundred men; rifles, heavy automatics, mortars, portable one-shot rocket-launchers, radios, medics; breaking into some kind of sweep formation, five files with small teams of specialists in each file. A gunship flew close hover-cover until we came to some low hills, then two more ships came along and peppered the hills until we'd passed safely through them. It was a beautiful operation. We played all morning until someone on the point got something—a "scout," they thought, and then they didn't know. They couldn't even tell for sure whether he was from a friendly tribe or not, no markings on his arrows because his quiver was empty, like his pockets and his hands. The captain thought about it during the walk back, but when we got to camp he put it in his report, "One VC killed"; good for the unit, he said, not bad for the captain either.

Search and Destroy, more a gestalt than a tactic, brought up alive and steaming from the Command psyche. Not just a walk and a firefight, in action it should have been named the other way around, pick through the pieces and see if you could work together a count, the sponsor wasn't buying any dead civilians. The VC had an ostensibly similar tactic called Find and Kill. Either way, it was us looking for him looking for us looking for him, war on a Cracker Jack box, repeated to diminishing returns.

A lot of people used to say that it got fucked up when they made it as easy for us to shoot as not to shoot. In I and II Corps it was "loose policy" for gunships to fire if the subjects froze down there, in the Delta it was to shoot if they ran or "evaded," either way a heavy dilemma, which would you do? "Air sports," one gunship pilot called it, and went on to describe it with fervor, "Nothing finer, you're up there at two thousand, you're God, just open up the flexies and watch it pee, nail those slime to the paddy wall, nothing finer, double back and get the caribou."

"Back home I used to fill my own cartridges for hunting," a platoon leader told me. "Me and my father and my brothers used to make a hundred a year between us maybe. I swear to God, I never saw anything like this."

Who had? Nothing like it ever when we caught a bunch of them out in the open and close together, we really ripped it then, volatile piss-off, crazed expenditure, Godzilla never drew that kind of fire. We even had a small language for our fire: "discreet burst," "probe," "prime selection," "constructive load," but I never saw it as various, just compulsive eruption, the Mad Minute for an hour. Charles really wrote the book on fire control, putting one round into the heart of things where fifty of ours might go and still not hit anything. Sometimes we put out so much fire you couldn't tell whether any of it was coming back or not. When it was, it filled your ears and your head until you thought you were hearing it with your stomach. An English correspondent I knew made a cassette of one of the heavy ones, he said he used it to seduce American girls.

Sometimes you felt too thin and didn't want to get into anything at all and it would land on you like your next-to-last breath. Sometimes your chops for action and your terror would reach a different balance and you'd go looking for it everywhere, and nothing would happen, except a fire ant would fly up your nose or you'd grow a crotch rot or you'd lie awake all night waiting for morning so you could get up and wait on your feet. Whichever way it went, you were covering the war, your choice of story told it all and in Vietnam an infatuation like that with violence wouldn't go unrequited for very long, it would come and put its wild mouth all over you.

"Quakin' and Shakin'," they called it, great balls of fire, Contact. Then it was you and the ground: kiss it, eat it, fuck it, plow it with your whole body, get as close to it as you can without being in it yet or of it, guess who's flying around about an inch above your head? Pucker and submit, it's the ground. Under Fire would take you out of your head and your body too, the space you'd seen a second ago between subject and object wasn't there anymore, it banged shut in a fast wash of adrenaline. Amazing, unbelievable, guys who'd played a lot of hard sports said they'd never felt anything like it, the sudden drop and rocket rush of the hit, the reserves of adrenaline you could make available to yourself, pumping it up and putting it out until you were lost floating in it, not afraid, almost open to clear orgasmic death-by-drowning in it, actually relaxed. Unless of course you'd shit your pants or were screaming or praying or giving anything at all to the hundred-channel panic that blew word salad all around you and sometimes clean through you. Maybe you couldn't love the war and hate it inside the same instant, but sometimes those feelings alternated so rapidly that they spun together in a strobic wheel rolling all the way up until you were literally

High On War, like it said on all the helmet covers. Coming off a jag like that could really make a mess out of you.

In early December I came back from my first operation with the Marines. I'd lain scrunched up for hours in a flimsy bunker that was falling apart even faster than I was, listening to it going on, the moaning and whining and the dull repetitions of whump whump whump and dit dit dit, listening to a boy who'd somehow broken his thumb sobbing and gagging, thinking, "Oh my *God*, this fucking thing is on a *loop*!" until the heavy shooting stopped but not the thing: at the lz waiting for choppers to Phu Bai one last shell came in, landing in the middle of a pile of full body bags, making a mess that no one wanted to clean up, "a real shit detail." It was after midnight when I finally got back to Saigon, riding in from Tan Son Nhut in an open jeep with some sniper-obsessed MP's, and there was a small package of mail waiting for me at the hotel. I put my fatigues out in the hall room and closed the door on them, I may have even locked it. I had the I Corps DT's, livers, spleens, brains, a blue-black swollen thumb moved around and flashed to me, they were playing over the walls of the shower where I spent a half-hour, they were on the bedsheets, but I wasn't afraid of them, I was laughing at them, what could they do to me? I filled a water glass with Armagnac and rolled a joint, and then I started to read my mail. In one of the letters there was news that a friend of mine had killed himself in New York. When I turned off the lights and got into bed I lay there trying to remember what he had looked like. He had done it with pills, but no matter what I tried to imagine, all I saw was blood and bone fragment, not my dead friend. After a while I broke through for a second and saw him, but by that time all I could do with it was file him in with the rest and go to sleep.

Between what contact did to you and how tired you got, between the farout things you saw or heard and what you personally lost out of all that got blown away, the war made a place for you that was all yours. Finding it was like listening to esoteric music, you didn't hear it in any essential way through all the repetitions until your own breath had entered it and become another instrument, and by then it wasn't just music anymore, it was experience. Life-as-movie, war-as-(war) movie, war-as-life; a complete process if you got to complete it, a distinct path to travel, but dark and hard, not any easier if you knew that you'd put your own foot on it yourself, deliberately and—most roughly speaking—consciously. Some people took a few steps along it and turned back, wised up, with and without regrets. Many walked on and just got blown off it. A lot went farther than they probably should have and then lay down, falling into a bad sleep of pain and rage, waiting for release, for peace, any kind of peace that wasn't just the absence of war. And some kept going until they reached the place where an inversion of the expected order happened, a fabulous warp where you took the journey first and then you made your departure.

Once your body was safe your problems weren't exactly over. There was the terrible possibility that a search for information there could become so exhausting that the exhaustion itself became the information. Overload was such a real danger, not as obvious as shrapnel or blunt like a 2,000-foot drop, maybe it couldn't kill you or smash you, but it could bend your aerial for you and land you on your hip. Levels of information were levels of dread, once it's out it won't go back in, you can't just blink it away or run the film backward out of consciousness. How many of those levels did you really want to hump yourself through, which plateau would you reach before you shorted out and started sending the messages back unopened?

Cover the war, what a gig to frame for yourself, going out after one kind of information and getting another, totally other, to lock your eyes open, drop your blood temperature down under the o, dry your mouth out so a full swig of water disappeared in there before you could swallow, turn your breath fouler than corpse gas. There were times when your fear would take directions so wild that you had to stop and watch the spin. Forget the Cong, the *trees* would kill you, the elephant grass grew up homicidal, the ground you were walking over possessed malignant intelligence, your whole environment was a bath. Even so, considering where you were and what was happening to so many people, it was a privilege just to be able to feel afraid.

So you learned about fear, it was hard to know what you really learned about courage. How many times did somebody have to run in front of a machine gun before it became an act of cowardice? What about those acts that didn't require courage to perform, but made you a coward if you didn't? It was hard to know at the moment, easy to make a mistake when it came, like the mistake of thinking that all you needed to perform a witness act were your eyes. A lot of what people called courage was only undifferentiated energy cut loose by the intensity of the moment, mind loss that sent the actor on an incredible run; if he survived it he had the chance later to decide whether he'd really been brave or just overcome with life, even ecstasy. A lot of people found the guts to just call it all off and refuse to ever go out anymore, they turned and submitted to the penalty end of the system or they just split. A lot of reporters, too, I had friends in the press corps who went out once or twice and then never again. Sometimes I thought that they were the sanest, most serious people of all, although to be honest I never said so until my time there was almost over.

"We had this gook and we was gonna skin him" (a grunt told me), "I mean he was already dead and everything, and the lieutenant comes over and says, 'Hey asshole, there's a re-porter in the TOC, you want him to come out and see that? I mean, use your fucking heads, there's a time and place for everything. . . .'"

"Too bad you wasn't with us last week" (another grunt told me, coming off a no-contact operation), "we killed so many gooks it wasn't even funny."

Was it possible that they were there and not haunted? No, not possible, not a chance, I know I wasn't the only one. Where are they now? (Where am I now?) I stood as close to them as I could without actually being one of them, and then I stood as far back as I could without leaving the planet. Dis-gust doesn't begin to describe what they made me feel, they threw people out of helicopters, tied people up and put the dogs on them. Brutality was just a word in my mouth before that. But disgust was only one color in the whole mandala, gentleness and pity were other colors, there wasn't a color left out. I think that those people who used to say that they only wept for the Vietnamese never really wept for anyone at all if they couldn't squeeze out at least one for these men and boys when they died or had their lives cracked open for them.

But of course we were intimate, I'll tell you how intimate: they were my guns, and I let them do it. I never let them dig my holes or carry my gear, there were always grunts who offered, but I let them do that for me while I watched, maybe for them, maybe not. We covered each other, an exchange of services that worked all right until one night when I slid over to the wrong end of the story, propped up behind some sandbags at an airstrip in Can Tho with a .30-caliber automatic in my hands, firing cover for a four-man reaction team trying to get back in. One last war story.

The first night of the Tet Offensive we were in the Special Forces C Camp for the Delta, surrounded, as far as we knew, and with nothing but bad news filtering in: from Hue, from Danang, from Qui Nhon, from Khe Sanh, from Ban Me Thuot, from Saigon itself, "lost" as we understood it at the moment, they had the embassy, they had Cholon, Tan Son Nhut was burning, we were in the Alamo, no place else, and I wasn't a reporter, I was a shooter.

In the morning there were about a dozen dead Vietnamese across the field there where we'd been firing. We sent a truck over to load them on and get them away. It all happened so fast, as they say, as everyone who has ever been through it has always said; we were sitting around smoking grass and listening to what we thought were Tet fireworks coming from the town, and then coming closer until we weren't stoned anymore, until the whole night had passed and I was looking at the empty clips around my feet behind the berm, telling myself that there would never be any way to know for sure. I couldn't remember ever feeling so tired, so changed, so happy.

Thousands of people died in Vietnam that night, the twelve across the field, a hundred more along the road between the camp and the Can Tho hospital compound where I worked all the next day, not a reporter or a shooter but a medic, unskilled and scared. When we got back to the camp that night I threw away the fatigues I'd been wearing. And for the next six years I saw them all, the ones I'd really seen and the ones I'd imagined, theirs and ours, friends I'd loved and strangers, motionless figures in a dance, the old dance. Years of thinking this or that about what happens to you when you pursue a fantasy until it becomes experience, and then afterward you can't handle the experience. Until I felt that I was just a dancer too.

From outside we say that crazy people think they hear voices, but of course inside they really hear them. (Who's crazy? What's insane?) One night, like a piece of shrapnel that takes years to work its way out, I dreamed and saw a field that was crowded with dead. I was crossing it with a friend, more than a friend, a guide, and he was making me get down and look at them. They were powdered with dust, bloodied like it had been painted on with a wide brush, some were blown out of their pants, just like they looked that day being thrown onto the truck at Can Tho, and I said, "But I've already seen them." My friend didn't say anything, he just pointed, and I leaned down again and this time I looked into their faces. New York City, 1975, when I got up the next morning I was laughing.

Hell Sucks

During the first weeks of the Tet Offensive the curfew began early in the afternoon and was strictly enforced. By 2:30 each day Saigon looked like the final reel of *On the Beach*, a desolate city whose long avenues held nothing but refuse, windblown papers, small distinct piles of human excrement and the dead flowers and spent firecracker casings of the Lunar New Year. Alive, Saigon had been depressing enough, but during the Offensive it became so stark that, in an odd way, it was invigorating. The trees along the main streets looked like they'd been struck by lightning, and it became unusually, uncomfortably cold, one more piece of freak luck in a place where nothing was in its season. With so much filth growing in so many streets and alleys, an epidemic of plague was feared, and if there was ever a place that suggested plague, demanded it, it was Saigon in the Emergency. American civilians, engineers and construction workers who were making it here like they'd never made it at home began forming into large armed bands, carrying .45's and grease guns and Swedish K's, and no mob of hysterical vigilantes ever promised more bad news. You'd see them at ten in the morning on the terrace of the Continental waiting for the bar to open, barely able to light their own cigarettes until it did. The crowds on Tu Do Street looked like Ensor processioners, and there was a corruption in the air that had nothing to do with government workers on the take. After seven in the evening, when the curfew included Americans and became total, nothing but White Mice patrols and MP jeeps moved in the streets, except for a few young children who raced up and down over the rubbish, running newspaper kites up into the chilling wind.

We took a huge collective nervous breakdown, it was the compression and heat of heavy contact generated out until every American in Vietnam got a taste. Vietnam was a dark room full of deadly objects, the VC were everywhere all at once like spider cancer, and instead of losing the war in little pieces over years we lost it fast in under a week. After that, we were like the character in pop grunt mythology, dead but too dumb to lie down. Our worst dread of yellow peril became realized; we saw them now dying by the thousands all over the country, yet they didn't seem depleted, let alone exhausted, as the Mission was claiming by the fourth day. We took space back quickly, expensively, with total panic and close to maximum brutality. Our machine was devastating. And versatile. It could do everything but stop. As one American major said, in a successful attempt at attaining history, "We had to destroy Ben Tre in order to save it." That's how most of the country came back under what we called control, and how it remained essentially occupied by the Viet Cong and the North until the day years later when there were none of us left there.

The Mission Council joined hands and passed together through the Looking Glass. Our general's chariot was on fire, he was taking on smoke and telling us such incredible stories of triumph and victory that a few high-level Americans had to ask him to just cool it and let them do the talking. A British correspondent compared the Mission posture to the captain of the *Titanic* announcing, "There's no cause for alarm, we're only stopping briefly to take on a little ice."

By the time I got back to Saigon on the fourth day a lot of information from around the country had settled, and it was bad, even after you picked out the threads of rumor: like the one about the "Caucasians," obviously Americans, fighting for the VC, or the one about thousands of NVA executions in Hue and the "shallow graves" in the flats outside the city, both of which proved true. Almost as much as the grunts and the Vietnamese, Tet was pushing correspondents closer to the wall than they'd ever wanted to go. I realized later that, however childish I might remain, actual youth had been pressed out of me in just the three days that it took me to cross the sixty miles between Can Tho and Saigon. In Saigon, I saw friends flipping out almost completely; a few left, some took to their beds for days with the exhaustion of deep depression. I went the other way, hyper and agitated, until I was only doing three hours of sleep a night. A friend on the *Times* said he didn't mind his nightmares so much as the waking impulse to file on them. An old-timer who'd covered war since the Thirties heard us pissing and moaning about how *terrible* it was and he snorted, "Ha, I love you guys. You guys are beautiful. What the fuck did you think it was?" We thought it was already past the cut-off point where every war is just like every other war; if we knew how rough it was going to get, we might have felt better. After a few days the air routes opened again, and we went up to Hue.

Going in, there were sixty of us packed into a deuce-and-a-half, one of eight trucks moving in convoy from Phu Bai, bringing in over 300 replacements for the casualties taken in the earliest fighting south of the Perfume River. There had been a harsh, dark storm going on for days, and it turned the convoy route into a mudbed. It was terribly cold in the trucks, and the road was covered with leaves that had either been blown off the trees by the storm or torn away by our artillery, which had been heavy all along the road. Many of the houses had been completely collapsed, and not one had been left without pitting from shell fragments. Hundreds of refugees held to the side of the road as we passed, many of them wounded. The kids would laugh and shout, the old would look on with that silent tolerance for misery that made so many Americans uneasy, which was usually misread as indifference. But the younger men and women would often look at us with unmistakable contempt, pulling their cheering children back from the trucks.

We sat there trying to keep it up for each other, grinning at the bad weather and the discomfort, sharing the first fear, glad that we weren't riding point or closing the rear. They had been hitting our trucks regularly, and a lot of the convoys had been turned back. The houses that we passed so slowly made good cover for snipers, and one B-40 rocket could have made casualties out of a whole truckload of us. All the grunts were whistling, and no two were whistling the same tune, it sounded like a locker room before a game that nobody wanted to play. Or almost nobody. There was a black Marine called Philly Dog who'd been a gang lord in Philadelphia and who was looking forward to some street fighting after six months in the jungle, he could show the kickers what he could do with some city ground. (In Hue he turned out to be incredibly valuable. I saw him pouring out about a hundred rounds of .30-caliber fire into a breach in the wall, laughing, "You got to bring some to get some"; he seemed to be about the only man in Delta Company who hadn't been hurt yet.) And there was a Marine correspondent, Sergeant Dale Dye, who sat with a tall yellow flower sticking out of his helmet cover, a really outstanding target. He was rolling his eyes around and saying, "Oh yes, oh yes, Charlie's got his shit together here, this will be *bad*," and smiling happily. It was the same smile I saw a week later when a sniper's bullet tore up a wall two inches above his head, odd cause for amusement in anyone but a grunt.

Everyone else in the truck had that wild haunted going-West look that said it was perfectly correct to be here where the fighting would be the worst, where you wouldn't have half of what you needed, where it was colder than Nam ever got. On their helmets and flak jackets they'd written the names of old operations, of girlfriends, their war names (FAR FROM FEARLESS, MICKEY'S MONKEY, AVENGER V, SHORT TIME SAFETY MOE), their fantasies (BORN TO LOSE, BORN TO

RAISE HELL, BORN TO KILL, BORN TO DIE), their ongoing information (HELL SUCKS, TIME IS ON MY SIDE, JUST YOU AND ME GOD—RIGHT?). One kid called to me, "Hey man! You want a story, man? Here man, write this: I'm up there on 881, this was May, I'm just up there walkin' the ridgeline like a movie star and this Zip jumps up smack into me, lays his AK-47 fucking right *into* me, only he's so *amazed* at my *cool* I got my whole clip off 'fore he knew how to thank me for it. Grease one." After twenty kilometers of this, in spite of the black roiling sky ahead, we could see smoke coming up from the far side of the river, from the Citadel of Hue.

The bridge was down that spanned the canal dividing the village of An Cuu and the southern sector of Hue, blown the night before by the Viet Cong, and the forward area beyond the far bank wasn't thought to be secure, so we bivouacked in the village for the night. It had been completely deserted, and we set ourselves up in empty hootches, laying our poncho liners out over broken glass and shattered brick. At dusk, while we all stretched out along the canal bank eating dinner, two Marine gunships came down on us and began strafing us, sending burning tracers up along the canal, and we ran for cover, more surprised than scared. "Way to go, motherfucker, way to pinpoint the fuckin' enemy," one of the grunts said, and he set up his M-60 machine gun in case they came back. "I don't guess we got to take *that* shit," he said. Patrols were sent out, guards posted, and we went into the hootches to sleep. For some reason, we weren't even mortared that night.

In the morning we crossed the canal on a two-by-four and started walking in until we came across the first of the hundreds of civilian dead that we were to see in the next weeks: an old man arched over his straw hat and a little girl who'd been hit while riding her bicycle, lying there with her arm up like a reproach. They'd been lying out like that for a week, for the first time we were grateful for the cold.

Along the Perfume River's south bank there is a long, graceful park that separates Hue's most pleasant avenue, Le Loi, from the riverfront. People will talk about how they'd sit out there in the sun and watch the sampans moving down the river, or watch the girls bicycling up Le Loi, past the villas of officials and the French-architected University buildings.

Many of those villas had been destroyed and much of the University permanently damaged. In the middle of the street a couple of ambulances from the German Mission had been blown up, and the Cercle Sportif was covered with bullet holes and shrapnel. The rain had brought up the green, it stretched out cased in thick white fog. In the park itself, four fat green dead lay sprawled around a tall, ornate cage, inside of which sat a small, shivering monkey. One of the correspondents along stepped over the corpses to feed it some fruit. (Days later, I came back to the spot. The corpses were gone, but so was the monkey. There had been so many refugees and so little food then, and someone must have eaten him.) The Marines of 2/5 had secured almost all of the central south bank and were now fanning out to the west, fighting and clearing one of the major canals. We were waiting for some decision on whether or not U.S. Marines would be going into the Citadel itself, but no one had any doubts about what that decision would be. We sat there taking in the dread by watching the columns of smoke across the river, receiving occasional sniper rounds, infrequent bursts of .50-caliber, watching the Navy LCU's on the river getting shelled from the wall. One Marine next to me was saying that it was just a damned shame, all them poor people, all them nice-looking houses, they even had a Shell station there. He was looking at the black napalm blasts and the wreckage along the wall. "Looks like the Imperial City's had the schnitz," he said.

The courtyard of the American compound in Hue was filled with puddles from the rain, and the canvas tops of the jeeps and trucks sagged with the weight of the water. It was the fifth day of the fighting, and everyone was still amazed that the NVA or the Cong had not hit the compound on the first night. An enormous white goose had come into the compound that night, and now his wings were heavy with the oil that had formed on the surface of the puddles. Every time a vehicle entered the yard he would beat his wings in a fury and scream, but he never left the compound and, as far as I knew, no one ever ate him.

Nearly 200 of us were sleeping in the two small rooms that had been the compound's dining quarters. The Army was not happy about having to billet so many of the Marines that were coming through, and they were absolutely furious about all the correspondents who were hanging around now, waiting until the fighting moved north across the river, into the Citadel. You were lucky to find space enough on the floor to lie down on, luckier if you found an empty stretcher to sleep on, and luckiest of all if the stretcher was new. All night long the few unbroken windows would rattle from the airstrikes across the river, and a mortar pit just outside fired incessantly. At two or three in the morning, Marines would come in from their patrols. They'd cross the room, not much caring whether they stepped on anyone or not. They'd turn their radios on and shout across the room to one another. "Really, can't you fellows show a bit more consideration?" a British correspondent said, and their laughter woke anyone who was not already up.

One morning there was a fire in the prison camp across the road from the compound. We saw the black smoke rising over the barbed wire that topped the camp wall and heard automatic weapons' fire. The prison was full of captured NVA and Viet Cong or Viet Cong suspects, the guards said that they'd started the fire to cover an escape. The ARVN and a few Americans were shooting blindly into the flames, and the bodies were burning where they fell. Civilian dead lay out on the sidewalks only a block from the compound, and the park by the river was littered with dead. It was cold and the sun never came out once, but the rain did things to the corpses that were worse in their way than anything the sun could have done. It was on one of those days that I realized that the only corpse I couldn't bear to look at would be the one I would never have to see.

It stayed cold and dark like that for the next ten days, and that damp gloom was the background for all the footage that we took out of the Citadel. What little sunlight there was caught the heavy motes of dust that blew up from the wreckage of the east wall, held it until everything you saw was filtered through it. And you saw things from unaccustomed angles, quick looks from a running crouch, or up from flat out, hearing the hard dry rattle of shrapnel scudding against the debris around you. With all of that dust blowing around, the acrid smell of cordite would hang in the air for a long time after firefights, and there was the CS gas that we'd fired at the NVA blowing back in over our positions. It was impossible to get a clean breath with all of that happening, and there was that other smell too that came up from the shattered heaps of stone wherever an airstrike had come in. It held to the lining of your nostrils and worked itself into the weave of your fatigues, and weeks later, miles away, you'd wake up at night and it would be in the room with you. The NVA had dug themselves so deeply into the wall that airstrikes had to open it meter by meter, dropping napalm as close as a hundred meters from our positions. Up on the highest point of the wall, on what had once been a tower, I looked across the Citadel's moat and saw the NVA moving quickly across the rubble of the opposing wall. We were close enough to be able to see their faces. A rifle went off a few feet to my right, and one of the running figures jerked back and dropped. A Marine sniper leaned out from his cover and grinned at me.

Between the smoke and the mist and the flying dust inside the Citadel, it was hard to call that hour between light and darkness a true dusk, but it was the time when most of us would open our C rations. We were only meters away from the worst of the fighting, not more than a Vietnamese city block in distance, and yet civilians kept appearing, smiling, shrugging, trying to get back to their homes. The Marines would try to menace them away at rifle point, shouting, "Di, di, *di*, you sorry-ass motherfuckers, go on, get the hell away from here!" and the refugees would smile, half bowing, and flit up one of the shattered streets. A little boy of about ten came up to a bunch of Marines from Charlie Company. He was laughing and moving his head from side to side in a funny way. The fierceness in his eyes should have told everyone what it was, but it had never occurred to most of the grunts that a Vietnamese child could be driven mad too, and by the time they understood it the boy had begun to go for their eyes and tear at their fatigues, spooking everyone, putting everyone really uptight, until a black grunt grabbed him from behind and held his arm. "C'mon, poor li'l baby, 'fore one a these grunt mothers shoots you," he said, and carried the boy to where the corpsmen were.

On the worst days, no one expected to get through it alive. A despair set in among members of the battalion that the older ones, the veterans of two other wars, had never seen before. Once or twice, when the men from Graves Registration took the personal effects from the packs and pockets of dead Marines, they found letters from home that had been delivered days before and were still unopened.

We were running some wounded onto the back of a half-ton truck, and one of the young Marines kept crying from his stretcher. His sergeant held both of his hands, and the Marine kept saying, "Shit, Sarge, I ain' gone make it. Oh damn, I'm gone die, ain't I?" "No you ain't gonna die, for Christ's sake," the sergeant said. "Oh yeah, Sarge, yeah, I am." "Crowley," the sergeant said, "you ain't hurt that bad. I want you to just shut the fuck up. You ain't done a thing except bitch ever since we got to this fucking Hue City." But the sergeant didn't really know. The kid had been hit in the throat, and you couldn't tell about those. Throat wounds were bad. Everyone was afraid of throat wounds.

We lucked out on our connections. At the battalion aid station we got a chopper that carried us and a dozen dead Marines to the base at Phu Bai, and three minutes after we landed there we caught a C-130 to Danang. Hitching in from the airfield, we found a Psyops officer who felt sorry for us and drove us all the way to the press center. As we came in the gate we could see that the net was up and the daily volleyball game between the Marines assigned to the press center was on.

"Where the hell have *you* guys been?" one of them asked. We looked pretty fucked up.

The inside of the dining room was freezing with air-conditioning. I sat at a table and ordered a hamburger and a brandy from one of the peasant girls who waited tables. I sat there for a couple of hours and ordered four more hamburgers and at least a dozen brandies. It wasn't possible, just not possible, to have been where we'd been before and to be where we were now, all in the same afternoon. One of the correspondents who had come back with me sat at another table, also by himself, and we looked at each other, shook our heads and laughed. I went to my room and took my boots and fatigues off and got into the shower. The water was incredibly hot, for a moment I thought I'd gone insane from it, and I sat down on the concrete floor for a long time, shaving there, soaping myself over and over. I dressed and went back to the dining room. The net was down now, one of the Marines said hello and asked me if I knew what the movie was going to be that night. I ordered a steak and another long string of brandies. When I left the correspondent was still sitting alone. I got into bed and smoked a joint. I was going back in the morning, it was understood, but why was it understood? All of my stuff was in order, ready for the five-o'clock wake-up. I finished the joint and shuddered off into sleep.

By the end of the week the wall had cost the Marines roughly one casualty for every meter taken, a quarter of them KIA. 1/5, which came to be known as the Citadel Battalion, had been through every tough battle the Marines had had in the past six months, they'd even fought the same NVA units a few weeks before between Hai Vanh Pass and Phu Loc, and now three of its companies were below platoon strength. They all knew how bad it was, the novelty of fighting in a city had become a nasty joke, everyone wanted to get wounded.

At night in the CP, the major who commanded the battalion would sit reading his maps, staring vacantly at the trapezoid of the Citadel. It could have been a scene in a Norman farmhouse twenty-five years ago, with candles burning on the tables, bottles of red wine arranged along damaged shelves, the chill in the room, the high ceilings, the heavy ornate cross on the wall. The major had not slept for five nights, and for the fifth night in a row he assured us that tomorrow would get it for sure, the final stretch of wall would be taken and he had all the Marines he needed to do it. And one of his aides, a tough mustang first lieutenant, would pitch a hard, ironic smile above the major's stare, a smile that rejected good news, it was like hearing him say, "The major here is full of shit, and we both know it."

Sometimes a company would find itself completely cut off,

and it would take hours for the Marines to get their wounded out. I remember one Marine with a headwound who finally made it to the Battalion CP when the jeep he was in stalled. He finally jumped out and started to push, knowing it was the only way out of there. Most of the tanks and trucks that carried casualties had to move up a long straight road without cover, and they began calling it Rocket Alley. Every tank the Marines had there had been hit at least once. An epiphany of Hue appeared in John Olson's great photograph for *Life*, the wounded from Delta Company hurriedly piled on a tank. Sometimes, on the way to the aid station the more seriously wounded would take on that bad color, the gray-blue fishbelly promise of death that would spread upward from the chest and cover the face. There was one Marine who had been shot through the neck, and all the way out the corpsmen massaged his chest. By the time they reached the station, though, he was so bad that the doctor triaged him, passed him over to treat the ones that he knew could still be saved, and when they put him into the green rubber body bag there was some chance that he was clinically alive. The doctor had never had to make choices like that before, and he wasn't getting used to it. During the lulls he'd step outside for some air, but it was no better out there. The bodies were stacked together and there was always a crowd of ARVN standing around staring, death-enthralled like all Vietnamese. Since they didn't know what else to do, and not knowing what it would look like to the Marines, they would smile at the bodies there, and a couple of ugly incidents occurred. The Marines who worked the body detail were overloaded and rushed and became snappish, ripping packs off of corpses angrily, cutting gear away with bayonets, heaving bodies into the green bags. One of the dead Marines had gone stiff and they had trouble getting him to fit. "*Damn*," one of them said, "this fucker had big feet. Didn't this fucker have big feet," as he finally forced the legs inside. In the station there was the youngest-looking Marine I'd ever seen. He'd been caught in the knee by a large piece of shrapnel, and he had no idea of what they'd do with him now that he was wounded. He lay out on the stretcher while the doctor explained how he would be choppered back to Phu Bai hospital and then put on a plane for Danang and then flown back to the States for what would certainly be the rest of his tour. At first the boy was sure that the doctor was kidding him, then he started to believe it, and then he knew it was true, he was actually getting out, he couldn't stop smiling, and enormous tears ran down into his ears.

It was at this point that I began to recognize almost every casualty, remember conversations we'd had days or even hours earlier, and that's when I left, riding a medevac with a lieutenant who was covered with blood-soaked bandages. He'd been hit in both legs, both arms, the chest and head, his ears and eyes were full of caked blood, and he asked a photographer in the chopper to get a picture of him like this to send to his wife.

But by then the battle for Hue was almost over. The Cav was working the northwest corner of the Citadel, and elements of the 101st had come in through what had formerly been an NVA re-supply route. (In five days these outfits lost as many men as the Marines had in three weeks.) Vietnamese Marines and some of the 1st ARVN Division had been moving the remaining NVA down toward the wall. The NVA flag that had flown for so long over the south wall had been cut down, and in its place an American flag had been put up. Two days later the Hoc Bao, Vietnamese Rangers, stormed through the walls of the Imperial Palace, but there were no NVA left inside. Except for a few bodies in the moat, most of their dead had been buried. When they'd first come into Hue the NVA had sat at banquets given for them by the people. Before they left, they'd skimmed all the edible vegetation from the surface of the moat. Seventy percent of Vietnam's one lovely city was destroyed, and if the landscape seemed desolate, imagine how the figures in that landscape looked.

There were two official ceremonies marking the expulsion of the NVA, both flag-raisings. On the south bank of the Perfume River, 200 refugees from one of the camps were recruited to stand, sullen and silent in the rain, and watch the GVN flag being run up. But the rope snapped, and the crowd, thinking the VC had shot it down, broke up in panic. (There was no rain in the stories that the Saigon papers ran, no trouble with the rope, and the cheering crowd numbered thousands.) As for the other ceremony, the Citadel was thought by most people to be insecure, and when the flag finally went up there was no one to watch it except for a handful of Vietnamese troops.

Major Trong bounced around in the seat of his jeep as it drove us over the debris scattered across the streets of Hue. His face seemed completely expressionless as we passed the crowds of Vietnamese stumbling over the fallen beams and powdered brick of their homes, but his eyes were covered by dark glasses and it was impossible to know what he was feeling. He didn't look like a victor, he was so small and limp in his seat I was afraid he was going to fly out of the jeep. His driver was a sergeant named Dang, one of the biggest Vietnamese I'd ever seen, and his English was better than the major's. The jeep would stall on rubble heaps from time to time, and Dang would turn to us and smile an apology. We were on our way to the Imperial Palace.

A month earlier the Palace grounds had been covered with dozens of dead NVA and the burned-over leavings of three weeks' siege and defense. There had been some reluctance about bombing the Palace, but a lot of the bombing nearby had done heavy damage, and there had been some shelling, too. The large bronze urns were dented beyond restoring, and the rain poured through a hole in the roof of the throne room, soaking the two small thrones where the old Annamese royalty had sat. In the great hall (great once you'd scaled it to the Vietnamese) the red lacquer work on the upper walls was badly chipped, and a heavy dust covered everything. The crown of the main gate had collapsed, and in the garden the broken branches of the old cay-dai trees lay like the forms of giant insects seared in a fire, wispy, delicate, dead. It was rumored during those days that the Palace was being held by a unit of student volunteers who had taken the invasion of Hue as a sign and had rushed to join the North Vietnamese. (Another rumor of those days, the one about some 5,000 "shallow graves" outside the city, containing the bodies from NVA executions, had just now been shown to be true.)

But once the walls had been taken and the grounds entered, there was no one left inside except for the dead. They bobbed in the moat and littered all the approaches. The Marines moved in then, and empty ration cans and muddied sheets from the *Stars and Stripes* were added to the litter. A fat Marine had been photographed pissing into the locked-open mouth of a decomposing North Vietnamese soldier.

"No good," Major Trong said. "No good. Fight here very hard, very bad."

I'd been talking to Sergeant Dang about the Palace and about the line of emperors. When we stalled one last time at the foot of a moat bridge, I'd been asking him the name of the last emperor to occupy the throne. He smiled and shrugged, not so much as if he didn't know, more like it didn't matter.

"Major Trong is emperor now," he said, and gunned the jeep into the Palace grounds.

Khe Sanh

I

During the bad maximum incoming days of the late winter of 1968 there was a young Marine at Khe Sanh whose Vietnam tour had run out. Nearly five of his thirteen months in-country had been spent there at the Khe Sanh Combat Base with the 26th Marines, who had been slowly building to full and then reinforced regimental strength since the previous spring. He could remember a time, not long before, when the 26th considered themselves lucky to be there, when the guys talked of it as though it were a reward for whatever their particular outfits had been through. As far as this Marine was concerned, the reward was for an ambush that fall on the Cam Lo–Con Thien road, when his unit had taken 40 percent casualties, when he himself had taken shrapnel in the chest and arms. (Oh, he'd tell you, but he had seen some shit in this war.) That was when Con Thien was the name everyone knew, long before Khe Sanh had taken on the proportions of a siege camp and lodged itself as an obsession in the heart of the Command, long before a single round had ever fallen inside the perimeter to take off his friends and make his sleep something indistinguishable from waking. He remembered when there was time to play in the streams below the plateau of the base, when all anybody ever talked about were the six shades of green that touched the surrounding hills, when he and his friends had lived like human beings, above ground, in the light, instead of like animals who were so spaced out that they began taking pills called Diarrhea-Aid to keep their walks to exposed latrines at a minimum. And on this last morning of his tour, he might have told you that he'd been through it all and hacked it pretty well.

He was a tall blond from Michigan, probably about twenty, although it was never easy to guess the ages of Marines at Khe Sanh since nothing like youth ever lasted in their faces for very long. It was the eyes: because they were always either strained or blazed-out or simply blank, they never had anything to do with what the rest of the face was doing, and it gave everyone the look of extreme fatigue or even a glancing madness. (And age. If you take one of those platoon photographs from the Civil War and cover everything but the eyes, there is no difference between a man of fifty and a boy of thirteen.) This Marine, for example, was always smiling. It was the kind of smile that verged on the high giggles, but his eyes showed neither amusement nor embarrassment nor nervousness. It was a little insane, but it was mostly esoteric in the way that so many Marines under twenty-five became esoterics after a few months in I Corps. On that young, nondescript face the smile seemed to come out of some old knowledge, and it said, "I'll tell you why I'm smiling, but it will make you crazy."

He had tattooed the name MARLENE on his upper arm, and up on his helmet there was the name JUDY, and he said, "Yeah, well, Judy knows all about Marlene. That's cool, there's no sweat there." On the back of his flak jacket he had once written, *Yea, though I walk through the Valley of the Shadow of Death I shall fear no Evil, because I'm the meanest motherfucker in the Valley*, but he had tried later, without much success, to scrub it off because, he explained, every damn dude in the DMZ had that written on their flak jackets. And he'd smile.

He was smiling on this last morning of his tour. His gear was straight, his papers in order, his duffel packed, and he was going through all of the last-minute business of going home, the back-slapping and goosing; the joshing with the Old Man ("Come on, you know you're gonna miss this place." "Yes sir. Oh wow!"); the exchanging of addresses; the odd, fragmented reminiscences blurted out of awkward silences. He had a few joints left, wrapped up in a plastic bag (he hadn't smoked them, because, like most Marines at Khe Sanh, he'd expected a ground attack, and he didn't want to be stoned when it came), and he gave these to his best friend, or, rather, his best surviving friend. His oldest friend had been blown away in January, on the same day that the ammo dump had been hit. He had always wondered whether Gunny, the company gunnery sergeant, had known about all the smoking. After three wars Gunny probably didn't care much; besides, they all knew that Gunny was into some pretty cool shit himself. When he dropped by the bunker they said goodbye, and then there wasn't anything to do with the morning but to run in and out of the bunker for a look at the sky, coming back in every time to say that it really ought to clear enough by ten for the planes to get in. By noon, when the goodbyes and take-cares and get-a-little-for-me's had gone on for too long by hours, the sun started to show through the mist. He picked up his duffel and a small AWOL bag and started for the airstrip and the small, deep slit trench on the edge of the strip.

Khe Sanh was a very bad place then, but the airstrip there was the worst place in the world. It was what Khe Sanh had instead of a V-ring, the exact, predictable object of the mortars and rockets hidden in the surrounding hills, the sure target of the big Russian and Chinese guns lodged in the side of CoRoc Ridge, eleven kilometers away across the Laotian border. There was nothing random about the shelling there, and no one wanted anything to do with it. If the wind was right, you could hear the NVA .50-calibers starting far up the valley whenever a plane made its approach to the strip, and the first incoming artillery would precede the landings by seconds. If you were waiting there to be taken out, there was nothing you could do but curl up in the trench and try to make yourself small, and if you were coming in on the plane, there was nothing you could do, nothing at all.

There was always the debris of one kind of aircraft or another piled up on or near the strip, and sometimes the damage would cause the strip to be closed off for hours while the Seabees or the 11th Engineers did the clearing. It was so bad, so predictably bad, that the Air Force stopped flying in their star transport, the C-130, and kept to the smaller, more maneuverable C-123. Whenever possible, loads were parachuted in on pallet drops from 1,500 feet, pretty blue-and-yellow chutes, a show, dropping down around the perimeter. But obviously, passengers had to be flown in or picked up on the ground. These were mostly replacements, guys going to or returning from R&R's, specialists of one kind or another, infrequent brass (most staff from Division and higher made their own travel arrangements for Khe Sanh) and a lot of correspondents. While a planeload of passengers tensed and sweated and made the run for the trench over and over in their heads, waiting for the cargo hatch to drop, ten to fifty Marines and correspondents huddled down in the trench, worked their lips futilely to ease the dryness, and then, at the exact same instant, they would all race, collide, stampede, exchanging places. If the barrage was a particularly heavy one, the faces would all distort in the most simple kind of panic, the eyes going wider than the eyes of horses caught in a fire. What you saw was a translucent blur, sensible only at the immediate center, like a swirly-chic photograph of Carnival, and you'd glimpse a face, a shell fragment cased in white sparks, a piece of gear somehow suspended in air, a drift of smoke, and you'd move around the flight crews working the heavy cargo strapping, over scout dogs, over the casually arranged body bags that always lay not far from the strip, covered with flies. And men would still be struggling on or off as the aircraft turned slowly to begin the taxi before the most accelerated take-off the machine had it in it to make. If you were on board, that first movement was an ecstasy. You'd all sit there with empty, exhausted grins, covered with the impossible red dust that laterite breaks down to, dust like scales, feeling the delicious afterchill of the fear, that one quick convulsion of safety. There was no feeling in the world as good as being airborne out of Khe Sanh.

On this last morning, the young Marine caught a ride from his company position that dropped him off fifty meters from the strip. As he moved on foot he heard the distant sound of the C-123 coming in, and that was all he heard. There was hardly more than a hundred-foot ceiling, scary, bearing down on him. Except for the approaching engines, everything was still. If there had been something more, just one incoming round, he might have been all right, but in that silence the sound of his own feet moving over the dirt was terrifying to him. He later said that this was what made him stop. He dropped his duffel and looked around. He watched the plane, his plane, as it touched down, and then he ran leaping over some discarded sandbags by the road. He lay out flat and listened as the plane switched loads and took off, listened until there was nothing left to listen to. Not a single round had come in.

Back at the bunker there was some surprise at his return, but no one said anything. Anyone can miss a plane. Gunny slapped him on the back and wished him a better trip the next time out. That afternoon he rode in a jeep that took him all the way to Charlie Med, the medical detachment for Khe Sanh that had been set up insanely close to the strip, but he never got himself past the sandbagging outside of the triage room.

"Oh no, you raggedy-assed bastard," Gunny said when he got back to the outfit. But he looked at him for a long while this time.

"Well," the kid said. "Well. . . ."

The next morning two of his friends went with him to the edge of the strip and saw him into the trench. ("Goodbye," Gunny said. "And that's an order.") They came back to say that he'd gotten out for sure this time. An hour later he came up the road again, smiling. He was still there the first time I left Khe Sanh, and while he probably made it out eventually, you can't be sure.

Such odd things happen when tours are almost over. It's the Short-Timer Syndrome. In the heads of the men who are really in the war for a year, all tours end early. No one expects much from a man when he is down to one or two weeks. He becomes a luck freak, an evil-omen collector, a diviner of every bad sign. If he has the imagination, or the experience of war, he will precognize his own death a thousand times a day, but he will always have enough left to do the one big thing, to Get Out.

Something more was working on the young Marine, and Gunny knew what it was. In this war they called it "acute environmental reaction," but Vietnam has spawned a jargon of such delicate locutions that it's often impossible to know even remotely the thing being described. Most Americans would rather be told that their son is undergoing acute environmental reaction than to hear that he is suffering from shell shock, because they could no more cope with the fact of shell shock than they could with the reality of what had happened to this boy during his five months at Khe Sanh.

Say that his legs just weren't working. It was clearly a medical matter, and the sergeant was going to have to see that something was done about it. But when I left, the kid was still there, sitting relaxed on his duffel and smiling, saying, "Man, when I get home, I'll have it knocked."

II

The terrain above II Corps, where it ran along the Laotian border and into the DMZ, was seldom referred to as the Highlands by Americans. It had been a matter of military expediency to impose a new set of references over Vietnam's older, truer being, an imposition that began most simply with the division of one country into two and continued—it had its logic—with the further division of South Vietnam into four clearly defined tactical corps. It had been one of the exigencies of the war, and if it effectively obliterated even some of the most obvious geographical distinctions, it made for clear communication, at least among members of the Mission and the many components of the Military Assistance Command, Vietnam, the fabulous MACV. In point of geographical fact, for example, the delta of Vietnam comprehends the Plain of Reeds and frames the Saigon River, but on all the charts and deep in all the sharp heads, it ended at the map line dividing III and IV Corps. Referentially, the Highlands were confined to II Corps, ending abruptly at the line which got drawn just below the coastal city of Chu Lai; everything between that and the DMZ was just I Corps. All in-country briefings, at whatever level, came to sound like a Naming of the Parts, and the language was used as a cosmetic, but one that diminished beauty. Since most of the journalism from the war was framed in that language or proceeded from the view of the war which those terms implied, it would be as impossible to know what Vietnam looked like from reading most newspaper stories as it would be to know how it smelled. Those Highlands didn't simply vanish at the corps border, but went all the way up into a section of North Vietnam that Navy fliers called the Armpit, running in a chain with the wonderful name of the Annamese Cordillera that spanned more than 1,700 miles from the Armpit to a point just below Pleiku, cutting through much of the North, through the DMZ, through the valley fastness (theirs) of the A Shau, and through the piedmont that was once the Marine Combat Base of Khe Sanh. And since the country it traversed was very special, with its special evocations, my insistence on placing Khe Sanh there is much more than some recondite footnote to a history of that sad place and the particular ways in which so many Americans suffered their part of the war there.

Because the Highlands of Vietnam are spooky, unbearably spooky, spooky beyond belief. They are a run of erratic mountain ranges, gnarled valleys, jungled ravines and abrupt plains where Montagnard villages cluster, thin and disappear as the terrain steepens. The Montagnards in all of their tribal components make up the most primitive and mysterious portion of the Vietnamese population, a population that has always confused Americans even in its most Westernized segments. Strictly speaking, the Montagnards are not really Vietnamese at all, certainly not *South* Vietnamese, but a kind of upgraded, demi-enlightened Annamese aborigine, often living in nakedness and brooding silence in their villages. Most Vietnamese and most Montagnards consider each other inferior, and while many Montagnards hired out as mercenaries to the American Special Forces, that older, racially based enmity often slowed down the Allied effort. Many Americans considered them to be nomadic, but the war had had more to do with that than anything in their temperament. We napalmed off their crops and flattened their villages, and then admired the restlessness

in their spirit. Their nakedness, their painted bodies, their re-
calcitrance, their silent composure before strangers, their benign savagery and the sheer, awesome ugliness of them
combined to make most Americans who were forced to associate with them a little uncomfortable over the long run. It
would seem fitting, ordained, that they should live in the
Highlands, among triple canopies, where sudden, contrary
mists offered sinister bafflement, where the daily heat and the
nighttime cold kept you perpetually, increasingly, on edge,
where the silences were interrupted only by the sighing of
cattle or the rotor-thud of a helicopter, the one sound I know
that is both sharp and dull at the same time. The Puritan belief
that Satan dwelt in Nature could have been born here, where
even on the coldest, freshest mountaintops you could smell
jungle and that tension between rot and genesis that all jungles give off. It is ghost-story country, and for Americans it
had been the scene of some of the war's vilest surprises. The
Ia Drang battles of late 1965 constituted the first and worst of
these surprises. They marked the first wholesale appearance of
North Vietnamese regulars in the South, and no one who was
around then can ever forget the horror of it or, to this day,
get over the confidence and sophistication with which entire
battalions came to engage Americans in a war. A few correspondents, a few soldiers back for second and third tours still
shuddered uncontrollably at what they remembered: impromptu positions held to the last man and then overrun;
Americans and North Vietnamese stiff in one another's death
embrace, their eyes wide open, their teeth bared or sunk deep
into enemy flesh; the number of helicopters shot down (relief
mission after relief mission after relief mission . . .); the NVA
equipment hauls which included the first AK-47 assault rifles,
the first RPG-7 rockets, the hundreds of aluminum grave
markers. No, a lot of the ones who saw that, the toughest of
them, didn't even like to talk about it. The very best of our
divisions, the 1st Air Cavalry, was blooded in the Ia Drang
that autumn, and while the official number of dead was released at around 300, I never met anyone who had been there,
including officers of the Cav, who would settle for less than
three or even four times that figure.

  There is a point of view that says that the United States got involved in the Vietnam War, commitments and interests aside, simply because we thought it would be easy. But after the Ia Drang, that first arrogance sat less and less well about the shoulders of the Command; it never vanished. There was never again a real guerrilla war after Ia Drang, except in the Delta, and the old Giap stratagem of interdicting the South through the Highlands, cutting the country in two, came to be taken seriously, even obsessively, by many influential Americans.

Oh, that terrain! The bloody, maddening uncanniness of it! When the hideous Battle of Dak To ended at the top of Hill 875, we announced that 4,000 of them had been killed; it had been the purest slaughter, our losses were bad, but clearly it was another American victory. But when the top of the hill was reached, the number of NVA found was four. Four. Of course more died, hundreds more, but the corpses kicked and counted and photographed and buried numbered four. Where, Colonel? And how, and why? Spooky. Everything up there was spooky, and it would have been that way even if there had been no war. You were there in a place where you didn't belong, where things were glimpsed for which you would have to pay and where things went unglimpsed for which you would also have to pay, a place where they didn't play with the mystery but killed you straight off for trespassing. The towns had names that laid a quick, chilly touch on your bones: Kontum, Dak Mat Lop, Dak Roman Peng, Poli Klang, Buon Blech, Pleiku, Pleime, Plei Vi Drin. Just moving through those towns or being based somewhere above them spaced you out, and every time I'd have that vision of myself lying dead somewhere, it was always up there, in the Highlands. It was enough to make an American commander sink to his knees and plead, "O God! Just *once*, let it be our way. We have the strength, give us the terms!" Not even the Cav, with their style and courage and mobility, were able to penetrate that abiding Highland face. They killed a lot of Communists, but that was all they did, because the number of Communist dead meant nothing, changed nothing.

Sean Flynn, photographer and connoisseur of the Vietnam War, told me that he once stood on the vantage of a firebase up there with a battalion commander. It was at dusk, those ghastly mists were fuming out of the valley floor, ingesting light. The colonel squinted at the distance for a long time. Then he swept his hand very slowly along the line of jungle, across the hills and ridges running into Cambodia (the Sanctuary!). "Flynn," he said. "Somewhere out there . . . is the *entire First NVA Division*."

O dear God, just once!

III

Somewhere Out There, within artillery range of the Khe Sanh Combat Base, within a twenty-mile radius, a day's march, assuming the "attack posture," concealed and silent and ominous, lay five full divisions of North Vietnamese Regulars. This was the situation during the closing weeks of 1967:

Somewhere to the southwest was the 304th NVA Division. Due east (somewhere) was the 320th. The 325C was deployed in an unknown fashion to the northwest, and the 324B (a cause for real alarm among enemy-division buffs) was somewhere to the northeast. There was also an unidentified division just the other side of the Laotian border, where their big artillery had been dug so deeply into the mountainsides that not even our B-52's could harm them. All of that terrain, all of that cover, ridge after ridge, murderous slides and gorges, all cloaked by triple canopy and thick monsoon mists. And whole divisions were out there in that.

Marine Intelligence (While I see many hoof-marks going in, I see none coming out), backed by the findings of increasing Air Force reconnaissance missions, had been watching and evaluating the build-up with alarm since spring. Khe Sanh had always been in the vicinity of major infiltration routes, "sat astride" them, as the Mission put it. That slight but definite plateau, rising abruptly from the foothills bridging Laos and Vietnam, had been of value for as long as the Vietnamese had been at war. The routes now used by the NVA had been used twenty years earlier by the Viet Minh. Khe Sanh's original value to the Americans might be gauged by the fact that in spite of the known infiltration all around it, we held it for years with nothing more than a Special Forces A Team; less than a dozen Americans and around 400 indigenous troops, Vietnamese and Montagnard. When the Special Forces first moved in there in 1962, they built their teamhouse, outbuildings, club and defenses over bunkers that had been left by the French. Infiltrating columns simply diverted their routes a kilometer or so away from the central Khe Sanh position. The Green Berets ran out regular, extremely cautious patrols. Since they were almost always surrounded by the infiltrators, Khe Sanh was not the most comfortable duty in Vietnam, but there was seldom anything more than the random ambush or the occasional mortaring that was standard for A Teams anywhere in-country. If the NVA had considered Khe Sanh tactically crucial or even important, they could have taken it at any time. And if we had thought of it as anything more than a token outpost—you can't have infiltrators running around without putting someone in there for a look—we could have created it as a major base. No one builds bases like Americans.

In the course of routine patrols during the early spring of 1966, Special Forces reported what appeared to be a significant increase in the number of enemy troops in the immediate Khe Sanh area, and a battalion of Marines was sent to reinforce the patrols. A year later, in April and May of 1967, during large but routine Search-and-Destroy operations, the Marines found and engaged battalion-strength units of North Vietnamese holding the tops of Hills 881 North and South, and a lot of people were killed on both sides. The battles grew into the bloodiest of the spring. The hills were taken and, weeks later, abandoned. The Marines that might have maintained the hills (Where better to observe infiltration than from a vantage of 881 meters?) were sent instead to Khe Sanh, where the 1st and 3rd Battalions of the 26th Marine Regiment rotated, increasing their harassment of the NVA, hoping, if not to drive them out of the sector, to at least force their movements into predictable patterns. The 26th, a hybrid regiment, was formed out of the TAOR of the 5th Marine Division, a numerical designation which remained on paper even after the actual command of the regiment became the responsibility of the 3rd Marine Division, headquartered at Dong Ha, nearby in the DMZ.

By summer, it became obvious that the battles for 881 North

and South had engaged a relatively small number of the enemy thought to be in the area. Patrols were stepped up (they were now thought to be among the most dangerous in I Corps), and additional elements of the 26th Marines were airlifted into what was now being called the Khe Sanh Combat Base. The Seabees laid down a 600-meter tarmac airstrip. A beer hall and an air-conditioned officers' club were built, and the regimental command set up its Tactical Operations Center in the largest of the deserted French bunkers. Yet Khe Sanh continued to be only a moderate, private concern of the Marine Corps. A few old hands in the press corps knew vaguely about the base and about the small ville of about a thousand Montagnards which lay four kilometers to the south. It was not until November, when the regiment had grown to full and then reinforced strength (6,000 Marines, not including units added from the 9th Marine Regiment), with 600 Vietnamese Rangers, two detachments of Seabees, a helicopter squadron and a small Special Forces Compound, that the Marines began "leaking" the rather remarkable claim that by building up the base we had lured an unbelievable number of enemy to the area.

It was at about this time that copies of the little red British paperback edition of Jules Roy's *The Battle of Dienbienphu* began appearing wherever members of the Vietnam press corps gathered. You'd spot them around the terrace bar of the Continental Hotel, in L'Amiral Restaurant and Aterbea, at the 8th Aerial Port of Tan Son Nhut, in the Marine-operated Danang Press Center and in the big briefing room of JUSPAO in Saigon, where every afternoon at 4:45 spokesmen conducted the daily war briefing which was colloquially referred to as the Five O'Clock Follies, an Orwellian grope through the day's events as seen by the Mission. (It was very hard-line.) Those who could find copies were reading Bernard Fall's Dien Bien Phu book, *Hell in a Very Small Place*, which many considered the better book, stronger on tactics, more businesslike, with none of the high-level staff gossip that made the Roy book so dramatic. And as the first Marine briefings on Khe Sanh took place in Marine headquarters at Danang or Dong Ha, the name Dien Bien Phu insinuated itself like some tasteless ghost hawking bad news. Marines who had to talk to the press found references to the old French disaster irritating and even insulting. Most were not interested in fielding questions about it, and the rest were unequipped. The more irritated they became, the more the press would flaunt the irritant. For a while it looked like nothing that had happened on the ground during those weeks seemed as thrilling and sinister as the recollection of Dien Bien Phu. And it had to be admitted, the parallels with Khe Sanh were irresistible.

To begin with, the ratio between attackers and defenders was roughly the same, eight to one. The terrain was hauntingly similar, although Khe Sanh was only two square miles inside its perimeter, as opposed to the sprawl of Dien Bien Phu. The weather conditions were the same, with the monsoons favoring the attackers by keeping American air activity at a minimum. Khe Sanh was now encircled, as Dien Bien Phu had been, and where the initial attacks of March 1954 had been launched from Viet Minh trenches, the NVA had begun digging a network of trenches that would soon approach to within a hundred yards of the Marine wire. Dien Bien Phu had been the master plan of General Vo Nguyen Giap; rumors splintered from American Intelligence suggested that Giap himself was directing the Khe Sanh operation from a post somewhere above the DMZ. Given the fact that a lot of Marine officers did not understand what we were doing at Khe Sanh in the first place, the repeated evocations of Dien Bien Phu were unnerving. But then, on what briefers liked to call "our side of the ledger," there were important differences.

The base at Khe Sanh was raised, if only slightly, on a plateau which would have slowed a ground attack and given the Marines a gentle vantage from which to fire. The Marines also had a massive reaction force to count on, or at least to hope for. For publication, this consisted of the 1st Air Cavalry Division and elements of the 101st Airborne, but in fact the force numbered almost a quarter of a million men, men at support firebases across the DMZ, planners in Saigon (and Washington) and, most important of all, pilots and crews from headquarters as far away as Udorn, Guam, and Okinawa, men whose energies and attentions became fixed almost exclusively on Khe Sanh missions. Air support was everything, the cornerstone of all our hopes at Khe Sanh, and we knew that once the monsoons lifted, it would be nothing to drop tens of thousands of tons of high explosives and napalm all around the base, to supply it without strain, to cover and reinforce the Marines.

It was a comfort, all of that power and precision and exquisitely geared clout. It meant a lot to the thousands of Marines at Khe Sanh, to the Command, to correspondents spending a few days and nights at the base, to officials in the Pentagon. We could all sleep easier for it: lance corporals and General Westmoreland, me and the President, Navy medics and the parents of all the boys inside the wire. All any of us had to worry about was the fact that Khe Sanh was vastly outnumbered and entirely surrounded; that, and the knowledge that all ground evacuation routes, including the vital Route 9, were completely controlled by the NVA, and that the monsoons had at least six weeks more to run.

There was a joke going around that went like this: "What's the difference between the Marine Corps and the Boy Scouts?" "The Boy Scouts have adult leadership." Dig it! the grunts would say, digging it just as long as they didn't have to hear it from outsiders, from "non-essential personnel" like the Army or the Air Force. For them it was only good as a joke when it also had that touch of fraternal mystery. And what a fraternity! If the war in I Corps was a matter for specialization among correspondents, it was not because it was inherently different as war, but because it was fought almost exclusively by the Marines, whose idiosyncrasies most reporters found intolerable and even criminal. (There was a week in the war, one week, when the Army lost more men killed, proportionately, than the Marines, and Army spokesmen had a rough time hiding their pride, their absolute glee.) And in the face of some new variation on old Marine disasters, it didn't much matter that you knew dozens of fine, fine officers. Something almost always went wrong somewhere, somehow. It was always something vague, unexplainable, tasting of bad fate, and the results were always brought down to their most basic element—the dead Marine. The belief that one Marine was better than ten Slopes saw Marine squads fed in against known NVA platoons, platoons against companies, and on and on, until whole battalions found themselves pinned down and cut off. That belief was undying, but the grunt was not, and the Corps came to be called by many the finest instrument ever devised for the killing of young Americans. There were always plenty of stories about entire squads wiped out (their mutilated bodies would so enrage Marines that they would run out "vengeance patrols" which often enough ended the same way), companies taking 75 percent casualties, Marines ambushing Marines, artillery and airstrikes called in on our own positions, all in the course of routine Search-and-Destroy operations. And you knew that, sooner or later, if you went with them often enough, it would happen to you too.

And the grunts themselves knew: the madness, the bitterness, the horror and doom of it. They were hip to it, and more: they savored it. It was no more insane than most of what was going down, and often enough it had its refracted logic. "Eat the apple, fuck the Corps," they'd say, and write it up on their helmets and flak jackets for their officers to see. (One kid tattooed it on his shoulder.) And sometimes they'd look at you and laugh silently and long, the laugh on them and on you for being with them when you didn't have to be. And what could be funnier, really, given all that an eighteen-year-old boy could learn in a month of patrolling the Z? It was that joke at the deepest part of the blackest kernel of fear, and you could die laughing. They even wrote a song, a letter to the mother of a dead Marine, that went something like, "Tough shit, tough shit, your kid got greased, but what the fuck, he was just a grunt. . . ." They got savaged a lot and softened a lot, their secret brutalized them and darkened them and very often it made them beautiful. It took no age, seasoning or education to make them know exactly where true violence resided.

And they were killers. Of course they were; what would anyone expect them to be? It absorbed them, inhabited them, made them strong in the way that victims are strong, filled them with the twin obsessions of Death and Peace, fixed them so that they could never, never again speak lightly about the Worst Thing in the World. If you learned just this much about them, you were never quite as happy (in the miserable-joyous way of covering the war) with other outfits. And, naturally, the poor bastards were famous all over Vietnam. If you spent some weeks up there and afterward joined an Army outfit of, say, the 4th or 25th Division, you'd get this:

"Where you been? We ain't seen you."

"Up in I Corps."

"With the *Marines*?"

"That's what's up there."

"Well, all I got to say is Good Luck! Marines. Fuck that."

"Khe Sanh is the Western Anchor of our defense," the Commanding General offered.

"Who told you that?" the Examining Angels replied.

"Why . . . everybody!"

No Marine ever called it that, not even those officers who believed in it tactically, just as no Marine ever called what happened there for seventy-six days a "siege." Those were MACV conceits, often taken up by the press, and they angered Marines. As long as the 26th Marines could maintain a battalion outside the wire (the garrison at Khesanville was withdrawn and the town bombed flat, but Marines still patrolled beyond the perimeter and lived on nearby hilltops), as long as planes could re-supply the base, it could not be a siege. Marines may get beleaguered, but not besieged. Whatever one chose to call it, by the time of the Tet Offensive, a week after the shelling of Khe Sanh began, it looked as though both sides had committed themselves on such a scale that engagement was inevitable. No one I knew doubted that it would come, probably in the form of a massive ground attack, and that when it came it would be terrible and great.

Tactically, its value to the Command was thought so great that General Westmoreland could announce that the Tet Offensive was merely Phase II of a brilliant Giap strategy. Phase I had been revealed in the autumn skirmishes between Loc Ninh and Dak To. Phase III ("the capstone," the general called it) was to be Khe Sanh. It seems impossible that anyone, at any time, even in the chaos of Tet, could have actually called something as monumental (and decisive?) as that offensive a mere diversion for something as negligible as Khe Sanh, but all of that is on record.

And by then, Khe Sanh was famous, one of the very few place names in Vietnam that was recognized by the American public. Khe Sanh said "siege," it said "encircled Marines" and "heroic defenders." It could be understood by newspaper readers quickly, it breathed Glory and War and Honored Dead. It seemed to make sense. It was good stuff. One can only imagine the anxiety which the Commander in Chief suffered over it. Lyndon Johnson said it straight out, he did not want "any damn Dinbinfoo," and he did something unprecedented in the history of warfare. The Joint Chiefs of Staff were summoned and made to sign a statement "for the public reassurance," asserting that Khe Sanh could and would be held at all costs. (Apparently, *Coriolanus* had never been required reading at the Point. Noncoms in the field, even grunts with no career ambitions, felt the professional indignity of the President's gambit, talked of it as something shameful.) Perhaps Khe Sanh would be held, perhaps not; the President had his statement now, and it was signed clearly. If Khe Sanh stood, he would presumably be available for a grin in the victory picture. If it fell, it would not be on his head.

More than any other Americans in Vietnam, Khe Sanh's defenders became hostages, nearly 8,000 Americans and Vietnamese who took their orders not from the regimental commander in the TOC, nor from General Cushman in Danang nor General Westmoreland in Saigon, but from a source which one Intelligence officer I knew always called "Downtown." They were made to sit and wait, and Marines defending are like antichrists at vespers. Somehow, digging in seems a soft thing to do, fighting from a hole is like fighting on your knees. ("Digging," General Cushman said, "is not the Marine way.") Most of the defenses against artillery were built entirely or substantially reinforced after the heavy shelling began, when the Tet Offensive diverted supply from the air and made Khe Sanh even more isolated. They were built on the scrounge and so haphazardly that the lines of sandbagging had a sensuous, plastic drift to them as they stretched away into the filtered light of mist and dust, the shapes growing dimmer in the distance. If all of the barbed wire and all of the sandbags were taken away, Khe Sanh would have looked like one of those Colombian valley slums whose meanness is the abiding factor, whose despair is so palpable that for days after you leave you are filled with a vicarious shame for the misery you have just tripped through. At Khe Sanh most bunkers were nothing more than hovels with inadequate overhead cover, and you could not believe that Americans were living this way, even in the middle of a war. The defenses were a scandal, and everywhere you could smell that sour reek of obsolescence that followed the Marines all over Vietnam. If they could not hear their own dead from Con Thien, only three months past, how could they ever be expected to hear the dead from Dien Bien Phu?

Not a single round had fallen inside the perimeter. The jungled slopes running up from the bowl of the base were not yet burned over and hung with the flare chutes that looked like infants' shrouds. Six shades of green, motherfucker, tell me that ain't something beautiful. There were no heaps of shredded, blood-soaked jungle fatigues outside the triage room, and the wires were not cluttered each dawn with their dead. None of it had happened yet when Khe Sanh became lost forever as a tactical entity. It is impossible to fix the exact moment in time when it happened, or to know, really, why. All that was certain was that Khe Sanh had become a passion, the false love object in the heart of the Command. It cannot even be determined which way the passion traveled. Did it proceed from the filthiest ground-zero slit trench and proceed outward, across I Corps to Saigon and on (taking the true perimeter with it) to the most abstract reaches of the Pentagon? Or did it get born in those same Pentagon rooms where six years of failure had made the air bad, where optimism no longer sprang from anything viable but sprang and sprang, all the way to Saigon, where it was packaged and shipped north to give the grunts some kind of reason for what was about to happen to them? In its outlines, the promise was delicious: Victory! A vision of as many as 40,000 of them out there in the open, fighting it out on our terms, fighting for once like men, fighting to no avail. There would be a battle, a set-piece battle where he could be killed by the numbers, killed wholesale, and if we killed enough of him, maybe he would go away. In the face of such a promise, the question of defeat could not even be considered, no more than the question of whether, after Tet, Khe Sanh might have become militarily unwise and even absurd. Once it was all locked in place, Khe Sanh became like the planted jar in Wallace Stevens' poem. It took dominion everywhere.

IV

When I think of it quickly, just seeing the name somewhere or being asked what it was like, I see a flat, dun stretch of ground running out in an even plane until the rim of the middle distance takes on the shapes and colors of jungled hills. I had the strangest, most thrilling kind of illusion there, looking at those hills and thinking about the death and mystery that was in them. I would see the thing I knew I actually saw: the base from the ground where I stood, figures moving across it, choppers rising from the pad by the strip, and the hills above. But at the same time I would see the other, too; the ground, the troops and even myself, all from the vantage of the hills. It was a double vision that came to me more than once there. And in my head, sounding over and over, were the incredibly sinister words of the song we had all heard for the first time only days before. "The Magical Mystery Tour is waiting to take you away," it promised, "Coming to take you away, dy-ing to take you away. . . ." That was a song about Khe Sanh; we knew it then, and it still seems so. Inside the bunker, one of the grunts has been saying hideous things in his sleep, laughing a bad laugh and then going more silent than even deep sleep permits before starting it up again, and it is more terrible in there than any place I can even imagine. I got up then and went outside, any place at all was better than this, and stood in the dark smoking a cigarette, watching the hills for a sign and hoping none would come because, shit, what could be revealed except more fear? Three in the morning, and my blood is intimate with the chill, host to it, and very willing too. From the center of the earth there is a tremor that shakes everything, running up through my legs and body, shaking my head, yet no one in the bunker wakes up. We called them "Archlights," he called them Rolling Thunder, and it was incessant during the nights. The bombs would release at 18,000 feet and the planes would turn and fly back to Udorn or Guam. Dawn seems to last until late morning, dusk falls at four. Everything I see is blown through with smoke, everything is on fire everywhere. It doesn't matter that memory distorts; every image, every sound comes back out of smoke and the smell of things burning.

Some of it, like smoke from an exploding round in the air, breaks cleanly and at a comfortable distance. Some of it pours out of large tubs of shit being burned off with diesel fuel, and it hangs, hangs, taking you full in the throat even though you are used to it. Right there on the strip a fuel ship has been hit, and no one who has heard that can kill the shakes for an hour. (What woke you? . . . What woke you?) A picture comes in, absolutely still for a moment, and then resumes the motion it once had: a heat tablet, burning in high intensity, covered by a tiny, blackened stove a Marine had made for me two weeks before in Hue out of the small dessert can from a ration box. From this little bit of light I can see the outlines of a few Marines, all of us in a bunker filling with the acrid smoke of the tablet, glad for it because the rations will be hot tonight, glad because we know how safe the bunker is and because we are both private and together, and find a lot of things to laugh about. I brought the tablets with me, stole them from a colonel's aide in Dong Ha, supercilious prick, and these guys hadn't had any in days, weeks. I also have a bottle. ("Oh man, you are welcome here. You are *def*initely welcome. Let's wait for Gunny.") The beef and potatoes, the meatballs and beans, the ham and Mothers, all that good stuff, will be hot tonight, and who really gives a fuck about tomorrow night anyway? Somewhere above ground now, in full afternoon light, there is a four-foot stack of C-ration cartons, the cardboard burned away from the metal binding wire, the cans and utility packs lying all around, and on top of it all there is the body of a young ARVN Ranger who had just come over to Bravo Recon to scrounge a few cans of American food. If he'd succeeded, he would have gone back to his unit a celebrity, but as it was he didn't make out. Three rounds had come in very quickly, neither killing nor wounding any of the Marines, and now two lance corporals are arguing. One wants to put the dead Ranger into a green body bag, the other just wants to cover the body somehow, anyhow, and run it over to the Dink compound. He's very pissed off. "We keep tellin' them fuckin' people to stay with their own fuckin' outfits," he says, over and over. Fires eat at everything. There are fires at night, the trees on hillsides kilometers away erupting in smoke, burning. At late morning, the sun burns off the last of the chill and early mist, making the base visible from above until late afternoon, when the chill and the mists return. Then it is night again, and the sky beyond the western perimeter is burning with slowly dropping magnesium flares. Heaps of equipment are on fire, terrifying in their jagged black massiveness, burning prehistoric shapes like the tail of a C-130 sticking straight up in the air, dead metal showing through the gray-black smoke. God, if it can do that to metal, what will it do to me? And then something very near me is smoldering, just above my head, the damp canvas coverings on the sandbags lining the top of a slit trench. It is a small trench, and a lot of us have gotten into it in a hurry. At the end farthest from me there is a young guy who has been hit in the throat, and he is making the sounds a baby will make when he is trying to work up the breath for a good scream. We were on the ground when those rounds came, and a Marine nearer the trench had been splattered badly across the legs and groin. I sort of took him into the trench with me. It was so crowded I couldn't help leaning on him a little, and he kept saying, "You motherfucker, you cocksucker," until someone told him that I wasn't a grunt but a reporter. Then he started to say, very quietly, "Be careful, Mister. Please be careful." He'd been wounded before, and he knew how it would hurt in a few minutes. People would just get ripped up in the worst ways there, and things were always on fire. Far up the road that skirted the TOC was a dump where they burned the gear and uniforms that nobody needed anymore. On top of the pile I saw a flak jacket so torn apart that no one would ever want it again. On the back, its owner had listed the months that he had served in Vietnam. *March, April, May* (each month written out in a tentative, spidery hand), *June, July, August, September, Octobler, Novembler, Decembler, Janurary, Feburary*, the list ending right there like a clock stopped by a bullet. A jeep pulled up to the dump and a Marine jumped out carrying a bunched-up fatigue jacket held out away from him. He looked very serious and scared. Some guy in his company, some guy he didn't even know, had been blown away right next to him, all over him. He held the fatigues up and I believed him. "I guess you couldn't wash them, could you?" I said. He really looked like he was going to cry as he threw them into the dump. "Man," he said, "you could take and scrub them fatigues for a million years, and *it would never happen.*"

I see a road. It is full of ruts made by truck and jeep tires, but in the passing rains they never harden, and along the road there is a two-dollar piece of issue, a poncho which had just been used to cover a dead Marine, a blood-puddled, mud-wet poncho going stiff in the wind. It has reared up there by the road in a horrible, streaked ball. The wind doesn't move it, only setting the pools of water and blood in the dents shimmering. I'm walking along this road with two black grunts, and one of them gives the poncho a vicious, helpless kick. "Go easy, man," the other one says, nothing changing in his face, not even a look back. "That's the American flag you gettin' your foot into."

During the early morning of February 7 something so horrible happened in the Khe Sanh sector that even those of us who were in Hue when we heard news of it had to relinquish our own fear and despair for a moment to acknowledge the horror and pay some tribute to it. It was as though the very worst dream any of us had ever had about the war had come true; it anticipated nightmares so vile that they could take you off shuddering in your sleep. No one who heard it was able to smile that bitter, secret survivor's smile that was the reflex to almost all news of disaster. It was too awful even for that.

Five kilometers southwest of the Khe Sanh Combat Base, sitting above the river which forms the border with Laos, there was a Special Forces A Camp. It was called Langvei, taking its name from the small Montagnard village nearby which had been mistakenly bombed a year before by the Air Force. The camp was larger than most Special Forces camps, and much better built. It was set on twin hills about 700 meters apart, and the vital bunkers holding most of the troops were on the hill nearest the river. It was manned by twenty-four Americans and over 400 Vietnamese troops. Its bunkers were deep, solid, with three feet of reinforced concrete overhead, seemingly impregnable. And sometime after midnight, the North Vietnamese came and took it. They took it with a style that had been seen only once before, in the Ia Drang, attacking with weapons and tactics which no one imagined they had. Nine light tanks, Soviet T-34's and 76's, were deployed east and west, closing on the camp so suddenly that the first sound of them was mistaken by the Americans for a malfunction of the camp generator. Satchel charges, bangalore torpedoes, tear gas and—ineffable horror—napalm were all hurled into the machine-gun slits and air vents of the bunkers. It took very little time. An American colonel who had come on an inspection visit to Langvei was seen charging the tanks with nothing but hand grenades before he was cut down. (He survived. The word "miracle" doesn't even apply.) Somewhere between ten and fifteen Americans were killed, and as many as 300 of the indigenous troops. The survivors traveled all night, most of them on foot through NVA positions (some were picked up later by choppers), arriving at Khe Sanh after dawn, and it was said that some of them had become insane. At the same time that Langvei was being overrun, Khe Sanh received the most brutal artillery barrage of the war: 1,500 rounds that night, six rounds a minute for more minutes than anyone could bear to count.

The Marines at Khe Sanh saw the Langvei survivors come in. They saw them and heard about them up in their Special Forces compound, holding off all visitors at rifle point, saw their faces and their unfocused stares, and they talked quietly among themselves about it. Jesus, they had tanks. Tanks! . . . After Langvei, how could you look out of your perimeter at night without hearing the treads coming? How could you patrol in the dark without remembering every story you ever heard about ghostly enemy helicopters flying the fringes of the Z? About the trails cut in the floor of the A Shau Valley, big enough to hold trucks? About the complete fanaticism of attackers who were doped to the eyeballs (sure they smoke dope, it gets them crazy), who ran pushing civilian shields forward, who chained themselves to their machine guns and died right there rather than fail, who had No Regard For Human Life?

Officially, the Marines admitted no relevance between the Langvei attack and Khe Sanh. Confidentially, they said something awful about Langvei having been bait—bait which the poor, desperate bastards took, exactly as we hoped they would. But everyone knew better, much better, and the majors and colonels who had to tell reporters about it were met with embarrassed silence. One hated to bring it up, one never really did, but there was a question that had everything in the world to do with Khe Sanh after Langvei fell. I wanted to ask it so badly that my hesitance made me mad for months. Colonel (I wanted to ask), this is purely hypothetical, I hope you understand. But what if all of those gooks that you think are out there are *really* out there? And what if they attack before the monsoons blow south, some mist-clogged night when our planes just cannot get up there? What if they really want Khe Sanh, want it so badly that they are willing to maneuver over the triple lines of barbed wire, the German razor wire too; over barricades formed by their own dead (a tactic, Colonel, favored by your gook in Korea), coming in waves, *human* waves, and in such numbers that the barrels of our .50-calibers overheat and melt and all the M-16's are jammed, until all of the death in all of the Claymore mines on our defenses has been spent and absorbed? What if they are still coming, moving toward the center of a base so smashed by their artillery that those pissy little trenches and bunkers that *your* Marines half got up are useless, coming as the first MIG's and IL-28's ever seen in this war bomb out the TOC and the strip, the med tent and the control tower (People's Army my ass, right, Colonel?), coming at you 20,000 to 40,000 strong? And what if they pass over every barricade we can put in their way . . . and kill every living thing, defending or retreating . . . and take Khe Sanh?

Some strange things would happen. One morning, at the height of the monsoons, the sun came up brightly at dawn and shone all day. The early-morning skies were a clean, brilliant blue, the only time before April that anyone saw that at Khe Sanh, and instead of waking and coming out shivering from their bunkers, the grunts stripped down to boots, pants and flak jackets; biceps, triceps and tattoos all out for breakfast. Probably because the NVA knew that American surveillance and bombers would be working overtime on a morning like this, there was almost no shelling, and we all knew we could count on it. For those few hours Khe Sanh had the atmosphere of reprieve. I remember passing a chaplain named Stubbe on the road and seeing his incredible pleasure at the miracle of this morning. The hills did not seem like the same hills that had given off so much fear the night before and all of the days and nights before that. In the early-morning light they looked sharp and tranquil, as though you could take some apples and a book and go up there for an afternoon.

I was walking around by myself in the 1st Battalion area. It was before eight in the morning, and as I walked I could hear someone walking behind me, singing. At first I couldn't hear what it was, only that it was a single short phrase being sung over and over at short intervals, and that every time someone else would laugh and tell the singer to shut up. I slowed down and let them catch up.

" 'I'd rather be an Oscar Mayer weiner,' " the voice sang. It sounded very plaintive and lonely.

Of course I turned around. There were two of them, one a big Negro with a full mustache that drooped over the corners of his mouth, a mean, signifying mustache that would have worked if only there had been the smallest trace of meanness anywhere on his face. He was at least six-three and quarterback thick. He was carrying an AK-47. The other Marine was white, and if I'd seen him first from the back I would have said that he was eleven years old. The Marines must have a height requirement; whatever it is, I don't see how he made it. Age is one thing, but how do you lie about your height? He'd been doing the singing, and he was laughing now because he'd made me turn around. His name was Mayhew, it was written out in enormous red letters across the front of his helmet: MAYHEW—*You'd better believe it!* I'd been walking with my flak jacket open, a stupid thing to do even on this morning, and they could see the stitched tag above my left breast pocket with the name of my magazine written on it.

"Correspondent?" the Negro said.

Mayhew just laughed. " 'I'd-a rather be—a Oscar Mayer . . . weenieeee,' " he sang. "You can write that, man, tell 'em all I said so."

"Don't pay no attention to him," the Negro said. "That's Mayhew. He's a crazy fucker, ain't you, Mayhew?"

"I sure hope so," Mayhew said. " 'I'd rather be a Oscar Mayer weiner. . . .' "

He was young, nineteen, he later told me, and he was trying to grow a mustache. His only luck with it so far was a few sparse, transparent blond clumps set at odd intervals across his upper lip, and you couldn't see that unless the light was right. The Negro was called Day Tripper. It was on his helmet, along with DETROIT CITY. And on the back, where most guys just listed the months of their tours, he had carefully drawn a full calendar where each day served was marked off with a neat X. They were both from Hotel Company of the 2nd Battalion, which was dug in along the northern perimeter, but they were taking advantage of the day to visit a friend of theirs, a mortar man with 1/26.

"The lieutenant ever hear 'bout this, he know what to do," Day Tripper said.

"Fuck the lieutenant," Mayhew said. "You remember from before he ain't wrapped too tight."

"Well, he wrapped tight enough to tear *you* a new asshole."

"Now what's he gonna do to me? Send me to Vietnam?"

We walked past the battalion CP, piled five feet high with sandbags, and then we reached a giant ring of sandbagging, the mortar pit, and climbed down. In the center was a large four-oh-deuce mortar piece, and the inside of the pit was stacked completely around with ammunition, piled from the ground to just below the sandbags. A Marine was stretched out in the dust with a war comic spread over his face.

"Hey, where's Evans?" Mayhew said. "You know a guy named Evans?"

The Marine took the comic off of his face and looked up. He'd been asleep.

"Shit," he said. "I thought you was the Old Man for a second. Beg your pardon."

"We're looking for this guy Evans," Mayhew said. "You know him?"

"I—uh—no, I don't guess so. I'm pretty new."

He looked it. He was the kind of kid that would go into the high-school gym alone and shoot baskets for the half-hour before the basketball team took it over for practice, not good enough yet for the team but determined.

"The rest of the crew'll be down here right away. You can wait if you want." He looked at all the rounds. "It's probably not too cool," he said, smiling. "But you can if you want."

Mayhew unbuttoned one of the pockets in the leg of his fatigues and took out a can of crackers and Cheddar-cheese spread. He took the P-38 opener from a band around his helmet and sat down.

"Might as well eat some shit while we wait. You get hungry, it ain't so bad. I'd give my left ball for a can of fruit now."

I always scrounged fruit from rear areas to bring forward, and I had some in my pack. "What kind do you like?" I asked.

"Any kind's good," he said. "Fruit cocktail's really good."

"No, man," Day Tripper said. "Peaches, baby, peaches. All that syrup. Now that's some good shit."

"There you go, Mayhew," I said, tossing him a fruit cocktail. I gave a can of peaches to Day Tripper and kept a can for myself.

We talked while we ate. Mayhew told me about his father, who "got greased in Korea," and about his mother, who worked in a department store in Kansas City. Then he started to tell about Day Tripper, who got his name because he was afraid of the night—not the dark, but the night—and who didn't mind who knew it. There wasn't anything he wouldn't do during daylight, but if there was any way at all to fix it he liked to be deep in his bunker by nightfall. He was always volunteering for the more dangerous daylight patrols, just to make sure he got in by dusk. (This was before daylight patrols, in fact almost all patrols around Khe Sanh, were discontinued.) There were a lot of white guys, especially junior officers trying to be cool, who were always coming on to Day Tripper about his hometown, calling it Dodge City or Motown and laughing. ("Why they think somethin's special about Detroit?" he said. "Ain't nothin' special, ain't nothin' so funny, neither.") He was a big bad spade gone wrong somehow, and no matter how mean he tried to look something constantly gentle showed. He told me he knew guys from Detroit who were taking mortars back, breaking them down so that each one could get a piece into his duffel and then reassembling them when they got together back on the block. "You see that four-oh-deuce?" he said. "Now, that'll take out a police station for you. I don't need all that hassle. But maybe nex' year I gonna need it."

Like every American in Vietnam, he had his obsession with Time. (No one ever talked about When-this-lousy-war-is-over. Only "How much time you got?") The degree of Day Tripper's obsession, compared with most of the others, could be seen in the calendar on his helmet. No metaphysician ever studied Time the way he did, its components and implications, its per-second per seconds, its shadings and movement. The Space-Time continuum, Time-as-Matter, Augustinian Time: all of that would have been a piece of cake to Day Tripper, whose brain cells were arranged like jewels in the finest chronometer. He had assumed that correspondents in Vietnam *had* to be there. When he learned that I had asked to come here he almost let the peaches drop to the ground.

"Lemmee . . . lemmee jus' hang on that a minute," he said. "You mean you don' *have* to be here? An' you're *here*?"

I nodded.

"Well, they gotta be payin' you some tough bread."

"You'd get depressed if I told you."

He shook his head.

"I mean, they ain' *got* the bread that'd get me here if I didn' have t' be here."

"Horse crap," Mayhew said. "Day Tripper loves it. He's short now, but he's comin' back, ain't you, Day Tripper?"

"Shit, my momma'll come over here and pull a tour before I fuckin' come back."

Four more Marines dropped into the pit.

"Where's Evans?" Mayhew demanded. "Any of you guys know Evans?"

One of the mortar men came over.

"Evans is over in Danang," he said. "He caught a little shit the other night."

"That right?" Mayhew said. "Evans get wounded?"

"He hurt bad?" Day Tripper asked.

"Not bad enough," the mortar man said, laughing. "He'll be back in ten days. Just some stuff in the legs."

"He's real lucky," another one said. "Same round got him killed a guy."

"Yeah," someone said. "Greene got killed." He wasn't talking to us, but to the crew, who knew it already. "Remember Greene?" Everyone nodded.

"Wow, Greene," he said. "Greene was all fixed to get out. He's jerkin' off thirty times a day, that fuckin' guy, and they's all set to give him a medical. And out."

"That's no shit," the other one said. "Thirty times a day. Dis*gus*ting, man. That sombitch had come all over his pants, that fuckin' Greene. He was waitin' outside to see the major about gettin' sent home, an' the major comes out to find him an' he's just sittin' there jerkin' off. Then he gets blown away the night before."

"Well," Day Tripper said quietly to Mayhew, "see what happens if you jerk off?"

A Chinook, forty feet long with rotors front and back, set down on the airstrip by Charlie Med, looking like a great, gross beast getting a body purchase on some mud, blowing bitter gusts of dust, pebbles and debris for a hundred yards around. Everywhere within that circle of wind men turned and crouched, covering their necks against the full violence of it. The wind from those blades could come up strong enough to blow you over, to tear papers from your hands, to lift tarmac sections weighing a hundred pounds in the air. But it was mostly the sharp fragments, the stinging dirt, the muddy, pissed-in water, and you acquired a second sense of when it would reach you, learned to give it only your back and your helmet. The Chinook had flown in with its rear hatch down and a gunner with a .50-caliber machine gun stretched out flat on his stomach peering over the edge of the hatch. Neither he nor the door gunners would relax their weapons until the chopper touched the strip. Then they let go, the barrels of the big guns dropping down like dead weights in their mounts. A bunch of Marines appeared on the edge of the strip and ran to the chopper, through the ring of harsh, filthy wind, toward the calm at the center. Three mortar rounds came in at three-second intervals, all landing in a cluster 200 meters down the strip. No one around the chopper stopped. The noise from the Chinook drowned out the noise of the rounds, but we could see the balls of white smoke blowing out away from the strip in the wind, and the men were still running for the chopper. Four full litters were carried at a run from the rear of the Chinook to the med tent. Some walking wounded came out and headed for the tent, some walking slowly, unaided, others moving uncertainly, one being supported by two Marines. The empty litters were returned and loaded with four poncho-covered figures, which were set down near some sandbagging in front of the tent. Then the Chinook reared up abruptly, dipped horribly, regained its flight and headed north and west, toward the covering hills.

"One-nine," Mayhew said. "I'll bet anything."

Four kilometers northwest of Khe Sanh was Hill 861, the hardest-hit of all the sector outposts after Langvei, and it seemed logical to everyone that the 1st Battalion of the 9th Marine Regiment should have been chosen to defend it. Some even believed that if anyone but 1/9 had been put there, 861 would never have been hit. Of all the hard-luck outfits in Vietnam, this was said to be the most doomed, doomed in its Search-and-Destroy days before Khe Sanh, known for a history of ambush and confusion and for a casualty rate which was the highest of any outfit in the entire war. That was the kind of reputation that takes hold most deeply among the men of the outfit itself, and when you were with them you got a sense of dread that came out of something more terrible than just a collective loss of luck. All the odds seemed somehow sharply reduced, estimates of your own survival were revised horribly downward. One afternoon with 1/9 on 861 was enough to bend your nerves for days, because it took only a few minutes up there to see the very worst of it: the stumbles, the simple motions of a walk suddenly racked by spasms, mouths sand-dry seconds after drinking, the dreamy smiles of total abdication. Hill 861 was the home of the thousand-yard stare, and I prayed hard for a chopper to come and get me away from there, to fly me over the ground fire and land me in the middle of a mortar barrage on the Khe Sanh pad—whatever! Anything was better than this.

On a night shortly after the Langvei attack an entire platoon of 1/9 was ambushed during a patrol and wiped out. Hill 861 had been hit repeatedly, once for three days straight during a perimeter probe that turned into a siege that really *was* a siege. For reasons that no one is certain of, Marine helicopters refused to fly missions up there, and 1/9 was cut off from support, re-supply or medical evacuation. It was bad, and they had to get through it any way they could, alone. (The stories from that time became part of the worst Marine legends; the story of one Marine putting a wounded buddy away with a pistol shot because medical help was impossible, or the story of what they did to the NVA prisoner taken beyond the wire— stories like that. Some of them may even have been true.) The old hostility of the grunt toward Marine Air became total on 861: when the worst of it was over and the first Ch-34 finally showed over the hilltop, the door gunner was hit by enemy ground fire and fell out of the chopper. It was a drop of over 200 feet, and there were Marines on the ground who cheered when he hit.

Mayhew, Day Tripper and I were walking near the triage tent of Charlie Med. In spite of all the shrapnel that had fallen into that tent, no way had been found to protect it. The sand-bagging around it was hardly more than five feet high, and the top was entirely exposed. It was one reason why grunts feared even the mildest of the Going Home wounds. Some-one ran out of the tent and took photographs of the four dead Marines. The wind from the Chinook had blown the ponchos from two of them, and one had no face left at all. A Catholic chaplain on a bicycle rode up to the entrance of the tent and walked inside. A Marine came out and stood by the flap for a moment, an unlighted cigarette hanging from his mouth. He had neither a flak jacket nor a helmet. He let the cigarette drop from his lips, walked a few steps to the sandbags and sat down with his legs drawn up and his head hanging down between his knees. He threw one limp arm over his head and began stroking the back of his neck, shaking his head from side to side violently, as though in agony. He wasn't wounded.

We were here because I had to pass this way to reach my bunker, where I had to pick up some things to take over to Hotel Company for the night. Day Tripper wasn't liking the route. He looked at the bodies and then at me. It was that look which said, "See? You see what it does?" I had seen that look so many times during the past months that I must have had it too now, and neither of us said anything. Mayhew wasn't letting himself look at anything. It was as though he were walking by himself now, and he was singing in an odd, quiet voice. " 'When you get to San Francisco,' " he sang, " 'be sure and wear some flowers in your hair.' "

We passed the control tower, that target that was its own aiming stake, so prominent and vulnerable that climbing up there was worse than having to run in front of a machine gun. Two of them had already been hit, and the sandbags running up the sides didn't seem to make any difference. We went by the grimy admin buildings and bunkers, a bunch of deserted "hardbacks" with crushed metal roofs, the TOC, the command latrine and a post-office bunker. There was the now roofless beer hall and the collapsed, abandoned officers' club. The Seabee bunker was just a little farther along the road.

It was not like the other bunkers. It was the deepest, safest, cleanest place in Khe Sanh, with six feet of timbers, steel and sandbags overhead, and inside it was brightly lit. The grunts called it the Alamo Hilton and thought it was candy-assed, while almost every correspondent who came to Khe Sanh tried to get a bed there. A bottle of whiskey or a case of beer would be enough to get you in for a few nights, and once you became a friend of the house, gifts like that were simply a token and very deeply appreciated. The Marines had set up a press "facility" very, very near the strip, and it was so bad that a lot of reporters thought there was a conscious conspiracy working to get some of us killed off. It was nothing more than a narrow, flimsily covered, rat-infested hole, and one day when it was empty an incoming 152 shell sewed part of it up.

I went down into the Seabee bunker, picked up a bottle of Scotch and a field jacket, and told one of the Seabees to give my rack to anyone who needed it that night.

"You ain't mad at us or anything?" he said.

"Nothing like that. I'll see you tomorrow."

"Okay," he said as I left. "If you think so."

As the three of us walked toward the 2/26 positions, two batteries of Marine artillery started firing 105's and 155's from

the other side of the base. Every time a round was fired I'd
flinch a little, and Mayhew would laugh.

"Them're outgoing," he said.

Day Tripper heard the deep sliding whistle of the other
shells first. "*That* ain' no outgoin'," he said, and we ran for
a short trench a few yards away.

"That ain't outgoing," Mayhew said.

"Now what I jus' say?" Day Tripper yelled, and we reached
the trench as a shell landed somewhere between the 37th
ARVN Rangers compound and the ammo dump. A lot of
them were coming in, some mortars too, but we didn't count
them.

"Sure was some nice mornin'," Day Tripper said. "Oh,
man, why they can' jus' leave us alone one time?"

" 'Cause they ain't gettin' paid to leave us alone," Mayhew
said, laughing. " 'Sides, they do it 'cause they know how it
fucks you all up."

"Tell me *you* ain' scared shit!"

"You'll never see *me* scared, motherfucker."

"Oh no. Three nights ago you was callin' out for your
momma while them fuckers was hittin' our wire."

"Boo-sheeit! I ain't never gettin' hit in Vietnam."

"Oh no? Okay, mothafucker, why not?"

" 'Cause," Mayhew said, "it don't exist." It was an old
joke, but this time he wasn't laughing.

By now, the trenchline circled the camp almost completely.
Most of the northern perimeter was held down by the 2nd
Battalion of the 26th Marine Regiment, and Hotel Company
was along this sector. In its westernmost part it was opposed
by North Vietnamese trenches that ended just 300 meters
away. Farther to the east it sat above a narrow river, and beyond that was Hill 950, three kilometers to the north, which
was held by the NVA and whose highest ridge ran exactly
parallel to the Khe Sanh airstrip. The bunkers and connecting
trenchworks sat on a rise that ran up from the riverbank, and
the hills began a couple of hundred meters from the far side
of the river. Two hundred meters away, facing the Marine
trenches, there was an NVA sniper with a .50-caliber machine

gun who shot at the Marines from a tiny spider hole. During
the day he fired at anything that rose above the sandbags, and
at night he fired at any lights he could see. You could see him
clearly from the trench, and if you were looking through the
scope of a Marine sniper's rifle you could even see his face.
The Marines fired on his position with mortars and recoilless
rifles, and he would drop into his hole and wait. Gunships
fired rockets at him, and when they were through he would
come up again and fire. Finally, napalm was called in, and for
ten minutes the air above the spider hole was black and orange
from the strike, while the ground around it was galvanized
clean of every living thing. When all of it cleared, the sniper
popped up and fired off a single round, and the Marines in
the trenches cheered. They called him Luke the Gook, and
after that no one wanted anything to happen to him.

Mayhew had a friend named Orrin from somewhere in Tennessee, from the mountains there where his family owned
three small trucks and did a short-haul business. On the
morning that Mayhew and Day Tripper had gone over to
1/26 to find Evans, Orrin received a letter from his wife. It
told him straight off that her pregnancy was not seven months
along, as he had believed, but only five. It made all the difference in the world to Orrin. She had felt so awful all the
time (she wrote) that she went to see the minister, and the
minister had finally convinced her that the Truth was God's
one sure key to a beautiful conscience. She would not tell him
who the father was (and Honey, don't you never, never try
and make me tell), except to mention that it was someone
Orrin knew well.

When we got back to the company, Orrin was sitting on
top of the sandbags above the trench, alone and exposed,
looking out toward the hills and Luke the Gook. He had a
beefy, sulky kid's face, a perpetual mean squint and a pouting
mouth that would break into a dull smile and then a dry,
soundless laugh. It was the face of someone who would hunt
the winter out and then let the meat go to rot, a mean Southland aberration of a face. He just sat there, working the bolt
of a freshly cleaned .45. No one in the trench would go near
him or say anything to him, except to yell out, "Come on

down, Orrin. You'll get greased for sure, motherfucker." Finally, the gunnery sergeant came along and said, "If you don't get your ass down off that berm I'll shoot you myself."

"Listen," Mayhew said. "Maybe you better go and see the chaplain."

"Real good," Orrin said. "What's that cocksucker gone do for me?"

"Maybe you could get an emergency leave."

"No," someone said. "There's gotta be a death in the family before you'll get out like that."

"Oh, don't worry," Orrin said. "There's gone be a death in my family. Just soon's I git home." And then he laughed.

It was a terrible laugh, very quiet and intense, and it was the thing that made everyone who heard it believe Orrin. After that, he was the crazy fucking grunt who was going to get through the war so he could go home and kill his old lady. It made him someone special in the company. It made a lot of guys think that he was lucky now, that nothing could happen to him, and they stayed as close to him as they could. I even felt some of it, enough to be glad that we would be in the same bunker that night. It made sense. I believed it too, and I would have been really surprised if I had heard later that anything had happened to him. But that was the kind of thing you seldom heard after you left an outfit, the kind of thing you avoided hearing if you could. Maybe he was killed or maybe he changed his mind, but I doubt it. When I remembered Orrin, all I could think of was that there was going to be a shooting in Tennessee.

Once on a two-day pass to Danang, Mayhew had gone off limits and into the black market looking for grass and an air mattress. He never found the grass, and he had been scared to death when he finally bought the mattress. He told me that nothing that had ever happened at Khe Sanh had scared him the way he had been scared that day. I don't know what he had been told the MP's would do to him if they caught him in the market, but as he told the story it had been the best adventure he'd had since the day two years back when the game warden had used a helicopter to chase him and a friend out of the woods after deer season had closed. We were sitting in the mingy damp of the eight-man bunker where Mayhew and Day Tripper both slept. Mayhew had been trying to make me use his mattress for the night and I'd refused it. He said that if I didn't sleep on it he was just going to take it and throw it outside into the trench and leave it there until morning. I told him that if I'd wanted an air mattress I could have picked one up anytime in Danang, and that the MP's wouldn't have even bothered me about it. I said I liked sleeping on the ground; it was good training. He said that that was all horsecrap (he was right), and he swore to God, the mattress would just lie out there all night with the rest of the rubbish that collects on trench floors. Then he got very mysterious and told me to think about it while he was gone. Day Tripper tried to find out where he was going, but Mayhew wouldn't tell him.

During those brief moments when the ground all around you was not rumbling, when there were no airstrikes on the hills, no incoming or outgoing or firing from the perimeter, you could sit inside and listen to the rats running across the bunker floor. A lot of them had been poisoned, shot, caught in traps or killed by the lucky toss of a combat boot, and they were here in the bunker too. There was the smell of urine, of old, old sweat, C-ration decay, moldy canvas and private crud, and that mixing up of other smells that were special to combat zones. A lot of us believed that exhaustion and fear could be smelled and that certain dreams gave off an odor. (We were regular Hemingway gypsies about some things. No matter how much wind a chopper would put out as it landed, you could always tell when there were body bags around an lz, and the tents where the Lurps lived smelled unlike any other tents anywhere in Vietnam.) This bunker was at least as bad as any I'd ever been in, and I gagged in there once, the first time. Because there was almost no light, you had to imagine most of what you smelled, and that became something like a pastime. I hadn't realized how black Day Tripper was until we walked inside the bunker.

"It *def*initely stinks somethin' fierce in here," he said. "I gotta be gettin' me a mo'—uh—ef*fec*tive deodorant."

He paused.

"Any kinda shit come up tonight, you jus' keep with me.

You be lucky Mayhew don' think you a Zip an' blast your fuckin' head off. He'll go pretty crazy sometimes."

"You think we'll be hit?"

He shrugged. "He might try an' do a probe. He did that number 'gainst us three nights ago an' kill one boy. Kill a Brother.

"But this here's a real good bunker. We took some shit right on top here. All kindsa dirt come down on top our heads, but we'se all right."

"Are guys sleeping in their flak jackets?"

"Some do. I don'. Mayhew, crazy fucker, he sleep bare-ass. He so tough, man, li'l fucker, the hawk is out, an' he's in here bare-ass."

"What's that? About the hawk?"

"That means it's a co-o-old Mother Fucker."

Mayhew had been gone for more than an hour now, and when Day Tripper and I stepped out on the ammo-crate planking that made the trench floor we saw him outside talking to some grunts. He started walking toward us, laughing, looking like a little boy dressed in a man's combat gear, swimming in his flak jacket, and the grunts sang after him, "Mayhew's a lifer. . . . 'Ray for him."

"Hey, Day Tripper!" he called. "Hey, you hear it, mother-fucker?"

"I hear *what*?"

"I just went over and extended."

The smile vanished on Day Tripper's face. He looked like he didn't understand for a second, and then he looked angry, almost dangerous.

"Say again?"

"Yeah," Mayhew said. "I just saw the Old Man about it."

"Uh-huh. How long you extend for?"

"Just four months."

"Jus' four months. Tha's real fine, Jim."

"Hey, man . . ."

"Don' talk to me, Jim."

"Oh come on, Day Tripper, don't be a hard-on. It gets me outta the Corps three months early."

"Whatever. Jim."

"Oh man, don't call me that." He looked at me. "Every

time he gets pissed off he calls me that. Listen, motherfucker, I get outta the *Marine Corps* early. And I get a home leave. The Old Man says I can go next month."

"You *can't* be talkin' to *me*. I jus' don' hear nonna that. I don' hear one word you sayin', Jim."

"Aw . . ."

"You jus' another dumb grunt. What I gotta talk to you for? It's like you never hear one word I say to you, ever. Not one word. An' I *know* . . . oh man, I jus' *know* you already sign that paper."

Mayhew didn't say anything. It was hard to believe that the two were around the same age.

"What I gonna do with you, poor fucker? Why . . . why you jus' don' go runnin' out over th' wire there? Let 'em gun you down an' get it over with. Here, man, here's a grenade. Why you jus' don' go up backa the shithouse an' pull the pin an' lie down on it?"

"You're fuckin' unbe*liev*able. Man, it's just four months!"

"Four months? Baby, four *seconds* in this whorehouse'll get you greased. An' after your poppa an' all that. An' you jus' ain' *learned*. You're the sorriest, *sorriest* grunt mother I ever seen. No, man, but the *sorriest*! Fuckin' Mayhew, man. I feel sorry for you."

"Day Tripper? Hey, it'll be okay. Y'know?"

"Sure, baby. Jus' don' talk to me right away. Clean your rifle. Write your momma. Do *somethin'*. Talk to me later."

"We can smoke some bullshit."

"Okay, baby. Say later." He walked back into the bunker and lay down. Mayhew took off his helmet and scratched out something written on the side. It had read *20 April and* OUTTA SIGHT!

Sometimes you'd step from the bunker, all sense of time passing having left you, and find it dark out. The far side of the hills around the bowl of the base was glimmering, but you could never see the source of the light, and it had the look of a city at night approached from a great distance. Flares were dropping everywhere around the fringes of the perimeter, laying a dead white light on the high ground rising from the piedmont. There would be dozens of them at once sometimes, trailing an intense smoke, dropping white-hot sparks, and it seemed as though anything caught in their range would be made still, like figures in a game of living statues. There would be the muted rush of illumination rounds, fired from 60-mm. mortars inside the wire, dropping magnesium-brilliant above the NVA trenches for a few seconds, outlining the gaunt, flat spread of the mahogany trees, giving the landscape a ghastly clarity and dying out. You could watch mortar bursts, orange and gray-smoking, over the tops of trees three and four kilometers away, and the heavier shelling from support bases farther east along the DMZ, from Camp Carrol and the Rockpile, directed against suspected troop movements or NVA rocket and mortar positions. Once in a while—I guess I saw it happen three or four times in all—there would be a secondary explosion, a direct hit on a supply of NVA ammunition. And at night it was beautiful. Even the incoming was beautiful at night, beautiful and deeply dreadful.

I remembered the way a Phantom pilot had talked about how beautiful the surface-to-air missiles looked as they drifted up toward his plane to kill him, and remembered myself how lovely .50-caliber tracers could be, coming at you as you flew at night in a helicopter, how slow and graceful, arching up easily, a dream, so remote from anything that could harm you. It could make you feel a total serenity, an elevation that put you above death, but that never lasted very long. One hit anywhere in the chopper would bring you back, bitten lips, white knuckles and all, and then you knew where you were. It was different with the incoming at Khe Sanh. You didn't get to watch the shells very often. You knew if you heard one, the first one, that you were safe, or at least saved. If you were still standing up and looking after that, you deserved anything that happened to you.

Nights were when the air and artillery strikes were heaviest, because that was when we knew that the NVA was above ground and moving. At night you could lie out on some sandbags and watch the C-47's mounted with Vulcans doing their work. The C-47 was a standard prop flareship, but many of them carried 20- and 7.62-mm. guns on their doors, Mike-Mikes that could fire out 300 rounds per second, Gatling style, "a round in every square inch of a football field in less than a minute," as the handouts said. They used to call it Puff the Magic Dragon, but the Marines knew better: they named it Spooky. Every fifth round fired was a tracer, and when Spooky was working, everything stopped while that solid stream of violent red poured down out of the black sky. If you watched from a great distance, the stream would seem to dry up between bursts, vanishing slowly from air to ground like a comet tail, the sound of the guns disappearing too, a few seconds later. If you watched at a close range, you couldn't believe that anyone would have the courage to deal with that night after night, week after week, and you cultivated a respect for the Viet Cong and NVA who had crouched under it every night now for months. It was awesome, worse than anything the Lord had ever put down on Egypt, and at night, you'd hear the Marines talking, watching it, yelling, "Get some!" until they grew quiet and someone would say, "Spooky understands." The nights were very beautiful. Night was when you really had the least to fear and feared the most. You could go through some very bad numbers at night.

Because, really, what a choice there was; what a prodigy of things to be afraid of! The moment that you understood this, really understood it, you lost your anxiety instantly. Anxiety was a luxury, a joke you had no room for once you knew the variety of deaths and mutilations the war offered. Some feared head wounds, some dreaded chest wounds or stomach wounds, everyone feared the wound of wounds, the Wound. Guys would pray and pray—Just you and me, God. Right?—offer anything, if only they could be spared that: Take my legs, take my hands, take my eyes, take my fucking *life*, You Bastard, but please, please, please, don't take *those*. Whenever a shell landed in a group, everyone forgot about the next rounds and skipped back to rip their pants away, to check, laughing hysterically with relief even though their legs might be shattered, their kneecaps torn away, kept upright by their relief and shock, gratitude and adrenaline.

There were choices everywhere, but they were never choices that you could hope to make. There was even some small chance for personal style in your recognition of the one thing you feared more than any other. You could die in a sudden bloodburning crunch as your chopper hit the ground like dead weight, you could fly apart so that your pieces would never be gathered, you could take one neat round in the lung and go out hearing only the bubble of the last few breaths, you could die in the last stage of malaria with that faint tapping in your ears, and that could happen to you after months of firefights and rockets and machine guns. Enough, too many, were saved for that, and you always hoped that no irony would attend your passing. You could end in a pit somewhere with a spike through you, everything stopped forever except for the one or two motions, purely involuntary, as though you could kick it all away and come back. You could fall down dead so that the medics would have to spend half an hour looking for the hole that killed you, getting more and more spooked as the search went on. You could be shot, mined, grenaded, rocketed, mortared, sniped at, blown up and away so that your leavings had to be dropped into a sagging poncho and carried to Graves Registration, that's all she wrote. It was almost marvelous.

And at night, all of it seemed more possible. At night in Khe Sanh, waiting there, thinking about all of them (40,000, some said), thinking that they might really try it, could keep you up. If they did, when they did, it might not matter that you were in the best bunker in the DMZ, wouldn't matter that you were young and had plans, that you were loved, that you were a noncombatant, an observer. Because if it came, it would be in a bloodswarm of killing, and credentials would not be examined. (The only Vietnamese many of us knew was the words "Bao Chi! Bao Chi!"—Journalist! Journalist! or even "Bao Chi Fap!"—French journalist!, which was the same as crying, Don't shoot! Don't shoot!) You came to love your life, to love and respect the mere fact of it, but often you became heedless of it in the way that somnambulists are heedless. Being "good" meant staying alive, and sometimes that was only a matter of caring enough at any given moment. No wonder everyone became a luck freak, no wonder you could wake at four in the morning some mornings and *know* that tomorrow it would finally happen, you could stop worrying about it now and just lie there, sweating in the dampest chill you ever felt.

But once it was actually going on, things were different.

You were just like everyone else, you could no more blink than spit. It came back the same way every time, dreaded and welcome, balls and bowels turning over together, your senses working like strobes, free-falling all the way down to the essences and then flying out again in a rush to focus, like the first strong twinge of tripping after an infusion of psilocybin, reaching in at the point of calm and springing all the joy and all the dread ever known, *ever* known by *everyone* who *ever* lived, unutterable in its speeding brilliance, touching all the edges and then passing, as though it had all been controlled from outside, by a god or by the moon. And every time, you were so weary afterward, so empty of everything but being alive that you couldn't recall any of it, except to know that it was like something else you had felt once before. It remained obscure for a long time, but after enough times the memory took shape and substance and finally revealed itself one afternoon during the breaking off of a firefight. It was the feeling you'd had when you were much, much younger and undressing a girl for the first time.

The Coleman lantern had been down to its minimum light for an hour, and now it was off for good. A lieutenant came in and flashed a sharp light around quickly, looking for someone who was supposed to be up on the wire. Then the canvas flap dropped shut, closing out the flarelight from the middle ground between their trenches and ours, and there were only cigarette ends and the light from Mayhew's radio.

"Let's talk about tracers," the announcer was saying. "Sure, they're fun to shoot. They light up the sky! But did you know that tracers leave *deposits* on your barrel? Deposits that often lead to mal*functions* and even *jamming* . . ."

"Hey Mayhew, turn that fuckin' thing off."

"Right after Sports," Mayhew said. He was naked now, sitting up in his bed and hunched over the radio as though the light and the voice were a miracle for him. He was cleaning his face with some Wash 'n Dri's.

"It's been proven!" someone said. "You take and put a Chevvy in a Ford and a Ford in a Chevvy and they *both* go faster. It's been proven!"

We were all ready for sleep. Mayhew was the only one with

his boots off. Two Marines that I hadn't even met before nightfall had gone out on the scrounge and come back with a new stretcher for me to sleep on, giving it to me without looking at me, as if to say, Shit, it ain't anything, we *like* walking around above ground. They were always doing things like that for you, the way Mayhew had tried to give me his mattress, the way grunts in Hue one day had tried to give me their helmets and flak jackets because I had turned up without my own. If you tore your fatigues on the wire or trying to crawl for cover, you'd have new or at least fresh ones within minutes and never know where they came from. They always took care of you.

". . . so next time," the announcer said, "*think* about it. It *might* just save your life." Another voice came on: "All right, then, moving right along here with our fabulous Sounds of the Sixties, AFVN, Armed Forces Radio Network, Vietnam, and for all you guys in the First of the Forty-fourth, and especially for the Soul Brother in the Orderly Room, here's Otis Redding—the *immortal* Otis Redding, singing 'Dock of the Bay.' "

"All right, my man," Day Tripper said.

"Listen," one of the Marines said. "When you think of all the guys in this fucked-up war, them casualties don't mean nothing. *Nothing!* Shit, your chances are better here than on the L.A. Freeway."

"Cold comfort," I muttered to myself.

Mayhew jumped up. "Hey, man, you cold? Whyn't you say so before? Here, my old lady sent me this. I ain't hardly used it." I didn't have a chance to say a word, he threw over a silvery square that fell against my hands like a sheet of India paper. It was a space blanket.

"Your ol' lady!" Day Tripper said.

"Yeah, my mother."

"Mayhew's momma," Day Tripper said. "What else your momma send you, Hand Job?"

"Well, she sent me them Christmas cookies that you scarfed up before I hardly got the fuckin' paper off."

Day Tripper laughed and lit another cigarette.

"Man," Mayhew said, "I'm so horny . . ." We waited for the rest of it, but there wasn't any.

"Hey, Mayhew," someone called, "you ever been laid? Your first don't count."

"Oh, yeah," Day Tripper said. "Mayhew got himself a little number down at China Beach, little chickie workin' the scivvie houses there, she jus' *love* Mayhew. Don't she?"

"That's a Rog," Mayhew said. He was grinning like an old illustration of Puck. "She loves it."

"Bullshit," Orrin said. "Ain't a Slope bitch in this whole fucked-up country that loves it."

"Okay, Jim," Mayhew said, and Day Tripper started to giggle.

The radio delivered a dramatized warning against losing pay vouchers and currency-exchange slips, and then the disc jockey came on again. "This one's a request for Hard-Core Paul and the Fire Team, and for our groovy CO, Fred the Head. . . ."

"Hey, Mayhew, turn that up. Turn it on up."

"Hey, cocksuck, you just tol' me to turn it off."

"Come on, man, that's an outtasight song."

Mayhew turned it up. It still wasn't very loud, but it filled the bunker. It was a song that had been on the radio a lot that winter.

> There's something happening here,
> What it is ain't exactly clear.
> There's a man with a gun over there,
> Tellin' me I've got to beware.
> I think it's time we stopped, children,
> What's that sound?
> Everybody look what's goin' down. . . .

"Know what I heard over at the captain's hootch?" Mayhew said. "Some kid tol' me the Cav's comin' in here."

"Right," someone said. "They're coming tomorrow."

"What *time* tomorrow?"

"All right," Mayhew said. "Don't believe me. This kid was a clerk. He's over to the TOC yesterday and he heard 'em talking."

"What's the Cav gonna do here? Make this a fuckin' parking lot for helicopters?"

The Marines did not like the Cav, the 1st Cavalry Division

(Airmobile), they liked them even less than they liked the rest of the Army, and at the same time members of the Cav were beginning to feel as though their sole mission in Vietnam was to bail out Marines in trouble. They had come to help the Marines a dozen times in the past six months, and the last time, during the battle of Hue, they had taken almost as many casualties as the Marines had. There had been rumors about a relief operation for Khe Sanh since February, and by now they were being taken about as seriously as the rumors of attack which would attach themselves to particular dates thought to be significant to the North Vietnamese. (March 13, the anniversary of the initial Dien Bien Phu attacks, was the only one of those dates which anyone believed in. No one wanted to be anywhere near Khe Sanh on that day, and, as far as I know, the only correspondent who stayed through it was John Wheeler of the Associated Press.) If the rumors involved attack, everyone chose to ignore them. If they involved relief, no matter how farfetched they seemed, the Marines would embrace them privately while laughing them away publicly.

"Man, ain' no Cav goin' anywhere *near* this motherfucker."

"Okay, I don' give a shit," Mayhew said. "I'm just tellin' you what this kid tol' me."

"Thanks, Mayhew. Now shut the fuck up and let's get some fuckin' sleep."

That's what we did. Sometimes, sleeping at Khe Sanh was like sleeping after a few pipes of opium, a floating and a drifting in which your mind still worked, so that you could ask yourself whether you were sleeping even while you slept, acknowledging every noise above ground, every explosion and every running tremor in the earth, cataloging the specifics of each without ever waking. Marines would sleep with their eyes open, with their knees raised and rigid, often standing up on the doze as though touched by a spell. You took no pleasure from sleep there, no real rest. It was a commodity, it kept you from falling apart, the way cold, fat-caked C rations kept you from starving. That night, probably sleeping, I heard the sound of automatic-weapons fire outside. I had no real sense of waking, only of suddenly seeing three cigarettes glowing in the dark without any memory of their having been lighted.

"Probe," Mayhew said. He was leaning over me, completely dressed again, his face almost touching mine, and for a second I had the idea that he might have run over to cover me from any possible incoming. (It would not have been the first time that a grunt had done that.) Everyone was awake, all of our poncho liners were thrown back, I reached for my glasses and helmet and realized that I'd already put them on. Day Tripper was looking at us. Mayhew was grinning.

"Listen to that fucker, listen to that, that fucker's gonna burn out the barrel for sure."

It was an M-60 machine gun and it was not firing in bursts, but in a mad, sustained manner. The gunner must have seen something; maybe he was firing cover for a Marine patrol trying to get back in through the wire, maybe it was a three- or four-man probe that had been caught in the flarelight, something standing or moving, an infiltrator or a rat, but it sounded like the gunner was holding off a division. I couldn't tell whether there was answering fire or not, and then, abruptly, the firing stopped.

"Let's go see," Mayhew said, grabbing his rifle.

"Don' you go messin' with that out there," Day Tripper said. "They need us, they be sendin' for us. Fuckin' Mayhew."

"Man, it's all over. Listen. Come on," he said to me. "See if we can get you a story."

"Give me a second." I put on my flak jacket and we left the bunker, Day Tripper shaking his head at us, saying, "Fuckin' Mayhew. . . ."

Before, the fire had sounded as though it were coming from directly above the bunker, but the Marines on watch there said that it had been from a position forty meters farther down the trenchline. We walked that way in the dark, figures appearing and disappearing in the mist around us, odd, floating presences; it seemed like a long walk and then Mayhew bumped helmets with someone.

"You wanna watch where the fuck you're goin'," he said.

"That's 'You want to watch where the fuck you're going, *Sir.*'" It was a lieutenant, and he was laughing.

"Sorry, Sir."

"Mayhew?"

"Yes, Sir."

"What the fuck are you doing over here?"

"We heard some shit."

"Who's that man? Where's his rifle?"

"He's a reporter, Sir."

"Oh . . . Hello."

"Hello," I said.

"Well," the lieutenant said, "you missed the good part. You should have been here five minutes ago. We caught three of them out there by the first wire."

"What were they trying to do?" I asked.

"Don't know. Maybe cut the wires. Maybe lay in a mine, steal some of our Claymores, throw grenades, harass us some, don't know. Won't know, now."

We heard then what sounded at first like a little girl crying, a subdued, delicate wailing, and as we listened it became louder and more intense, taking on pain as it grew until it was a full, piercing shriek. The three of us turned to each other, we could almost feel each other shivering. It was terrible, absorbing every other sound coming from the darkness. Whoever it was, he was past caring about anything except the thing he was screaming about. There was a dull pop in the air above us, and an illumination round fell drowsily over the wire.

"Slope," Mayhew said. "See him there, see there, on the wire there?"

I couldn't see anything out there, there was no movement, and the screaming had stopped. As the flare dimmed, the sobbing started up and built quickly until it was a scream again.

A Marine brushed past us. He had a mustache and a piece of camouflaged parachute silk fastened bandana-style around his throat, and on his hip he wore a holster which held an M-79 grenade-launcher. For a second I thought I'd hallucinated him. I hadn't heard him approaching, and I tried now to see where he might have come from, but I couldn't. The M-79 had been cut down and fitted with a special stock. It was obviously a well-loved object; you could see the kind of work that had gone into it by the amount of light caught from the flares that glistened on the stock. The Marine looked serious, dead-eyed serious, and his right hand hung above the holster, waiting. The screaming had stopped again.

"Wait," he said. "I'll fix that fucker."

His hand was resting now on the handle of the weapon. The sobbing began again, and the screaming; we had the pattern now, the North Vietnamese was screaming the same thing over and over, and we didn't need a translator to tell us what it was.

"Put that fucker away," the Marine said, as though to himself. He drew the weapon, opened the breach and dropped in a round that looked like a great swollen bullet, listening very carefully all the while to the shrieking. He placed the M-79 over his left forearm and aimed for a second before firing. There was an enormous flash on the wire 200 meters away, a spray of orange sparks, and then everything was still except for the roll of some bombs exploding kilometers away and the sound of the M-79 being opened, closed again and returned to the holster. Nothing changed on the Marine's face, nothing, and he moved back into the darkness.

"Get some," Mayhew said quietly. "Man, did you *see* that?"

And I said, Yes (lying), it was something, really something.

The lieutenant said he hoped that I was getting some real good stories here. He told me to take her easy and disappeared. Mayhew looked out at the wire again, but the silence of the ground in front of us was really talking to him now. His fingers were limp, touching his face, and he looked like a kid at a scary movie. I poked his arm and we went back to the bunker for some more of that sleep.

v

On the higher levels of Command, the Khe Sanh situation was being regarded with great optimism, the kind that had seen us through Tet, smiling in the shambles. This often led to misunderstandings between the press and ranking Marine officers, particularly when it caused heavy casualties to be announced as light, routs and ambushes to be described as temporary tactical ploys, and filthy weather to be characterized as good and even excellent. It is hard to be there in the coastal warmth of Danang and be told by some Marine PIO that the

DMZ, from which you have just that day returned, is enjoying the same warmth, especially when a hot shower and a change of clothes have failed to remove the damp chill of three days from your buttocks. You don't have to be a seasoned tactician to realize that your ass is cold.

Interviews with the commander of the 26th Marine Regiment, Colonel David Lownds, seemed to reveal a man who was utterly insensible to the gravity of his position, but Lownds was a deceptively complicated man with a gift (as one of his staff officers put it) for "jerking off the press." He could appear as a meek, low-keyed, distracted and even stupid man (some reporters referred to him privately as "The Lion of Khe Sanh"), as though he had been carefully picked for just these qualities by a cynical Command as a front for its decisions. When confronted with the possible odds against a successful defense of Khe Sanh, he would say things like "I do not plan on reinforcements" or "I'm not worried. I've got Marines." He was a small man with vague, watery eyes, slightly reminiscent of a rodent in a fable, with one striking feature: a full, scrupulously attended regimental mustache.

His professed ignorance of Dien Bien Phu drove correspondents crazy, but it was a dodge. Lownds knew very well about Dien Bien Phu and what had happened there, knew more about it than most of the interviewers. When I first met him, I brought a two-week-old message to Khe Sanh from his son-in-law, a Marine captain whom I'd met in Hue. He had been badly wounded in the fighting along the canals southwest of the Citadel, and the message amounted to little more than personal regards. Being a colonel commanding a regiment, Lownds of course had all the current information on the captain's condition, but he seemed glad for the chance to talk to someone who'd been there, who had seen him. He was proud of his son-in-law and very touched by the remembrance. He was also growing tired of reporters and of the criticism which most of the questions addressed to him implied, and I couldn't help but feel a sympathy for him. There were policies and attitudes at Khe Sanh that were getting grunts killed, but I doubted that they were the colonel's. He was really sort of a grunt himself, he had been there for a long time now, and it was beginning to tell on his face. The stories published about him never bothered to mention his personal courage or the extreme and special caution with which he risked the lives of his men.

No, to find the really mindless optimism, the kind that rejected facts and killed grunts wholesale and drove you into mad, helpless rages, you had to travel outward from Khe Sanh. The morale of the men at Khe Sanh was good (they were surviving, most of them; they were hacking it), but that didn't give any general the right to claim that they were anxious for a fight, eager for the attack to come. During a five-day trip across the DMZ at the end of February and the beginning of March, that seemed to be the only kind of talk that any of them was capable of. "Excellent," "real fine," "outstanding," "first rate": talk like that poured over you until it was all you could do to keep from seizing one graying crew-cut head or another and jamming it deep into the nearest tactical map.

On that trip I traveled with Karsten Prager of *Time*. Prager was in his early thirties and had been covering the war on and off for over three years. He was a German who had come to the States to attend college, and had lost all traces of his original accent. What replaced it was a gruff, clipped, Brooklyn-docks way of speaking. I once asked him how it was that he had been speaking English for such a short time and yet lost his German accent. "Well," he said, "I got dis tuhriffic eah fuh langwidjis." He had tough, shrewd eyes that matched his voice and a disdain for Command bravado that could be unsettling in an interview.

We flew the DMZ together from Quang Tri to Camp Carrol and the Rockpile, hitting each of the firebases that had been set up or converted to firing missions supporting Khe Sanh. We flew in beat-up Marine choppers, clumsy H-34's (Screw metal fatigue, we decided; the 34 had a lot of heart), over the cold, shattered, mist-bound hills, the same hills that had received over 120,000,000 pounds of explosives from B-52 raids in the previous three weeks, terrain like moonscapes, cratered and pitted and full of skilled North Vietnamese gunners. From past experience and the estimates of our meteorologists, the monsoons should be ending now, blowing south, clearing the DMZ skies and leaving the hills warm, but it wasn't happening, the monsoon held ("The weather?" some

colonel would say. "The weather is increasingly advanta-
geous!"), we were freezing, you could barely piss on those
hilltop firebases, and the ceilings were uniformly low before
noon and after three. On the last part of the trip, flying into
Dong Ha, the aluminum rod that held the seats broke, spilling
us to the floor and making the exact sound that a .50-caliber
round will make when it strikes a chopper, giving us all a bad
scare and then a good, good laugh. A couple of times the
pilots thought they saw something moving on the hilltops and
we went down, circling five or six times while we all groaned
and giggled from fear and the cold. The crew chief was a
young Marine who moved around the chopper without a
safety line hooked to his flight suit, so comfortable with the
rolling and shaking of the ship that you couldn't even pause
to admire his daredevil nerve; you cut straight through to his
easy grace and control, marveling as he hunkered down by
the open door to rig the broken seat up again with pliers and
a length of wire. At 1,500 feet he stood there in the gale-
sucking door (Did he ever think about stepping off? How
often?), his hands resting naturally on his hips, as though he
were just standing around on a street corner somewhere, waiting. He knew he was good, an artist, he knew we were digging
it, but it wasn't for us at all; it was his, private; he was the
man who was never going to fall out of any damn helicopter.

At Dong Ha, after days without a bath or a shave or a
change of fatigues, we went to the headquarters of the 3rd
Marine Division, where Prager requested an immediate interview with General Tompkins, the commander. The general's
aide was a brisk dude of a first lieutenant, scrubbed and shaved
and polished to a dull glow, and he stared at us in disbelief.
That initial distaste was mutual, and I didn't think we'd ever
get beyond it, but a moment later he led us reluctantly into
the general's office.

General Tompkins was seated behind his desk dressed in an
OD sweatshirt, and he gave us a smile that made us feel
slightly lunatic, standing there in our stubble and dirt and
wrecked fatigues. When the lieutenant left the room, it was
as though a great door had been slammed against the chill,
and the general asked us to be seated. In spite of his hard
good health and his taut, weathered face, he reminded me of

Everett Dirksen. It was something sly and amused in his smile, a lurking wit behind the eyes, a soft gravel in his voice, each sentence rounding out in a grand deliberateness. Behind him several flags hung in their standards, and across the length of one entire wall there was a remarkable relief map of the DMZ, with several small sectors covered over, obscured from the eyes of unauthorized personnel.

We sat down, the general offered us cigarettes (by the pack) and Prager began the questioning. It was all stuff I'd heard before, a synthesis of everything Prager had gotten together during the past four days. I'd never seen any point in asking generals heavy questions about anything; they were officials too, and the answers were almost always what you expected them to be. I half listened, tuning in and out, and Prager began a long, involved question dealing with weather variants, air capability, elevation and range of our big guns, his big guns, problems of supply and reinforcement and (apologetically) disengagement and evacuation. The general touched his fingertips together as the question developed, smiled and nodded as it went into its third minute, he looked impressed by Prager's grasp of the situation and, finally, when the question ended, he placed his hands on the desk. He was still smiling.

"What?" he said.

Prager and I looked at each other quickly.

"You'll have to excuse me, boys. I'm a little hard of hearing. I don't always catch it all."

So Prager did it again, speaking unnaturally loud, and my mind went back to the map, into it really, so that the sound of outgoing artillery beyond the general's windows and the smell of burning shit and wet canvas brought in on the cold air put my head back at Khe Sanh for a moment.

I thought about the grunts who had sat in a circle one night with a guitar, singing "Where Have All the Flowers Gone?" Jack Laurence of CBS News had asked them if they knew what that song meant to so many people, and they said, Yes, yes, they knew. I thought about the graffiti that John Wheeler had discovered on a latrine wall there, "I think I'm falling in love with Jake," and about the grunts who had gone running up the trenchline to find a stretcher for me to sleep on, about Mayhew's space blanket, about the kid who had mailed a gook ear home to his girl and could not understand now why she had stopped writing to him. I thought of the thirteen Marine maneuver battalions deployed across the Z and of the brutality and sweetness they contained, all the ways they had of saying their thanks, even though they knew you were crazy for being there. I thought about the Marines at Khe Sanh on this night; it would be about the forty-fifth night of the shelling, the Flood had not lasted this long. Prager was still talking, the general was still nodding and touching his fingertips together and the question was almost finished. "General," Prager said, "what I want to know is, *what if* he decides to attack at Khe Sanh and, at the same time, he attacks at every single base the Marines have set up to support Khe Sanh, all across the DMZ?"

And I thought, Please, General, say "God forbid!" Let your hands fly up, let involuntary shudders rack your spare, tough frame. Remember Langvei. Remember Mayhew.

The general smiled, the crack trapper anticipating something good, past all doubting. "*That* . . . is *exactly* . . . what we . . . *want* him to do," he said.

We thanked him for his time and cigarettes and went out to look for a place to sleep that night.

On the afternoon of the day that we returned to Danang an important press conference was held at the Marine-operated, Marine-controlled press center, a small compound on the river where most correspondents based themselves whenever they covered I Corps. A brigadier general from III MAF, Marine Headquarters, was coming over to brief us on developments in the DMZ and Khe Sanh. The colonel in charge of "press operations" was visibly nervous, the dining room was being cleared for the meeting, microphones set up, chairs arranged, printed material put in order. These official briefings usually did the same thing to your perception of the war that flares did to your night vision, but this one was supposed to be special, and correspondents had come in from all over I Corps to be there. Among us was Peter Braestrup of the *Washington Post*, formerly of *The New York Times*. He had been covering the war for nearly three years. He had been a captain in the Marines in Korea; ex-Marines are like ex-Catholics or off-duty

Feds, and Braestrup still made the Marines a special concern of his. He had grown increasingly bitter about the Marines' failure to dig in at Khe Sanh, about their shocking lack of defenses against artillery. He sat quietly as the colonel introduced the general and the briefing began.

The weather was excellent: "The sun is up over Khe Sanh by ten every morning." (A collective groan running through the seated journalists.) "I'm glad to be able to tell you that Route Nine is now open and completely accessible." (Would you drive Route 9 into Khe Sanh, General? You bet you wouldn't.)

"What about the Marines at Khe Sanh?" someone asked.

"I'm glad we've come to that," the general said. "I was at Khe Sanh for several hours this morning, and I want to tell you that those Marines there are *clean*!"

There was a weird silence. We all knew we'd heard him, the man had said that the Marines at Khe Sanh were clean ("Clean? He said 'clean,' didn't he?"), but not one of us could imagine what he'd meant.

"Yes, they're bathing or getting a good wash every other day. They're shaving every day, every single day. Their mood is good, their spirits are fine, morale is excellent and there's a twinkle in their eye!"

Braestrup stood up.

"General."

"Peter?"

"General, what about the defenses at Khe Sanh? Now, you built this wonderful, air-conditioned officers' club, and that's a complete shambles. You built a beer hall there, and *that's* been blown away." He had begun calmly, but now he was having trouble keeping the anger out of his voice. "You've got a medical detachment there that's a disgrace, set up right on the airstrip, exposed to hundreds of rounds every day, and *no* overhead cover. You've had men at the base since July, you've expected an attack at least since November, they've been shelling you heavily since January. General, why haven't those Marines *dug in*?"

The room was quiet. Braestrup had a fierce smile on his face as he sat down. When the question had begun, the colonel had jerked suddenly to one side of his chair, as though he'd been shot. Now, he was trying to get his face in front of the general's so that he could give out the look that would say, "See, General? See the kind of peckerheads I have to work with every day?" Braestrup was looking directly at the general now, waiting for his answer—the question had not been rhetorical—and it was not long in coming.

"Peter," the general said, "I think you're hitting a small nail with an awfully big hammer."

VI

The door gunner was leaning out, looking down, and he started to laugh. He wrote out a note and handed it to me. It read, "We sure brang some pee down to bear on them hills."

The monsoons were breaking, a hard heat was coming back to I Corps and the ordeal at Khe Sanh was almost over. Flying across the westernmost stretches of the DMZ, you could read the history of that terrible winter just by looking at the hills.

For most of the time that the North Vietnamese had controlled Route 9 and kept the Marines isolated at Khe Sanh, all that anyone could see of the hills had been what little the transient mists allowed, a desolated terrain, cold, hostile, all colors deadened by the rainless monsoon or secreted in the fog. Now they were full and voluptuous in the new spring light.

Often you'd hear Marines talking about how beautiful those hills must have been, but that spring they were not beautiful. Once they had been the royal hunting grounds of the Annamese emperors. Tigers, deer and flying squirrels had lived in them. I used to imagine what a royal hunt must have been like, but I could only see it as an Oriental children's story: a conjuring of the emperor and empress, princes and princelings, court favorites and emissaries, all caparisoned for the hunt; slender figures across a tapestry, a promise of bloodless kills, a serene frolic complete with horseback flirtations and death-smiling game. And even now you could hear Marines comparing these hills with the hills around their homes, talking about what a pleasure it would be to hunt in them for anything other than men.

But mostly, I think, the Marines hated those hills; not from time to time, the way many of us hated them, but constantly, like a curse. Better to fight the war in the jungles or along the dry flats that lined the Cua Viet River than in those hills. I heard a grunt call them "angry" once, probably something he'd picked up from a movie or a television series, but from his point of view he was right, the word was a good one. So when we decimated them, broke them, burned parts of them so that nothing would ever live on them again, it must have given a lot of Marines a good feeling, an intimation of power. They had humped those hills until their legs were in an agony, they'd been ambushed in them and blown apart on their trails, trapped on their barren ridges, lain under fire clutching the foliage that grew on them, wept alone in fear and exhaustion and shame just knowing the kind of terror that night always brought to them, and now, in April, something like revenge had been achieved.

We never announced a scorched-earth policy; we never announced any policy at all, apart from finding and destroying the enemy, and we proceeded in the most obvious way. We used what was at hand, dropping the greatest volume of explosives in the history of warfare over all the terrain within the thirty-mile sector which fanned out from Khe Sanh. Employing saturation-bombing techniques, we delivered more than 110,000 tons of bombs to those hills during the eleven-week containment of Khe Sanh. The smaller foothills were often quite literally turned inside out, the steeper of them were made faceless and drawless, and the bigger hills were left with scars and craters of such proportions that an observer from some remote culture might see in them the obsessiveness and ritual regularity of religious symbols, the blackness at the deep center pouring out rays of bright, overturned earth all the way to the circumference; forms like Aztec sun figures, suggesting that their makers had been men who held Nature in an awesome reverence.

Once on a Chinook run from Cam Lo to Dong Ha, I sat next to a Marine who took a Bible from his pack and began reading even before we took off. He had a small cross sketched in ballpoint on his flak jacket and another, even less obtrusive, on his helmet cover. He was an odd-looking guy for a combat Marine in Vietnam. For one thing, he was never going to tan, no matter how many months he spent in the sun. He would just go red and blotchy, even though his hair was dark. He was also very heavy, maybe twenty pounds over-weight, although you could see from his boots and fatigues that he'd humped it a lot over here. He wasn't a chaplain's assistant or anything, just a grunt who happened to be fat, pale and religious. (You didn't meet that many who were deeply religious, although you expected to, with so many kids from the South and the Midwest, from farms and small rural towns.) We strapped in and he started reading, getting very absorbed, and I leaned out the door and looked at the endless progression of giant pits which were splashed over the ground, at the acre-sized scars where napalm or chemical spray had eaten away the cover. (There was a special Air Force outfit that flew defoliation missions. They were called the Ranch Hands, and their motto was, "Only we can prevent forests.") When I held out some cigarettes to offer him one, he looked up from the Bible and shook his head, getting off that quick, pointless laugh that told me for sure that he'd seen a lot of action. Maybe he had even been at Khe Sanh, or up on 861 with the 9th. I don't think he realized that I wasn't a Marine, I had on a Marine flak jacket which covered the correspon-dent's identification tags sewn on my fatigues, but he saw the offer of a cigarette as a courtesy and he wanted to return it. He passed over the open Bible, almost giggling now, and pointed to a passage. It was Psalms 91:5, and it said,

Thou shalt not be afraid for the terror by night; nor for the arrow that flieth by day.

Nor for the pestilence that walketh in darkness; nor for the destruction that wasteth at noonday.

A thousand shall fall at thy side, and ten thousand at thy right hand; but it shall not come nigh thee.

Okay, I thought, that's good to know. I wrote the word "Beautiful!" out on a piece of paper and handed it back to him, and he jerked his thumb up, meaning that he thought so too. He went back to the book and I went back to the door, but I had a nasty impulse all the way into Dong Ha to run through Psalms and find a passage which I could offer him, the one that talked about those who were defiled with their own works and sent a-whoring with their own inventions.

The relief of Khe Sanh began on April 1. It was code-named Operation Pegasus, and while it included over 10,000 Marines and three full battalions of ARVN, it took its name and its style from the 1st Cavalry Division (Airmobile). A week earlier, 18,000 members of the Cav had left their base at Camp Evans, near Dong Ha, and moved to a point in a river valley eleven miles northeast of Khe Sanh, just beyond the range of the big guns that were dug into the Laotian mountains. The Cav had plenty of helicopters, choppers were what the Cav was all about; and Sky Cranes lifted in earth-moving equipment, Chinooks brought in the heavier artillery pieces, and within days there was a forward operational base that looked better than most permanent installations in I Corps, complete with a thousand-meter airstrip and deep, ventilated bunkers. They named it LZ Stud, and once it was finished Khe Sanh ceased to be the center of its own sector; it became just another objective.

It was almost as though the war had ended. The day before Pegasus began, President Johnson had announced the suspension of airstrikes against the North and put a closing date on his own Administration. The Marines' 11th Engineers had begun moving down Route 9, deactivating mines and repairing bridges, and they had met with no resistance. The shelling of Khe Sanh had become a matter of a few scattered rounds a day, and it had been more than two weeks now since General Westmoreland had revealed that, in his opinion, the attack on Khe Sanh would never come. The 304th NVA Division had left the area, and so had the 325C. Now, it seemed that all but a token force of NVA had vanished. And now, everywhere you went, you could see the most comforting military insignia in all of Vietnam, the yellow-and-black shoulder patch of the Cav. You were with the pro's now, the elite. LZ's and firebases were being established at a rate of three and four a day, and every hour brought them closer to Khe Sanh.

Really, it was almost too good, and by the third day something odd attended Pegasus. As an operation, it revealed the tastes of the Cav's commander, Major General John Tolson, a general of uncommon intelligence and subtlety. Its precision and speed were unbelievable, especially to anyone who had just spent the better part of three months with the Marines. Pegasus was almost elegant in its tactics and scope. Stendhal would have loved it (he would have called it "an affair of outposts"), but it soon came to look more like a spectacle than a military operation, a non-operation devised to non-relieve the non-siege of Khe Sanh. When I told General Tolson that I had no real grasp of what the Cav was doing, he laughed and told me that I was probably brighter about it than I knew. Pegasus was objectiveless, he said. Its purpose was to engage. But engage what?

Perhaps, as we claimed, the B-52's had driven them all away, broken the back of their will to attack. (We claimed 13,000 NVA dead from those raids.) Maybe they'd left the Khe Sanh area as early as January, leaving the Marines pinned down, and moved across I Corps in readiness for the Tet Offensive. Many people believed that a few battalions, clever enough and active enough, could have kept the Marines at Khe Sanh inside the wire and underground for all of those weeks. Maybe they'd come to see reasons why an attack would be impossible, and gone back into Laos. Or A Shau. Or Quang Tri. Or Hue. We didn't know. They were somewhere, but they were not around Khe Sanh anymore.

Incredible arms caches were being found, rockets still crated, launchers still wrapped in factory paper, AK-47's still packed in Cosmoline, all indicating that battalion-strength units had left in a hurry. The Cav and the Marines above Route 9 were finding equipment suggesting that entire companies had fled. Packs were found on the ground in perfect company formations, and while they contained diaries and often poems written by the soldiers, there was almost no information about where they had gone or why. Considering the amount of weapons and supplies being found (a record for the entire war), there were surprisingly few prisoners, although one prisoner did tell his interrogators that 75 percent of his regiment had been killed by our B-52's, nearly 1,500 men, and that the survivors were starving. He had been pulled out of a spider hole near Hill 881 North, and had seemed grateful for his capture. An American officer who was present at the interrogation actually said that the boy was hardly more than seventeen or eighteen, and that it was hideous that the North was feeding such young men into a war of aggression. Still, I don't remember anyone, Marine or Cav, officer or enlisted, who was not moved by the sight of their prisoners, by the sudden awareness of what must have been suffered and endured that winter.

For the first time in eleven weeks, Marines at Khe Sanh left their perimeter, walked two miles to Hill 471, and took it, after what amounted to the one serious battle of those weeks. (LZ's, including Stud, were sporadically rocketed and mortared; the Cav lost some ships to NVA gunners; there were small often sharp firefights almost every day. One or two body bags waited for removal at most landing zones on most afternoons, but it was different, and that was the trouble. After the slaughter of the winter, you were afraid of this unaccustomed mercy, afraid of becoming lax or afraid of having the Joke played on you. It was one thing, if it had to happen, to have it happen in Hue or Khe Sanh, but something else to be one of the few. WHY ME? was a common piece of helmet graffiti.) You'd hear a trooper of the Cav say something like, "I hear the Marines stepped into the shit above Route Nine," but what he really meant was, Of *course* the Marines stepped into the shit, what *else* would they be doing in this war? The Cav's attitude acknowledged that they might die too, but never the way the Marines did. A story circulated around the Pegasus TAOR about a Marine who had been staked to a hillside by the NVA: Marine choppers refused to pick him up, so the Cav went down and got him. Whether it was true or not, it revealed the complexities of the Marine–Cav rivalry, and when the Cav sent an outfit to relieve the Marines on 471, it killed off one of the last surviving romances about war left over from the movies: there was no shouting, no hard kidding, no gleeful obscenities, or the old "Hey, where you from? Brooklyn!? No kiddin'! Me too!" The departing and arriving files passed one another without a single word being spoken.

The death of Martin Luther King intruded on the war in a way that no other outside event had ever done. In the days that followed, there were a number of small, scattered riots, one or two stabbings, all of it denied officially. The Marine recreational facility in China Beach in Danang was put off-limits for a day, and at Stud we stood around the radio and listened to the sound of automatic-weapons fire being broadcast from a number of American cities. A southern colonel on the general's staff told me that it was a shame, a damn shame, but I had to admit (didn't I?) that he'd been a long time asking for it. A black staff sergeant in the Cav who had taken me over to his outfit for dinner the night before cut me dead on the day that we heard the news, but he came over to the press tent later that night and told me that it shouldn't happen that way. I got a bottle of Scotch from my pack and we went outside and sat on the grass, watching the flares dropping over the hillside across the river. There were still some night mists. In the flarelight it looked like heavy snow, and the ravines looked like ski trails.

He was from Alabama and he had all but decided on a career in the Army. Even before King's murder he had seen what this might someday mean, but he'd always hoped to get around it somehow.

"Now what I gonna do?" he said.

"I'm a great one to ask."

"But dig it. Am I gonna take 'n' turn them guns aroun' on my own people? Shit!"

That was it, there was hardly a black NCO anywhere who wasn't having to deal with that. We sat in the dark, and he told me that when he'd walked by me that afternoon it had made him sick. He couldn't help it.

"Shit, I can't do no twenny in this Army. They ain' no way. All's I hope is I can hang back when push comes t' shove. An' then I think, Well, fuck it, why should I? Man, home's jus' gonna be a hassle."

There was some firing on the hill, a dozen M-79 rounds and the dull bap-bap-bap of an AK-47, but that was over there, there was an entire American division between that and us. But the man was crying, trying to look away while I tried not to look.

"It's just a bad night for it," I said. "What can I tell you?"

He stood up, looked at the hill and then started to leave. "Oh, man," he said. "This war gets old."

At Langvei we found the two-month-old corpse of an American stretched out on the back of a wrecked jeep. This was on the top of the small hill that opposed the hill containing the Special Forces bunkers taken by the NVA in February. They were still in there, 700 meters away. The corpse was the worst thing we'd ever seen, utterly blackened now, the skin on the face drawn back tightly like stretched leather, so that all of his teeth showed. We were outraged that he had not been buried or at least covered, and we moved away and set up positions around the hill. Then the ARVN moved out toward the bunkers and were turned back by machine-gun fire. We sat on the hill and watched while napalm was dropped against the bunkers, and then we set up a recoilless rifle and fired at the vents. I went back to Stud. The next day a company of the Cav tried it, moving in two files on high and low ground approaching the bunkers, but the terrain between the hills offered almost no cover, and they were turned back. That night they were rocketed heavily, but took no serious casualties. I came back on the third day with Rick Merron and John Lengle of the Associated Press. There had been heavy airstrikes against the bunkers that night, and now two tiny helicopters, Loaches, were hovering a few feet above the slits, pouring in fire.

"Man, one Dink with a forty-five could put a hurtin' on those Loaches they'd never come back from," a young captain said. It was incredible, those little ships were the most beautiful things flying in Vietnam (you had to stop once in a while and admire the machinery), they just hung there above those bunkers like wasps outside a nest. "That's sex," the captain said. "That's pure sex."

One of the Loaches rose suddenly and flew over the hill, crossed the river and darted into Laos. Then it circled quickly, dipped, flew directly over us and hung there. The pilot radioed the captain.

"Sir, there's a gook di-di-ing down the trail into Laos. Permission to kill him."

"Permission given."

"Thank you," the pilot said, and the ship broke its suspended motion and sped toward the trail, clearing its guns.

A rocket whistled by, missing the hill, and we ran for the
bunkers. Two more came in, both missing, and then we
moved out for the opposite hill one more time, watching the
machine-gun slits for fluttering blips of light with one eye and
checking the ground for booby traps with the other. But they
had abandoned it during the night, and we took it without a
shot, standing on top of the bunkers, looking down into Laos,
past the remains of two bombed-out Russian tanks, feeling
relieved, victorious and silly. When Merron and I flew back to
Stud that afternoon, the two-month-old corpse rode with us.
No one had covered him until ten minutes before the chopper
had picked us up, and the body bag swarmed with flies until
the motion of the rising chopper shook them off. We got out
at Graves Registration with it, where one of the guys opened
the bag and said, "Shit, this is a *gook*! What'd they bring him
here for?"

"Look, Jesus, he's got on our uniform."

"I don't give a fuck, that ain't no American, that's a fucking
gook!"

"Wait a minute," the other one said. "Maybe it's a
spade. . . ."

The chopper that brought us back to Khe Sanh had barely
touched the strip, and we were running again. I must have
seen the Marines playing softball there, lounging around,
hanging up laundry, but I rejected it and ran anyway. It was
the only way I knew to behave there. I knew where the trench
was, and went for it.

"Must be Airborne trainin'," some grunt called, and I
slowed down.

"Ain' no hurry-up no more," a black Marine said. They all
had their fatigue shirts off, there must have been hundreds of
them, all around the field. It didn't seem possible, but I knew
it must be all right; I had noticed the weight of my flak jacket
and pack as I'd run. Nearly 500 Vietnamese Rangers sat near
the strip with all of their gear around them. One of them ran
up to an American, probably an advisor, and embraced him
tightly. They were being taken out that morning. Colonel

Lownds' replacement was due at the base any hour now, and some of the 26th had already been lifted out and moved to Hoi An, south of Danang. The new Charlie Med triage room had just been completed, deep underground and well lighted, but only a few men a day were being treated there. I went over to Hotel Company's position, but they were gone; a company of the Cav was there instead. They had cleaned out the trench floor all along the perimeter there, and the old bunker smelled now as though it had been dug that morning. It was no wonder that the Marines called the Cav dudes and got uncomfortable whenever they were around. I was relieving myself on the ground by one of the dumps when a Marine sergeant came up to me.

"You wanna please use the piss tube next time," he said.

It hadn't even occurred to me; I couldn't remember ever having seen a piss tube at Khe Sanh.

"Has the Cav taken over most of the perimeter?" I asked.

"Hmmmm."

"It must be a relief not to have to worry about that anymore."

"Shit, I'd feel a whole lot better if we had *Marines* here still. Damn Cav, all's they do is sleep on watch."

"Have you seen that?"

"No, but that's what they do."

"You don't like the Cav much?"

"I wouldn't say that."

Far up the strip, 400 meters away, there was a man sitting on some ammo crates. He was by himself. It was the colonel. I hadn't seen him in nearly six weeks, and he looked tired now. He had the same stare that the rest of the Marines here had, and the corners of his mustache had been rolled tortuously into two tight points that were caked with dried creamed coffee. Yes, he said, it sure would be good to get out of this place. He sat there looking at the hills, and I think that he was all but hypnotized by them now; they were not the same hills that had surrounded him for most of the past ten months. They had held such fearful mystery for so long that when they were suddenly found to be peaceful again, they were transformed as greatly as if a flood had swept over them.

A token American force was kept at Khe Sanh for the next

month, and the Marines went back to patrolling the hills, as they had done a year before. A great many people wanted to know how the Khe Sanh Combat Base could have been the Western Anchor of our Defense one month and a worthless piece of ground the next, and they were simply told that the situation had changed. A lot of people suspected that some kind of secret deal had been made with the North; activity along the DMZ all but stopped after Khe Sanh was abandoned. The Mission called it a victory, and General Westmoreland said that it had been "a Dien Bien Phu in reverse." In early June engineers rolled up the airstrip and transported the salvaged tarmac back to Dong Ha. The bunkers were filled with high explosives and then blown up. The sandbagging and wire that remained were left to the jungle, which grew with a violence of energy now in the Highland summer, as though there was an impatience somewhere to conceal all traces of what had been left by the winter.

POSTSCRIPT: CHINA BEACH

It was a great curving stretch of beachfront that faced the Bay of Danang. Even during the monsoons the afternoons were warm and clear, but now, in August, the dry, hot winds blew the sharp grit of the sand across the beach, into your eyes, hurling it stinging against your skin. Every Marine in I Corps got to spend a few days at China Beach at least once during their thirteen-month tours. It was a place where they could go swimming or surfing, get drunk, get stoned, get laid, get straight, groove in the scivvie houses, rent sailboats, or just sleep on the beach. Sometimes it was just an in-country R&R, a vacation, and sometimes it was a reward for outstanding service, exceptional bravery. Some Marines, the ones who were more than just good in a firefight, would get here as often as once a month because their company commanders did not like having them around between operations. With their medals and commendations, they would get three days out, a reprieve that promised them hot food, hot showers, time to goof and miles of beach. Sometimes choppers from the Cav would fly low along the beach, buzzing the Marines, and once, when a beautiful girl in a bikini was sighted, one of them actually landed. But you saw very few women here, mostly just Marines, and on some days there were thousands of them. They would splash in the surf, giggling and shouting, riding beach disks along the shoreline, playing like kids. Sometimes they would just lie asleep, half in the water and half in the sand. This was not the war for such images, you knew better, but they were Marines, and there was something terrible about seeing them there, limp in the wash of the tide.

Up from the beach there was a long, airless concrete building that served as a cafeteria. It had the best jukebox in Vietnam, and black Marines would spend more time there than on the beach, jiving around the room, carrying stacks of greasy hamburgers, dank french fries, giant paper cups full of malted milk, grape drink or (because it was so pretty, one of them told me) tomato juice. You'd sit at the tables there listening to the music, glad to be out of the sun, and every once in a while some grunts would recognize you from an operation and come over to talk. It was always nice to see them, but it always brought bad news, and sometimes the sight of what the war had done to them was awful. The two who came up to me now looked all right.

"You're a reporter, ain't you?"

I nodded.

"We seen you one time at Khe Sanh."

They were from the 26th Marines, Hotel Company, and they told me all about what had happened to the outfit since April. They weren't from the same platoon as Orrin and Day Tripper, but they knew that both of them had made it home. One of the guys who had run out to bring me a stretcher to sleep on was in a big hospital in Japan. I couldn't remember the name of the one grunt I most wanted to hear about, I was probably afraid of what they'd say, but I described him. He was a little cat with blond hair, and he was trying to grow a mustache.

"Oh, you mean Stoner."

"No, it wasn't that. He was always hanging out with Day Tripper. The guy I mean extended back in March. A crazy, funny little guy."

They looked at each other, and I was sorry I'd asked.

"I know the guy you mean," one of them said. "He was

always running around singing real crazy shit? Yeah, I know. He got killed. What was that little fucker's name?"

"I don't know which one," the other Marine said.

"Shit, yes, he got greased out on that *brilliant* fuckin' operation down from Hoi An. 'Member, in May?"

"Oh yeah. Him."

"Took a fuckin' RPG round right in the chest. God *damn*, I'll think of his name."

But I already remembered it now, and I sat there playing with a bottle of suntan lotion.

"It was Montefiori," one of them said.

"No, but it started with an M," the other one said.

"Winters!"

"No, dumb shit, now does Winters start with an M?"

"That kid Morrisey."

"You're just fuckin' with me now. Morrisey got sent home last week. . . ."

They went on like that, they really couldn't remember it. It was just a matter of pride or politeness for them to come up with the name of a dead buddy, they were going to try, but when they thought I wasn't watching, they looked at each other and smiled.

Illumination Rounds

We were all strapped into the seats of the Chinook, fifty of us, and something, someone was hitting it from the outside with an enormous hammer. How do they do that? I thought, we're a thousand feet in the air! But it had to be that, over and over, shaking the helicopter, making it dip and turn in a horrible out-of-control motion that took me in the stomach. I had to laugh, it was so exciting, it was the thing I had wanted, almost what I had wanted except for that wrenching, resonant metal-echo; I could hear it even above the noise of the rotor blades. And they were going to fix that, I knew they would make it stop. They had to, it was going to make me sick.

They were all replacements going in to mop up after the big battles on Hills 875 and 876, the battles that had already taken on the name of one great battle, the battle of Dak To. And I was new, brand new, three days in-country, embarrassed about my boots because they were so new. And across from me, ten feet away, a boy tried to jump out of the straps and then jerked forward and hung there, his rifle barrel caught in the red plastic webbing of the seat back. As the chopper rose again and turned, his weight went back hard against the webbing and a dark spot the size of a baby's hand showed in the center of his fatigue jacket. And it grew—I knew what it was, but not really—it got up to his armpits and then started down his sleeves and up over his shoulders at the same time. It went all across his waist and down his legs, covering the canvas on his boots until they were dark like everything else he wore, and it was running in slow, heavy drops off of his fingertips. I thought I could hear the drops hitting the metal strip on the chopper floor. Hey! . . . Oh, but this isn't anything at all, it's not real, it's just some *thing* they're going through that isn't real. One of the door gunners was heaped up on the floor like a cloth dummy. His hand had the bloody raw look of a pound of liver fresh from the butcher paper. We touched down on the same lz we had just left a few minutes before, but I didn't know it until one of the guys shook my shoulder, and then I couldn't stand up. All I could feel of my legs was their shaking, and the guy thought I'd been hit and helped me up. The chopper had taken eight hits, there was shattered plastic all over the floor, a dying pilot up front, and the boy was hanging forward in the straps again, he was dead, but not (I knew) really dead.

It took me a month to lose that feeling of being a spectator to something that was part game, part show. That first afternoon, before I'd boarded the Chinook, a black sergeant had tried to keep me from going. He told me I was too new to go near the kind of shit they were throwing around up in those hills. ("You a reporter?" he'd asked, and I'd said, "No, a writer," dumbass and pompous, and he'd laughed and said, "Careful. You can't use no eraser up where you wanna go.") He'd pointed to the bodies of all the dead Americans lined in two long rows near the chopper pad, so many that they could not even cover all of them decently. But they were not real then, and taught me nothing. The Chinook had come in, blowing my helmet off, and I grabbed it up and joined the replacements waiting to board. "Okay, man," the sergeant said. "You gotta go, you gotta go. All's I can say is, I hope you get a clean wound."

The battle for Hill 875 was over, and some survivors were being brought in by Chinook to the landing strip at Dak To. The 173rd Airborne had taken over 400 casualties, nearly 200 killed, all on the previous afternoon and in the fighting that had gone on all through the night. It was very cold and wet up there, and some girls from the Red Cross had been sent up from Pleiku to comfort the survivors. As the troops filed out of the helicopters, the girls waved and smiled at them from behind their serving tables. "Hi, soldier! What's your name?" "Where you from, soldier?" "I'll bet some hot coffee would hit the spot about now."

And the men from the 173rd just kept walking without answering, staring straight ahead, their eyes rimmed with red from fatigue, their faces pinched and aged with all that had happened during the night. One of them dropped out of line and said something to a loud, fat girl who wore a Peanuts sweatshirt under her fatigue blouse and she started to cry. The rest just walked past the girls and the large, olive-drab coffee urns. They had no idea of where they were.

A senior NCO in the Special Forces was telling the story: "We was back at Bragg, in the NCO Club, and this schoolteacher comes in an' she's real good-lookin'. Dusty here grabs her by the shoulders and starts runnin' his tongue all over her face like she's a fuckin' ice-cream cone. An' you know what she says? She says, 'I like you. You're different.'"

At one time they would have lighted your cigarette for you on the terrace of the Continental Hotel. But those days are almost twenty years gone, and anyway, who really misses them? Now there is a crazy American who looks like George Orwell, and he is always sleeping off his drinks in one of the wicker chairs there, slumped against a table, starting up with violence, shouting and then going back to sleep. He makes everyone nervous, especially the waiters; the old ones who had served the French and the Japanese and the first American journalists and OSS types ("those noisy bastards at the Continental," Graham Greene called them) and the really young ones who bussed the tables and pimped in a modest way. The little elevator boy still greets the guests each morning with a quiet *"Ça va?"* but he is seldom answered, and the old baggage man (he also brings us grass) will sit in the lobby and say, "How are you tomorrow?"

"Ode to Billy Joe" plays from speakers mounted on the terrace's corner columns, but the air seems too heavy to carry the sound right, and it hangs in the corners. There is an exhausted, drunk master sergeant from the 1st Infantry Division who has bought a flute from the old man in khaki shorts and pith helmet who sells instruments along Tu Do Street. The old man will lean over the butt-strewn flower boxes that line the terrace and play "Frère Jacques" on a wooden stringed instrument. The sergeant has bought the flute, and he is playing it quietly, pensively, badly.

The tables are crowded with American civilian construction engineers, men getting $30,000 a year from their jobs on government contracts and matching that easily on the black market. Their faces have the look of aerial photos of silicone pits, all hung with loose flesh and visible veins. Their mistresses were among the prettiest, saddest girls in Vietnam. I always wondered what they had looked like before they'd made their arrangements with the engineers. You'd see them at the tables there, smiling their hard, empty smiles into those rangy, brutal, scared faces. No wonder those men all looked alike to the Vietnamese. After a while they all looked alike to me. Out on the Bien Hoa Highway, north of Saigon, there is a monument to the Vietnamese war dead, and it is one of the few graceful things left in the country. It is a modest pagoda set above the road and approached by long flights of gently rising steps. One Sunday, I saw a bunch of these engineers gunning their Harleys up those steps, laughing and shouting in the afternoon sun. The Vietnamese had a special name for them to distinguish them from all other Americans; it translated out

to something like "The Terrible Ones," although I'm told
that this doesn't even approximate the odium carried in the
original.

There was a young sergeant in the Special Forces, stationed
at the C Detachment in Can Tho, which served as the SF
headquarters for IV Corps. In all, he had spent thirty-six
months in Vietnam. This was his third extended tour, and he
planned to come back again as soon as he possibly could after
this current hitch was finished. During his last tour he had
lost a finger and part of a thumb in a firefight, and he had
been generally shot up enough times for the three Purple
Hearts which mean that you don't have to fight in Vietnam
anymore. After all that, I guess they thought of him as a combat liability, but he was such a hard charger that they gave
him the EM Club to manage. He ran it well and seemed
happy, except that he had gained a lot of weight in the duty,
and it set him apart from the rest of the men. He loved to
horse around with the Vietnamese in the compound, leaping
on them from behind, leaning heavily on them, shoving them
around and pulling their ears, sometimes punching them a
little hard in the stomach, smiling a stiff small smile that was
meant to tell them all that he was just being playful. The
Vietnamese would smile too, until he turned to walk away.
He loved the Vietnamese, he said, he really *knew* them after
three years. As far as he was concerned, there was no place in
the world as fine as Vietnam. And back home in North Carolina he had a large, glass-covered display case in which he
kept his medals and decorations and citations, the photographs taken during three tours and countless battles, letters
from past commanders, a few souvenirs. The case stood in the
center of the living room, he said, and every night his wife
and three kids would move the kitchen table out in front of
it and eat their dinner there.

At 800 feet we knew we were being shot at. Something hit
the underside of the chopper but did not penetrate it. They
weren't firing tracers, but we saw the brilliant flickering blips
of light below, and the pilot circled and came down very fast,
working the button that released fire from the flex guns

mounted on either side of the Huey. Every fifth round was a tracer, and they sailed out and down, incomparably graceful, closer and closer, until they met the tiny point of light coming from the jungle. The ground fire stopped, and we went on to land at Vinh Long, where the pilot yawned and said, "I think I'll go to bed early tonight and see if I can wake up with any enthusiasm for this war."

A twenty-four-year-old Special Forces captain was telling me about it. "I went out and killed one VC and liberated a prisoner. Next day the major called me in and told me that I'd killed fourteen VC and liberated six prisoners. You want to see the medal?"

There was a little air-conditioned restaurant on the corner of Le Loi and Tu Do, across from the Continental Hotel and the old opera house which now served as the Vietnamese Lower House. Some of us called it the Graham Greene Milk Bar (a scene in *The Quiet American* had taken place there), but its name was Givral. Every morning they baked their own baguettes and croissants, and the coffee wasn't too bad. Sometimes, I'd meet there with a friend of mine for breakfast.

He was a Belgian, a tall, slow-moving man of thirty who'd been born in the Congo. He professed to know and love war, and he affected the mercenary sensibility. He'd been photographing the Vietnam thing for seven or eight years now, and once in a while he'd go over to Laos and run around the jungles there with the government, searching for the dreaded Pathet Lao, which he pronounced "Paddy Lao." Other people's stories of Laos always made it sound like a lotus land where no one wanted to hurt anyone, but he said that whenever he went on ops there he always kept a grenade taped to his belly because he was a Catholic and knew what the Paddy Lao would do to him if he were captured. But he was a little crazy that way, and tended to dramatize his war stories.

He always wore dark glasses, probably even during operations. His pictures sold to the wire services, and I saw a few of them in the American news magazines. He was very kind in a gruff, offhanded sort of way, kindness embarrassed him, and he was so graceless among people, so eager to shock, that he couldn't understand why so many of us liked him. Irony was the effect he worked for in conversation, that and a sense of how exquisite the war could be when all of its machinery was running right. He was explaining the finish of an operation he'd just been on in War Zone C, above Cu Chi.

"There were a lot of dead VC," he said. "Dozens and dozens of them! A lot of them were from that same village that has been giving you so much trouble lately. VC from top to bottom—Michael, in that village the fucking *ducks* are VC. So the American commander had twenty or thirty of the dead flown up in a sling load and dropped into the village. I should say it was a drop of at least two hundred feet, all those dead Viet Congs, right in the middle of the village."

He smiled (I couldn't see his eyes).

"Ah, Psywar!" he said, kissing off the tips of his fingers.

Bob Stokes of *Newsweek* told me this: In the big Marine hospital in Danang they have what is called the "White Lie Ward," where they bring some of the worst cases, the ones who can be saved but who will never be the same again. A young Marine was carried in, still unconscious and full of morphine, and his legs were gone. As he was being carried into the ward, he came out of it briefly and saw a Catholic chaplain standing over him.

"Father," he said, "am I all right?"

The chaplain didn't know what to say. "You'll have to talk about that with the doctors, son."

"Father, are my legs okay?"

"Yes," the chaplain said. "Sure."

By the next afternoon the shock had worn off and the boy knew all about it. He was lying on his cot when the chaplain came by.

"Father," the Marine said, "I'd like to ask you for something."

"What, son?"

"I'd like to have that cross." And he pointed to the tiny silver insignia on the chaplain's lapel.

"Of course," the chaplain said. "But why?"

"Well, it was the first thing I saw when I came to yesterday, and I'd like to have it."

The chaplain removed the cross and handed it to him. The Marine held it tightly in his fist and looked at the chaplain.

"You lied to me, Father," he said. "You cocksucker. You lied to me."

His name was Davies, and he was a gunner with a helicopter group based at Tan Son Nhut airport. On paper, by the regulations, he was billeted in one of the big "hotel" BEQ's in Cholon, but he only kept his things there. He actually lived in a small two-story Vietnamese house deeper inside of Cholon, as far from the papers and the regulations as he could get. Every morning he took an Army bus with wire-grille windows out to the base and flew missions, mostly around War Zone C, along the Cambodian border, and most nights he returned to the house in Cholon where he lived with his "wife" (whom he'd found in one of the bars) and some other Vietnamese who were said to be the girl's family. Her mamma-san and her brother were always there, living on the first floor, and there were others who came and went. He seldom saw the brother, but every few days he would find a pile of labels and brand names torn from cardboard cartons, American products that the brother wanted from the PX.

The first time I saw him he was sitting alone at a table on the Continental terrace, drinking a beer. He had a full, drooping mustache and sharp, sad eyes, and he was wearing a denim workshirt and wheat jeans. He also carried a Leica and a copy of *Ramparts*, and I just assumed at first that he was a correspondent. I didn't know then that you could buy *Ramparts* at the PX, and after I'd borrowed and returned it we began to talk. It was the issue that featured left-wing Catholics like Jesus Christ and Fulton Sheen on the cover. *"Catholique?"* one of the bar girls said later that night. *"Moi aussi,"* and she kept the magazine. That was when we were walking around Cholon in the rain trying to find Hoa, his wife. Mamma-san had told us that she'd gone to the movies with some girl-friends, but Davies knew what she was doing.

"I hate that shit," he said. "It's so uncool."

"Well, don't put up with it."

"Yeah."

Davies' house was down a long, narrow alley that became

nothing more than a warren at the end, smelling of camphor smoke and fish, crowded but clean. He would not speak to Mamma-san, and we walked straight up to the second floor. It was one long room that had a sleeping area screened off in an arrangement of filmy curtains. At the top of the stairs there was a large poster of Lenny Bruce, and beneath it, in a shrine effect, was a low table with a Buddha and lighted incense on it.

"Lenny," Davies said.

Most of one wall was covered with a collage that Davies had done with the help of some friends. It included glimpses of burning monks, stacked Viet Cong dead, wounded Marines screaming and weeping, Cardinal Spellman waving from a chopper, Ronald Reagan, his face halved and separated by a stalk of cannabis; pictures of John Lennon peering through wire-rimmed glasses, Mick Jagger, Jimi Hendrix, Dylan, Eldridge Cleaver, Rap Brown; coffins draped with American flags whose stars were replaced by swastikas and dollar signs; odd parts clipped from *Playboy* pictures, newspaper headlines (FARMERS BUTCHER HOGS TO PROTEST PORK PRICE DIP), photo captions (*President Jokes with Newsmen*), beautiful girls holding flowers, showers of peace symbols; Ky standing at attention and saluting, a small mushroom cloud forming where his genitalia should have been; a map of the western United States with the shape of Vietnam reversed and fitted over California and one large, long figure that began at the bottom with shiny leather boots and rouged knees and ascended in a microskirt, bare breasts, graceful shoulders and a long neck, topped by the burned, blackened face of a dead Vietnamese woman.

By the time Davies' friends showed up, we were already stoned. We could hear them below, laughing and rapping with Mama, and then they came up the stairs, three spades and two white guys.

"It sure do smell *peculiar* up here," one of them said.

"Hi, you freaky li'l fuckers."

"This grass is Number Ten," Davies said. "Every time I smoke this grass over here it gives me a bad trip."

"Ain' nuthin' th' matter with that grass," someone said. "It ain't the grass."

"Where's Hoa?"

"Yeah, Davies, where's your ole lady at?"

"She's out hustling Saigon tea, and I'm fucking sick of it." He tried to look really angry, but he only looked unhappy.

One of them handed off a joint and stretched out. "Hairy day today," he said.

"Where'd you fly?"

"Bu Dop."

"Bu Dop!" one of the spades said, and he started to move toward the joint, jiving and working his shoulders, bopping his head. "Bu Dop, budop, bu dop dop *dop*!"

"Funky funky Bu Dop."

"Hey, man, can you OD on grass?"

"I dunno, baby. Maybe we could get jobs at the Aberdeen Proving Grounds smokin' dope for Uncle Sugar."

"Wow, I'm stoned. Hey, Davies, you stoned?"

"Yeah," Davies said.

It started to rain again, so hard that you couldn't hear drops, only the full force of the water pouring down on the metal roof. We smoked a little more, and then the others started to leave. Davies looked like he was sleeping with his eyes open.

"That goddamn pig," he said. "Fuckin' whore. Man, I'm paying out all this bread for the house and those people downstairs. I don't even know who they are, for Christ's sake. I'm really . . . I'm getting sick of it."

"You're pretty short now," someone said. "Why don't you cut out?"

"You mean just split?"

"Why not?"

Davies was quiet for a long time.

"Yeah," he finally said. "This is bad. This is really bad. I think I'm going to get out of here."

A bird colonel, commanding a brigade of the 4th Infantry Division: "I'll bet you always wondered why we call 'em Dinks up in this part of the country. I thought of it myself. I'll tell you, I never *did* like hearing them called Charlie. See, I had an uncle named Charlie, and I liked him too. No, Charlie was just too damn good for the little bastards. So I just thought, What are they *really* like? and I came up with rinky-dink. Suits 'em just perfect, Rinky-Dink. 'Cept that was too long, so we cut it down some. And that's why we call 'em Dinks.''

One morning before dawn, Ed Fouhy, a former Saigon bureau chief for CBS, went out to 8th Aerial Port at Tan Son Nhut to catch the early military flight to Danang. They boarded as the sun came up, and Fouhy strapped in next to a kid in rumpled fatigues, one of those soldiers you see whose weariness has gone far beyond physical exhaustion, into that state where no amount of sleep will ever give him the kind of rest he needs. Every torpid movement they make tells you that they are tired, that they'll stay tired until their tours are up and the big bird flies them back to the World. Their eyes are dim with it, their faces almost puffy, and when they smile you have to accept it as a token.

There was a standard question you could use to open a conversation with troops, and Fouhy tried it. "How long you been in-country?" he asked.

The kid half lifted his head; that question could *not* be serious. The weight was really on him, and the words came slowly.

"All   fuckin'   day," he said.

"You guys ought do a story on me suntahm," the kid said. He was a helicopter gunner, six-three with an enormous head that sat in bad proportion to the rest of his body and a line of picket teeth that were always on show in a wet, uneven smile. Every few seconds he would have to wipe his mouth with the back of his hand, and when he talked to you his face was always an inch from yours, so that I had to take my glasses off to keep them dry. He was from Kilgore, Texas, and he was on his seventeenth consecutive month in-country.

"Why should we do a story about you?"

" 'Cause I'm so fuckin' good," he said, " 'n' that ain' no shit, neither. Got me one hunnert 'n' fifty-se'en gooks kilt. 'N' fifty caribou." He grinned and stanched the saliva for a second. "Them're all certified," he added.

The chopper touched down at Ba Xoi and we got off, not

unhappy about leaving him. "Lis'n," he said, laughing, "you git up onna ridgeline, see y' keep yer head down. Y'heah?"

"Say, how'd you get to be a co-respondent an' come ovah to this raggedy-ass motherfucker?"

He was a really big spade, rough-looking even when he smiled, and he wore a gold nose-bead fastened through his left nostril. I told him that the nose-bead blew my mind, and he said that was all right, it blew everybody's mind. We were sitting by the chopper pad of an lz above Kontum. He was trying to get to Dak To, I was heading for Pleiku, and we both wanted to get out of there before nightfall. We took turns running out to the pad to check the choppers that kept coming in and taking off, neither of us was having any luck, and after we'd talked for an hour he laid a joint on me and we smoked.

"I been here mor'n eight months now," he said. "I bet I been in mor'n twenny firefights. An' I ain' hardly fired back once."

"How come?"

"Shee-it, I go firin' back, I might kill one a th' Brothers, you dig it?"

I nodded, no Viet Cong ever called *me* honky, and he told me that in his company alone there were more than a dozen Black Panthers and that he was one of them. I didn't say anything, and then he said that he wasn't just a Panther; he was an agent for the Panthers, sent over here to recruit. I asked him what kind of luck he'd been having, and he said fine, real fine. There was a fierce wind blowing across the lz, and the joint didn't last very long.

"Hey, baby," he said, "that was just some shit I tol' you. Shit, I ain' no Panther. I was just fuckin' with you, see what you'd say."

"But the Panthers have guys over here. I've met some."

"Tha' could be," he said, and he laughed.

A Huey came in, and he jogged out to see where it was headed. It was going to Dak To, and he came back to get his gear. "Later, baby," he said. "An' luck." He jumped into the chopper, and as it rose from the strip he leaned out and laughed, bringing his arm up and bending it back toward him, palm out and the fist clenched tightly in the Sign.

One day I went out with the ARVN on an operation in the rice paddies above Vinh Long, forty terrified Vietnamese troops and five Americans, all packed into three Hueys that dropped us up to our hips in paddy muck. I had never been in a rice paddy before. We spread out and moved toward the marshy swale that led to the jungle. We were still twenty feet from the first cover, a low paddy wall, when we took fire from the treeline. It was probably the working half of a crossfire that had somehow gone wrong. It caught one of the ARVN in the head, and he dropped back into the water and disappeared. We made it to the wall with two casualties. There was no way of stopping their fire, no room to send in a flanking party, so gunships were called and we crouched behind the wall and waited. There was a lot of fire coming from the trees, but we were all right as long as we kept down. And I was thinking, Oh man, so this is a rice paddy, yes, wow! when I suddenly heard an electric guitar shooting right up in my ear and a mean, rapturous black voice singing, coaxing, and when I got it all together I turned to see a grinning black corporal hunched over a cassette recorder. "Might's well," he said. "We ain' goin' *no*where till them gunships come."

That's the story of the first time I ever heard Jimi Hendrix, but in a war where a lot of people talked about Aretha's "Satisfaction" the way other people speak of Brahms' Fourth, it was more than a story; it was Credentials. "Say, that Jimi Hendrix is my main man," someone would say. "He has *de*finitely got his shit together!" Hendrix had once been in the 101st Airborne, and the Airborne in Vietnam was full of wiggy-brilliant spades like him, really mean and really good, guys who always took care of you when things got bad. That music meant a lot to them. I never once heard it played over the Armed Forces Radio Network.

I met this kid from Miles City, Montana, who read the *Stars and Stripes* every day, checking the casualty lists to see if by some chance anybody from his town had been killed. He didn't even know if there was anyone else from Miles City in Vietnam, but he checked anyway because he knew for sure that if there *was* someone else and they got killed, he would be all right. "I mean, can you just see *two* guys from a rag-gedy-ass town like Miles City getting killed in Vietnam?" he said.

The sergeant had lain out near the clearing for almost two hours with a wounded medic. He had called over and over for a medevac, but none had come. Finally, a chopper from another outfit, a LOH, appeared, and he was able to reach it by radio. The pilot told him that he'd have to wait for one of his own ships, they weren't coming down, and the sergeant told the pilot that if he did not land for them he was going to open fire from the ground and fucking well *bring* him down. So they were picked up that way, but there were re-percussions.

The commander's code name was Mal Hombre, and he reached the sergeant later that afternoon from a place with the call signal Violent Meals.

"God *damn* it, Sergeant," he said through the static, "I thought you were a professional soldier."

"I waited as long as I could, Sir. Any longer, I was gonna lose my man."

"This outfit is perfectly capable of taking care of its own dirty laundry. Is that clear, Sergeant?"

"Colonel, since when is a wounded trooper 'dirty laundry'?"

"At ease, Sergeant," Mal Hombre said, and radio contact was broken.

There was a spec 4 in the Special Forces at Can Tho, a shy Indian boy from Chinle, Arizona, with large, wet eyes the color of ripe olives and a quiet way of speaking, a really nice way of putting things, kind to everyone without ever being stupid or soft about it. On the night that the compound and the airstrip were hit, he came and asked me if there was a chaplain anywhere around. He wasn't very religious, he said, but he was worried about tonight. He'd just volunteered for a "suicide squad," two jeeps that were going to drive across

the airstrip with mortars and a recoilless rifle. It looked bad,
I had to admit it; there were so few of us in the compound
that they'd had to put me on the reaction force. It might be
bad. He just had a feeling about it, he'd seen what always
happened to guys whenever they got that feeling, at least he
thought it was that feeling, a bad one, the worst he'd ever had.

I told him that the only chaplains I could think of would
be in the town, and we both knew that the town was cut off.

"Oh," he said. "Look, then. If I get it tonight . . ."

"It'll be okay."

"Listen, though. If it happens . . . I think it's going to
. . . will you make sure the colonel tells my folks I was looking for a chaplain anyway?"

I promised, and the jeeps loaded and drove off. I heard
later that there had been a brief firefight, but that no one had
been hurt. They didn't have to use the recoilless. They all
drove back into the compound two hours later. The next
morning at breakfast he sat at another table, saying a lot of
loud, brutal things about the gooks, and he wouldn't look at
me. But at noon he came over and squeezed my arm and
smiled, his eyes fixed somewhere just to the right of my own.

For two days now, ever since the Tet Offensive had begun,
they had been coming by the hundreds to the province hospital at Can Tho. They were usually either very young or very
old or women, and their wounds were often horrible. The
more lightly wounded were being treated quickly in the hospital yard, and the more serious cases were simply placed in
one of the corridors to die. There were just too many of them
to treat, the doctors had worked without a break, and now,
on the second afternoon, the Viet Cong began shelling the
hospital.

One of the Vietnamese nurses handed me a cold can of beer
and asked me to take it down the hall where one of the Army
surgeons was operating. The door of the room was ajar, and
I walked right in. I probably should have looked first. A little
girl was lying on the table, looking with wide dry eyes at the
wall. Her left leg was gone, and a sharp piece of bone about
six inches long extended from the exposed stump. The leg
itself was on the floor, half wrapped in a piece of paper. The

doctor was a major, and he'd been working alone. He could not have looked worse if he'd lain all night in a trough of blood. His hands were so slippery that I had to hold the can to his mouth for him and tip it up as his head went back. I couldn't look at the girl.

"Is it all right?" he said quietly.

"It's okay now. I expect I'll be sick as hell later on."

He placed his hand on the girl's forehead and said, "Hello, little darling." He thanked me for bringing the beer. He probably thought that he was smiling, but nothing changed anywhere in his face. He'd been working this way for nearly twenty hours.

The Intel report lay closed on the green field table, and someone had scrawled "What does it all mean?" across the cover sheet. There wasn't much doubt about who had done that; the S-2 was a known ironist. There were so many like him, really young captains and majors who had the wit to cut back their despair, a wedge to set against the bitterness. What got to them sooner or later was an inability to reconcile their love of service with their contempt for the war, and a lot of them finally had to resign their commissions, leave the profession.

We were sitting in the tent waiting for the rain to stop, the major, five grunts and myself. The rains were constant now, ending what had been a dry monsoon season, and you could look through the tent flap and think about the Marines up there patrolling the hills. Someone came in to report that one of the patrols had discovered a small arms cache.

"An arms cache!" the major said. "What happened was, one of the grunts was out there running around, and he tripped and fell down. That's about the only way we ever find any of this shit."

He was twenty-nine, young in rank, and this was his second tour. The time before, he had been a captain commanding a regular Marine company. He knew all about grunts and patrols, arms caches and the value of most Intelligence.

It was cold, even in the tent, and the enlisted Marines seemed uncomfortable about lying around with a stranger, a correspondent there. The major was a cool head, they knew that; there wasn't going to be any kind of hassle until the rain stopped. They talked quietly among themselves at the far end of the tent, away from the light of the lantern. Reports kept coming in: reports from the Vietnamese, from recon, from Division, situation reports, casualty reports, three casualty reports in twenty minutes. The major looked them all over.

"Did you know that a dead Marine costs eighteen thousand dollars?" he said. The grunts all turned around and looked at us. They knew how the major had meant that because they knew the major. They were just seeing about me.

The rain stopped, and they left. Outside, the air was still cool, but heavy, too, as though a terrible heat was coming on. The major and I stood by the tent and watched while an F-4 flew nose-down, released its load against the base of a hill, leveled and flew upward again.

"I've been having this dream," the major said. "I've had it two times now. I'm in a big examination room back at Quantico. They're handing out questionnaires for an aptitude test. I take one and look at it, and the first question says, 'How many kinds of animals can you kill with your hands?' "

We could see rain falling in a sheet about a kilometer away. Judging by the wind, the major gave it three minutes before it reached us.

"After the first tour, I'd have the goddamndest nightmares. You know, the works. Bloody stuff, bad fights, guys dying, *me* dying . . . I thought they were the worst," he said. "But I sort of miss them now."

Colleagues

I

There's a candle end burning in a corner of the bunker, held to the top of a steel helmet by melted wax, the light guttering over a battered typewriter, and the Old Guy is getting one off: "Tat-tat-tat, tatta-tatta-tat like your kid or your brother or your sweetheart maybe never wanted much for himself never asked for anything except for what he knew to be his some men have a name for it and they call it Courage when the great guns are still at last across Europe what will it matter maybe after all that this one boy from Cleveland Ohio won't be coming back-a-tat-tat." You can hear shellfire landing just outside, a little gravel falls into the typewriter, but the candle burns on, throwing its faint light over the bowed head and the few remaining wisps of white hair. Two men, the Colonel and the Kid, stand by the door watching. "Why, Sir?" the Kid asks. "What makes him do it? He could be sitting safe in London right now." "I don't know, son," the Colonel says. "Maybe he figures he's got a job to do, too. Maybe it's because he's somebody who really cares. . . ."

I never knew a member of the Vietnam press corps who was insensible to what happened when the words "war" and "correspondent" got joined. The glamour of it was possibly empty and lunatic, but there were times when it was all you had, a benign infection that ravaged all but your worst fears and deepest depressions. Admitting, for argument's sake, that we were all a little crazy to have gone there in the first place, there were those whose madness it was not to know always which war they were actually in, fantasizing privately about other, older wars, Wars I and II, air wars and desert wars and island wars, obscure colonial actions against countries whose names have since changed many times, punitive wars and holy wars and wars in places where the climate was so cool that you could wear a trench coat and look good; in other words, wars which sounded old and corny to those of us for whom the war in Vietnam was more than enough. There were correspondents all around who could break you up with their bad style and self-consciousness, but those aberrations were hardly ever beyond your understanding. Over there, all styles grew in their way out of the same haunted, haunting romance. Those Crazy Guys Who Cover The War.

In any other war, they would have made movies about us too, *Dateline: Hell!*, *Dispatch from Dong Ha*, maybe even *A Scrambler to the Front*, about Tim Page, Sean Flynn and Rick Merron, three young photographers who used to ride in and out of combat on Hondas. But Vietnam is awkward, everybody knows how awkward, and if people don't even want to hear about it, you know they're not going to pay money to sit there in the dark and have it brought up. (*The Green Berets* doesn't count. That wasn't really about Vietnam, it was about Santa Monica.) So we have all been compelled to make our own movies, as many movies as there are correspondents, and this one is mine. (One day at the battalion aid station in Hue a Marine with minor shrapnel wounds in his legs was waiting to get on a helicopter, a long wait with all of the dead and badly wounded going out first, and a couple of sniper rounds snapped across the airstrip, forcing us to move behind some sandbagging. "I *hate* this movie," he said, and I thought, "Why not?") My movie, my friends, my colleagues. But meet them in context:

There was a ridge called Mutter's Ridge that ran the crest of one of those DMZ hills which the Americans usually named according to height in meters, Hill Three Hundred Whatever. The Marines had been up there since early morning, when Kilo Company and four correspondents were choppered into a sparse landing zone on the highest rise of the ridge. If this had been an Army operation, we would have been digging now, correspondents too, but the Marines didn't do that, their training taught them more about fatal gesture than it did about survival. Everyone was saying that Charlie was probably just over there on the next hill scoping on us, but the grunts were keeping it all in the open, walking out along the ridge "coordinating," setting up positions and cutting out a proper lz with battery-powered saws and chunks of explosive. Every few minutes one or another of them would shag down to the spot below the lz where the correspondents were sitting and warn us indifferently about the next blast, saying, "Uh, listen, there's fire in the hole, so you guys wanna just turn your backs and sort of cover over your heads?" He'd hang in there for a moment to give us a good look, and then run back up to the lz site to tell the others about us.

"Hey, see them four guys there? Them're reporters."

"Bullshit, reporters."

"Okay, motherfucker, go on down and see. Next time we blast."

There were some Marines stretched out a few feet from us, passing around war comics and talking, calling each other Dude and Jive, Lifer and Shitkick and Motherfucker, touching this last with a special grace, as though it were the tenderest word in their language. A suave black grunt, identified on his helmet cover as LOVE CHILD, was studying an exhausted copy of *Playboy*, pausing to say, "Oh . . . *man!* She can sure come sit on my face *any*time. Any . . . time . . . at . . . all." But none of them were talking to us yet, they were sort of talking for us, trying to make us out, maintaining that odd delicacy of theirs that always broke down sooner or later. It was like a ritual, all the preliminary forms had to be observed and satisfied, and it wasn't simply because they were shy. As far as any of them knew, we were crazy, maybe even dangerous. It made sense: They *had* to be here, they knew that. We did *not* have to be here, and they were sure enough of that too. (The part that they never realized until later was that our freedom of movement was a door that swung both ways; at that very moment, the four of us were giving each other that Nothing Happening look and talking about getting out.) A GI would walk clear across a firebase for a look at you if he'd never seen a correspondent before because it was like going to see the Geek, and worth the walk.

Besides, there were four of us sitting there in a loose professional knot, there was another one flying in the command helicopter trying to get a long view of the operation, and a sixth, AP photographer Dana Stone, was walking up the hill now with a platoon that had been chosen to scout the trail. It was one thing for a lone reporter to join an outfit before an operation because the outfit, if it was a company or larger, could absorb him and the curiosity that his presence always set working, and when the operation was over most of the troops would never even know that he'd been along. But when six correspondents turned up on the eve of an operation, especially when it fell during a long period of light contact, the effect was so complicated that the abiding ambivalence of all troops and commanders toward all reporters didn't even begin to explain it. Everyone from the colonel to the lowest-ranking grunt felt a new importance about what he was going into, and to all appearances, as far as they were in touch with it, they were glad to see you. But our presence was also unnerving, picking at layers of fear that they might never have known about otherwise. ("Why us? I mean, *six* of those bastards, where the hell are we *going*?") When it came all the way down to this, even the poorest-connected free-lancer had the power on him, a power which only the most pompous and unfeeling journalists ever really wanted, throwing weird career scares into the staff and laying a cutting edge against each Marine's gut estimates of his own survival. Then, it didn't matter that we were dressed exactly as they were and would be going exactly where they were going; we were as exotic and as fearsome as black magic, coming on with cameras and questions, and if we promised to take the anonymity off of what was about to happen, we were also there to watchdog the day. The very fact that we had chosen *them* seemed to promise the most awful kind of engagement, because they were all certain that war correspondents never wasted time. It was a joke we all dug.

It was August now, when the heat in I Corps forgave nothing. That year the northern monsoons had been almost dry (so many stories had run the phrase "grim reminders of a rainless monsoon" that it became a standard, always good for a laugh), and across the raw spaces between hills you could see only the faintest traces of green in the valleys and draws, the hills rising from pale brown to sunbleached yellow and gaping like dark, dried sores wherever the winter airstrikes had torn their sides out. Very little had happened in this sector since early spring, when an odd disengagement had been effected at Khe Sanh and when a multi-division operation into the A Shau Valley had ended abruptly after two weeks, like a speech cut at mid-sentence. The A Shau held the North's great supply depot, they had tanks and trucks and heavy anti-aircraft guns dug in there, and while the American Mission had made its reflexive claims of success for the operation, they were made for once without much enthusiasm, indicating that even the Command had to acknowledge the inviolability of that place. It was admitted at the time that a lot of our helicopters had been shot down, but this was spoken of as an expensive equipment loss, as though our choppers were crewless entities that held to the sky by themselves, spilling nothing more precious than fuel when they crashed.

Between then and now, nothing larger than company-size

sweeps had worked the western Z, generally without contact. Like all of the war's quieter passages, the spring-summer lull had left everyone badly strung out, and a lot of spooky stories began going around, like the ones about NVA helicopters (a Marine patrol supposedly saw one touch down on the abandoned Marine base at Khe Sanh and wait while a dozen men got out and walked around the perimeter, "like they was just checking things out"). It had been a mild season for Vietnam correspondents too (the lull aside, home offices were beginning to make it clear to their Saigon bureaus that the story was losing the old bite, what with Johnson's abdication, the spring assassinations and the coming elections), and we were either talking about how the Vietnam thing was really finished or bitching about getting shot at only to wind up on page nine. It was a good time to cruise the country, a day here and a week there, just hanging out with troops; a good time to make leisurely investigations into the smaller, darker pockets of the war. Now word had come down that a large mass of NVA was moving across the DMZ, possibly building for a new offensive against Hue, and battalions of the 5th Marines were deploying in rough conjunction with battalions of the 9th to find and kill them. It had the feel of what we always called a "good operation," and the six of us had gone up for it.

But there was nothing here now, no dreaded Cong, no shelling, no pictures for the wires, no stories for the files, no sign that anyone had been on this scalding ridge for at least six months. (A few miles north and a little east, a company of the 9th was in the middle of an evil firefight that would last until nightfall, leaving eleven of them dead and nearly thirty wounded, but we knew nothing about that now. If we had, we might possibly have made an effort at getting to it, some of us at least, explaining it later in cold professional terms and leaving all the other reasons unspoken, understood between us. If a Marine had ever expressed a similar impulse, we would probably have called him psychotic.) The only violence on Mutter's Ridge was in the heat and whatever associations with that terrible winter you could take from the view, from Cam Lo, Route 9 into Khe Sanh, the Rockpile. A few more Marines had joined the group around us, but they were being cool, pausing to read the tags sewn on our fatigue shirts as though to themselves, but out loud, just to show us that they knew we were here.

"Associated Press, yeah, and UPI, uh-huh, and *Esquire*, wow, *they* got a guy over here, what the fuck for, you tell 'em what we're wearing? And—hey, man, what's *that* supposed to be?" (Sean Flynn had only the words "Bao Chi" on his tags, Vietnamese for "journalist.") "That's pretty far out, what's that, in case you're captured or something?"

Actually, Bao Chi was all the affiliation that Flynn needed or wanted in Vietnam, but he didn't go into that. Instead, he explained that when he had first begun taking pictures here in 1965, most operations had been conducted by the South Vietnamese, and reporters would identify themselves this way so that they would not be mistaken for American advisors and shot by the ARVN during the routine hysteria of routine retreats.

"Boy, if that ain't just like the Slopes," one of the Marines said, walking away from us.

Flynn was cleaning his camera lens with a length of Australian sweat scarf that he always wore into the field, but the least movement sent up a fine-grained dust that seemed to hang there without resettling, giving the light a greasy quality and caking in the corners of your eyes. The Marines were looking hard at Flynn and you could see that he was blowing their minds, the way he blew minds all over Vietnam.

He was (indeed) the Son of Captain Blood, but that didn't mean much to the grunts since most of them, the young ones, had barely even heard of Errol Flynn. It was just apparent to anyone who looked at him that he was what the Marines would call "a dude who definitely had his shit together." All four of us on the ridge looked more or less as though we belonged there; the AP's John Lengle had covered every major Marine operation of the past eighteen months, Nick Wheeler of UPI had been around for two years, I'd had the better part of a year in now, we were all nearly young enough to be mistaken for grunts ourselves, but Flynn was special. We all had our movie-fed war fantasies, the Marines too, and it could be totally disorienting to have this outrageously glamorous figure intrude on them, really unhinging, like looking up to see that you've been sharing a slit trench with John Wayne or William Bendix. But you got used to that part of Flynn quickly.

When he'd first arrived in Vietnam in the summer of 1965, he had been considered news himself, and a lot of stories were written about his early trips into combat. Most of them managed to include all the clichés, all of them called him "swashbuckling." There were still a lot of easy things to say about him, and a lot of people around who were more than willing to say them, but after you knew him all of that talk just depressed you. There were a number of serious (heavy) journalists who could not afford to admit that anyone who looked as good as Flynn looked could possibly have anything more going for him. They chose not to take him as seriously as they took themselves (which was fine with Sean), and they accused him of coming to Vietnam to play, as though the war was like Africa had been for him, or the South of France or one of the places he'd gone to make those movies that people were always judging him by. But there were a lot of people in Vietnam who were playing, more than the heavies cared to admit, and Flynn's playing was done only on the most earnest levels. He wasn't much different from the rest; he was deeply fascinated by war, by *this* war, but he admitted it, knew where he stood in it, and he behaved as though it was nothing to be ashamed of. It gave him a vision of Vietnam that was profound, black and definitive, a knowledge of its wildness that very few of his detractors would have understood. All of this was very obvious in his face, particularly the wildness, but those people only saw it as handsome, making you realize that, as a group, newspapermen were not necessarily any more observant or imaginative than accountants. Flynn moved on and found his friends among those who never asked him to explain himself, among the GI's and the Apaches of the press corps, and he established his own celebrity there. (There would be occasional intrusions: embarrassingly deferential information officers, or a run-in with Colonel George Patton, Jr., who put him through one of those my-father-knew-your-father trials.) The grunts were always glad to see him. They'd call him "Seen," a lot of them, and tell him that they'd caught one of his flicks on R&R in Singapore or Taiwan, something that only a grunt could bring up and get away with, since all of that was finished for Flynn, the dues-paying and the accommodations, and he didn't like to talk about it. Sometime during his years in Vietnam, he realized that there really were people whom he cared for and could trust, it must have been a gift he'd never expected to have, and it made him someone who his father, on the best day he ever had, could have envied.

It was still a little too soon for the Marines to just sit down and start talking, they would have to probe a little more first, and we were getting bored. By the time they had finished cutting the lz there was no cover left from the sun, and we were all anxious for the scouting platoon to reach the top so that we could get together with Dana Stone, put a little pressure on for a helicopter and get out. The trip back to the press center in Danang could take two hours or two days, depending on what was flying, but it was certain to go faster with Stone along because he had friends at every airfield and chopper pad in I Corps. Danang was Soul City for many of us, it had showers and drinks, flash-frozen air-freighted steaks, air-conditioned rooms and China Beach and, for Stone, a real home—a wife, a dog, a small house full of familiar possessions. Mutter's Ridge had sickening heat, a rapidly vanishing water supply and boredom, so there really wasn't any choice. Judging by the weathered, blackened bits of ammunition casing (theirs and ours) that littered the ground around us, the ridge also had a history, and Dana had told us something about it.

Stone was a lapsed logger from Vermont (he always spoke about going back to that, especially after a bad day in the field, screw all this bullshit), twenty-five years old with sixty-year-old eyes set in deep behind wire-rimmed glasses, their shrewdness and experience almost lost in the lean anglings of his face. We knew for certain that he would be walking well ahead of the rest of the platoon on the trail, standard Dana and a break for the Marines, since he was easily the best-equipped man in the party for spotting booby traps or ambushes. But that had nothing to do with his being on point. Dana was the man in motion, he just couldn't slow himself down; he was the smallest man on the trail, but his engines would drive him up it as though the incline ran the other way. GI's who had forgotten his name would describe him for you as "that wiry little red-headed cat, *crazy* motherfucker, funny as a bastard," and Stone *was* funny, making you pay for every laugh he gave you. Hard mischief was his specialty—a thumb stuck abruptly into your egg yolk at breakfast or your brandy at dinner, rocks lobbed onto the metal roof of your room at the press center, flaming trails of lighter fluid rampaging across the floor toward you, a can of ham and limas substituted for peaches in syrup when you were practically dying of thirst—all Dana's way of saying hello, doing you good by doing you in. He'd wake you at dawn, shaking you violently and saying, "Listen, I need your glasses for just a minute, it's really important," splitting with them for an hour. He also took beautiful pictures (he called them "snaps" in accordance with the wire-service ethic which said you must never reveal your pride in good work) and in almost three years as a combat photographer he'd spent more time on operations than anyone else I knew, getting his cameras literally blown off his back more than once but keeping otherwise unhurt. By now, there was nothing that could happen around him in the field that he hadn't seen before, and if his joking was belligerent and even ghastly, you knew at least where it came from, saw the health that it carried. And that morning, waiting by the base-camp airstrip for the assault to begin, he started to tell us about the other time he'd been up on Mutter's Ridge, in the days before it even had a name. It had been, in fact, two years ago *to the day*, he'd said, on that *exact same ridge*. He'd gone up there with the 9th that time, and they'd *really stepped in deep shit*. (It was true, we all knew it was true, he was doing it to us again, and a smile showed for just an instant on his face.) They had been pinned down on the ridge all night long without support or re-supply or medevac, and the *casualties* had been *unbelievable*, running somewhere around 70 percent. Flynn laughed and said, "Dana, you bastard," but Stone would have gone on like that in his flat Vermont voice, telling it to those of us about to go up there as though it were nothing more than the history of a racehorse, except that he looked up and saw that we weren't alone; a few of the guys from Kilo Company had come over to ask questions about our cameras or something, and they'd heard some of it. Stone turned a deep red, as he always did when he realized that he'd gone a little too far. "Aw, that was just a bunch of shit, I never even been *near* that ridge," he said, and he pointed to me. "I was just trying to get him uptight because this is his last operation, and he's already fucked up about it." He laughed, but he was looking at the ground.

Now, while we waited for him, a Marine came up to Lengle and me and asked if we'd like to look at some pictures he'd taken. Marines felt comfortable around Lengle, who looked like a college basketball star, six-seven and very young (actually, he was thirty), a Nevadan who'd parlayed a nice-kid image into a valuable professional asset. The pictures were in a little imitation-leather folder, and you could tell by the way the Marine stood over us, grinning in anticipation as we flipped over each plastic page, that it was among his favorite things. (He'd also taken some "number-one souvenirs," he said, leaving the details to our imaginations.) There were hundreds of these albums in Vietnam, thousands, and they all seemed to contain the same pictures: the obligatory Zippo-lighter shot ("All right, let's burn these hootches and move out"); the severed-head shot, the head often resting on the chest of the dead man or being held up by a smiling Marine, or a lot of heads, arranged in a row, with a burning cigarette in each of the mouths, the eyes open ("Like they're *lookin'* at you, man, it's scary"); the VC suspect being dragged over the dust by a half-track or being hung by his heels in some jungle clearing; the very young dead with AK-47's still in their hands ("How old would you say that kid was?" the grunts would ask. "Twelve, thirteen? You just can't tell with gooks"); a picture of a Marine holding an ear or maybe two ears or, as in the case of a guy I knew near Pleiku, a whole necklace made of ears, "love beads" as its owner called them; and the one we were looking at now, the dead Viet Cong girl with her pajamas stripped off and her legs raised stiffly in the air.

"No more boom-boom for that mamma-san," the Marine said, that same, tired remark you heard every time the dead turned out to be women. It was so routine that I don't think he even realized that he'd said it.

"You posed that one," Lengle said.

"Not me," the Marine said, laughing.

"Now come on, you rascal. You mean you found her just like that?"

"Well, some other guy fixed her that way, and it was funny, 'cause that guy got zapped later on the same day. But look, look at that bitch there, cut right in half!"

"Oh, that's a honey," John said, "really terrific."

"I was thinkin' about sending some in to the *Stars and Stripes*. You think the *Stripes* would run 'em?"

"Well . . ." We were laughing now, what could you do? Half the combat troops in Vietnam had these things in their packs, snapshots were the least of what they took after a fight, at least pictures didn't rot. I'd talked to a Marine who'd taken a lot of pictures after an operation on the Cua Viet River, and later, when he was getting short and nervous about things, he'd brought them to the chaplain. But the chaplain had only told him that it was forgivable and put the pictures in his drawer and kept them.

A couple of Marines were talking to Flynn and Wheeler about their cameras, the best place to buy this lens, the right speed to use for that shot, I couldn't follow any of it. The grunts were hip enough to the media to take photographers more seriously than reporters, and I'd met officers who refused to believe that I was really a correspondent because I never carried cameras. (During a recent operation, this had almost gotten me bumped from the Command chopper because the colonel, for reasons of his own, was partial to photographers. On that one, a company of his battalion had made contact with a company of Viet Cong and forced them out on a promontory, holding them there between their fire and the sea for the gunships to kill. This particular colonel loved to order the chopper in very low so that he could fire his .45 into the Cong, and he'd always wanted pictures of it. He was doubly disappointed that day; I'd not only turned up without a camera, but by the time we got there all the VC were dead, about 150 of them littered across the beach and bobbing in and out with the waves. But he fired off a few clips anyway, just to keep his piece working.)

Marines were all around us now, about fifteen of them, and one, a short, heavy kid with a flat, dark face and the bearing of an overdeveloped troll, came up and looked hard at us.

"You guys're reporters, huh? Boy, you really get it all fucked up," he said. "My old man sends me stuff from the papers, and he thinks you're all full of shit."

A couple of Marines booed him, most of them laughed. Lengle laughed too. "Well, podner, what can I tell you? I mean, we try, we really take a shot at it."

"Then why can't you guys just tell it right?"

"Fuckin' Krynski," someone said, hitting the kid hard on the back of the head. According to his helmet, it was the Avenger himself, and he'd come to work for us now, just in time. He looked like a freshman in divinity school—clear blue eyes, smooth snub nose, cornsilk hair and a look of such trust and innocence that you hoped there would always be someone around to take care of him. He seemed terribly embarrassed about what had just been said to us.

"Don't you listen to that asshole," he said. "God *damn*, Krynski, you don't know any fuckin' thing about it. These guys are number-one dudes, and that's no shit."

"Thank you, friend," Lengle said.

"I didn't mean nothin'," Krynski said. "Don't go gettin' your balls in an uproar."

But the Avenger wasn't letting it go. "Man, these guys take plenty of chances, they eat C's just like us, and sleep in the mud, and all that good shit. They don't have to stand around here and listen to you bitch. They don't even have to be here at all!"

"Now what's *that* supposed to mean?" Krynski said, looking really puzzled. "You mean you guys *volunteer* to come over here?"

"Well, dumb shit, what'd you think?" the Avenger said. "You think they're just some dumb grunt like you?"

"Oh man, you *got* to be kidding me. You guys *asked* to come here?"

"Sure."

"How long do you have to stay?" he asked.

"As long as we want."

"Wish *I* could stay as long as *I* want," the Marine called Love Child said. "*I'd* been home las' March."

"When did you get here?" I asked.

"Las' March."

The lieutenant who had been supervising the blasting looked down from the lz and yelled for someone named Collins.

"Yes Sir?" the Avenger said.

"Collins, get your bod up here."

"Yes Sir."

There was some movement on the lz now, the platoon had reached the clearing. Stone came out first, backing out very fast with his camera up, referring quickly to the ground just behind him between shots. Four Marines came out next, carrying a fifth on an improvised litter. They brought him to the center of the clearing and set him down carefully on the grass. We thought at first that he was dead, taken off by a booby trap on the trail, but his color was much too awful for that. Even the dead held some horrible light that seemed to recede, vanishing through one layer of skin at a time and taking a long time to go completely, but this kid had no color about him anywhere. It was incredible that anything so motionless and white could still be alive.

"Collins," the lieutenant said, "you go find the Old Man. Tell him we've got a real serious heat casualty here. Remember, tell him serious."

"Yes Sir," the Avenger said, starting at a slow run along the ridge toward the CP.

Dana took a few more pictures and then sat down to change film. His fatigues were completely darkened with sweat, but except for that he showed no signs of exertion. The rest of the column was coming off of the trail now, dropping in the clearing like sniper victims, the packs going first, staggering a few feet and falling. A few were smiling up at the sun like happy dreamers, more went face down and stopped moving except for some twitching in their legs, and the radio man made it all the way across the clearing to the commo section, where he eased the equipment from his back slowly, set his helmet very carefully on the ground for a pillow after picking his spot, and immediately fell asleep.

Stone ran over and photographed him. "You guys know something?" he said.

"What's that?"

"It's hotter than a bastard."

"Thanks."

We could see the colonel approaching, a short, balding man with flinty eyes and a brief black mustache. He was trussed up tightly in his flak jacket, and as he came toward us small groups of Marines broke and ran to get their flak jackets on too, before the colonel could have the chance to tell them about it. The colonel leaned over and looked hard at the unconscious Marine, who was lying now in the shade of a poncho being held over him by two corpsmen, while a third brushed his chest and face with water from a canteen.

Well hell, the colonel was saying, there's nothing the matter with that man, feed some salt into him, get him up, get him walking, this is the Marines, not the goddamned Girl Scouts, there won't be any damned chopper coming in *here* today. (The four of us must have looked a little stricken at this, and Dana took our picture. We were really pulling for the kid; if he stayed, we stayed, and that meant all night.) The corpsmen were trying to tell the colonel that this was no ordinary case of heat exhaustion, excusing themselves but staying firm about it, refusing to let the colonel return to the CP. (The four of us smiled and Dana took a picture. "Go away, Stone," Flynn said. "Hold it just like that," Stone said, running in for a closeup so that his lens was an inch away from Flynn's nose. "One more.") The Marine looked awful lying there, trying to work his lips a little, and the colonel glared down at the fragile, still form as though it was blackmailing him. When the Marine refused to move anything except his lips for fifteen minutes, the colonel began to relent. He asked the corpsmen if they'd ever heard of a man dying from something like this.

"Oh, yes Sir. Oh, wow, I mean he really needs more attention than what we can give him here."

"Mmmmmm . . ." the colonel said. Then he authorized the chopper request and strode with what I'm sure he considered great determination back to his CP.

"I think it would have made him feel better if he could have shot the kid," Flynn said.

"Or one of us," I said.

"You're just lucky he didn't get you last night," Flynn said.

The evening before, when Flynn and I had arrived together at the base camp, the colonel had taken us into the Command bunker to show us some maps and explain the operation, and a captain had given us some coffee in Styrofoam cups. I'd carried mine outside and finished it while we talked to the colonel, who was being very hale and friendly in a way I'd seen before and didn't really trust. I was looking around for some place to toss the empty cup, and the colonel noticed it.

"Give it here," he offered.

"Oh, that's okay, Colonel, thanks."

"No, come on, I'll take it."

"No, really, I'll just find a—"

"Give it to me!" he said, and I did, but Flynn and I were afraid to look at each other until he'd returned underground, and then we broke up, exchanging the worst colonel stories we knew. I told him about the colonel who had threatened to court-martial a spec 4 for refusing to cut the heart out of a dead Viet Cong and feed it to a dog, and Flynn told me about a colonel in the American Division (which Flynn always said was sponsored by General Foods) who believed that every man under his command needed combat experience; he made the cooks and the clerks and the supply men and the drivers all take M-16's and go out on night patrol, and one time all of his cooks got wiped out in an ambush.

We could hear the sound of our Chinook coming in now, and we were checking to see if we had all of our gear, when I took a sudden terrible flash, some total dread, and I looked at everyone and everything in sight to see if there was some real source. Stone had been telling the truth about this being my last operation, I was as strung out as anybody on a last operation, there was nothing between here and Saigon that didn't scare me now, but this was different, it was something else.

"Fuckin' heat . . . ," someone said. "I . . . oh, man, I just . . . can't . . . fuckin' . . . *make it!*"

It was a Marine, and as soon as I saw him I realized that I'd seen him before, a minute or so ago, standing on the edge of the clearing staring at us as we got ourselves ready to leave.

He'd been with a lot of other Marines there, but I'd seen him much more distinctly than the others without realizing or admitting it. The others had been looking at us too, with amusement or curiosity or envy (we were splitting, casualties and correspondents this way out, we were going to Danang), they were all more or less friendly, but this one was different, I'd seen it, known it and passed it over, but not really. He was walking by us now, and I saw that he had a deep, running blister that seemed to have opened and eaten away much of his lower lip. That wasn't the thing that had made him stand out before, though. If I'd noticed it at all, it might have made him seem a little more wretched than the others, but nothing more. He stopped for a second and looked at us, and he smiled some terrifying, evil smile, his look turned now to the purest hatred.

"You fucking guys," he said. "You guys are *crazy!*"

There was the most awful urgency to the way he said it. He was still glaring, I expected him to raise a finger and touch each of us with destruction and decay, and I realized that after all this time, the war still offered at least one thing that I had to turn my eyes from. I had seen it before and hoped never to see it again, I had misunderstood it and been hurt by it, I thought I had finally worked it out for good and I was looking at it now, knowing what it meant and feeling as helpless under it this last time as I had the first.

All right, yes, it had been a groove being a war correspondent, hanging out with the grunts and getting close to the war, touching it, losing yourself in it and trying yourself against it. I had always wanted that, never mind why, it had just been a thing of mine, the way this movie is a thing of mine, and I'd done it; I was in many ways brother to these poor, tired grunts, I knew what they knew now, I'd done it and it was really something. Everywhere I'd gone, there had always been Marines or soldiers who would tell me what the Avenger had told Krynski, *You're all right, man, you guys are cool, you got balls.* They didn't always know what to think about you or what to say to you, they'd sometimes call you "Sir" until you had to beg them to stop, they'd sense the insanity of your position as terrified volunteer-reporter and it would seize them with the giggles and even respect. If they dug you, they always saw that you knew that, and when you choppered out they'd say goodbye, wish you luck. They'd even thank you, some of them, and what could you say to that?

And always, they would ask you with an emotion whose intensity would shock you to please tell it, because they really did have the feeling that it wasn't being told for them, that they were going through all of this and that somehow no one back in the World knew about it. They may have been a bunch of dumb, brutal killer kids (a lot of correspondents privately felt that), but they were smart enough to know that much. There was a Marine in Hue who had come after me as I walked toward the truck that would take me to the airstrip, he'd been locked in that horror for nearly two weeks while I'd shuttled in and out for two or three days at a time. We knew each other by now, and when he caught up with me he grabbed my sleeve so violently that I thought he was going to accuse me or, worse, try to stop me from going. His face was all but blank with exhaustion, but he had enough feeling left to say, "Okay, man, you go on, you go on out of here you cocksucker, but I mean it, you tell it! You tell it, man. If you don't tell it . . ."

What a time they were having there, it had all broken down, one battalion had taken 60 percent casualties, all the original NCO's were gone, the grunts were telling their officers to go die, to go fuck themselves, to go find some other fools to run up those streets awhile, it was no place where I'd have to tell anyone not to call me "Sir." They understood that, they understood a lot more than I did, but nobody hated me there, not even when I was leaving. Three days later I came back and the fighting had dropped off, the casualties were down to nothing and the same Marine flashed me a victory sign that had nothing to do with the Marine Corps or the fading battle or the American flag that had gone up on the Citadel's south wall the day before, he slapped me on the back and poured me a drink from a bottle he'd found in one of the hootches somewhere. Even the ones who preferred not to be in your company, who despised what your work required or felt that you took your living from their deaths, who believed that all of us were traitors and liars and the creepiest kinds of parasites,

even they would cut back at the last and make their one con-
cession to what there was in us that we ourselves loved most:
"I got to give it to you, you guys got balls." Maybe they
meant just that and nothing more, we had our resources and
we made enough out of that to keep us going, turning the
most grudging admissions into decorations for valor, making
it all all right again.

But there was often that bad, bad moment to recall, the
look that made you look away, and in its hateful way it was
the purest single thing I'd ever known. There was no wonder
left in it anywhere, no amusement, it came out of nothing so
messy as morality or prejudice, it had no motive, no conscious
source. You would feel it coming out to you from under a
poncho hood or see it in a wounded soldier staring up at you
from a chopper floor, from men who were very scared or who
had just lost a friend, from some suffering apparition of a
grunt whose lip had been torn open by the sun, who just
couldn't make it in that heat.

At first, I got it all mixed up, I didn't understand and I felt
sorry for myself, misjudged. "Well fuck you too," I'd think.
"It could have been me just as easily, I take chances too, can't
you see that?" And then I realized that that was exactly what
it was all about, it explained itself as easily as that, another of
the war's dark revelations. They weren't judging me, they
weren't reproaching me, they didn't even mind me, not in
any personal way. They only hated me, hated me the way
you'd hate any hopeless fool who would put himself through
this thing when he had choices, any fool who had no more
need of his life than to play with it in this way.

"You guys are *crazy!*" that Marine had said, and I know
that when we flew off of Mutter's Ridge that afternoon he
stood there for a long time and watched us out of sight with
the same native loathing he'd shown us before, turning finally
to whoever was around, saying it maybe to himself, getting
out what I'd actually heard said once when a jeepload of correspondents had just driven away, leaving me there alone, one
rifleman turning to another and giving us all his hard, cold
wish:

"Those fucking guys," he'd said. "I hope they die."

II

Name me someone that's not a parasite,
And I'll go out and say a prayer for him.
—BOB DYLAN, "Visions of Johanna"

I keep thinking about all the kids who got wiped out by seventeen years of war movies before coming to Vietnam to get wiped out for good. You don't know what a media freak is until you've seen the way a few of those grunts would run around during a fight when they knew that there was a television crew nearby; they were actually making war movies in their heads, doing little guts-and-glory Leatherneck tap dances under fire, getting their pimples shot off for the networks. They were insane, but the war hadn't done that to them. Most combat troops stopped thinking of the war as an adventure after their first few firefights, but there were always the ones who couldn't let that go, these few who were up there doing numbers for the cameras. A lot of correspondents weren't much better. We'd all seen too many movies, stayed too long in Television City, years of media glut had made certain connections difficult. The first few times that I got fired at or saw combat deaths, nothing really happened, all the responses got locked in my head. It was the same familiar violence, only moved over to another medium; some kind of jungle play with giant helicopters and fantastic special effects, actors lying out there in canvas body bags waiting for the scene to end so they could get up again and walk it off. But that was some scene (you found out), there was no cutting it.

A lot of things had to be unlearned before you could learn anything at all, and even after you knew better you couldn't avoid the ways in which things got mixed, the war itself with those parts of the war that were just like the movies, just like *The Quiet American* or *Catch-22* (a Nam standard because it said that in a war everybody thinks that everybody else is crazy), just like all that combat footage from television ("We're taking fire from the treeline!" "Where?" "There!" "*Where*?" "Over *there*!" "Over WHERE?" "Over THERE!!") Flynn heard that go on for fifteen minutes once; we made it

an epiphany), your vision blurring, images jumping and falling
as though they were being received by a dropped camera,
hearing a hundred horrible sounds at once—screams, sobs,
hysterical shouting, a throbbing inside your head that threatened to take over, quavering voices trying to get the orders
out, the dulls and sharps of weapons going off (Lore: When
they're near they whistle, when they're really near they crack),
the thud of helicopter rotors, the tinny, clouded voice coming
over the radio, "Uh, that's a Rog, we mark your position,
over." And out. Far out.

That feedback stalked you all over Vietnam, it often threatened you with derangement, but somehow it always left you
a little saner than you had any right to expect. Sometimes its
intrusions could be subtle and ferocious. One afternoon during the battle for Hue, I was with David Greenway, a correspondent for *Time*, and we found it necessary to move from
one Marine position to another. We were directly across from
the south wall of the Citadel and airstrikes had dropped much
of it down into the street, bringing with it torn, stinking portions of some North Vietnamese who had been dug in there.
We had to make a run of something like 400 meters up that
street, and we knew that the entire way was open to sniper
fire, either from the standing sections of the wall on our right
or from the rooftops on our left. When we'd run to our present position an hour earlier, David had gone first, and it was
my turn now. We were crouching among some barren shrub-
bery with the Marines, and I turned to the guy next to me,
a black Marine, and said, "Listen, we're going to cut out now.
Will you cover us?" He gave me one of those amazed, penetrating looks. "You can go out there if you want to, baby,
but shee-it . . ." and he began putting out fire. David and I
ran all doubled over, taking cover every forty meters or so
behind boulder-sized chunks of smashed wall, and halfway
through it I started to laugh, looking at David and shaking
my head. David was the most urbane of correspondents, a
Bostonian of good family and impeccable education, something of a patrician even though he didn't care anything about
it. We were pretty good friends, and he was willing to take
my word for it that there was actually something funny, and
he laughed too.

"What is it?" he said.

"Oh man, do you realize that I just asked that guy back there to *cover us*?"

He looked at me with one eyebrow faintly cocked. "Yes," he said. "Yes, you did. Oh, isn't that *marvelous*!"

And we would have laughed all the way up the street, except that toward the end of it we had to pass a terrible thing, a house that had been collapsed by the bombing, bringing with it a young girl who lay stretched out dead on top of some broken wood. The whole thing was burning, and the flames were moving closer and closer to her bare feet. In a few minutes they were going to reach her, and from our concealment we were going to have to watch it. We agreed that anything was better than that and we finished the run, but only after David spun around, dropped to one knee and took a picture of it.

A few days after that, David's file from Hue appeared in *Time*, worked over into that uni-prose which all news magazines and papers maintained, placed somewhere among five or six other Vietnam stories that had come in that week from the five or six other reporters *Time* kept in Vietnam. About five months after that, a piece I'd written about the battle appeared in *Esquire*, turning up like some lost dispatch from the Crimea. I saw it in print for the first time on the day that we returned from Mutter's Ridge, while the issue of *Time* which carried David's story was on sale in Saigon and Danang within a week of the events described. (I remember that issue in particular because General Giap was on the cover and the South Vietnamese would not allow it to be sold until a black X was scrawled over each copy, disfiguring but hardly concealing Giap's face. People were doing weird things that Tet.) What all of this means is that, no matter how much I love the sound of it, there's no way that I can think of myself as a war correspondent without stopping to acknowledge the degree to which it's pure affectation. I never had to run back to any bureau office to file (or, worse, call it in from Danang over the knotted clot of military wires, "Working, operator, I said working, hello, working. . . . Oh, you moron, *working*!"). I never had to race out to the Danang airfield to get my film on the eight-o'clock scatback to Saigon; there wasn't any bu-reau, there wasn't any film, my ties to New York were as slight as my assignment was vague. I wasn't really an oddity in the press corps, but I was a peculiarity, an extremely privileged one. (An oddity was someone like the photographer John Schneider, who fixed a white flag to his handlebars and took a bike from the top of Hill 881 North over to Hill 881 South during a terrible battle, in what came to be known as Schnei-der's Ride; or the Korean cameraman who had spent four years in Spain as a matador, who spoke exquisite, limpid Cas-tilian and whom we called El Taikwando; or the Portuguese novelist who arrived at Khe Sanh in sports clothes, carrying a plaid suitcase, under the impression that field gear could be bought there.)

I'd run into Bernie Weinraub in Saigon, on his way to *The New York Times* bureau carrying a bunch of papers in his hand. He'd be coming back from a meeting with some of "the beautiful people" of the Joint U.S. Public Affairs Office, and he'd say, "I'm having a low-grade nervous breakdown right now. You can't really see it, but it's there. After you've been here awhile, you'll start having them too," laughing at the little bit of it that was true as much as at the part of it that had become our running joke. Between the heat and the ug-liness and the pressures of filing, the war out there and the JUSPAO flacks right here, Saigon could be overwhelmingly depressing, and Bernie often looked possessed by it, so gaunt and tired and underfed that he could have brought out the Jewish mother in a Palestinian guerrilla.

"Let's have a drink," I'd say.

"No, no, I can't. You know how it is, we on the *Times* . . ." He'd start to laugh. "I mean, *we* have to file every day. It's a terrible responsibility, there's so little time. . . . I hope you'll understand."

"Of course. I'm sorry, I just wasn't thinking."

"Thank you, thank you."

But it was fine for me to laugh; he was going back to work, to write a story that would be published in New York hours later, and I was going across the street to the terrace bar of the Continental Hotel for a drink, possibly to write a few leisurely notes, probably not. I was spared a great deal, and except for a small handful of men who took their professional responsibilities very solemnly, no one ever held that against me. Whatever they came to know about the war was one thing; I know how they tried to get it into their stories, how generous they were as teachers and how embittering it all could become.

Because they worked in the news media, for organizations that were ultimately reverential toward the institutions involved: the Office of the President, the Military, America at war and, most of all, the empty technology that characterized Vietnam. There is no way of remembering good friends without remembering the incredible demands put on them from offices thousands of miles away. (Whenever the news chiefs and network vice-presidents and foreign editors would dress up in their Abercrombie & Fitch combat gear and come by for a firsthand look, a real story would develop, Snow In The Tropics, and after three days of high-level briefings and helicopter rides, they'd go home convinced that the war was over, that their men in the field were damned good men but a little too close to the story.) Somewhere on the periphery of that total Vietnam issue whose daily reports made the morning papers too heavy to bear, lost in the surreal contexts of television, there was a story that was as simple as it had always been, men hunting men, a hideous war and all kinds of victims. But there was also a Command that didn't feel this, that rode us into attrition traps on the back of fictional kill ratios, and an Administration that believed the Command, a cross-fertilization of ignorance, and a press whose tradition of objectivity and fairness (not to mention self-interest) saw that all of it got space. It was inevitable that once the media took the diversions seriously enough to report them, they also legitimized them. The spokesmen spoke in words that had no currency left as words, sentences with no hope of meaning in the sane world, and if much of it was sharply queried by the press, all of it got quoted. The press got all the facts (more or less), it got too many of them. But it never found a way to report meaningfully about death, which of course was really what it was all about. The most repulsive, transparent gropes for sanctity in the midst of the killing received serious treatment in the papers and on the air. The jargon of Progress got blown into your head like bullets, and by the time you waded through all the Washington stories and all the Saigon stories, all the Other War stories and the corruption stories and the stories about brisk new gains in ARVN effectiveness, the suffering was somehow unimpressive. And after enough years of that, so many that it seemed to have been going on forever, you got to a point where you could sit there in the evening and listen to the man say that American casualties for the week had reached a six-week low, only eighty GI's had died in combat, and you'd feel like you'd just gotten a bargain.

If you ever saw stories written by Peter Kann, William Tuohy, Tom Buckley, Bernie Weinraub, Peter Arnett, Lee Lescaze, Peter Braestrup, Charles Mohr, Ward Just or a few others, you'd know that most of what the Mission wanted to say to the American public was a psychotic vaudeville; that Pacification, for example, was hardly anything more than a swollen, computerized tit being forced upon an already violated population, a costly, valueless program that worked only in press conferences. Yet in the year leading up to the Tet Offensive ("1967—Year of Progress" was the name of an official year-end report) there were more stories about Pacification than there were about combat—front page, prime time, just as though it was really happening.

This was all part of a process which everyone I knew came grudgingly to think of as routine, and I was free of it. What an incredible hassle it would have been, having to run out to the airport to watch the Mayor of Los Angeles embrace Mayor Cua of Saigon. (L.A. had declared Saigon its Sister City, dig it, and Yorty was in town to collect. If there had been no newspapers or television, Cua and Yorty never would have met.) I never had to cover luncheons given for members of the Philippine Civic Action Group or laugh woodenly while the Polish delegate to the International Control Commission lobbed a joke on me. I never had to follow the Command to the field for those interminable get-togethers with the troops. ("Where are you from, son?" "Macon, Georgia, Sir." "Real fine. Are you getting your mail okay, plenty of hot meals?" "Yes, Sir." "That's fine, where you from, son?" "Oh, I don't know, God, I don't know, I don't *know!*" "That's fine, real fine, where you from, son?") I never had to become familiar with that maze of government agencies and sub-agencies, I never had to deal with the Spooks. (They were from the real Agency, the CIA. There was an endless Vietnam game played between the grunts and the Spooks, and the grunts always lost.) Except to pick up my mail and get my accreditation renewed, I never had to frequent JUSPAO unless I wanted to. (That office had been created to handle press relations and psychological warfare, and I never met anyone there who seemed to realize that there was a difference.) I could skip the daily briefings, I never had to cultivate Sources. In fact, my concerns were so rarefied that I had to ask other correspondents what they ever found to ask Westmoreland, Bunker, Komer and Zorthian. (Barry Zorthian was the head of JUSPAO; for more than five years he *was* Information.) What did anybody ever expect those people to *say*? No matter how highly placed they were, they were still officials, their views were well established and well known, famous. It could have rained frogs over Tan Son Nhut and they wouldn't have been upset; Cam Ranh Bay could have dropped into the South China Sea and they would have found some way to make it sound good for you; the Bo Doi Division (Ho's Own) could have marched by the American embassy and they would have characterized it as "desperate"—what did even the reporters closest to the Mission Council ever find to write about when they'd finished their interviews? (My own interview with General Westmoreland had been hopelessly awkward. He'd noticed that I was accredited to *Esquire* and asked me if I planned to be doing "humoristical" pieces. Beyond that, very little was really said. I came away feeling as though I'd just had a conversation with a man who touches a chair and says, "This is a chair," points to a desk and says, "This is a desk." I couldn't think of anything to ask him, and the interview didn't happen.) I honestly wanted to know what the form was for those interviews, but some of the reporters I'd ask would get very officious, saying something about "Command postures," and look at me as though I was insane. It was probably the kind of look that I gave one of them when he asked me once what I found to talk about with the grunts all the time, expecting me to confide (I think) that I found them as boring as he did.

And just-like-in-the-movies, there were a lot of correspondents who did their work, met their deadlines, filled the most preposterous assignments the best they could and withdrew, watching the war and all its hideous secrets, earning their cynicism the hard way and turning their self-contempt back out again in laughter. If New York wanted to know how the troops felt about the assassination of Robert Kennedy, they'd go out and get it. ("Would you have voted for him?" "Yeah, he was a real good man, a real good man. He was, uh, young." "Who will you vote for now?" "Wallace, I guess.") They'd even gather troop reflections on the choice of Paris as the site of the peace talks. ("Paris? I dunno, sure, why not? I mean, they ain't gonna hold 'em in Hanoi, now are they?"), but they'd know how funny that was, how wasteful, how profane. They knew that, no matter how honestly they worked, their best work would somehow be lost in the wash of news, all the facts, all the Vietnam stories. Conventional journalism could no more reveal this war than conventional firepower could win it, all it could do was take the most profound event of the American decade and turn it into a communications pudding, taking its most obvious, undeniable history and making it into a secret history. And the very best correspondents knew even more than that.

There was a song by the Mothers of Invention called "Trouble Comin' Every Day" that became a kind of anthem among a group of around twenty young correspondents. We'd play it often during those long night gatherings in Saigon, the ashtrays heaped over, ice buckets full of warm water, bottles empty, the grass all gone, the words running, "You know I watch that rotten box until my head begin to hurt, From checkin' out the way the newsmen say they get the dirt" (bitter funny looks passing around the room), "And if another woman driver gets machine-gunned from her seat, They'll send some joker with a Brownie and you'll see it all complete" (lip-biting, flinching, nervous laughter), "And if the place blows up, we'll be the first to tell, 'Cause the boys we got downtown are workin' hard and doin' swell . . ." That wasn't really about *us*, no, we were *so* hip, and we'd laugh and wince every time we heard it, all of us, wire-service photographers and senior correspondents from the networks and special-

assignment types like myself, all grinning together because of
what we knew together, that in back of every column of print
you read about Vietnam there was a dripping, laughing death-
face; it hid there in the newspapers and magazines and held
to your television screens for hours after the set was turned
off for the night, an after-image that simply wanted to tell you
at last what somehow had not been told.

On an afternoon shortly before the New Year, a few weeks
before Tet, a special briefing was held in Saigon to announce
the latest revisions in the hamlet-rating system of the Pacification program, the A-B-C-D profiling of the country's security and, by heavy inference, of the government's popular
support "in the countryside," which meant any place outside
of Saigon, the boonies. A lot of correspondents went, many
because they had to, and I spent the time with a couple of
photographers in one of the bars on Tu Do, talking to some
soldiers from the 1st Infantry Division who had come down
from their headquarters at Lai Khe for the day. One of them
was saying that Americans treated the Vietnamese like animals.

"How's that?" someone asked.

"Well, you know what we do to animals . . . kill 'em and
hurt 'em and beat on 'em so's we can train 'em. Shit, we don't
treat the Dinks no different than that."

And we knew that he was telling the truth. You only had
to look at his face to see that he really knew what he was
talking about. He wasn't judging it, I don't think that he was
even particularly upset about it, it was just something he'd
observed. We mentioned it later to some people who'd been
at the Pacification briefing, someone from the *Times* and
someone from the AP, and they both agreed that the kid from
the Big Red One had said more about the Hearts-and-Minds
program than they'd heard in over an hour of statistics, but
their bureaus couldn't use his story, they wanted Ambassador
Komer's. And they got it and you got it.

I could let you go on thinking that we were all brave, witty,
attractive and vaguely tragic, that we were like some in-
comparable commando team, some hot-shit squadron, the
Dreaded Chi, danger-loving, tender and wise. I could use it
myself, it would certainly make for a prettier movie, but all

of this talk about "we" and "us" has got to get straightened out.

At the height of the Tet Offensive alone, there were between 600 and 700 correspondents accredited to the Military Assistance Command, Vietnam. Who all of them were and where all of them went was as much a mystery to me and to most of the correspondents I knew as it was to the gentle-tempered bull-faced Marine gunnery sergeant assigned to the department of JUSPAO which issued those little plastic-coated MACV accreditation cards. He'd hand them out and add their number to a small blackboard on the wall and then stare at the total in amused wonder, telling you that he thought it was all a fucking circus. (He's the same man who told a television star, "Hold on to your ass awhile. You people from the electronic media don't scare me anymore.") There was nothing exclusive about that card or its operational match, the Bao Chi credential of the Republic of South Vietnam; thousands of them must have been issued over the years. All they did was admit you to the Vietnam press corps and tell you that you could go out and cover the war if you really wanted to. All kinds of people have held them at one time or another: feature writers for religious organs and gun magazines, summer vacationers from college newspapers (one paper sent two, a Hawk and a Dove, and we put it down because it hadn't sent a Moderate over as well), second-string literary figures who wrote about how they hated the war more than you or I ever could, syndicated eminences who houseguested with Westmoreland or Bunker and covered operations in the presence of Staff, privileges which permitted them to chronicle fully our great victory at Tet, and to publish evidence year after year after year that the back of the Cong had been broken, Hanoi's will dissolved. There was no nation too impoverished, no hometown paper so humble that it didn't get its man in for a quick feel at least once. The latter tended to be the sort of old reporter that most young reporters I knew were afraid of becoming someday. You'd run into them once in a while at the bar of the Danang press center, men in their late forties who hadn't had the chance to slip into uniform since V-J Day, exhausted and bewildered after all of those briefings and lightning visits, punchy from the sheer volume of

facts that had been thrown on them, their tape recorders broken, their pens stolen by street kids, their time almost up.
They'd been to see Cam Ranh Bay and quite a bit of the
countryside (Mission diction, which meant that they'd been
taken out to look at model or "New Life" hamlets), a crack
ARVN division (where?), even some of our boys right there
at the front (where?), and a lot of Military Information Office
people. They seemed too awed by the importance of the
whole thing to be very clear, they were too shy to make
friends, they were all alone and speechless, except to say,
"Well, when I came over here I thought it was pretty hopeless,
but I have to admit, it looks like we've gotten things pretty
much under control. I must say, I've been awfully impressed
. . ." There were a lot of hacks who wrote down every word
that the generals and officials told them to write, and a lot for
whom Vietnam was nothing more than an important career
station. There were some who couldn't make it and left after
a few days, some who couldn't make it the other way, staying
year after year, trying to piece together their very real hatred
of the war with their great love for it, that rough reconciliation
that many of us had to look at. A few came through with the
grisliest hang-ups, letting it all go every chance they got, like
the one who told me that he couldn't see what all the fuss
had been about, *his* M-16 never jammed. There were Frenchmen who'd parachuted into Dien Bien Phu during what they
loved to call "the First Indochina War," Englishmen sprung
alive from *Scoop* (a press-corps standard because it said that if
the papers didn't get it, it didn't happen), Italians whose only
previous experience had been shooting fashion, Koreans who
were running PX privileges into small fortunes, Japanese who
trailed so many wires that transistor jokes were inevitable,
Vietnamese who took up combat photography to avoid the
draft, Americans who spent all their days in Saigon drinking
at the bar of L'Amiral Restaurant with Air America pilots.
Some filed nothing but hometowners, some took the social
notes of the American community, some went in the field only
because they couldn't afford hotels, some never left their hotels. Taken all together, they accounted for most of the total
on Gunny's blackboard, which left a number of people, as
many as fifty, who were gifted or honest or especially kind and

who gave journalism a better name than it deserved, particularly in Vietnam. Finally, the press corps was as diffuse and faceless as any regiment in the war, the main difference being that many of us remained on our own orders.

It was a characteristic of a lot of Americans in Vietnam to have no idea of when they were being obscene, and some correspondents fell into that, writing their stories from the daily releases and battlegrams, tracking them through with the cheer-crazed language of the MACV Information Office, things like "discreet burst" (one of those tore an old grandfather and two children to bits as they ran along a paddy wall one day, at least according to the report made later by the gunship pilot), "friendly casualties" (not warm, not fun), "meeting engagement" (ambush), concluding usually with 17 or 117 or 317 enemy dead and American losses "described as light." There were correspondents who had the same sensibility concerning the dead as the Command had: Well, in a war you've got to expect a little mud to get tracked over the carpet, we took a real black eye but we sure gave Charlie a shitstorm, we consider this a real fine kill ratio, real fine. . . . There was a well-known correspondent of three wars who used to walk around the Danang press center with a green accountant's ledger. He'd sit down to talk and begin writing everything you'd say, entering it in, so to speak. The Marines arranged for a special helicopter (or "fragged a chopper," as we used to call it) to take him in and out of Khe Sanh one afternoon, weeks after it had become peaceful again. He came back very cheerful about our great victory there. I was sitting with Lengle, and we recalled that, at the very least, 200 grunts had been blown away there and around 1,000 more wounded. He looked up from his ledger and said, "Oh, two hundred isn't anything. We lost more than that in an hour on Guadalcanal." We weren't going to deal with that, so we sort of left the table, but you heard that kind of talk all the time, as though it could invalidate the deaths at Khe Sanh, render them somehow less dead than the dead from Guadalcanal, as though light losses didn't lie as still as moderate losses or heavy losses. And these were American dead they were talking about; you should have heard them when the dead were Vietnamese.

So there we all were, no real villains and only a few heroes, a lot of adventurers and a lot of drudges, a lot of beautiful lunatics and a lot of normals, come to report what was ultimately the normals' war; and somehow, out of all that, a great number of us managed to find and recognize each other. You could be hard about it and deny that there was a brotherhood working there, but then what else could you call it? It wasn't just some wartime clique of buddies, it was too large in number for that, including members of at least a dozen cliques, some of them overlapping until they became indistinguishable, others standing in contemptuous opposition to one another; and it was far too small to incorporate the whole bloated, amorphous body of the Vietnam press corps. Its requirements were unstated because, other than sensibility and style, it had none. Elsewhere, it would have been just another scene, another crowd, but the war gave it urgency and made it a deep thing, so deep that we didn't even have to like one another to belong. There was a lot that went unsaid at the time, but just because it was seldom spoken didn't mean that we weren't very much aware of it or that, in that terrible, shelterless place, we weren't grateful for each other.

It made room for correspondents who were themselves members of Saigon's American Establishment, it included young marrieds, all kinds of girl reporters, a lot of Europeans, the Ivy-League-in-Asia crowd, the Danang bunch, the Straights and the Heads, formals and funkies, old hands (many of whom were very young) and even some tourists, people who wanted to go somewhere to screw around for a while and happened to choose the war. There was no way of thinking about "who we were" because we were all so different, but where we were alike we were really alike. It helped if you went out on operations a lot or if you were good at your work, but neither was very necessary as long as you knew something of what the war was (as opposed to what the Mission and MACV told you it was), and as long as you weren't a snob about it. We were all doing terribly upsetting work, it could often be very dangerous, and we were the only ones who could tell, among ourselves, whether that work was any good. Applause from home meant nothing next to a nice word from a colleague. (One reporter loved to call his New York superiors "those leg motherfuckers," taking from Airborne the term for anyone who was not jump-qualified; if you can appreciate the 4th Division Lurp who called himself "The Baptist" even though he was an Episcopalian, you get the idea.) We were all studying the same thing, and if you got killed you couldn't graduate.

We were serious enough about what we were doing over there, but we were also enchanted by it (not even the most uncomplicated farmboy pfc can go through a war without finding some use for it), and even when you got tired, felt you'd had too much, grown old in an afternoon, there were ways to take that and work it back into the style that we all tried to maintain. Things had to get really bad before you saw the war as clearly as most troops came to see it, but those times were rare enough and we (Those Crazy Guys . . .) were incorrigible. Most of us had times when we swore that we'd never go near any of it again if we could only be allowed out this once, everybody made those deals, but a few days in Danang or Saigon or even Hong Kong or Bangkok would get you over that, and the choice to go back was still there, still yours, priceless option, property of the press corps.

Friendships were made directly, with none of the clutter that had once seemed so necessary, and once they were made they outvalued all but your oldest, most special friendships. Your scene before Vietnam was unimportant, nobody wanted to hear about it, and we often seemed a little like those Green Berets out in their remote, harassed outposts, groups of eight or twelve Americans commanding hundreds of local mercenaries who could be as hostile as the Cong, who often *were* Cong; living together this way for months at a time without ever learning each other's first names or hometowns. You could make friends elsewhere, a Special Forces captain in the Delta, a grunt up in Phu Bai, some decent, witty (and usually suffering) member of the Embassy Political Section. But whether you hung out with them or with other correspondents, all you ever talked about anyway was the war, and they could come to seem like two very different wars after a while. Because who but another correspondent could talk the kind of mythical war that you wanted to hear described? (Just hearing the way Flynn pronounced the word "Vietnam," the tenderness and respect that he put in it, taught you more about the beauty and horror of the place than anything the apologists or explainers could ever teach you.) Who could you discuss politics with, except a colleague? (We all had roughly the same position on the war: we were in it, and that was a position.) Where else could you go for a real sense of the war's past? There were all kinds of people who knew the background, the facts, the most minute details, but only a correspondent could give you the exact mood that attended each of the major epochs: the animal terror of the Ia Drang or the ghastly breakdown of the first major Marine operation, code-named Starlight, where the Marines were dying so incredibly fast, so far beyond the Command's allowance, that one of them got zipped into a body bag and tossed to the top of a pile of KIA's while he was still alive. He regained consciousness up there and writhed and heaved until his bag rolled to the ground, where some corpsmen found him and saved him. The Triangle and Bong Son were as remote as the Reservoir or Chickamauga, you had to hear the history from somebody you could trust, and who else could you trust? And if you saw some piece of helmet graffiti that seemed to say everything, you weren't going to pass it along to some colonel or tell it to a Psyops official. "Born to Kill" placed in all innocence next to the peace symbol, or "A sucking chest wound is Nature's way of telling you that you've been in a firefight" was just too good to share with anyone but a real collector, and, with very few exceptions, those were all correspondents.

We shared a great many things: field gear, grass, whiskey, girls (that Men Without Women trip got old all the time), sources, information, hunches, tips, prestige (during my first days there bureau chiefs from *Life* and CBS took me around to introduce everyone they could think of, and somebody did as much for other new arrivals), we even shared each other's luck when our own seemed gone. I was no more superstitious than anyone else in Vietnam, I was very superstitious, and there were always a few who seemed so irrefutably charmed that nothing could make me picture them lying dead there; having someone like that with you on an operation could become more important than any actual considerations about what might be waiting on the ground for you. I doubt whether anything else could be as parasitic as that, or as intimate.

And by some equation that was so wonderful that I've never stopped to work it out, the best and the bravest correspondents were also usually the most compassionate, the ones who were most in touch with what they were doing. Greenway was like that, and so were Jack Laurence and Keith Kay, who worked together as a reporter-camera team for CBS for nearly two years. And there was Larry Burrows, who had been photographing the war for *Life* since 1962, a tall, deliberate Englishman of about forty with one of the most admirable reputations of all the Vietnam correspondents. We were together on one of the lz's that had been built for the operation that was supposedly relieving Khe Sanh, and Burrows had run down to take pictures of a Chinook that was coming in to land. The wind was strong enough to send tarmac strips flying fifty feet across the lz and he ran through it to work, photographing the crew, getting the soldiers coming down the incline to board the chopper, getting the kids throwing off the mailbags and cartons of rations and ammunition, getting the three wounded being lifted carefully on board, turning again to get the six dead in their closed body bags, then the rise of the chopper (the wind now was strong enough to tear papers out of your hand), photographing the grass blown flat all around him and the flying debris, taking one picture each of the chopper rearing, settling and departing. When it was gone he looked at me, and he seemed to be in the most open distress. "Sometimes one feels like such a bastard," he said.

And that was one more thing we shared. We had no secrets about it or the ways it could make you feel. We all talked about it at times, some talked about it too much, a few never seemed to talk about anything else. That was a drag, but it was all in the house; you only minded it when it came from outside. All kinds of thieves and killers managed to feel sanctimonious around us; battalion commanders, civilian businessmen, even the grunts, until they realized how few of us were making any real money in it. There's no way around it, if you photographed a dead Marine with a poncho over his face and got something for it, you were *some* kind of parasite.

But what were you if you pulled the poncho back first to make a better shot, and did that in front of his friends? Some other kind of parasite, I suppose. Then what were you if you stood there watching it, making a note to remember it later in case you might want to use it? Those combinations were infinite, you worked them out, and they involved only a small part of what we were thought to be. We were called thrill freaks, death-wishers, wound-seekers, war-lovers, hero-worshipers, closet queens, dope addicts, low-grade alcoholics, ghouls, communists, seditionists, more nasty things than I can re-member. There were people in the military who never forgave General Westmoreland for not imposing restrictions against us when he'd had the chance in the early days. There were officers and a lot of seemingly naïve troops who believed that if it were not for us, there would be no war now, and I was never able to argue with any of them on that point. A lot of the grunts had some of that sly, small-town suspicion of the press, but at least nobody under the rank of captain ever asked me whose side I was on, told me to get with the program, jump on the team, come in for the Big Win. Sometimes they were just stupid, sometimes it came about because they had such love for their men, but sooner or later all of us heard one version or another of "My Marines are winning this war, and you people are losing it for us in your papers," often spoken in an almost friendly way, but with the teeth shut tight behind the smiles. It was creepy, being despised in such casual, offhanded ways. And there were plenty of people who be-lieved, finally, that we were nothing more than glorified war profiteers. And perhaps we were, those of us who didn't get killed or wounded or otherwise fucked up.

Just in the regular course of things, a lot of correspondents took close calls. Getting scratched was one thing, it didn't mean that you'd come as close as you could have, it could have been closer without your even knowing it, like an early-morning walk I took once from the hilltop position of a Special Forces camp where I'd spent the night, down to the teamhouse at the foot of the hill, where I was going to have some coffee. I walked off the main trail onto a smaller trail and followed it until I saw the house and a group of eight giggling, wide-eyed Vietnamese mercenaries, Mikes, pointing at me and talking very excitedly. They all grabbed for me at once when I reached the bottom, and as it was explained to me a moment later, I'd just come down a trail which the Special Forces had rigged out with more than twenty booby traps, any one of which could have taken me off. (Any One Of Which ran through my head for days afterward.) If you went out often, just as surely as you'd eventually find yourself in a position where survival etiquette insisted that you take a weapon ("You know how this thang works 'n' airthang?" a young sergeant had to ask me once, and I'd had to nod as he threw it to me and said, "Then git some!", the American banzai), it was unavoidable that you'd find yourself almost getting killed. You expected something like that to happen, but not exactly that, not until events made things obvious for you. A close call was like a loss of noncombatant status: you weren't especially proud of it, you merely reported it to a friend and then stopped talking about it, knowing in the first place that the story would go around from there, and that there wasn't really anything to be said about it anyway. But that didn't stop you from thinking about it a lot, doing a lot of hideous projecting from it, forming a system of pocket metaphysics around it, getting it down to where you found yourself thinking about which *kind* of thing was closer: that walk down the hill, the plane you missed by minutes which blew apart on the Khe Sanh airstrip an hour later and fifty miles away, or the sniper round that kissed the back of your flak jacket as you grunted and heaved yourself over a low garden wall in Hue. And then your *Dawn Patrol* fantasy would turn very ugly, events again and again not quite what you had expected, and you'd realize that nothing ever came closer to death than the death of a good friend.

In the first week of May 1968, the Viet Cong staged a brief, vicious offensive against Saigon, taking and holding small positions on the fringes of Cholon and defending parts of the outlying areas that could be retaken only from the Y Bridge, from the racetrack grounds, from Plantation Road and the large French graveyard that ran for several hundred yards into a grove and a complex of Viet Cong bunkers. The offensive's value as pure revolutionary terror aside (those results were always incalculable, our good gear notwithstanding), it was more or less what MACV said it was, costly to the VC and largely a failure. It cost the Friendlies too (between Saigon and the A Shau, it was the week that saw more Americans killed than any other in the war), a lot more damage was done to the city's outskirts, more homes were bombed out. The papers called it either the May Offensive, the Mini-Offensive (you know I'm not making that up), or the Second Wave; it was the long-awaited Battle of Algiers-in-Saigon that had been manically predicted by the Americans for practically every weekend since the Tet Offensive had ended. In its early hours, five correspondents took a jeep into Cholon, past the first files of refugees (many of whom warned them to turn back), and into a Viet Cong ambush. One of them escaped (according to his own story) by playing dead and then running like an animal into the crowds of Cholon. He said that they had all yelled, "Bao Chi!" a number of times, but that they had been machine-gunned anyway.

It was more like death by misadventure than anything else, as if that mattered, and of the four dead correspondents, only one had been a stranger. Two of the others were good acquaintances, and the fourth was a friend. His name was John Cantwell, an Australian who worked for *Time*, and he had been one of the first friends I'd made in Vietnam. He was a kind, congenial mock-goat whose talk was usually about the most complex, unimaginable lecheries, architectural constructions of monumental erotic fantasies. He had a Chinese wife and two children in Hong Kong (he spoke fluent Chinese, he'd take it through the Cholon bars for us sometimes), and he was one of the few I knew who really hated Vietnam and the war, every bit of it. He was staying only long enough to earn the money to settle some debts, and then he was going to leave for good. He was a good, gentle, hilarious man, and to this day I can't help thinking that he wasn't *supposed* to get killed in Vietnam, getting killed in a war was not John's scene, he'd made no room for that the way some others had. A lot of people I had liked a lot, GI's and even some correspondents, had already died, but when Cantwell got murdered it did more than sadden and shock me. Because he was a friend, his death changed all the odds.

In that one brief period of less than two weeks it became a war of our convenience, a horrible convenience, but ours. We could jump into jeeps and minimokes at nine or ten and drive a few kilometers to where the fighting was, run around in it for a few hours and come back early. We'd sit on the Continental terrace and wave each other in, get stoned early and stay up late, since there was no question of 5:30 wake-ups. We'd been scattered all over Vietnam for months now, friends running into friends now and again, and this put everyone together. There was no other time when that was needed so badly. A day after John and the others died, a strange, death-charged kid named Charlie Eggleston, a UPI photographer, got killed at the Cemetery, reportedly while returning fire at a Viet Cong position. (He willed everything he had to Vietnamese charities.) A Japanese photographer was killed later that same day, a Brazilian lost a leg the day after that and somewhere in there another correspondent was killed; by then everyone had stopped counting and worked at keeping it away. Again in the Cemetery, a bullet tore through Co Rentmeester's hand and lodged under the eye of another photographer, Art Greenspahn. A Frenchman named Christien Simon-Pietrie (known as "Frenchy" to his movie-warped friends) was hit above the eye by some shrapnel from the same round which crippled General Loan; not a serious wound but one more out of too many, more than correspondents had ever received at one time. By the fifth day, eight had died and more than a dozen others had been wounded. We were driving toward the racetrack when an MP stepped in front of our car to ask for identification.

"Listen," he said, "I saw those four other guys and I never want to see any more like that. You know those guys? Then what the fuck do you want to go in there for? Don't you people ever learn? I mean, I *saw* those guys, believe me, it ain't worth it."

He was firm about not letting us through, but we insisted and he finally gave up.

"Well, I can't really stop you. You *know* I can't stop you. But if I could, I would. You wouldn't be driving up to no shit like those four guys."

In the early evenings we'd do exactly what correspondents

did in those terrible stories that would circulate in 1964 and
1965, we'd stand on the roof of the Caravelle Hotel having
drinks and watch the airstrikes across the river, so close that a
good telephoto lens would pick up the markings on the
planes. There were dozens of us up there, like aristocrats view-
ing Borodino from the heights, at least as detached about it
as that even though many of us had been caught under those
things from time to time. There'd be a lot of women up there,
a few of them correspondents (like Cathy Leroy, the French
photographer, and Jurati Kazikas, a correspondent of great,
fashion-model beauty), most of them the wives and girls of
reporters. Some people had tried hard to believe that Saigon
was just another city they'd come to live in; they'd formed
civilized social routines, tested restaurants, made and kept ap-
pointments, given parties, had love affairs. Many had even
brought their wives with them, and more often than not it
worked out badly. Very few of the women really liked Saigon,
and the rest became like most Western women in Asia: bored,
distracted, frightened, unhappy and, if left there too long,
fiercely frantic. And now, for the second time in three months,
Saigon had become unsafe. Rockets were dropping a block
from the best hotels, the White Mice (the Saigon police) were
having brief, hysterical firefights with shadows, you could hear
it going on as you dropped off to sleep; it was no longer
simply a stinking, corrupt, exhausting foreign city.

At night, the rooms of the Continental would fill with correspondents drifting in and out for a drink or a smoke before
bed, some talk and some music, the Rolling Stones singing,
"It's so very lonely, You're two thousand light years from
home," or "Please come see me in your Citadel," that word
putting a chill in the room. Whenever one of us came back
from an R&R we'd bring records, sounds were as precious as
water: Hendrix, the Airplane, Frank Zappa and the Mothers,
all the things that hadn't even started when we'd left the
States. Wilson Pickett, Junior Walker, *John Wesley Harding*,
one recording worn thin and replaced within a month, the
Grateful Dead (the name was enough), the Doors, with their
distant, icy sound. It seemed like such wintry music; you
could rest your forehead against the window where the air-
conditioner had cooled the glass, close your eyes and feel the

heat pressing against you from outside. Flares dropped over
possible targets three blocks away, and all night long, armed
jeeps and massive convoys moved down Tu Do Street toward
the river.

When we were down to a hard core of six or seven, we'd
talk tired, stoned talk about the war, imitating commanders
who were always saying things like, "Well, Charlie's dug in
there pretty good, but when we can get him out where we
can see him we find we're getting some real decent kills, we
got Charlie outgunned for sure, only thing is we can't kill him
if we can't see 'cause Charlie's always running. Come on, we'll
take you up and get you shot at." We talked about a disco-
theque we were going to open in Saigon, the Third Wave,
with a stainless-steel dance floor, blow-ups of the best war
photographs on the walls, a rock group called Westy and the
KIA's. (Our talk had about as much taste as the war did.) And
we'd talk about LZ Loon, the mythical place where it got dark
so fast that by the time you realized that there wouldn't be
another chopper in until morning, you'd already picked a
place to sleep for the night. Loon was the ultimate Vietnam
movie location, where all of the mad colonels and death-
spaced grunts we'd ever known showed up all at once, saying
all the terrible, heartbreaking things they always said, so nonchalant about the horror and fear that you knew you'd never
really be one of them no matter how long you stayed. You
honestly didn't know whether to laugh or cry. Few people
ever cried more than once there, and if you'd used that up,
you laughed; the young ones were so innocent and violent,
so sweet and so brutal, beautiful killers.

One morning, about twenty-five correspondents were out
by the Y Bridge working when a dying ARVN was driven by
on the back of a half-ton pick-up. The truck stopped at some
barbed wire, and we all gathered around to look at him. He
was nineteen or twenty and he'd been shot three times in the
chest. All of the photographers leaned in for pictures, there
was a television camera above him, we looked at him and then
at each other and then at the wounded Vietnamese again. He
opened his eyes briefly a few times and looked back at us. The
first time, he tried to smile (the Vietnamese did that when
they were embarrassed by the nearness of foreigners), then it

left him. I'm sure that he didn't even see us the last time he looked, but we all knew what it was that he'd seen just before that.

That was also the week that Page came back to Vietnam. *A Scrambler to the Front* by Tim Page, *Tim Page* by Charles Dickens. He came a few days before it started, and people who knew about his luck were making jokes blaming the whole thing on his return. There were more young, apolitically radical, wigged-out crazies running around Vietnam than anybody ever realized; between all of the grunts turning on and tripping out on the war and the substantial number of correspondents who were doing the same thing, it was an authentic subculture. There were more than enough within the press corps to withstand a little pressure from the upright, and if Flynn was the most sophisticated example of this, Page was the most extravagant. I'd heard about him even before I came to Vietnam ("Look him up. If he's still alive"), and between the time I got there and the time he came back in May, I'd heard so much about him that I might have felt that I knew him if so many people hadn't warned me, "There's just no way to describe him for you. Really, no way."

"Page? That's easy. Page is a child."

"No, man, Page is just crazy."

"Page is a crazy child."

They'd tell all kinds of stories about him, sometimes working up a passing anger over things he'd done years before, times when he'd freaked a little and become violent, but it always got softened, they'd pull back and say his name with great affection. "Page. Fucking Page."

He was an orphan boy from London, married at seventeen and divorced a year later. He worked his way across Europe as a cook in the hotels, drifting east through India, through Laos (where he claims to have dealt with the Spooks, a little teen-age espionage), into Vietnam at the age of twenty. One of the things that everybody said about him was that he had not been much of a photographer then (he'd picked up a camera the way you or I would pick up a ticket), but that he would go places for pictures that very few other photographers were going. People made him sound crazy and ambitious, like the Sixties Kid, a stone-cold freak in a country where the madness raced up the hills and into the jungles, where everything essential to learning Asia, war, drugs, the whole adventure, was close at hand.

The first time he got hit it was shrapnel in the legs and stomach. That was at Chu Lai, in '65. The next time was during the Buddhist riots of the 1966 Struggle Movement in Danang: head, back, arms, more shrapnel. (A *Paris-Match* photograph showed Flynn and a French photographer carrying him on a door, his face half covered by bandages, *"Tim Page, blessé à la tête."*) His friends began trying to talk him into leaving Vietnam, saying, "Hey, Page, there's an airstrike looking for you." And there was; it caught him drifting around off course in a Swift boat in the South China Sea, blowing it out of the water under the mistaken impression that it was a Viet Cong vessel. All but three of the crew were killed, Page took over 200 individual wounds, and he floated in the water for hours before he was finally rescued.

They were getting worse each time, and Page gave in to it. He left Vietnam, allegedly for good, and joined Flynn in Paris for a while. He went to the States from there, took some pictures for Time-Life, got busted with the Doors in New Haven, traveled across the country on his own (he still had some money left), doing a picture story which he planned to call "Winter in America." Shortly after the Tet Offensive, Flynn returned to Vietnam, and once Page heard that, it was only a matter of time. When he got back in May, his entrance requirements weren't in order, and the Vietnamese kept him at Tan Son Nhut for a couple of days, where his friends visited him and brought him things. The first time I met him he was giggling and doing an insane imitation of two Vietnamese immigration authorities fighting over the amount of money they were going to hold him up for, "Minh phung, auk nyong bgnyang gluke poo phuc fuck fart, I mean you should have *heard* those beastly people. Where am I going to sleep, who's got a rack for Page? The Dinks have been mucking about with Page, Page is a *very* tired boy."

He was twenty-three when I first met him, and I can remember wishing that I'd known him when he was still young. He was bent, beaten, scarred, he was everything by way of being crazy that everyone had said he was, except that you could tell that he'd never get really nasty again when he flipped. He was broke, so friends got him a place to sleep, gave him piastres, cigarettes, liquor, grass. Then he made a couple of thousand dollars on some fine pictures of the Offensive, and all of those things came back on us, twice over. That was the way the world was for Page; when he was broke you took care of him, when he was not he took care of you. It was above economics.

"Now, would Ellsworth Bunker like the Mothers of Invention?" he'd say. (He wanted to rig loudspeakers around the Lower House and along the park facing it and play the freakiest music he could find as loud as the equipment would permit.)

"On your head, Page," Flynn would say.

"No. I ask you, would William C. Westmoreland dig the Mothers or wouldn't he?"

His talk was endlessly referential, he mixed in images from the war, history, rock, Eastern religion, his travels, literature (he was very widely read and proud of it), but you came to see that he was really only talking about one thing, Page. He spoke of himself in the third person more than anyone I ever knew, but it was so totally ingenuous that it was never offensive. He could get very waspish and silly, he could be an outrageous snob (he was a great believer in the New Aristocracy), he could talk about people and things in ways that were nearly monstrous, stopping short of that and turning funny and often deeply tender. He carried all kinds of clippings around with him, pictures of himself, newspaper stories about the times he'd been wounded, a copy of a short story that Tom Mayer had written about him in which he got killed on an operation with the Korean Marines. He was especially vain about that story, very proud and completely spooked by it. That first week back, he'd had things brought around to where he could remember them again, remembering that you could get killed here, the way he almost had those other times, the way he had in the story.

"*Look* at you," he'd say, coming into the room at night. "Every one of you is *stoned*. Look at you, what are you doing there if it isn't rolling a joint? Grinning, Flynn, grinning is sinning. Dope is hope. Help! Give us a bit of that, will you? I ain't doin' no evil, give us just a toke. Ahhhhh, yesh! It *can't* be my turn to change the record because I've only just come in. Are any birds coming by? Where are Mimsy and Poopsy? [His names for two Australian girls who dropped over some evenings.] Women is good, women is necessary, women is definitely good for business. Yesh."

"Don't smoke that, Page. Your brain is already about the consistency of a soggy quiche lorraine."

"Nonsense, utter nonsense. Why don't you roll a five-handed joint while I prepare a steamboat for this ugly, filthy roach?" He'd jab his misshapen left index finger at you to underline key words, taking the conversation wherever his old child's whimsey took his thoughts, planning projects which ranged from full-scale guerrilla ops in New York City to painting the front of the hotel in Day-Glo colors in the belief that the Vietnamese would love it. "They're all stoned all the time anyway," he'd say. If any girls showed up, he'd tell them lurid stories about the war, about the Middle East (both he and Flynn had caught a couple of days of the June War, flying down from Paris for it), about venereal diseases he'd had, talking to them the way he'd talk to anybody. He only had one way of speaking, it could have been to me or the Queen, it didn't matter. ("What do you mean, of *course* I love the Queen. The Queen's a very lovable bird.") If he was too absorbed to talk, he'd stand in front of a full-length mirror and dance to the Doors for an hour at a time, completely lost in it.

When Saigon became quiet again during the third week of May, it seemed as though the war had ended. Nothing was happening anywhere, and I realized that after seven months straight of this I needed some time out. Saigon was the place where you always noticed how tired your friends looked anyway; a place needs a lot of character for that, and in Saigon you could look perfectly marvelous one day and then perfectly terrible the next, and friends were telling me about it. So while Flynn went up for a month with the 4th Division Lurps, walking point on unearthly four-man night patrols through the Highlands (he came back from that one with three rolls of exposed film), I left for a month in Hong Kong, followed by practically everyone I knew. It was like moving my scene intact to more pleasant surroundings, a recess session. Page came over to buy expensive toys: more cameras, a fish-eye lens, a Halliburton. He stayed for a week and talked of nothing but how awful Hong Kong was, how Singapore was much, much groovier. When I got back to Vietnam in early July, he and I spent ten days in the Delta with the Special Forces, and then we went to Danang to meet Flynn. (Page called Danang "Dangers," with a hard g. In a war where people quite seriously referred to Hong Kong as "Hongers" and spoke of running over to Pnompers to interview Sukie, a British correspondent named Don Wise made up a Vietnam itinerary: Canters, Saigers, Nharters, Quinners, Pleikers, Quangers, Dangers and Hyoo-beside-the-Sea.)

Page's helmet decor now consisted of the words HELP, I'M A ROCK! (taken from another Zappa song) and a small Mao button, but he didn't have much chance to wear it. Things were still quiet everywhere, fini la guerre, I wanted to leave in September and it was already August. We went out on operations, but all of them were without contact. That was fine with me, I didn't want contact (what the hell for?), that month in Hong Kong had been good in a lot of ways, one of them being the leisure it offered me to recall with some precision just how awful Vietnam could be. Away from it, it was a very different place. We spent most of August on China Beach sailing and goofing, talking to Marines who'd come down for in-country R&R, coming back in the late afternoons to the press center by the Danang River. It was perfectly peaceful, better than any vacation could be, but I knew that I was going home, I was short, and a kind of retrospective fear followed me everywhere.

In the bar of the press center, Marines and members of the Naval Support Activity, all information specialists, would gather after a long day in the IO Shop to juice a little until it got dark enough for the movie to start outside. They were mostly officers (no one under E-6 was allowed in the bar, including a lot of combat grunts whom many of us had tried to bring in for drinks over the past year), and there was a constant state of mistrust between us. The Marines from the Combat Information Bureau seemed to like most civilian reporters about as well as they liked the Viet Cong, maybe a little less, and we grew sick of their constant attempts to impose Marine order on our lives there. That winter, you'd return to the press center from places that were too terrible to believe, and a lot of our tack would become impaired in transit, causing stupid quarrels over things like tee shirts and shower clogs in the dining room and helmets worn in the bar. We'd walk in now from China Beach and they'd all look at us, wave, laugh harshly and ask us how it was going.

"We're winning," Flynn would say cryptically, smiling pleasantly, and they'd smile back uncertainly.

"Look how nervous Page makes them," Flynn said. "He really makes the Marines nervous."

"Freak," Page said.

"No, honest to God, I mean it. Look, the minute he walks in they sort of shy like ponies, they move just a little closer together. They don't like your hair, Page, and you're a foreigner, and you're insane, you really spook the shit out of them. They might not be sure of how they feel about this war, some of them may even think it's wrong, some of them may dig Ho a little bit, they're not sure about a lot of things, but they're sure about you, Page. You're the enemy. 'Kill Page!' You wait, man. Wait, Page."

Just before I went back to Saigon to begin arrangements for flying home, the three of us met at a place called Tam Ky, near the mouth of the Perfume River, where Page was trying out his fish-eye lens on the airboats that had just come back to Vietnam after an earlier failure in the war. We rode around on those for a day and then took a boat downriver to Hue, where we met Perry Dean Young, a reporter for UPI who came from North Carolina. (Flynn called him "the fullest flowering of southern degeneracy," but the closest to degeneracy any of us ever came was in our jokes about it, about what bad, dope-smoking cats we all were. We were probably less stoned than the drinkers in our presence, and our livers were holding up.) Perry had a brother named Dave who ran the small Naval detachment that had been set up during the battle, directly across from the south wall of the Citadel. For months now, Flynn and I had been living vicariously off of each other's war stories, his Ia Drang stories and my Hue stories, and Perry's brother got a Navy truck and drove us around the city while I gave a running commentary which would have been authoritative if only I'd been able to recognize any of it now. We were sitting on the back of the truck on folding chairs, bouncing around in the heat and dust. Along the park that fronted the river we passed dozens of lovely young girls riding their bicycles, and Page leaned over and leered at them, saying, "Good mornin', little schoolgirl, I'm a li'l schoolboy too."

When I'd been here before, you couldn't let yourself be seen on the riverbank without machine guns opening upon you from the opposite bank, you couldn't breathe anywhere in Hue without rushing somebody's death into your bloodstream, the main bridge across the river had been dropped in the middle, the days had been cold and wet, the city had been composed seemingly of destruction and debris. Now it was clear and very warm, you could stop by the Cercle Sportif for a drink, the bridge was up and the wall was down, all the rubble had been carted away.

"It *couldn't* have been *that* bad," Page said, and Flynn and I laughed.

"You're just pissed because you missed it," Flynn said.

"That's you you're talking about boy, not Page."

And I was realizing for the first time how insanely dangerous it had been, seeing it in a way I hadn't in February.

"No," Page said. "It got awfully exaggerated, Hue. I know it couldn't have been that bad, I mean look around. I've seen worse. Much, much worse."

I meant to ask him where, but I was already in New York when I thought of it.

III

Back in the World now, and a lot of us aren't making it. The story got old or we got old, a great deal more than the story had taken us there anyway, and many things had been satisfied. Or so it seemed when, after a year or two or five, we realized that we were simply tired. We came to fear something more complicated than death, an annihilation less final but more complete, and we got out. Because (more lore) we all knew that if you stayed too long you became one of those poor bastards who had to have a war on all the time, and where was that? We got out and became like everyone else who has been through a war: changed, enlarged and (some things are expensive to say) incomplete. We came back or moved on, keeping in touch from New York or San Francisco, Paris or London, Africa or the Middle East; some fell into bureaus in Chicago or Hong Kong or Bangkok, coming to miss the life so acutely (some of us) that we understood what amputees went through when they sensed movement in the fingers or toes of limbs lost months before. A few extreme cases felt that the experience there had been a glorious one, while most of us felt that it had been merely wonderful. I think that Vietnam was what we had instead of happy childhoods.

During my first month back I woke up one night and knew that my living room was full of dead Marines. It actually happened three or four times, after a dream I was having those nights (the kind of dream one never had in Vietnam), and that first time it wasn't just some holding dread left by the dream, I knew they were there, so that after I'd turned on the light by my bed and smoked a cigarette I lay there for a moment thinking that I'd have to go out soon and cover them. I don't want to make anything out of this and I certainly don't want sympathy; going to that place was my idea to begin with, I could have left anytime, and as those things go I paid little enough, almost nothing. Some guys come back and see their nightmares break in the streets in daylight, some become inhabited and stay that way, all kinds of things can trail after you, and besides, after a while my thing went away almost completely, the dream, too. I know a guy who had been a combat medic in the Central Highlands, and two years later he was still sleeping with all the lights on. We were walking across 57th Street one afternoon and passed a blind man carrying a sign that read, MY DAYS ARE DARKER THAN YOUR NIGHTS. "Don't bet on it, man," the ex-medic said.

Of course coming back was a down. After something like that, what could you find to thrill you, what compared, what did you do for a finish? Everything seemed a little dull, heaviness threatened everywhere, you left little relics lying around to keep you in touch, to keep it real, you played the music that had been with you through Hue and Khe Sanh and the May Offensive, tried to believe that the freedom and simplicity of those days could be maintained in what you laughingly referred to as "normal circumstances." You read the papers and watched television, but you knew what those stories were really all about beforehand, and they just got you angry. You missed the scene, missed the grunts and the excitement, the feelings you'd had in a place where no drama had to be invented, ever. You tried to get the same highs here that you'd had there, but none of that really worked very well. You wondered whether, in time, it would all slip away and become like everything else distant, but you doubted it, and for good reason. The friendships lasted, some even deepened, but our gatherings were always stalked by longing and emptiness, more than a touch of Legion Post Night. Smoking dope, listening to the Mothers and Jimi Hendrix, remembering compulsively, telling war stories. But then, there's nothing wrong with that. War stories aren't really anything more than stories about people anyway.

In April I got a call telling me that Page had been hit again and was not expected to live. He had been up goofing somewhere around Cu Chi, digging the big toys, and a helicopter he was riding in was ordered to land and pick up some wounded. Page and a sergeant ran out to help, the sergeant stepped on a mine which blew his legs off and sent a two-inch piece of shrapnel through Page's forehead above the right eye and deep into the base of his brain. He retained consciousness all the way to the hospital at Long Binh. Flynn and Perry Young were on R&R in Vientiane when they were notified, and they flew immediately to Saigon. For nearly two weeks, friends at Time-Life kept me informed by telephone from their daily cables; Page was transferred to a hospital in Japan and they said that he would probably live. He was moved to Walter Reed Army Hospital (a civilian and a British subject, it took some doing), and they said that he would live but that he'd always be paralyzed on his left side. I called him there, and he sounded all right, telling me that his roommate was this very religious colonel who kept apologizing to Page because he was only in for a check-up, he hadn't been wounded or anything fantastic like that. Page was afraid that he was freaking the colonel out a little bit. Then they moved him to the Institute for Physical Rehabilitation in New York, and while none of them could really explain it medically, it seemed that he was regaining the use of his left arm and leg. The first time I went to see him I walked right past his bed without recognizing him out of the four patients in the room, even though he'd been the first one I'd seen, even though the other three were men in their forties and fifties. He lay there grinning his deranged, uneven grin, his eyes were wet, and he raised his right hand for a second to jab at me with his finger. His head was shaved and sort of lidded now across the forehead where they'd opened it up ("What did they find in there, Page?" I asked him. "Did they find that quiche lorraine?") and caved in on the right side where they'd removed some bone. He was emaciated and he looked really old, but he was still grinning very proudly as I approached the bed, as if to say, "Well, didn't Page step into it this time?" as though two inches of shrapnel in your brain was the wiggiest goof of them all, that wonderful moment of the Tim Page Story where our boy comes leering, lurching back from death, twin brother to his own ghost.

That was that, he said, *fini Vietnam*, there could be no more odds left, he'd been warned. Sure he was crazy, but he wasn't *that* crazy. He had a bird now, a wonderful English girl named Linda Webb whom he'd met in Saigon. She'd stayed with him in the Long Binh hospital even though the shock and fear of seeing him like that had made her pass out fifteen times on the first evening. "I'd really be the fool, now, to just give that one up, now, wouldn't I?" he said, and we all said, Yes, man, you would be.

On his twenty-fifth birthday there was a big party in the apartment near the hospital that he and Linda had found. Page wanted all of the people to be there who, he said, had bet him years ago in Saigon that he'd never make it past twenty-three. He wore a blue sweat suit with a Mike patch, black skull and bones, on his sleeve. You could have gotten stoned just by walking into the room that day, and Page was so happy to be here and alive and among friends that even the strangers who turned up then were touched by it. "There's Evil afoot," he kept saying, laughing and chasing after people in his wheelchair. "Do no Evil, think ye no Evil, smoke no Evil. . . . Yesh."

A month went by and he made fantastic progress, giving up the chair for a cane and wearing a brace to support his left arm.

"I've a splendid new trick for the doctors," he said one day, flinging his left arm out of the brace and up over his head with great effort, waving his hand a little. Sometimes he'd stand in front of a full-length mirror in the apartment and survey the wreckage, laughing until tears came, shaking his head and saying, "Ohhhhh, fuck! I mean, just *look* at that, will you? Page is a fucking hemi-plegic," raising his cane and stumbling back to his chair, collapsing in laughter again.

He fixed up an altar with all of his Buddhas, arranging prayer candles in a belt of empty .50-caliber cartridges. He put in a stereo, played endlessly at organizing his slides into trays, spoke of setting out Claymores at night to keep "undesirables" away, built model airplanes ("Very good therapy, that"), hung toy choppers from the ceiling, put up posters of Frank Zappa and Cream and some Day-Glo posters which Linda had made of monks and tanks and solid soul brothers smoking joints in the fields of Vietnam. He began talking more and more about the war, often coming close to tears when he remembered how happy he and all of us had been there.

One day a letter came from a British publisher, asking him to do a book whose working title would be "Through with War" and whose purpose would be to once and for all "take the glamour out of war." Page couldn't get over it.

"Take the glamour out of war! I mean, how the bloody hell can you do *that*? Go and take the glamour out of a Huey, go take the glamour out of a Sheridan. . . . Can *you* take the glamour out of a Cobra or getting stoned at China Beach? It's like taking the glamour out of an M-79, taking the glamour out of Flynn." He pointed to a picture he'd taken, Flynn laughing maniacally ("We're winning," he'd said), triumphantly. "Nothing the matter with *that* boy, is there? Would you let your daughter marry that man? Ohhhh, war is *good* for you, you can't take the glamour out of that. It's like trying to take the glamour out of sex, trying to take the glamour out of the Rolling Stones." He was really speechless, working his hands up and down to emphasize the sheer insanity of it.

"I mean, you *know* that, it just *can't be done!*" We both shrugged and laughed, and Page looked very thoughtful for a moment. "The very *idea!*" he said. "Ohhh, what a laugh! Take the bloody *glamour* out of bloody *war!*"

Breathing Out

I am going home. I have seen a lot of Vietnam in 18 months. May Lord help this place. DEROS 10 Sept 68.

Mendoza was here. 12 Sept 68. Texas.

Color me gone. (Mendoza is my buddy.)

Release graffiti on the walls at Tan Son Nhut airport, where Flynn, almost overtly serious for a second, gave me a kind of blessing ("Don't piss it all away at cocktail parties") and Page gave me a small ball of opium to eat on the flight back; stoned dreaming through Wake, Honolulu, San Francisco, New York and the hallucination of home. Opium space, a big round O, and time outside of time, a trip that happened in seconds and over years; Asian time, American space, not clear whether Vietnam was east or west of center, behind me or somehow still ahead. "Far's I'm concerned, this one's over the day I get home," a grunt had told us a few weeks before, August 1968, we'd been sitting around after an operation talking about the end of the war. "Don't hold your breath," Dana said.

Home: twenty-eight years old, feeling like Rip Van Winkle, with a heart like one of those little paper pills they make in China, you drop them into water and they open out to form a tiger or a flower or a pagoda. Mine opened out into war and loss. There'd been nothing happening there that hadn't already existed here, coiled up and waiting, back in the World. I hadn't been anywhere, I'd performed half an act; the war only had one way of coming to take your pain away quickly.

It seemed now that everybody knew someone who had

been in Vietnam and didn't want to talk about it. Maybe they just didn't know how. People I'd meet would take it for granted that I was articulate, ask me if I minded, but usually the questions were political, square, innocent, they already knew what they wanted to hear, I'd practically forgotten the language. Some people found it distasteful or confusing if I told them that, whatever else, I'd loved it there too. And if they just asked, "What was your scene there?" I wouldn't know what to say either, so I'd say I was trying to write about it and didn't want to dissipate it. But before you could dissipate it you had to locate it, Plant you now, dig you later: information printed on the eye, stored in the brain, coded over skin and transmitted by blood, maybe what they meant by "blood consciousness." And transmitted over and over without letup on increasingly powerful frequencies until you either received it or blocked it out one last time, informational Death of a Thousand Cuts, each cut so precise and subtle you don't even feel them accumulating, you just get up one morning and your ass falls off.

There was a black grunt with the 9th Division who called himself the Entertainer. When I asked him why he said, " 'Cause I rock and I roll," and flipped the selector switch on his 16 back and forth between semi and full. He walked away, moving almost in two sections like his ass was stalking his chest, so that his dog tags flopped hard against him. He spun on his heel and did it backward for a few yards. Then he stopped and reached over his head. When he pulled his arm down a heavy rain came pouring in. "I been here so long I can call these motherfuckers in on the *dime*." He put a lot of energy and care into his jive, it had made him a star in his unit, but he wasn't just some feets-do-yo-stuff spade. So when he told me that he saw ghosts whenever they went on night patrol I didn't laugh, and when he said that he'd started seeing his own out there I think I freaked a little. "Naw, that's cool, that's cool, motherfucker was be*hind* me," he said. "It's when he goes and moves up in front that you're livin' in a world of hurt." I tried to say that what he probably had seen was the phosphorescence that gathered around rotting tree trunks and sent pulsing light over the ground from one damp spot to another. "Crazy," he said, and, "Later."

They were bulldozing a junction into Route 22 near Tay Ninh and the old Iron Triangle when the plows ran into some kind of VC cemetery. The bones started flying up out of the ground and forming piles beside the furrows, like one of those films from the concentration camps running backward. Insta-matic City, guys racing like crazy with their cameras, taking snaps, grabbing bones for souvenirs. Maybe I should have taken one too; three hours later back in Saigon I wasn't that sure whether I'd really seen it or not. While we were there and the war seemed separate from what we thought of as real life and normal circumstance, an aberration, we all took a bad flash sooner or later and usually more than once, like old acid backing up, residual psychotic reaction. Certain rock and roll would come in mixed with rapid fire and men screaming. Sit-ting over a steak in Saigon once I made nasty meat connec-tions, rot and burning from the winter before in Hue. Worst of all, you'd see people walking around whom you'd watched die in aid stations and helicopters. The boy with the huge Adam's apple and the wire-rimmed glasses sitting by himself at a table on the Continental terrace had seemed much more nonchalant as a dead Marine two weeks before at the Rockpile than he did now, wearing the red 1st Division patch, trying to order a Coke from the waiter while a couple of margouilla lizards chased each other up and down the white column be-hind his head. I thought for a second that I was going to faint when I saw him. After a fast second look I knew that he wasn't a ghost or even a double, there actually wasn't much resem-blance at all, but by then my breath was gummed up in my throat and my face was cold and white, shake shake shake. "Nothing to worry about boy," Page said. "Just your nine-teenth nervous breakdown."

They were always telling you that you mustn't forget the dead, and they were always telling you that you shouldn't let yourself think about them too much. You couldn't re-main effective as a soldier or a reporter if you got all hung up on the dead, fell into patterns of morbid sensitivity, entered per-petual mourning. "You'll get used to it," people would say, but I never did, actually it got personal and went the other way.

Dana used to do a far-out thing, he'd take pictures of us

under fire and give them to us as presents. There's one of me on the ramp of a Chinook at Cam Lo, only the blur of my right foot to show that I'm not totally paralyzed, twenty-seven pushing fifty, reaching back for my helmet and the delusion of cover. Behind me inside the chopper there's a door gunner in a huge dark helmet, a corpse is laid out on the seat, and in front of me there's a black Marine, leaning in and staring with raw raving fear toward the incoming rounds; all four of us caught there together while Dana crouched down behind the camera, laughing. "You fuck," I said to him when he gave me the print, and he said, "I thought you ought to know what you look like."

I don't have any pictures of Dana, but there's not much chance I'll forget what he looked like, that front-line face, he never got anything on film that he didn't get on himself, after three years he'd turned into the thing he came to photograph. I have pictures of Flynn but none by him, he was in so deep he hardly bothered to take them after a while. Definitely off of media, Flynn; a war behind him already where he'd confronted and cleaned the wasting movie-star karma that had burned down his father. In so far as Sean had been acting out, he was a great actor. He said that the movies just swallowed you up, so he did it on the ground, and the ground swallowed him up (no one I ever knew could have dug it like you, Sean), he and Dana had gone off somewhere together since April 1970, biking into Cambodia, "presumed captured," rumors and long silence, MIA to say the least.

There it is, the grunts said, like this: sitting by a road with some infantry when a deuce-and-a-half rattled past with four dead in the back. The tailgate was half lowered as a platform to hold their legs and the boots that seemed to weigh a hundred pounds apiece now. Everyone was completely quiet as the truck hit a bad bump and the legs jerked up high and landed hard on the gate. "How about that shit," someone said, and "Just like the motherfucker," and "There it is." Pure essence of Vietnam, not even stepped on once, you could spin it out into visions of laughing lucent skulls or call it just another body in a bag, say that it cut you in half for the harvest or came and took you under like a lover, nothing ever made the taste less strong; the moment of initiation where you get down and bite off the tongue of a corpse. "Good for your work," Flynn would say.

Those who remember the past are condemned to repeat it too, that's a little history joke. Shove it along, dissolve your souvenirs: a pair of fatigues that started to fit about a week before I left, an ashtray from the Continental, a pile of snaps, like one of me on the top of a hill called Nui Kto, one of the Seven Sisters in the Delta, standing around with some Cambodian mercenaries (bandits actually, every squad carried pliers for pulling gold teeth), all looking like we're having a great time waiting for the choppers to come and take us off, only way out; we had the entire base and the top, but everything in between was all full up with Viet Cong. A *National Geographic* map of Indochina with about a hundred pencil marks, every place I ever went there, dots and crosses and big crosses even, wherever I'd been in or near combat and my vanity had told me I'd pulled through, not "scathed"; attached to every mark and the complex of faces, voices and movements that gathered around each one. Real places, then real only in the distance behind me, faces and places sustaining serious dislocation, mind slip and memory play. When the map fell apart along the fold lines its spirit held together, it landed in safe but shaky hands and one mark was enough, the one at LZ Loon.

At dark they finished the perimeter, doubled the guard and sent half the company out on patrols; a brand-new no-name Marine lz in the heart of Indian country. I slept like a morphine sleeper that night, not knowing which was awake or asleep, clocking the black triangle of the raised tent flap as it turned dark blue, fog white, sun yellow, and it felt okay to get up. Just before I flew back to Danang they named it LZ Loon, and Flynn said, "That's what they ought to call the whole country," a more particular name than Vietnam to describe the death space and the life you found inside it. When we rebuilt Loon on China Beach that day we laughed so hard we couldn't sit up.

I loved the door, loved it when the ship would turn a little and tilt me toward the earth, flying at a hundred feet. A lot of people thought it opened you to some kind of extra danger, like ground fire spilling in on you instead of just severing the hydraulic system or cutting off the Jesus nut that held the rotor on. A friend of mine said he couldn't do it, it put him close to rapture of the deep, he was afraid he'd flip the latch on his seat belt and just float out there. But I was afraid anyway, more afraid closed in, better to see, I didn't go through all of that not to see.

At midnight over Vinh Long, the gunship made seven or eight low runs above a company of Viet Cong on the eastern edge of the city. At first the tracers just snapped away into the dark, spending themselves out in sparks or skipping once or twice on the ground. Then flares showed a lot of men running out in the open, and our tracer lights began disappearing abruptly. The smoke from white phosphorus was so bright against the darkness that you had to squint a little to look at it. By four, half the city was on fire. Reporters weren't allowed on gunships, but this was the second night of the Tet Offensive, total hysteria and no rules. I never got to ride in one again.

A gunship flew on either side of us going into Hue, escorting a Chinook that carried a slingload of ammunition. We followed the river and headed into the Citadel through a narrow slot with heavy trees on the right and a cemetery on the left. At a hundred feet we began drawing fire. Groundfire reflex, clench your ass and rise up in your seat a few inches. Pucker, motherfucker; you used muscles you didn't even know you had.

Once I was in a chopper that took a hit and dropped about 300 feet until the pilot pumped his pedals into auto-rotate, restoring us to the air and the living. Dragging back to base camp, we passed over three ships shot down close together, two of them completely smashed and the third almost intact, surrounded by the bodies of the crew and the brigade commander, all killed after they'd reached the ground.

Later that day I went out on a joypop in a Loach with the Cav's star flier. We flew fast and close to the ground, contour flying, a couple of feet between the treads and the ground, treetops, hootch roofs. Then we came to the river where it ran through a twisting ravine, the sides very steep, almost a canyon, and he flew the river, taking us through blind turns like a master. When we cleared the ravine he sped straight toward the jungle, dipping where I'd been sure he would rise, and I felt the sharp freezing moment of certain death. Right in there under the canopy, a wild ship-shaking U turn in the jungle, I couldn't even smile when we broke clear, I couldn't move, everything looked like images caught in a flash with all the hard shadows left in. "That dude can fly 'em right up his own ass," someone said back at the lz, and the pilot came over and said, "Too bad we didn't get shot at. I'd like to've shown you my evade."

In the Special Forces A Camp at Me Phuc Tay there was a sign that read, "If you kill for money you're a mercenary. If you kill for pleasure you're a sadist. If you kill for both you're a Green Beret." Great sounds at Me Phuc Tay, the commander dug the Stones. At An Hoa we heard "Hungry for those good things baby, Hungry through and through," on the radio while we tried to talk to an actual hero, a Marine who'd just pulled his whole squad back in from deep serious, but he was sobbing so hard he couldn't get anything out. "Galveston oh Galveston I'm so afraid of dying," at LZ Stud, two kids from Graves having a quarrel. "He's all haired off 'cause they won't let him sew Cav patches on the bags," one said, and the other, pouting heavily, said, "Fuck you. I mean it man, fuck you. I think it looks real sharp." Only one song from Hue, "We gotta get out of this place if it's the last thing we ever do"; a reporter friend looking totally mind-blown, he woke up that morning and heard two Marines lying near him making love. "Black is black I want my baby back," at China Beach with IGOR FROM THE NORTH, every card in his deck an ace of spades. He wore a sombrero and a serape and his face went through about as many changes as a rock when a cloud passes over it. He almost lived on the beach, every time he added to the count they'd send him down as reward. He spoke twice in an hour in a spooky clipped language of his own like slow rounds, finally he got up and said, "Got to go Dong Ha kill more," and went. "I said shot-gun, shoot 'em 'fore they run now," at Nha Trang, talking to a man just starting his second tour. "When I come home I seen how scared you all was. I mean it wasn't no damn combat situation or nothing like that, but believe you me, you was scared. I seen it here and I seen it there, so what the fuck? I come back." No sounds at all on the road out of Can Tho, twenty of us in a straight line that suddenly ballooned out into a curve, wide berth around a Vietnamese man who stood without a word and held his dead baby out to us. We made tracks and we made dust in our tracks, I swore to God I'd get out soonest, all it took was eight more months.

Out on the street I couldn't tell the Vietnam veterans from the rock and roll veterans. The Sixties had made so many casualties, its war and its music had run power off the same circuit for so long they didn't even have to fuse. The war primed you for lame years while rock and roll turned more lurid and dangerous than bullfighting, rock stars started falling like second lieutenants; ecstasy and death and (of course and for sure) life, but it didn't seem so then. What I'd thought of as two obsessions were really only one, I don't know how to tell you how complicated that made my life. Freezing and burning and going down again into the sucking mud of the culture, hold on tight and move real slow.

That December I got a Christmas card from a Marine I'd known in Hue. It showed a psychotic-art Snoopy in battered jungle fatigues, a cigarette clenched in his teeth, blasting away with an M-16. "Peace on Earth, Good Will Toward Men," it read, "and Best Wishes for a Happy One-Niner-Six-Niner."

Maybe it was classic, maybe it was my twenties I was missing and not the Sixties, but I began missing them both before either had really been played out. The year had been so hot that I think it shorted out the whole decade, what followed was mutation, some kind of awful 1969-X. It wasn't just that I was growing older, I was leaking time, like I'd taken a frag from one of those anti-personnel weapons we had that were so small they could kill a man and never show up on X-rays. Hemingway once described the glimpse he'd had of his soul after being wounded, it looked like a fine white handkerchief drawing out of his body, floating away and then returning. What floated out of me was more like a huge gray 'chute, I hung there for a long time waiting for it to open. Or not. My life and my death got mixed up with their lives and deaths, doing the Survivor Shuffle between the two, testing the pull of each and not wanting either very much. I was once in such a bad head about it that I thought the dead had only been spared a great deal of pain.

Debriefed by dreams, friends coming in from the other side to see that I was still alive. Sometimes they looked 500 years old and sometimes they looked exactly as I'd known them, but standing in a strange light; the light told the story, and it didn't end like any war story I'd ever imagined. If you can't find your courage in a war, you have to keep looking for it anyway, and not in another war either; in where it's old and jammed until the rocks start moving around, a little light and air, long time no see. Another frequency, another information, and death no deterrent to receiving it. The war ended, and then it really ended, the cities "fell," I watched the choppers I'd loved dropping into the South China Sea as their Vietnamese pilots jumped clear, and one last chopper revved it up, lifted off and flew out of my chest.

I saw a picture of a North Vietnamese soldier sitting in the same spot on the Danang River where the press center had been, where we'd sat smoking and joking and going, "Too much!" and "Far out!" and "Oh my God it gets so freaky out there!" He looked so unbelievably peaceful, I knew that somewhere that night and every night there'd be people sitting together over there talking about the bad old days of jubilee and that one of them would remember and say, Yes, never mind, there were some nice ones, too. And no moves left for me at all but to write down some few last words and make the dispersion, Vietnam Vietnam Vietnam, we've all been there.

MAPS

CHRONOLOGY

BIOGRAPHICAL NOTES

NOTE ON THE TEXTS

NOTES

GLOSSARY

INDEX

SOUTH VIETNAM
Provinces and Military Regions

SOUTH VIETNAM

- ·—··— International boundaries
- ··········· Provincial boundaries
- ▬ ▬ ▬ Military regions boundaries

| 0 | 50 | 100 | 150 km |
| 0 | 50 | 100 | 150 miles |

Chronology, 1940–1995

1940   Defeat of France by Germany, May 10–June 22, increases vulnerability of French Indochina to Japanese expansionism. (Indochinese Union, formed in 1887, consists of five states: Cambodia, a French protectorate since 1863; Cochin China, a French colony since 1867; Annam and Tonkin, French protectorates since 1883; and Laos, a French protectorate since 1893.) Japanese forces attack French posts along the Chinese border in northern Tonkin, September 22–24; fighting ends after French governor-general agrees to allow Japanese to station troops and use airfields in Tonkin.

1941   Indochinese Communist Party holds conference in northern Tonkin in May under chairmanship of Nguyen Ai Quoc ("Nguyen the Patriot"), the party's founder, and establishes the Viet Nam Doc Lap Dong Minh (Vietnam Independence League) as a united front organization opposed to French and Japanese rule. Vichy French sign agreement on July 22 giving Japanese military control of Cochin China, including air and naval bases that can be used to attack Malaya, the Dutch East Indies, and the Philippines. Japan begins war against the United States and Great Britain on December 8 (December 7 in the U.S.).

1942–43   Vo Nguyen Giap, a Communist activist since the 1930s, begins recruiting and training Viet Minh guerrilla forces in mountains along the Chinese frontier. Nguyen Ai Quoc is arrested during visit to southern China in 1942 and is imprisoned by Chinese Nationalists until 1943. After his release he adopts Ho Chi Minh ("He Who Enlightens") as new political pseudonym and works in southern China with the Vietnam Revolutionary League, an anti-Japanese front controlled by the Chinese Nationalists. Free French movement led by Charles de Gaulle declares in December 1943 that Indochina will assume a new "political status within the French community" after the defeat of Japan.

1944   Ho Chi Minh returns to Vietnam in August and begins planning for a general uprising under Viet Minh leadership

771

following the defeat of Japan. Giap leads small Viet Minh force in successful attacks on two French outposts on December 24.

1945   Japanese demands for rice and other crops cause severe famine in northern and central Vietnam (as many as two million Vietnamese die from hunger by 1946). Japanese overthrow French administration in Indochina on March 9 and install Bao Dai, heir to dynasty that ascended to the throne in 1802, as emperor of puppet Vietnamese state with authority over Annam and Tonkin. Viet Minh form army in April with Giap as its commander, and work with the Office of Strategic Services, American special operations organization, to collect intelligence and rescue downed Allied airmen in Indochina. Allies divide Indochina at the 16th parallel into Chinese Nationalist and British occupation zones for the purpose of disarming and repatriating Japanese troops following the surrender of Japan. Emperor Hirohito announces Japanese surrender on August 15. Ho Chi Minh issues call for general uprising on August 16. Viet Minh seize power in Hanoi on August 19 and control most of Tonkin by August 22. Bao Dai abdicates on August 23 and uprising spreads to Saigon on August 25. Provisional government of the Democratic Republic of Vietnam is formed with Ho as its president. Ho declares Vietnam independent at mass rally in Hanoi on September 2. Chinese Nationalist army enters northern Vietnam in early September. British, Indian, and French troops begin landing at Saigon on September 12. French seize key buildings in Saigon on September 23; fighting spreads throughout Cochin China as French, British, Indian, and rearmed Japanese troops attempt to suppress Viet Minh resistance. Indochinese Communist Party is officially dissolved in November as Ho, seeking to conciliate Chinese Nationalists, negotiates with other Vietnamese nationalist factions to form new coalition government in Hanoi (Communist Party apparatus continues to control Viet Minh).

1946   French military command declares Cochin China pacified in early February. Agreement signed by Ho and French emissary Jean Sainteny on March 6 provides for French recognition of Democratic Republic of Vietnam as a "free State" within the French Union, allows the French to station 25,000 troops in northern Vietnam for five years, and calls for a plebiscite to determine the status of Cochin China. Nationalist Chinese troops begin withdrawing from Vietnam after signing of Sino-French agreement on March 14 (withdrawal is completed in October; last British forces leave Vietnam in April). Ho holds further talks on status of Vietnam in France, June–September, that leave major issues unresolved. Viet Minh suppress rival nationalist parties in the north. Ho returns to Vietnam on October 20. Clashes between Viet Minh and French in Haiphong lead to bombardment of the city by the French navy on November 23 in which as many as 6,000 Vietnamese civilians are killed. Viet Minh begin offensive against French in Tonkin on December 19.

1947–48   French gain control of major towns in Annam and Tonkin by spring of 1947 as main Viet Minh forces and leadership retreat into the Viet Bac, mountainous region north of Hanoi. Major French offensive in the Viet Bac using paratroops and armored columns inflicts heavy casualties but fails to destroy the Viet Minh, October–November 1947. Guerrilla warfare continues throughout Vietnam as French concentrate on holding the Red River and Mekong deltas, major rice-growing regions in Tonkin and Cochin China. Using captured French and Japanese weapons, Viet Minh build army made up of local village militia, regional guerrilla units, and main-force infantry battalions; by the end of 1948 Viet Minh regain control of the Viet Bac and establish base areas along the central coast and in remote regions of southern Vietnam.

1949   Bao Dai signs agreement with French on March 8 consolidating Cochin China, Annam, and Tonkin into the State of Vietnam, an "associated state" within the French Union; under its terms, Bao Dai will serve as chief of state, with the French retaining control of Vietnamese foreign policy, finances, and defense. Agreements making Laos and Cambodia associated states are signed in July and November. French Expeditionary Corps in Indochina now numbers 150,000, and is composed of troops from France, Algeria, Morocco, Tunisia, Senegal, units of the Foreign Legion, and Indochinese recruits (for political reasons, French government does not send conscripts to serve in Indochina). Communist Chinese troops begin arriving along northern Vietnamese border on December 15 following defeat of Nationalists in the Chinese civil war.

1950   Ho Chi Minh declares Democratic Republic of Vietnam to be the sole Vietnamese government on January 14. After China and the Soviet Union extend diplomatic recognition to the Democratic Republic of Vietnam, the United States recognizes the Associated States of Vietnam, Laos, and Cambodia on February 7. Viet Minh use bases in southern China to organize, train, and equip regular infantry divisions and receive new weapons, including machine guns, mortars, and recoilless rifles, from the Chinese. President Truman approves sending $15 million in military assistance to French forces in Indochina on March 10. Aid is rapidly increased after Korean War begins on June 25 (U.S. will send $2 billion in military aid to Indochina by 1954). Viet Minh regulars overrun French outpost at Dong Khe, September 16–18, opening major offensive along northeastern Vietnamese-Chinese border. French abandon Lang Son, October 18, and retreat from northeastern border region after losing 6,000 men killed or captured in border battles. During autumn French build line of fortifications around Red River delta as Giap plans general offensive designed to capture Hanoi. French sign agreement with Bao Dai regime on December 8 establishing Vietnamese National Army.

1951   Viet Minh lose more than 10,000 men killed in three major attacks on Red River delta, January–June, before abandoning general offensive (French inflict many casualties with air-dropped napalm during Red River battles). Vietnamese Communist Party is overtly reestablished in February as the Lao Dong (Workers') Party. French drop paratroops on Hoa Binh, 40 miles west of Hanoi, on November 14, beginning campaign intended to draw Viet Minh into open battle against superior French firepower.

1952   Both sides suffer heavy losses in fighting around Hoa Binh before French withdraw on February 24. French give Vietnamese National Army increasing role in counter-guerrilla operations in southern and central Vietnam as French Expeditionary Corps is concentrated in northern Vietnam for operations against Viet Minh regulars. Viet Minh begin successful offensive on October 11 in highlands northwest of Hanoi but fail to overrun fortified airfield at Na San, November 23–December 1. Major French incursion into the Viet Bac, October 29–December 1, fails to significantly disrupt Viet Minh logistics.

1953   Viet Minh begin receiving trucks, anti-aircraft artillery, and heavy mortars from the Soviet Union. Armistice is signed in Korean War on July 27. French command decides to reoccupy abandoned airstrip at Dien Bien Phu, village in valley near the Laotian border over 180 miles west of Hanoi, and use it as a base to block Viet Minh operations into Laos. Dien Bien Phu operation begins with successful French parachute assault on November 20. Giap orders major reinforcements to Dien Bien Phu and begins planning siege of French base. French command reinforces Dien Bien Phu in hopes of inflicting major defeat on Viet Minh.

1954   Viet Minh surround Dien Bien Phu garrison of 10,000 men with force of 40,000 regulars and achieve three-to-one superiority over French in howitzers and heavy mortars. Intense bombardment of Dien Bien Phu begins on March 13; by March 17 Viet Minh capture three of the eight strongpoints held by the French forces. Eisenhower administration considers, and then rejects, proposals for the U.S. to launch airstrikes in support of the French garrison. Viet Minh overrun Dien Bien Phu on May 7 and capture 6,500 prisoners; more than 2,000 French troops and 8,000 Viet Minh are killed during the battle.

International conference on Indochina opens in Geneva on May 8, attended by delegations from France, Great Britain, the U.S., the Soviet Union, Communist China, the Democratic Republic of Vietnam, the State of Vietnam, Laos, and Cambodia. Ngo Dinh Diem becomes premier of the State of Vietnam on July 7. Cease-fire agreement is signed in Geneva July 21 between representatives of Viet Minh army and the French Expeditionary Corps; it provides for the exchange of prisoners and the "regrouping" of the opposing armies within 300 days north and south of a "provisional military demarcation line" near the 17th parallel. Separate cease-fire agreements are signed for Laos and Cambodia that call for the withdrawal of Viet Minh forces from both countries. The "Final Declaration" of the conference, which calls for holding internationally supervised general elections throughout Vietnam in July 1956, is not signed by any of the delegations, and the U.S. and the State of Vietnam refuse to "associate" themselves with it. Cease-fire goes into effect throughout Indochina by August 11. French Expeditionary Corps loses 75,000 men killed, including 21,000 from metropolitan France, during the Indochina War, while the Viet Minh lose at least 200,000 dead.

French withdraw from Hanoi in October as Lao Dong Party takes control of North Vietnam. Over 900,000 refugees, most of them Roman Catholic, move south from North Vietnam by May 1955, and between 50,000 and 90,000 Viet Minh move north, while about 10,000 Viet Minh remain in South Vietnam with instructions to engage in "political struggle" toward reunification. Authority of Diem is challenged within South Vietnam by the Cao Dai and Hoa Hao, politically powerful religious sects, and the Binh Xuyen, criminal organization that controls much of Saigon.

1955   Troops loyal to Diem drive Binh Xuyen from Saigon in intense fighting, April 28–30, and begin successful campaign against military forces of the Cao Dai and Hoa Hao. Diem declares on July 6 that South Vietnam is not bound by the Geneva agreements to hold national elections in 1956. Land reform campaign conducted by the Lao Dong Party in North Vietnam results in widespread denunciations, arrests, and executions. Diem ousts Bao Dai as head of state and on October 26 proclaims himself the first president of the Republic of Vietnam. U.S. establishes Military Assistance and Advisory Group Vietnam on November 1 to train and equip South Vietnamese army (new group succeeds MAAG-Indochina, which was established in 1950 to convey aid to the French).

1956   Diem regime begins repressive campaign aimed at Viet Minh in South Vietnam that results in the death or imprisonment of thousands of suspected Viet Minh supporters by the end of the 1950s. Last French troops leave South Vietnam on April 28. Land reform campaign in North Vietnam ends in November after resulting in 10,000–15,000 deaths.

1957–58   Former Viet Minh in South Vietnam begin forming small armed units and assassinating government officials, sometimes working with remnants of the Binh Xuyen, Cao Dai, and Hoa Hao military forces. (Communist-led insurgents in South Vietnam will become known as Viet Cong, from Viet Nam Cong San, "Vietnamese Communists," a term applied to them by the Diem regime.)

1959   Lao Dong Party leadership decides to use "armed struggle" as well as "political struggle" to overthrow Saigon government and reunify Vietnam. In May North Vietnamese organize secret transportation group to infiltrate cadre who "regrouped" north in 1954 back into South Vietnam along the Truong Son Strategic Route ("Ho Chi Minh Trail"), a network of paths running through the mountains of southeastern Laos. North Vietnamese also organize transportation groups for infiltration of men and supplies into South Vietnam by sea, and for sending supplies to Laos after fighting breaks out in July between the Communist Pathet Lao movement and the Royal Lao army. Viet Cong assassinations and ambushes increase (Communist forces assassinate more than 30,000 people in South Vietnam between 1957 and 1972).

1960   Military coup in Laos on August 9 leads to increased outside involvement in the Laotian civil war, with the U.S. supplying and training rightist forces and the Soviet Union airlifting military equipment to the Pathet Lao and its neutralist allies. Formation of National Liberation Front, an alliance of opponents of Diem regime, is announced in Hanoi on December 20 (insurgency in South Vietnam remains under control of the Lao Dong Party). U.S. military personnel serving in South Vietnam total 900 by the end of the year.

1961   U.S. Central Intelligence Agency begins arming Hmong (Meo) tribesmen to fight Pathet Lao in Laotian mountains and sending teams of South Vietnamese into North Vietnam on sabotage missions. Cease-fire is declared in Laotian civil war on May 11 and international conference on Laos convenes in Geneva on May 16. In response to requests by Diem for more American assistance in fighting the Viet

Cong, President John F. Kennedy decides in November to increase the number of U.S. military personnel in South Vietnam and expand their role in counter-guerrilla operations. In December U.S. helicopter units begin carrying South Vietnamese troops on operations and American pilots begin flying combat missions in attack aircraft with Vietnamese aircrew onboard (flights are officially described as training missions). American military personnel in South Vietnam total 3,200 by the end of the year.

1962   General Paul D. Harkins becomes first commander of U.S. Military Assistance Command Vietnam (MACV), new headquarters established in Saigon on February 8 to control buildup of U.S. advisers and support personnel. U.S. special forces begin organizing paramilitary units among Montagnards in Central Highlands. With U.S. assistance, Diem regime launches strategic hamlet program designed to protect rural population from Viet Cong coercion. American helicopters and armored personnel carriers increase mobility of government troops in counter-guerrilla operations and allow the South Vietnamese to make offensive sweeps into Viet Cong base areas. Geneva conference on Laos ends on July 23 with signing of accords under which the U.S. and North Vietnam agree to observe the neutrality of Laos and refrain from using Laotian territory for military purposes. North Vietnam fails to withdraw its troops from Laos by October 7 deadline and continues to use Ho Chi Minh Trail to infiltrate men into the South. U.S. curtails overt military aid to Laotian government in compliance with Geneva agreement, but continues covert support of the Royal Lao army and the Hmong. Viet Cong begin forming battalion-sized main-force units in South Vietnam. American military personnel in South Vietnam total 11,300 by the end of the year.

1963   Viet Cong main-force troops repulse attack by numerically superior South Vietnamese force equipped with helicopters, armored personnel carriers, and heavy artillery at Ap Bac on January 2 before withdrawing from the battlefield; engagement is hailed as major victory by Viet Cong propagandists and increases doubts among some American advisers and journalists about fighting ability of South Vietnamese army. Organized Buddhist opposition to

Diem regime increases after South Vietnamese troops kill nine persons during Buddhist celebration in Hue on May 8. Buddhist monk commits suicide by self-immolation in Saigon on June 11, the first of seven protest suicides by Buddhists in 1963. Paramilitary forces commanded by Ngo Dinh Nhu, Diem's brother and chief adviser, raid Buddhist temples in several major cities on August 21 as Diem imposes martial law. Kennedy administration loses confidence in ability of Diem to prevent Communist takeover in South Vietnam and secretly informs generals plotting to overthrow Diem that the U.S. would not oppose a coup. Group of military commanders led by General Duong Van Minh overthrow Diem on November 1, and Diem and Nhu are murdered on November 2 by officers participating in coup. Kennedy is assassinated on November 22 and Vice-President Lyndon B. Johnson becomes president. Lao Dong Party leadership decides in December to intensify military operations in South Vietnam by supplying new Chinese and Soviet weapons to the Viet Cong and by sending North Vietnamese cadre to the South. Strategic hamlet program declines. American military personnel in South Vietnam total 16,300 by the end of the year.

1964   General Nguyen Khanh overthrows ruling military committee in bloodless Saigon coup on January 30 (until February 1965 Khanh will remain central figure in period of continued South Vietnamese political turmoil). In February 1964 President Johnson authorizes raids against the North Vietnamese coast by South Vietnamese naval commando units operating under U.S. control. North Vietnamese undertake major expansion of Ho Chi Minh Trail network, building roads capable of bearing heavy truck traffic and extending trail into northeastern Cambodia (eventually a force of 50,000 North Vietnamese soldiers will guard and maintain the roads, supply depots, and anti-aircraft defenses of the trail). American pilots working for the CIA begin flying fighter-bomber missions over Laos in late May as Laotian fighting intensifies, and two U.S. navy jets flying reconnaissance missions over Laos are shot down in early June. General William Westmoreland succeeds Harkins as commander of MACV on June 20. Fighting in South Vietnam intensifies in July as Viet Cong increase attacks against government outposts.

U.S. destroyer *Maddox* is attacked by North Vietnamese torpedo boats in the Gulf of Tonkin on August 2 while on an electronic intelligence-gathering mission. On the night of August 4 the *Maddox* and another destroyer, *C. Turner Joy*, report a second attack by North Vietnamese torpedo boats (evidence indicates that reports of August 4 attack were probably the result of false radar contacts caused by tropical weather conditions). Johnson responds to reports of second attack by ordering first U.S. airstrikes against North Vietnam, and on August 5 navy aircraft attack five military targets. Administration submits Tonkin Gulf Resolution to Congress; it authorizes the president to "take all necessary measures to repel any armed attack against the forces of the United States and to prevent further aggression" in Southeast Asia. Resolution is passed by the House of Representatives, 416–0, and the Senate, 88–2, on August 7.

Rioting breaks out in Saigon and other cities, August 21–29, in response to unsuccessful attempt by Khanh to assume the presidency. Viet Cong kill five Americans in mortar attack on Bien Hoa airbase, November 1; U.S. does not respond with airstrikes against North Vietnam. Johnson is elected president on November 3. U.S. air force and navy aircraft begin bombing northern Laos on November 14 (raids will be publicly described as "armed reconnaissance"). North Vietnamese infantry regiments begin moving into South Vietnam. American military personnel in South Vietnam total 23,300 by the end of the year; more than 260 Americans have died in combat since the conflict began.

1965   South Vietnamese army loses 200 men killed in Viet Cong ambush near village of Binh Gia, 40 miles from Saigon, in early January. Viet Cong kill eight Americans in attack on U.S. bases at Pleiku on February 7. Johnson orders retaliatory airstrikes against North Vietnam, February 7–8. Viet Cong blow up barracks at Qui Nhon on February 10, killing 23 Americans; U.S. aircraft bomb North Vietnam on February 11. American aircraft begin intensive bombing of Viet Cong targets in South Vietnam on February 19 (raids are no longer required to be flown with South Vietnamese personnel onboard). General Khanh is removed from power on February 21 by military coup that leaves Phan Huy Quat, a civilian, serving as premier of South Vietnam.

U.S. begins sustained bombing of North Vietnam on March 2, using navy aircraft based on carriers in the South China Sea and air force planes based in Thailand and South Vietnam. First American ground combat units are deployed to South Vietnam on March 8 as marines land at Danang to protect its airbase against Viet Cong attack. U.S. begins sustained bombing of Ho Chi Minh Trail in Laos on April 3. Johnson authorizes marines to conduct offensive ground operations around Danang base on April 6. U.S. and South Vietnam begin naval interdiction operations off Vietnamese coast (patrols will significantly reduce maritime flow of supplies to Communist forces in South Vietnam). First national demonstration against U.S. intervention in Vietnam, held in Washington, D.C., on April 17, draws 20,000 protestors. American paratroopers begin guarding Bien Hoa airbase on May 5 as first U.S. army ground combat units are deployed to South Vietnam. North Vietnamese plan major offensive in Central Highlands with objective of capturing Pleiku and Qui Nhon and inflicting decisive defeat on South Vietnamese. Viet Cong defeat South Vietnamese forces in heavy fighting in Quang Ngai and Phouc Long provinces in late May and early June, inflicting over 1,200 casualties. Westmoreland warns his superiors that the South Vietnamese army is on the brink of collapse. Military government takes power in Saigon on June 19 with Air Vice-Marshal Nguyen Cao Ky serving as premier and General Nguyen Van Thieu as chief of state.

Johnson decides in late July to send up to 200,000 U.S. troops to South Vietnam to avert defeat of Saigon government, but does not order mobilization of the reserves or the national guard, forcing a major increase in monthly draft calls. Johnson also limits U.S. ground operations to South Vietnam, and will consistently reject proposals to invade North Vietnam or launch ground attacks against Communist supply routes and bases in Laos and Cambodia. U.S. aircraft continue bombing North Vietnam, concentrating on transportation targets in attempt to interdict flow of supplies into South Vietnam. Effectiveness of bombing campaign is limited by the increasing strength and complexity of North Vietnamese air defenses, which

are equipped with Soviet-made anti-aircraft artillery, surface-to-air missiles, jet fighters, and radar control systems,
and by changing series of restrictions on targets and tactics
imposed by Johnson administration in effort to avoid Soviet or Chinese intervention in the war.

Marines conduct first major American ground operation, attacking Viet Cong regiment massed near Chu Lai
airbase, August 18–24; 45 marines and more than 600 Viet
Cong are killed in the fighting. About 100,000 demonstrators protest American intervention in marchs and rallies held in cities and on campuses throughout the U.S.,
October 15–16. U.S. special forces begin secret cross-border reconnaissance missions into southern Laos (missions
continue until early 1971, and are also carried out in eastern
Cambodia, 1967–70). North Vietnamese begin Central
Highlands offensive with attack on Plei Me special forces
camp in Pleiku province on October 19. Westmoreland
sends American "airmobile" troops heavily equipped with
helicopters to Pleiku in late October, beginning first major
battle between American and North Vietnamese forces.
Heaviest fighting occurs in two separate engagements in
the Ia Drang Valley, November 14–18, in which 234 Americans and more than 1,000 North Vietnamese are killed.
Campaign ends when North Vietnamese retreat into Cambodia and Americans return to base camp at An Khe in
late November; U.S. victory increases confidence of American commanders that superior mobility and firepower of
U.S. troops will give them decisive advantage in battles
with North Vietnamese and main-force Viet Cong units.
Johnson decides to extend Christmas bombing halt begun
on December 24 in hopes of starting negotiations with
the North Vietnamese. Over 184,000 American military
personnel are in South Vietnam by the end of the year,
and more than 1,300 Americans are killed in combat during 1965.

1966   Buildup of U.S. forces continues, with American combat
troops deployed both to defend bases, installations, and
roads, and to begin conducting offensive operations aimed
at finding and destroying North Vietnamese and main-
force Viet Cong units (U.S. commanders do not have sufficient combat troops to hold permanently large amounts
of territory, and the majority of South Vietnamese forces
are deployed to defend towns and cities). During the year

most major U.S. army combat operations are conducted in the region between Saigon and the Cambodian border, especially Binh Long, Tay Ninh, and Hau Nghia provinces; in Kontum and Pleiku provinces in the Central Highlands; and in the northern coastal plains in Binh Dinh province. Most ground operations by U.S. marines are initially directed at securing populated areas around major bases at Phu Bai, Danang, and Chu Lai. U.S. resumes bombing of North Vietnam on January 31.

Ky government dismisses General Nguyen Chanh Thi, South Vietnamese commander in I Corps, on March 10, leading to rebellion against Saigon regime in northern cities of South Vietnam. Forces loyal to Ky retake Danang, May 15–24, and Hue, June 15–23.

U.S. aircraft bomb targets close to Hanoi and Haiphong for the first time on June 29, beginning campaign directed at petroleum and oil storage sites (Johnson continues to forbid bombing of Haiphong harbor or central Hanoi). Campaign against oil targets continues until September 4 and succeeds in destroying most major storage sites, but fails to create significant fuel shortage because of widespread dispersion of oil storage undertaken by North Vietnamese since 1965; focus of bombing shifts back to transportation targets.

North Vietnamese army begins moving in strength across the Demilitarized Zone (DMZ) into northern Quang Tri province in early July. Marines deploy along southern boundary of the DMZ, where they fight North Vietnamese in series of infantry engagements and begin constructing series of fortified combat bases and outposts. U.S. incursion into War Zone C, major Viet Cong base area in Tay Ninh province, results in heavy fighting, November 3–15, in which 155 Americans and as many as 1,000 Viet Cong are killed. Determined Viet Cong resistance leads American commanders to plan further attacks on Communist base areas in hopes of forcing the Viet Cong and North Vietnamese into battle. (American efforts to wage successful war of attrition are made difficult by ability of Viet Cong and North Vietnamese to evade many offensive sweeps; to fight many engagements at close range and from dug-in positions, thereby reducing the effectiveness of American airstrikes and artillery fire; and to withdraw successfully their surviving forces from the battlefield after most engagements.) More than 385,000 American military personnel are in South Vietnam by the end of the year, and more than 5,000 Americans are killed in combat during 1966.

1967   American ground combat units begin operations in the Mekong delta. U.S. forces launch major operation in War Zone C on February 22; over 280 Americans and at least 2,000 Viet Cong and North Vietnamese are killed by April 1. Disruption caused by offensive contributes to increasing use of base areas inside Cambodia by Communist forces, who purchase large amounts of Cambodian rice and receive arms shipped through port of Kompong Som (Sihanoukville) with the collusion of the Cambodian government and army. American troops continue operations against North Vietnamese and Viet Cong units in the Central Highlands and in Binh Dinh, Quang Ngai, Quang Tin, and Quang Ngai provinces. North Vietnamese begin shelling U.S. outposts along the DMZ with long-range Soviet artillery.

Senator Robert F. Kennedy gives speech on March 2 calling for a halt in the bombing of North Vietnam and the opening of peace negotiations. U.S. aircraft begin bombing major North Vietnamese industrial sites and electric power plants in early March. Campaign continues until May, when priority is again given to interdiction targets. Johnson administration internally debates continued bombing of the North as Robert S. McNamara, the secretary of defense since 1961, loses confidence in American policy. Anti-war march in New York City on April 15 draws at least 125,000 people; speakers at rally include Dr. Martin Luther King Jr. and pediatrician Dr. Benjamin Spock.

U.S. marines attack North Vietnamese troops entrenched in hills near Khe Sanh combat base, April 24–May 11; 155 Americans and 900 North Vietnamese are killed before North Vietnamese withdraw into Laos (heavy fighting continues in northern Quang Tri province during the spring and summer).

Civil Operations and Revolutionary Development Support (CORDS) program is established in May to consolidate pacification efforts of the U.S. military, CIA, Agency for International Development, and the State Department.

Lao Dong Party leadership decides during summer to stage "General Offensive–General Uprising" in South Vietnam. North Vietnamese begin planning widespread attacks on towns and cities using Viet Cong forces with goal of inflicting major defeat on the South Vietnamese army and causing a widespread revolutionary uprising among the urban population.

Nguyen Van Thieu is elected president and Nguyen Cao Ky vice-president of South Vietnam on September 3, winning 35 per cent of the vote out of field of 11 electoral slates.

Giap initiates series of major battles along borders of South Vietnam as first phase of General Offensive–General Uprising with objective of drawing U.S. combat forces away from major South Vietnamese cities. North Vietnamese begin heavy shelling of Con Thien, marine outpost along the DMZ, on September 11; siege lasts until October 31 as U.S. forces respond with prolonged bombardment involving coordinated use of heavy artillery, naval gunfire, fighter-bombers, and B-52 heavy bombers.

March on Pentagon on October 22 draws 50,000 people.

Viet Cong lose 900 killed in unsuccessful attack on Loc Ninh in northern Binh Long province, October 29–November 3. U.S. and North Vietnamese fight series of engagements in Central Highlands near Dak To, November 3–December 1; almost 300 Americans and at least 1,000 North Vietnamese are killed before North Vietnamese units withdraw into Cambodia.

Johnson administration seeks to counter growing public and Congressional opposition to the war by stressing "progress" being made in Vietnam. In speech given in Washington on November 21, Westmoreland states that American forces have reached "an important point where the end begins to come into view" and that "the enemy's hopes are bankrupt." Resignation of McNamara, effective February 29, 1968, is announced by Johnson on November 29. Senator Eugene McCarthy announces on November 30 that he will oppose Johnson in 1968 Democratic presidential primaries and calls for a negotiated settlement in Vietnam. Over 485,000 American military personnel are in South Vietnam by the end of the year, and more than 9,300 Americans are killed in combat during 1967.

1968   North Vietnamese mass large number of troops around Khe Sanh combat base and its garrison of 6,000 U.S. marines. Westmoreland and Lieutenant General Frederick C.

Weyand, American field commander in III Corps, decide on January 10 to move significant number of American combat troops away from the Cambodian border and closer to Saigon to guard against possible attacks in the capital region. North Vietnamese bombard Khe Sanh with heavy rocket and mortar fire on January 21, beginning 77–day siege. U.S. forces respond with sustained bombing and shelling of North Vietnamese positions in surrounding area, using intelligence from aerial reconnaissance and from signals sent by hundreds of seismic and acoustic sensors (U.S. also uses recently developed sensors to target airstrikes against the Ho Chi Minh Trail in Laos).

North Vietnamese and Viet Cong open second phase of General Offensive–General Uprising with ground attacks on over 100 cities and towns throughout South Vietnam during the Tet holiday truce, when many South Vietnamese soldiers are home on leave. Communist forces attack Danang and six other cities in I and II Corps in early hours of January 30. U.S. and South Vietnamese commanders cancel remainder of Tet truce, but are still surprised by intensity and extent of main wave of Tet attacks, which begin in early hours of January 31. Viet Cong and North Vietnamese troops capture much of Hue; during their occupation, Viet Cong murder at least 2,800 residents. In the Saigon area Viet Cong attack several key installations, including the presidential palace, the government radio station, the U.S. embassy, the South Vietnamese Joint General Staff headquarters, Bien Hoa airbase, the U.S. army base at Long Binh, and Tan Son Nhut airbase, the site of MACV headquarters, where heavy fighting takes place between a large Viet Cong force and American base security troops, South Vietnamese paratroopers, and U.S. armored cavalry. Viet Cong in Saigon region fail to capture or hold any of their major objectives, and fail throughout the country to start popular uprisings or to cause South Vietnamese units to defect.

Lang Vei special forces camp, five miles from Khe Sanh, is overrun on February 7 as North Vietnamese use tanks in South Vietnam for the first time. By mid-February South Vietnamese and U.S. forces have retaken all of the cities attacked during Tet except for Saigon, where fighting continues in Cholon section, and Hue, where U.S. and South Vietnamese troops engage in house-to-house combat until city is recaptured on February 25. More than

1,700 Americans are killed in action during the Tet offensive, while South Vietnamese lose about twice as many men (20,000 South Vietnamese soldiers are killed in combat during 1968); Communist forces lose as many as 40,000 killed, most of them Viet Cong, including many veteran cadre.

Johnson asks Clark Clifford, who succeeds McNamara as secretary of defense on March 1, to conduct reassessment of U.S. policy in Vietnam after administration receives proposal from the military to send as many as 206,000 more troops to Vietnam by the end of 1968. Clifford becomes strong advocate for a major change in policy, arguing that a military victory in Vietnam is unachievable and that the U.S. must limit its commitment to South Vietnam. Johnson authorizes sending 13,500 more troops to Vietnam. McCarthy wins 42 per cent of the vote in the New Hampshire Democratic primary on March 12. Robert Kennedy announces on March 16 that he will seek the Democratic presidential nomination.

American infantry company murders between 200 and 500 unarmed South Vietnamese villagers at My Lai, hamlet in Quang Ngai province, on March 16. (U.S. army begins investigation of the atrocity in the spring of 1969, and the first press reports of the massacre appear in November 1969.)

North Vietnamese begin withdrawing some of their troops from the Khe Sanh area after suffering heavy casualties from sustained U.S. bombing and shelling. Johnson meets on March 26 with group of senior advisers, most of whom recommend reducing American involvement in Vietnam. In speech delivered on March 31, Johnson announces a partial halt in the bombing of North Vietnam in effort to start negotiations and declares that he will not seek reelection.

American forces begin major operation to relieve Khe Sanh on April 1. Bombing of North Vietnam is halted above the 20th parallel. North Vietnamese government announces on April 3 its willingness to meet with U.S. representatives. Assassination of Martin Luther King Jr. on April 4 is followed by widespread rioting in American cities and increase in racial tension among U.S. forces in Vietnam. Siege of Khe Sanh ends on April 8, though heavy fighting continues in region around base through June. U.S. begins major program to expand South Vietnamese armed forces and to provide them with modern equipment. North Vietnamese attack near Dong Ha begins series of engagements along eastern end of DMZ. Viet Cong launch two waves of attacks in Saigon area, May 5–13 and May 25–June 4, resulting in renewed fighting in Cholon and near Tan Son Nhut airbase in which South Vietnamese troops play a major role. Fighting is also intense in Quang Nam province, and over 100 towns and military bases in South Vietnam are hit by mortar and rocket attacks during May "mini-Tet" offensive. U.S. and North Vietnamese negotiators meet in Paris on May 13, but talks soon deadlock over North Vietnamese demand for an end to all U.S. bombing of the North. American combat deaths in May total more than 2,000, the highest loss of any month of the war.

Robert Kennedy is assassinated on June 5. General Creighton Abrams succeeds Westmoreland as commander of MACV on July 3. Marines abandon Khe Sanh base on July 5 in shift toward using more mobile tactics in defense of northern Quang Tri. North Vietnamese stage last wave of 1967–68 General Offensive in late August, launching unsuccessful ground attacks on city of Tay Ninh and the Duc Lap special forces camp in Quang Duc province. Heavy casualties suffered by Viet Cong during General Offensive, and its failure to bring a rapid end to the war, cause permanent decline in Viet Cong strength and force Communist commanders to send North Vietnamese replacements to serve with Viet Cong main-force units.

Police and protestors repeatedly clash in Chicago streets as Democratic National Convention meets, August 26–29, and nominates Vice-President Hubert H. Humphrey for president. U.S. and South Vietnamese troops continue combat operations designed to protect urban areas against further ground attack or rocket bombardment. Johnson announces complete halt in bombing of North Vietnam on October 31 as part of agreement to begin negotiations involving the U.S., North and South Vietnam, and the National Liberation Front. (Over 900 U.S. aircraft, most of them modern jets, are shot down over North Vietnam, 1965–68.) Republican candidate Richard M. Nixon wins presidential election on November 5. Negotiations in Paris deadlock over procedural issues. Over 536,000 American military personnel are in South Vietnam by the end of the year, and more than 14,500 Americans are killed in combat during 1968.

1969   First session of four-party peace talks is held in Paris on January 18. Nixon is inaugurated as president on January 20. U.S. marines conduct operation along Laotian border in western Quang Tri province, January 22–March 18, with aim of disrupting North Vietnamese supply system. (Capture of arms and food caches and protection of populated rural areas increasingly become major objectives of American operations during 1969 as less emphasis is placed on engaging large North Vietnamese and Viet Cong units in ground combat.) U.S. bombing of Ho Chi Minh Trail in Laos is increased as consequence of bombing halt over North Vietnam.

North Vietnamese and Viet Cong begin new offensive across South Vietnam on February 23; in effort to avoid high casualties suffered during 1967–68 General Offensive, Communist ground attacks on U.S. installations are increasingly carried out by small "sapper" units armed with explosive charges and trained in night infiltration tactics. More than 1,100 Americans are killed in action in first three weeks of the offensive, and heavy fighting continues for months in region between Saigon and the Cambodian border and in northern coastal plains. Nixon orders first in series of B-52 raids on Communist base areas in eastern Cambodia on March 18 (bombing is not disclosed to Congress or the American public). American troop strength in South Vietnam reaches peak level of 543,000 men in April; "Free World" forces in South Vietnam also include 50,000 troops from South Korea, 11,500 from Thailand, and more than 8,000 from Australia.

National Liberation Front delegation in Paris calls on May 8 for an unconditional U.S. withdrawal from Vietnam and the creation of a coalition government in Saigon; Nixon responds on May 14 by proposing the phased mutual withdrawal of American and North Vietnamese troops from South Vietnam. American troops conducting sweep through the A Shau Valley, a major North Vietnamese stronghold along the Laotian border 25 miles southwest of Hue, capture Hill 937 ("Hamburger Hill") on May 20 after ten-day battle in which at least 56 Americans and more than 500 North Vietnamese are killed. Engagement causes controversy in press and Congress over American tactics in Vietnam.

Nixon announces on June 8 that 25,000 American troops will be withdrawn from Vietnam as South Vietnamese armed forces assume greater role in the war (further withdrawals involving another 85,000 men will be announced on September 16 and December 15). National Liberation Front forms Provisional Revolutionary Government for South Vietnam on June 10. Nixon administration instructs Abrams in August to "hold down" U.S. casualties. Ho Chi Minh dies on September 2 after several years of poor health. Small group of senior officials, including Lao Dong Party general secretary Le Duan, premier Pham Van Dong, defense minister Vo Nguyen Giap, and party ideologist Truong Chinh, assume collective leadership of North Vietnam. Hmong forces drive North Vietnamese troops from the Plain of Jars in September as ground fighting in northern Laos intensifies.

Series of anti-war demonstrations held across the U.S. on October 15 draw large crowds, and 250,000 protestors attend rally in Washington on November 15. First draft lottery is held on December 1 as Selective Service moves to reduce number of draft deferments. U.S. forces in Vietnam suffer increasingly from declining morale, insubordination, racial tension, and drug use; breakdown in discipline is generally more severe among support troops in rear areas than in combat units. Control of Viet Cong "shadow government" over rural areas is reduced as aid administered through CORDS program increases size and effectiveness of village-based South Vietnamese paramilitary forces, and as U.S. and South Vietnamese forces achieve increasing success in capturing or killing Viet Cong political cadre. American military personnel serving in South Vietnam total 475,000 at the end of the year; more than 9,400 Americans are killed in action in 1969.

1970   U.S. air force uses B-52 bombers over northern Laos for the first time on February 17 as North Vietnamese overrun Hmong postions on the Plain of Jars. National security adviser Henry Kissinger holds first in series of secret negotiating sessions in Paris with Le Duc Tho, a senior member of the Lao Dong Party leadership, on February 21.

Prince Norodom Sihanouk is ousted as chief of state of Cambodia on March 18 in coup led by General Lon Nol, who also demands that all North Vietnamese and Viet Cong troops leave the country. South Vietnamese troops begin series of raids into Communist base areas in Cambodia on March 27. North Vietnamese begin attacking Cambodian army outposts in the border region on March 29. Hundreds of ethnic Vietnamese are murdered in Cambodia in April as Lon Nol regime incites anti-Vietnamese hatred. U.S. continues airstrikes against Communist forces in Cambodia and begins covertly sending weapons to the Cambodian army. Nixon announces on April 20 that an additional 150,000 U.S. troops will be withdrawn from Vietnam by the spring of 1971. After intense debate within the administration, Nixon approves "incursion" into North Vietnamese base areas inside Cambodia on April 26 and announces operation on April 30. American troops cross border on May 1. Four students are shot to death by National Guardsmen during demonstration at Kent State University in Ohio on May 4. As widespread protests continue across the U.S., Nixon announces on May 8 that all American troops will be withdrawn from Cambodia by June 30. U.S. and South Vietnamese forces capture large amounts of weapons, ammunition, and rice as North Vietnamese and Viet Cong troops retreat into Cambodia (U.S. troops are restricted from going further than 35 kilometers across the border). Demonstration by construction workers in support of Nixon draws 100,000 people in New York City on May 20. South Vietnamese troops continue ground operations in Cambodia after June 30 with American air support. By the end of July North Vietnamese and Viet Cong occupy most of eastern Cambodia and begin organizing Cambodian insurgents to fight the Lon Nol regime.

U.S. participation in ground combat in South Vietnam decreases as most remaining American combat units prepare to withdraw and South Vietnamese army assumes responsibility for defending border areas against North Vietnamese incursions. Land reform program instituted by Thieu increases support for government in rural areas. North Vietnamese work to reestablish supply system in Cambodia.

U.S. special forces raid camp at Son Tay in North Vietnam on November 21 in attempt to rescue 70 American prisoners of war, but discover that camp has been abandoned. Congress passes amendment to defense appropriations bill on December 22 forbidding deployment of U.S. troops or advisers in Laos and Cambodia. By the end of the year more than 334,000 U.S. military personnel remain in South Vietnam; more than 4,200 Americans are killed in action in 1970.

1971   South Vietnamese troops cross border into southern Laos west of Khe Sanh on February 8 in offensive designed to destroy North Vietnamese supplies and disrupt Ho Chi Minh Trail. U.S. provides extensive air support for operation, but recently passed legislation prevents U.S. advisers from accompanying South Vietnamese units on the ground. Advance is slowed by lack of coordination among South Vietnamese commanders. North Vietnamese begin series of counterattacks on February 18, using tanks, heavy artillery, and mass infantry assaults, and subjecting American supply helicopters to intense anti-aircraft fire. South Vietnamese enter town of Tchepone on March 6, then begin retreating from Laos on March 9. Operation ends on April 6 after South Vietnamese lose at least 1,700 men killed, many of them from elite airborne, marine, and ranger units. Encouraged by results of Laotian battle, North Vietnamese continue planning for major conventional offensive in South Vietnam.

The New York Times publishes on June 13 the first in series of excerpts from secret Defense Department study of U.S. involvement in Vietnam, prepared in 1967–68 on instructions from McNamara. Nixon administration obtains court order stopping publication of the "Pentagon Papers," but Supreme Court lifts injunction in 6–3 decision on June 30. (Attempt by Nixon administration to discredit Daniel Ellsberg, a former government official who gave the study to the press, results in illegal break-in in September 1971 conducted by operatives later involved in 1972 Watergate burglary.)

Thieu is relected president of South Vietnam on October 3, receiving 94 per cent of the vote after major opposition candidates withdraw from the race. Fighting in northern Laos continues as CIA hires increasing number of Thai soldiers to replace Hmong casualties. Cambodian army suffers series of defeats in engagements with North Vietnamese and Viet Cong troops, October–December. Nixon announces on November 12 that U.S. troops in Vietnam have ended offensive ground operations. More than 156,000 American military personnel remain in South Vietnam by the end of the year, and more than 1,300 Americans are killed in action in 1971.

1972   North Vietnamese launch massive invasion of South Vietnam ("Easter Offensive") on March 30, using hundreds of tanks, truck-drawn heavy artillery pieces, and surface-to-air missiles in cross-border attacks into Quang Tri, Binh Long, and Kontum provinces. Quang Tri offensive begins on March 30 and drives South Vietnamese from their bases along the DMZ by April 2. Binh Long offensive begins with capture of Loc Ninh, April 4–6. U.S. resumes bombing North Vietnam below the 20th parallel on April 6. North Vietnamese move south from Loc Ninh and surround An Loc on April 7. South Vietnamese hold defensive line along Cam Lo and Cau Viet rivers and halt offensive in Quang Tri on April 9. Offensive in Kontum province begins on April 12 with attacks on South Vietnamese bases at Tan Canh and Dak To. South Vietnamese repulse attack on An Loc on April 13 with intense U.S. air support. Nixon orders air attacks on Hanoi and Haiphong on April 16.

North Vietnamese resume offensive in Quang Tri on April 23 and overrun Tan Canh and Dak To on April 24. South Vietnamese troops abandon Quang Tri City on May 1 and retreat south of the My Canh river toward Hue on May 2. Major General Ngo Quang Truong assumes command of I Corps and organizes successful defense of Hue with heavy American air and naval gunfire support.

Nixon announces mining of North Vietnamese ports on May 8 while offering to withdraw all U.S. forces from Vietnam within four months after the signing of a cease-fire and the release of American prisoners. U.S. expands bombing of North Vietnam on May 10, attacking targets in the Hanoi-Haiphong area as well as rail lines and roads leading to the Chinese border; ability of American aircraft to destroy bridges and military targets in populated areas is greatly increased by use of new laser-guided bombs. (New air campaign operates under fewer political restrictions than the bombing carried out between 1965 and 1968.)

South Vietnamese repulse attacks on An Loc, May 11–14, and city of Kontum, May 14–30; air support controlled by American advisers includes helicopters firing new wire-guided anti-tank missiles and close-in B-52 strikes.

"Easter Offensive" ends in June after North Vietnamese lose as many as 100,000 men killed, wounded, or captured; on all three fronts, North Vietnamese operations suffer from poor coordination among artillery, tanks, and infantry, and from supply difficulties that prevent the quick exploitation of initial successes. General Frederick Weygand succeeds Abrams as commander of MACV. South Vietnamese begin counteroffensive north of Hue on June 28. Siege of An Loc is broken on July 11 as heavy fighting continues in Quang Tri province. South Vietnamese recapture Quang Tri City on September 15; counteroffensive in I Corps ends with North Vietnamese still holding much of the territory captured by them during the spring.

In meeting with Kissinger on October 8 Le Duc Tho drops previous North Vietnamese demand that a coalition government be formed in South Vietnam as part of any peace agreement; by October 12 negotiators have agreed on general terms of an agreement. Thieu strongly objects to proposed terms in series of meetings with Kissinger, October 18–23. Nixon halts bombing of North Vietnam above the 20th parallel on October 23. North Vietnamese make terms of tentative agreement public on October 26 and call for its signing by October 31. Kissinger holds press conference on October 26 during which he says "peace is at hand" while stating that many details in agreement remain to be worked out. Nixon wins reelection as president on November 7. Negotiations in Paris between Kissinger and Le Duc Tho over final agreement break down on December 13. Nixon orders renewed bombing of Hanoi and Haiphong. Bombing begins on December 18 with first B-52 raids of the war against Hanoi and continues, with 36-hour pause at Christmas, until December 29 as B-52s and other aircraft attack railroad yards, power plants, airfields, and military storage areas. U.S. loses 26 aircraft, including 15 B-52s, in raids, while more than 1,300 persons are killed in Hanoi during December bombing. Nixon halts bombing above 20th parallel on December 29 after North Vietnamese announce willingness to resume negotiations.

1973   Negotiations resume in Paris on January 8. Nixon halts all bombing of North Vietnam on January 15. Final agreement is initialed by Kissinger and Le Duc Tho on January 23 and formally signed in Paris by representatives of the

U.S., North Vietnam, South Vietnam, and the Provisional Revolutionary Government on January 27. Agreement calls for a cease-fire in place, the withdrawal of foreign troops from Vietnam, the release of prisoners of war, the establishment of a Council of National Reconciliation in South Vietnam, and the holding of elections under international supervision; under its terms, the North Vietnamese are not to reinforce their troops in South Vietnam or to seek reunification by other than peaceful means. Fighting continues after cease-fire goes into effect on January 28 as both sides attempt to seize control of disputed areas. (At the time of the cease-fire, Saigon government controls most of the population and the territory of South Vietnam, although the North Vietnamese occupy significant border areas in the northern provinces, in the Central Highlands, and along the Cambodian border north of Saigon.) Withdrawal of remaining 23,400 American troops in South Vietnam begins. Military draft is ended in the United States.

Cease-fire goes into effect in Laos on February 22 following the formation of a new coalition government. War in Cambodia between Lon Nol government and Communist insurgents (Khmer Rouge) continues. Thieu declares that he will not surrender any territory to the Communists, form a coalition government, negotiate with the Communists, or permit Communist political agitation. North Vietnamese continue to send reinforcements and new equipment into South Vietnam. General Van Tien Dung, who replaced Giap as commander of the North Vietnamese army after the failure of the 1972 spring offensive, orders major expansion of Communist supply system within South Vietnam.

Last U.S. troops are withdrawn from South Vietnam on March 29. North Vietnamese complete release of 566 military and 25 civilian American prisoners on April 1. Heavy U.S. bombing continues in Cambodia as Khmer Rouge advance on Phnom Penh. Congress passes legislation on June 30 prohibiting funding of combat operations in Cambodia, Laos, and North and South Vietnam after August 15. Khmer Rouge advance on Phnom Penh is halted in early August. Bombing of Cambodia ends on August 15 (American military aid to Lon Nol government continues; by the end of 1973 the Khmer Rouge control most of Cambodia but are unable to overrun government enclaves around the major cities). Fighting in South Vietnam increases as Lao Dong Party leadership decides that Thieu government can be overthrown only by "revolutionary violence."

1974   North Vietnamese launch series of local attacks in South Vietnam designed to protect new supply routes and to position their troops for general offensive planned for 1976. Inflation and cuts by Congress in American aid program cause increasing shortages of fuel, ammunition, and spare parts among South Vietnamese forces. Nixon resigns as president on August 9 to avoid impeachment and Vice-President Gerald Ford becomes president. North Vietnamese continue construction of new roads, fuel pipelines, and radio and telephone networks within South Vietnam. Dung reorganizes North Vietnamese army to increase coordination among infantry, artillery, and tank forces. Widespread fighting continues in South Vietnam (more than 50,000 South Vietnamese soldiers are killed in action in 1973 and 1974). North Vietnamese begin offensive in Phouc Long province on December 13.

1975   Khmer Rouge launch new offensive in Cambodia on January 1.

     North Vietnamese complete capture of Phouc Long province on January 6. Lack of American military response encourages Lao Dong Party leadership, who approve plans for a major offensive in the Central Highlands in 1975. Offensive begins on March 4 as North Vietnamese troops block roads around Ban Me Thuot in Darlac province. North Vietnamese assault Ban Me Thuot on March 10 and capture town on March 11. Thieu decides to withdraw troops from much of I and II Corps and on March 14 orders South Vietnamese forces to evacuate Kontum and Pleiku, move to the coast, and then recapture Ban Me Thuot. Evacuation of Central Highlands begins on March 16; retreating columns come under intense North Vietnamese attack (of the 60,000 troops who leave the Highlands, only 20,000 reach the coast at Tuy Hoa on March 27). Redeployment of elite airborne troops from Quang Tri to Saigon region weakens South Vietnamese forces in I Corps. North Vietnamese overrun Quang Tri province on March 19. Refugee flight and concern of soldiers for safety of their families undermine morale of South Vietnamese troops in northern provinces. Hue is abandoned on March 25 as soldiers and refugees flee toward Danang in hope of being evacuated by sea or air. North Vietnamese capture Danang on March 30 and Nha Trang on April 1.

Khmer Rouge close Mekong River to supply convoys and begin intense rocket bombardment of Phnom Penh and its airport.

Dung redeploys North Vietnamese army in preparation for "Ho Chi Minh campaign" aimed at capture of Saigon. North Vietnamese attack on Xuan Loc on April 9 is repulsed by determined South Vietnamese resistance.

Khmer Rouge capture Phnom Penh on April 17 and forcibly evacuate its population into countryside as war in Cambodia ends.

Thieu resigns on April 21 and goes into exile. North Vietnamese capture Xuan Loc on April 22 and complete encirclement of Saigon on April 27. Duong Van Minh, leader of 1963 coup against Diem, becomes president of South Vietnam on April 28. U.S. evacuates several thousand Americans and South Vietnamese by helicopter from Saigon, April 29–30. North Vietnamese army enters Saigon on morning of April 30 as Minh orders South Vietnamese forces to surrender.

Pathet Lao troops enter Vientiane on August 23, and People's Democratic Republic of Laos is proclaimed on December 2. Communists establish "reeducation" camps in South Vietnam, where more than 200,000 persons are eventually sent to perform forced labor and undergo ideological indoctrination under harsh conditions.

1976   Socialist Republic of Vietnam is proclaimed in Hanoi on July 2 as North and South Vietnam are formally united.

1977   President Jimmy Carter pardons Vietnam-era draft resisters and evaders. Fighting begins along Vietnamese-Cambodian border in late April after Khmer Rouge stage major raid into Vietnam. Pathet Lao and Vietnamese troops attack Hmong villages inside Laos (over 300,000 people flee Laos after 1975). Refugees continue to leave Vietnam by boat (over 900,000 Vietnamese, many of them ethnic Chinese, become refugees between 1975 and 1988, in addition to the 140,000 who fled the country during the Communist victory in 1975).

1978   Vietnamese-Chinese relations worsen as Vietnam forms
              closer ties with the Soviet Union. Vietnamese army in-
              vades Cambodia on December 25.

1979   Vietnamese capture Phnom Penh on January 7 and install
              new regime. Khmer Rouge retreat into western Cambodia
              and begin guerrilla warfare against Vietnamese, using Chi-
              nese weapons supplied through Thailand. Chinese invade
              border region of northern Vietnam on February 17; fight-
              ing causes heavy casualties on both sides before Chinese
              withdraw on March 16. U.S. refuses to recognize new
              Cambodian government and tightens economic embargo
              imposed on Vietnam in 1975.

1982   Vietnam Veterans Memorial is dedicated in Washington,
              D.C., on November 13.

1986   Le Duan dies. Nguyen Van Linh becomes general secre-
              tary of the Communist Party and begins extensive pro-
              gram of economic reform.

1989   Vietnamese troops withdraw from Cambodia.

1994   President Bill Clinton lifts embargo on trade with Vietnam
              in response to increased Vietnamese cooperation in re-
              solving cases of American servicemen missing in action.

1995   United States establishes full diplomatic relations with
              Vietnam on July 11.

———

More than 58,000 American military personnel died in
Indochina between 1959 and 1975; of these deaths, more
than 47,000 were the result of hostile action. Battle deaths
by service were approximately 31,000 in the army, 13,000
in the marines, 1,700 in the air force, and 1,600 in the
navy.

South Korea lost 4,400 men killed in action in Vietnam.
Australia and New Zealand lost almost 500 dead. Thai
losses in Vietnam and Laos are not known. The number
of persons killed in the fighting in Laos is not known,
although it is estimated that 30,000 Hmong died during
the war. Cambodia lost at least 180,000 dead between

1970 and 1975, and at least one million Cambodians were executed, starved, or worked to death under the Khmer Rouge between 1975 and 1978; the number of Cambodians and Vietnamese killed in Cambodia since 1979 is not known. South Vietnam lost at least 220,000 military dead and at least 300,000 civilian dead during the war, and tens of thousands of Vietnamese refugees died at sea after 1975. It is estimated that at least 50,000 civilians were killed by American bombing in North Vietnam. In 1995 the Vietnamese government stated that 1,100,000 North Vietnamese and Viet Cong soldiers died between 1954 and 1975.

Biographical Notes

T. D. ALLMAN (October 16, 1944–) Born Timothy D. Allman in Tampa, Florida. Educated at Harvard University, graduating in 1966; worked as reporter for *Anchorage Daily News* and *Philadelphia Bulletin* while in college. Served as a Peace Corps volunteer in Nepal for two years beginning in 1966, then reported from Southeast Asia as a freelance journalist, 1968–70. Later worked as foreign correspondent for London *Guardian* and *Le Monde Diplomatique* (1971–75), and senior editor for Pacific News Service, San Francisco, (1977–82), contributing editor of *Harper's* (1977–84), foreign correspondent for *Vanity Fair* (1987–95), and staff writer for *The New Yorker* (1995–97). Author of *Unmanifest Destiny* (1984) and *Miami: City of the Future* (1987).

STEWART ALSOP (May 17, 1914–May 26, 1974) Born in Avon, Connecticut. Graduated from Yale University in 1936. After college worked as editor at Doubleday Doran & Company in New York. Volunteered for service in U.S. Army in World War II; rejected for medical reasons, joined British Army in 1942 and served as infantry officer in Italy. Volunteered for American Office of Strategic Services in 1944; parachuted into France after D-Day to join underground Maquis. From 1945 to 1957, wrote syndicated column "Matter of Fact" with brother Joseph Alsop. Became contributing editor of *The Saturday Evening Post* in 1962; later Washington editor. Contributed column to *Newsweek* beginning in 1968. Author of *Sub Rosa: The O.S.S. and American Espionage* (with Thomas Braden, 1946), *We Accuse! The Story of the Miscarriage of American Justice in the Case of J. Robert Oppenheimer* (with Joseph Alsop, 1954), *The Reporter's Trade* (with Joseph Alsop, 1958), *Nixon & Rockefeller: A Double Portrait* (1960), *The Center: People and Power in Political Washington* (1968), and *Stay of Execution: A Sort of Memoir* (1973). Died in Bethesda, Maryland.

PETER ARNETT (November 13, 1934–) Born in Riverton, New Zealand. Began career in 1951 as reporter for New Zealand newpapers *Southland Times* and *The Standard*. Moved to Sydney, Australia, in 1956, working briefly for *Sydney Sun* and *TV Preview*. After travel in Southeast Asia, took job in 1958 as reporter for *Bangkok World*; joined Associated Press in 1959 as stringer. Started paper *Vientiane World* in 1960. In 1961, hired as Associated Press Jakarta correspondent; expelled for anti-government stories. From 1962 until fall of Saigon in 1975, served as AP Vietnam correspondent, winning Pulitzer Prize in 1966. After war, continued to work for AP in New York; naturalized as U.S. citizen in 1979. Joined Cable News Network in 1981 as global correspondent, reporting from El Salvador, Iran, Lebanon, the Soviet Union, and Panama.

Covered 1991 Gulf War from Baghdad. Memoir *Live from the Battlefield: From Vietnam to Baghdad, 35 Years in the World's War Zones* published in 1994.

KEYES BEECH (August 13, 1913–February 15, 1990) Born in Pulaski, Tennessee. Began career at St. Petersburg, Florida, *Evening Independent* as copyboy, 1931–36. In 1937 took job as reporter for *Akron Beacon Journal*, remaining until 1942, when he enlisted in the U.S. Marines. Served as combat correspondent until 1945; after the war, worked as Washington correspondent for *The Honolulu Star-Bulletin* (1945–47). From 1947 to 1977 was Far East correspondent for Chicago *Daily News*. Won Pulitzer Prize for Korean War reporting, 1951. Moved to Saigon in mid-1960s, remaining until 1975. Subsequently reported from Bangkok for the *Los Angeles Times*, retiring in 1983. Books include *The U.S. Marines on Iwo Jima* (1945, with Raymond Henri and other marine combat correspondents), *Uncommon Valor: Marine Divisions in Action* (1946), *Tokyo and Points East* (1954), and *Not without the Americans: A Personal History* (1971). Died in Washington, D.C.

PETER BRAESTRUP (June 8, 1929–August 10, 1997) Born in New York City. After graduation from Yale University in 1951 joined U.S. Marines in Korea; discharged in 1953 following battle wound. Began career in journalism as staff writer for *Time* (1953–57). Later worked for the New York *Herald Tribune* as reporter (1957–59), for *The New York Times* as correspondent in Algiers, Bangkok, and Paris, and for *The Washington Post* as reporter and Saigon bureau chief (1968–73). Founded *Wilson Quarterly* in 1975; also worked as senior editor and director of communications for the Library of Congress (1989–97). Author of *Big Story: How the American Press and Television Reported and Interpreted the Crisis of Tet 1968 in Vietnam and Washington* (1977) and *Battle Lines: Report of the Twentieth Century Fund Task Force on the Military and the Media* (1985). Died in Rockport, Maine.

MALCOLM W. BROWNE (April 17, 1931–) Born Malcolm Wilde Browne in New York City; attended Swarthmore College and New York University, graduating in 1952. After college worked for four years as a chemist and technical writer. Drafted in 1956; began journalism career as reporter for *Pacific Stars and Stripes* in Korea. On return to U.S., hired as newsman and copy editor for Middletown (New York) *Daily Record*; moved to Baltimore bureau of Associated Press two years later, in 1960. Worked in Vietnam as chief AP Indochina correspondent (1961–65) and Saigon correspondent for the American Broadcasting Corporation (1965–66). Shared 1964 Pulitzer Prize for coverage of fall of Diem regime. After two years as a freelance correspondent and writer, joined staff of *The New York Times* in 1968, serving as correspondent in Buenos Aires, South Asia (1971–73), and Eastern Europe (1973–77). Since 1977 has been *Times* science correspondent and writer; edited *Discover* for three years beginning in 1981. His books include *The New Face of War* (1965) and memoir *Muddy Boots and Red Socks* (1993).

TOM BUCKLEY (January 2, 1930–   )   Born Thomas F.S. Buckley in Chatham, New York. Graduated from Columbia University in 1950, after which he served for two years in U.S. Army. Joined *The New York Times* in 1953, working as copy editor, rewrite man, and reporter (in Vietnam, 1966–68). Worked as staff writer for *The New York Times Magazine* from 1968 to 1973, and later as columnist and special writer. Since 1980 has been a freelance writer. Author of *Violent Neighbors: El Salvador, Central America, and the United States* (1984).

FOX BUTTERFIELD (July 8, 1939–   )   Born in Lancaster, Pennsylvania; educated at Harvard University (B.A. 1962, M.A. 1964; graduate study 1964–69). Joined *The New York Times* as Vietnam correspondent in 1969; also reported from Japan, Hong Kong, and China. Was co-recipient of Pulitzer Prize in 1971 for role in publication of the Pentagon Papers. Since 1984, has been chief of *Times* Boston bureau. Author of *China: Alive in the Bitter Sea* (1982) and *All God's Children: The Bosket Family and the American Tradition of Violence* (1985).

PHILIP CAPUTO (June 10, 1941–   )   Born in Chicago; graduated from Loyola University in 1964, after which he served as officer with U.S. Marines in Vietnam, 1965–66. Joined staff of the *Chicago Tribune* in 1968, working as foreign correspondent from 1972 until 1977, when he published memoir *A Rumor of War*. Has also written novels *Horn of Africa* (1980), *DelCorso's Gallery* (1983), *Indian Country* (1987), *Means of Escape* (1991), *Equation for Evil* (1996), and *Exiles: Three Short Novels* (1997).

FRED J. COOK (March 8, 1911–   )   Born Fred James Cook in Point Pleasant, New Jersey; graduated from Rutgers University in 1932. After college worked as reporter (1933–36) and city editor (1938–44) for *Asbury Park Press* (Asbury Park, New Jersey); also edited *New Jersey Courier* (Toms River, N.J.), 1936–37. Was a feature writer for *New York World-Telegram* from 1944 to 1959; afterwards worked as freelance journalist and author. His books include *The Girl in the Death Cell* (1953), *The Girl on the Lonely Beach* (1954), *What Manner of Men: Forgotten Heroes of the American Revolution* (1959), *The Welfare State* (1962), *Barry Goldwater: Extremist of the Right* (1964), *The FBI Nobody Knows* (1964), *The Corrupted Land: The Social Morality of Modern America* (1966), *The Secret Rulers* (1966), *The Plot Against the Patient* (1967), *What So Proudly We Hailed* (1968), *The Nightmare Decade* (1971), *The Demagogues* (1972), *The Muckrakers: Crusading Journalists Who Changed America* (1972), *Mafia!* (1973), *American Political Bosses and Machines* (1973), *Dawn over Saratoga: The Turning Point of the Revolutionary War* (1973), *Julia's Story: The Tragedy of an Unnecessary Death* (1976), *Mob, Inc.* (1977), *Storm Before Dawn* (1978), *City Cop* (1979), *The Ku Klux Klan: America's Recurring Nightmare* (1980), *The Crimes of Watergate* (1981), *The Great Energy Scam: Private Billions vs. Public Good* (1983), and *Maverick: Fifty Years of Investigative Reporting* (1984).

GLORIA EMERSON (May 19, 1930–) Born in New York City. Began career in journalism in 1957, assigned to women's page of *The New York Times*; later worked in Paris and London bureaus. Covered war in Vietnam from 1970 to 1972; won George Polk Award for foreign reporting, 1971. Her books include *Winners & Losers: Battles, Retreats, Gains, Losses and Ruins from a Long War* (National Book Award, 1978), *Some American Men* (1985), and *Gaza: A Year in the Intifada* (1990).

GEORGE ESPER (September 16, 1932–) Born in Uniontown, Pennsylvania; educated at West Virginia University (B.S. 1953). Joined the Associated Press in 1958. Reported from Vietnam for AP for ten years, beginning in 1965, later becoming bureau chief; expelled five weeks after Communist victory. Returned to Vietnam in 1993 to reopen AP bureau; also served as AP bureau chief during 1991 Gulf War, covering 1991 Iraqi armistice negotiations, and reported from Somalia and Bosnia on U.S. interventions. Author of *The Eyewitness History of the Vietnam War* (1983).

KARL FLEMING (August 30, 1927–) Born in Newport News, Virginia; grew up in church orphanage. Began career as police and court reporter for Wilson, North Carolina, *Daily Times* and reporter for *Atlanta Constitution*. Joined *Newsweek* in 1960 as civil rights correspondent. In 1965 became Los Angeles bureau chief; seriously injured while reporting on Watts riots. Covered campaigns and political conventions for *Newsweek*. From 1978 to 1985 worked in television, as managing editor and on-air political editor for KNXT in Los Angeles; produced documentary *Watts Revisited* for CBS. From 1985 to 1987 was editor and publisher of *California Business*. Since 1988 has been president of Prime Time Communications, a media consulting firm. Author of *The First Time* (1975, with Anne Taylor Fleming).

ZALIN GRANT (April 17, 1941–) Born Zalin B. Grant in Cheraw, South Carolina. Graduated from Clemson University in 1963; during college, worked as stringer for Associated Press. After two years of service in Saigon and Danang as U.S. Army intelligence officer and Vietnamese linguist, joined staff of *Time* magazine; reported on Vietnam from 1965 to 1967, and later from Washington and New York. Became Southeast Asia correspondent for *The New Republic* in 1968. Beginning in 1971, has been a freelance writer, living in Spain and France; has served as editorial director of Pythia Press since 1995. His books include *Survivors* (1975), *Over the Beach* (1986), *Facing the Phoenix* (1992), and *Flying Smart* (1995).

FRANCINE DU PLESSIX GRAY (September 25, 1930–) Born Francine du Plessix in the French Embassy in Warsaw; immigrated to the United States in 1941. Attended Bryn Mawr College; graduated from Barnard College in 1952. After college worked as reporter for United Press International and as book editor for *Art in America*. Married Cleve Gray, 1957. Began publishing fiction and political essays in *The New Yorker* and other periodicals in the 1960s.

Author of nonfiction works *Divine Disobedience: Profiles in Catholic Radicalism* (1970), *Hawaii: The Sugar-Coated Fortress* (1972), *Adam & Eve in the City: Selected Nonfiction* (1987), *Soviet Women: Walking the Tightrope* (1990), *Rage and Fire: A Life of Louise Colet* (1994), and *At Home with the Marquise de Sade: A Life* (1998), and novels *Lovers and Tyrants* (1976), *World without End* (1981), and *October Blood* (1985).

H. D. S. GREENWAY (May 8, 1935–   )   Born Hugh Davids Scott Greenway in Boston, Massachusetts; educated at Yale (B.A. 1958) and Oxford (1960–62). Began career as correspondent for *Time*, reporting from London (1962–63), Washington, D.C. (1963–64), Boston (1964–66), Saigon (1967–68), Bangkok (1968–70), and the United Nations (1970–72). Later worked for *The Washington Post* in Hong Kong (1973–76) and Jerusalem (1976–78), and *The Boston Globe*, as associate editor for national and foreign news (1978–91), senior associate editor (1991–93), and editorial page editor (1994–   ).

WILLIAM GREIDER (August 6, 1936–   )   Born Cincinnati, Ohio; graduated from Princeton University, 1958. Began career in 1960 as reporter for *Wheaton Daily Journal* (Wheaton, Illinois). Later worked as reporter and Washington correspondent for Louisville *Courier-Journal and Times* (1962–68), as reporter for *The Washington Post* (1968–82), and since 1982 as columnist and national affairs editor for *Rolling Stone*. Won George Polk Award, 1982. Author of *The Education of David Stockman and Other Americans* (1982), *Secrets of the Temple: How the Federal Reserve Runs the Country* (1988), *The Trouble with Money: A Prescription for America's Financial Fever* (1989), *Who Will Tell the People: The Betrayal of American Democracy* (1992), and *One World, Ready or Not: The Manic Logic of Global Capitalism* (1997).

MICHAEL HERR (April 13, 1940–   )   Born in Syracuse, New York; attended Syracuse University. Began career in journalism as an editor and freelance writer for *Holiday* magazine in the early 1960s. Went to Vietnam in November 1967 as freelance correspondent for *Esquire*; reports later included in *Dispatches* (1977). Other books include *The Big Room* (1984) and *Walter Winchell* (1990); also co-authored screenplays for *Apocalypse Now* (1979) and *Full Metal Jacket* (1987).

SEYMOUR M. HERSH (April 8, 1937–   )   Born in Chicago, Illinois; educated at University of Chicago. Began journalistic career as police reporter for City News Bureau of Chicago, 1959–60. Later United Press International correspondent in Pierre, South Dakota, 1962–63; Associated Press correspondent in Chicago and Washington, 1963–67, at the Pentagon beginning in 1966. Resigned AP position in 1967 after piece on biological warfare was drastically edited; briefly served as press secretary for Eugene McCarthy's New Hampshire primary campaign. Won 1970 Pulitzer Prize for reporting of My Lai massacre. Author of *Chemical and Biological Warfare: America's Hidden Arsenal* (1969), *My Lai 4: A Report on the Massacre and Its Aftermath* (1970),

The Price of Power: Kissinger in the Nixon White House (1983), *The Target Is Destroyed: What Really Happened to Flight 007* (1986), *The Samson Option: Israel's Nuclear Arsenal and America's Foreign Policy* (1991), and *The Dark Side of Camelot* (1998).

ARNOLD R. ISAACS (February 6, 1941–   )   Born in New York City. Graduated from Harvard University in 1961. From 1962 to 1981 worked as reporter, Washington correspondent, foreign correspondent, and editor at *The Baltimore Sun*. Covered Vietnam for *Sun*, 1972–75; after war was based in Hong Kong for three years. Since 1981 has been a freelance journalist, author, and educator. His books include *Without Honor: Defeat in Vietnam and Cambodia* (1983) and *Vietnam Shadows: The War, Its Ghosts, and Its Legacy* (1997); co-authored *Pawns of War* (1987).

PETER R. KANN (December 13, 1942–   )   Born Peter Robert Kann in New York City. Began newspaper career in high school as copyboy for *The Princeton Packet*. Graduated from Harvard University, where he was political editor of *The Harvard Crimson*, in 1964. Joined *The Wall Street Journal* as staff reporter in 1964, working in Pittsburgh and Los Angeles bureaus. Covered Vietnam war as resident correspondent from 1967 to 1969; later served as Hong Kong-based Asia correspondent, 1969–76. Won Pulitzer Prize for 1971 coverage of India-Pakistan war. Named first publisher and editor of *The Asian Wall Street Journal* in 1976. In 1979 returned to United States as associate publisher of *The Wall Street Journal* and vice-president of Dow Jones & Company; appointed chief executive officer and chairman of Dow Jones in 1991.

DORIS KEARNS (January 4, 1943–   )   Born Doris Helen Kearns in Rockville Centre, New York. Educated at Colby College and Harvard University (Ph.D. 1968). Served as special assistant to President Lyndon Johnson, 1968. Appointed assistant professor at Harvard in 1969; associate professor of government beginning in 1972. Was special consultant to President Lyndon Johnson from 1969 to 1973. Married Richard Goodwin, 1975. Books include *Lyndon Johnson and the American Dream* (1976), *The Fitzgeralds and the Kennedys* (1986), *No Ordinary Time: Franklin and Eleanor Roosevelt—The Home Front in World War II* (1994, winner of 1995 Pulitzer Prize), and *Wait Till Next Time: A Memoir* (1997).

MICHAEL KINSLEY (March 9, 1951–   )   Born in Detroit, Michigan. Graduated from Harvard University, where he was vice-president of the *Harvard Crimson*, in 1972, and from Harvard Law School in 1977; also attended Oxford University, 1972–74. Has worked as managing editor of *Washington Monthly* (1975), managing editor, editor, and senior editor of *The New Republic* (1976–96), editor of *Harper's* (1981–83), co-host of CNN's *Crossfire* (1989–96). In 1996, became editor of internet magazine *Slate*.

DONALD KIRK (May 7, 1938–   )   Born in New Brunswick, New Jersey; educated at Princeton (B.A. 1959), the Indian School of International Studies,

New Delhi (1962–63), and the University of Chicago (M.A. 1965). Began career as a reporter for the *Chicago Sun-Times* (1960–61) and the *New York Post* (1961–64). Covered Vietnam as a freelance correspondent beginning in 1965, and later for *The Evening Star*, Washington, D.C. (1967–70), and the *Chicago Tribune* (1971–74). Received George Polk Award for foreign reporting, 1975. After war, reported from New York and the United Nations for the *Tribune* (1975–76), wrote for *Time* (1977–78), was special correspondent based in Tokyo for *The Observer*, London (1978–82), and special correspondent for *USA Today* (1982–90). Since 1991 has been a freelance writer; his books include *Wider War: The Struggle for Cambodia, Thailand, and Laos* (1971), *Tell It to the Dead: Memories of a War* (1975), *Korean Dynasty: Hyundai and Chung Ju Yung* (1994), and *Looted: The Philippines after the Bases* (1998).

JOSEPH KRAFT (September 4, 1924–January 10, 1986)   Born in South Orange, New Jersey. Began journalism career at 14, covering high school sports for New York *World-Telegram*. Served as cryptographer in army during the Second World War, after which he studied at Columbia University (B.A. 1947) and Princeton (1948–51). Joined staff of *The Washington Post* in 1951 as editorial writer; later staff writer for *The New York Times* (1953–57), Washington correspondent for *Harper's* (1962–65), columnist for Field Newspapers (1965–80), and columnist for the Los Angeles Times Syndicate (1980–85). Won 1958 and 1972 Overseas Press Club Award for foreign reporting. His books include *The Struggle for Algeria* (1961), *The Grand Design: From Common Market to Atlantic Partnership* (1962), *Profiles in Power: A Washington Insight* (1963), and *The Chinese Difference* (1973).

LE KIM DINH (July 1, 1934–   )   Born in Hanoi; immigrated to South Vietnam after signing of Geneva Accords in 1954. After graduate education at Université de Saigon (1960), was drafted into South Vietnamese Army, serving until 1965. Worked as war correspondent for United Press International in Vietnam from 1965 to 1967, and later as reporter and assistant to *The New York Times* Saigon bureau chiefs (1968–75). After fall of Saigon joined staff of *Times* in New York City (1975–87). Moved to California in 1989; contributed articles to *The Orange County Register* and the *Los Angeles Times*. Currently a consultant and contributing editor for *CN* magazine, national monthly publication of Vietnamese-American community.

FLORA LEWIS   Born in Los Angeles, California; educated at UCLA (B.A. 1941) and the Columbia University School of Journalism (M.S. 1942). Began career as reporter for the *Los Angeles Times* (1942) and the Associated Press (New York, Washington, and London, 1942–46). From 1946 to 1958 worked as a freelance journalist. Later served as bureau chief in Bonn and London for *The Washington Post* (1958–66) and syndicated columnist for *Newsday* (1967–72). Joined *The New York Times* as Paris bureau chief (1972–80), foreign affairs columnist (1980–90), and senior columnist (1990–   ). Books include *A Case History of Hope: The Story of Poland's Peaceful Revolutions* (1958), *Red*

Pawn: The Story of Noel Field (1964), *One of Our H-Bombs Is Missing* (1967), *Europe: A Tapestry of Nations* (1987), *Europe: A Road to Unity* (1992).

JOHN S. MCCAIN III (August 29, 1936–) Born in Panama Canal Zone; graduated from U.S. Naval Academy in 1958. Shot down over Hanoi in 1967 and held as prisoner of war for five and a half years. After attending National War College, served as director of Navy-Senate Liaison Office until retirement from service in 1981. A Republican from Arizona, he was elected to two terms as U.S. Representative (1982–86), and to U.S. Senate in 1986 and 1992. In 1993 was appointed chairman of the International Republican Institute; chairs Senate Commerce, Science, and Transportation Committee.

PHILIP A. MCCOMBS (July 20, 1944–) Born in Ogdensburg, New York; educated at Yale University (B.A. 1966) and the School of Advanced International Studies at Johns Hopkins (M.A. 1968). Drafted into the army in 1969, he served as Saigon bureau chief of *Pacific Stars and Stripes*; covered allied invasion of Cambodia. Joined staff of *The Washington Post* in 1970, becoming Saigon bureau chief in 1973; currently a reporter for *Post* Style section. Author of novel *The Typhoon Shipments* (with Kevin Klose, 1974).

JAMES A. MICHENER (February 3, 1907–October 16, 1997) Born in New York City; raised in Doylestown, Pennsylvania. Graduated from Swarthmore College in 1929; received a master's degree from the University of North Colorado in 1937. Taught at the George School, Newtown, Pennsylvania, and worked briefly as a textbook editor for Macmillan in New York before enlisting in the navy in 1941. Collection of stories, *Tales of the South Pacific* (1947, winner of 1948 Pulitzer Prize and adapted as musical *South Pacific*), became bestseller. Also published *The Fires of Spring* (1949), *Return to Paradise* (1951), *The Voice of Asia* (1951), *The Bridges at Toko-Ri* (1953), *Sayonara* (1954), *Floating World* (1955), *The Bridge at Andau* (1957), *Hawaii* (1959), *Caravans* (1963), *The Source* (1965), *Iberia* (1968), *Kent State* (1971), *Centennial* (1974), *Sports in America* (1976), *Chesapeake* (1978), *Space* (1982), *Poland* (1983), *Texas* (1985), *Legacy* (1987), *Alaska* (1988), *Caribbean* (1989), *Journey* (1989), *The Novel* (1991), *Mexico* (1992), *The World Is My Home: A Memoir* (1992), *Literary Reflections* (1993), *Recessional* (1994), *Miracle in Seville* (1995), and *This Noble Land* (1996).

RUDOLPH S. RAUCH (July 5, 1943–) Born in Bryn Mawr, Pennsylvania. After graduating from Princeton University in 1965, served for two years as policy assistant at Radio Free Europe. Joined *Time* in 1969, working in New York bureau and as European economic correspondent before assignment to Saigon in July 1971. After 15 months in Saigon, assigned to Rio de Janeiro (1973–74), Buenos Aires (1974–76), and Atlanta (1976–79). Became deputy chief of correspondents for Time-Life News Service in 1979; in 1980 was Edward R. Murrow Fellow, Council on Foreign Relations. Held various positions at Time, Inc. from 1981 to 1987, and was managing editor of *Consti-*

tution magazine from 1991 to 1994. Currently serves as managing director of the Metropolitan Opera Guild in New York City.

JOHN SAAR (June 4, 1939–)   Born in London; educated at London Northwestern Polytechnic (1961–63), and served for two years in the British Army (1959–61). Began journalism career in England, working for Barnet Press in London (1957–59, 1961–63), *Farmers Weekly* (1963–64), and *Soldier Magazine* (1964–67). Moved to New York in 1967 as correspondent for *Life*; covered Vietnam for *Life* from 1968 to 1972. Later worked for *The Washington Post* as reporter (1972–75) and northeast Asia correspondent (1975–78), as a freelance writer (1978–81), as writer and senior editor at *People* (1981–92), and as senior editor at Time International and Time, Inc. (1992–98). Currently managing editor of *Cartoon News*.

SYDNEY H. SCHANBERG (January 17, 1934–)   Born Sydney Hillel Schanberg in Clinton, Massachusetts. Graduated from Harvard University in 1955. Served in U.S. Army, 1956–58. Joined staff of *The New York Times* in 1959, becoming reporter in 1960; served as Albany, New York, bureau chief (1967–69), New Delhi bureau chief (1969–73), Southeast Asia correspondent (1973–75), metropolitan editor (1977–80), and columnist (1981–85). Became associate editor and columnist for New York *Newsday* in 1986. Won Pulitzer Prize for international reporting, 1976, Overseas Press Club Award in 1971 and 1975, and 1972 George Polk Award for foreign reporting. 1980 *New York Times Magazine* article "The Death and Life of Dith Pran" was basis for film *The Killing Fields* (1984); author of *The Killing Fields: The Facts behind the Film* (1984, with Dith Pran).

ROBERT SHAPLEN (March 22, 1917–May 15, 1988)   Born Robert Modell Shaplen in Philadelphia; educated at University of Wisconsin (B.A. 1937). After receiving master's in journalism from Columbia University (1938), worked as reporter for New York *Herald Tribune* (1937–43). Covered Pacific war for *Newsweek*, 1943–45; on return served as Far East bureau chief (1946–47). Left *Newsweek* to be Nieman Fellow at Harvard (1947–48), writer for *Fortune* (1948–50), and Asia correspondent for *Collier's* (1950–52). Joined staff of *The New Yorker* in 1952, where he worked until his death; from 1962 to 1978 he was magazine's Far East correspondent. His books include *A Corner of the World* (1949), *Free Love and Heavenly Sinners: The Story of the Great Henry Ward Beecher Scandal* (1954), *A Forest of Tigers* (novel, 1956), *Kreuger: Genius and Swindler* (1960), *The Lost Revolution* (1965), *Time out of Hand: Revolution and Reaction in Southeast Asia* (1969), *The Road from War: Vietnam 1965–1970* (1970), *A Turning Wheel* (1979), and *Bitter Victory* (1986).

JAMES P. STERBA (May 1, 1943–)   Born James Paul Sterba in Detroit, Michigan; graduated from Michigan State University in 1966. Began career as reporter for *The Evening Star* in Washington, D.C. (1966–67); later joined staff of *The New York Times*, working as assistant to columnist James Reston (1967–68), war correspondent in Vietnam (1969–70), and foreign and national correspondent (1970–81). Moved to *The Wall Street Journal* in 1982 as assistant foreign editor; later foreign and senior correspondent.

BOB TAMARKIN (November 5, 1937–   ) Born Robert Allen Tamarkin in St. Louis, Missouri. Graduated from Washington University in 1961 and from the University of Missouri School of Journalism in 1963. Began career as business reporter for Fairchild Publications in Chicago (1963–66); later stock market columnist and financial writer for Chicago *Daily News* (1966–68), *Daily News* reporter in Saigon (1973–74) and Saigon bureau chief (1975), bureau chief in Bangkok (1975–76) and Nairobi (1976–77), editor and founder of *Generation* magazine (1968–71), senior editor at *Forbes* (1978–81), special writer for *The Wall Street Journal* (1983–84), writer for *Crain's Illinois Business*, host of "Inside Business," National Public Radio (1982–83), and managing editor of *Intermarket Magazine* (1987–   ). Author of *Young Executive Today* (1972), *The New Gatsbys: Fortunes and Misfortunes of Commodity Traders* (1985), *The Merc: The Emergence of a Global Financial Powerhouse* (1993), and *Rumor Has It: A Curio of Lies, Hoaxes, and Hearsay* (1993).

HUNTER S. THOMPSON (July 18, 1939–   ) Born Hunter Stockton Thompson in Louisville, Kentucky. Studied journalism at Columbia University. Served with the U.S. Air Force from 1956 to 1958; wrote for base magazine. Worked as Caribbean correspondent for *Time* and New York *Herald Tribune* (1959–60), South American correspondent for *The National Observer* (1961–63), West Coast correspondent for *The Nation* (1964–66), columnist for *Ramparts* (1967–68) and *Scanlan's Monthly* (1969–70), national affairs editor for *Rolling Stone* (1970–84), *High Times* global correspondent (1977–82), and media critic for the *San Francisco Examiner* (1985–90). Author of *Hell's Angels: A Strange and Terrible Saga* (1966), *Fear and Loathing in Las Vegas: A Savage Journey in the Heart of the American Dream* (1972), *Fear and Loathing on the Campaign Trail '72* (1973), *The Great Shark Hunt: Strange Tales from a Strange Time* (1979), *The Curse of Lono* (1983), *Generation of Swine: Tales of Shame and Degradation in the '80s* (1988), *Songs of the Doomed: More Notes on the Death of the American Dream* (1990), *Better than Sex: Confessions of a Campaign Junkie* (1993), and *The Proud Highway: Saga of a Desperate Southern Gentleman* (1997).

PAUL VOGLE (March 18, 1932–   ) Born in Anadarko, Oklahoma; educated at Sacred Heart Seminary, Detroit. Served in U.S. Army in Vietnam from 1955 to 1958 as Vietnamese language interpreter; later taught English at University of Hue. In 1961 joined editorial staff of *Saigon Daily News*. Worked as stringer for United Press International in Vietnam from 1968 until 1975. Remained with UPI after fall of South Vietnam on staff of bureaus in Bangkok and Hong Kong (1975–83), and Detroit (1983–91).

BERNARD WEINRAUB (December 19, 1937–   ) Born in New York City; graduated from City College in 1959. After two years of service in the U.S. Army, joined staff of *The New York Times* as copyboy. Reported from Vietnam for *Times* in 1968 and 1969; later based in London, New Delhi, and Washington, D.C., and, beginning in 1993, in Los Angeles. Author of *Bylines* (1983), a novel.

JOHN E. WOODRUFF (January 20, 1939–May 12, 1996) Born in Greenville, Michigan, and raised in Ann Arbor. Studied history at Williams College, graduating in 1960. After college, joined staff of *Williamstown News* as reporter; later worked for *Springfield Union*. Moved to *The Baltimore Sun* in 1965, covering police beat and city hall. Reported from Vietnam for *Sun*, 1969–70; subsequently served as bureau chief in Hong Kong (1970–73), Beijing (1982–87), and Tokyo (1988–93), and in Baltimore as deputy editorial page editor, city editor, and weekend editor. Served as Fellow at University of Michigan School of Journalism (1973–74), and later as Visiting Professor of Communication (1987–88). In 1989, published *China in Search of Its Future: Reform vs. Repression, 1982–1989.*

Note on the Texts

This volume collects newspaper and magazine articles, book excerpts, and the book *Dispatches* by Michael Herr, written between 1969 and 1977 and dealing with events connected with the Vietnam War in the period between November 1969 and May 1975. Newspaper and magazine articles have been taken from their original printings; excerpts from books are taken from first editions. Original wire copy for the three wire service articles included in this volume is not known to be extant; these articles have been taken from the most complete versions available. *Dispatches*, portions of which appeared originally in different form in *New American Review #7, Esquire,* and *Rolling Stone,* is reprinted here from the first edition, published by Alfred A. Knopf in 1977.

The following is a list of the sources of the texts included in this volume, listed alphabetically by author. For untitled pieces and untitled book excerpts, a title is supplied and is enclosed in quotation marks.

T. D. Allman. Yesterday's Prisoners Lie Dead in Bloody Cambodian Schoolyard: *The Washington Post*, April 18, 1970; The Aftermath of a Massacre: *The Washington Post*, April 20, 1970. Copyright © 1970 The Washington Post.

Stewart Alsop. The American Class System: *Newsweek*, June 29, 1970. Copyright © 1970 by Newsweek, Inc. All rights reserved. Reprinted by permission.

Peter Arnett. U.S. Embassy Looted: Associated Press wire copy, May 1, 1975. As reprinted in The Associated Press, *Twentieth Century America: A Primary Source Collection from the Associated Press.* Vol. 8: *The Crisis of National Confidence, 1974–1980* (Danbury, Connecticut: Grolier Educational Corporation, 1995). Copyright © 1975 by The Associated Press. Reprinted by permission.

Keyes Beech. We Clawed for Our Lives!: *Chicago Daily News*, May 1, 1975. Copyright © 1975 by The Chicago Sun-Times. Reprinted by permission.

Peter Braestrup. Quangtri: Anything But Easy: *The Washington Post*, July 9, 1972; Viet Soldier Serves Officer, Not Nation: *The Washington Post*, July 10, 1972. Copyright © 1972 The Washington Post. Reprinted by permission.

Malcolm W. Browne. Tenderness, Hatred and Grief Mark Saigon's Last Days: *The New York Times*, May 6, 1975. Copyright © 1975 by The New York Times Company. Reprinted by permission.

Tom Buckley. Portrait of an Aging Despot: *Harper's*, April 1972. Copyright © 1972 by Tom Buckley. Reprinted by permission.

Fox Butterfield. Who Was This Enemy?: *The New York Times Magazine*, February 4, 1973. Copyright © 1973 by The New York Times Company. Reprinted by permission.

Philip Caputo. One Small Act in a Bloody Drama—S. Viet Rangers Prove They Can Fight: *Chicago Tribune*, April 11, 1975; S. Viets Take Skeleton of City: *Chicago Tribune*, April 14, 1975; Running Again—the Last Retreat: *Chicago Tribune*, April 28, 1975. © Copyrighted Chicago Tribune Company. All rights reserved. Used with permission.

Fred J. Cook. Hard-Hats: The Rampaging Patriots: *The Nation*, June 15, 1970. Copyright © 1970 by *The Nation*. Reprinted by permission.

Le Kim Dinh. For Those Who Flee, Life Is "Hell on Earth": *The New York Times*, April 2, 1975. Copyright © 1975 by The New York Times Company. Reprinted by permission.

Gloria Emerson. At Border Crossing into Laos, the Litter of Troops and History: *The New York Times*, February 18, 1971; Copters Return from Laos with the Dead: *The New York Times*, March 3, 1971; Spirit of Saigon's Army Shaken in Laos: *The New York Times*, March 28, 1971. Copyright © 1971 by The New York Times Company. Reprinted by permission. We Are All "Bui Doi": *Playboy* magazine, June 1973. Copyright © 1973 Gloria Emerson.

George Esper. Communists Enter Saigon: Associated Press wire copy, May 1, 1975. As reprinted in The Associated Press, *Twentieth Century America: A Primary Source Collection from the Associated Press*. Vol. 8: *The Crisis of National Confidence, 1974–1980* (Danbury, Connecticut: Grolier Educational Corporation, 1995). Copyright © 1975 by The Associated Press. Reprinted by permission.

Karl Fleming. The Homecoming of Chris Mead: *Newsweek*, March 29, 1971. Copyright © 1971 by Newsweek, Inc. All rights reserved. Reprinted by permission.

Zalin Grant. "Don't Sell Your Soul": *Survivors* (New York: W. W. Norton, 1975), pp. 284–301. Copyright © 1975 by Claude Renee Boutillon. Reprinted by permission of W. W. Norton & Company.

Francine du Plessix Gray. The Moratorium and the New Mobe: *The New Yorker*, January 3, 1970. Copyright © 1970 by Francine du Plessix Gray. Reprinted by permission of Georges Borchardt, Inc., for the author.

H. D. S. Greenway. A Night with the Vietcong: *The Washington Post*, March 15, 1973; Last GIs Leave South Vietnam: *The Washington Post*, March 30, 1973. Copyright © 1973 The Washington Post.

William Greider. Viet Vets: A Sad Reminder: *The Washington Post*, March 30, 1974. Copyright © 1974 The Washington Post.

Michael Herr. *Dispatches* (New York: Alfred A. Knopf, 1977). Copyright © 1968, 1969, 1970, 1977 by Michael Herr. Reprinted by permission of Alfred A. Knopf, Inc. Permission was not granted by rights holders in two instances to reproduce song lyrics included in the first edition of *Dispatches*. These song lyrics (nineteen words from the "Lil' Red Riding Hood," by Ronald Blackwell and seven words from "Fire," by Jimi Hendrix) have been omitted, and the author has consented to the revision of two sentences involved (at 571.26–28 and 700.20–21 in this volume). Acknowledgments, as updated in 1998, for other copyrighted material included in the Alfred A. Knopf edition are indicated in below (page and line numbers refer to the present volume).

Grateful acknowledgment is made to the following for permission to reprint previously published song lyrics: ABKCO Music, Inc.: Specified eleven words from the song "2000 Light Years from Home" by Mick Jagger and Keith Richards (743.29–30). Copyright © 1967 by ABKCO Music, Inc. Also, specified seven words from the song "Citadel" by Mick Jagger and Keith Richards (743.30). Copyright © 1967 by ABKCO Music, Inc. All rights reserved. International copyright secured. Reprinted by permission. MCA Music Publishing and Spirit Two Music: Specified two lines from the song "San Francisco (Be Sure to Wear Some Flowers in Your Hair)" by John Phillips (653.7–8). Copyright © 1967 (renewed) by MCA Music Publishing, a division of Universal Studios, Inc., and Honest John Music. All rights controlled and administered by MCA Music Publishing. International copyright secured. All rights reserved. Used by permission. Arc Music Corp.: Specified ten words from the song "Good Morning, Little Schoolgirl" by Sonny Boy Williamson (751.8–9). Copyright © 1964 by Arc Music Corp. All rights reserved. Used by permission. Sony/ATV Music Publishing: Specified twenty words from the song "Magical Mystery Tour" by John Lennon and Paul McCartney (640.21–23). Copyright © 1967 by Sony/ATV Songs LLC (Renewed). All rights administered by Sony/ATV Music Publishing, 8 Music Square West, Nashville, TN 37203. All rights reserved. Used by permission. Cotillion Music, Inc.: Specified eleven words from the song "The Tighten Up" by Archie Bell & The Drells; (559.17–18). Copyright © 1968 by Cotillion Music, Inc., and Orellia Publishing Co. Also, specified seven lines from the song "For What It's Worth" by Stephen Stills (665.23–29). Copyright © 1966 by Cotillion Music, Inc., Springalo Toones and Ten-East Music. All rights reserved. Used by permission. Dwarf Music: Specified two lines of lyrics from the song "Visions of Johanna" by Bob Dylan (723.2–3). Copyright © 1966 by Dwarf Music. All rights reserved. Used by permission. Frank Zappa Music, Inc.: Specified six lines of lyrics from the song "Trouble Comin' Every Day" by Frank Zappa and the Mothers of Invention (730.29–37). Copyright © 1965 by Frank Zappa Music, Inc. All rights reserved. Used by permission. Jobete Music Co., Inc.: Specified eight words from the song "Galveston" by Jimmy Webb (762.21). Copyright © 1968 by Jobete Music Co., Inc. Also, specified ten words from the song "Shotgun" by Autry Dewalt (762.37–38). Copyright © 1965 by Jobete Music Co., Inc. All rights reserved. Used by permission. Painted Desert Music Corporation: Specified two lines of lyrics from the song "Ring of Fire" by June Carter and Merle Kilgore (563.21, 563.27–28). Copyright © 1962, 1963 by Painted Desert Music Corporation. International copyright secured. All rights reserved. Used by permission. Robert Mellin Music Publishing Corp.: Specified eight words from the song "Black Is Black" by Los Bravos (762.29). Copyright © 1965 by Robert Mellin Music Publishing Corp. Screen Gems-EMI Music, Inc.: Specified fifteen words from the song "We Gotta Get Out Of This Place," words and music by Barry Mann and Cynthia Weil (762.26–27). Copyright © 1965 by Screen

Gems-EMI Music, Inc. Also, specified ten words from the song "Hungry," words and music by Barry Mann and Cynthia Weil (762.16–17). Copyright © 1966 by Screen Gems-EMI, Inc. All rights reserved. Used by permission.

Seymour M. Hersh. Lieutenant Accused of Murdering 109 Civilians: *St. Louis Post-Dispatch*, November 13, 1969; Hamlet Attack Called "Point-Blank Murder": *St. Louis Post-Dispatch*, November 20, 1969; Ex-GI Tells of Killing Civilians at Pinkville: *St. Louis Post-Dispatch*, November 25, 1969. Copyright © 1969 *St. Louis Post-Dispatch*.

Arnold R. Isaacs. War Lingers in Hamlets as Cease-Fire Hour Passes: *Baltimore Sun*, January 29, 1973. Courtesy of *The Baltimore Sun* and Arnold Isaacs.

Peter R. Kann. A Long, Leisurely Drive through Mekong Delta Tells Much of the War: *The Wall Street Journal*, November 10, 1969; Vietnamese Alienate Cambodians in Fight Against Mutual Enemy: *The Wall Street Journal*, July 2, 1970. Copyright © 1969, 1970 Dow Jones & Company, Inc. Reprinted by permission. All rights reserved.

Doris Kearns. From Who *Was* Lyndon Baines Johnson?: Who *Was* Lyndon Baines Johnson?, *The Atlantic Monthly*, May 1976 (sections 3, 4, 6, 7, 8). Copyright © 1976 Doris Kearns.

Mike Kinsley. "I think we have a very unhappy colleague-on-leave tonight": *The Harvard Crimson*, May 19, 1970. (Title appeared originally in quotation marks.) Copyright © 1970 by The Harvard Crimson. Reprinted with permission of Michael Kinsely.

Donald Kirk. Who Wants To Be the Last American Killed in Vietnam?: *The New York Times Magazine*, September 19, 1971. Copyright © by The New York Times Company. Reprinted by permission; "I Watched Them Saw Him 3 Days": *Chicago Tribune*, July 14, 1974. (Title appeared originally in quotation marks.) © Copyrighted Chicago Tribune Company. All rights reserved. Used by permission.

Joseph Kraft. Letter from Hanoi: *The New Yorker*, August 12, 1972. Copyright © 1972 The New Yorker Magazine, Inc. All rights reserved. Reprinted by permission.

Flora Lewis. Vietnam Peace Pacts Signed; America's Longest War Halts: *The New York Times*, February 4, 1973. Copyright © 1973 by The New York Times Company. Reprinted by permission.

John S. McCain III. How the POW's Fought Back: *U.S. News & World Report*, May 14, 1973. Copyright © 1973 by U.S. News & World Report. Reprinted by permission.

Philip A. McCombs. Scars of Delta Savagery: *The Washington Post*, March 26, 1974. Copyright © 1974, The Washington Post. Reprinted by permission.

James A. Michener. What Happened on Monday: Michener, *Kent State: What Happened and Why*. (New York: Random House, 1971), pp. 327–43; Letters to the Editor: *Kent State*, pp. 434–46. Copyright © 1971 by Random House, Inc. and the Reader's Digest Association, Inc. Reprinted by permission of Random House, Inc. The map on pp. 62–63 of this volume is taken from the endpapers of *Kent State: What Happened and Why*.

Don Oberdorfer. Dawn at Memorial: Nixon, Youths Talk: *The Washington Post*, May 10, 1970. Copyright © 1970, The Washington Post. Reprinted by permission.

Rudolph Rauch. A Record of Sheer Endurance: *Time*, June 26, 1972. Copyright © 1972 by Time, Inc. Reprinted by permission.

John Saar. You Can't Just Hand Out Orders. *Life*, October 23, 1970; A Frantic Night on the Edge of Laos. *Life*, February 19, 1971; Report from the Inferno: *Life*, April 28, 1972. Copyright © 1970, 1971, 1972 by Time, Inc. Reprinted by permission.

Sydney H. Schanberg. Many Troops Fleeing from Quang Tri: *The New York Times*, May 3, 1972; "It's Everyone for Himself" as Troops Rampage in Hue: *The New York Times*, May 4, 1972; The Saigon Follies, or, Trying to Head Them Off at Credibility Gap: *The New York Times Magazine*, November 12, 1972; Bomb Error Leaves Havoc in Neak Luong: *The New York Times*, August 9, 1973; In a Besieged Cambodian City; *The New York Times*, March 29, 1975; Cambodia Reds Are Uprooting Millions As They Impose a "Peasant Revolution": *The New York Times*, May 9, 1975; American's Brief Brush With Arrest and Death: *The New York Times*, May 9, 1975; Grief and Animosity in an Embassy Haven: *The New York Times*, May 9, 1975; Evacuation Convoy to Thailand: Arduous Trip Through the Secret Cambodia: *The New York Times*, May 9, 1975. Copyright © 1972, 1973, 1975 by The New York Times Company. Reprinted by permission.

Robert Shaplen. We Have Always Survived: *The New Yorker*, April 15, 1972. Copyright © 1972 by The Estate of Robert Shaplen. All rights reserved. Reprinted by permission.

James P. Sterba. Scraps of Paper from Vietnam: *The New York Times Magazine*, October 18, 1970. Copyright © 1970 by The New York Times Company. Reprinted by permission.

Bob Tamarkin. Diary of S. Viet's Last Hours: *Chicago Daily News*, May 6, 1972. Copyright © 1975 The Chicago Sun-Times. Reprinted by permission.

Hunter S. Thompson. From *Fear and Loathing: On the Campaign Trail '72*. Thompson, *Fear and Loathing: On the Campaign Trail '72*. (San Francisco: Straight Arrow, 1973), pp. 381–92. Copyright © 1973 Hunter S. Thompson. Reprinted by permission.

Paul Vogle. "A Flight into Hell": UPI wire copy, March 29, 1975. As reprinted in Alan Dawson, *55 Days: The Fall of South Vietnam* (Englewood Cliffs, New Jersey: Prentice-Hall, 1977), pp. 182–84.

Bernard Weinraub. A Highlands Mother Escapes, but Pays a Terrible Toll: *The New York Times*, March 19, 1975. Copyright © 1975 by The New York Times Company. Reprinted by permission.

John E. Woodruff. CIA Alliance Brings Ruin to Proud Race: *Baltimore Sun*, February 21, 1971; U.S. Finances Victor to Refugee Transit: *Baltimore Sun*, February 22, 1971; A War Exhausted People Seek a Way Out: *Baltimore Sun*, February 23, 1971. Courtesy of *The Baltimore Sun*.

The map on page 767 in this volume is taken from Arnold R. Isaacs, *Without Honor: Defeat in Vietnam and Cambodia* (Baltimore: Johns Hopkins

This volume presents the texts listed here without change except for the correction of typographical errors, but it does not attempt to reproduce features of their typographic design. The following is a list of typographic errors, cited by page and line number: 8.17, forcig; 14.17, Dispute; 19.34, GIs'; 19.37, the report; 20.3, Berkhardt; 21.2, Utah. Then; 27.1–2, Meadlo; 52.11, that he has; 52.13, unhaven; 52.13, placed; 52.32, Shianouk; 54.11, I; 54.29, policeman; 56.2–3, We . . . them.; 56.8–9, Prince . . . sympathetic.; 89.17, threshhold; 89.24, ond; 89.37, behaver; 92.24, 33, Averill; 92.34, appreciately; 92.36, Eliot; 93.31, actics; 94.13, Eliot; 94.26, advise; 96.26, Japan; 98.7, assistant; 98.20, late.; 144.18, beautiful."; 172.7, place."; 191.33, thatn; 193.32, American; 196.3, sill; 196.39, perserve; 217.29, eatting; 229.19, a a; 355.1, briefly, 1968; 355.1, Cinnamon; 355.26, comander; 355.32, get-/getting; 357.39, Dnang; 359.13, Siagon; 359.16, 1970; 359.28, well from; 360.10, question"; 360.14, helicopter; 360.38, GI; 361.17, "difficult"; 361.17–18, "political directives"; 361.19, "unable . . . situation."; 361.24, divisions; 361.37, command for; 361.40, (GI); 362.26, Hunghia; 362.27, Binhfinh; 362.27, provinces. inces; 362.29, forces; 365.12, units; 365.18, batallion; 367.20, recoiless; 367.25, ob; 367.27 Khuhon; 412.22, *indocrination*; 426.3, a Tuong; 426.31, secruity; 427.7, Thon; 427.29, networks's; 455.26, Caddis; 465.18, em-/embassy; 466.5, outside; 467.8, That; 467.30, 865; 467.32, rockpile; 469.8, occured; 475.10, It; 480.15, compaints; 480.34, shouted "Money,"; 490.34, civilian."; 490.36, explosion; 491.1, yerar; 497.24, aboard."; 497.25, Let's; 500.7, reidgeline; 501.13, concial; 501.25, devasted; 502.39, But; 523.8, were; 526.9, begain; 527.10, 1 the; 528.6, scrapping; 533.26, side." Why; 535.32, Anyway; 539.19, third-county; 542.29, La Guex; 552.23, life; 588.39, COORDS; 594.15, Landsdale; 660.38, B-25's; 687.37, March,; 728.12, Touhy; 742.19–20, Rentmeister.

Notes

In the notes below, the reference numbers denote page and line of this volume (the line count includes headings). No note is made for material included in standard desk-reference books such as Webster's *Collegiate, Biographical,* and *Geographical* dictionaries. Biblical references are keyed to the King James Version. Footnotes and bracketed editorial notes within the text were in the originals. For historical background see Chronology in this volume. For weapons and military terms not identified in the notes, see Glossary in this volume. For further historical background and references to other studies, see Stanley Karnow, *Vietnam: A History* (revised edition; New York: Viking Penguin, 1991); Harry G. Summers Jr., *Vietnam War Almanac* (New York: Facts on File Publications, 1985); and *Encyclopedia of the Vietnam War,* ed. Stanley I. Kutler (New York: Macmillan Reference USA, 1996). For further background on Vietnam war journalism, see Clarence R. Wyatt, *Paper Soldiers: The American Press and the Vietnam War* (New York: W. W. Norton, 1993). For more detailed maps, see Harry G. Summers Jr., *Historical Atlas of the Vietnam War* (Boston: Houghton Mifflin, 1995).

2.37–38   Nixon's troop-withdrawal] See Chronology, June 1969.

3.14–15   "Saigon tea"] Cold tea or soda which customers in a bar had to purchase in order to talk with a hostess.

9.28   Popular . . . Force] People's Self Defense Force.

10.9–10   U.S.-controlled . . . (PRU)] The Provincial Reconnaissance Units were organized and directed by the Central Intelligence Agency.

13.23   murder . . . Green Berets] The army announced on August 6, 1969, that Colonel Robert Rheault, the former commander of the Fifth Special Forces Group, and seven men who had served under his command had been charged with the murder on June 20, 1969, of a Vietnamese intelligence agent whom they suspected of working for the Communists as well as the United States. The charges were dismissed on September 29, 1969, after the CIA refused to release documents pertaining to the case.

16.7–8   men who . . . Calley] See page 22.13–22 in this volume.

20.37   copyright story] The story was written by Joe Eszterhas, a reporter for the *Plain Dealer.* Haeberle later sold the photographs to *Life* for $19,550; they appeared in the magazine on December 5, 1969.

21.30   helicopter pilot]   Hugh Thompson Jr., an observation helicopter
pilot with the 123rd Aviation Battalion.

21.34   pilot was killed]   Glenn Andreotta, the crew chief on Thompson's
helicopter, was killed in action on April 8, 1968. Thompson reported what he
had witnessed at My Lai to his superior officers on March 16 and to Colonel
Oran Henderson, commander of the 11th Brigade, on March 18, 1968; he later
testified at Calley's court-martial, as did his door gunner, Lawrence Colburn.
In 1998 Thompson, Colburn, and Andreotta were awarded the Soldier's
Medal by the U.S. army for having saved the lives of at least ten villagers at
My Lai.

23.18–24   Medina . . . Calley]   Medina was court-martialed for murder
and acquitted on September 22, 1971. Mitchell was court-martialed for assault
with intent to commit murder and was acquitted on November 20, 1970.
Calley was convicted of premeditated murder on March 29, 1971, and sentenced
to life imprisonment. On April 1, 1971, President Nixon ordered that Calley
be released from the stockade and placed under house arrest at Fort Benning,
Georgia, while his conviction was appealed. Calley's sentence was reduced on
administrative appeal to 20 years imprisonment in August 1971 and to ten years
in April 1974; he was paroled on November 9, 1974. Ten other soldiers from
Charlie Company were charged for crimes committed at My Lai; one was
acquitted at court-martial and the charges against the other nine were dismissed. Colonel Oran Henderson, the former commander of the 11th Brigade,
was court-martialed for his role in concealing the massacre and acquitted on
December 17, 1971. Similar charges brought against 13 other officers, including
Major General Samuel Koster, the former commander of the Americal Division, were dismissed.

24.6   17 M-16 . . . clip]   To reduce the risk of misfeeds, American soldiers
often loaded only 17 or 18 rounds into a 20-round M-16 magazine.

32.36   New Hampshire primary]   See Chronology, March 1968.

33.16   Bayard Rustin's]   Rustin was a civil rights and anti-war activist who
worked closely with A. Philip Randolph and with King.

34.22   SANE]   Committee for a Sane Nuclear Policy, founded in 1957.

35.40–36.1   Galbraith . . . Goodwin]   Galbraith, a professor of economics
at Harvard, had served as U.S. ambassador to India, 1961–63; Goodwin, a
former speechwriter in the Johnson administration, had worked for the 1968
presidential campaigns of Robert Kennedy and Eugene McCarthy.

37.39   S.D.S.]   Students for a Democratic Society, founded in 1962.

38.7   Goodell]   Republican senator from New York.

38.18–19   Allard Lowenstein's]   Lowenstein served in Congress, 1969–71,
representing a district on Long Island, New York. Before his election in 1968
he had played a major role in organizing opposition within the Democratic
Party to the renomination of Lyndon Johnson.

39.16   Dick Gregory] A comedian who had been active in the civil rights movement since the early 1960s.

43.28   Student National . . . Committee] Student Non-violent Coordinating Committee.

44.20   George Wald] Biochemist and professor of biology at Harvard University, and a co-recipient of the 1967 Nobel Prize in physiology.

45.18–19   Chicago . . . defendants] Abbie Hoffman, Jerry Rubin, David Dellinger, Rennie Davis, Tom Hayden, Bobby Seale, Lee Weiner, and John Froines were indicted in March 1969 on federal charges of having conspired to incite a riot during the 1968 Democratic National Convention in Chicago. Their trial, which began in September 1969, was marked by frequent outbursts in the courtroom, and in early November Judge Julius Hoffman declared a mistrial in Seale's case. Abbie Hoffman, Rubin, Dellinger, Davis, and Hayden were found guilty in February 1970, but their convictions were overturned on appeal, and the charges against Seale were eventually dropped.

45.36–37   clean-for-Gene] Phrase used to describe young people who adopted a more conservative personal appearance while campaigning for Eugene McCarthy in 1968.

46.11   John W. Dean III] Dean later served as White House counsel, 1970–73, and became a major participant in the Watergate scandal.

46.13   Lindsay] The mayor of New York, elected in 1965 and reelected in 1969.

47.32   Kim Agnew] The 14-year-old daughter of Vice-President Spiro Agnew, who reportedly had been prevented by her father from participating in the October 1969 Moratorium.

47.33   Snobs for Peace] In a speech delivered on October 19, 1969, Vice-President Agnew described leaders of the anti-war movement as an "effete corps of impudent snobs."

49.6–7   Nixon's . . . speech] In his televised address, Nixon announced that his administration had adopted a plan for the eventual complete withdrawal of all U.S. ground combat forces from Vietnam and asked for the support of "the great silent majority of my fellow Americans."

52.11–12   catastrophe . . . March 18] See Chronology, March–April 1970.

53.21   Thursday] April 16, 1970.

57.3   *Kent State . . . Why*] In his afterword to *Kent State*, Michener described the book as a collaboration with a team of researchers that included Andrew Jones, John Hubbell, Leslie Laird, Nathan Adams, Eugene Methvin, Mari Yoriko Sabusawa, Linda Peterson, Ben Post, Jeff Sallot, Larry Rose, Scott Mueller, John P. Hayes, Howard Ruffner, and John Filo.

57.13   confusion on campus]   The ROTC building on the Kent State campus was destroyed by arson on the evening of Saturday, May 2, 1970, as a large crowd of student demonstrators watched. Units of the Ohio National Guard arrived on campus later that night, and on Sunday night, May 3, student demonstrators and Guardsmen clashed during rioting on campus and in the town of Kent.

57.21   Satrom]   LeRoy Satrom, the mayor of Kent, Ohio.

61.34   Eszterhas and Roberts]   Joe Eszterhas and Michael D. Roberts, in *13 Seconds: Confrontation at Kent State* (1970).

68.21–22   Alewitz . . . later]   Alewitz, a member of the Trotskyist Young Socialist Alliance, had been tear-gassed earlier in the confrontation and was running toward Johnson Hall so that he could wash the irritants from his eyes. After seeing the Guard he retreated to the fence and then passed through a small hole in it.

72.40   the Guard]   In a report issued on October 16, 1970, a special state grand jury stated that the Guardsmen had fired their weapons "in the honest and sincere belief that they would suffer bodily injury had they not done so" and therefore were not subject to criminal prosecution.

73.2–4   Walker . . . Filo]   Walker and Filo were Kent State students who photographed the events of May 4. Filo was awarded the Pulitzer Prize for Spot News Photography for his photograph of 14-year-old Mary Vecchio kneeling beside the body of Jeffrey Miller.

80.1–2   construction . . . New York]   See pp. 101–7 in this volume.

81.12–13   silent majority . . . snobs]   See notes 49.6–7 and 47.33 in this volume.

81.14   'bums']   During a visit to the Pentagon on May 1, 1970, Nixon had praised American troops in Vietnam and then said: "You know, you see these bums, you know, blowing up the campuses."

85.2–3   *"I think . . . tonight"*]   This article appeared in the Harvard *Crimson* with a head note that read: "This is the second of a two-part feature about a group of distinguished senior faculty members—most former presidential advisers—who went to Washington, D.C., May 8, to lobby against the war. When last seen, Our Heroes were crossing Lafayette Park toward the White House for a meeting with their once-and-future Harvard colleague—and special assistant to the President for National Security Affairs—Henry Kissinger."

85.5   FRANCIS BATOR]   Professor of political economy at the John F. Kennedy School of Government, Harvard University.

85.21–22   special assistant . . . Affairs.]   Bator served from 1965 until 1967, with responsibility for foreign economic policy and European relations.

85.25   Rostow's] Walt Rostow, chairman of the Policy Planning Council of the Department of State, 1961–66, and national security adviser to President Johnson, 1966–69.

86.17   Dean May] Ernest May was the dean of Harvard College, 1969–71.

87.28   SALT] Strategic Arms Limitation Talks. The negotiations, which began in 1969, resulted in the signing in 1972 of major U.S.-Soviet agreements limiting defensive and offensive nuclear weapons.

88.35   Bundy] McGeorge Bundy, presidential national security adviser, 1961–66, and former dean of Harvard College, 1953–61.

90.7   Undersecretary of State] Undersecretary of Defense.

90.14–15   Friday] May 8, 1970.

91.11   Reston's] James Reston, columnist for *The New York Times.*

92.27   Scotty] James Reston.

92.35–36   Elliot Richardson] Richardson later served as Secretary of Health, Education, and Welfare (1970–73), Secretary of Defense (1973), and Attorney General (1973). In October 1973 he resigned after refusing an order from Nixon to fire Archibald Cox, the Watergate special prosecutor.

93.9   Herb Klein] White House director of communications.

94.39   CFIA] Center for International Affairs.

96.5   yesterday] May 9, 1970.

97.16–17   Merriman Smith] Smith had been a White House correspondent for United Press International.

109.22   Watts . . . flames] During rioting in Los Angeles in 1965.

118.4   Supreme Court ruling] *Welsh* v. *United States.*

119.19   Secretary Laird] Melvin Laird served as Secretary of Defense during the first Nixon administration, 1969–73.

119.39   Life . . . last year] The photographs appeared in *Life* on June 27, 1969.

124.20   Guam Doctrine] At a press briefing held on Guam on July 25, 1969, Nixon had said that the United States would no longer provide ground troops to defend Asian countries against Communist subversion and insurgencies.

131.17   *New Life Development*] A pacification program.

139.19   MOS] Military Occupation Specialty.

140.14   *Robert Rheault*] See note 13.23 in this volume.

142.14   rome plow]   A special bulldozer used for clearing paths in the
jungle.

147.14   lema]   A telephone line.

148.24   50 ammo]   Ammunition for a .50 caliber heavy machine gun.

149.2   the major's . . . the colonel]   Identified in *Into the Storm: A Study
in Command*, by Tom Clancy with Fred Franks Jr. (1997), as Major Fred
Franks, operations officer of the Second Squadron, 11th Armored Cavalry, and
Colonel Donn Starry, commander of the 11th Armored Cavalry. Franks
eventually had his left leg amputated below the knee, but remained on active
duty and commanded the VII Corps in Saudi Arabia and Iraq during the 1991
Gulf War.

150.11   Sonmy]   The village in which the hamlet of My Lai is located.

152.7   *A.C.R.*]   Armored Cavalry Regiment.

154.4   Nixon's . . . cease-fire]   In a televised address on October 7, 1970,
Nixon proposed an internationally supervised "cease-fire in place" throughout
Indochina and the convening of an Indochina peace conference.

154.14   Hamburger Hill]   See Chronology, May 1969.

163.37–38   Robert McNamara]   Secretary of Defense from January 1961 to
February 1968.

170.21   Fulbright]   Democratic senator from Arkansas and chairman of the
Senate Foreign Relations Committee.

171.26   Galbraiths]   See note 35.40–36.1 in this volume.

171.27–28   Burnet Cave]   Near Burnet, Texas, about 30 miles from Johnson's childhood home.

174.33   first bombing pause]   May 13–17, 1965.

174.38   Senator Morse]   Democrat Wayne Morse of Oregon, one of two
senators to vote against the Tonkin Gulf Resolution in 1964.

175.1   Clark . . . Church]   Democratic senators Joseph Clark of Pennsylvania, Mike Mansfield of Montana, and Frank Church of Idaho.

175.2   Dobrynin]   Anatoli Dobrynin, the Soviet ambassador to the United
States.

175.4   Rusk . . . Clifford]   Dean Rusk served as Secretary of State, 1961–
69. Clark Clifford served as an unofficial presidential adviser before becoming
Secretary of Defense in 1968.

175.7   ordered a pause]   From December 24, 1965, until January 30, 1966.

176.26   Henry Fowler]   Secretary of the Treasury, 1965–68.

177.6   Geneva Accords]   See Chronology, 1954.

177.33   elections . . . 1967?] The presidential and senate elections held on September 3, 1967, in which 83 percent of the registered voters were reported to have voted.

181.6   Larry Burrows] British photographer for *Life* who had covered the Vietnam War since 1962. Burrows was killed on February 10, 1971, when his helicopter was shot down over Laos.

193.32   Continental Air Services] Charter airline that flew missions on contract for the CIA and the Agency for International Development.

197.38   agency that preceded] United States Operations Mission.

200.6–8   Vang Pao . . . country] Vang Pao was evacuated from Laos on May 14, 1975, and later became an American citizen.

202.39   Phou Pha Thi] Mountain, over 5,500 feet high, in northeastern Laos, 160 miles west of Hanoi. In late 1967 the U.S. air force built a secret radar installation near the summit that was used to guide aircraft bombing North Vietnam in bad weather and at night. The installation, which was supplied by helicopter and guarded by Hmong soldiers, was overrun by the North Vietnamese on March 11, 1968; 11 air force technicians were killed during the attack.

206.16   Hotel 2] A South Vietnamese artillery base.

208.32   Wednesday] March 24, 1971.

209.31   Brigade A] Possibly a mistranslation of Battery A.

215.13   amphibious "duck"] An amphibious truck equipped with a propeller and a rudder.

220.38–40   brigade commander . . . defoliant] Brigadier General John Donaldson was accused in June 1971 of murdering six Vietnamese civilians in 1968–69; the charges were dropped in December 1971. In October 1970 *Time* magazine reported that units of the Americal Division were continuing to disperse Agent Orange despite an April 15, 1970, order suspending its use in Vietnam.

221.2   attack . . . firebase] Fire Base Mary Ann was attacked on the night of March 27–28, 1971, by North Vietnamese sappers who infiltrated through the perimeter without being detected and then killed 30 American soldiers before withdrawing.

242.28   mercenaries . . . Asia] American aid paid for the deployment of Thai and South Korean troops in South Vietnam.

243.10   Hué . . . hundreds] At least 2,800 people were murdered by the Viet Cong in Hue during the Tet Offensive in 1968.

244.2   Tansonhut] The headquarters of the South Vietnamese Joint General Staff were at Tan Son Nhut air base.

246.1   prize money]   Eddie Adams was awarded the Pulitzer Prize for
Spot News Photography for his photograph of General Loan shooting the
Viet Cong suspect.

247.12   *"vite" . . . "moins vite"*]   Fast; less fast.

247.17–18   Sainteny's . . . *Manquée*]   Book (1953) by Jean Sainteny, who
negotiated an agreement on the status of Vietnam with Ho Chi Minh in 1946;
see Chronology.

249.38   *The Strawberry Statement*]   *The Strawberry Statement: Notes of a
College Revolutionary* by James Simon Kunen (1969), an account of the student unrest at Columbia University in 1968.

254.11   Open Arms]   Chieu Hoi; see Glossary.

256.1–6   "Come on . . . fun."]   From "Feel Like I'm Fixin' to Die Rag"
by Country Joe McDonald (1967).

256.7   Sterba]   James Sterba, a correspondent for *The New York Times*.

264.2   *"Don't . . . Soul"*]   This excerpt from the book *Survivors* describes
events that took place in a prison camp in Hanoi called "The Plantation" and
"Plantation Gardens" by American POWs.

264.4   *Harker*]   David Harker, an army rifleman captured in South Vietnam on January 8, 1968, and held by the Viet Cong in a jungle camp in
western Quang Nam province until February 1971, when the surviving American prisoners in the camp were marched north along the Ho Chi Minh Trail
into North Vietnam.

264.20   Kushner]   Captain Floyd Kushner, an army doctor who was captured after his helicopter crashed in November 1967 and held in the Quang
Nam camp until 1971.

265.24   Peace Committee]   Name used in "The Plantation" for a group
of five (later eight) American prisoners, all of whom were army or marine
enlisted men who had been captured in South Vietnam.

265.25   *Guy . . . Elliott*]   Lieutenant Colonel Ted Guy, an air force F-4
pilot, was shot down over Laos on March 11, 1968. Major Artice Elliott was
captured near Dak To in 1970 while serving as an adviser with the South
Vietnamese army.

268.4   *McMillan . . . Anzaldua*]   Ike McMillan, an army mortarman, was
captured on March 12, 1968, and held in the Quang Nam camp until 1971.
Anzaldua, a marine POW, was brought to the Quang Nam camp in February
1970.

268.10–11   Riate . . . Kavanaugh]   Al Riate, Bob Chenoweth, and Larry
Kavanaugh were members of the Peace Committee.

268.20   Cheese] Prisoners' name for Le Van Vuong, a lieutenant in the North Vietnamese army.

269.36   *Daly*] James Daly, an army rifleman captured on January 9, 1968, and held in the Quang Nam camp until 1971.

272.14   Anton] Frank Anton, an army helicopter pilot, captured on January 5, 1968, and held in the Quang Nam camp until 1971.

272.20   *Davis*] Tom Davis, an army mortarman captured on March 12, 1968, also a prisoner in the Quang Nam camp until 1971.

274.19–20   article . . . *Times*] The article appeared December 24, 1971.

275.21   Sontay raid] See Chronology, November 1970.

278.21   *Young*] John Young, a member of the Peace Committee, was a sergeant in the special forces captured near Khe Sanh on January 30, 1968.

279.32   my religion] Daly, who was raised as a Baptist, considered himself a Jehovah's Witness but had been unable to obtain conscientious-objector status.

280.11   Elbert] A marine prisoner who had assumed a false identity while in the Quang Nam camp.

280.15   the PCs] After their release in 1973 Colonel Guy brought charges against Riate, Chenoweth, Kavanaugh, Young, Daly, Elbert, and the two other members of the Peace Committee. The military dismissed the charges after Kavanaugh committed suicide on June 27, 1973.

292.5   Pentagon Papers] See Chronology, June 1971.

298.4   "Guernica"-like] Painting (1937) by Pablo Picasso, inspired by bombing of the town of Guernica during the Spanish Civil War.

303.21–22   book . . . voyage] *History of a Voyage to the China Sea*.

309.28–29   Sûreté headquarters] French police headquarters and prison.

323.12   pro-Kuomintang] Supporters of the Chinese Nationalists.

325.9   "Hansel and Gretel"] Three-act opera (1893) by Engelbert Humperdinck, with libretto by Adelheid Wette.

327.27   first coup] The coup attempt, staged by disaffected army officers on November 11–12, 1960, failed.

328.26   Pham Xuan An] An worked for the Reuters news agency before becoming a staff correspondent for *Time* magazine. He remained in Vietnam in 1975, and later revealed that he had served as a Viet Cong intelligence officer from 1960 onward.

336.7–8   "Freedom's . . . lose] From "Me and Bobby McGee" by Kris Kristofferson, recorded by Janis Joplin for her album *Pearl* (1971).

337.36   tac air]   Tactical air support by fighter-bombers.

340.30   fire . . . Bastogne]   The fire base had been built by the U.S. 101st
Airborne Division and named after the Belgian town defended by the division
during the Battle of the Bulge in December 1944.

342.19   enemy offensive]   See Chronology, March–May 1972.

350.15   An Loc]   See Chronology, April–July 1972.

352.31   Tan Canh]   The South Vietnamese regiment defending Tan Canh,
a combat base 25 miles north of Kontum, broke and fled on April 24, 1972,
after the North Vietnamese launched a tank attack.

356.32   draftee division]   Conscripts served in the 11 regular infantry divisions of the South Vietnamese army, but not in the all-volunteer airborne and
marine divisions.

358.3   Carmine De Sapio]   Leader of the New York City Democratic
Party, 1949–61.

360.30–31   end of May]   End of March.

361.34   Ky, Big Minh]   Both Vice-President Nguyen Cao Ky and Duong
Van Minh, the general who led the 1963 coup against Diem, were presidential
candidates in 1971 before they withdrew from the race and charged Thieu with
rigging the election. (Minh was called "Big Minh" by some Americans because of his six-foot height.)

372.2–3   anti-personnel bombs]   See CBU in Glossary.

372.31–32   use anti-personnel bombs]   Anti-personnel cluster bombs were
used by American aircraft over North Vietnam to attack anti-aircraft artillery
batteries and surface-to-air missile sites.

378.6   *Pravda*]   Official newspaper of the Soviet Communist Party.

381.3–4   "*J'ai . . . Paris*]   I have two loves / My country and Paris.

381.10   Yevtushenko]   Russian poet Yevgeny Yevtushenko.

382.13–14   Aeroflot]   Soviet airline.

383.8   *Izvestia*]   Official newspaper of the Soviet government.

385.29   San Diego]   The 1972 Republican National Convention was originally scheduled to be held in San Diego, but was moved to Miami for security
reasons.

385.30–31   Five weeks . . . McGovern]   The 1972 Democratic National
Convention was held in Miami, July 10–14, and nominated Senator George
McGovern for president.

390.17 Pete McCloskey] Republican congressman from California who had received 20 percent of the vote running as an anti-war candidate against Nixon in the 1972 New Hampshire presidential primary.

392.7 Ron Kovic] Later author of the memoir *Born on the Fourth of July* (1976).

392.23–393.2 last year . . . fence] On April 23, 1971, members of the Vietnam Veterans Against the War threw their medals over a fence onto the steps of the Capitol.

395.27–28 "protective reaction" attacks] Airstrikes against North Vietnamese air defense sites during the 1968–72 bombing halt, carried out to protect U.S. reconnaissance aircraft flying over North Vietnam.

431.17 Coleman lantern] A gasoline-fueled lantern.

435.24 name . . . birth] The only information a prisoner of war is obliged to give under the Geneva Convention.

436.20 father . . . admiral] John S. McCain Jr., who served as commander of U.S. forces in the Pacific, 1968–72.

438.10–11 Vietnamese Workers Party] Official name of the Vietnamese Communist Party.

440.6–9 Day . . . recaptured] After his release in 1973 Day was awarded the Medal of Honor for his escape attempt and his determined resistance to interrogation.

441.34 Ernie . . . civilian pilot] Brace flew for Air America, the CIA-owned airline that provided logistical support for anti-Communist forces in Laos.

443.13 Code of Conduct] The Code of Conduct for Members of the Armed Forces of the United States, first issued in 1955.

443.19 Alvarez] Everett Alvarez, a navy pilot shot down over North Vietnam on August 5, 1964.

447.37 Fort Hood Three] Three soldiers who were court-martialed for refusing to go to Vietnam after completing basic training at Fort Hood, Texas, in June 1966. They each served two years in prison.

448.29–30 Capt. Dick Stratton] Stratton, a naval officer, held the rank of commander when he was shot down on January 5, 1967.

449.6 press conference] Held on March 6, 1967. A photograph of Stratton bowing at the conference appeared in *Life* on April 7, 1967.

454.23 Capt. Jeremiah Denton] A naval officer.

457.1–2 Senator Brooke] Edward W. Brooke, a Republican from Massachusetts.

457.6   Ramsey Clark]   Clark had served as Attorney General in the Johnson administration, 1967–69. He visited North Vietnam in July 1972.

459.11   China . . . Russia]   Nixon visited China in February 1972 and
signed agreements on strategic arms during his visit to the Soviet Union in
May 1972.

461.27   Kissinger . . . Hanoi]   In February 1973.

462.1   International Control Commission]   See page 423.26–29 in this
volume.

464.13   Joint Military Commission]   The commission, established under
the Paris Accords and composed of delegations from the U.S., South Vietnam,
North Vietnam, and the Viet Cong, supervised the withdrawal of the remaining American and South Korean troops from South Vietnam and the exchange
of prisoners of war. It was succeeded on March 29, 1973, by the Joint Military
Team.

470.5   Monday]   August 6, 1973.

489.9–10   recent surge . . . Highlands]   See Chronology, March 1975.

493.6–7   Hac . . . Panthers).]   An elite company of the 1st Division.

500.12   Tuesday]   April 8, 1975.

501.25   Sunday]   April 13, 1975.

504.4–6   *Cambodia . . . Revolution*]   This story appeared in *The New
York Times* with a headnote that read: "The writer of the following dispatch
remained in Cambodia after the American evacuation and was among the
foreigners who arrived in Thailand last Saturday. His dispatches were withheld,
under an agreement among all the confined correspondents, until the remaining foreigners were transported to safety yesterday."

510.23–29 Long Boret . . . executed.]   Long Boret, Sisowath Sirik Matak, and Lon Non were executed by the Khmer Rouge.

511.21   Congress . . . aid]   President Gerald Ford requested $222 million
in supplemental military aid for Cambodia on January 28, 1975, but Congress
did not approve any additional funds.

516.38   Dith Pran]   Pran was forced to leave the French embassy compound on April 20, 1975, and was sent by the Khmer Rouge to the countryside,
where he pretended to be a former Phnom Penh taxi driver. He escaped across
the border into Thailand on October 3, 1979, and immigrated to the United
States. Sydney Schanberg wrote about his experiences in an article, "The
Death and Life of Dith Pran," published in *The New York Times Magazine*
on January 20, 1980, which became the basis for the film *The Killing Fields*
(1984).

531.4   Tuesday]   April 29, 1975.

535.35   Graham Martin] U.S. ambassador to South Vietnam, 1973–75.

537.19   H. G. Summers] Harry G. Summers Jr., later the author of *On Strategy: A Critical Analysis of the Vietnam War* (1982).

543.36   Thomas Polgar] CIA station chief in Saigon, 1973–75.

548.19–21   bronze plaque . . . wall] The plaque had been removed from the wall on April 29 by Captain Stuart Herrington (see pp. 537–38 in this volume), who had intended to take it with him but changed his mind after being ordered to leave before the last Vietnamese at the embassy were evacuated. In his book *Peace with Honor?* (1983), Herrington wrote: "Disgusted at what I was about to do, I canceled my plans to rescue the plaque. ('Those guys would roll over in their graves if they could see what's happening now!')"

559.17–18   "C'mon now . . . Up. . . ."] From "The Tighten Up" (1968), by Archie Bell and The Drells.

560.3   La Vida Loca] The crazy life.

561.7   Willy Peter] White phosphorus.

562.10   banana clips] Curved magazines.

563.21   *I fell . . . fire*] From "Ring of Fire" (1962), by June Carter and Merle Kilgore, recorded by Johnny Cash.

563.27–28   *and it . . . burns*] From "Ring of Fire."

581.10   seals, recondos] SEALs (from "Sea-Air-Land") were members of the U.S. navy special forces; recondos (from "recon" and "commando") were men trained at special schools in South Vietnam to conduct long-range reconnaissance patrols.

582.31   *dakini*] A female deity in Hindu and Buddhist mythology and iconography.

589.13–14   Leonard Wood or Andrews] Army base in Missouri; air force base in Maryland.

590.25   *Fort Apache*] Western (1948) directed by John Ford.

592.17   A Camps] Camps used by 12-man special forces A Teams.

593.4   Trail of Tears] Route taken by the eastern Cherokees when they were forcibly removed from Georgia by the U.S. army and sent to the Indian Territory (Oklahoma) in 1838–39.

593.12   a novel] *The Quiet American* (1955), by Graham Greene.

594.15   Edward Lansdale] In 1954–56 Lansdale headed a special CIA team based in Saigon that conducted covert operations against the Communists in North Vietnam and in support of the Diem regime in the South. Lansdale later served as a special assistant to the U.S. ambassador to South Vietnam, 1965–68.

594.31   Deuxième Bureau]   French military intelligence.

598.25   *sin loi*]   Vietnamese: "Sorry about that."

599.25   Huey Newton]   Co-founder of the Black Panther Party.

601.35   *Nevada Smith*]   Western (1966) directed by Henry Hathaway.

608.16   C Camp]   A special forces headquarters.

609.24   *On the Beach*]   Film (1959) about the aftermath of nuclear war,
directed by Stanley Kramer.

610.28–30   American major . . . it."]   In his February 7, 1968, story about
the fighting in Ben Tre, Associated Press correspondent Peter Arnett quoted
an unnamed U.S. major as saying: "It became necessary to destroy the town
to save it."

611.28–39   deuce-and-a-half]   Two-and-a-half-ton truck.

614.13   2/5]   Second Battalion, Fifth Marine Regiment.

614.21   Navy LCU's]   Landing craft.

618.18   1/5]   First Battalion, Fifth Marine Regiment.

618.35   mustang]   An officer promoted from the ranks.

624.27   V-ring]   The innermost part of a rifle target.

632.27–28   hills . . . abandoned]   The marines withdrew from Hill 881
North, but held Hill 881 South throughout the 1968 siege.

634.38   Udorn]   Airbase in Thailand.

640.4   Wallace Stevens' poem]   "Anecdote of the Jar," published in *Har-
monium* (1923).

640.21–23   "The Magical . . . away,"]   From "Magical Mystery Tour"
(1967) by John Lennon and Paul McCartney, recorded by the Beatles.

640.37   "Archlights,"]   Arc Light was the code name for B-52 missions
flown against targets in South Vietnam.

653.7–8   'When you . . . hair.']   From "San Francisco (Be Sure to Wear
Some Flowers in Your Hair)" (1967), by John Phillips, recorded by Scott
McKenzie.

665.23–29   There's . . . goin' down]   From "For What It's Worth"
(1966), by Stephen Stills, recorded by Buffalo Springfield.

669.38   PIO]   Public Information Officer.

674.27   III MAF]   III Marine Amphibious Force, the corps-level headquarters in Danang that controlled marine operations in the northern provinces of South Vietnam.

679.1–3   the one . . . inventions.]   Cf. Psalm 106:39.

696.17   Cleaver . . . Brown]   Cleaver was a Black Panther leader and author of *Soul on Ice* (1968); Brown, a Black Power advocate, succeeded Stokely Carmichael as chairman of the Student Non-violent Coordinating Committee in May 1967.

697.3   Saigon tea]   See note 3.14–15 in this volume.

701.10   LOH]   Light Observation Helicopter.

703.16   S-2]   Intelligence officer for a battalion or regiment.

706.1   *The Green Berets*]   Film (1968) starring and co-directed by John Wayne.

711.18   those movies]   Sean Flynn appeared in *The Son of Captain Blood* (1962), *Duel at the Rio Grande* (1962), *Stop Train 349* (1964), *The Temple of the White Elephant* (1965), and *Singapore, Singapore* (1968).

725.17   David's file . . . *Time*]   On February 16, 1968.

725.22–23   piece . . . *Esquire*]   "Hell Sucks" appeared in August 1968.

730.24–25   Mothers . . . Every Day"]   By Frank Zappa and the Mothers of Invention (1965).

733.27   *Scoop*]   Novel (1938) by Evelyn Waugh.

737.11–12   Marine operation . . . Starlight]   Operation Starlite, the marine offensive near Chu Lai in August 1965; see Chronology.

737.18–19   the Reservoir or Chickamauga]   The Chosin Reservoir in North Korea, where the 1st Marine Division broke out of a Chinese encirclement in December 1950; Chickamauga Creek in northwestern Georgia, scene of a Confederate victory in the Civil War, September 19–20, 1863.

740.29   *Dawn Patrol*]   Films (1930, 1938) about World War I aviators; the 1938 version starred Errol Flynn.

743.10   Jurati Kazikas]   Jurate Kazickas.

743.29–30   "It's so very . . . Citadel,"]   From "2000 Light Years from Home" and "Citadel" (1967), by Mick Jagger and Keith Richards, recorded by the Rolling Stones.

743.35   *John Wesley Harding*]   Album (1968) by Bob Dylan.

746.14   Swift boat]   A small patrol boat 50 feet in length, usually manned by a crew of five or six.

748.20   June War]   June 1967.

749.4   Halliburton]   Brand of metal camera carrying case.

749.36   E-6]   Rank of staff sergeant.

751.8–9   "Good mornin' . . . too."] From "Good Morning, Little Schoolgirl" (1964), by Sonny Boy Williamson.

755.33   Sheridan] An American light tank.

756.5   Page] Tim Page resumed his career as a photographer in the 1970s. With Horst Faas, a photographer who covered the Vietnam War for the Associated Press, he edited *Requiem* (1997), a collection of photographs by 135 photographers who died or disappeared while covering the wars in Indochina, Vietnam, Cambodia, and Laos.

756.10   *DEROS*] Date of Estimated Return from Overseas.

759.25–27   he and Dana . . . MIA] Sean Flynn and Dana Stone disappeared along Route 1 in the Parrot's Beak area of Cambodia on April 6, 1970. In the late 1980s Tim Page began investigating their fate using information from declassified CIA documents. In *Requiem* Page wrote that after two visits to Kompong Cham province in eastern Cambodia, he concluded that Flynn and Stone were captured by Communist forces and held prisoner for 13 months before being beaten to death by the Khmer Rouge.

762.16–17   "Hungry for . . . through,"] From "Hungry" (1966) by Barry Mann and Cynthia Weil, recorded by Paul Revere and the Raiders.

762.26–27   "We gotta get out . . . do"] From "We Gotta Get Out of This Place" (1965) by Barry Mann and Cyntha Weil, recorded by The Animals.

762.29   "Black is black . . . back,"] From "Black Is Black" (1965) by Los Bravos.

762.37–38   "I said shot-gun . . . now,"] From "Shotgun" (1965) by Autry Dewalt, recorded by Junior Walker.

Glossary of Military Terms

Notes on U.S. military organization appear at the end of the Glossary.

Air America]   Charter airline covertly owned by the Central Intelligence Agency that operated in Southeast Asia from 1959 until 1976. It was especially active in providing logistical support to American-backed forces in Laos.

AK-47]   Soviet rifle, also manufactured in Communist China, that fired a 7.62 mm. bullet and was capable of both semiautomatic and full automatic fire. It was fed from a 30-round magazine, had an effective range of 330 yards, weighed 10.5 pounds when loaded, and proved to be a highly reliable weapon under combat conditions.

Americal]   American infantry division formed in Vietnam in September 1967 and deactivated in November 1971. It was named after the Americal (from "Americans in New Caledonia") Division formed in the Southwest Pacific in 1942.

APC]   Armored personnel carrier. The American M-113 was capable of transporting 11 troops, weighed 12 tons, had a maximum speed of 40 mph, and was often armed with three machine guns. Although its armor gave protection against bullets and shell fragments, the M-113 proved vulnerable to rocket-propelled grenades and large land mines.

ARVN]   Army of the Republic of Vietnam; the South Vietnamese army.

B-40]   Soviet rocket-propelled grenade, also manufactured in Communist China. The grenade had a diameter of 82 mm. and an effective range of 150 yards; it was fired from a shoulder-carried tube launcher, and contained a shaped charge that could penetrate armor plate.

B-52]   Eight-engined jet heavy bomber. The B-52 had a crew of six, a cruising speed of 520 mph, and was armed with four .50 caliber machine guns mounted in the tail; the B-52D, used in Southeast Asia in 1966–73, could carry a bombload of up to 60,000 pounds, while the B-52G, which was used along with the B-52D in 1972, could carry a bombload of 20,000 pounds. B-52 crews usually bombed from an altitude of 30,000 feet after using electronic equipment to locate their targets.

C-47]   Twin piston-engined American transport aircraft, the military version of the DC-3 passenger plane.

C-123]   Twin piston-engined transport aircraft designed for use on short runways.

C-130]   Four-engined turboprop transport aircraft.

C-141]   Four-engined jet transport aircraft.

Carbine]   A short rifle. The American M-1 carbine, first used in World War II, was a semiautomatic weapon with a 15- or 30-round magazine; it fired a .30 caliber bullet, had an effective range of 300 yards, and weighed six pounds. Another model, the M-2, was capable of both semiautomatic and full automatic fire.

CBU]   Cluster Bomb Unit, a bomb canister that broke apart in mid-air and dispersed smaller "bomblets" over a wide area. The CBU-24 anti-personnel weapon contained 600 bomblets, each of which scattered 300 steel balls at high velocity when detonated. Other CBUs dispersed land mines or shaped-charge armor-piercing bomblets.

CH-34]   Transport helicopter capable of carrying 16–18 troops.

CH-53]   Transport helicopter capable of carrying up to 38 troops.

Chieu Hois]   Defectors from the Viet Cong or the North Vietnamese army, so-called after the Chieu Hoi ("Open Arms") amnesty program begun in 1963 to encourage defections.

Chinook]   Twin-rotor transport helicopter that could carry 33 troops or up to 16,000 pounds of cargo.

Claymore]   American anti-personnel mine detonated from a remote position by sending an electric signal to the weapon. It fired 700 steel balls in a fan-shaped pattern with an 80° arc and had a lethal range of 50 yards.

Cobra]   Name for the AH-1G helicopter gunship introduced into service in Vietnam in late 1967. It had a crew of two, a cruising speed of 166 mph, and carried a variety of weapons, including multi-barreled 7.62 mm. machine guns and 20 mm. cannon, 40 mm. automatic grenade launchers, and 2.75-inch diameter rockets.

CORDS]   Civil Operations and Revolutionary (later, Rural) Development Support.

C-rations]   American canned field rations that could be eaten hot or cold.

CS]   Tear gas.

8-inch howitzer]   American howitzer that fired a 200-pound shell 8 inches in diameter, with a maximum range of more than ten miles (18,370 yards).

82 mm. mortar]   Soviet mortar, also manufactured in Communist China. It fired a 6.7 pound shell 82 mm. in diameter and had a range of almost two miles (3,300 yards).

F-4]   Jet fighter and fighter-bomber used by both the navy and the air force. The "Phantom" had a crew of two, a maximum speed of 816 mph at sea level, and could carry up to 16,000 pounds of bombs. When used as an escort fighter it could carry up to four heat-seeking and four radar-guided air-to-air missiles; in 1967 air force F-4s also began carrying a rapid-firing 20 mm. cannon mounted in an external pod.

F-100] Single-seat air force jet fighter-bomber. The "Super Sabre" had a cruising speed of 590 mph, was armed with four rapid-firing 20 mm. cannon, and could carry up to 7,000 pounds of bombs.

F-105] Single-seat air force jet fighter-bomber. The "Thud" had a maximum speed of 839 mph at sea level, was armed with a rapid-firing 20 mm. cannon, and usually carried 6,000 pounds of bombs on missions against North Vietnam. A two-seat version was used as a "Wild Weasel" aircraft to locate and attack surface-to-air missile sites.

.50 caliber] American heavy machine gun that was mounted on armored personnel carriers, tanks, and other vehicles. It fired a .50 caliber bullet and had an effective range of over 2,000 yards.

.51] American name for Soviet heavy machine gun frequently used by the North Vietnamese as an anti-aircraft weapon. It fired a 12.7 mm. bullet and had an effective range of over 1,600 yards.

4.2] U.S. mortar that fired a 24-pound shell 4.2 inches in diameter, with a maximum range of over 2.5 miles (4,500 yards).

Gatling guns] Name used in Vietnam for multi-barreled 7.62 mm. and 20 mm. guns capable of firing up to 6,000 rounds per minute.

Grease gun] American M-3 submachine gun. It fired a .45 caliber bullet, had a 30-round magazine, an effective range of 100 yards, and weighed 10 pounds.

Howitzer] An artillery gun capable of having its barrel elevated past 45°.

Huey] Popular name for the UH-1 Iroquois, the most widely used helicopter of the Vietnam War. The Huey could carry 8–12 troops or 3,000 pounds of supplies into assault landing zones and was also used for medical evacuation missions; gunship versions carried a variety of weapons, including multi-barreled 7.62 mm. machine guns, multi-tubed launchers for firing 2.75-inch diameter rockets, and 40 mm. automatic grenade launchers.

IL-28] Soviet jet bomber supplied to the North Vietnamese air force but never used in combat by them.

JUSPAO] Joint United States Public Affairs Office.

Lee Enfield] Bolt-action, magazine-fed British rifle.

Loach] Name for the OH-6 light observation helicopter introduced into service in Vietnam early in 1968. It had a crew of three, a maximum speed of 150 mph, and was armed with a multi-barreled 7.62 mm. machine gun.

M-1 rifle] Standard U.S. infantry rifle of World War II. A semiautomatic weapon, it fired a .30 caliber bullet, held eight rounds in its magazine, had an effective range of 550 yards, and weighed over nine pounds.

M-16]   American rifle firing a 5.56 mm. bullet and capable of both semi-automatic and full automatic fire. It was fed by a 20-round magazine, had an effective range of 430 yards, and weighed seven pounds. The M-16 frequently jammed under combat conditions in 1965–67, but modifications to its design, the widespread issue of cleaning kits, and improved training significantly reduced problems with the weapon after 1968.

M-48]   American tank. It weighed 52 tons, had a four-man crew, a maximum speed of 30 mph, armor with a maximum thickness of 120 mm., and was armed with a 90 mm. gun.

M-60]   American light machine gun, known as "The Pig," issued to the weapons squad of infantry platoons and usually operated by a two-man team, although it could be fired by one man. It fired a 7.62 mm. bullet, was fed by a metal belt, weighed 23 pounds, and had an effective range of 1,100 yards when used with its bipod mount. The M-60 was also used by door gunners on Huey helicopters and was often mounted on M-113 armored personnel carriers.

M-79]   Single-shot grenade launcher that fired a projectile 40 mm. in diameter. It weighed six and a half pounds and had a maximum range of 400 yards.

MACV]   Military Assistance Command Vietnam; the headquarters that commanded American forces in South Vietnam, 1962–73.

MiG]   Soviet single-seat jet fighter used for air defense by the North Vietnamese. The MiG-17 had a maximum speed of 661 mph at sea level and was armed with one 37 mm. and two 23 mm. rapid-firing cannon, while the MiG-21 had a maximum speed of 684 mph at sea level and was armed with one 30 mm. cannon and two heat-seeking air-to-air missiles; both aircraft were highly maneuverable in aerial combat.

MK-82]   A 500-pound bomb.

NVA]   North Vietnamese Army.

105]   American howitzer that fired a 33-pound shell 105 mm. in diameter, with a maximum range of almost seven miles (12,200 yards).

122-millimeter rockets]   Soviet rocket with a 41-pound warhead 122 mm. in diameter and a maximum range of almost seven miles (12,000 yards). The rocket, launching tube, and tripod mount could be carried to its firing position and set up by a six-man crew.

130-mm]   Soviet artillery gun that fired a 74-pound shell 130 mm. in diameter, with a maximum range of almost 17 miles (29,700 yards).

152]   Soviet howitzer that fired an 96-pound shell 152 mm. in diameter, with a maximum range of over 11 miles (19,600 yards).

155]   American howitzer that fired a 95-pound shell 155 mm. in diameter, with a maximum range of over nine miles (16,000 yards).

Patton]   See M-48.

Phantom]   See F-4.

People's Self Defense Force]   South Vietnamese hamlet-based militia.

Popular Forces]   South Vietnamese village-based militia.

Provisional Revolutionary Government]   Government formed by the National Liberation Front in June 1969 and later represented at the Paris peace talks. It was dissolved in 1976 when North and South Vietnam were formally united.

PT-76]   Soviet amphibious light tank. It weighed 14 tons, had a three-man crew, a maximum speed of 27 mph, armor 14 mm. thick, and was armed with a 76.2 mm. gun.

Regional Forces]   South Vietnamese provincial militia.

RPG]   Rocket-propelled grenade. See B-40.

SAC]   Strategic Air Command.

SAMs]   Surface-to-air missile. The Soviet SA-2 used by the North Vietnamese was a two-stage missile with a range of 25 miles and a 288 pound warhead; it could accelerate to a maximum speed of Mach 3 and was guided by a radio beam linked to a tracking radar.

60 mm. mortar]   U.S. mortar firing 60 mm. shell weighing 3.1 pounds, with a maximum range of over one mile (1,985 yards). The Viet Cong and North Vietnamese used a similar weapon manufactured in China with a shorter range (1,670 yards).

Sky Crane]   Transport helicopter capable of carrying over 20,000 pounds of cargo in an underslung load.

Skyhawk]   Name for the A-4 single-seat, carrier-based jet fighter-bomber. It had a maximum speed of 670 mph, was armed with two rapid-firing 20 mm. cannon, and could carry up to 8,200 pounds of bombs.

Skyraider]   Name for the A-1 single piston-engined fighter-bomber used by both the navy and the air force. It had a maximum speed of 325 mph, a crew of one, was armed with four rapid-firing 20 mm. cannon, and could carry up to 8,000 pounds of bombs or air-to-ground rockets.

Smart bomb]   Name for bombs equipped with sensors, control fins, and computers that homed in on their targets, guided either by a television image or by reflected light from a laser beam focused on the target by a designator aircraft. First introduced into combat in Southeast Asia in 1967, they were extensively used over North Vietnam in 1972.

Swedish K]   Name for the Swedish Carl Gustav M-45 submachine gun ("kulspruta" is Swedish for "machine gun"). It fired a 9 mm. bullet, had a 36-round magazine, weighed over nine pounds, and had an effective range of over 100 yards.

T-34]   Soviet medium tank, first used in World War II. It weighed 35 tons, had a five-man crew, a maximum speed of 34 mph, armor ranging in thickness from 20 mm. to 90 mm., and was armed with a 85 mm. gun.

T-54]   Soviet medium tank. It weighed 36 tons, had a four-man crew, a maximum speed of 31 mph, armor with a maximum thickness of 100 mm., and was armed with a 100 mm. gun.

TAOR]   Tactical Area of Operational Responsibility.

TOC]   Tactical Operations Center.

USARV]   U.S. Army, Republic of Vietnam.

Vulcan]   Six-barreled 20 mm. cannon capable of firing 6,000 rounds per minute.

U.S. ARMY AND MARINE ORGANIZATION

Platoon]   Unit of about 40 men at full strength, commanded by a second lieutenant.

Company]   Unit made up of three rifle platoons and one weapons platoon, and other troops, usually commanded by a captain. The equivalent unit in the air and armored cavalry is a troop.

Battalion]   Unit usually made up of four rifle companies, one support company, and a headquarters company, usually commanded by a lieutenant colonel. The equivalent unit in the cavalry is a squadron.

Regiment]   In the marines and the armored cavalry, a formation made up of three battalions or squadrons plus supporting troops, commanded by a colonel. During the Vietnam War army infantry battalions were identified by the names of their historic regimental affiliations, but were operationally organized into brigades.

Brigade]   Formation made up of between two and four battalions plus supporting troops, commanded by either a colonel or a brigadier general.

Division]   Formation made up of three brigades (in the marines, three regiments) plus supporting troops. American divisions in Vietnam had between 15,000 and 22,000 men and were commanded by a major general. By 1969 the U.S. had seven army and two marine divisions in Vietnam, along with four separate brigades and an armored cavalry regiment.

Index

839

Route 13, 341, 350–52, 362–63, 401
Route 15, 529
Route 21, 490
Route 22, 758
Route TL-1, 137
Roy, Jules, 633
Royal Lao Army, 196
Rucker, Spec. 4 Earl, 158
Rue Catinat (Saigon), 259, 283, 327,
    310–11, 469. *See also* Tu Do Street.
Rumbull, Wes, 452
Rumsfeld, Donald, 98
Rusk, Dean, 175
Rustin, Bayard, 33

Saar, John, *153–60, 181–85, 335–41*
Saigon River, 303, 327, 469, 547–48,
    627
Saint-John Perse. *See* Perse, St. John
Sainteny, Jean, 247
Salt Lake City, Utah, 18
Sam Neua province, Laos, 193,
    197–99
Sam the Sham, 571
Sam Thong, Laos, 200, 203
Samuels, Howard, 44
San Antonio, Texas, 188
San Dec Province, South Vietnam, 1,
    11
San Diego, California, 385, 392
San Francisco, California, 558, 578, 752,
    756
Sanchez, Manolo, 97
Sanguon Preap, 484
Santa Monica, California, 288, 706
Sapper, Douglas A., 3d, 521–22
Sarun (driver), 516
Satrom, LeRoy, 57
Saxton, Phillip, 215
Sayaboury Province, Laos, 201, 202
Schanberg, Sydney H., *342–49, 394–*
    407, 470–73, 486–88, 504–26
Schell, Jonathan, 249
Schelling, Thomas, 85–95
Scheuer, Sandra Lee, 71, 82
Schneider, John, 726
Schroder, Staff Sgt. ——, 135
Schroeder, William K., 71
Schryner, Harold, 101, 103
Schwalm, Pfc. Floyd, 149

Schwartz, Richard, 107–8
Seabees, U.S. Navy, 633, 653
Second Battalion, Fifth Marine
    Regiment, U.S., 614
Second Battalion, Twenty-sixth
    Marine Regiment (Hotel
    Company), 647, 652–54, 685, 687
Second Battalion, 16th Infantry, First
    Infantry Division, 144
Second Division, South Vietnamese,
    354, 362
Second Marine Artillery Battalion,
    South Vietnamese, 209–10
Second Squadron, 11th Armored
    Cavalry Regiment, 147
Second Squadron, 107th Armored
    Cavalry Regiment (Troop G), Ohio
    National Guard, 60, 61, 68
Secret Service, U.S., 97
Sedler, Pfc. Duane, 156–57
Selective Service Administration, U.S.,
    118
Senate, U.S., 87, 106, 168, 479–80;
    Judiciary Committee, 194, 200;
    Veterans Affairs Subcommittee, 480
Senegal, 239
Seven Sister mountains, South
    Vietnam, 6, 8, 760
Seventh Air Force, U.S., 395
Seventh Division, South Vietnamese,
    358
Seventh Fleet, U.S., 544
Seventh Marine Regiment, U.S., 582
Seymour, Whitney North, Jr., 109
Sgambati, Sgt. Jim, 158
Shakespeare, William, 275
Shalala, Nancy, 98
Shan plateau, Burma, 192
Shannon, Sgt. John, 138
Shaplen, Robert, *281–334*
Sheen, Fulton, 695
Sheridan, Maj. Robert, 344
Sherman, Gen. William Tecumseh, 80,
    588
Shroeder, William K., 82
Shufro, Edward, 104
Shuster, Alvin, 259
Siem Reap, Cambodia, 505
Sihanouk, Prince Norodom, 52, 122,
    124, 512
Simon-Pietrie, Christien, 742

Library of Congress Cataloging-in-Publication Data

Reporting Vietnam
    p.   cm. — (The Library of America ; 104–105)
    Includes indexes.
    Contents: pt. 1. American journalism 1959–1969 — pt. 2. American
journalism 1969–1975.
    ISBN 1–883011–58–2 (alk. paper : v. 1). — ISBN 1–883011–59–0
(alk. paper : v. 2)
    1. Journalism—United States—History—20th century.
2. Vietnamese Conflict, 1961–1975—Press coverage—United States.
I. Title: Reporting Vietnam.   II. Series.
PN4867.R45   1998
070.4'499597043—dc21   98–12267
                                                      CIP

THE LIBRARY OF AMERICA SERIES

*This book is set in 10 point Linotron Galliard,
a face designed for photocomposition by Matthew Carter
and based on the sixteenth-century face Granjon. The paper is
acid-free Ecusta Nyalite and meets the requirements for permanence
of the American National Standards Institute. The binding
material is Brillianta, a woven rayon cloth made by
Van Heek-Scholco Textielfabrieken, Holland.
The composition is by The Clarinda
Company. Printing and binding by
R.R.Donnelley & Sons Company.
Designed by Bruce Campbell.*

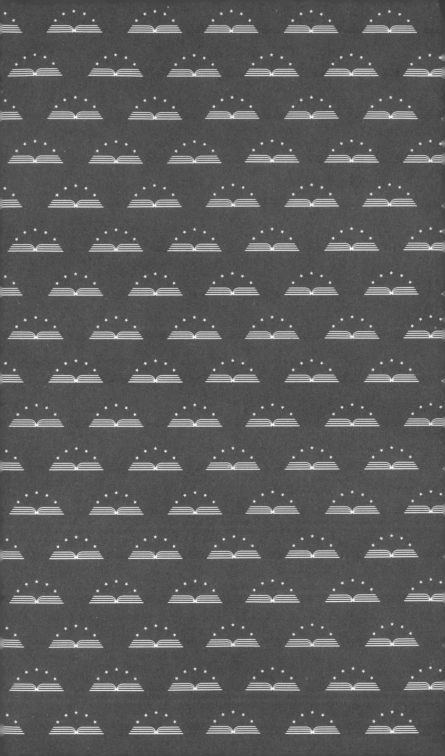